Modern World History

Made Simple

The Made Simple series
has been created
especially for self-education
but can equally well
be used as
an aid to group study.
However complex the subject,
the reader is taken
step by step
clearly and methodically,
through the course. Each volume
has been prepared by experts,
taking account of
modern educational requirements,
to ensure the most
effective way of
acquiring knowledge

In the same series

Modern World History

Made Simple

Keith Perry BA, MA, AR Hist. S.

MADE SIMPLE
BOOKS

Made Simple Books
An imprint of Heinemann Professional Publishing Ltd
Halley Court, Jordan Hill, Oxford OX2 8EJ

OXFORD LONDON MELBOURNE AUCKLAND SINGAPORE
IBADAN NAIROBI BABORNE KINGSTON

First published 1990

British Library Cataloguing in Publication Data
Perry, K. (Keith), *1937–*
    Modern world history made simple.
    1. World, 1900–
    I. Title
    909.82
ISBN 0 434 91514 9

Contents

Preface

The year 1988 had its usual crop of disasters on the international scene but was in many ways a time of hope; it witnessed *glasnost* in Russia, Russian withdrawal from Afghanistan, arms limitation agreements between two more cordial superpowers, China building more bridges with the West and moving towards better relations with India for the first time since the border war of 1962, hopes of a return to democracy in Pakistan after Benazir Bhutto's election victory, an edging towards a modus vivendi in troubled Kampuchea, an end to the Iran–Iraq war and the acceptance by the leaders of the Palestine Liberation Organisation of the need to relinquish terrorism.

It would be naive indeed to believe that all these hopeful developments will come to fruition in the next decade, but the list of advances is in itself significant; all the advances are fundamentally extra-European in nature and illustrate one of the chief themes of this book – the shift in power during the twentieth century from Europe to other parts of the world, firstly to North America and latterly to the Pacific. Therefore the author makes no excuses for making his treatment of the first decades of the century Euro-centred before giving over the bulk of the latter half of the book to treatment of the superpowers and the emergence of Asian nations.

It is well at this point to make a disclaimer; the task of encompassing all aspects of world history in the twentieth century is an impossible one in a relatively short book and therefore at times some pruning has been necessary in the sense that some areas of the world receive scant treatment where their impact on international politics has been relatively small.

This book will be of value to students and teachers in schools, colleges and universities, as it covers the syllabuses of GCSE and GCE 'A' Level courses as well as degree courses at university level. It should also be of interest to any lay person seeking a greater understanding of the world in which he/she lives.

I gladly express my thanks to those at Heinemann with whom I have associated over this project, in particular Jacquie Shanahan and Douglas Fox. I also wish to thank the library staff at the Dorset

Institute; in the course of building up a fine learning resources centre and also moving premises, they nonetheless have always found time to give help in a courteous and friendly fashion.

My deepest debt of gratitude is to my wife, whose life has, if possible, become even busier in the last two years as she successfully pursues her own professional career yet has still given unfailing encouragement. Those mixed blessings, my three daughters, must also be thanked for conspiring, on most occasions, to cheer me up when the job of writing the book taxed the spirits!

Keith Perry

1

The world scene in 1900: Imperialism, European global domination and the origins of the First World War

(1) The new Imperialism

(a) The extent of expansion

In 1900 Europe was truly the mighty continent, and Europeans and their descendants who had settled in the Americas, Australasia and Africa seemed close to dominating the globe. As J. A. S. Grenville suggests, two main factors explain Europe's global domination in this period – her technological superiority arising from industrialisation and her huge combined population. One in every four human beings lived in Europe, some 400 million people out of a total world population of 1600 million. If to this figure is added Europeans in the colonies and those of European descent in the USA, then more than one in every three human beings was European or of European descent. The Europeans ruled a great world empire, with the subject peoples in Asia, Africa and the Americas numbering nearly 500 million.

Yet during the first three-quarters of the nineteenth century the interest of European states in overseas expansion reached its lowest point in several centuries. By 1800 France had lost most of her old empire, Great Britain had lost the thirteen American colonies and early in the nineteenth century Spain and Portugal lost their possessions in South America. Only France of the great powers undertook serious colonisation in the 50 years after 1815, acquiring Cochin China, Algeria and Tahiti. Great Britain also acquired large territories, for example New Zealand and Australia, but only with reluctance when intrepid settlers made it inevitable. British governments regarded the growing empire as an encumbrance, and their attitude has been well summed up by Disraeli. 'These wretched colonies', he wrote in 1852, 'will all be independent in a few years and are millstones round our necks.' Only India was accepted as a predestined duty, but elsewhere effective access was preferred to formal control because of the expense of direct rule.

But between 1870 and 1900 the states of Europe began to extend their control over vast areas of the world. About 10 million square miles and 150 million people were brought under imperial rule, usually by the waging of aggressive wars in one-sided conflicts which Bismarck sardonically called 'sporting wars'. Any territory overseas, whether desert or swamp, was considered worthy of annexation. 'Expansion is everything,' said Cecil Rhodes. 'I would annex the planets if I could.' What was strikingly novel about the new imperialism was its concentration upon two continents – Africa and eastern Asia, the only two important areas of the globe uninfluenced by Europe before 1870. Africa and Asia were opened up more than ever before to the benefits as well as to the evils of European civilisation.

In 1875 less than one-tenth of Africa had been annexed by European states, yet by 1895 only one-tenth remained unappropriated. Between 1871 and 1900 Britain added 4½ million square miles and 66 million people to her empire, France added 3½ million square miles and 26 million people, Russia half a million square miles and 6½ million people. Germany acquired a new empire of 1 million square miles and 13 million people and Belgium and Italy also gained considerable territory in Africa. By the end of the nineteenth century much of the international tension was caused by questions of empire; undoubtedly a phenomenon of the greatest importance had taken place.

(b) The motives behind Imperialism

The most comprehensive explanation of imperialism is that which concentrates on economic factors. This thesis was first developed by J. A. Hobson in 1902 and later by Lenin. Hobson's interest in imperialism stemmed from a visit he made to South Africa as a correspondent of the *Manchester Guardian* just before the Boer War, and he became a severe critic of British policy there. In his view the 'disastrous folly' of imperial wars was partly on account of certain sectional interests – the armaments firms, manufacturers relying on exports, the shipping trade, the armed forces and the professions generally. They all benefited from imperialism because it was a creator of job opportunities, and so Hobson quotes James Mill's description of colonies as 'a vast system of outdoor relief for the upper classes'.

But to Hobson the most important factor in imperialism was investment. British capital invested abroad in 1893 represented about 15 per cent of the total wealth of the United Kingdom; in his view this profoundly influenced the actions of government and he claimed that 'the modern foreign policy of Great Britain is primarily a struggle for profitable markets of investment'. Imperialists in European countries as well as the United States justified imperialism as a necessity because large savings of capital were made which could not find profitable use in the mother country and colonies were required as fields of investment. This need for investment, says Hobson, is the 'economic taproot of imperialism'. He saw imperialism as motivated only by selfish forces which would manipulate the idealism of missionaries and politicians.

Lenin's views on imperialism were contained in a pamphlet written in 1916 called 'Imperialism, the Highest Stage of Capitalism'. He saw imperialism arising out of modern capitalism, which had become dominated by monopolistic combines. These combines found difficulty in investing at home because the European market was saturated and they were also anxious to control all sources of raw materials. The direct acquisition of colonies was the solution, for 'colonial possession alone gives complete guarantee of success to the monopolies against all the risks of the struggle with competitors'. Free markets would become a thing of the past under imperialism, which was 'the monopoly stage of capitalism'. In Lenin's view the action of European powers in dividing the world between them to safeguard investments increased tension and inevitably led to war.

The Marxist thesis is very one-sided and can be refuted when the actual evidence is analysed. The export of capital in fact seems to have had little connection with imperial expansion. There was much British investment abroad before 1875 when imperialism was out of vogue, and the rate of growth in foreign investment fell away in the period between 1875 and 1895 when imperial aggrandisement was at its height. Nor did a large proportion of this investment go into the new colonies. In 1913 Britain had more money invested in the United States than any colony; less than half her total export of capital was to her empire and most of this was in such old white dominions as Canada, New Zealand and Australia, not in the new acquisitions in Africa or Asia. France sent most of her capital to Russia and other European countries, investing under 7 per cent of her foreign capital in her colonies. Germany in 1913 had only 3 per cent of her foreign investment in Africa and Asia, and only a small proportion of this amount was invested in her own colonies. Three of the most important imperial nations, Russia, Italy and Japan, were nations with too little capital for domestic requirements to send any significant amount abroad, Russia in particular borrowing heavily from France.

Nor can the urge for colonial markets and raw materials have been a crucial factor in imperialism. The great industrial countries obtained only a fraction of their raw materials from the colonies, and the colonial trade in general played a relatively unimportant part in the total foreign commerce of the industrial nations because of the low purchasing power of the natives. The industrial nations were each other's best customers despite the international rivalry, whereas trade and investment in Africa and Asia had a high risk content which made them unattractive.

Lenin's view of European industry under the domination of huge combines also fails to square with reality. Only in Germany had the trust movement made much headway by 1914; it came much later in other countries, even in England, the state which controlled the largest empire. The combines that did exist did not support their country's foreign policy as one might expect. During the Bosnian crisis of 1908, when France should have been supporting Russia, Franco-German talks were held over Moroccan mining rights. The talks were inspired by the two great combines Schneider–Creusot and Krupps, and are proof that international capitalism could combine as well as compete. If big business had controlled government, it would have stopped the coming of war in 1914 because it resulted in the destruction of its best customers and sources of supply. Schumpeter went as far as asserting that capitalism was anti-imperialist because it regarded imperial adventures as a distraction from the realities of economic activity.

In fact it was the politicians who were the prophets of imperial expansion, and the new imperialism was a nationalistic, not an economic, phenomenon. It grew out of the diplomatic situation in Europe after the Franco-Prussian war, when the French government sought prestige abroad as consolation for the loss of Alsace-Lorraine. This Bismark encouraged in the interests of Franco-German friendship, giving France a free hand in Tunis. He also had in mind the hope that England and Italy would be alienated, as indeed they were. Britain, already in possession of a great empire, was now apprehensive of the growing interest of other countries in imperialism and sought to take measures to safeguard it. Her concern for the security of the routes to India led her to occupy Egypt. To other powers envious of the British Empire, British action did not seem to aim at security only but at ever greater empire. France and Russia were particularly hostile to consolidation of the British position in the Eastern Mediterranean. The scramble for Africa was under way.

Once the imperial movement had started, it generated its own momentum. Often territories were absorbed not for their present value but as an insurance against the future. Baumont described this process as 'taking as much as possible without knowing what to do with it, taking what others want because they want it and to prevent them getting it'. Lord Rosebery in 1893 told the Colonial Institute that the government was pegging out claims for the future, implying that otherwise Britain would be left out of the partition of the rest of the world. Many like him admitted that the colonies were not worth much at present, but dwelt on the future commerical advantages because these were easier to justify than the real strategic and political motives.

Considerations of national prestige played a large part in the imperial saga. Governments accepted, often uncritically, the words of Gambetta that 'to remain a great nation or to become one, you must colonise'. When he became head of the French government in 1881 Jules Ferry remarked, 'It is a question of fifty or a hundred years' time . . . of the future heritage of our children.' The imperial scramble was more than a vogue; it became a mania, a process which possessed, says Hannah Arendt, its own 'inherent insanity'.

Another vital political factor was the relation between imperialism and democracy in Western Europe. The industrial and white-collar classes were gradually being enfranchised in the late nineteenth century. Politicians could no longer ignore their opinions and if colonial adventures satisfied the craving of the masses for excitement, then it was political wisdom to follow a 'forward' policy in imperial affairs. Gladstone's Liberal party was out of office for most of the period from 1885 to 1905 because its policy of Home Rule for Ireland was against the spirit of the times, while the Conservative party, which supported imperialism, enjoyed a secure period of power. Thus C. J. H. Hayes concludes that in the last analysis it was the nationalistic masses who made imperialism possible and who most vociferously applauded and most constantly backed it. It possessed inherent attractions, and Marxists have given insufficient attention to the psychological ingredients in imperialism. Imperial adventure was exciting and a change from dull routine for workers confined in ugly cities. They could identify with the nation's colonial victories and prestige and feel a share in them. When Mafeking was relieved during the Boer War, the London public went wild. Feeling was as intense in other countries. The Italian pubic fervently supported its government's imperial adventures in Africa because, as Christopher Seton-Watson phrases it, they brought back the poetry to national life and were a vivid contrast to the humdrum prose of parliamentary life. Critics of imperialism such as G. P. Gooch condemned it as the equivalent of bread and circuses in Roman times.

Whatever the psychological factors, imperialism became a great theme on which pressure groups, the press, men of letters and even the song-writers went into eulogies. Politicians could not remain immune to the pressure of patriots, whether those of the Primrose League in Britain or the Colonial Society in Germany. Even the revisionist socialists gave guarded support for imperialism. Eduard Bernstein stressed its humanitarian aspects and saw materials benefits in it for the working classes. 'A certain tutelage of the civilized peoples over the uncivilized is a necessity,' he asserted.

The imperialism of the period was one aspect of a revolution which was challenging the ideas of earlier generations. Relations between states were now based on fresh assumptions about the nature of men and society. These assumptions included the belief in the duty of the advanced peoples to bring civilisation to the backward ones. This need for idealistic devotion to duty was enshrined in Kipling's 'The White Man's Burden'. Obviously at times such thoughts were hypocritical but imperial administration furnished many examples of dedicated governors sincerely desirous of bringing benefits to their colonies – for example Cromer in Egypt, Karl Peters in German East Africa and Marshal Lyautey in Morocco.

The most profound of the ideas underlying imperialism was Social Darwinism, which took Charles Darwin's ideas on evolution and applied them to international relations. It viewed relations between states as a perpetual struggle for existence in which only the strongest survived. Living meant fighting, for the international scene was, like nature itself, a vast field of carnage. In practice it encouraged the naked use of force and a glorification of the military life. It also led to a belief that states must expand or decline; they must increase their empires or be overtaken by others. Joseph Chamberlain said in 1902, 'The future is with the great Empires and there is no greater Empire than the British Empire.' The law of the survival of the fittest came to be seen almost as a revelation of the Divine Will on earth, and the act of obstructing the growth of the nation's empire was disobedience to the will of God! Perhaps the definition of imperialism given by John McManners is the most appropriate; it was not the highest stage of capitalism but the highest stage of nationalism.

In addition to international tensions, the two other factors deciding the timing of imperialism were exploration and technology. The work of such explorers as Peters, Livingstone and Stanley opened up the hitherto dark continent of Africa. Livingstone crossed the Kalahari Desert, explored the River Zambesi and penetrated into what became Nyasaland and Tanganyika. After his death in 1873 Stanley explored the area around Lake Victoria and reached the River Congo. The continent could be exploited by this period through the development of railways and the steamship. The indigenous population could not prevent this because of the vast superiority in weaponry possessed by the Europeans, so that in Africa and Asia a handful of European soldiers could control vast territories. The reason was wittily summed up in Hilaire Belloc's couplet:

> 'Thank the Lord that we have got
> The Gatling gun and they have not.'

This superiority in weaponry encourages K. R. Minogue to suggest a technological theory of imperialism. Europe expanded when the use of force was easy, but imperialism ceased when the natives acquired guns, for the game now cost more than it was worth.

These considerations – the political rivalries, the popularity of imperialism with the masses, its Social Darwinism and its technological aspects – all demonstrate that the Marxist interpretation is an over-simplification. Yet it would be unwise to attempt to eliminate the economic factor altogether. Profits were made out of imperial development by munitions manufacturers and traders in such raw materials from the colonies as ivory and rubber. There were examples of gross exploitation, possibly the worst example being the activities of Leopold, King of the Belgians, in the Congo. Imperial expansion provided jobs for soldiers and administrators, and economic pressure groups at times played a considerable part in persuading the governments of Europe to embark on colonial expansion, for example in Germany.

Yet if one thinks in terms of pressure groups, it is equally fair to say that missionary societies played as important a role as financial interests. In both France and Britain the anti-slavery movement campaigned for government intervention in Africa; it was an impressive campaign, too, dramatised by the work of Livingstone and publicised by church leaders such as Cardinal Lavigerie. Indeed the late nineteenth century was perhaps the greatest period of missionary work in the history of the Christian Church. About 40,000 Roman Catholic and 20,000 Protestant missionaries went over to Asia and Africa, making the conversion of the whole world seem, for a short time anyway, a real possibility. The activities of the church facilitated a political take-over later. Lavigerie's Society of African Missionaries extended its work from Algeria into Tunisia in 1875, easing the task of the French government in taking over Tunis in 1881. Gambetta said of Lavigerie, 'His presence in Tunisia is worth an army for France.' The presence of the Church could also furnish pretexts for government intervention. It was the murder of two German missionaries in China in 1897 which gave the German government the excuse to seize the port of Kiao-Chow.

Enthusiasm for imperial adventures began to decline from 1905 after a series of crises. Spain suffered losses in the war of 1898 with the United States, ceding Cuba and the Philippines. The British, victorious in the Sudan at the Battle of Omdurman in 1898, were soon to be deflated by the outbreak of the costly Boer War in 1899. Faith in imperial invincibility was shaken by two other clashes which showed that it was not inevitable that Asians and Africans must always be defeated in any encounter with the West. In 1896 the defeat of the Italian army at Adowa in Abyssinia caused the fall of the Italian prime minister Crispi. Even more astonishing were the setbacks on land and sea that befell the Russians during the Russo-

Japanese war of 1904–5, which precipitated the 1905 Revolution. The great age of imperialism was drawing to a close.

There were few more acquisitions to be made, and the expense of empire was beginning to appear disproportionate to the gains. Already demands for political rights and independence were being made in the colonies, for, as K. R. Minogue points out, 'modern Europeans carried with them the boot that would eventually send them packing – the nationalistic belief that anything else but self-government is a kind of slavery'. In addition, European knowledge had been taken to other parts of the world and non-European peoples were adept at learning European military and industrial techniques. The subject peoples not only became less easily policed but proved that industrial productivity was not a Western monopoly. Indeed the Japanese and others were able to become more competitive than Western countries. Thus the spread both of European ideas and knowledge undermined the bases of European control of the world. Europe's demographic domination and economic superiority declined as the century progressed and the European empires collapsed soon after the Second World War (see Chapter 11).

(2) Industrial change and the challenge of socialism

(a) The development of the industrial society

The Industrial Revolution that gave Europe its temporary world domination started in Britain, but by 1850 had penetrated into Belgium, France and Germany and by 1900 had extended to Italy and Russia. This revolution was based on the exploitation of hitherto untapped sources of energy such as coal, oil, gas and electricity. Key basic industries developed, notably textiles, iron and steel and railway construction; common to all was the new mode of production – power-driven machinery located in new urban factories.

So many innovations took place in the late nineteenth century that the price of manufactures fell steadily. By this period Germany had become an industrial giant, taking the lead in new steel-making processes, chemicals and electrical products. David Landes admires this initiative. 'In technical virtuosity and aggressive enterprise, this leap to hegemony, almost to monopoly, has no parallel. It was Imperial Germany's greatest industrial achievement.'

From 1850 to 1914 there was an unprecedented increase in the European population, from 266 million to over 468 million. The increase was caused by a fall in the death rate, owing to cheaper food, improved medicine and a rise in real incomes from 1850. There was a rapid acceleration in the growth of the urban population, which by the late nineteenth century was beginning to outstrip the rural population. Such advances were mainly experienced in Western Europe; to the East agrarian, indeed feudal, societies changed only slowly.

The excess of births over deaths in most parts of Europe was one of the chief causes of mass migration. The motives for this phenomenon were complex but both the 'push' of adverse conditions at home and the 'pull' of better prospects overseas were major factors. Between 1841 and 1880 13 million Europeans emigrated, mostly from Britain, Ireland and Germany. From 1871 to 1914 another 34 million Europeans left for the New World, the biggest contingents from 1885 coming from east and south Europe. This European emigration was probably the greatest transfer of population in the history of mankind.

(b) The challenge of socialism

The rapid evolution of an urban society possibly aggravated and certainly highlighted political and social inequalities and stimulated the rise of a radical new political ideology – socialism. It had its roots in the French Revolution, but its crucial formative years were between 1830 and 1848, when the work of the French socialists – St Simon, Fourier and Louis Blanc – transformed it from a doctrine into a movement.

Two major elements developed within socialism after 1848 – Marxism and anarchism. Karl Marx was born in the Rhineland of middleclass Jewish parents in 1818. In 1843 he went to Paris and met working-class socialists, including Friedrich Engels, who was to become his major collaborator. By 1845 Marx was a dedicated socialist who aimed at the organisation of an international socialist movement.

When the 1848 Revolutions broke out in a number of European states, Marx published 'The Communist Manifesto'. In it he asserted his theory of Historical Materialism, that economic factors are the cause of all historical change and that all history is the history of class struggles. He pointed to the growing gulf between middle-class owners of capital and the exploited proletariat, and claimed that the capitalist system would be undermined by crises which would inevitably end in its overthrow by the growing ranks of the proletariat. In 1867 Marx elaborated the theory behind 'The Communist Manifesto' in his great work, *Das Kapital*. By then he had helped to create the first International Working Men's Association in 1864.

Insufferably arrogant, Marx despised anyone with different views to his own. The rise of another branch of socialism (Proudhonism or anarchism) led to conflict in the International. Pierre Joseph Proudhon was born in 1809 at Besançon. His pamphlet 'What is Property?' published in 1840, produced one of the most famous revolutionary phrases of the nineteenth century – 'Property is theft'. Proudhon opposed traditional forms of government. In his opinion centralised government was a tyranny that must be broken by the workers and the bourgeoisie through organising syndicates which they would run. The syndicates would be the basis of a new society in which people would rule themselves in a system of non-government or anarchism. Thus Proudhon preached a doctrine of federation, in which society would consist of small communities running their own affairs with little or no central administration. His ideas spread because of the impact of a professional Russian revolutionary, Michael Bakunin.

Between Marx and Bakunin there was no possibility of compromise. Marx called the anarchist programme an empty rigmarole, fearing Bakunin's inspiring oratory in public meetings. While Marx wanted an organisation to capture political power, Bakunin worked for a loose federal organisation to stimulate insurrections and dissolve authority. Marx saw no future except in the capture of the state and the setting up of the dictatorship of the proletariat, after which he believed the state would wither away. Proudhon and Bakunin detested the centralised state and aimed at extreme decentralisation and democracy.

Bakunin also conflicted with Marx over which classes were the right revolutionary material. He believed that true revolutionaries were those with nothing to lose, for example the landless agricultural labourers of Spain or Russia. Marx maintained that it was the industrial proletariat in advanced societies who would be the spearhead of the next revolution. Bakunin said that they were already enjoying the benefits of economic progress and therefore had a stake which they would not throw away.

Bakunin went further than Marx in his belief in the need for violence to sweep away existing institutions. This anarchy should be started by young educated individuals who would inspire the people to similar acts of terrorism and revolution. This need for an elite is similar to Marx's, but the two men came to loathe each other personally as well as each repudiating the other's ideas. The rift between the two factions split the international movement at its 1869 and 1872 conferences and contributed to a decline in Marx's final years before his death in 1883.

Marx's influence on European and world thought was immense. His doctrine of the class struggle and of the inevitable triumph of the working class made it immediately appealing to industrial workers. In his view changes in the mode of production at each stage of historical development would cause a new class to take over. Thus the bourgeoisie had taken over from the feudal aristocracy and in time the bourgeoisie would make way for the proletariat, enabling a new era of social justice to begin.

Marx believed that this process was inevitable because of certain features of the capitalist state. Firstly, the payment of low wages for long hours would be resented by the workers. Secondly, as industrialisation continued, small firms would be driven out as markets became dominated by a few large firms. Thus the ranks of the working classes would be swelled by elements formerly among the middle class. Thirdly, capitalism would be incapable of making the system work. Commercial crises would occur, each one worse than the last because of the competition for profit. In the end catastrophic slumps would lead to the final collapse of the capitalist system.

The validity of Marx's analysis has continued to be a matter of fierce debate. Surely in any issue factors other than economic play a significant part – political or religious motives, human talent, geography, even sheer chance. Secondly, Marx's assumption that individuals usually stay loyal to their own class has proved unfounded. When the First World War broke out, socialists in every warring state found that their nationalism was stronger than their class solidarity.

Marx's belief in the inevitability of class warfare was at best a half-truth. Even in his lifetime measures had been taken at government and factory level to improve the lot of the workers. In the twentieth century mixed economies – private enterprise and state socialism – have achieved considerable success. Proletarian revolutions have occurred in precisely those countries which Marx assumed would be least susceptible to revolution, such as Russia and China, where no bourgeois industrialisation had taken place as a necessary prerequisite. The dictatorship of the proletariat in communist countries has not resulted in the withering away of the state, as Marx believed, but on the contrary it has led to the creation of new forms of totalitarian government.

Nevertheless Marxism has had the messianic power and driving force of a great religion. Marx's analysis of capitalism had a veneer of objectivity, but in reality it was, in Schumpeter's phrase, 'preaching in the garb of analysis'. It became a substitute religion because working men could look forward to ultimate victory and a socialist millenium. Marx's promise of sure salvation had tremendous appeal for the underprivileged across the world in the twentieth century.

In the years immediately following his death, however, it seemed unlikely that Marx's ideas would be so influential. Many socialists such as Edouard Bernstein in Germany, perceived that despite Marx's prediction of its imminent collapse, the capitalist system was making continued progress. They turned to revisionism, a policy of working within the system to pursue gradual rather than revolutionary change. Such thinking was condemned by such orthodox Marxists as Lenin.

Despite this division on tactics, a new international organisation was started in 1889, the Second International. However, it became as badly divided as the First International. For years it exhorted all socialists against fighting brother workers should war break out between the great powers. When war did break out in 1914, socialists demonstrated national loyalty rather than class solidarity, with the exception of a courageous minority, including Keir Hardie and Bernstein. The Second International did not survive the war.

Despite this failure, socialism was a formidable mass movement, imposing enough to alarm governments. It was fear of its internal enemies, the socialists, that partly explains Germany's aggressive stance in the July crisis of 1914. By then the German government perceived that a victorious war against its external enemies (France and Russia) would strengthen its hands against the rising Social Democratic Party at home. (see Chapter 1, Sections 3 and 4).

(3) The Great Powers in 1900

(a) Germany

In 1900 Imperial Germany appeared to symbolise success. Created in three victorious wars (against Denmark in 1864, Austria in 1866 and France in 1870), Germany had replaced France as the premier military power in Europe. Her success was on many levels – in education, technology, science and industry. The organisation and hard work of her 67 million inhabitants had made Germany the dominant industrial nation in Europe. Unlike Britain, which she was now overtaking, Germany was transformed by industrial development in a relatively short period from the middle of the nineteenth century on.

Unfortunately Germany's political development was in contrast much slower. In 1871 the Prussian prime minister Bismarck became Imperial Chancellor and ensured that real power remained with Prussia and the landowning class (the junkers). Germany became a federation of twenty-five states and each state possessed its own parliament, but Prussia was dominant because she possessed three-fifths of the population. Constitutionally Prussian domination was secured in two ways. Firstly, the King of Prussia was to be hereditary Emperor (Kaiser) of the German Empire, controlling civil administration through the chancellor and the army through a military council. He had great power, as he could appoint and dismiss the chancellor, in addition to being supreme commander of the armed forces and the final arbiter of war and peace. Secondly, Prussia had sufficient voting power in the upper house (the Reichsrat or Federal Council) to block any unwelcome constitutional amendments. She possessed 17 out of the 58 votes and could in practice secure a majority.

The Reichstag (the German parliament) was elected by manhood suffrage and in theory had considerable power. However, German parliamentarians failed after 1871 to exploit the potential of the Reichstag as an instrument for political change. In practice only the Reichsrat drafted legislation and the Reichstag even failed to exercise much control over expenditure.

The nature of the Prussian state government also assisted authoritarianism. The King's position was buttressed by an entrenched ruling class which held many of the top positions in the civil service and armed forces. The junkers also dominated the Prussian parliament because of the three class franchise, which, by making an elector's voting strength dependent on the amount of taxes he paid, produced a permanent right-wing majority. Open voting also permitted the use of intimidation.

Although the Reichstag was by no means a cypher, the constitution did permit Prussian authoritarianism, and Max Weber, Germany's leading sociologist, described the system set up by Bismarck as 'sham-constitutionlism'. It did not reflect the actual distribution of power in German society even in 1871, as it ignored the aspirations of rising new urban groups. However, in the final decades of the nineteenth century, as Germany rapidly industrialised, a further growth occurred in the industrial and commercial bourgeoisie as well as in the rise of a large industrial proletariat. Neither the bourgeoisie nor the proletariat were content with a constitution which gave the Kaiser and the landed aristocracy a power which bore little relation to the declining economic importance of the old agrarian elites. Therefore there was growing pressure for reform which the Kaiser and his advisers met by a policy of stubborn preservation of the status quo. The voters therefore turned to parties that advocated radical change, and by 1912 millions of them were voting for the Social Democratic Party (SPD), which became the largest party in the Reichstag with 110 seats out of a total of 391. This development in turn frightened the conservatives, who came to believe almost hysterically that revolution was just round the corner. The SPD was denounced as revolutionary by conservatives in the government when, despite its Marxist origins, it had become reformist and was operating within the law.

William II, who became Kaiser in 1890, did not have the strength or commonsense to lead Germany in the right direction. Unsure of himself, he tried to be all things to all men, at one moment wishing to be a social reformer and then a stern authoritarian the next, at one moment wishing to be the Kaiser of peace, the next the Kaiser who would make Germany a world as well as a European power. Those around him, in particular military figures, were able to play on his vanity.

That Germany contrived to entangle herself in war in 1914 is partly explained by the uneasy relation between the civil and military authorities. The chief of the general staff in practice ranked equally with the chancellor as adviser to the Kaiser. William also detached the Naval High Command from the Imperial Admiralty on his accession and placed it directly under his command. The chief beneficiary of this naval reorganisation was Tirpitz, chief of staff to the Naval High Command and soon to be minister of marine. Tirpitz played on his master's vanity in naval matters. The policy of reducing civilian control of the armed forces widened the breach between the army and sections of the public.

More seriously the army pursued independence in matters of high policy. In 1891 Count Alfred von Schlieffen became chief of the general staff. Up to this point German plans for a war on two fronts had assigned the bulk of the army to the Russian front, where an offensive would be launched while defensive action was undertaken against France. Schlieffen reversed these roles to concentrate in the West, believing that France could be knocked out of the war in a few weeks so that German forces could concentrate on the harder task of defeating Russia. The only way of defeating France quickly was by an outflanking movement through Belgium and Luxembourg, two countries guaranteed by the powers, Germany included. By 1897 the Schlieffen Plan had been amended to take in these countries, yet no politician objected to it, despite the plan being in Ritter's words, 'a daring, indeed an overdaring, gamble whose success depended on many lucky accidents'. For politicians to raise objections to a plan worked out by the General Staff amounted in the Kaiser's Germany to unwarranted interference in a foreign sphere.

The military domination of government became ever more dangerous as 1914 approached. By 1912 the military clique around William were filled with deep pessimism about the future, despite all the evidence proving Germany's success. To their fear of democratic revolution was added apprehension at the creation of the Triple Entente and in particular Russian military reform after 1905. In December 1912 a war council discussed the desirability of waging a preventive war against France and Russia. While it was decided that war should be postponed, a consensus concluded that Germany must make war soon, while she still retained some chance of winning, and in 1913 military spending was increased. A successful war would also, it was hoped, strengthen the hands of the government against its internal enemies, the SPD. Thus by 1914 there was a pronounced drift to war in Germany. International and internal pressures explain the attitude of the German government during the July Crisis of 1914 in supporting Austrian action against Serbia.

(b) France

If Germany symbolised progress and discipline to contemporaries, the French Third Republic was viewed as a divided nation, ruled by inept politicians and riddled with scandal. Yet this perception was superficial; in everyday life France was a stable, well-ordered country enjoying economic growth in the period before 1914.

To be sure, the Third Republic faced many problems after 1871. It was born in the misery of defeat in the Franco-Prussian War of 1870, which toppled the regime of Napoleon III's Second Empire. Defeat by Prussia led to the loss of Alsace-Lorraine by the 1871 Treaty of Frankfurt, and was compounded by the tragedy of the Commune, a revolt by radical and proletarian elements in Paris, which the Provisional Government put down ferociously, 20,000 Communards being killed in the fighting and by subsequent executions.

The affair led to a permanent rift between the new regime and the working classes, but other groups too were hostile to the Third Republic. For much of the period there seemed to be some possibility of a royalist restoration, as parties supporting the Bourbon and Orleans families continued to plot though harmlessly, against Republican government. The Republic's anti-clerical campaigns under Jules Ferry (1879–85) and Emile Combes (1902–5) alienated the Church.

The new regime failed to provide strong government. Fearful of a return to Napoleon III's authoritarian rule, the creators of the French constitution ensured that the president had little real power, as he was to be elected by parliament and deputies would only vote for mediocrities. The lack of a two-party system meant that the political labels that a man used in order to get himself elected as a deputy were often no guide to how he would behave in parliament. Deputies could behave irresponsibly by voting against a government, because parliaments ran their full term and deputies did not risk losing their seats. Weak coalition governments were the rule, and there were fifty changes of government in the first 40 years of the Republic.

At the close of the century the regime was beset by three outbreaks of excitement which appeared to point to the Republic's instability. In 1889 a popular general, Georges Boulanger, had the opportunity to overthrow the Republic, but his nerve failed and he fled to Brussels, where he committed suicide in 1891. Then occurred the Panama Scandal. In 1879 Ferdinand de Lesseps had floated the Panama Canal Company, which ran into difficulties, and in 1888 the Assembly voted for the company to be helped by a large public loan. Nevertheless the company went into liquidation in 1892, and it was revealed that one-third of its capital had been spent on bribing politicians to keep quiet about its difficulties so that the public would still invest in the company.

Most notorious of all the scandals was the Dreyfus Affair. In 1894 a Jew, Alfred Dreyfus, was accused of passing secrets to the Germans, and he was subsequently found guilty after an irregular trial and sentenced to life imprisonment on Devil's Island. Despite evidence being later produced that he was innocent, the military authorities refused to consent to a retrial or grant a pardon. The Affair bitterly divided French society; the anti-Dreyfusards stood for old conservative monarchical France and believed that Dreyfus should be sacrificed in order to preserve the army's honour. The Dreyfusards stood for radicalism and the ideals of the French Revolution. Only in 1906 was Dreyfus reinstated. The whole incident had shown up the limitations of the French legal system, in which the odds were loaded against the accused; it obscured social problems for a decade and widened existing tensions in French society, especially anti-Semitism (as Dreyfus was a Jew) and anti-clericalism (as the Roman Church clearly supported the original verdict). One consequence of the Affair was the stimulus it gave to chauvinism in France. In 1899 came the formation of a group under Charles Maurras which believed that a strong government would not have allowed the humiliations which the Affair had heaped on France. By 1905 the group was fully established as Action Française. It was anti-Semitic, violently nationalistic and may truly be called a precursor of later French fascist groups.

The years before 1914 also saw the growth of a united socialist party under the able and conciliatory Jean Jaurès, and a more militant trade union organisation, the Confédération Générale du Travail (CGT). With the hostility of previously mentioned groups, it is tempting to believe that the Third Republic was in a state of crisis, attacked on all sides by its enemies. Yet this is a false picture, because France was more stable than she appeared and had recovered her position as a great power by 1914 despite defeat in 1870 and economic inferiority to Germany. The country remained deeply conservative, partly because it did not experience rapid population growth or rapid industrialisation. In 1906 43 per cent of the population still worked on the land and much French industry remained small scale. Nevertheless productivity in agriculture and industry rose with the development of new industries, such as the electrical, chemical and car sectors. Living standards rose to comparability with Germany's.

On the diplomatic front France sought a deterrent against further German aggression, and found her way out of diplomatic isolation through the 1894 alliance with Russia, which was cemented by French loans for Russia's industrial development. From the 1880s French colonial policy was expansionist, and the French Empire was extended in West Africa, North Africa (Tunis and Morocco) and East Asia (Indo-China). When Raymond Poincaré became premier in 1912, French foreign policy acquired a new determination. In 1913 service in the French army was lengthened from two to three years, and Poincaré himself made it clear that France would honour her obligations as an ally if a matter of vital interest to Russia was at stake in the Balkans.

(c) Italy

As Grenville perceptively comments, Italy provides an interesting test case, most relevant for Third World countries today, of what happens when a parliamentary constitution is imposed on an under-developed society. The country had been fully united by 1870, with the acquisition of Rome during the Franco-Prussian War, but the main Italian initiatives came from the Kingdom of Piedmont. Its rulers now became the rulers of Italy and imposed parliamentary government over the whole of the Italian peninsula. Such government failed to attract the mass of the Italian people, as unity seemed to bring few real benefits.

One factor causing disillusionment was the nature of parliamentary government itself. Power remained in the hands of two coalitions of parties, the Left and the Right. But there was no essential difference between these groupings, and therefore no possibility of constructive debate or alternation of power. In practice politicians avid for office kept themselves in power by the technique of *transformismo*. They disregarded party labels and made bargains with deputies from both the Left and Right to create a parliamentary majority. The chief practitioners of this method were Depretis, Crispi and Giolitti.

Parliament became an amorphous mass of deputies led by ministries whose members changed constantly. Between 1871 and 1914 there were thirty-one different ministers of finance alone. As parliamentary government appeared to have little relevance to Italy's real problems, public apathy towards parliament resulted, and one-third of the electorate habitually abstained from voting even though only 2.6 per cent of the population had the vote. Apathy turned to contempt as Italy seemed determined to equal France in parliamentary scandal. The Banco Romana scandal occurred at the same time as the Panama Scandal. The bank had to be liquidated because of malpractices and both Crispi and Giolitti were implicated in the affair.

Under this system the problem of the South was not tackled with sufficient vigour. Southerners resented the new centralised administration, which brought with it conscription and higher taxation. The problem was partly psychological: Northern Italians were urban and did not understand the problems of a backward rural society, believing that the South was potentially a land of milk and honey which was being wasted by feckless Southerners. Yet the poverty of the South was all too real; it had little industry and its agriculture was held back by the absence of fertile land. Consequently much of the huge emigration from Italy in this period was from the South, and in 1913 alone, 873,000 people left Italy, mainly for the USA. As Christopher Seton-Watson explains, emigration helped the South. 'It provided a safety-valve by drawing off surplus labour from the land, thus performing the function which in the North was performed by industrialisation.'

The problems of relations with the Church continued to embarrass Italian governments. The Papacy disliked the new united Italy for its liberalism and was not reconciled to the loss of Rome. It tried to prevent Catholics from participating in politics and only in 1904 did this policy begin to change, when Catholics were allowed to vote in areas where there might be a socialist victory. A new socialist party had been founded in 1892 by the dedicated moderate Turati. But a more extreme wing grew up in the party under Antonio Labriola, and this contributed to growing violence in national life at the end of the century. In 1898 riots in Milan led to the death of eighty people and in 1900 an anarchist murdered King Humbert in revenge for the Milan incident.

There was no relief from domestic issues in the field of foreign and imperial affairs. Though she joined the Triple Alliance in 1882, Italy was still regarded as a second-class power by the genuine great powers of Europe. Her colonial ambitions led her to fruitless scrambling after territory in Africa – arid Eritrea and part of the Somaliland. It also led to a humiliating defeat at the Battle of Adowa by the Abyssinians in 1896. Seton-Watson believes that this left a lasting mark on modern Italy, a disgrace that could only be expunged through a victorious war. The real lesson – that imperial gambles were a waste of precious resources – was soon forgotten. Indeed the years before 1914 saw the rise of a group of nationalist writers and politicians who anticipated in their ideas and tactics much of Mussolini's later fascism. Gabriele D'Annunzio, a poet and playwright who lived for sensation and glorified violence, won some influence over Italian youth. He despised Giolitti's humdrum Italy and sang the praises of war. The second great figure of the nationalist movement, Enrico Corradini, lamented that Italy was a proletarian nation which could only become a true nation by a victorious war in Africa or the Mediterranean.

It would be misleading, however, to view the early decades of the united Italy as a complete failure. Italy did gain experience in parliamentary government, and for all its limitations the experiment in liberal government was maintained, with extensions to the franchise in 1882 and 1912. Real efforts were made under Giolitti after 1901 to help the South, and Italian unity was consolidated. An improvement in the quality of life went hand in hand with the development of the economy. After 1880 the pace of industrialisation increased.

Heavy investment in railways helped to bind the country together, and with the rise of important new companies – Pirelli in rubber, Fiat in motor cars and Olivetti in office machinery – industrial production increased by 87 per cent between 1901 and 1913. Unfortunately Italy's entry into the First World War against the wishes of the majority of her citizens interrupted Italy's progress towards mature liberal government.

(d) Russia

In the light of the 1917 Revolution and Stalin's later totalitarianism, it is difficult to look objectively at Russian history in the final decades of Tsarist rule. Russia was a huge underdeveloped country with a backward peasant population and an inefficient autocratic government. The survival of such a system was always open to question, and historians have disagreed on its progress towards stability in the period before 1914. Gerschenkron has argued that genuine modernisation occurred after 1880 and only the onset of war frustrated the continuation of promising political and economic trends. However, other historians, such as George Kennan and Lionel Kochan, while accepting that real attempts were made to tackle Russia's difficulties, argue that Russia was approaching a new and possibly insoluble crisis with or without war by 1914.

The difficulties facing Russian rulers were immense. Tsarist Russia was a multi-national state. Two centuries of expansion had brought with it an accumulated diversity of nationalities that constantly challenged the idea of uniform bureaucratic centralisation which was the tsarist objective. The first proper census in 1897 revealed that 55 per cent of the people were non-Russian. To attempt to impose uniformity on the diverse nationalities was futile and often cruel, but this policy of Russification was followed, especially on the Poles and the Jews.

The futility was inevitable, given the inability of the government to pursue any policy of repression rigorously. As Norman Stone has shown, many sections of the Russian bureaucracy were painfully understaffed because there was not enough money to pay officials. Thus the Security Police in Moscow consisted of six officials in the 1850s, and even in 1900 the situation had not improved much. The inefficiency of the system was highlighted by defeat by Japan in 1904–5. Transport to Manchuria was very slow, as the Trans-Siberian railway was single track with a hole in the middle, so that troops had to detrain at Lake Baikal and march to the other side of the lake to entrain. Bronze artillery was still used, because it was cheaper than steel, even if it was heavier and less accurate. The average age of the generals was 69, and half of them had not reached fourth form standard at school. (Ironically the army was a field of opportunity for the lower classes, but this meant that many officers came from peasant families which had enjoyed little access to education.)

The defeats at the hands of Japan reduced the prestige of the regime at home. Violence flared in the countryside and in the main urban centres, such as St Petersburg, to the extent that the disturbances have been termed 'the Revolution of 1905'. On Bloody Sunday in January 1905 a peaceful procession seeking redress of grievances from the Tsar was attacked by Cossack cavalry and nearly 1,000 people perished. The myth of the beneficent Tsar, the 'little father' of his people, was broken for ever.

Not that the last Tsar of all the Russias was the man to cope with the gathering crisis. Nicholas II (1894–1917) has often been described as a good family man who was too shy and gentle to be a firm autocrat. He was in fact densely self-assured and determined to remain an autocrat; in addition he was anti-Semitic and untrustworthy, especially in terms of giving honest support to his ministers. The Revolution of 1905 led to renewed demands for a central parliament and gave Nicholas the opportunity of transforming Russia into a constitutional state by collaborating with moderate liberal opinion. This chance he effectively spurned. Although a parliamentary assembly (duma) was created in 1906, Nicholas changed the electoral rules to ensure that it was conservative and powerless. Yet before 1914 the revolutionary groups in Russia had little support among urban workers or peasants. Therefore constitutional change along Western lines was still feasible, and, if implemented, would have prevented the violence of 1917 and the horrors of Stalinism.

In contrast genuine efforts at economic modernisation were made from the 1890s by Sergei Witte and Peter Stolypin. Witte was anxious to promote Russian industrialisation for the maintenance of Russia's great power status. The resources for state investment in new industries were gained by loans from France and heavy taxation of the peasantry. Railway development was spectacular and high tariffs excluded foreign competition. Stolypin rightly perceived that a solution of the peasant problem was essential. In 1900 80 per cent of the population were peasants, and although they had been emancipated from serfdom in 1861, the rising population had caused growing land hunger to the point where the peasants had become a revolutionary force by 1900. Therefore Stolypin brought in several important measures. In 1905 the peasants' redemption payments for the land they farmed were cancelled and peasants could now become the legal proprietors of their land. However, the village commune (mir) controlled many aspects of village life, including farm methods, and therefore between 1906 and 1911 laws were passed to facilitate the redistribution of land into consolidated sectors (as opposed to the former strip system). Peasants also gained the right to secede from the commune. Behind Stolypin's thinking was a desire to create a strong class of rich peasants (kulaks) who would support the regime.

Such reforms were, however, only a beginning and did not mollify the growing opposition to the regime in Russia. In addition to the liberals, Marxist groups arose in Russia and a united Marxist party, the Social Democratic Labour Party, was formed in 1898. it split in 1903, the Bolshevik group under Lenin insisting that the party should aim at forming an elite of dedicated revolutionaries while the Mensheviks under Martov wished to create a mass party. A third party, the Social Revolutionary Party under Victor Chernov, was found in 1901; its aim was land distribution to the peasants, and one of its key tactics was political assassination.

But perhaps the greatest threat to Tsarism came from the rapid industrialisation, which led to an increase in the size of the proletariat. Many of the new urban workers had not wished to leave the land, to which they were still emotionally attached. They missed the cohesion of village life and felt a sense of alienation in the cities. They lived in appallingly overcrowded tenements and experienced horrifyingly dangerous conditions at work. Unlike sections of the peasantry, urban workers did not experience an improvement in their lot in the boom period after 1906, when inflation outstripped wage rises and heavy taxation further eroded living standards.

Their harsh experiences as much as left-wing propaganda made the new urban working class more politically aware than the peasants and more capable of revolutionary organisation. In the unrest of 1905 workers formed themselves into soviets (workers' councils), not at the behest of any political party but on their own initiative. Though dispersed eventually, the potential of the soviets for future revolutionary activity was great, as Lenin appreciated.

Strikes by urban workers became more numerous and more political in nature after 1905. In 1909 only 340 strikes occurred; in 1914 the number had risen to 3,574. The government's only response was repression, which led to tragedy in the Lena goldfields in 1912 when troops killed 170 miners.

By 1914 Russia was becoming increasingly ungovernable and the royal family's personal prestige even lower. Nicholas and his wife Alexandra had fallen under the sway of a monk, Gregory Rasputin, after 1905, despite his capacity for drunken orgies and rape, because they believed that he could alleviate the Tsarevitch's haemophilia.

(e) Austria–Hungary

The growth of the Austrian Empire, ruled by the House of Habsburg, illustrated how essential was monarchy as a unifying force. The Emperor's possessions evolved into a formidable empire over more than four centuries, but in a haphazard way, with different territories having no common interest or history. Therefore the dynasty along with the army and bureaucracy performed a vital role in holding the territories together. Austria became a multi-national agglomeration which had evolved partly through war, mainly at Turkey's expense, but more through dynastic marriage and diplomatic shrewdness. As the fifteenth-century Hungarian wit Matthias Corvinus had put it, 'Let other powers make war! Thou, happy Austria, marry.'

However, this multinational state was ill-suited to a century which saw the growth of nationalism. In A. J. P. Taylor's words it was 'a collection of entailed estates, not a state and the Habsburgs were landlords, not rulers'. Inside the Empire were many important nationalities, including Germans, Magyars, Czechs, Italians, Slovaks, Ruthenes, Poles, Serbs, Croats and Slovenes. The supporters of the monarchy were well aware that, as nationalism and liberalism developed, the dissolution of the Habsburg lands might be imminent. Metternich, Austrian chancellor from the Napoleonic wars to 1848, was obsessed by this threat, and referred to his task as that of 'propping up the mouldering edifice'. The onset of industrialisation provided a further threat to imperial rule through the growth of an urban socialist movement.

Yet it has perhaps been too easy for historians to emphasise the ramshackle nature of the Empire and to assume that its disintegration in 1918 was inevitable. Industrialisation was a positive force in the Empire and was stimulated by a large internal free-trade market, while the socialism which grew with industrial expansion called for an allegiance which cut across the ethnic differences of nationality.

The monarchy was still popular because rule by one man was comprehensible to ordinary people, and it was still widely believed that only a hereditary monarch could rise above sectional interests and govern for the general good of all groups in society. Emperor Francis Joseph won the affection of his subjects, partly by the longevity of his rule. He had come to the throne in 1848, when Austria was in the throes of revolution, and his personal life was tragic. His son, Crown Prince Rudolf, committed suicide at Mayerling in 1889 and his wife Elizabeth was assassinated in 1898. Over time the Emperor became venerated, as he developed a patriarchal dignity and possessed a high sense of duty. Thus despite bringing in Russian troops to defeat Hungarian rebels in 1849 and losing the major wars in which Austria was engaged in the period (against France and Italy in 1859 and against Prussia in 1866), he remained as a unifying force.

A further element of stability had been provided by settlement of the Magyar problem in Hungary. The main threat to the Empire had been Magyar demands for Hungarian independence, but the Compromise of 1867 created the Dual Monarchy of Austria–Hungary. It placed Hungary on an equal footing with Austria and granted to each half of the Empire its own government, with control of internal affairs. The Magyars were reconciled to the unity of the Empire under Francis Joseph and the Compromise lasted until 1918, a long time by central European standards.

The Empire was well governed by an efficient, honest bureaucracy, and its more favoured regions, such as Bohemia, enjoyed a fast rate of industrial growth. The period before 1914 was also one of great cultural achievements. Vienna was, in the words of Robert Musil, a home for genius – for example Freud, Kokoschka and Mahler.

Thus the Austro-Hungarian Empire possessed some real resilience, despite its internal problems, and, as Grenville has shown, the destruction of the Empire was not seriously wanted by any of the major national groups before 1914. The Germans in Austria and the Magyars in Hungary enjoyed their dominant position. The Poles of Galicia enjoyed more freedom than their fellow Poles in Germany and Russia. The Jews found cultural opportunities in Vienna, and for the other subject nationalities – Czechs and South Slavs – imperial rule was seen as protection against a worse oppression. Agitation for independence was largely the work of a small minority among the more educated; the great majority of the Emperor's subjects were content to see the Empire continue.

However, the national groups did differ bitterly on the kind of Empire they wanted, and Francis Joseph failed to attack the nationality problem constructively. In the words of the Austrian satirist Karl Kraus, the Emperor was a Daemon of mediocrity and lacked ideas and imagination. After the 1867 Compromise he set his face against further reform and followed a policy of divide and rule. The result was some alienation of the loyalty of the non-German and non-Magyar majority of the Habsburg peoples. As C. A. Macartney has stressed, 'He simply did not appreciate the nature and the strength of the new forces which had grown larger since he was a younger man.' For example, the industrialised and prosperous Czechs resented German domination in Austria and believed that the Emperor had promised to turn the Dual Monarchy into a Triple Monarchy by elevating Bohemia into the same position as Austria and Hungary. To Czech disappointment the Emperor reneged on this promise in 1871 in the face of Magyar and German opposition.

By the end of the century a new virulence had entered Austrian politics, exacerbated by the rise of new parties. Georg von Schönerer's Pan-German movement preached the racial superiority of the Germans over the Slavs. Under Karl Lueger a new Christian Socialist party developed; in some ways it was progressive, for example in its demands for social insurance for workers, but it was also anti-Semitic. Both von Schönerer and Lueger were admired by the young Hitler. National groups increased their agitation and the government was forced to rely on its emergency powers as parliamentary life became paralysed.

In Hungary the Magyars monopolised political power more fully than the Germans in Austria. Only one ethnic group – the Croats – avoided complete domination, because they had remained loyal to the Emperor in 1848. Other nationalities in Hungary – Rumanians, Serbs and Slovaks – were forced to endure a policy of Magyarisation, with the Magyar language made compulsory in government, education, the law and even on the railways. The Emperor did consider suffrage reform in 1906 but again he backed away from change.

The Empire as a whole lagged behind the more advanced European states in economic development. The perennial lack of funds meant that the armed forces, composed of many nationalities and led by an incompetent general staff, were inadequate for the Empire's status as a great power. But the forces holding the Empire together – the centripetal forces, as Jaszi terms them – were many. In addition to the monarchy, the aristocracy, Church, army, civil service and even the nationalities to a greater or lesser extent supported the Empire. Only a devastating war and defeat broke Habsburg power and finally splintered the cohesion of the Empire.

(f) Britain

There is a persisting image that Britain in the late nineteenth and early twentieth centuries enjoyed a period of confidence and security only ended by the outbreak of war in 1914. On the face of it such an image seems accurate. Britain had successfully adapted to the conditions brought about by the Industrial Revolution. Her parliamentary system had been developed by extension of the suffrage in 1832, 1867 and 1884, while an act in 1872 brought in the secret ballot. Governments, both Conservative and Liberal, had extended the responsibilities of the state in the fields of education and social reform. The economy had passed peacefully through the difficult years after 1873, and, as Ashworth has stressed, real economic development did occur then despite some lost opportunities. Britain's Empire in India and Africa was the largest in the world and was defended by the world's most powerful navy. Superficially the Edwardian age was elegant and opulent, Edward VII himself giving a lead to fashionable society.

Nonetheless the image of a strong confident Britain is erroneous, because by the 1900s a new mood of apprehension about the future had arisen in British circles. Behind this apprehension lay four particular concerns – the rise of competitor nations, imperial problems, the stagnation of the British economy and doubts about national unity at home.

By the 1890s Britain faced a more competitive world. Her traditional rivals in the nineteenth century had been Russia and France, but German colonial and naval policy added a third potential threat. Thus by 1914 the most striking aspect of Britain's world position was the contrast between the appearance of her world power and its reality. The British Empire might cover a world map with many blobs of red but in practice this meant that a crisis anywhere in the world would threaten to involve Britain. Even with the world's largest navy there was no guarantee that the British in all eventualities would have the resources to protect the whole Empire. The reality that British resources were overstretched was demonstrated by the Boer War, and a policy of alliances replaced 'splendid isolation' in the 1890s.

The search for allies was accelerated by worries over imperial unity. The possibility that existing colonies would go the way of the American Colonies in 1776 in demanding and obtaining independence had to be faced. Already dominion status – self-government only a step short of total independence – had been granted to Canada in 1867, to New Zealand in 1876, to Australia in 1901 and South Africa in 1909. The bright jewel of the Empire, India, was no longer seen as a secure possession. The Indian Mutiny of 1857 was not forgotten, while in 1885 the first Indian National Congress had met and, though it admired aspects of British influence, its long-term objective was Indian independence.

The twin concerns of growing Anglo-German hostility and doubts about imperial solidarity led to fears of a German invasion and a belief in the reality of the ubiquitous German spy. A new genre of spy stories developed. Examples include Erskine Childers' *Riddle of the Sands* and William Le Queux's *The Invasion of 1910*. As David French has shown, spy fever was aroused to such an extent in the first decade of the twentieth century that in 1911 it led to an amendment of the Official Secrets Act.

The period saw more and more pessimism over the steady erosion of Britain's former dominance of world trade and industry. In 1872 Britain had been responsible for 32 per cent of world output but by 1900 her share had fallen to 19 per cent. It was appreciated that British industry was lagging behind that of the USA and Germany. In addition, industrial rivals would continue to rise from the less developed world, and by 1914 some British industries, in particular textiles, were feeling the strength of Indian and Japanese competition. True the traditional industries – steel, coal and textiles – continued to grow strongly and Britain remained the world's financial centre. However, she was less strongly represented in the new growth industries of the 'second' Industrial Revolution (chemicals, cars, electrical goods) and her relative decline seemed likely to continue.

In the face of foreign threats and economic strains, would national unity hold? The period saw the rise of a new working-class party, the Labour Party, while the British trade union movement revealed a new militancy in the 1900s. The unions were furious at the 1900 Taff Vale legal decision which made a union liable for damages caused by a strike even when it was unofficial. The unions were also disappointed by Liberal government policies after 1906 and their real

wages were eroded by rising inflation. Consequently an unprecedented number of strikes in 1911 and 1912 threatened industrial
peace. At the same time the growth of the suffragette movement led
to spectacular demonstrations and acts of violence to gain the vote for
women.

But the very unity of the United Kingdom itself was threatened by
the problem of Ireland. British policy in Ireland had been characterised by the giving of too little too late on Irelands' political, religious
and economic grievances. By the 1880s Irish national feeling had
grown to such a pitch that the Liberal prime minister Gladstone
became convinced of the need for Irish Home Rule. His attempts to
give Ireland self-government within the Empire were, however,
defeated in 1886 and 1893. In 1912 Asquith introduced a third Home
Rule bill into the Commons, a move that infuriated Ulster Protestants, who wished to remain within the United Kingdom. Both the
Ulstermen and Sinn Fein, the Irish republican movement which
wanted an independent Ireland, raised private armies. Britain was
therefore threatened with civil war, and only the outbreak of the First
World War allowed Asquith the opportunity of postponing the
confrontation.

Despite such problems, the period before 1914 saw some creative
reform by British governments. The Conservative government of
1902–5 introduced educational reform and the Liberals after 1906
introduced measures which laid the foundations of the Welfare State
– old age pensions and national insurance, for example – and also
limited the power of the House of Lords after a prolonged struggle in
1911. For all her internal divisions, Britain with her Empire entered
the First World War united.

(g) The United States

After the thirteen original American Colonies had won their independence from Britain between 1775 and 1783, the new United States
of America followed George Washington's dictum of no entangling
alliances. The main lines of direction in national life in the nineteenth
century were the development of national institutions, the expansion
of national territory by westward emigration (the moving frontier),
economic development and the preservation of unity. In contrast the
twentieth century was to see the USA emerge as a superpower, and
probably no nation has ever exercised so much global influence as did
the USA in the two or three decades after 1945.

The roots of American world power were demographic and economic. In 1880 the American population was only 50 million, 5 million
more than that of Germany. But from then on the USA outdistanced
all European states except Russia, and by 1930 the American population had risen to 122 million. A crucial factor in this population

growth was large-scale emigration from Europe. Both 'push' and 'pull' influences were at work. Many Europeans were driven from their original homes by poverty and political or religious persecution, and the USA was a beacon of hope for a better life. More than 13 million people flooded into the USA between 1900 and 1914, mainly from central and southern Europe. These 'new' immigrants (to distinguish them from the 'old' immigrants from Northern Europe) settled in the major cities and contributed to economic expansion. More than 1 million were Jews fleeing from pogroms in Russia.

The USA was attractive to these immigrants not only because of its economic opportunities but also because American society was in many ways more egalitarian than Europe's. The USA was the country where the accident of social status mattered less than elsewhere in the Western world. The great exceptions to this rule were the cases of the indigenous Indian population (which was largely wiped out by the whites) and the blacks brought over as slaves to work the cotton plantations. Though negroes were granted emancipation from slavery in 1865, they remained second-class citizens.

American economic growth was explosive; the years 1900 to 1914 saw industrial production double and manufacturing overtake agriculture as the main source of national wealth. Before 1900 America had still been a nation of farmers, artisans and small businessmen but the America of the twentieth century was industrial and urban, with industry dominated by such giant corporations as Rockefeller's Standard Oil.

The explosive growth in the American economy was facilitated by the abundant labour, the enterprising nature of the population and by the opening up through railway development of a continent singularly blessed with natural resources – fertile farm land, forests, coal, iron and oil. Their simultaneous successful development caused a rate of economic growth that no European nation could match, and meant that the USA was less dependent on imports and exports than other advanced countries. The Americans were pioneers of new forms of business techniques (Taylor's time and motion study, for example) and were foremost in the creation of new industries that maintained the economic lead of the USA – chemicals, electricity and the car industry.

Americans were too prone to think of their country as uniquely different to Europe in the sense that the USA enshrined liberty, progress and manifest destiny. One of the chief founding fathers of the nation, John Adams, had written in his diary in 1765, 'America was designed by providence for the theatre in which Man is to make his true figure.' Certainly the descendants of the founding fathers saw a unique destiny opening up for the new nation in the nineteenth century, with its society enjoying more wealth and equality of opportunity than the old societies of Europe. This view was not an unreasonable one; the new nation had the most democratic institutions in the world, established firmly by the Federal Constitution, which laid down the powers of the President and the role of the two houses of Congress – the Senate (the upper house) and the House of Representatives (the lower house).

However, soon after the middle of the nineteenth century Americans began to meet problems with which other nations were only too familiar. Between 1861 and 1865 a bitter civil war took place over the right of the Southern states to secede from the Union, and underpinning the quarrel was the slave status of the negroes of the Southern plantations. In 1890 the Bureau of Census declared that the frontier (the zone of land available for settlement), which had been moving westward since 1607, was now closed. In 1893 the USA experienced a severe economic depression and looked much less like the land of opportunity. Finally, in 1898 the USA went to war with Spain, emerged victorious and became a colonial power in the European sense by the acquisition of overseas colonies.

The nation now experienced many of the same political and social tensions that had plagued Europe. The gap between rich and poor widened and successful industrialists were viewed less as captains of industry and more in the role of robber barons. Western farmers often were caught in the Catch 22 situation that farmers all over the world have faced. A good harvest would drive down the price ruinously, while a poor harvest would mean that the farmers had little to sell. Their plight, they claimed, was made worse by high interest rates on their loans, a result of a government policy over-influenced by the industrial East. In the South economic growth was relatively slow, as the economy there failed to diversify sufficiently and cotton was no longer as profitable as before the Civil War.

No new left-wing party emerged to challenge the monopoly of power enjoyed by the Republican and Democratic parties, nor was the American trade union movement, the American Federation of Labour, able to recruit a large percentage of workers or defeat employers backed by the Federal government. Yet the period between 1901 and 1917 has been called the Progressive Era, and a Progressive Movement which aimed to clean up political corruption and the domination of politics by big business did have some success. Theodore Roosevelt, president from 1901 to 1909, did reduce restrictive practices in business, especially in the transport sector, and helped to win higher wages for miners. The development of a new group of journalists who accepted what was meant to be an insulting description of their work – the Muckrakers – meant that social evils were more publicised. In many states this helped to lead to laws which improved the working conditions of women and children. Yet in the main the Progressive Movement failed because its supporters were divided over methods of reform and their influence was undercut by the massive emigration, which made any improvement in the working man's lot difficult.

Theodore Roosevelt was one of the most nationalistic of American presidents, and his adage 'Speak softly and carry a big stick' denotes his interest in a large navy as a protector of American interests. He was one of a growing number of Americans who feared the future direction of European imperialism. In particular they were worried that Spanish influence in Cuba might give way to British or German control. Therefore an aggressive strain entered American foreign policy. In 1898 the USA picked a war with Spain – 'a splendid little war' in John Hay's phrase – and after crushing victories over the Spaniards acquired Puerto Rico and the Philippines and obtained the independence of Cuba from Spain.

The motives for the war were largely defensive. Yet as S. E. Morison has shown, the war pulled the USA into world politics. 'Responsibility for the Philippines made the USA a power in the Far East, involved her in Asian power politics and made an eventual war with Japan probable. Annexing the Philippines was a major turning-point in American history.' Though Americans came to accept growing engagement in world politics with considerable reluctance, the potential for the exercise of world influence now existed and the clock could not be turned back.

(4) The road to war, 1890–1914

(a) The Franco-Russian entente

The fall of Bismarck (summarily dismissed by William II) in March 1890 was a great turning point in European diplomacy. Ever since 1871 he had followed a policy of restraint, and he bequeathed to Germany a strong international position. Given astute handling, his system was workable, but it was doomed once William II ascended the throne in 1888. By 1907 Germany's diplomatic position was no longer secure: a coalition had drawn together against her, forged by a series of German blunders as well as by the designs in German world policy.

The first blunder was not long in coming. William was much influenced by Holstein, who was anti-Russian. German foreign policy now aimed at friendship with Britain as well as with Austria-Hungary, and because William disliked the complexity of Bismarck's alliances, a more open style of diplomacy was attempted. Accordingly, when the Russian foreign secretary Shuvalov in March 1890 proposed the renewal of the Reinsurance Treaty for 6 years, he was astonished at German rejection of the proposal on the grounds that it would offend British and German public opinion. The non-renewal of the treaty restored to Russia a freedom of action which at the time was not desired. Russian suspicion of German aims was further aroused in July by the Anglo-German colonial agreement, by which Germany gained Heligoland in return for giving up her rights in Zanzibar and limiting her rights in East Africa. Good in itself, the agreement made both the Russians and the French believe that a virtual Anglo-German alliance had come into existence.

Fear of isolation gradually drew Russia and France together, yet the process was slow and certainly not inevitable. The reactionary Alexander III was reluctant to make any firm alliance with a republican government, and it was left to the French to press hard for negotiations, alarmed at the renewal of the Triple Alliance in May 1891, and the erratic personality of William II. Yet Alexander himself resented the drawing together of Britain and the Triple Alliance and was acutely aware of his country's need for French loans, which might be withheld if he refused an alliance with France. Therefore in July 1891 a French squadron visited Kronstadt and the tsar even stood bare-headed to listen to the Marseillaise.

Serious negotiations now began. A major difficulty was that France wanted an alliance directed primarily against Germany, but the Russians wanted an alliance directed mainly against Britain. The Russians still had reservations at the idea of an alliance and wanted a general agreement which would in practice leave them with freedom of action. In contrast, the French wanted specific guarantees of Russian help if they were embroiled in a conflict with the Triple Alliance powers or Britain. In August the two powers agreed to consult on necessary measures if one of the parties were menaced by aggression. Though it was a vague arrangement, this new entente was a turning point in the history of Europe, and it was soon given military teeth. In December 1893 a military convention was signed, the two partners pledging themselves to give each other assistance in the event of any attack by Germany. The general staffs of the two countries were to hold talks and mobilisation would take place if any of the Triple Alliance powers mobilised, the French supplying 1,200,000 troops and the Russians not less than 700,000. The alliance was now a reality. Its aim was to keep Germany neutral while the two partners pursued their ambitions overseas. In most crises diplomatic support was all that the new allies were to give each other and it was a passive alliance as late as the Russo-Japanese war of 1904–5. 'All the same', remarks A. J. P. Taylor, 'it was a weapon loaded only against Germany.'

The Germans at the time did not take this new development very seriously. Indeed they believed that it might improve their position by forcing Britain into the Triple Alliance. The new alliance did have an anti-British aspect, for both powers would be better placed to defeat Britain when there was a collision of colonial interests, say in Egypt or the Far East.

(b) The British position

The British reaction to the new alliance was one of apprehension. In a Europe divided into two blocs, at a time when European interests had become global, Britain came to feel more and more isolated, especially in view of the tone of German diplomacy. The Germans aimed at bringing Britain into the Triple Alliance but mistakenly believed that they would achieve this by blackmail and threats. The peremptory tone of German diplomats irritated British statesmen, as the German historian Brandenburg admits. 'The way in which German policy invariably opened fire at once with its biggest guns was extremely antipathetic to English statesmen who were more tranquil and tolerant, and very sensitive to threat.'

The weakness of the British position became very clear from 1895, when a series of diplomatic crises forced the British to seek allies. Their isolation became very evident in the Far East, now assuming great importance in European diplomacy. Britain had long been accustomed to a dominant position in China, but this state of affairs was now threatened by other European powers, especially Russia. But a new power had arisen in the Far East itself.

Japan, from being a medieval state earlier in the nineteenth century, was by the 1890s in the course of being transformed into a modern industrial state, and the Japanese were determined to make their country a great power. They particularly coveted Korea and were fearful of being forestalled there by the Russians. In September 1894 they waged a successful war against China and the Chinese government was forced to sign the Treaty of Shimonoseki in April 1895. By the treaty Korea became independent and Japan gained Port Arthur and the Liaotung Peninsula, the keys to Manchuria and North China. The Russians were furious at Japanese success and organised a joint protest, being joined by Germany and France. The Japanese government was forced to 'bear the unbearable' and return its gains to China. It was a cynical move by the European powers, for they were soon to extract concessions from China themselves. For Britain the affair was novel and humiliating. The other powers had simply elbowed her aside in an area which had formerly been a British preserve.

Further British embarrassment occurred in South Africa. The existence there of independent Boer republics, especially the Transvaal, hampered the British objective of a united South Africa which would give security at the Cape. In December 1895 Dr Jameson, an agent of Cecil Rhodes, prime minister of Cape Colony, launched an abortive raid into the Transvaal in the hope of provoking an uprising of the Uitlanders (white non-Boers). The raid, in which Joseph Chamberlain was implicated, was a fiasco and gave an opportunity to the Germans to thrust themselves forward as champions of Boer independence. In January 1896 William II sent a telegram to Kruger, the Boer president, congratulating him on having preserved the independence of his country 'without appealing to the help of friendly powers'. This was a gross miscalculation; the British responded strongly by organising a flying squadron, a powerful and fast naval force, which made it ridiculous for the Germans to imply that they could defend the Transvaal. Langer is right to refer to William's diplomacy as 'amateurish jockeyings' and calls the telegram one of the greatest blunders in the history of modern diplomacy. The Kaiser later sent Queen Victoria a letter, explaining rather lamely that the telegram was sent in the name of peace. It had, however, crystallised British resentment of German economic rivalry and aroused similar feelings against Britain in Germany, where pressure for the development of a strong navy grew. Unfortunately William did not learn from the affair; he was to make similar errors in the future.

African affairs continued to trouble the British. In 1898 they clashed with France over control of the Sudan. The French had no alternative but to give way because the Dreyfus Affair was pulling France towards civil war, and in any case the British possessed a superior navy and already had an army in the disputed area. The quarrel aroused the furious anglophobia of the French public, but paradoxically the affair encouraged Delcassé the French foreign minister to aim at a reconciliation with Britain.

British self-satisfaction over the result of the Sudan incident was short-lived. In October 1899 came the outbreak of the Boer War, which proved to be a much tougher campaign than the British expected, 300,000 troops being required to crush the resistance of 60,000 Boers. The war was an uncomfortable demonstration of Britain's lack of allies as well as proof of the limitations of the British army. On the continent public opinion strongly favoured the Boers, and there was much talk of a continental league against Britain, though this necessarily remained talk, because the decisive factor in the situation was the British navy; but if British security at home was never in doubt, Britain's interests elsewhere certainly were, because both the armed forces were fully extended by the war.

(c) German world policy

In the late 1890s the opportunities for peace in Europe were considerable, for in April 1897 came an Austro-Russian agreement to maintain the status quo in the Middle East. For the next decade the Balkans were relatively quiet and in 1897 no burning issue in Europe threatened peace. It was singularly unfortunate therefore that 1897 marked a distinct change of course in German policy – the promotion of a thrusting, forward attitude in world affairs. It was motivated by a craving for prestige, a 'place in the sun', as befitted a nation of Germany's rank, but it was also a ruse to divert public attention away from difficulties at home. The flaw in the policy was that Germany could not play a world role; she was a European power with two hostile neighbours, and the clumsiness of her diplomacy was to add Britain to the number of her potential enemies.

The German government came to see that for purposes of world greatness a strong navy must be developed. William, influenced by Tirpitz, became enthusiastic at the idea of Germany possessing a formidable battle fleet and in March 1898 the German Navy Code was enacted. Behind German thinking was the belief that the possession of a strong navy would force Britain into an alliance with Germany, and at the same time break Britain's worldwide predominance. It was dangerously like blackmail and the British resented it. The Germans failed to comprehend the British feeling that such a development undermined their security as an island state with a scattered empire. As Winston Churchill put it, the British fleet was a necessity and the German fleet was a luxury. Germany was already the most powerful military state; against whom would she wish to use a powerful navy? The answer to the British could only be – the greatest naval power. The German attitude to these fears was unsympathetic, as E. L. Woodward has demonstrated:

> In public discussions and in official negotiations, the German people and their rulers took little account of English susceptibilities and fears. They were inclined to complain of exaggerated suspicions and unreasonable anxiety. They did not pay enough attention to the fair and logical deductions which might be made not merely from their words but from the steady increase in the number of their ships.

At first the German challenge did not appear very serious, for despite a further increase in the German fleet in 1900, the British lead appeared unassailable. In 1906, however, the British admiralty launched the *Dreadnought*, the first all big-gun ship, which made all existing battleships obsolete. The British now had to reconstruct their lead and an expensive naval arms race began. British suggestions that the naval programmes be cut in 1908 were turned down by the Germans. Public opinion in Britain now backed the government in its naval development. 'We want eight and we won't wait', was the cry of the public in 1909 when the Germans were thought to be catching the British up. German naval policy gradually estranged Britain while serving no important national interest whatsoever. If the Germans had abandoned their unnecessary naval programme, they might well have won British neutrality in the war, and, with the extra resources available, have won it as well. When war did come, the German fleet, despite its quality, proved to be a white elephant, fighting only one major engagement. The naval rivalry pushed Britain and France towards an informal alliance which Grey, foreign secretary from 1906, came to regard as a morally binding commitment, so that in the event of war it would be difficult for Britain to keep out.

The second aspect of German world policy was the new willingness of the German government to make unexpected incursions into any international issue. By 1897 the issue that overshadowed all others was the Far East. In Taylor's phrase China had taken the place of Turkey as the pre-eminent Sick Man; and between 1897 and 1905 the future of China determined the relations of the great powers. The Germans helped to provoke a period of crisis in Far Eastern affairs by seizing Kiao-Chow in November 1897, thus precipitating the seizure of Chinese territory by other powers. The Russians took over Port Arthur and the British gained Wei-Hai-wei, an insufficient sop to the British public, which termed it Woe-Woe-Woe. This degree of foreign aggression stimulated the growth of a nationalistic Chinese organisation called the Society of the Harmonious Fists (the Boxers). In June 1900 came the Boxer Rising which led to the siege of the European legations in China. Though the legations were saved by a joint European military expedition, the troubles gave Russia a pretext for invading Manchuria, and British interests in the Far East appeared even more precarious.

(d) The creation of new alliances, 1902–7

The conclusion of the Franco-Russian alliance, German pressure and the strain of her global commitments made Britain seek closer relations with several powers after 1894. In January 1898 the British sought some deal over the Far East with Russia but the Russians broke off negotiations and seized Port Arthur as a base to exploit Manchuria and challenge British trade in China. The British therefore turned to Germany and three main attempts were made in 1898, 1899 and 1901 to form an alliance, but to no avail.

The course of events was now influenced by Japan. The Japanese had viewed the European gains in China in 1897 and 1898 with impotent rage and felt that their stake in Korea was being increasingly threatened by Russia. In 1901 they sought desperately for an alliance with either Russia or Britain. The Russians would not compromise over the Korean question but the British, engaged in the Boer War and anxious to safeguard their Far Eastern interests, came to an agreement with Japan in January 1902. The treaty recognised Korea as Japan's special sphere of influence and provided for intervention by one partner if the other partner went to war with two powers. Now Japan could go to war with Russia confident that Britain would keep France neutral, while Britain could afford to concentrate more of the fleet in home waters with an ally in the Far East to protect her interests there. In a European context the alliance confirmed rather than ended Britain's isolation, for she could now stay aloof of European powers, especially with a recent improvement in her naval strength.

Nevertheless Britain's relations with France since the Sudan quarrel had started to improve, while Anglo-German relations had continued to deteriorate. The British refused to contribute capital required by German entrepreneurs for the construction of the Berlin to Bagdad railway, thus delaying its completion until 1914. Meanwhile an Anglo-French rapprochement was worked at by Delcassé. The influence of Edward VII was useful in promoting a more cordial relationship between the two countries, and in 1903 he visited Paris for the first time as king. Hard negotiations between Delcassé and Lansdowne came to fruition in April 1904 with the signing of an Anglo-French entente. It settled minor disputes over Siam and Newfoundland fishing rights but the main issues were Egypt and Morocco. Britain agreed that Morocco was a French sphere of influence, while the French in their turn admitted British supremacy in Egypt. The two powers agreed to give each other support in the event of any modification in the status quo in those two areas.

At the time it was the French who appeared to have conceded most; they renounced in Egypt an area of proven worth while Morocco's value, great in the future, was an unknown quantity in 1904. The French hand was to some extent forced by the outbreak of the Russo-Japanese war in February, which made them anxious to limit the area of conflict to the Far East. In the long run they were aiming at more than a mere settling of colonial disputes; they wanted a firm alliance with Britain as further protection against Germany. Perhaps the British did not quite realise this, as they wished to live in peace with other countries and did not foresee how the entente would become a more binding commitment. The German government was sure that Britain had taken a firm stand with France against the Triple Alliance and was soon to put pressure on the new entente.

German opportunities to do so were created by the new developments in the Far East. The Russian refusal to compromise over Korea finally exhausted Japanese patience. In February 1904 Japan precipitated war by a surprise attack on Port Arthur. The war had an epic quality, with clear-cut victories in major engagements for the Japanese and chivalry shown on both sides. Port Arthur after siege by land and sea fell in January 1905, and on the other major front the Japanese won the Battle of Mukden in March. The Russians in desperation sent their Baltic fleet round the world to the Far East and on the way it caused a row with Britain by firing in panic on British fishing boats on the Dogger Bank in October. The Japanese admiral, Togo, worked out the course which the Russian fleet would take and was able to annihilate it at Tsushima in May, only two out of forty ships escaping destruction. The Japanese victories were gained by superior command and organisation, by the advantage of shorter supply lines and fervent public support for the war. After such defeats the Russian government, with a revolution at home, was forced to sue for peace and it found Japan willing to negotiate, for the war had strained Japanese resources as well. Therefore in September 1905 the Treaty of Portsmouth was signed, the Russians recognising Korea as a Japanese sphere of influence and ceding the Liaotung Peninsula and the southern half of Sakhalin.

In the long run the war was to alter the course of history, and as the French ambassador to Britain, Paul Cambon, remarked, it was to 'weigh upon the whole century'. Japan was now a great power in the Far East and it was significant that in 1905 her alliance with Britain was modified so that in the future one partner would help the other in the event of attack by one or more powers. Japan was now on the road to confrontation with the United States and she had destroyed the myth of the White Man's invincibility, thus stimulating the growth of Asian nationalism.

Russia no longer counted as a great power until the military reforms after 1905 began to take effect. Her relations with Japan now improved and further agreements on spheres of influence took place in 1907 and 1910. Russia in fact kept control of Manchuria, and the emphasis of her foreign policy after defeat in the Far East shifted back to the Balkans, with fateful consequences for European peace.

The destruction of Russian power presented the Germans with a unique opportunity to change the European balance of power in their favour. They had two alternative lines of action. They could maintain friendly neutrality in the war to win Russian support or they could attack France while her major ally was helpless. In fact the Germans muddled along, trying to do both. During the war a series of telegrams passed between the Tsar and the Kaiser, known as the Willy–Nicky correspondence. William tried to persuade the Tsar that British neutrality in the war was really anti-Russian. In July 1905 he met Nicholas II on a Baltic yachting cruise and they signed the Treaty of Bjorko, a defensive alliance against attack by an European power in Europe. William hoped that the French would have to join the alliance and would thus be separated from their new partner, Britain. In practice the treaty became a dead letter almost immediately. The Russians soon realised that the alliance would be of no military value in the Far East. Nor would it even keep Britain neutral in the event of a second Russo-Japanese war, for Britain in August pledged herself to help Japan if war broke out. The alliance also offended the French and threatened the supply of French loans which were so necessary for Russian recovery.

The second German move during the Russo-Japanese war was interference in the affairs of Morocco to show the world that Germany could not be ignored in any international issue and perhaps to shake the Anglo-French entente. In March 1905 William was induced by Holstein and Bulow to break his Mediterranean cruise by landing at Tangier. He assured the Sultan of Morocco that he regarded him as a free and independent sovereign, thus repudiating the Anglo-French agreement on Morocco. The Germans next demanded a conference on the question and won the first round of the dispute because Delcassé who opposed surrender to the German demand found the rest of the French cabinet against him and resigned. The conference met at Algeciras in January 1906 and went very differently to German expectations. At the conference not only Britain supported French claims in Morocco but also Russia, Spain, Italy and the United States. Imperial Germany was unaccustomed to such a rebuff, which ended Holstein's career. The Germans had not been aiming at war and they had a good case on the Moroccan question, over which they had never been consulted. But the brusque stupidity of their diplomacy ruined their case and strengthened, rather than weakened, the Anglo-French entente. Grey, the new British foreign secretary, authorised conversations between the British and French general staffs.

The Moroccan crisis also contributed to a reconciliation between Britain and Russia. The British for years had wanted to settle various questions which kept them at loggerheads with the Russians. After their defeat by Japan, the Russians were more willing to negotiate than before. Izvolsky, who became Russian foreign minister in 1906, favoured a rapprochement with Britain, and in August 1907 the main areas of friction were settled. Tibet was made a buffer state and the Russians renounced direct contact with Afghanistan, so that India's north-west frontier became more secure. The main question was Persia, which was to be divided into three zones, the north becoming a Russian sphere of interest and the south-east adjacent to India a British sphere of interest, with a neutral zone in the centre.

As with the Anglo-French entente, the agreement was an elimination of differences, not an alliance. Relations between the two countries remained uneasy because of continued Russian advances in Persia and the hostility of liberal opinion in Britain towards agreement with autocratic Russia. 'If the Germans had kept quiet', notes A. J. P. Taylor, 'the triple entente might soon have dissolved; instead their actions turned it into a reality.' The Germans came to believe that Britain was following a deliberate policy of encircling Germany when in fact the British moves were purely precautionary. After 1907 fear of encirclement undermined any remaining commonsense in German policy that might have checked the drift to war.

(e) The growth of tension, 1908–14

The Austro-Russian agreement of 1897 had in Taylor's phrase put the Balkans 'on ice' for a decade, though it still remained a problem area. The years after 1897 saw a sharp decline in Austro-Serb relations. Austro-Hungarian treatment of Slavs inside the Empire angered the Serbs, who dreamt of a Great Yugoslavia. In 1903 the pro-Austrian Alexander of Serbia was murdered and Peter Karageorge, who favoured closer relations with Russia, became king. The Serbian prime minister, Pasich, tried to break Serbia's economic dependence on Austria by finding new markets in the Balkans, and French capital helped the growth of Serb armaments. As Turner indicates, Serbia became 'potentially the most explosive element in the Balkans and she regarded covetously Austria-Hungary's Slav provinces – Bosnia, Croatia and Dalmatia'. Behind this nationalistic thinking was a strategic motive – the desire to gain an outlet on to the Adriatic.

But if Serb ambitions threatened peace in the Balkans, so did those of Austria-Hungary. With the appointment of Aerenthal as foreign minister and Conrad von Hotzendorff as army chief in 1906, a gambling spirit entered Austrian diplomacy. Austrian policy now aimed at the elimination of Serbia, because it was believed to be the nucleus of a South Slav state which would stimulate unrest among the Croats and Serbs within the Empire.

The opportunity for action in the Balkans came with a revolt in Turkey in 1908 by the Young Turk movement, which aimed at more liberal efficient government. The arrogant Aerenthal saw in Turkey's discomfiture a chance to restore the prestige of the monarchy by annexing Bosnia–Herzegovina, which in any case had been administered by the Austrians since 1878. In September 1908 he secured consent of the Russian foreign minister Izvolsky to the annexation, in return for Austrian support for a revision of the Treaty of Berlin by reopening the Straits to Russian warships. Izvolsky was led to believe that a formal conference of the powers would approve the annexation, but instead Aerenthal issued a unilateral declaration on the matter and Izvolsky felt that he had been cheated. Stolypin and Nicholas II, who felt that Izvolsky had in any case exceeded his instructions, were furious and so of course were the Serbian and Turkish governments. Grey expressed the British view that the annexation 'struck at the roots of all good international order'. Even the Germans were annoyed at the Austrian action, for they had received little notice of Aerenthal's intentions. However, when the Russians demanded a conference on the question, the Austrians were able to reject it because of a promise of military support from Germany. Moltke, the chief of the general staff, with the approval of William and Bulow said that Germany would mobilise as soon as Russia did. Convinced of Russian weakness, the Germans went further and demanded in March 1909 that Russia recognise the annexation of Bosnia–Herzogovina and make Serbia do the same. The demand contained a scarcely veiled threat of military action and the Russians, who could not be sure of any support from Britain or France, were forced to give way.

Aerenthal's vanity had screwed up tension in the Balkans, which became once more in Anderson's phrase 'the powder-keg of European politics'. The Russians accelerated their military reforms, conscious that if they were forced to surrender in any future confrontation, they would lose all credibility as a great power. The German attitude in 1909 boded ill for the future. Convinced that the balance of power in Europe was turning against them, they felt obliged to support Austria-Hungary, their only reliable ally. This clear case of the tail wagging the dog would have disgusted Bismarck. The crisis indicated that the German army would always be on hand to support Austrian adventures and the Austrians knew it. Yet even if Austrian objectives were gained, the only result would be to increase the number of dissident Slavs within the Empire. The crisis foreshadowed that of July 1914 in all its essentials.

Tension in Europe was made even more acute by a second row over Morocco. Franco-German relations over this issue improved after 1905, with agreements in 1908 and 1909. In April 1911 the French were able to extend their control in Morocco by answering the appeal of the sultan for assistance in crushing a revolt in Fez. The Germans would have been well advised to ignore this development but in the propaganda of the Pan-German League Morocco had been built up as a great economic prize. The new German foreign secretary, Kiderlen-Wachter, had drafted the aggressive note to Russia in 1909 and believed that similar tactics over Morocco would split the Triple Entente powers. Therefore he persuaded Bethmann-Hollweg and William to declare the French action a violation of the treaty of Algeciras and also to send a warship, the *Panther*, to Agadir ostensibly to protect German lives and property.

The result of this inept move was only too predictable. In Winston Churchill's words, 'all the alarm bells throughout Europe began to quiver'. The British response was particularly startling, for they believed, though mistakenly, that the Germans were planning to establish a naval base on the West Atlantic. It was particularly striking that Lloyd George, a pacifist during the Boer War, should refer in a speech at the Mansion House to Britain's resolve 'at all hazards to maintain her place and her prestige'. In the end Kiderlen-Wachter, who had demanded all the French Congo as compensation for Germany, had to be content with a slice of it in return for recognising a French protectorate in Morocco.

The Agadir crisis was of profound importance in the events leading up to the war. In France it cemented a previously divided public

opinion against Germany and France's new determination was symbolised by the accession of the hard-liner Poincaré to the premiership
in 1912. The Germans, who had wanted to check French control in
Morocco, had failed to do so and had received another diplomatic
rebuff. Their injured pride rather than world policy would mean that
in future crises they could not back down again. Anglo-German
relations dipped sharply, and the Conservative leader Heydebrand
was cheered when he said in the Reichstag that the incident showed
who the real enemy was. Tirpitz was able to persuade the German
Goverment to plan further increases in the navy, and these went
ahead despite Haldane's visit to Berlin in 1912 to try to limit the naval
race. As a result the British and French naval staffs held talks and
decided that the French fleet would safeguard the Mediterranean
while the British fleet would concentrate on the Channel and North
Sea. The Anglo-French entente was now virtually a military alliance.
All over Europe there was the feeling that war was just a matter of
time.

One of the many unfortunate results of the Agadir crisis was the
way in which it incited the Italians to attack Tripoli in 1911 in order to
gain compensation for the French acquisition of Morocco. The Italian
aggression in turn excited the ambitions of the small Balkan states
bordering Turkey. A Balkan League was formed in 1912 consisting of
Serbia, Bulgaria, Greece and Montenegro, and its objective was to
drive Turkey out of Europe. The League had the support of Russia
and France, because a Slav victory would undermine Austrian security. The risk of the war becoming general was considered worth
taking. In October 1912 the League powers attacked Turkey,
Adrianople fell, and the Turks were forced to make peace. Germany
and Austria-Hungary had stood aside, assuming that Turkey would
be victorious, when in fact the victory of Balkan nationalism was a
disaster for them. By the Treaty of London of May 1913 Turkey was
left with Constantinople and its environs, Albania was reserved for
disposal by the great powers and the rest of the mainland was left for
the members of the League to distribute among themselves.

But war now broke out among the victors over division of the
spoils, when Bulgaria, encouraged by the Austrians, attacked Serbia
in June. The attack was routed and the Bulgarians now found Turkey
in the field against them as well as Serbia. Finally, by the Treaty of
Bucharest of August 1913, Bulgaria was forced to cede her gains in
Macedonia to Serbia and Greece, while Eastern Thrace and Adrianople were returned to Turkey. The Serbs also wanted Albania as an
outlet to the sea and insisted on keeping troops there despite the
disapproval of the great powers. In October they had to yield to an
Austrian ultimatum, again backed by Germany, William declaring
grandiloquently that he would draw his sword whenever Austria
needed help.

Nevertheless Austria-Hungary's strategic position had declined sharply as a result of the two Balkan Wars, for Serbia was now a formidable Balkan power capable of putting 400,000 troops into the field. Indeed both the Central Powers were worried at the way in which the military balance of power appeared to be turning against them. Austria's army had a peace-time strength of 475,000 and Germany's 651,000, but these numbers appeared inadequate compared to France's army of 600,000 and Russia's, which numbered 1,300,000 men and was expected to become a force of 2 million men by 1917. The British were expected to join in a general war by the Germans and Moltke admitted that they were opponents 'not to be underestimated'. This situation appears to have created a sense of fatalism in the minds of the German leaders. William, Bethmann and Moltke were pessimistic about Germany's chances in a general war, but felt that time would only serve to make the position more hopeless. When war broke out in 1914, the German plan of campaign, as Corelli Barnett demonstrates, was not at all an aggression plotted by a general staff conscious of great power, but a desperate sally by men haunted by numerical weakness.

By 1914 any crisis was likely to precipitate war because of military considerations. The French and the Russians were well aware of the implications of the Schlieffen Plan and had their own plans to dislocate it, the French by attacking Lorraine, the Russians by launching a major offensive against East Prussia. All the plans hinged on rapid mobilisation, which, once started, would accelerate the whole tempo of any crisis, leaving diplomacy with little hope of solving it.

(f) The July Crisis and the outbreak of war

On 28 June the Archduke Francis Ferdinand, nephew of Francis Joseph, was murdered by a Bosnian extremist, Princep, while on a visit to Sarajevo. The group to which Princep belonged had been encouraged by Colonel Dimitrievich, one-time Chief of Intelligence and leader of a Serb Terrorist organisation, the Black Hand. The Serb prime minister Pasich had known of the plot and had sent a vague warning to the Austrian government, which had yet neglected to give the archduke proper protection. Despite the fact that the Serbian government was not guilty of complicity in the plot, most members of the Austrian government felt that strong action was needed, and indeed on 5 July the Germans urged them to make war on Serbia, though it should be said that the German government hoped that the conflict would be localised.

On 23 July an Austrian ultimatum was sent to Serbia, deliberately framed by the Austrian foreign secretary Berchtold in terms that no self-respecting state could accept. It demanded the suppression of all anti-Austrian societies in Serbia, the dismissal of all officials to whom Austria objected and the entry of Austrian police and officials into Serbia to ensure that all the demands were being carried out. The Russian government, which had conferred with Poincaré earlier in the month was now confident of its army's capabilities and of French support; this time the Russians were not going to give way and they initiated military preparations. Therefore Serbia, confident of Russian support, replied in an evasive way to the ultimatum, and Austria declared war on her on 28 July. By now the danger of Franco-Russian intervention was clear, and Bethmann-Hollweg and others in the German government must be blamed for not restraining the Austrians in a situation where there was little hope of localising the dispute. Bethmann's attempts to warn off the Russians came to nothing, for they mobilised on 30 July. Only then did Bethmann join Grey in urging restraint on Austria, impressed by Grey's clear warning that Britain would not find it practicable to stand aside in the event of a general war; but while Bethmann urged caution, Moltke urged quite the opposite course on the Austrians.

On 31 July the German government, worried by Russian mobilisation, demanded that Russia should cease her military preparations and in the absence of any reply declared war on 1 August. The French were asked for a promise of neutrality in a Russo-German war, and as no such French promise was received, Germany declared war on France on 3 August. On the same day they sent an ultimatum to the Belgian government demanding free passage through Belgium to attack France. The Belgians refused and German troops crossed the Belgian frontier on 4 August. It was this moral issue of the violation of Belgian neutrality, guaranteed by the powers under the 1839 treaty, that united opinion in Britain and led her to declare war on Germany. A general war which was to transform Europe and its place in the world was under way.

Explanations of why war broke out have been many and varied. Underlying its outbreak was a total lack of comprehension of the implications of total war. On all sides it was assumed that the war would be short and would not destroy the fabric of civilisation. In Russia and Austria it was seen as an escape from domestic difficulties, for it was hoped that a successful war would restore the prestige of the monarchy. Lack of any great statesmanship during the July crisis was another factor. 'Again and again in the July crisis', comments James Joll, 'one is confronted with men who suddenly feel themselves trapped, caught up in a fate they are unable to control.' The disproportion between the talents of the politicians and the gravity of the problems is perhaps symbolised by Bethmann's answer to Bulow soon after the outbreak of war. Bulow asked how the war had come about. 'If only I knew,' was the anguished reply. No one planned a general war in 1914. Therefore the coming of war was in one sense a tragedy of miscalculation. Germany's miscalculation lay in the brusqueness and insensitivity of her diplomacy, which had created the Triple Entente, and it was German support which allowed the Austrians to choose to wage war on Serbia. Yet German hegemony of Europe could have been achieved without war; in fact it had already been achieved by the early years of the twentieth century through economic advance and the defeat of Russia in the Far East.

But of all the powers it was Austria who did most to provoke war in 1914. She had reopened the difficult Balkan question in 1908 and her ultimatum in July 1914 raised her quarrel with Serbia to the level of a grave international crisis. Finally it was Austria who, ignoring German calls for caution during that crisis, was the first power to resort to force by attacking Serbia.

The question of responsibility for the war has been an explosive issue since the guilt clause in the Versailles Treaty of 1919 put the whole blame on Germany and her allies. After this many historians came to agree with Lloyd George that all the nations had 'stumbled into war' and that therefore all nations were in part to blame. In recent years the debate has again aroused strong feelings, with the work of Fritz Fischer, who maintained that Germany had specific expansionist aims and that German leaders not only prepared for a major war from 1911 but provoked it in 1914. His views were sharply challenged by other German historians, notably Gerhard Ritter, who stressed that Germany was only partly to blame for the war, the responsibility of the German government lying in its surrender of all political reasoning to military planning.

FURTHER READING

Bergahn, V. R., *Germany and the Approach of War 1914*, Macmillan, London, 1973

Cobban, A., *A History of Modern France*, Volume 3, Penguin, Harmondsworth, 1970

Fischer, F., *The War of Illusions: German Policy 1911–1914*, Chatto and Windus, London, 1975

Grenville, J. A. S., *A World History of the Twentieth Century* Volume I, Fontana, London, 1980

Joll, J., *Europe Since 1870*, Penguin, London, 1970

Joll, J., *Origins of the First World War*, Longmans, London, 1984

Kennedy, P., *The Rise and Fall of the Great Powers*, Unwin Hyman, London, 1988

Morison, S. E., Commager, H. and Leuchtenburg, W. E., *The Growth of the American Republic* (7th Edition), Oxford University Press, Oxford, 1980

Read, Donald, *England 1868–1914*, Longmans, London, 1979

Roberts, J. M., *Europe 1880–1945*, Longmans, London, 1972

Ryder, A. J., *Twentieth Century Germany from Bismarck to Brandt*, Macmillan, London, 1973

Seton-Watson, C., *Italy from Liberalism to Fascism*, Methuen, London, 1973

Seton-Watson, H., *The Russian Empire 1801–1917*, Oxford University Press, Oxford, 1967

Stone, N., *Europe Transformed 1878–1919*, Fontana, London, 1983

QUESTIONS

1. How important were economic factors in the scramble for colonies after 1880?
2. Assess the threats to the stability of the Russian Empire before 1914.
3. 'An interesting test case of what happens when a parliamentary constitution is imposed on an underdeveloped country.' How far does this statement explain Italy's difficulties between 1870 and 1914?
4. Why had a new mood of apprehension entered British political life by 1900?
5. Assess the effects of colonial rivalries upon great power relations in the period 1890 to 1914.
6. How far was the First World War caused by Germany's grasp after world power?

2
The First World War and the Versailles Settlement, 1914–25

(1) The First World War, 1914–18

(a) The character of the war

Nothing is more extraordinary to later generations than the rapture with which the onset of war was greeted in major cities all over Europe. Many people no doubt felt the war would bring colour and heroism to their drab, humdrum lives and glory and profit to the nation. In the excitement of the hour old enmities were forgotten in the general patriotic reaction, and even the socialists turned from opposition to support. Popular hysteria demonstrated that this was the greatest of all wars of nationality.

The disillusionment was to be swift and terrible. The war was expected, even by the generals, to be short and mobile, and few could have conceived of a conflict lasting 4 years, bringing with it untold millions of casualties and leaving Europe sadly weakened. It was a war dominated by military technology that made defence stronger than ever before. The new strength of the defence lay in increased fire-power provided by the magazine rifle and the machine-gun. This fire-power employed by men in trenches behind barbed wire ended the possibility of the cavalry retaining any military significance and made infantry attacks suicidal. Therefore heavy artillery was required to prepare the attack by pulverising barbed-wire entanglements and well-prepared machine-gun emplacements in an elaborate trench system. The howitzers employed expended shells at an unprecedented rate, and demand soon far outran supply.

The shell shortage of the early years of the war was symbolic of the failure to anticipate the nature of modern warfare. There were many other examples: the French army of 1914 went into action in red trousers which made their wearer an easy target, while on both sides the doctrine of the offensive at all costs still dominated military thinking in a new situation when such offensives would be futile and costly in men's lives.

Once the deadlock of trench warfare was appreciated, ways round the deadlock were sought. In 1915 the German action in using poison gas was soon copied by their enemies, and in 1917, partly through Churchill's prompting, the British threw the first tanks into battle at Cambrai. Some old weapons, such as the mortar and grenade, were revived but in the end the deadlock was only broken by the exhaustion of the Central Powers rather than by military innovations.

The misery endured by millions of ordinary men in the trenches of the Western front for nearly 4 years must be without parallel in recorded history. It demonstrated the truth of Dostoievski's observation that, 'Man is an animal that can become accustomed to anything.' Great armies faced each other across a shattered No-Man's-land and were smashed by shell-fire, shot, burnt and gassed. Wounded men hung for days on the barbed wire until they died and millions were mown down in the futile offensives.

One of the most acidly realistic accounts of life in Flanders was *Good-bye to All That* by Robert Graves. The author describes the relative comfort of the officers' dugouts compared to the dismal holes, often full of water, in which the ordinary ranks served. All men, however, shared the same dangers and hoped for the 'lucky wound' which might secure release from more fighting.

(b) The Western Front, 1914–16

In 1914 the Germans hoped to win the war in the West by a knockout blow against France launched through Belgium, after which Paris would be surrounded as the German armies crossed the Seine to the north-west of the capital. The French armies attacking Alsace-Lorraine could then be taken in the rear. It was a plan of Napoleonic audacity, for it committed nearly seven-eighths of the German forces in the west to the pincer movement while only one eighth would be left in Germany to counter the French offensive. Yet as Ritter and Liddell Hart have shown, the Schlieffen Plan had its weaknesses. It was hardly feasible in 1914 for German soldiers advancing on foot with horse-drawn artillery and rounding the circumference of the circle to move more quickly than the French, who were able to switch troops by rail across the chord of the circle. Moreover the French would have time to destroy bridges and railways in the path of the invasion. Schlieffen's failure to appreciate such factors leads one to conclude that he has enjoyed an exaggerated reputation as a war strategist.

For all that, the Plan came near to success. When the German offensive was launched, the French military under Joffre underestimated the weight of the attack through Belgium and soon the French armies and the British Expeditionary Force under Sir John French were forced to retreat to a more defensible position on the River

Marne. Their survival was aided by a number of German errors. Four German divisions in Belgium were sent to East Prussia to help check the Russian offensive, so that the right-wing princer movement was weakened. More seriously the advance of the Second Army of von Bülow and the First Army under von Kluck had been so rapid that they lost contact and a gap appeared between them. To regain contact von Kluck veered south-east and exposed his right flank. Joffre seized the opportunity to counter-attack in September and the Germans retreated. In the crisis Joffre had shown admirable coolness and ability to improvise new strategy, though his triumph at the Marne was to be his one outstanding victory. The crisis had also demonstrated the quality of the British Expeditionary Force, which by its stubborn resistance at Mons in August had prevented the Germans from outflanking the French left.

Erick Von Falkenhayn replaced Moltke as supreme commander of the German army and both sides attempted to outflank each other to the north in a race for the Channel ports. Dogged French and British resistance prevented the Germans breaking through, but the losses at the first battle of Ypres in November were enormous. After this both sides dug in and by the end of the year an elaborate system of trenches ran from the Channel to the Swiss frontier.

In 1915 the Germans were content to remain on the defensive for the most part as Falkenhayn was committed to a major offensive in the east; their attack on the British at the second battle of Ypres was notable for the first use of poison gas. The French and British launched major assaults after this, in Champagne and at Loos respectively, though they did not gain more than 3 miles at any one point. Yet the war was to take on a more monstrous grimness in 1916, with the most formidable battle of the war, Verdun, which lasted from February to December. Alistair Horne in *The Price of Glory* writes:

> Of all battles of the First World War, Verdun was the one in which most Frenchmen had taken part. Something like seven-tenths of the whole French army passed through Verdun. The combined casualties of both sides reached the staggering total of over 700,000. It is probably no exaggeration to call Verdun the 'worst battle' in history.

The French were unprepared for the German onslaught because Joffre failed to discern the German objective in undertaking so titanic an offensive far from Paris. But Falkenhayn was not really attempting a break-through at Verdun but rather trying to bleed the French army to death through its determination to defend at any cost a city so rich in historical associations. Joffre had not prepared Verdun sufficiently, despite the warnings of its commander of its unpreparedness and from military intelligence about German preparations.

When the offensive started, the German artillery wreaked deadly damage, the aim being to create, in Pétain's phrase, 'a zone of death'. Especially lethal were the monstrous 420 mm 'Big Bertha' mortars. Yet the French would not yield Verdun and when the military wished to abandon the Verdun salient, Briand insisted that it be held, for otherwise a grave blow would be struck at French morale. The cold conservative Pétain was brought in to command a new Army of Verdun, and he rotated the divisions which had to endure the German shelling. French heroism meant that the Germans did not pass and the battle of Verdun was a heavy strain on both sides.

On the British sector, in an attempt to relieve the French at Verdun, an assault along the line of the Somme by fourteen British divisions and five French in July was a disaster. On the first day the British lost nearly 60,000 men, including 19,000 dead, and Kitchener's volunteer army was destroyed. The reward for this slaughter was an advance of no more than 5 miles.

(c) The Eastern Front, 1914–16

In August 1914 the mobilisation of the Russian armies was swifter than expected and by the end of the month there were 2 million Russians under arms. Eight Russian corps were deployed against five German corps in East Prussia, while in Galicia eighteen Russian corps faced twelve Austrian corps. The Russians responded bravely to the French plea for an immediate offensive against the Central Powers to relieve the pressure on Russia's allies in the West. The Russian commander-in-chief, the Grand Duke Nicholas, ordered the Russian armies into action before they were fully equipped and a second disadvantage was the mutual hostility of the two generals, Rennenkampf and Samsonov, who were to invade East Prussia from the east and the south to effect a juncture.

The Russian advance was an unmitigated disaster. Two German generals, Ludendorff and Hindenburg, were able to exploit the gap between the two Russian armies. Samsonov's army was surrounded at Tannenberg in August and 90,000 prisoners were taken, the commander committing suicide. In September Hindenburg was able to gain a victory over Rennenkampf's isolated forces at the battle of the Masurian Lakes and East Prussia was cleared of Russian troops.

Better fortune attended Russian arms in the south. Here the Serbs had parried the Austrian thrust after ferocious battles and had expelled the invaders from Serbia. The Austrian general Hötzendorff could not devote his main strength against the Serbs, for he wished to launch an offensive against Russian Poland to divert the Russians while the Schlieffen Plan was put into operation in the west; but the

Russians took the offensive first in Galicia and in September took 100,000 prisoners at Lemberg.

This proof of Austrian military incapacity meant that friction between Austria and Germany grew as early as 1914. It also required Falkenhayn in 1915 to help the Austrians by an offensive in the east. In May Mackensen, on a plan suggested by Hötzendorff, broke through the Russian line at Gorlice in Galicia, taking over 100,000 prisoners, and by August Warsaw had fallen. The Russian defeats led to the entry of Bulgaria into the war on the side of the Central Powers and the annihilation of the Serb armies.

In 1916, with the German pressure at Verdun, the Western allies appealed to Russia for a new offensive. In June came a magnificent Russian response – the great Brusilov offensive which broke the Austrian front and by October had led to the capture of 400,000 prisoners and 500 guns. It was to be the last great feat of arms of the Russian Empire.

(d) War aims and the search for allies

The deadlock after the first battles drove the Powers to consider their war aims. As Taylor has pointed out, 'no power had entered the war with any defined aim except to win. Victory was expected to provide a policy; in fact victory was the policy'. Austria-Hungary was the only power, on the outbreak of war, with a specific objective – the crushing of South Slav nationalism by conquest. The Germans lacked war aims when the war started and sought to work out concrete objectives which once gained would destroy all the forces facing them. In September 1914 Bethmann-Hollwegg's Memorandum showed clearly what this would entail; the loss by France of territory with strategic and economic value, German protectorates over Belgium and Luxembourg, German leadership of a central European customs union and fresh colonial acquisitions for Germany in Central Africa.

As the war continued, German war aims in Eastern Europe became ever more ambitious, and resemble Hitler's later demand for 'living-space' in the East. In 1917 at a meeting at Kreuznach attended by Bethmann, William and the Supreme Command, it was decided that Belgium, Poland, Lithuania and Courland should be fully incorporated into Germany. By March and May 1918, when the Central Powers concluded punitive peace treaties with Russia at Brest-Litovsk and with Rumania at Bucharest, it was clear that the Germans wanted complete domination of Eastern Europe.

For the Allies, the general objective sought was the destruction of German militarism and the war was presented as a war for democracy and security. For Britain this meant the destruction of the German fleet and an end to German colonialism; for France it meant the acquisition of Alsace-Lorraine, the Saar and territory on the left bank of the Rhine. The Russians had no specific territorial demands to make of Germany, for any territory gained would add to the number of dissident Poles in the Empire; it was the destruction of Austria-Hungary that Russia sought.

Yet the problem of war aims was intimately bound up with the question of alliances, and Allied aims developed markedly once Turkey entered the war on the side of the Central Powers and Italy on the side of the Allies. The Turks entered the war in October 1914 because they feared partition at the hands of Russia if the Allies won the war; in any case they were confident of German victory and German influence in Turkey was strong. Two battle cruisers, the *Goeben* and the *Breslau*, had fled to Constantinople for safety from the Mediterranean in August, and in October they entered the Black Sea to attack Russian ports and shipping. At the same time the Turkish action in closing the Straits to commercial traffic led to the Triple Entente declaring war. This was a crucial development and brought nearer the destruction of both the Russian and Turkish Empires. The Turks committed a blunder in joining the war; they could have stayed neutral with complete security, for Russia would be fully occupied fighting the Central Powers. The closing of the Straits was a fatal blow to Russia; without the essential supplies from her Western allies her war effort soon came near to collapse and she was to stand on the defensive in 1915.

The Turkish entry into the war soon led to a Russian demand for the Straits and the adjoining territory to be included in the Empire at the end of the War. France and Britain agreed by April 1915, because this was the only way in which they could stimulate the Russian war effort now that direct help was impossible. 'Diplomacy had to make up for the failures of strategy', says A. J. P. Taylor, 'and a promise for the future was the cheapest coin in which to pay.' By 1916 the Russians were demanding Armenia and Kurdistan, while Britain and France settled their share by the Sykes–Picot agreement of January 1916. France was to have Syria with an extensive hinterland while Britain would gain Mesopotamia, Transjordan and Southern Palestine.

Meanwhile the Allies had attempted to entice the most valuable of the uncommitted nations, Italy, into the war. It had been no surprise to the other powers when Italy in August 1914 had declared her neutrality in a war which the Italian government regarded as being caused by an Austrian attack on Serbia, for Italy, since an agreement of 1902 with France, had been only a nominal member of the Triple Alliance. Both sides offered inducements, but the Allies could offer more, since the main territories which Italy coveted were Austrian. By the secret treaty of London in April 1915 Italy was promised, at Austria's expense, Trentino, the Tyrol up to the Brenner Pass,

Trieste, Istria and North Dalmatia, and at Turkey's expense Adalia and extensions of territory in Libya.

The Italian intervention in May 1915 gave the war an anti-Habsburg character which otherwise it lacked. Dismemberment of the Austro-Hungarian Empire became an even clearer war aim in 1916 with the promises made to Rumania by the treaty of Bucharest in August, which awarded her Transylvania, Bukovina and the Banat of Temesvar. It was ironic that a war originally waged by the Allies for the destruction of German militarism had been transmuted by wartime diplomacy into a war waged for the elimination of the Turkish and Austro-Hungarian Empires.

(e) The Balkans and Arabia

The futile bloodshed of the Western front created divisions in the Allied governments on strategy. In Britain several important men in the government became 'Easterners', convinced that the war would be won by opening new fronts in the Balkans, where the campaigns would be more mobile and likely to win the support of the neutral Balkan states. When therefore Grand Duke Nicholas requested relief from the Turkish armies in the Caucasus, Winston Churchill proposed an expedition to force open the Dardanelles Straits so that a lifeline would be opened to munitions-starved Russia.

The Dardanelles campaign was a series of missed opportunities. A partial attack was launched in February 1915 by the Anglo-French fleets, but delays meant that the full assault was not attempted until March, by which time the advantage of surprise had been lost and the Turks had stationed four divisions along the waterway. By the time an Allied army arrived in April Liman von Sanders and Mustafa Kemal had organised the Turkish defences, which now numbered six divisions. The Allied forces – British, French, Australians and New Zealanders – performed prodigies of valour but were pinned down on a narrow beachhead at Gallipoli, and in November Kitchener decided to abandon the enterprise. The fiasco caused 214,000 British Commonwealth casualties and had important effects at home, being a factor in the overturning of the Asquith government and the total eclipse of Churchhill's career. It led to a suspicion of army 'sideshows' diverting resources from the Western front, and it encouraged Bulgarian intervention in the war in October 1915 on the side of the Central Powers. The sole consolation in the campaign was that it obliged Turkey to divert forces from the Russian front, thus enabling the Russian armies to hold out longer.

The British and the Turks also clashed in Mesopotamia when a British force under Townshend advanced towards Bagdad in 1915 only to be defeated at Kut in April 1916. The British, however, were able to make more capital out of an Arab revolt against the Turks in 1916, seeing in the revolt an opportunity to strike at the Turkish Empire from its vulnerable southern flank. Ronald Storns and Captain T. E. Lawrence were sent on a mission to the Hejaz area of Arabia to help Hussein, the sherif of Mecca and his son Feisal, who were leading the revolt. Lawrence already knew the area well and his grasp of strategy, his courage and stamina enabled him to give a great stimulus to the Arab uprising. He persuaded Feisal to attack the Turkish lifeline, the Damascus to Medina railway, by hit-and-run tactics which were admirably suited to the mobile, brave but undisciplined Arabs. While they could be provisioned by the British from the sea, the Turks suffered from malnutrition as they tried to defend the railways. Lawrence's full realisation of this strategy proved his genius and his tactics were later used by, among others, Giap in Vietnam.

In May 1917 Lawrence and Sheik Adudu Abu Taya led the Huwaitat tribesmen across the desert to attack the fort of Aqaba on the eastern coast of the Sinai peninsula. The Turks were taken completely by surprise, and with Aqaba as a base Feisal's army could now function as the east wing of a British advance from Egypt into Palestine. By October 1917 General Sir Edmund Allenby was laying seige to Jerusalem, and it was while Lawrence was trying to cut the railway between Jerusalem and Damascus that he was captured, tortured by the Turks and yet was able to effect an escape.

After the capture of Jerusalem in December, Allenby went on to win the battle of Megiddo in North Palestine, which was considered by Liddell Hart to be the 'strategic masterpiece' of the First World War. This victory, won by Australian and Indian cavalry divisions, opened the way to Damascus, which was taken in October 1918. At Versailles a system of mandates was created for the Arabs lands. Lawrence was disgusted by the decision and retired into anonymity.

(f) The war at sea

Technology had transformed naval operations by 1914, with the coming of the torpedo, the mine and the submarine. Guns were bigger, the latest British battleships possessing 15-inch weapons. The latest dreadnoughts, driven by improved turbines and oil-firing, were faster and more armour-plated than their predecessors. On the outbreak of war, Britain possessed the strongest navy the world had ever seen, with twenty-seven of the new dreadnoughts, including cruisers, compared to Germany's sixteen, and the cruisers could reach a speed of 25 knots.

When the war started, the British public hoped for a great sea battle with a Nelson-style victory, but as the grand fleet could be lost in one encounter with the enemy or torpedoes by submarines, caution was the watchword. Churchill appreciated this position when he said of the commander of the British Grand Fleet, 'Jellicoe was the only man on either side who could lose the war in an afternoon.' Therefore British naval strategy was more concerned with maintaining the sea lanes than defeating the German fleet. The Germans, conscious of their inferiority in numbers of ships, also wished to avoid battle and aimed at the piecemeal destruction of the British fleet through mines and torpedoes.

The early years of the war then saw no great battles but in 1916 came the collision of the two fleets at Jutland, the only major confrontation of dreadnoughts in the history of sea warfare. Not surprisingly the battle occurred by accident. The German Admiral Scheer attempted to lure the British into a trap by sending part of his fleet to sail off the Norwegian coast. This ruse, he hoped, would draw out the southern section of the British Grand Fleet under Beatty, which the bulk of the German fleet would then destroy, but the British intercepted a wireless signal and Jellicoe's force set out from Scapa Flow as well.

The British battle-cruisers, hit repeatedly by the Germans, were shown to be inferior in the accuracy of their fire, the quality of their shells and in the design of their magazines which were not protected from the danger of cordite-flash. Jellicoe at one point late in the battle had the opportunity to destroy most of the German fleet but refused to take risks with night coming on. The British lost three battle-cruisers, three armoured cruisers, eight destroyers and over 6,000 men killed; the Germans lost one battleship, one battle-cruiser, four light cruisers and five destroyers and only 2,500 men. Yet though the battle conferred tactical credit on the Germans, the strategic advantage was gained by Britain, for the German High Seas Fleet stayed in port for the remainder of the war and its crews mutinied in 1918. Jellicoe was criticised for failing to display the Nelson touch, but he wisely maintained an aloof silence on the controversy.

After Jutland British control of sea communications was challenged only by the submarine. Its menace was seen as early as September 1914, when one submarine sunk three old British cruisers in the space of a few hours. The Germans did not make full use of the new weapon early in the war for fear of offending American opinion. After Jutland they neglected the fleet and concentrated on submarine attacks on shipping, the jugular vein of the British Empire. Supplies of ships and essential imports began to run short in 1916, and when Germany renewed unrestricted submarine warfare in 1917 with more submarines, Britain came near to defeat. In April one out of four ships leaving British ports was sunk, and in that month alone 1 million tons of shipping was lost. The British reserve of wheat dwindled to 6 weeks' supply, and the supply of pit props from Norway was so interrupted that coal production was threatened.

The Admiralty in this crisis was reluctant to adopt new methods, such as the convoy system, and Lloyd George took over and forced the measure through, retiring Jellicoe when he was slow to implement it. The adoption of the convoy system was Lloyd George's most decisive achievement of the war and enabled Britain to survive. Losses in convoy were under 1 per cent, and by the end of the war British and American yards were building more ships than were being sunk. The German policy of unrestricted submarine warfare boomeranged. It not only failed to bring Britain to her knees but provoked the entry of the United States into the war in April 1917. Meanwhile the British navy exercised a fatal silent blockade of Germany which had undermined health and morale there by 1918.

(g) Air warfare

With the use of aircraft a new dimension was added to combat during the First World War. When hostilities began, aircraft served largely for reconnaissance, but by 1918 they had evolved into a weapon of long-range attack. On several occasions air reconnaissance made crucial observations of the enemy's movements, for example Von Kluck's swerve to the south-east, which enabled the Allied victory at the Marne to take place. The development of the camera and aerial photography greatly increased the accuracy of artillery spotting by the British Royal Flying Corps.

The Germans responded with attempts to stop observation aircraft, and thus air combat developed. Methods were primitive: pilots lobbed hand grenades and took potshots at their antagonists with pistols. The Germans produced better fighter planes in 1915 and achieved a great break-through in air fighting by perfecting a fixed machine-gun which could shoot forward through the propeller, a technique pioneered by Anthony Fokker. The Allies had to resort to formation flying and safety in numbers to match the deadly Fokker fighter, and so team fighting developed and great daylight air battles took place. Air warfare had a glamour which could not survive in the grim attrition of the trenches and air aces emerged. The most famous, Baron Manfred von Richthofen, was killed in action in 1918.

The Allies were goaded into trying to break German air supremacy. They invented the practice of strafing ground troops and developed new fighter planes to match the Fokkers and the Halberstadts. By 1917 Allied air dominance was achieved with such fighters as the Sopwith Camel and the de Havilland D. H. Robbed of their previous ascendancy over the battlefields, the Germans intensified long-range bombing of Britain, which had started in 1914. The British retaliated with the use of the de Havilland 9A and Handley-Page bombers, and there was a debate over the practicality of such bombing. Winston Churchill, now back as minister of munitions, opposed saturation bombing of German cities in 1917, but though he was correct in asserting that area bombing would not break enemy morale, his opinion did not prevail.

In April 1918 Lord Trenchard won Parliamentary consent to unite the Royal Flying Corps and the Royal Navy Air Service into one service, the Royal Air Force. During the last year of the war planes were used extensively for long-range naval reconnaissance and anti-submarine patrols. With the first blockbuster bombs in use and the British, French and Germans possessing 3,300, 4,500 and 2,400 planes respectively, air warfare was no longer in its infancy.

(h) Allied setbacks, 1917–18

The year 1917 brought the Allies nearer to defeat than at any point since September 1914. At sea, losses of merchant ships threatened Britain with starvation, while on three major fronts the Allies experienced a series of calamities. Joffre's successor, Nivelle, was confident that one sharp offensive would break the German lines; as a preliminary to the main area of operations the British attacked at Arras, but with only one success, the taking of Vimy Ridge by the Canadians. The Germans were ready for the French offensives on the Aisne, which were repelled with heavy losses. Mutinies now spread among four French armies during May and June, but they were so effectively suppressed by the French command that Ludendorff admitted later hearing little about them at the time. The quelling of the mutinies was the work of Pétain; he called a halt to further offensives, improved conditions generally and meted out ruthless punishment to the mutineers. French official sources stated that only 23 were executed but Haig noted in his dairy that there were 30,000 cases to be dealt with.

The failure of Nivelle's offensive left Haig free to determine his own strategy regardless of the French, and he insisted on a great offensive in Flanders. It was launched in July at what was officially called the third battle of Ypres, popularly Passchendaele. The preliminary bombardment churned the Flanders plain into impassable mud, especially as August was the wettest for many years. In this offensive British casualties numbered 324,000 and three British soldiers were killed for every two Germans. The sole gleam of hope was the victory at Cambrai in November, which was won with the use of tanks.

The Italian task was equally unenviable. Italy went to war on the most difficult front in Europe; it was 400 miles long through precipitous mountains, and whenever the Italians attacked, they had to fight uphill and were very vulnerable to counter-attack. Cadorna, the Italian commander, enjoyed a numerical superiority of two to one, but the Austrian defences were formidable. The Italians fought courageously, but, lacking training, artillery and machine-guns, lost

66,000 killed and 100,000 wounded in 7 months in 1915. In 1916 the Italian offensive also failed and Conrad initiated a counter-attack which destroyed the Italian centre and seemed likely to envelop the whole Italian army. Cadorna showed his calibre as a commander at this point by stemming the Austrian advance, but the reality of invasion was a grave blow to Italian morale.

Early in 1917 the French and British suggested that they give help to a plan for a knock-out blow on the Italian front. Because the Italians were lukewarm about the plan, it was shelved. 'This', affirms Christopher Seton-Watson, 'proved the most serious blunder that the Italians committed during the whole war; they threw away the chance of seizing the military initiative and thus forestalling Caporetto.' Their allies went on to plan the offensive under Nivelle on the Western front, leaving the Italians to face a more powerful enemy now that German troops were available to help the Austrians after the Russian Revolution. Early Italian victories in 1917 persuaded the German High Command to send seven divisions, while the Austrians themselves sent eight, swelling the total number of divisions facing the Italians from twenty-one to thirty-six. Now the Italians no longer had numerical superiority, and in October the German offensive at Caporetto split the Italian armies in two and Cadorna was forced into a 50-mile headlong retreat. Cadorna was dismissed as commander-in-chief and eleven British and French divisions were sent to help the Italians, though the front was stabilised by the time they arrived.

On the Eastern front the Russian war effort lurched to an end in 1917. Russia sustained more casualties than any other belligerent – at least 4 million dead and conceivably twice this figure. The 'human wave' infantry charges often by troops equipped with bayoneted rifles but no cartridges had taken a ghastly toll. The Russian shortages of all armaments prevented any successful exploitation of Brusilov's 1916 offensive, which had cost 1 million casualties.

Nicholas II contributed to the military debacle by dismissing Grand Duke Nicholas as commander-in-chief and assuming control himself. At home his neurotic wife and Rasputin interfered in the running of the war, Rasputin relaying the Russian plans to the Germans. By March 1917 the Russian people had had enough and forced the Tsar to abdicate. The March Revolution was received with delight in the West, for it was hoped that the new parliamentary regime would prosecute the war with more vigour and encourage American entry into the war. Yet the Provisional Government failed to appreciate the Russian people's yearning for peace and in July 1917, prompted by the Western allies, Brusilov launched another offensive which made some initial headway against the Austrians; but only one soldier in six possessed a rifle and the Austrian and German counter-attack in August drove the Russians out of Galicia and Bukovina. The army was now demoralised and receptive to Bolshevik propaganda. 'Why fight any more? Take your gun and go home and seize your parcel of land.' When the Bolsheviks seized power in November, they began immediate negotiations for an armistice with the Central Powers, and a truce was concluded in December, followed by the Carthaginian peace treaty of Brest-Litovsk in March 1918. The Russians lost Poland, the three Baltic provinces, Finland and the Ukraine. They were deprived of 40 per cent of their industry, 70 per cent of their coalfields, 25 per cent of their arable land and one-third of their railways and population. Perhaps the robber peace indicates the type of peace which the German government, now completely influenced by the military, would have extorted in the West in the event of its victory. Certainly it makes the Versailles Treaty appear moderate in comparison. Only the Allied victory in November 1918 nullified the Brest-Litovsk treaty, and justifies the observation of Hugh Seton-Watson that it was Marshal Foch who saved Russia, not Lenin or Trotsky!

(i) The collapse of the Central Powers

If 1917 was a dark hour for the Allies, it was yet in this year that powerful compensating factors appeared. In France military defeat was compounded by a series of scandals, the most notorious being the activities of Mata Hari, who was suspected of seducing prominent personages to extract secrets from them. A mood of defeatism grew and strong leadership was required. The hour brought forth the man. Only Clemenceau could rally the nation and in November 1917 he became prime minister. His motto was 'I wage war' and he was true to his word. He visited the front weekly and became a symbolic figure promising victory. He purged the government of defeatists like Caillaux, who had been in touch with the enemy, and had spies like Mata Hari executed. In the great German spring offensive of 1918 he showed coolness as the military situation grew critical and backed his commander-in-chief Marshal Foch when the cry went up for a scape-goat.

An even more crucial factor was the entry of the United States into the war in April 1917. On the outbreak of war President Wilson had issued a formal declaration of neutrality and his government assumed that, owing to the large English, German, Jewish and Irish elements in the population, the nation could never take part on either side without bringing on civil war at home. In any case, it was classical American policy not to become embroiled in European affairs. Events, however, made real neutrality difficult. Though the Americans disliked British seizure of war contraband on neutral ships bound for Germany or Holland, sympathy with the Allied cause grew, so that early in the war President Wilson estimated that 90 per cent of American citizens were on the side of the Allies. The German invasion of Belgium meant that from the first Germany forfeited any moral case for her policy, whereas the Allies were given a morally irrefutable case for taking a firm stand against aggression. American indignation grew when the Germans answered the British blockade in 1915 with a counter-blockade using U-boats. 'England wants us to starve,' said Tirpitz. 'We can play the same game.' This policy led to the torpedoing of the *Lusitania* in May 1915 in which 1,198 people died, including 139 Americans, mostly women and children. American determination to stay out of the war at any cost diminished from that day.

For a while Bethmann-Hollwegg managed to restrict U-boat warfare and 1915 and 1916 passed by without German–American relations deteriorating further, but in this period more submarines had been constructed and Hindenburg and Ludendorff were now ascendant in the German government. They shared Tirpitz's belief that full use of the U-boat was Germany's last hope of victory, and they believed that it would starve Britain into surrender before any significant American aid could reach Europe. Therefore in February 1917 the German government announced that its submarines would sink without warning all ships including neutrals, within a broad zone round Britain, France, Italy and the eastern Mediterranean. Wilson now severed diplomatic relations with Germany.

The German foreign secretary, Zimmermann, attempted to pin down the United States by entangling her in a conflict with Mexico. In March his telegram to the German minister in Mexico City was intercepted by British naval intelligence and divulged to Wilson. In his cable Zimmermann instructed the minister to propose an alliance to the Mexican government in which Germany would support Mexican reconquest of Texas, New Mexico and Arizona. When Wilson released the note for publication, it caused a wave of anti-German sentiment in America. Later in March the Germans sank three American ships without warning, and in April the United States declared war on Germany.

The way for such a declaration had been cleared in March as the Russian Revolution removed the only obstacle for believing that the European conflict was a struggle between autocracy and freedom. In any case, as F. R. Dulles has shown, 'real neutrality had gone by the board long before Germany adopted unrestricted submarine warfare'. While trade with the Central Powers had dwindled away, the United States had extended vital economic aid to the Allies through the increasing flow of munitions and food. Interruption of this trade would not only have undermined the Allied war effort, it would have had disastrous consequences on many branches of the American economy. By 1917 most Americans feared that a German victory would threaten the United States, and they felt that the Allies stood for the things in which they themselves believed.

The American intervention in the war was not a negligible factor, as the Germans had fondly imagined. By the end of the war 2 million American troops were in Europe and supplies of essential materials increased. Great psychological encouragement was given to the Allies even when the number of Americans in the fighting was still small in 1917. Wilson's declaration that the war was one fought for democracy seemed to transform it into a crusade which might yet make the tragedies of the previous years worthwhile. For these reasons, and as Ludendorff himself admitted, 'America became the deciding factor in the war.'

The winter of 1917–18 was a long and hard one in central Europe. By January 1918 the flour ration in Vienna was reduced to 165 grams a day. Left-wing opposition to the war had begun to grow even while German armies were still successful in 1916. In 1918 it combined with the general exhaustion and reached a revolutionary pitch, fostered by three events. The Russian Revolution meant that the war could no longer be represented as a struggle against tsarist barbarism, and it encouraged German workers to hope for similar changes in Germany. The annexationist peace of Brest-Litovsk alienated permanently a large section of the working class, and it responded with a wave of strikes in April 1918 which undermined preparations for Ludendorff's spring offensive. The strikers demanded a peace based on 'no annexations', encouraged by President Wilson's enunciation in January of the fourteen points which he believed would be the basis of a just peace. His statement had a particularly powerful appeal for the subject races of the Austro-Hungarian Empire, because of its insistence on national self-determination.

With the domestic situation deteriorating so rapidly and with American aid growing inexorably, the German military leadership pinned its last hopes on a great offensive on the Western front in Spring 1918. In March thirty-five German divisions attacked the British on the Somme, driving them back 40 miles. A second offensive in April in Flanders scored a complete breakthrough and was contained only with great difficulty. In May a third German offensive broke through the French on the Aisne river and advanced to within 37 miles of Paris. But the German army had now shot its bolt and Allied morale had held. Survival was aided by the belated decision of the Allies to agree to a system of unified command under Marshal Foch. Allied generals had learned the art of elastic defence by holding the front line with a thin screen of troops and conserving their strength for a crushing counter-attack. In July the French drove the Germans from their salient near Paris and on 8 August, the 'black day' of the German army, as Ludendorff termed it, the British Fourth Army with large Canadian and Australian contingents, over 600 tanks and heavy air support, broke the Germans at Amiens. In September the Americans and Belgians struck at Verdun and Ypres respectively. Foch succeeded in concerting the separate national thrusts into a grand strategy of offence which took full advantage of Germany's lack of reserves as well as her advanced front-line positions.

The final Austrian offensive on the Italian front took place in June, but Austrian determination could not offset their lack of reserves. In October the Italians' counter-offensive led to a rout of the Austrian forces at Vittorio Veneto. By now the Habsburg Empire was already in process of disintegration, Czech leaders taking over in Prague, Serb and Croat leaders proclaiming the establishment of a Yugoslav state and Karolyi asserting Hungary's independence.

In Germany Hindenburg and Ludendorff realised that the war was lost by 29 September. They therefore abdicated their power, leaving the Reichstag as the responsible body for making the peace. In November, after the Kaiser had abdicated, a new Cabinet under Ebert was formed, and it negotiated an armistice with the Allies on 11 November, it being understood by the Germans that Wilson's fourteen points would be the basis of peace terms.

(j) The results of the war

The First World War had enormous consequences for Europe and the rest of the world. It was, as Lenin said, a mighty accelerator of events, and it destroyed the Hohenzollern, Romanov and Habsburg dynasties and the Ottoman Empire. Republics were created in eleven countries, but democracy had only shallow roots in these states and in the turbulent postwar world it was replaced by totalitarian rule.

Another factor which promoted postwar instability was finance. The war had to be paid for and the device most used was borrowing at home and from abroad. Foreign loans came mostly from allies and were used to pay for imports from one's allies. Therefore by the end of the war there was a structure of inter-allied war debts to be paid off, with the Western allies deeply indebted to the United States. This was to vitiate international financial affairs after the war, as governments sought to pay back loans to citizens and other governments. It was a temptation to print more paper money, and this hastened the inflation which had already begun during the war. Britain was the only country which sought to finance by increasing direct taxation to any significant degree.

The cost of the war in human and material terms was staggering. Total casualties were 22 million dead and 21 million wounded, thus making the war Europe's cruellest scourge since the Black Death. The casualties were selective, since it was the able-bodied, the 'lost generation', who were singled out for combat and death. The optimism of the nineteenth century, with its belief in automatic progress, could scarcely survive a war which left 10 million widows and orphans.

The war had a levelling effect on customs and manners. A partial compensation for the hardships which women endured was the sudden availability of men's jobs in industry and agriculture. Conscription created labour shortages which had to be filled at once, and women soon dispelled many anti-feminist myths as they proved their capacity to do hard physical jobs in the factories and on the farm. Girls in the munitions industry subjected to poisonous dust and fumes found that their skins turned yellow and that in consequence they were ostracised. Yet the world's largest minority group gained a degree of self-reliance which was reflected in their successful demands for the vote in postwar Britain, Germany, Russia and many other countries. If women edged nearer to some kind of equality, the same was even more true of organised labour in nearly all the belligerent countries. For government to mobilise manpower in the war, the cooperation of the trade union movement was essential and by the end of the war unions were in a much stronger position after collaboration with government.

Total war affected the civilian populations, which soon began to suffer from food shortages and diseases caused by malnutrition. The inhabitants of Belgium, Germany and Austria suffered most, for they were subjected to the slow restriction of the blockade, which continued well into 1919. After years of poor diet, influenza killed off thousands of civilians in Central Europe in August 1918, finding easy victims among peoples worn down by the hardships of war.

It is true that some of the grossest extremes of poverty were eradicated by the growth of planned economies and the inception of the early welfare state. But the power of the state increased vastly during the war, and was one factor facilitating the postwar growth of totalitarian governments. In liberal Britain, as in Imperial Germany, the war forced the growth of state intervention into all aspects of life. Walter Rathenau in Germany created a kind of war socialism which directed labour, brought in rationing and allocated resources to the various industries competing for scarce raw materials. Everything was subordinated to the needs of state. Britain more reluctantly gave up its attempt to run the war on 'laissez-faire' principles, but Lloyd George helped to transform the British economy by his work at the ministry of munitions. Nothing was sacred: even the opening hours of public houses were restricted and the beer was weakened!

The war weakened the world's centre, Europe, and strengthened the periphery – North America, Russia and Asia. Another war would accentuate this trend by making the United States and Russia emerge as superstates. Europe's primacy was at an end, and its future looked bleak, for the aftermath of war presented huge problems – the finding

of employment for demobilised soldiers, the feeding of the populations, the conversion of industry from wartime to peaceful purposes
and the danger of incipient revolt. Normal conditions were restored
in central Europe because the government machinery – the civil
service and the police – continued to function. 'One of the most
important achievements of the Habsburg and Hohenzollern monar-
chies', says F. L. Carsten, 'was the creation of large and well-
functioning bureaucracies; they outlived the disappearance of their
masters, in complete contrast with Soviet Russia where revolution
and civil war destroyed the government machinery totally and irre-
vocably.' Central Europe avoided the civil war that raged in Russia
for years after the revolution, but it did not achieve stability. During
the war millions of men had become accustomed to systematic
violence. Many soldiers found it impossible to return to normal
civilian life and, when the opportunity occurred, eagerly enlisted in
paramilitary organisations like the Freikorps or the Heimwehr. Violence and insecurity were to be endemic in Central European affairs
after 1919.

Finally the European War had developed by 1918 into a World
War. In 1917 when the French armies mutinied, large sections of the
most important front depended on British contingents, among which
were 100,000 Canadians, 150,000 Australians and New Zealanders,
as well as Indians and South Africans. By 1918 there were 270,000
Indians in the battleline. Their immense contribution in turn made
the war a stage in the decline of colonialism. British rule in India soon
faced new demands for independence from the Indian nationalist
party. Similar demands for self-determination were to also make the
Middle East a storm centre of politics after 1919.

(2) The Versailles Settlement, 1914–25

(a) The difficulties of peacemaking

The postwar settlement of Europe provoked furious controversy at
the time and has continued to do so ever since. Winston Churchill
was able to affirm that Germany got off lightly, but in Germany the
Versailles Treaty was assailed as a vindictive dictated peace, designed
to cripple Germany permanently. Of course the Allies were bound to
demand harsher terms after the German treatment of the Russians at
Brest-Litovsk. It was also inevitable that after a war of such terrible
cost that the victor powers should seek to increase their resources and
territories at the expense of the defeated. Only an optimist could
have assumed that a benevolent peace would have followed such
devastation, especially when it was assumed, as stated in Article 231
of the Versailles Treaty, that German aggression had caused the war.

John Maynard Keynes was to write in his book *The Economic Consequences of the Peace* that nearly all the major decisions of the treaties were wrong, but he underrated the immense difficulties facing the statesmen of 1919. When these difficulties are borne in mind, the Versailles Settlement appears a more reasonable achievement, despite several serious errors and its failure to establish a permanent order.

One problem that soon emerged was a lack of unity of purpose between the great powers. The self-righteous and idealistic Wilson came to Europe almost in the guise of a prophet and expected his colleagues to make sacrifices in the interests of a just peace. It was easy for him to do this; his country had not been invaded nor had American losses been heavy. The French press turned upon him and subjected him to bitter ridicule which he found difficult to stomach. In contrast Clemenceau was bound to consider only one objective; French security. Twice in just over 40 years France had been invaded by the Germans. Germany must be permanently weakened so that never in the future would she be able to mount an invasion of France. Lloyd George, though restricted by unwise election pledges, was able at Paris to display his talents for conciliation; again, it was relatively easy for him to do this. Britain's security problem had already been solved by the surrender of the German fleet and colonies.

Commitments made during the war added to the complexity of the negotiations. Promises made to Italy in 1915 to entice her into the war were clearly at odds with the principles of the fourteen points enunciated by Wilson in January 1918, on which the peace treaties were to be based. The former gave to Italy territory with a large German population, while Wilson had emphasised the principle of national self-determination.

More seriously, the statesmen were under considerable pressure from their respective publics. In the United States opinion was turning against further involvement in Europe. In Europe nationalism had become a Frankenstein monster. Popular passions were roused and strident demands were made for a treaty of vengeance on Germany. Lloyd George was no doubt mistaken to promise in the British election of 1918 to 'hang the Kaiser', to 'make Germany pay the whole cost of the war' and to 'squeeze the lemon until the pips squeak'. When he tried to limit reparations during the negotiations of 1919, he received a telegram from 370 MPs holding him to his election promises. In Britain popular feelings were whipped up by the Northcliffe press. The *Daily Mail* carried such headlines as 'Hun food snivel', and demands for a harsh dictated peace. Even the narrow patriotism of Clemenceau seemed too moderate for the French. He was later to be refused the Presidency of the Republic partly because of the compromises made during the peace settlement. It was a mistake to choose Paris as the venue for the Conference. Wire-netting was required to guard the German delegates from the fury of the mob, and when the Allied delegates arrived, they had pinned to their coat-tails posters with slogans on them like 'Hang the Kaiser' and 'Make them pay'. This pressure of public opinion must not be discounted. As Harold Nicolson has noted, democratic diplomacy 'possesses one supreme disadvantage: the representatives are obliged to reduce the standards of their own thoughts to the level of other people's feelings'.

In any case the sheer immensity of the task of reconstructing Europe was appalling. The continent was in chaos and the statesmen faced an impossible task in attempting to appraise a situation which deteriorated daily while the Conference deliberated. By 1918 the Austro-Hungarian Empire was broken up. National committees had been set up in exile during the war by several of its subject nationalities. The Czechs under Thomas Masaryk and Eduard Benes were proclaiming their independence in October 1918. A similar Yugoslav committee under Trumbic represented the Croats and the Slovenes. It agreed in July 1917 with the Serbian government to form a united Yugoslavia under the Serbian monarchy. The statesmen were therefore faced with a *fait accompli* in a part of Europe where the question of national boundaries was most complex. Wilson was astounded by the deluge of national claims which he received from racial goups of whom he had never even heard. In such a situation errors were inevitable. Wilson, for example, agreed to the cession of the Tyrol to Italy, not realising at the time that the area in question contained 230,000 Germans.

The fear of Communism did not make for calm deliberation at Paris. By 1919 the red flag waved over the government buildings in Munich and Budapest. It was feared that the menace would spread further – to Berlin or Vienna or even to Italy. In fact the regimes of Kurt Eisner in Bavaria and Bela Kun in Hungary were short-lived, but their existence added to the pressure for a quick peace.

Harold Nicolson as a member of the British peace delegation has described the strains of the conference with its 'scurrying cacophony', and 'sense of riot in a parrot house'. Behind all the negotiations was felt 'the ache of exhaustion and despair'. There was, explains Nicolson, a drift away from 'our early peaks of aspiration towards the low countries where figures laboured hurriedly together in a gathering fog'. Nicolson came to believe that the treaties were neither just nor wise but vindictive, and he underestimates the achievements. Considering the conditions, the statesmen did well. As Gilbert White, a member of the American delegation put it, 'It is not surprising that they made a bad peace: what is surprising is that they made peace at all.'

Although most attention has been focused on the treaty with Germany, it was only one part of a reconstruction of Europe which took 5 years. In June 1919 the Treaty of Versailles with Germany was worked out. Then came the treaties of St Germain with Austria and Neuilly with Bulgaria. In 1920 the treaty of Sèvres was signed with Turkey and that of the Trianon with Hungary. In a resettlement with Turkey a new treaty was signed at Lausanne in 1923.

(b) The Treaty of Versailles

The territorial requirements imposed on Germany were moderate and she did not suffer partition, as after the Second World War. She lost Alsace-Lorraine to France, West Prussia and Posen to Poland, North Schleswig after a plebiscite to Denmark, and the three small areas of Eupen, Moresnet and Malmèdy to Belgium, a move justified on grounds of nationality. All German colonies, which were a liability anyway, were confiscated on the plea that the Germans were unfit to govern backward peoples, and the colonies were turned into mandates for the Allied powers. The separation of East Prussia from the rest of Germany was particularly resented, as was the clause forbidding the union of Germany and Austria unless expressly sanctioned by the powers.

Yet in the main there was respect for the principle of nationality and self-determination. Plebiscites were held in the East Prussian districts of Marienwerder and Allenstein, where the vote went in Germany's favour. The compromise by which Danzig, a German port dominating the commerce of Poland's greatest river, the Vistula, was made into a German municipality with a Polish foreign policy, was a reasonable one. The same solution was found for Memel on the River Niemen. Upper Silesia, a great industrial area, was at first assigned outright to Poland. At Lloyd George's insistence a plebiscite was held there and eventually Poland was given only half the area, though with more of the mineral wealth, while more Poles were left under German rule than Germans under Polish sovereignty. Opportunities in the future were given to Germany in the arrangements over the Saar. It was to be under international control for 15 years with a military force of occupation and French control of the mines. A plebiscite was then to be held. This was duly fulfilled and the Saar was fully restored to Germany in 1935.

The military clauses were more stringent. The army was reduced to 100,000 and volunteers were to enlist for 12 years to prevent the training of reserves by a period of short service. Its armaments were strictly limited. There was to be no military or naval air force and the size of the navy was to be limited to six battleships, six cruisers, twelve destroyers and twelve torpedo boats. The rest of the fleet was to be surrendered to the Allies. In fact the German crews as a last act of defiance scuttled their ships at Scapa Flow. The French obtained a further guarantee against German aggression – the demilitarisation of the Rhineland. This was seen by the French as a pledge for good behaviour. If a third war broke out between themselves and the Germans, it would be fought on German, not French, soil.

Much less wise was Article 231, which raised violent German objections. This was the War Guilt clause, which blamed Germany and her allies for planning and provoking the war. It was bitterly resented in Germany because it meant admitting under duress that all Germans who had died in the war had died for an unjust cause. It was also used to justify a demand for compensation for all damage done to the civilian population of the Allies. Lloyd George, supported by Clemenceau, suggested that war pensions should be classed as civilian damages and Wilson gave way on the point. The inclusion of pensions doubled the charge which would be placed on Germany, though to be fair to Wilson he had earlier refused a French and British proposal that Germany should pay the total cost of the war, i.e. military and civilian damages. No definite figure was fixed at Versailles and a Reparations Commission was established to determine by 1921 the total amount of Germany's obligations. After prolonged haggling the Commission fixed Germany's liability at £6,600 million, with immediate down payments in cash and in kind in the form of coal and shipping. The attempts to extract payment from Germany were to poison the international atmosphere throughout the 1920s.

The question divided Britain and France, for while the British desired the rehabilitation of the German economy, the French, in their desire to cripple Germany permanently, occupied the Ruhr in 1923, the pretext being provided by the failure of the Germans to keep up to date with their payments. The occupation triggered off the collapse of the German currency, which had an immense social impact in Germany. In 1924 the Dawes Plan and in 1929 the Young Plan proposed revised schemes of reparations, but when the reparations question was brought to an end by the Lausanne Conference of 1932, it is doubtful whether Germany had paid much in the way of reparations at all. Keynes was right to condemn the economic clauses as unworkable and their effect on Europe as unsettling.

The Treaty of Versailles was signed in the Hall of Mirrors in June 1919. The German delegates had not been allowed to discuss the Allied proposals, only to submit observations in writing, which, apart from the notable exception of the plebiscite question in Upper Silesia, were ignored. Discussion might well have softened some of the harsher aspects of the treaty. The absence of discussion allowed the Germans to claim in the future that as the treaty was a Diktat it was not morally binding. Indeed the treaty could have been improved by a little more consideration for German susceptibilities. The attempt to extradite the Kaiser from Holland and the prosecution of twelve war criminals was bound to keep antagonisms alive. So were the many petty provisions in the treaty, which must have galled the Germans, who, for instance, were forced to return astronomical instruments taken during the Boxer Rising of 1900, and the skull of an East African Sultan.

But in conclusion the underlying leniency of the terms must again be stressed. The balance of power was not restored, for Germany still dominated Europe. Her steel production by 1925 was twice that of Britain's. Only dismemberment could have destroyed German predominance, and this was felt to be impracticable. Machiavelli no doubt would have attributed the failure of the Versailles treaty to the fact that it ignored the rule that an intelligent victor does one of two things to the defeated: he crushes or conciliates. The Versailles treaty did neither. It irritated the Germans but did not deprive them of the means of retaliation. But it would be as fair to say that French policy after 1919, obsessed by the need for security, undermined the Versailles treaty. Versailles failed, says Gerhard Schulz, 'not because the treaties were worthless, not because mistakes were made, but primarily because there was no timely or far-sighted attempt to revise these treaties and to continue the necessarily unfinished work of the Paris Peace Conference'.

(c) The Treaties with Austria, Hungary and Bulgaria

The peace treaties of 1919 and 1920 merely formalised a process that had been generating for a long time, the dissolution of the Austro-Hungarian Empire. For the minorities in central and eastern Europe the war strengthened the hitherto incipient desire for national independence. The statesmen of 1919 were determined to respect these feelings but they brushed aside the request of the Austrian delegation, led by Karl Renner, that a new republic of Austria was as new a creation as Czechoslovakia and should not therefore be saddled with responsibility for the war. Both Austria and Hungary, the core of the old empire, were to have treaties imposed on them and were to pay reparations.

At St Germain Austria yielded Bohemia and Moravia, with a population of 10 millions, to the new Czechoslovakia. Dalmatia and Bosnia-Herzegovina went to Yugoslavia, Bukovina to Rumania and Galicia to Poland. The Trentino, South Tyrol as far as the Brenner Pass, and Istria with Trieste were gained by Italy. The population of Austria was reduced from 22 million to 6½ million, and one-third of the German-speaking population was assigned to other states. Vienna, with a population of 2 million, was left with an agricultural hinterland which could not easily support it, though the Burgenland, which had been Hungarian, was allotted to Austria, as its population was mainly German. No longer was Austria the centre of a free trade area with a population of over 50 million, and this caused considerable problems in the future. Yet if Vienna appeared a city that had lost its *raison d'être*, Austria was not regarded with the same hate as Germany and in the 1920s was frequently given economic assistance by the powers and the League of Nations.

Hungary's fate was all too similar to that of Austria's. She lost Croatia and Slovenia to Yugoslavia, and Slovakia and Ruthenia to Czechoslovakia. To Rumania was ceded Transylvania and the Banat of Temesvar. Hungary's population fell from 21 million to 7.5 million, with a rather greater reduction in territory. Hungary remained an island of feudalism looking out over a sea of peasant states which were not only former Hungarian territory but also states in which were absorbed over 3 million Magyars. The failure to consult all parties on central and east European questions was most unfortunate, because the frontier problems were more complicated and the ignorance of the Conference leaders greater. When Lloyd George spoke to the House of Commons on the subject of a territorial dispute between Czechoslovakia and Poland, he was honest enough to admit that he had never heard of the area.

In drawing up the new Bulgarian boundaries in the Treaty of Neuilly, the Allies were influenced primarily by the desire to reduce Bulgaria's capacity to wage another offensive war. Accordingly she was forced to cede to Yugoslavia four strategic salients in North Macedonia, while Western Thrace was given to Greece, which meant the loss of any outlet on to the Aegean Sea. The Dobrudja was returned to Rumania. The Bulgarians complained bitterly that nearly a million of their people were contained in neighbouring states.

(d) The settlement with Turkey

By the Treaty of Sèvres of August 1920 Turkey was forced to cede Eastern Thrace, her Aegean Islands and Smyrna with its hinterland to the Greeks. Armenia was to become independent and the Straits were to be put under the control of an international commission which would keep them open at all times. Syria was to become a French mandate, and Palestine, Transjordan and Iraq British mandates. It was a harsh peace, which reflected the Turcophobe opinions of Lloyd George.

Yet the delay in the settlement had crucial consequences because it made possible a remarkable growth of Turkish nationalism from the spring of 1919. The revival was caused by the landing of Greek troops in May 1919 at Smyrna, a move authorised by the allies to put pressure on the Turks and also to forestall any Italian seizure of Smyrna. The defeat at the hands of the British and French had been seen as a disaster by the Turks but not a dishonourable event, which the Greek invasion certainly was. A national revival took place, led by Mustapha Kemal who, though a successful military leader in the war at the Dardanelles and in Syria, had opposed government policy and was therefore free in the public mind of any association with the collapse of 1918. Kemal's nationalist movement, which was to oust the Sultan in 1923 and lay the foundations of a new Turkey, built up its armed strength and demanded the recognition by the Allies of the integrity of Turkish territory, which implied the end of Greek occupation and continued Turkish control of Armenia. None of the Allies had sufficient military presence in the Middle East to crush Kemal, and their rivalries in the area prevented any real cooperation over the problem.

In April 1920 the Turks reached an agreement with Soviet Russia for a joint attack on Armenia. By March 1921 a peace treaty was signed between the two countries which settled the Russo-Turkish frontiers in the Caucasus. Turkey returned Batum but retained the adjacent Kars-Ardahan salient. Kemal now turned to his main task, the expulsion of the Greeks from Anatolia. This was achieved by August 1922, for the Greeks were discredited by internal excesses, which meant that only Lloyd George among the Allied leaders wished to give aid, and he fell from power over the issue.

New peace terms now had to be worked out at Lausanne in 1923. Turkish success at the Conference was due to the stubborn, shrewd diplomacy of Ismet. The British representative Curzon attempted to use what the American observer Child called Star Chamber tactics to bully Ismet, but the Turk stood his ground, using his deafness to ignore proposals which he disliked! He was prepared to make concessions over the Straits because the British still had warships at Istanbul as well as troops in Mosul. The Straits were made free to commercial vessels at all times except when Turkey was at war, but there was only limited right of passage for foreign warships. The Turks were to demilitarise zones on both shores of the Dardanelles, and administration of the area was to be under an international commission. The Turks, however, regained East Thrace and the islands of Imbros and Tenedos from Greece. The special legal privileges of foreign governments and individuals in Turkey, known as the capitulations, had been a source of grievance to the Turkish nationalists, and were abolished. Turkey was freed from 40 per cent of the public debt of the Ottoman Empire, and no longer had to suffer the indignity of foreign supervision of her finances.

The Lausanne settlement faced facts, and its realism enabled it to be a permanent solution of the Turkish problem. Turkey was no longer contracting, for she was now an ethnically Turkish unit. Free of pressure from stronger rivals, she was now truly independent, balanced between Russia and the West. The Eastern Question was at an end. For a century or more it had been the most permanent of all sources of international conflict; and yet, as Anderson has stressed, sterility had been its keynote because 'these rivalries were too often fruitless and too often irrelevant to the real interests of the states concerned'.

(e) Some general considerations of the Settlement

One of the consequences of the war was to bring democratic ideals and institutions to peoples who had not known them before. But democracy as a rule only works satisfactorily when created by an evolutionary process; the sudden creation of democratic regimes caused by the revolutionary changes in the war and peace settlements was therefore to be yet another factor promoting instability after 1919. Large areas of Europe were committed to a political regime in whose working they were wholly without experience, and which ran counter to their historical traditions. The liberal assumption that this form of government was in some mystic way appropriate for all Europe was soon proved to be ill-founded and optimistic. Experience was to confirm in Italy, Germany, and elsewhere the thesis of Socrates that democracy may all too easily become the parent of tyranny.

The second main strand of the postwar settlements was the vogue for national self-determination. But to apply the principle meant its violation, for, in the words of Gathorne-Hardy, 'in the racial and linguistic jig-saw of Eastern Europe there are no clear-cut lines of demarcation'. Wilson's later regret at his pronouncements about self-determination are worth recalling. 'When I gave utterance to these words', he said, 'I said them without the knowledge that nationalities existed which are coming to us day after day.' Therefore a new patchwork of national minorities replaced the old one. Czechoslovakia, for example, had a total population of 14 million, of whom 4.5 million were Poles, Ruthenes, Magyars and Germans. Poland's population of 32 million included nearly 1 million Germans, 6 million White Russians and 3 million Jews. Rumania now included 1.5 million Magyars. The result was highly unsettling for postwar Europe because it divided the continent into some states which wished to uphold the Versailles Settlement and some which were determined to revise it.

The greatest of the revisionist powers was Germany. Only the continued collaboration of Britain, the United States and France could have guaranteed the settlement against her. The French appeared to have gained an Anglo-American guarantee of military assistance in the event of a German attack, but the British–French agreement was contingent on the ratification of the American–French treaty. Unfortunately the American government failed to secure ratification of the Versailles treaty by Congress and abandoned the guarantee to France. This had grave consequences for the future. The burden of maintaining the Versailles Settlement now lay on the French, who felt that they had been deceived, for in return for the Anglo-American guarantee they had given up claims on Germany. The British still attempted to work with the French, but they did not ratify the military guarantees which the French so earnestly desired. British interests were still global, and Britain sought to avoid entanglements on the continent. Yet the failure to give the military guarantees provoked the French into punitive anti-German policies which undermined the hopes of lasting peace.

The failure of so much of the Settlement has obscured its valid virtues. The terms of the Versailles treaty were so moderate as to be a diplomatic defeat for France. Clemenceau had hoped to detach the left bank of the Rhine from Germany but failed to do so. And despite the minorities problem in several of the new states, the treaty marked the triumph of nationalism in the sense that a larger proportion of European people than ever before were ruled by governments to which they would voluntarily pay allegiance and over which they had some direct control. The disaffected minorities probably numbered only 3 per cent of the population of Europe.

The Germans were wont to claim after the Settlement that it was radically different from the one promised to them as laid down in Wilson's fourteen points of January 1918. In fact only a few of the fourteen points actually concerned Germany, and these were fulfilled. Point 5 stated the intention to adjust colonial claims in the interests of the populations concerned, and this clearly implied the loss by Germany of her colonies. Points 7 and 8 provided for the evacuation of Belgium territory and the return to France of Alsace-Lorraine. Point 13 provided for the creation of an independent Poland with 'frcc and secure access to the sea', which meant that West Prussia would have to be ceded by Germany.

When the armistice was concluded in November 1918, the Germans were informed that they would have to compensate the civilian populations of their enemies for damage done. Many of the remaining clauses in the fourteen points were implemented in the Versailles Settlement. Point 10 referred to the right to self-determination of the peoples of Austria-Hungary and the Settlement ratified the creation of Yugoslavia and Czechoslovakia. Point 11 provided for the freedom of Serbia, Montenegro and Rumania, and Point 12 for the independence of the peoples under Turkish rule outside Turkey proper. Point 14 expressed the hope that a general association of nations would be formed to guarantee international order. Wilson's persistence here led to the creation of the League of Nations, the necessary machinery for the revision of the treaties. Therefore the fourteen points and the Versailles Treaty were not part of a massive Allied confidence trick. On the contrary, they demonstrate the underlying idealism of the Settlement.

(f) The French alliance system

France emerged from the war, suggests Gathorne-Hardy, rather in the situation of a boxer who has laid out the former champion by a well-placed blow but who is still too dazed to be certain whether his opponent has been or will be counted out. To a point the metaphor is valid, but the French in fact were only too well aware that the opponent had not in fact been counted out and that true security had not yet been attained because Germany might yet struggle off the canvas. Conscious that Germany possessed twice as many men of military age and lacking the Anglo-American guarantee or faith in the collective security of the League of Nations, the French attempted to provide their own security.

Three main techniques were used. The French tried to use, or rather abuse, the reparations system so as to strengthen themselves and weaken Germany. Secondly, there was reliance on military methods. The French insisted on keeping the largest military establishment on the continent and were determined to use force if they deemed it necessary, as they did in 1923 when they occupied the Ruhr. They also bolstered their strength through the traditional diplomacy of alliances. A treaty of mutual support was signed with Belgium in 1920, but the area of chief concern was Eastern Europe. A fundamental purpose of the peace settlement of 1919 had been to create a *cordon sanitaire* of new states between the two dangerous powers, Germany and Soviet Russia. As Hugh Seton-Watson has shown, 'the permanent nightmare of Western statesmen during the first decade after the Armistice was an alliance of Germany with Russia'. It was not an unlikely development, for the left was strong in Germany and both powers were aggrieved at the Versailles Settlement. The fears of the West were given confirmation by the signing of the Treaty of Rapallo between Germany and Russia in 1922. Provision was made in the treaty for recognition of Russia and the expansion of Russo-German trade.

The Rapallo treaty had two consequences. It hardened the French attitude towards Germany and made Poincaré seize the opportunity to occupy the Ruhr in 1923; it also intensified the French search for new allies in Eastern Europe. An alliance had already been reached with Poland in 1921. Between 1924 and 1927 treaties were signed with the 'Little Entente' powers of Czechoslovakia, Rumania and Yugoslavia. These alliances remained the fundamental features of the East European political situation until the rise of Hitler. France granted her allies financial and military assistance, and the French bloc was able to dominate Europe and the League of Nations in the 1920s. Real progress in economic cooperation was made and for a season an illusion of security was created.

But it proved to be a chimera. The alliance of the Little Entente powers had come into existence originally because of a common fear of Hungarian revisionism. When this fear receded, the individual preoccupations of each power became prominent. Yugoslavia looked upon Italy as her chief threat, while Rumania and Czechoslovakia were most apprehensive of Russia and Germany respectively. In any case no combination of small powers could equal one great state. The strength of the French system, as Cobban has stressed, was the stength of France. It would survive while France had the strength and the will to defend her allies and herself. As German and Soviet strength returned, however, that of France relatively declined, and with it the value of the alliances concluded with the East European states. By 1930 the French had again become acutely aware of their weakness and begun to construct a chain of fortifications known as the Maginot Line along the French-German frontier. But this implied a defensive mentality which was incompatible with the maintenance of France's network of alliances, which had formed the cornerstone of her security system since the war.

(g) Locarno

This process of decline in the French alliance system was fore-shadowed at the Locarno meeting of 1925, although the meeting appeared to usher in a new era of more cordial relations in Western Europe. After the chaos caused by the invasion of the Rhur, the more conciliatory Briand replaced Poincaré and worked for a rap-prochement with Germany. One rapid result was the Dawes Plan of April 1924, which reduced reparations and made a loan of 800 million gold marks to Germany.

This new French attitude had the approval of the British foreign secretary, Austen Chamberlain, and was reciprocated by the German government now that Gustav Stresemann was foreign minister. Stresemann was able and courageous; he came from a nationalistic businessman's world and hated the losses of German territory in Eastern Europe. In February 1925 he made it known that Germany was prepared to conclude a settlement guaranteeing Germany's western boundaries. Stresemann believed that a guarantee of Ger-many's western frontier was an essential preparation for revision of her eastern frontier.

His initiative led to the signing of the Locarno treaties of October 1925. The frontiers of France and Belgium with Germany were guaranteed not only by these states but by Italy and Britain. Ger-many also signed arbitration treaties with France, Belgium, Poland and Czechoslovakia. The agreements induced a mood of euphoria in Europe, which was given more substance in the following year when Germany became a member of the League of Nations. Locarno seemed the turning point between the years of war and the years of peace. The treaties were the result of genuine collaboration between the British, German and French governments during 1924 and 1925, for Stresemann had established a close rapport with Aristide Briand and Chamberlain. The three succeeded in creating an atmosphere in which Germany could again feel an equal partner in the family of European nations. Locarno raised hopes that more revision of the Versailles Settlement could take place, so that Germany's aims could be satisfied peacefully, and as Britain was linked to the Locarno agreement, French confidence in Britain's concern for European security was in some measure restored.

But the treaties were criticised at the time and have been ever since on the grounds that they made one set of European frontiers more inviolable than the others. Britain and Italy were bound to act only if Germany or France tried to change the western boundaries arranged at Versailles. The East was to be the concern only of Germany, France and the Eastern states. The French had of course tried to extract full guarantees of Germany's eastern frontiers, but Britain and Italy refused to assume any obligations in that area. Austen Chamberlain defined the British position: 'For the Polish Corridor no British government ever will or ever can risk the bones of a British grenadier.' But the very fact that certain sections of the Versailles settlement were given a privileged position weakened the rest of it. The illusion of security was soon to be shattered. Locarno in a sense reflected the brief period of relative prosperity which Europe enjoyed up to 1929. This prosperity died with the Wall Street crash and so did the Locarno spirit. Even in 1925 Stresemann had been attacked for his conciliation by the nationalists in Germany. With the years of depression, extremism was to triumph in Germany and end the prospects of European peace.

FURTHER READING

Ferro, M., *The Great War*, Routledge, London, 1987

Henig, R., *Versailles and After*, Methuen, London, 1984

Horne, A., *The Price of Glory: Verdun*, Macmillan, London, 1962

Kennedy, P., *The Rise and Fall of the Great Powers*, Unwin Hyman, London, 1988

Liddell Hart, B., *The History of the First World War*, Pan Books, London, 1972

Marks, S., *The Illusion of Peace*, Macmillan, London, 1976

Sontag, R., *A Broken World 1919–1939*, Harper Torchbooks, New York, 1971

Stone, N., *Europe Transformed 1878–1919*, Fontana, London, 1983

Stone, N., *The Eastern Front*, Hodder and Stoughton, London, 1985

Terraine, J., *White Heat: the New Warfare*, Sidgwick, London, 1975

QUESTIONS

1. Account for the deadlock on the Western Front during the First World War.
2. How and why did Allied war aims change during the First World War?
3. What were the chief causes of Allied victory in 1918?
4. Critically analyse the most important consequences of the First World War.
5. 'Germany got off lightly.' How far do you agree with Churchill's view of the Versailles Treaty?
6. What were the objectives of French foreign policy after 1919 and how did French governments seek to implement them?

3
Russia, 1914–39: The revolutions of 1917 and the establishment of communism

(a) The war and the fall of Tsarism

The domestic situation in Russia, deprived of Stolypin's strong hand, had been deteriorating before the outbreak of war. Real power was vested in the hands of the court, and ministers were appointed at the whim of Rasputin, who was free to advance incompetent individuals to important posts. Treadgold terms this situation a 'psychopathic tragicomedy', and it lasted until December 1916, when Rasputin was assassinated by a group of courtiers led by Prince Yusupov.

The outbreak of war led to strong demonstrations of loyalty to tsar and country and the Duma voted war credits enthusiastically, but disillusion was swift. Russia was unprepared for war and, unlike Britain and the United States, was incapable of carrying out the necessary planning. The whole economy was strained. The mobilisation of men and the inroads of war in the west diminished the food supply, and the railway network, which was not properly maintained, became even more inadequate for wartime emergencies. The lack of comprehension in government circles of the nature of the new crisis is evident in the advice to industry to cut production, as it was believed that demand would decrease.

The commander-in-chief of the army was Grand Duke Nicholas, who was popular with the soldiers, but the weaknesses in the army were beyond the wisdom of any one man to repair. Russian troops lacked proper training, equipment and munitions. The problems of supplying them in a theatre of war which was mobile and distances vast were never overcome. The offensives of 1914 and 1915 produced staggering casualties – 2 million in 1915 alone. As the army retreated, a refugee problem was created, for 3 million civilians retreated with the soldiers.

The calamities did produce some exertions at government level. In 1915 special councils were established for defence, transport, fuel and food. The government also promised Poland autonomy at the end of the war, and some of the reactionary ministers were dismissed for opposing this policy. In September the formation of a Progressive Bloc of parties in the Duma was announced, and the bloc demanded more share in the government. Most ministers would have welcomed this, but not Goremykin, who persuaded the Tsarina to goad the Tsar into dissolving the Duma. Two days later Nicholas committed another error by dismissing his uncle and assuming command at the front himself. This led to a further deterioration at home as the Tsarina and Rasputin now had complete control of government. In February 1916 Goremykin was replaced by the even more mediocre Boris Stürmer, who was himself dismissed in favour of an old man, Golitsyn. A new minister of the interior, A. D. Protopopov, was appointed, despite the fact that he was virtually insane. At the same time the Russian offensives in 1916 cost a million more casualties and the morale of the army began to crumble.

Therefore the final crisis began to develop by late 1916. In November the Duma was reconvened and the Cadet leader, Paul Miliukov, angrily denounced government failures and asked, 'Is this stupidity or treason?' In December, in a macabre night of horror, Prince Yusupov and other desperate members of the nobility managed with some difficulty to dispose of Rasputin. The monk was poisoned and shot yet was still alive when he was thrown into the River Neva. By 1917 most thoughtful observers foresaw the likelihood of revolution, but when it broke out in Petrograd in March, its spontaneity took everyone by surprise. Three factors gave the Revolution its first impetus. There were 400,000 workers in Petrograd and by March they were hungry. Demonstrations on 8 March over bread shortages led to riots which merged with processions celebrating International Women's Day and a strike at the Putilov armaments factory. Unlike the Revolution of 1905, the Cossacks openly sided with the rioters, and the situation became serious.

The apathy of the Tsar at this point is astounding. He was warned by both the Petrograd garrison commander and the President of the Duma, Rodzianko, that a grave crisis had arisen. He commented, 'This fat Rodzianko has written me some nonsense to which I will not even reply.' He did, however, write to his wife, expressing how much he missed his game of patience every evening and stating his intention to take up dominoes again in his spare time! The riots continued and the only move the Tsar made was to dissolve the Duma on 11 March. It met in defiance of the order and elected a provisional committee composed of members of the Progressive Bloc with the idea of restoring order, but it was too late. Discipline had broken down and on 12 March the Taurida Palace was invaded by the workers, who set up a workers' soviet modelled on the institutions that had proved their worth in 1905. On 13 March most of the ministers were arrested, and on 15 March the Tsar himself was persuaded to abdicate in favour of his brother, Grand Duke Michael. As Michael refused to take the throne, the Romanov dynasty ended without even a whimper. Nicholas renounced power, calmly enjoying the crisp cold weather and reading the works of Julius Caesar.

The last years of Tsarism had seen a number of promising developments in Russian life, particularly in education and industry. It was Russia's tragedy that these developments were soon to be stifled by a new totalitarian regime committed to the monolithic unity of all aspects of life. Tsarist government had stunted political growth but it had left other aspects of life, for example the arts, to develop freely. Yet with the pressures of twentieth-century warfare, revolution became more and more likely. The Russian economy and bureaucracy could not cope, and by 1916 there were severe food shortages, with meat rising in price 149 per cent and vegetables 228 per cent between 1916 and 1917. Russian casualties in the war were enormous and difficult to quantify, but it would be safe to say that 8 million Russians had been killed. The loyalty of the Russian people was at last eroded by such disasters and the regime was seen to have outlived its usefulness. As the poet Mayakovsky expressed it,

> 'Like the chewed stump of a fag
> We spat their dynasty out.'

(b) The Provisional Government and the Bolshevik seizure of power

After the abdication of the Tsar, real power was divided between the Provisional Committee of the Duma and the Petrograd Soviet of Workers Deputies. It was a situation which prevented any possibility of effective government, and Adam Ulam is right to describe it as 'a perfect prescription for anarchy'. The Provisional Committee was now formed into the Provisional Government, with Prince George Lvov as prime minister. He and the foreign minister, Paul Miliukov, were Cadets, Alexander Guchkov, the Octobrist, was services minister, and Alexander Kerensky, a Social Revolutionary, was minister of justice.

Government was difficult, for the Taurida Palace was like a madhouse and the Petrograd Soviet, dominated by Mensheviks and Social Revolutionaries, allowed the Provisional Government to exist only on sufferance. The Executive Committee of the Petrograd Soviet soon issued an order providing for the setting up in every army unit of elective committees, and announced that the military orders of the Provisional Government were only to be obeyed if they did not conflict with Soviet orders. This opened the way for a further breakdown of discipline in the army. The relative inertia of the Petrograd Soviet is mainly to be explained by the Menshevik theory of history, according to which the bourgeois liberals should first hold power.

The Provisional Government faced other difficulties. The postponement of a Constituent Assembly caused mounting public impatience,
and an early dispute about continuing the war led to the resignation
of Miliukov and Guchkov in May. Meanwhile exiled revolutionary
leaders were returning to Russia – the Social Revolutionary Victor
Chernov and Joseph Stalin from Siberia, but most notably Lenin,
who arrived at the Finland Station in Petrograd in April after his
journey in the famous 'sealed train', which the Germans had allowed
through in the hope that its cargo would weaken the Russian war
effort. He condemned the war as imperialistic and demanded that the
Bolsheviks oppose the Provisional Government and uphold the
slogan 'All Power to the Soviets'. This appeared at the time a
disinterested action, as the Mensheviks and Social Revolutionaries
rather than the Bolsheviks dominated the Soviets, and the immediate
effect was to further weaken the prestige of the Provisional Government.

In May a newly formed cabinet included six socialists, including
Chernov as minister of agriculture. The strong man in this coalition
was Kerensky, who believed that a new offensive was necessary so
that Russia could demand a victorious peace. He managed to kindle
some enthusiasm for the task, and even the Petrograd Soviet gave
grudging assent. The offensive began in July, but, after initial successes, it collapsed and the complete demoralisation of the army resulted. Troops now began to flee home in large numbers, and in
Petrograd violence erupted spontaneously, with the Bolsheviks most
prominent. The urban masses were puzzled because the Menshevik
and Social Revolutionary leaders had not seized office and one
demonstrator shouted at Chernov, 'Take power, you son of a bitch,
when they offer it to you.'

Later in the month Lvov resigned and Kerensky became prime
minister in a cabinet which now contained a majority of socialists.
Kerensky was alarmed by the Bolshevik threat, which after the July
disorders was seen to be a reality. The government therefore accused
Lenin of being a German agent and arrested Trotsky and Kamenev,
Lenin being forced to flee to Finland. Kerensky also attempted to
gather support by creating his own forum of public opinion. In August
he convened a conference composed of Duma deputies, representatives of the Soviets and members of the unions. At the same time he
appointed General Lavr Kornilov in place of Brusilov as commander-
in-chief of the army, and he managed to stabilise the front after the
collapse of the offensive.

The latter move, however, led to another fatal fiasco. In September Kornilov decided that in view of the weakness of the government
he would send a force to the capital to effect a governmental
reconstruction. Through a mediator it was suggested that he should
become prime minister, with Kerensky still a member of the cabinet,

but Kerensky arrested the mediator and tried to dismiss Kornilov, who refused to accept the order. By then his troops were already on their way to Petrograd, and Kerensky was forced to free Bolshevik captives and use their help in suppressing Kornilov's mutiny, which they did by mobilising their Red Guards and by sending agitators who persuaded Kornilov's troops to abandon him. The general, who was forced to surrender, was probably only trying to strengthen the Provisional Government rather than overthrow it, but the whole affair helped the final collapse of discipline in the army and peasants streamed home hoping for land and liberty.

The illegal seizure of land by the peasantry had already started, and the legal owners, the gentry, usually left for their own good. Yet the peasant action did not meet the approval of the party which claimed to stand for peasant interests, the Social Revolutionaries, who declared that their programme was not the same as the arbitrary seizure of land for personal advantage. Chernov, their leader and also a member of the government, told a Soviet of Peasant Deputies in May that the solution of the land question must await the decision of the Constituent Assembly, and also that the war must go on. The peasants ignored him and continued their illegal division of land.

In the towns bitter rivalry grew up between the factory committees, increasingly under Bolshevik control, and the unions, influenced by the Mensheviks and Social Revolutionaries. The government did little to restrain prices, and as the Mensheviks and the Social Revolutionaries had participated in the government, they received much of the blame. Donald Treadgold puts much of the responsibility for government inaction on Kerensky, whose weakness was that 'oratory became a substitute for action'. Only the Bolsheviks, who had consistently refused to collaborate with the government, seemed to possess a credible set of policies which might solve the crisis.

By the autumn the Bolsheviks had gained in both membership and popular support. The membership now exceeded 200,000 and control of the factory committees had been gained. Bolshevik policies, mainly developed by Lenin, had a realism which the policies of other parties lacked. Bolsheviks urged the immediate seizure of land by the peasants, a rapid conclusion of the war and all power to the soviets. These ideas won them support away from the Social Revolutionaries and Mensheviks, although, as E. H. Carr reminds us, even in November their 'independent power in the countryside was still negligible'.

The Bolsheviks were more tightly organised than other socialist parties. Kerensky, nominally a Social Revolutionary, demanded loyalty from his party, but, as he would not follow party decisions himself, that loyalty was not forthcoming. In contrast, Lenin could count on the unswerving support of his party, a vindication of his insistence on a small group of really committed members. By October he was able to declare to the Bolshevik Central Committee that the time was ripe for action. Zinoviev and Kamenev, who opposed such a policy, leaked it to the party press, thereby revealing the plot to the public, but the government took no action, harassed as it was by desertions from the army, peasant violence and strikes in the cities.

The man who did the most to plan a Bolshevik take-over was Leon Trotsky, born Bronstein, the son of a wealthy Jewish farmer. He stressed that a rising against the government would have more chance of success if it were made under the auspices of a soviet action against a counter-revolutionary plot than if it were done openly in the name of the Bolshevik party. Working through the Petrograd Soviet, the Bolsheviks challenged Kerensky's right to order troop movements in the capital. This goaded the premier into a denunciation of their tactics and into an attempt to arrest Lenin. Now the Bolsheviks could claim to be resisting counter-revolution, and on the night of 6–7 November they seized key points in Petrograd and arrested the minister of the Provisional Government. Kerensky tried to rally loyal troops outside the capital, failed to do so and fled into exile. Lenin formed a new government, with himself as premier, Trotsky as commissar for foreign affairs and Stalin as commissar for nationalities. Gradually Bolshevik control spread to the other chief urban centres of Russia.

Lenin now attempted to implement Bolshevik policies as well as to ward off attacks by units loyal to the Provisional Government. Private property in land was abolished, and all private and church lands were transferred to land committees and soviets of peasant deputies for distribution. In December, after an armistice had been agreed, Trotsky began negotiations with the Germans. As Lenin insisted that they needed a breathing space, the Bolsheviks signed in March the punitive treaty of Brest-Litovsk, by which they ceded Poland, the Baltic States of Esthonia, Latvia and Lithuania, the Ukraine, Finland, much of Belorussia and part of Transcaucasia. A total area of 1,300,000 square miles was detached, and the loss in population was 62 millions, a third of the entire population. One-third of the railways and three-quarters of coal and iron resources were lost.

Three centuries of Russian expansion were undone but Ulam sees the treaty as a blessing in disguise for Lenin's regime. The terms, by stripping Russia of its borderlands, made the Bolsheviks concentrate on dealing with opposition in Russia proper without trying to cope with the militant nationalism of the Poles, Finns and Ukrainians. Lenin's wisdom on the matter was in time vindicated and he was now seen as 'the providential leader of the Party and the state, without whom the regime would disintegrate'. There is no doubt that Lenin's concessions to Germany were necessary, for any attempt to continue the war would have caused violent opposition in Russia generally.

Yet the treaty was denounced even by some Bolsheviks, and a Social Revolutionary murdered the German ambassador Count Mirbach in an attempt to provoke a renewal of hostilities. In August Lenin was seriously wounded by Social Revolutionaries, who killed two other Communist leaders.

The Bolshevik response was swift and ruthless. A Red Terror was launched through the Cheka, the Bolshevik secret police. It was the first of a series of moves to destroy the old state and build a new one. Members of the Provisional Government were deported, and the zemstvos (local councils) and municipal councils in Petrograd and Moscow were dissolved. The Russian Orthodox Church was attacked, and the separation of church and state was proclaimed in February 1918. The Constituent Assembly, for which elections were held in November, returned a Social Revolutionary majority, but met only once, and then was dispersed by Bolshevik troops.

The task of establishing a new political and social order was immense, for the country was in a state of chaos. It was clear that a new army would be necessary to assist the regime, and in 1918 Trotsky began to create the Red Army, based on conscription, authority and discipline. The death penalty for desertion was restored and the election of officers ceased. Trained officers were required, and Trotsky accepted volunteer officers from the old armies and recruited unwilling officers, warning them that desertion would result in harm to their families. About 50,000 officers of the old army were used in the civil war that was about to start. Political commissars were appointed to keep an eye on officers and to carry out propaganda among the recruits. The soldiers fought with devotion for their cause, for they were told that death and torture awaited them if they were captured by the Whites, a piece of propaganda which had considerable foundation in truth.

To grapple with the deteriorating economy, the government decided to establish 'Committees of Poor Peasants' all over Russia to requisition grain from the kulaks (rich peasants) to feed the cities. In fact, as E. H. Carr suggests, there were far fewer poor peasants than the Bolsheviks had assumed, and therefore Bolsheviks from the cities did much of the requisitioning, thus arousing deep anger among the peasantry in general. A number of peasant risings occurred in the summer of 1918, which, with similar events in some cities, contributed to the murder of the Tsar and his family at Ekaterinburg by local Bolsheviks in July.

(c) The Civil War

In the early months of Bolshevik rule there had been little in the way of organised opposition, partly because other parties failed to appreciate what the nature of Bolshevik control would be. After Brest-

Litovsk, however, anti-Bolshevik leaders began to resist the new regime more vigorously. They fell into three groups: (1) non-Bolshevik politicians (2) former officers of the Imperial army and (3) nationalists seeking independence for their particular minority. As the nationalists were only interested in their own lands and the politicians disliked working with conservative officers, the real core of the opposition were the military commanders.

The Whites (the anti-Bolsheviks) were immensely encouraged by the uprising of the Czechoslovak Brigade and its seizure of the area around Omsk in central Siberia in May. The Czechs were troops who had been fighting with the Allies in the European war in the hope of an independent Czechoslovakia after the war. Their action sparked off Allied intervention on a new scale. The Allies had already intervened at Archangel and Vladivostock on the pretext of safe-guarding war supplies. Now the scale of the intervention was stepped up by British, French, Americans and Japanese in the hope that the Bolsheviks would be overthrown and replaced by a regime willing to continue the war. The Allied intervention gave the Whites opportunities which they were unable to grasp, but it was in the main counter-productive, as the Bolsheviks, posing as good patriots, were able to undermine White support by using slogans of defence of the home-land against the foreigners. In contrast, the Whites received only half-hearted Allied support, particularly when the November armis-tice eliminated the need for Russian help against Germany.

The Whites at Omsk were also weakened by internal disunity, for the Social Revolutionaries, Cadets and right-wing elements formed a most uneasy coalition. In November 1918 the conservatives carried out a coup d'état and made Admiral Kolchak, former commander of the Black Sea Fleet, dictator of all forces in Russia. In Esthonia General Yudenich organised an army with British help and the stage was set for the decisive battles of the Civil War in 1919, as Denikin and Kolchak attempted to link up their forces.

Denikin struck north from Azov and won major victories as he advanced on Moscow. Kolchak's disadvantages were, however, too much for him. He was not a competent general and had few able men to assist him. Rival generals and Social Revolutionaries refused to obey his orders, and swift advance was difficult in the periphery of the country, which lacked industry and communications. After some advances in 1919 his forces were rolled back by a Red offensive in June. Denikin's march on Moscow was halted in October, while Yudenich's attempt to take Petrograd also failed. From this point on the Whites collapsed. Decisive factors in their failure were bad relations with the minorities and the brutality used on the peasantry. The American commander in Siberia commented acidly that the Whites killed 100 people in Eastern Siberia to every one killed by the Bolsheviks.

Nevertheless 1920 was a year of crisis for the Bolsheviks. The new Polish government under Pilsudski was determined to recreate the Poland of 1722, and in April Polish troops swept into Kiev. The Bolsheviks, facing a traditional enemy, were again able to invoke nationalistic slogans, and attracted to their side ex-tsarist generals like Brusilov. As a result, they were able to throw back the Poles and advanced towards Warsaw, but the Poles initiated a counter-offensive which routed the Red Army. The Bolsheviks were forced to sign the Treaty of Riga in March 1921, which left some of Belorussia and the Ukraine in Polish hands.

(d) Lenin and the New Economic Policy

The miseries of the Russian people were immensely increased by the carnage and destruction of the Civil War and the terrorism of the Bolshevik dictatorship. In 1920 famine caused the death of about 3 million people and industrial production was only about one-eighth of the 1913 level. As the Red Army was demobilised in 1920, peasant risings erupted in southern and eastern Russia. The climax of the anti-Communist unrest, which included workers as well as the peasantry, came in March 1921 with a revolt at Kronstadt, the naval base, which had been a centre of Bolshevik power in 1917. The revolt was ruthlessly crushed but made a deep impression on Lenin. As always the supreme realist, he realised the need for a Brest-Litovsk, or breathing-space, on the economic front and he adopted the so-called New Economic Policy (NEP).

The essence of this policy was acceptance of a compromise with the peasantry. Peasants were no longer forced into collective farms, and the ruthless requisitioning of agricultural produce was abandoned in favour of a tax in kind on a fixed percentage of the production. The peasant was free to sell as much of the remainder as he wished. Lenin's analysis of the peasantry had in fact been incorrect. The poor peasants had not helped the Communists against the rich peasants, and in fact, as E. H. Carr had demonstrated, there had occurred 'a striking equalization of the size of the unit of production'. As a result, the middle peasants had become the majority of the Russian people and it was they with whom Leinin had to compromise. The compromise was a tactical manoeuvre: the long-term aim of collective farming was not abandoned.

Private enterprise on a small scale was allowed in industry and trade, though the state still retained control over the essentials of the economy. These 'commanding heights' were the banks, heavy industry, transport, and foreign trade, such as it was. Some factories were actually handed back to private owners, but state industries employed four-fifths of the industrial labour force. What galled doctrinaire Communists was the use in state factories of capitalist devices like piece-work rates, preferential rations and bonuses. Bourgeois experts had to be employed but, as Lenin pointed out, 'No price will be too high if we learn intelligently.'

Gradually the Russian economy recovered, helped by the toughness of the Russian people and the enthusiasm of the Communist hierarchy, especially Lenin, who had to goad his followers into implementing the policies. The currency was stabilised and by 1928 the Communists felt able to claim that levels of industrial and agricultural production had overtaken those of 1913.

Meanwhile groups opposing Lenin's policies in the party were disbanded in 1921, and a nationwide purge of the party resulted in the expulsion of one-third of party members. The Cheka was abolished and its place was taken by the GPU, which had the important power, not possessed by the Cheka, to arrest party members. These were, however, the last important moves to be initiated by Lenin. In 1921 and 1922 he suffered strokes which forced his virtual retirement, and he found it impossible to keep in touch with what was going on in government as his colleagues began to intrigue for power. Lenin died in January 1924, and the deep admiration which ordinary Russians felt for him was demonstrated by the millions who came to pay their respects to his embalmed corpse.

That Lenin was a political genius there can be little doubt. He was close to the average Russian and could influence audiences by the straightforward and clear exposition of his ideas. He was also a humane man, who, said Maxim Gorky, declared war on human misery. Two characteristics dominated Lenin's career. The first was his complete dedication to revolution and the subordination of his life to that end. This overwhelming sense of service accounted for the modesty of his demeanour and, as E. H. Carr remarks, 'he set an example of austerity and impersonality which long remained a standard of conduct for the party'. Despite his lack of personal vanity or ambition, he possessed the unwavering conviction that he alone was capable of leading the party. From this conviction sprang the ability to carry colleagues with him at times of crisis, as in the seizure of power in 1917 or the adoption of NEP. Therefore, to Trotsky, Lenin's greatness lay in his capacity for effective action and he was 'the greatest engine-driver of revolution'. The second major characteristic was a unique realism, which led Lenin to make correct decisions on a number of vital issues – on the nature of the party, on the question of party's policies in 1917 and the tactics by which it was able to take power. These issues reveal Lenin as a great political strategist.

On the other hand, Lenin's lifework boded ill for the future of Russia and indeed the whole world. He had forecast that the state would wither away after revolution, yet the reverse occurred. The élite that had led the revolution added to its power and the result was dictatorship. Lenin may be criticised for his obsessional persecution of opponent after victory had been gained, even when they had begun to support his regime, for in this way he contributed to making terror a permanent feature of Russian life. Adam Ulam writes:

> It must be an indelible stain on Lenin's record that for all his humane instincts he allowed this cult, a veritable mystique of terror, to develop. While he was quick to intervene when an individual case of injustice was brought to his attention, he allowed mass terror not only to be practised, but to become legitimate and respectable.

(c) The emergence of Stalin

Lenin's stroke threw everything into confusion and uncertainty. The governing body had been the Politburo (the Political Bureau of the Central Committee), and its members were Lenin, Trotsky, Kamenev, Stalin, Bukharin, Tomsky and Zinoviev. It settled policy, and it was then left to the Orgburo to implement decisions reached by the Politburo. The liaison between the two bureaux had fallen to Stalin, who was now general secretary of the Central Committee.

Stalin was born Joseph Djugashvili in 1879, the son of Georgian peasants. He was educated in a theological seminary at Tiflis, a period which Isaac Deutscher sees as decisive in his intellectual development, because he reacted against the repressive teaching and absorbed forbidden socialist ideas. Unlike most of the revolutionary leaders, he was not from the middle class, and his class hatred was all-consuming. By 1904 he had become a Bolshevik, and his gifts as an administrator led to his gradual rise in the party. In 1921 he was Commissar for Nationalities and a member of the Politburo as well as general secretary. This concentration of power worried Lenin, who after his second stroke made a will in which he pointed to the danger of a clash between Trotsky and Stalin. He also mentioned Stalin's rudeness and capacity for stirring up trouble in the party. Lenin was actually preparing an attack with Trotsky's help on Stalin when a third stroke immobilised him in March 1923.

'Stalin', affirms Ulam, 'was a man of uncommonly good sense and unusually vile as well as brooding temper.' He had great gifts as a committee man: brevity and the ability to get to the point. As well as being on the major committees, he was also on most of the important sub-committees, such as the editorial board of *Pravda* and the committee to deal with the Ukrainian question. It was a strength of Stalin's that he was willing to undertake such tasks, which on the face of it were unglamorous and unrewarding. Many Communists liked him because he was not a middle-class intellectual like Lenin or Trotsky but was a coarse peasant like themselves. His skilful administrative work explains only in part his rise to power. By the mid-1920s he had become a superb politician, possessing an excellent sense of timing, simple but effective oratory and an apparent but misleading joviality. As commissar for nationalities, he was able to take most of the credit for the constitutional reform by which in 1922 a Union of Soviet Socialist Republics was established. He claimed that this achievement was as important as the creation of the Red Army in the Civil War, implying that he was the equal of Trotsky.

With Lenin now incapacitated, a Truimvirate of Zinoviev, Kamenev and Stalin now began to act together against Trotsky, whose brilliant achievements made him appear a potential Napoleon. His partners underestimated Stalin, as did Trotsky, who on Lenin's death failed to act with any decisiveness, as he was ill himself. When Lenin's will was read out in May 1924, Zinoviev said that Lenin's fears about Stalin were groundless, a remark he was soon to regret. This was a decisive moment in Stalin's progress, for Trotsky did not seize on the will as a weapon with which to attack him. He was mainly concerned with the hostility of Kamenev and Zinoviev, who clashed with him on such major issues as the question of permanent revolution, while Stalin remained in the background. In January 1925 his enemies persuaded the Central Committee to dismiss Trotsky from his post as war commissar. Trotsky was too loyal to the party to resort to the only expedient left to him – the use of the Red Army. In 1926 he lost his seat on the Politburo, in 1927 he was expelled from the party and in 1929 was expelled from Russia.

Zinoviev and Kamenev soon found that though they had defeated Trotsky, they were not in control of the situation. By 1925 Stalin had gained new allies on the Politburo – Bukharin, Rykov and Tomsky. The new commissar of war, Voroshilov, was also his man. Now Stalin was able to move against his partners in the Triumvirate, and both Zinoviev and Kamenev were expelled from the party in 1927. Bukharin, Rykov and Tomsky, who had supported Stalin against Zinoviev and Kamenev, were forced out of the Politburo by 1930 and Stalin's ascendancy was now complete.

(f) Stalin's totalitarianism

After 1928 Stalin began to unleash the apparatus of terror against the mass of the population, and to carry out a purge of party members in order to revolutionise the economic and social system and to consolidate his own power. By the late 1930s he had built up a totalitarian dictatorship which was more complete and efficient than that in Nazi Germany, and which was based on three institutions – the party organisation, the secret police and the army.

Donald Treadgold sees Soviet totalitarianism as having seven major objectives: (1) to preserve and strengthen Communist power and stifle any political opposition, (2) to plan the entire economic system, rooting out any individual enterprise, (3) to stamp out nationalism in the borderlands and to subject the minority nationalities to Moscow's control, (4) to control academic and artistic work and crush it if it ran counter to the currently applied ideological line in the arts and sciences, (5) to crush organised religion and, when that proved difficult, to confine its activities, (6) to create a pervading atmosphere of fear which would quell the independence of political non-conformists and (7) to prepare the way for the extension of Soviet power abroad whenever the opportunity might arise.

In seeking total control of all facets of Russian life Stalin had to be a working dictator, unlike Hitler, who left vast areas of government to others. 'Stalin', asserts Ulam, 'displayed jealous proprietary feelings for power in all its aspects and details.' As his power grew, the politician in him receded and he had become vindictively tyrannical by 1927. This reality was carefully hidden from the Russian people. Stalin was a consummate actor and to the masses he seemed a godlike figure, endowed both with iron resolution and genial paternal qualities. He built up this image skilfully and came to represent both the party and the state, thus commanding loyalty almost amounting to worship.

Up to 1927 the Russian people under NEP had been for the most part left alone to lead their own lives. The peasantry believed that they had more freedom as they had obtained land; in their eyes the two were synonymous. Some political criticism had been allowed and even those imprisoned for too outspoken anti-Communist views received light sentences. It seemed that the majority of the people preferred what Bukharin called 'the creep at a snail's pace' towards socialism. Stalin's sudden decision to industrialise rapidly both the city and the countryside by converting the peasantry into a landless proletariat shocked the nation. To achieve this, state power required strengthening, and therefore the first Five Year Plan inaugurated a new phase in Russian history in which government began to invade every area of life in a manner unparalleled in the history not only of Russia but of any other country up to that time. Thus the first Five Year Plan marked the real beginning of Soviet totalitarianism.

The secret police, the OGPU, an agency increasingly at Stalin's disposal, extended its work. It arrested or bullied independent minds in the party and kept watch on industry and the armed forces. It spied on all foreigners in Russia. It acquired special troops of its own, some of whom ran the concentration camps for political prisoners. From 1928 on it began to arrest private entrepreneurs, kulaks and members of the intelligentsia, who were often brought before 'show trials'. In July 1934 the OGPU was changed to the NKVD, or People's Commissariat for Internal Affairs. In the 1930s it became the biggest employer in the Soviet Union and was entrusted with over one-sixth of new construction work by 1941. By then the prison labour force which it controlled numbered about 10 million people.

The NKVD became a state within a state and its operations extended into every branch of government. It became a web for collecting information, exerting control and cross-spying, and all the threads reposed ultimately in Stalin's hands. A powerful state or party figure could be sure that somewhere in the NKVD there was a man reporting on his policies and performance. Spying became a way of life. Nor was the moulding of youth neglected. A number of youth organisations were developed – the Little Octobrists for children aged from 8 to 11, the Pioneers for children aged from 10 to 16, and the Komsomol (the Communist Union of Youth) for young people over the age of 15. Russian youth was to be conditioned to obey the Communist Party unquestioningly.

(g) The economic changes

With the inception of the first Five Year Plan in 1928, Stalin laid down an extremely ambitious programme. Industrial production, including consumer goods, was to be increased by 250 per cent, agricultural production by 130 per cent and a major start was to be made on the collectivisation of peasant farms. Stalin's motives were not merely economic. The main objective was to convert the entire labour force, rural as well as urban, into employees of state-controlled enterprises, and it would then be easier for the government to exert control over the masses. A second objective derived from one of Stalin's obsessions. He felt that the kulak was the main enemy of Communism, and that the peasantry as a whole was barring Russia's path to industrialisation and socialism. As Ulam puts it, 'a kingdom of darkness must be conquered before the Soviet Union could become the promised land'. A third objective stemmed from Stalin's vision of himself as a modern Ivan the Terrible or Peter the Great. Like them, he wished to modernise Russia for the purposes of great power status, and was obsessed with the need for a mighty Russia which would overtake other European states and even the United States. It was a tragedy for Russia that Stalin was profoundly ignorant on economic matters and launched policies which brought economic disaster by the mad speed which characterised them.

By 1928 the peasantry owned 96 per cent of the land, and Stalin ordered that the kulaks (rich peasants) were to be destroyed as a class by collectivisation of agriculture. The government met with the violent opposition of many peasants, especially in the Ukraine and the Caucasus, but opposition was ruthlessly crushed. OGPU agents and army units would surround villages and machine-gun the inhabitants into surrender, transporting those left alive to concentration camps. Peasants still found ways of retaliation; they ate or sold their livestock rather than put them into a common pool, and by 1933 livestock production had fallen to half the 1928 figure. This, combined with the loss of managerial talent, helped to exacerbate the effect of three bad harvests in the years 1931 to 1933, when over 5 million people died of famine and government action.

Some concessions had to be made to the peasants, and they were allowed to keep their own garden plots, but the basic drive for collectivisation continued. By 1940 the 25 million peasant holdings had been replaced by nearly a quarter of a million collective farms on which lived about 75 million people. Individual farms were rare, and an immense technical and administrative revolution had been carried out. Russian farming became the most mechanised in Europe, particularly in the use of tractors. Large fields replaced small arable strips and by 1940 the wheat crop was 80 per cent higher than in 1914. The collective farms were to feed the growing population of the towns even during the Second World War, when Russia might not otherwise have withstood the German onslaught. More efficient methods meant that much labour was released for use in industry, and it is certainly true that before 1928 the agricultural population was so huge as to encourage wasteful employment, especially as it was a characteristic of the Russian peasant, as Nove has noted, to produce mainly for subsistence. The increased production of grain allowed more to be exported, and this furnished extra capital for industrial development.

Against these advantages must be set the human cost, which is self-evident, and certain economic weaknesses. The process of collectivisation caused lasting damage to Russian agriculture; the 1928 level of livestock production was not reached again until 1953. Nor were collective farms always efficient, for they were often too large and suffered unduly from the interference of central government. The heavy taxation of the peasant was basic to the system; collectives were left with only about half their produce, and this was a serious disincentive to hard work. When Stalin died in 1953, the average income per head of the farm worker was only half that of the industrial worker.

For industry the first Five Year Plan envisaged a vast programme of investment, especially in the capital goods industries, to raise production by 20 per cent a year. Targets set for particular industries were unrealistic, and that decided for pig-iron was only reached in 1941. Nevertheless some industries did well, especially machine-making and electrical goods. The standard of living probably declined after 1928 as the state amassed the necessary capital by the intensive exploitation of the Russian people. Nevertheless it would be fair to pay tribute to the epic nature of the events. Vast projects were begun. One such was Magnitogorsk in the Urals, a great new metallurgical centre created out of a wilderness. Many of the workers and technicians striving in conditions of extreme hardship seemed to have been fired by a real faith in the future.

On the other hand, Stalin's stated aim to make up the difference between Russia and the West in 10 years was optimism run riot. His fear of foreign states is no excuse for attempting the impossible. Targets were set beyond practical possibility and, as Alec Nove has demonstrated, 'the rush, strain, shortages, pressures became intolerable and caused disorganisation'. This made the government tighten its control even more over resource allocation, physical output and credit, but it could not make uneducated peasants into skilled craftsmen overnight.

By the time the Second Five Year Plan was framed, a more realistic attitude had developed in government which now called for production increases of 14 per cent instead of 20 per cent. The second plan was carried out more smoothly than the first one, as unskilled labourers hurriedly pulled into the factories were acquiring more competence and government control of labour intensified. It is difficult to state the degree of success of the plan because of the unreliability of Soviet production figures, which tend to overstate reality! Certainly the plans for consumer goods, housing and real wages were not fulfilled. With the accession to power of Hitler in 1933, emphasis was placed on armaments, which nearly trebled in the years 1933 to 1938. Excellent growth rates were also achieved in the engineering and metal-working sectors, which diminished Russia's dependence on foreign countries for its capital goods and relieved the strain on the balance of payments. Other industries made considerable gains, e.g. coal and electricity, even if they did not fulfil the forecasts of the planners. The oil, textile and iron ore extraction industries were disappointing.

The third Five Year Plan was overshadowed even more than its predecessor by the growing threat of Germany and the consequent need for more rearmament. The plan called for an annual increase of production of 12 per cent, but it ran into difficulties, including labour shortages and the disorganisation created by Stalin's purges. According to Nove, progress was exceedingly uneven, with good performances in chemicals, machinery and engineering (including armaments) but with stagnation in oil and steel and an actual decline in sugar output. New plant was located far to the east in the Urals and Siberia, partly to cope with the problem of over-large units and also to reduce the long haul of raw materials from remote areas of Russia. However, the strategic factor was the overriding consideration: the further to the east that Russian industry lay, the more secure it was from German aggression.

Despite all the errors and waste, Russia succeeded in the 10 years beginning in 1928 in creating the industrial basis for a powerful arms industry. The production of coal, pig-iron and steel were quadrupled in this period and Russia became a great industrial nation. The base was, however, still too weak to enable civilian investment and consumer programmes to survive the effects of a redoubling of arms spending.

One major problem in the cities was the high labour turnover as the peasant workers, conscripted from the collectives, rootless and bewildered by their new surroundings, wandered around in search of better things. To maintain stable employment, unemployment relief was ended in 1930, and in 1937 workers found guilty of absenteeism were to be dismissed and deprived of their houses, which the régime admitted might mean starvation. In 1930 legislation provided that the worker should go where he was sent by the authorities, and the passport system adopted by the tsars to catch runaway serfs was restored. The Soviet worker was closely subjected to state control, and collective agreements and strikes were abolished.

Despite this coercion, productivity in the economy rose substantially for three reasons: (1) incentives were made much more effective by the recasting of the wage scales and widening differentials, (2) training schemes at all levels began to transform the quality of the labour force, and (3) a new movement called the Stakhanovite movement developed. Stakhanov was a coalminer who by hard work and intelligence achieved an output fourteen times the norm. The party took up the example to encourage others to emulate Stakhanov, and those who did were rewarded with higher pay and honours. These three factors also tended to help the creation of a new élite, an intelligentsia of about 10 million people who were highly favoured on matters of pay, housing and medical treatment to an extent that a visiting Spanish Communist, Delgado, wondered at the nerve of the Soviet government in calling Russia a classless society.

(h) Cultural life, 1917–39

Lenin had stated that the arts should play an important role in the new Russia and that the state would determine developments, but, unlike Stalin later, he did not enforce his conservative preferences. Many writers and artists in the early years were able to make an uneasy peace with the regime, and a few, like the Futurist Mayakovsky, were enthusiastic Bolsheviks.

Original creative work was virtually doomed under the Soviet regime once Stalin took control. The arts became controlled by the Soviet government as a vehicle for fulfilling its propaganda needs. Writers now had to write novels about the five year plans or stop writing, so that a growing output of politically motivated trash resulted. In the 1930s the pressure on artists mounted, and some important writers, such as Isaac Babel, disappeared in the purges; others, like Mayakovsky, committed suicide.

Some creative work of quality somehow survived the onslaught. Michael Sholokhov's *The Quiet Don* was a novel of genuine realism about the Civil War, while Boris Pasternak and Anna Akhmatova did at least survive the Stalinist period, though their work was restricted. In film-making the Soviets could boast a genuine giant, Sergei Eisenstein, whose films *Potemkin* and *Alexander Nevsky* set new standards and won world acclaim. In the field of music both Sergei Prokofiev and Dmitri Shostakovich continued to compose, though the latter was roundly condemned in 1936 for the harsh discord in his music.

Lenin had objected to religious belief in principle, and he believed that religion as the opium of the people was therefore a prop for the old autocracy. However, he always urged caution on the ecclesiastical question in the hope that the Church would wither away. In fact peasants and urban workers held fast to the Orthodox Church. Despite the arrest of its leaders and seizure of its property and wealth, the Church was still functioning on nearly the same scale as 1917 in 1927. But the youth in the cities had been affected by Communist propaganda and the Church was also weakened by division; some leaders wished to cooperate fully with the regime while others wished to retain some independence on doctrinal matters at least.

When Stalin gained power, he prepared to launch a full offensive against the Church, despite Lenin's warning. Many churches and monasteries were closed and a continuous work week ended Sunday as a public holiday. A League of the Militant Godless, started in 1929 to attack religion, claimed a membership of over 5 million in 1932. The number of parishes fell from nearly 50,000 in 1914 to 31,000 in 1930, and a number of the clergy were liquidated in the purges. Nevertheless religious belief probably remained strong in Russia, for the 1937 census was not published, as it had contained a question on religion and 40 per cent of the population had declared their religious belief.

In some aspects life in Russia improved. Though the consumer was neglected and clothing and other commodities remained drab and expensive, the social services were developed to provide free medical attention and social insurance. Education became compulsory and free, with a reduction in illiteracy, though the relatively progressive ideas of the 1920s gave way to a more traditional discipline, with an emphasis on ideological goals. Education became indoctrination intended to produce 'new Soviet man'. Students and teachers were subjected to close scrutiny by the party and the secret police. As they threatened Stalin's totalitarian control, the minority nationalities faced the same repression.

(i) The purges

In 1932 Stalin's second wife, Nadezhda Allilueva, spoke up against the misery that Russia was now suffering. Stalin abused her and that same night she died, apparently by suicide; but she had merely voiced the concern of many leading Communists at the cost of the economic changes. The murder of Sergei Kirov, a member of the Politburo, in December 1934 triggered off a wave of purges in the party against any potential opposition. Kruschev stated in 1956 that Stalin had arranged Kirov's murder himself, a view upheld by Robert Conquest in his book *The Great Terror*. Stalin, it is said, was jealous of Kirov's popularity in the party and needed a pretext to liquidate important rivals. The truth of the matter is difficult to establish.

What is certain is that the punishment of Kirov's murderers in 1935 was merely a curtain-raiser for the main drama. In 1936 came the public trial of sixteen Old Bolsheviks, including Kamenev and Zinoviev, who were both executed; and in 1938 twenty-one leaders of the Right were brought to trial. Tomsky committed suicide and both Bukharin and Rykov were eliminated. But Stalin had done to death many ordinary people who were utterly loyal and therefore no threat to his power. As Ulam remarks, 'never since the outbreak of the Black Death in the fourteenth century could so many people have felt so alone and afraid'. Why did Stalin initiate such slaughter?

Perhaps he believed that under a totalitarian regime anyone is potentially disloyal and therefore the regime could only be secure if everyone was so terrorised as to become incapable of independent action. Part of the explanation surely lies in a deterioration in Stalin's character, for by the 1930s the strains of office had made him even more mean and sadistic. The show trials stand as a monument to his vindictiveness. As Ulam points out, 'many despots of the past killed their victims and desecrated their memories. Stalin in addition killed his victims' self respect'. This was done by making the prisoner either sign a written confession or announce his guilt in public. To extract such confessions, the use of torture was necessary, and as failure to obtain such a confession was a black mark against an NKVD interrogator, he would throw himself into the task with dedication.

Stalin's purge of the army in 1937–8 vividly demonstrates the extent to which he had become omnipotent. Three out of the first five marshals of the Soviet Union, including the commander-in-chief Tukhachevsky, three of the four full generals, all the twelve lieutenant-generals, sixty out of sixty-seven corps commanders and 136 of the 199 divisional commanders were shot. The purge was even more extreme in the navy. The liquidations were a hideous insult, as the armed forces had always fought loyally for Russia. The architect of the purges carefully dissociated himself from these events by not appearing at the trials. Instead in 1936 he presented a new Constitution, anxious to appear as a philosopher statesman. Probably about 8 million people were arrested during the purges, many of whom were shot or sent to concentration camps, though when in 1938 Beria replaced Yezhov (later shot) as chief of the secret police, the show trials stopped.

(j) Foreign policy, 1917–35

Hostility towards capitalist states was built into Soviet ideology, and western intervention in the Civil War merely intensified an existing attitude. The Communists regarded themselves as the agents of a world revolution which could not be long delayed because of the inherent rottenness of the democracies. Lenin himself believed that the democracies could be brought down by ending imperialism, and therefore Russian support was forthcoming for any anti-western nationalist movement, such as those of Kemal Ataturk in Turkey or Chiang Kai-shek in China. Yet it would be unwise to concentrate on this aspect of Russian foreign policy alone, for the Communists inherited an expansionist nationalism from the tsars. In his desire for Russian territorial expansion, Stalin was consciously following in the footsteps of Ivan the Terrible and Peter the Great. By 1945 he had achieved what the tsarist regime had striven for but never achieved – an Eastern Europe under Russian domination. It is therefore clear, as Adam Ulam stresses, that there was 'a strong continuity between the old and the new regime'.

Communist hopes in 1917 that world revolution was imminent were soon shown to be absurd by the course of events. The punitive treaty of Brest-Litovsk, the Civil War and the Polish war left Russia in such a state of chaos that the first task was survival. Though the long-term objective of world revolution was never abandoned, tactics had to be flexible, and a period of coexistence between the Soviet Union and capitalist states had to be tolerated. Meanwhile the security of the infant Soviet state could best be protected by exploiting the rivalries between the various capitalist states, especially those between Britain and Germany and between the United States and Japan. In perceiving the latter area of rivalry, Lenin demonstrated his ability to analyse situations realistically, for in the First World War Japan and the United States had been allies.

The Soviet government refused to give up the revolutionary propaganda which it believed had brought power in Russia. To disseminate the propaganda on a world scale, the Third International or Comintern was inaugurated in March 1919. With Zinoviev as its head until 1925, the Comintern was a branch of the Soviet state, though its policies were not fully coordinated with Soviet foreign policy for some years. In 1920 Lenin laid down the rules which all foreign Communist parties wishing to join the Comintern would be required to follow. They were to avoid any collaboration with moderate socialists and to support the Soviet republic legally and illegally. They were to exploit parliamentary institutions and unions, and to accept as binding all decisions of the Comintern.

The importance of the Comintern must not be exaggerated. In the 1920s the Soviet government was mainly absorbed in domestic affairs, in the attempt to implement 'socialism in one state'. World revolution was no longer expected in the near future, though it continued to be used as a kind of advertising slogan. From 1921 on, a new pattern of Soviet foreign relations evolved, with other countries recognising the Soviet government as uneasy co-existence evolved, which caused a great debate in the party. The Communists maintained relations with most European states while at the same time directing within those same countries movements which were designed to overthrow the governments. When accused of such subversion, the Soviet government blandly replied that the Comintern was a private organisation, a fiction which it maintained resolutely. No change, however, occurred in Soviet hostility towards the League of Nations, which was regarded as a robber league because it was dominated by Britain and France.

When Stalin came to power, the Russian diplomats were more firmly controlled than before through tight organisation and purges. Stalin differed from Lenin, Zinoviev or Trotsky, all of whom had been willing to make sacrifices of Soviet state interest for the sake of revolution abroad. Foreign Communism was now regarded only as an extension of the power of the Soviet Union, and eventually as an extension of the power of the dictator. Stalin's cold-blooded realism in foreign affairs was, says Ulam, 'unaccompanied by any lingering ideological compunctions', as his alliance with Hitler was to demonstrate.

The two main areas of concern in Russian foreign policy in the 1920s were Germany and the Far East, for they were regarded as the weak spots in the world order. Initially the Soviet government hoped that a Communist revolution would occur in Germany in 1919, but even when that failed, the two countries had much in common. Both were revisionist powers whose common enemy was Poland and whose needs were complementary. Germany was weak militarily as a result of the Versailles stipulations on armaments, while Soviet Russia was weak economically. Both states were diplomatically isolated. In April 1922 the Treaty of Rapallo, signed between Russia and Germany, restored full diplomatic relations between the two countries and provided for an increase in trade. Both sides emerged from isolation with a diplomatic partner to play off against Britain and France. Later military contacts were developed. Russia provided bases for German military experiments and in return the Germans erected armaments factories in Russia and shared in their output.

The foundations were laid for the rapid recovery of Germany's military predominance in the 1930s, which would not have occurred so rapidly without the German army's training on Soviet soil in the previous decade.

The alliance itself was fraught with difficulties. Not unnaturally the Weimar government resented Soviet encouragement of a Communist coup in 1923, even though the coup itself fizzled out. The Soviet government for its part was disappointed at the German rapprochement with the West at Locarno, which represented a Russian defeat even though the Rapallo agreement was renewed for a further 5 years in 1926. Russia's diplomatic position worsened in this period, as Communist aid to the General Strike and a raid by police on the Soviet trade mission in London led to a breach of diplomatic relations with Britain. Stalin with his usual skill exploited the situation by a propaganda campaign explaining to the Russian people that their isolation and suffering was caused by Western saboteurs and spies. Foreign policy, like everything else in Russia, was being integrated into Stalin's totalitarian scheme.

Russian foreign policy in China was many-sided. In one respect it resembled tsarist imperialism, as, by a treaty of 1924 with the Chinese Republican government, a virtual protectorate was gained over Outer Mongolia and the Chinese Eastern Railway in Manchuria. The most promising ally was the Kuomintang (Nationalist) party, which, the Russians believed, would most weaken Western influence in China. It was assumed that the Chinese Communist party could not at this stage be a mass party, because China was still too rural and a large proletariat had not yet evolved. Therefore the Chinese Communists were told to cooperate with the Kuomintang in 1922 and gain influence in it by stealth. In the next 3 years, with the help of Michael Borodin, the Soviet's political adviser to the Kuomintang, the Communists did grow more influential in the party and helped to make it more anti-western in attitude. 'We must squeeze the Kuomintang like a lemon', said Stalin, 'and then throw it away.'

His policy in China, however, collapsed in 1927. The Kuomintang leader, Chiang Kai-shek, saw the trend of events and, having captured Shanghai with Communist help, he promoted the massacre of large numbers of Communists. The Russians then attempted to mobilise the left wing of the Kuomintang against Chiang but the move failed. Ulam's comment that by 1928 'Soviet policy in China was a shambles' is a fair one. Chiang had beaten the Communists at their own game, and Stalin's analysis of the whole Chinese situation was faulty. He failed to understand the true potential of Mao Tse-Tung's Communist party, which was to be based on peasant support rather than the proletariat.

When Japan invaded Manchuria in 1931, the Russians became even more apprehensive about the security of their Far Eastern possessions. They reacted with a mixture of firmness and conciliation. The Russian army was strengthened in the Far East to show Japan that war with Russia would be costly, but unlike the Western powers, Russia made no criticism of Japanese aggression. The Soviets even offered Japan a non-aggression pact, and sold the Chinese Eastern Railway to Japanese Manchukuo in 1935. This was appeasement, but appeasement without illusions and from a position of strength. To deflect Japan away from Russia, it was essential that the Japanese armies should be fully engaged in China. Therefore Soviet policy again performed some veritable diplomatic acrobatics in 1932 by restoring relations with Chiang Kai-shek, who since 1927 had been the arch-enemy of Communism. For the same reason, the Soviet government urged the Chinese Communists to declare war on Japan, which they did in 1932.

Soviet policy in the Far East was intimately related to developments in Europe. The Soviet government evinced grim satisfaction at the mass unemployment in Germany from 1929, as it appeared to demonstrate that capitalism was bankrupt and only one obstacle stood in the way of Communist power, the socialist party. Therefore the German Communists were ordered to avoid any collaboration with the socialists, and the net result of their activity between 1930 and 1933 was that they contributed to the failure of the Left and assisted Hitler's coming to power. They regarded the Nazi leader as merely a tool of the Right who would soon lose support to the Communist party. But in 1934, as Hitler's energetic regime tightened its grip in Germany, the Nazi threat to Russia became evident and caused what Ulam has described as an 'agonizing reappraisal of Soviet foreign policy'. Faced by the menace of Japan in the Far East and Nazism in Europe, the Soviet government was forced into a radically different attitude towards the democracies and the League of Nations. Russia entered the League in 1934 and had a permanent seat on the League Council. In 1933 formal relations were established with the United States, and in 1935 a treaty of mutual assistance was signed with France. Even the Comintern was forced to share in the diplomatic acrobatics. Instead of unrelenting hostility towards socialist parties, Communist parties in Europe were now exhorted to support them in a Popular Front against Fascism in 1935.

FURTHER READING

Carr, E. H., *The Russian Revolution from Lenin to Stalin*, Macmillan, London, 1980

Conquest, R., *The Harvest of Sorrow*, Hutchinson, London, 1986

Hosking, G., *A History of the Soviet Union*, Fontana, London, 1985

McCauley, M., *The Soviet Union Since 1917*, Longmans, London, 1981

Nove, A., *An Economic History of the U.S.S.R.*, Penguin, Harmondsworth, 1972

Stone, N., *October 1917*, Cambridge University Press, 1980

Treadgold, D., *Twentieth Century Russia*, Rand McNally, Chicago, 1972

QUESTIONS

1. Why did revolution break out in Russia rather than Western Europe in 1917?
2. Was the Bolshevik success in Russia due more to Marxist ideology or political opportunism?
3. 'A political genius.' How far do you agree with this estimate of Lenin?
4. Why did Stalin emerge victorious in the power struggles after Lenin's death?
5. Critically analyse the motives behind Stalin's creation of a totalitarian dictatorship in Russia.

4
The rise of fascism

(a) Towards a definition of fascism

The rise of fascist movements in many European countries was the great political surprise of the first half of the twentieth century. Fascism remains as one of the most important historical problems of our time, and yet its essence is still elusive 40 years after the destruction of Hitler's Germany. Perhaps, as S. B. Woolf suggests, the word 'fascism' should be banned, at least temporarily, from our political vocabulary, because its meaning has become so blurred. Communists use 'fascist' as a smear word to discredit any group which appears to be hindering communist purposes, and the word is too often used as a term of abuse by woolly minded persons of left-wing views, to pillory anyone with views that are remotely right wing.

Another problem is that of deciding which countries were fascist. The term is appropriate for Mussolini's Italy but may be considered less so for Nazi Germany. Nazism can certainly be viewed as an aberration from fascist norms, a movement unique unto itself, impelled to nihilistic extremes by the mood of a nation in despair. Without the German experience, fascism would be more acceptable to civilised men. Neither should fascism be considered a singularly German or Italian experience, for several European nations contrived their own expression of the phenomenon, while in others right-wing dictatorships have been mistakenly called fascist.

Interpretations of fascism have been many and varied and it is only possible in a book of this length to give the gist of a few of them. The Marxists saw fascism as a bourgeois device to prevent the collapse of capitalism and maintain class dictatorship. They fail to explain why, if they were mere agents of the bourgeoisie, the fascists were able to win mass support from peasants and workers. Obviously fascist movements provided emotional satisfaction for the masses to compensate them for the insecurity of the times, and therefore an understanding of fascism requires a psychological dimension. Erich Fromm in *Fear of Freedom* saw in the lower middle and working classes a desire to give up their freedom, which in a period of war and unemployment bred insecurity. They wished to leave decisions to others but at the same time they also craved for power and for domination. They were able to satisfy both desires by joining fascist movements.

Later scholars saw meaningful comparisons between Nazi Germany and Soviet Russia and would define fascism as non-Marxist totalitarianism. The foundations of this new kind of dictatorship lay, they argued, in certain modern developments in technology, ideology and urban growth which enabled total control over man to develop. To Hannah Arendt the essential driving forces of the totalitarian system were ideology and terror, as exemplified in the racial theories of the Nazis. Total terror was the essence of totalitarian government, the means by which the masses could be made to conform. But Arendt's thesis only applies to Nazi Germany and not the other fascist movements, which were not totalitarian or guilty of mass murder.

The Arendt thesis appealed to the imagination of the generation of writers working during the worst period of the Cold War, as it gave meaning to the great power confrontation between the United States and Russia. In the 1960s, as relations between the two power blocs eased somewhat, a number of writers repudiated the idea that fascism was totalitarian and identified it as a radical form of traditional political protest. Seymour Lipset in his book *Political Man* asserted that fascism was a middle-class reaction. Certain groups of white-collar workers, such as teachers and small traders, who normally supported the liberal centre felt trapped between the unions and big business on the one hand, and between the state and their 'social inferiors the workers' on the other. Therefore they supported fascism, which can be defined as an 'extremism of the centre'. Finally the anti-Marxism of fascism is emphasised by Ernst Nolte, who, while pointing to certain similarities between the two ideologies, also stresses the nationalistic elements in fascism.

The author finds aspects which commend themselves in several of the above interpretations and would not restrict himself to any single approach to a complex problem. A clearer understanding may emerge by an analysis of the following characteristics of fascism:

   (i) ultra-nationalism and racialism,
  (ii) mass support,
 (iii) the leader principle and the élite,
 (iv) the ambivalent relationship with socialism, and
  (v) autarchy and the corporate state

(i) Nationalism was a springboard for the development of fascism in three ways. A number of countries emerged from the war with a profound sense of grievance. In Germany the peace treaties were stigmatised as a Diktat, while in Italy dissatisfaction with Italian gains made nationalists refer to the 'mutilated victory'. This national frustration was a major factor assisting the rise of Hitler and Mussolini, because they vigorously condemned the peace settlement. Secondly, in states where there appeared to be a serious threat of communist subversion and violent revolution, nationalists flocked to support fascist parties that promised to keep their countries free from the socialist menace.

One of the worst consequences of the war was the creation of a horde of ex-servicemen who could not settle down to civilian life. Their disappointed patriotism made them natural recruits for the new fascist movements, which fully shared their nationalistic aims. A number of paramilitary organisations supporting fascism grew up, e.g. the SA (Brownshirts) in Germany and the Legion of the Archangel Michael in Rumania. In France the Croix de Feu, founded in 1927 under de la Rocque, was an ex-serviceman's organisation. Alan Bullock has demonstrated the importance of Ernst Rohm, the leader of the Brownshirts, in the rise of Hitler. 'Rohm was the indispensable link in securing for Hitler the protection or at least the tolerance of the Army ... without the Army's patronage, Hitler would have found the greatest difficulty in climbing the first steps of his political career.'

Behind the intense nationalism was the underlying assumption of racial superiority, a constituent part of fascist ideology. The forerunner of Italian fascism, D'Annunzio, wrote in 1895, 'I glory in the fact that I am a Latin: and I recognise a barbarian in every man of non-Latin blood.' The notion of German racial superiority had its roots deep in the nineteenth century; it was developed in the work of Gobineau and H. S. Chamberlain, who conceived of a hierarchy of races, with the Aryan (German) race at the top. By the end of the First World War racial doctrines had become respectable, especially those of Oswald Spengler, who, in his book *The Decline of the West*, tried to persuade western civilisation to avoid its fate at the hands of inferior races.

The most sinister component of the racial myth was anti-Semitism. It was in the late nineteenth century that anti-Jewish feelings, long held in many countries, were erected into a comprehensive doctrine in the work of Chamberlain and Duhring, who stated that Jews corrupted the purity of the German race. Thus Germany replaced Russia as the fatherland of modern anti-Semitism, and Hitler's later mass murder of Jews was foreshadowed. The collapse of Germany in the war gave a new impetus to such extreme views as anti-Semitism, and it was now that Anton Drexler founded the Nazi Party and adopted a policy of systematic anti-Semitism, which attracted important recruits like Ludendorff.

In certain countries – Italy, Belgium, Holland and France – fascist movements paid little attention to anti-Semitism until the eve of the

Second World War. It was in central and eastern Europe that anti-Semitism was an integral part of fascist ideology, for there the Jews were more numerous and in Rumania and Hungary a dominant section of the middle class. Hitler has told of his disgust at meeting Jews in Vienna, and his reactions may well have been typical. As George Mosse has explained, in the Jews 'fascism had an enemy who could be singled out as symbolising the forces which must be overcome'. The Jews were large enough to be a credible target, but not strong enough to resist.

In a time of insecurity the middle and lower classes seized on the Jew as a scapegoat for their distress. Four additional factors encouraged this hostility. There existed the old Christian hatred of the Jews as Christ's enemies. The Jews were prominent in international business and finance and could be seen as the national enemy. Social and cultural differences existed, and the Jews accentuated them by their tight family circles, Saturday Sabbaths and their willingness to help fellow Jews in financial trouble. Finally, by seizing on the fact that many of the avant-garde thinkers in Germany were Jewish, the Nazis were able to exploit the sentiments of the religious and conformist elements in German society.

The assumption of racial superiority boded ill for the hopes of international peace. It was a fundamental supposition of most fascists that their state could do no wrong and that might was right. Fascist foreign policy was therefore to be aggressive and expansionist.

(ii) Fascism has often been identified as merely a reactionary movement, but this definition is unsatisfactory, because the fascist movements won support from all classes. Fascist leaders themselves came from every class. Quisling, the Norwegian fascist, was an army officer, whereas Mussolini was the son of a blacksmith. As we have seen, fascism had a strong nationalistic appeal which, with its uniforms, flags and historic symbols (the fasces and the swastika) won the support of ex-servicemen. But the war had undermined the economic stability of Europe and brought about social mobility which induced a sense of insecurity in many classes. 'Fascism', says Trevor-Roper, 'was born of fear, the fear of a proletarian revolution,' and the normally moderate middle class supported fascism.

Fascism had a special appeal for youth, which welcomed the opportunity for action and rebellion. Fascist ideas seemed new, vital and patriotic and no other party had such an attraction for young people, who formed an important element in a number of fascist movements – Antonio's Falange in Spain, Degrelle's Rexists in Belgium and the Jeunesses Patriotes in France. In both Italy and Germany the fascists had their youthful martyrs. The Nazis made a hero out of Horst Wessel, killed in 1930 in a brawl with the Communists over a prostitute, and the Horst Wessel song became the anthem of the Nazi Party. In Italy the fascist youth organisation was called after the boy hero Balilla, who had thrown a rock at the Austrian police in the eighteenth century.

The fundamental violence of fascism appealed to the socially uprooted and maladjusted. By joining fascist movements, they could vent their frustration by causing trouble and beating up opponents. A. J. P. Taylor in reviewing Kirkpatrick's study of Mussolini called Mussolini the first of the Rockers. 'Mussolini and the Rockers had much in common: blackshirts, a love of speed and violent gesture, a persistent craze to race after nothing in particular.'

(iii) In the nineteenth century Hegel had affirmed the need for leaders to stand out from the multitude, and the ideas of Gobineau and Pareto supported and triggered off interest in élites. The leading figure in the establishment of the theory of the élite and the leader was, however, Nietzsche. 'God is dead,' he wrote, and proclaimed the need for man to fuse his passion and self-discipline. Then a new race of supermen would be created and redemption would only come through them. In also expressing the need for new breeding methods and violence, Nietzsche anticipated two other parts of the Nazi doctrine. In France élitist ideas were subscribed to by Sorel and Déroulède, although Sorel looked to the proletariat for his élite. The fascists seized on the concept of the élite and proclaimed their desire to establish a new hierarchy. This policy proved to be a significant asset, for potential recruits could be convinced that they would become important cogs in the new order.

Soon after the war charismatic leaders began to emerge. In a period of insecurity they were a focus of loyalty, especially in Germany, where the expulsion of the imperial family had left a vacuum in national life. At a time when liberal government had patently failed, many Germans and Italians wanted to feel that there was a strong hand at the helm. But the real genius of these leaders lay primarily in their ability to play on the emotions of their followers. Mack Smith calls Mussolini 'an artist in propaganda', able to create, for some years at least, an image of himself as the strong, efficient but cultivated leader. Albert Speer has recalled how at party gatherings Goebbels and Hitler were able to rouse the workers, bourgeoisie and students, and mould them into a new unity. In its frenzy the mob demanded victims and Hitler provided them in the form of Jews or socialists.

(iv) Most of the fascist leaders had been socialist earlier in their career, including Mussolini, Mosley, Deat, Doriot and Quisling. Fascist programmes had a considerable socialist content, particularly in Germany through the influence of Hitler's rivals in the Nazi Party, the Strasser brothers. Fascism was therefore able to offer nationalism and socialism together, a combination which produced a tremendous appeal.

But at the same time fascism was born out of fear of socialism. The threat of Bolshevik revolution frightened the European middle and upper classes and swung them over to support fascist parties, which promised to contain the socialist threat. In several countries valuable financial aid was donated to the fascists by leading industrialists. It was after the success of the socialists in the elections of 1919 in Italy that fascism became a political force. Hitler's rise to power followed the world depression of 1929–32, when revolution again appeared to be dangerously close. Therefore before all else fascism was anti-communist and it was anti-communism that was the true uniting factor in a heterogeneous movement.

(v) The central principle in fascist economics was autarchy (economic self-sufficiency). In the nineteenth century the concept had been developed by St Simon and List, and during the First World War by Naumann, who supported the idea of a Mitteleuropa which would allow Germany to be self-reliant and dominate Europe. To pursue autarchy implied the need for state direction and extra living space. From this need was derived the concept of the corporate state, i.e. a system of government in which all national life would be concentrated in the hands of the state. In practice fascist economic policy became a series of improvisations rather than a system, though fascism did seem to provide an answer to some of the contemporary economic problems, such as unemployment. However, to rule effectively and dynamically and to implement the promised improvements called for internal and foreign aggression – the spoliation of the Jews at home and conquest abroad.

(b) The First World War and the undermining of Italian Liberalism

On the outbreak of the First World War Italy's initial attitude was careful neutrality. The government feared Germany's power and did not wish to antagonise Austria-Hungary for fear of prejudicing its chances of compensation in the Trentino or Albania. Its decision pleased the majority of the Italian public, but neutrality had its dangers. Whichever side won the war would have scant regard for Italian ambitions, especially the Central Powers, who felt that the Allied victory at the Marne was due to the removal by the French of ten of their divisions from the Italian frontier. Therefore Salandra's government bargained with both sides to extract generous terms by which Italy might enter the war. The Allies were able to offer more, and in April 1915 the signing of the Treaty of London committed Italy to enter the war on the side of the Entente. Italy was promised South Tyrol, Trentino, Trieste, Istria, Dalmatia, Valona and the Dodecanese.

During the negotiations a great debate on intervention had blown up in Italy, but those favouring intervention – nationalists, liberals and a few socialists like Mussolini – were more successful in organising aggressive demonstrations. This ardent minority rather than parliament imposed its will on the country. Parliament suffered another blow to its prestige and the country entered the war deeply divided below the surface.

Italy went to war on the most difficult front in Europe. It was 400 miles long and so mountainous that wherever the Italians attacked, they had to fight uphill. Despite Cadorna, the Italian commander, enjoying a numerical superiority of two to one, no progress was made because the enemy defences were formidable and Italy lacked artillery and machine-guns. In the first seven months 66,000 Italians were killed and 100,000 wounded. Great efforts were made for an offensive in 1916 but the results were negligible. Then in May Conrad initiated a counter-attack which destroyed the Italian centre and brought the Italian war effort near complete collapse. It was in this crisis that Cadorna showed his calibre as a commander by stemming the Austrian advance, but the public was shocked into recognition of the true nature of the war and resentment at failure led to the fall of Salandra's government.

A major blunder was made by Italy in January 1917. Her Western allies suggest a plan for a major offensive on the Italian Front with their help. The Italian government, probably out of motives of prestige, was lukewarm and the plan was shelved. 'This proved the most serious blunder that the Italians committed during the whole war,' asserts Seton-Watson. 'They threw away the chance of seizing the military initiative and thus forestalling Caporetto.' When the heroism of the Italian armies resulted in some advances, the German High Command decided that action was required to save its ally from collapse. Seven German divisions and eight more Austrian divisions were sent to the Italian front. The offensive by the Central Powers at Caporetto in October led to the collapse of the Italian armies and the dismissal of Cadorna by a new government under Orlando.

By the spring of 1918 Diaz had managed to reorganise the army, and he did not rush into any premature offensives. In October he was able to launch an offensive around Vittorio Veneto, with the Austrian armies already in virtual dissolution.

A belated victory could not make up for the years of defeat or for the cost of the war. Over 5 million men had been mobilised and 680,000 had been killed. Italy found at the peace conference that her defeats had depreciated her stock in the eyes of her Allies. In any case the United States refused to be bound by the Treaty of London and therefore Italy was disappointed over her claims to Fiume, Dalmatia and African territory. This was galling when Italian gains were set beside those of Britain and France, and seemed puny in comparison. The considerable gains which were made, including the disappearance of Austria-Hungary, were overlooked. As Seton-

Watson points out, 'What was not achieved loomed larger than what was, and more and more Italians came to believe that victory had been mutilated and the war fought in vain.'

A second factor undermined national life – the impact of the war on the standard of living and social stability. The war had strained government finances and the public debt had risen nearly sevenfold. The war hit the middle classes – small landowners, tradesmen and members of the professions – whom Chabod describes as 'the real backbone, in the political sense, of the Italian State'. They suffered from higher taxation and the decline through inflation of the real value of their incomes and pensions. The cost of living rose sharply because of the decline in the value of the lira. In 1914 the dollar was worth 5 lire but by 1920 it was worth 28 lire, a serious factor, since Italy had to import huge quantities of coal, wheat and oil. Between 1914 and 1921 the cost of living rose 560 per cent. The 2½ million demobilised soldiers added to the ranks of the discontented.

The immediate postwar years were therefore characterised by social unrest. In 1919 18.8 million workdays were lost by strikes and the figure was almost as high in 1920. The Italian trade unions called for workers' control of factories, and when Alfa Romeo implemented a lock-out in August, 280 factories were taken over by workers in Milan. Giolitti followed a deliberate policy of allowing the workers their head to discover for themselves the difficulty of running factories. The policy had begun to work in 1921, for the number of days lost by strikes had been halved. Nevertheless the fear of a Bolshevik revolution remained strong in the minds of the middle and upper classes, and was a factor which an able leader might exploit.

A third factor undermined the hopes of effective liberal government. In 1919 proportional representation had been introduced, and it helped the creation of two mass parties, the Socialist Party and the Catholic Popular Party. Neither could on its own provide the nucleus of a stable coalition. The socialists were averse to parliamentary procedures anyway, and were fragmented by disputes over whether to work within the system or not. In 1921 the extremists broke away to form a communist party. The Popular Party also lacked unity, for its members ranged from clerical reactionaries to Christian Democrat radicals. The two parties were too far apart ideologically to allow the moderates of each to create a coalition. Between 1918 and 1922 there were five governments, with constant cabinet reshuffles between the major changes. Therefore by 1922 there was a power vacuum at the heart of Italian politics and a demagogue arose to exploit it.

(c) Mussolini and the fascist seizure of power

Mussolini was born in 1883 at Dovia, the son of a socialist blacksmith and a schoolmistress. He hated his education at a seminary because as a poor child he was forced to sit at a segregated table for meals and eat inferior food. He was expelled from the seminary for stabbing a fellow student. Developing a violent style of socialism which bordered on anarchism, he went into journalism and became chief editor of the Socialist Party newspaper *Avanti* in 1912. When the First World War began, Mussolini broke with the official socialist line of opposition to intervention in the war, a move which he justified on the grounds that the Allies represented the Left. The Socialists expelled him from the party and from his job as editor of *Avanti*, so he started a new paper, *Il Popolo d'Italia*.

At the end of the war Mussolini searched for new means of self-aggrandisement. Influenced by Sorel, Corradini and D'Annunzio, he felt a need for constant action. Mussolini was not, however, merely a thug; he had some genuine political talent. As Chabod has pointed out, 'his strength lay in large part in his undeniable ability to rouse the masses by means of an oratory which was always polemical and violent, often vulgar, but never obscure or colourless'.

After the armistice, with the encouragement of the syndicalist Michele Bianchi and a few Arditi (daredevil military corps), Mussolini summoned a meeting in Milan and with Marinetti proclaimed the birth of the Fascio di Combattimento. The term 'fascio' derived from the insignia that the lictors of ancient Rome carried (a bundle of rods with an axe blade protruding, symbolising authority and discipline). In the elections of 1919 not one Fascist was elected, despite the movement boasting the names of Marinetti and Toscanini. Mussolini was still hoping to be the Lenin of Italy, but the extremism of his policies alienated respectable people, while the workers regarded Mussolini as a renegade.

In 1920 Mussolini therefore moderated his policies, cutting down his tirades against the Church, the monarchy and capitalism. But it was the scare brought about by the occupation of the factories by the workers that brought widespread support for the Fascists, who claimed to be the saviours of the nation in the face of the socialist menace. The industrialists began to give financial support, which formed about three-quarters of Fascist revenue. Important contributors included Giovanni Agnelli of Fiat, Alberto Pirelli, the tyre magnate, and the Perrone brothers of the armaments firm Ansaldo. The largest sum, the equivalent of £1.5 million, came from the Banking Association. These contributors were not fascist by conviction; they were simply anxious to protect their interests by any means possible. As Dennis Mack Smith put it, they 'evidently put riches and comfort before liberty'. Mussolini meanwhile tailored his programme to please his industrial backers, and by January 1921 was advocating a return to private enterprise, with a minimum of state interference. By this stage fascism was also bidding for the support of the landowners, for fascist action squads were moving into the countryside and attacking socialists with liberal doses of castor oil and muggings. Mussolini clearly rejected the policy of land for the peasants, and stated that the land rightly belonged to the person investing in it, not the persons working on it.

Events began to play into Mussolini's hands, for in January 1921 the Socialist party split. The Communists formed their own separate party and the consequence of the breach was that membership of both parties was halved in 1921. In May Giolitti, the prime minister, sprang elections on the country in the hope of breaking the Socialist and Popular Parties, and he included the Fascists in a new coalition 'National Bloc'. This gave the stamp of respectability to the Fascists, and Mussolini with 34 of his colleagues was elected after an election campaign characterised by the violence of the fascist squads.

Despite a peace pact with the Socialists in August 1921, violence continued, and opposition from his own ranks forced Mussolini to denounce the pact in November and launch a new campaign against the Socialists. The violence used was connived at by many sectors of public opinion, and by late 1921 the Fascists had a considerable measure of mass support. An analysis of about half its membership of 320,000 shows that 18,000 landowners, 14,000 tradesmen, 4,000 manufacturers, 10,000 from the professions, 7,000 state employees, 15,000 private employees, 36,000 agricultural labourers and 23,000 industrial workers supported the party. The fascist ranks therefore contained many of the lower middle class who felt caught between capital and labour. There were, says Seymour Lipset, 'the displaced masses of the newly industrialising countries' who in their insecurity turned for protection to the radical forces outside the traditional Left or Right. Thus the popular support that fascism gained was 'an extremism of the centre', and, able demagogue that he was, Mussolini was able to exploit the lower middle-class neurosis.

With large sections of the army and police also approving his 'stand' against socialism, Mussolini now required the benevolent neutrality of the Church and monarchy. In 1922 direct approaches were made to the Vatican, and in September Mussolini made a speech in which he indicated that he was now ready to renounce his republican ideas and support the House of Savoy. By October the Fascists had the scent of real power in their nostrils. In August a general strike had been called for by the socialists as part of a counter-attack, but it was such a failure that it became known as 'the Caporetto of Italian socialism'. It gave Mussolini an even better claim for standing as the bulwark against the Red menace, and the Fascists took control in Milan. As Giolitti had retired in June 1921, the government under Facta lacked both firmness and wisdom.

In October Mussolini at last nerved himself to implement what extremists like Farinacci had long desired, a move towards power: 50,000 Blackshirts began to converge on Rome, with many of the political leaders still failing to realise the danger. When Facta asked the king to sign a proclamation of martial law in the emergency, Victor Emmanuel refused. Instead the king sought to entrust the task of forming of a new government to Salandra and Mussolini. When Mussolini refused, the king invited him to come to Milan on 29 October to form a new government.

What is striking about these developments is the way in which the various authorities stood aside and connived at the Fascist victory. The police and the army made no move to stop the Blackshirts, and when they entered Rome, it was not a battle, merely a parade. Victor Emmanuel III's motives for not giving a lead require explanation. He appears to have doubted Facta's determination or ability to resist Mussolini. Moreover he was uncertain whether the army would support the government in proclaiming martial law. But he was already half disposed to accept the Fascists anyway, for he feared the possibility of losing his throne to his ambitious cousin, the Duke of Aosta, who enjoyed great popularity because of his war record and could be sure of Fascist backing if the king was difficult. Finally the Queen Mother Margherita, an iron reactionary, was by 1922 a fervent Fascist supporter.

The influence of the Roman Catholic Church too was being used on behalf of the Fascists. Pius XI saw the Fascists as a lesser evil than the socialists, and assumed that in power they would grow more responsible. Accordingly the Pope ordered all priests to withdraw from politics on the eve of the March on Rome, and gave no support to the Popular Party. It is clear that, as Alan Cassels demonstrates, 'by 1922 there was hardly any section of the Italian establishment not ready to collaborate with Fascism either for nationalistic or anti-bolshevik reasons or both'.

(d) The implementing of dictatorship

Mussolini now announced the formation of a coalition cabinet, including members from the Liberals, Nationalists, Popular and Socialist Parties. Technically he had come to power legally and his government was a compromise arrangement. True revolution was only to come in January 1925. Meanwhile Mussolini moved carefully in the direction of more totalitarian power, lulling the opposition into believing that he was not really different from past premiers. More rigid control of the press was brought in and local Fascist party bosses, the 'ras', acquired more control in many areas than the government-appointed prefects. In 1923 Acerbo drafted a new electoral law, enacted in November. It provided that whichever party received the largest number of votes would obtain two-thirds of the seats in the Chamber. Fascist violence in the election campaign of April 1924 ensured that the party obtained 64 per cent of the votes.

An important development was the formation of the Blackshirts into a permanent Fascist militia, the Volunteer Militia for National Security (MVSN), which swore allegiance to Mussolini not to the king and whose support was to help Mussolini stay in power during the great crisis of 1924.

In May of that year a young socialist, Giacomo Matteotti, denounced Fascist abuses during the election and challenged the validity of the results. In June he was kidnapped by fascists in Rome and stabbed to death. When his body was found later, a great storm of indignation arose, and for the next 6 months Mussolini faced a political crisis with which he could not cope. He had not in fact ordered the murder but the gang responsible had worked for Rossi, head of Mussolini's press bureau, and as Mussolini had given instructions that life should be made difficult for socialists, he was morally guilty.

With public revulsion against fascism now so great, there was a supreme opportunity for the opposition to unseat Mussolini. They failed to grasp it. A substantial minority of socialists and popularists withdrew from parliament, an action dubbed the Aventine secession, as it recalled the last stand of Caius Gracchus and his followers on the Aventine Hill. Amendola, the head of this movement, hoped to topple Mussolini's regime by making it completely isolated. It was hoped that Victor Emmanuel would dismiss Mussolini, but the king refused to act. As the Aventine lacked such key figures as Salandra and Giolitti, its action merely weakened parliament and helped Mussolini's political survival. Finally the attitude of the Church was again of assistance. In 1923 the Pope had forced the resignation of the Popular Party's most determined figure, Sturzo, and in 1924, after Matteotti's murder, he condemned the Popular Party itself and ordered all priests to resign from it. Pius XI saw the fascists as the only force capable of resisting socialism, but as S. B. Woolf notes, 'by these successive acts the Papacy destroyed the only popular movement which might have outbidden Mussolini'.

Mussolini gradually regained his composure, and in January 1925 was able to launch his regime on a truly dictatorial path. All pretence at collaboration was now ended. Amendola was beaten up and died soon after. The political parties, Masonic lodges and opposition newspapers were all suppressed. In December a decree made Mussolini head of the Fascist Grand Council, and he was no longer accountable to parliament. Only the king had the power to dismiss him. Mussolini decided what questions might be debated in parliament, which was now a cypher. The bureaucracy was filled only with his appointees and a secret police (OVRA) was established.

Individual liberty was now circumscribed and Italians were deprived of their citizenship if the government wished. One of the first victims was Professor Salvemini of the University of Florence. A special tribunal was set up to judge political crimes in 1927. Between then and 1943 some 5,000 people were sentenced by this court, but its severity is put into perspective when one considers that only twenty-nine death sentences were passed. Many political cases were still heard in the regular courts, where the accused could often obtain a fair hearing.

The Acerbo law of 1923 was replaced by a new law in 1928. There was one list for which candidates were to be nominated by the labour syndicates and other organisations. For the list the Fascist Grand Council would choose 400 and present them to the electorate for approval. In effect this law ended the liberal system and replaced it with a rubber-stamp plebiscite. The right to vote depended on membership of a Fascist syndicate, a rule which disqualified 3 million people. Italy was now a one-party state under the dictatorship of Mussolini, and in practice the Grand Council merely approved what he had already decided.

(e) The corporate state

Since the war Mussolini had been intrigued by the possibility of instituting a system of representation that would rest on the national syndicates instead of the old parliamentary system. This was not a new idea, for it was derived from two currents of thought. Catholic supporters of corporativism looked back with nostalgia to a revival of the medieval guilds or corporations in which there would be cooperation between employer and workers, even profit-sharing and part-ownership. The second current was syndicalism which had been most cogently argued by Georges Sorel. Originally syndicalists had supported the idea of class warfare and government based on labour syndicates alone, but some moderation of this view had taken place. Some syndicalists had become friendly with Mussolini during the war and one of them, Edmondo Rossoni, conceived of a syndicalist organisation which would include producer syndicates as well as the labour unions. It was argued that if the government coordinated the work of the syndicates, it would end class warfare at a stroke while at the same time preserving capitalism. In practice in Italy capital was to be treated more leniently than labour, and therefore the corporative system can be seen as designed to win the support of employers. In this sense Woolf is right to call Italian fascism 'a mass party of reaction', because it employed its power in the interests of capitalism.

Mussolini had set up a committee made up of members of the employers' federation and the fascist labour syndicates in 1923 to study the issue, and in 1925 the employers' federation agreed to deal only with Rossoni's fascist labour syndicates. The rival Socialist and Catholic labour unions were to be outlawed. The government would choose the officials of the labour syndicates rather than allow workers to do so, whereas the employers' federation was free to choose its own representatives. In 1926 the minister of justice, Alfredo Rocco, who was perhaps the most coherent thinker in the government, began his attempt to subordinate all elements in the country to the state. Strikes and lock-outs were prohibited and the syndicalist state came into existence; the state, acting as umpire, recognised producers' and workers' syndicates in six fields of the economy (industry, agriculture, commerce, maritime and air transport, land and inland-waterway transport and banking). In 1934 the system underwent further change when twenty-two corporations were set up for particular fields of economic activity, for example wine and textiles. In each corporation the PNF, employers and employees were represented, and in 1939 a Central Committee of Corporations replaced the Chamber of Deputies.

The theory behind the corporate state was very fine: it would bring about social justice and real planning of the economy. In practice it had two essential features. It was a device through which the political dictatorship of the PNF could be exercised, and it ensured the pre-eminent position of employer over employees. Ironically, even the industrialists began to lose faith in Mussolini in the years when the system was created. There was too much bureaucratic bungling and perhaps even more graft, and the system was no answer to Italy's economic problems.

(f) The economy

As with many parts of their programme, the fascists had kept their ideas on the economy rather vague before taking office. Their period of power was to see an initial liberal phase in economic policy which was followed by a growth in state intervention and a programme of autarchy.

Under the liberal economist De Stefani, who was minister of finance from 1922 to 1925, Italy's finances recovered from the strain of the previous years. De Stefani brought in a simpler tax system, and attracted foreign capital by exemptions from taxation. He also sought to withdraw government from business wherever possible and abolished price-fixing, rent controls and subsidies. By his reductions in government expenditure he achieved a budget surplus for the first time since the war. With a revival in trade there was a fall in unemployment from over 500,000 to 122,000. 'This recovery from the deep depression of the postwar years', says Clough, 'was remarkable and greatly aided the Fascists in winning favour and in establishing themselves in power.'

Mussolini could not leave well alone, and at the behest of some industrialists dismissed his minister in 1925. His policy in the next few years was based on considerations of prestige rather than the economic welfare of Italy. In August 1926 he made a speech in which he declared, 'I shall defend the Italian lira to my last breath – to my last drop of blood.' The lira was revalued at 90 to the £ instead of 100 to the £, but this made it more difficult for Italy to export and pushed the country towards depression, 2 years before the Wall Street Crash. Not until 1936 did Mussolini devalue the lira, and meanwhile unemployment rose to 1.1 million by 1932, with perhaps half the total labour force underemployed. The government added to the deflationary spiral by cutting the wages of public employees by 12 per cent, and raising tariffs, which led to foreign retaliation. A reduction in the number of foreign tourists owing to the world depression aggravated the balance of payments problem.

Another government response was to attempt a policy of national self-sufficiency, especially in food production. Mussolini called for a victory in the 'battle for grain', an attempt to reduce Italian wheat imports by the bringing into cultivation of marginal land and better methods. Wheat imports were cut by 75 per cent between 1925 and 1935, but the resources deployed in this effort would have been more productive in the cultivation of other crops. The serious problems of agriculture were not tackled, and the real wages of agricultural labourers fell by about 50 per cent.

In industry the worst phase of the depression was reached in 1932. The depression years saw an increasing tendency towards monopoly in industry, with small firms swallowed by large concerns with government blessing. The large firms were able to act like cartels in matters of price-fixing and production quotas. In 1933 the government organised the Institute for Industrial Reconstruction to provide subsidies for firms in difficulty, with the result that by 1940 the government held a 20 per cent interest in Italian industry. Thus state capitalism was encouraged by Fascism, and was conspicuous in shipbuilding, aviation and petroleum production.

In 1934 the government reduced the working week to 40 hours to spread out employment, but, as hourly pay was not increased, workers took a cut in their real income. No real attempt was made to raise purchasing power as a means of combating depression, though the government did spend considerable sums on public works. Land reclamation to increase arable land and reduce malaria had some success, notably the draining of the Pontine Marshes. The electrification of the railways was begun and a new development in roadbuilding, the autostrada, was pioneered. In Rome itself new archaeological projects opened up the area around the Coliseum, and many new government buildings were constructed, usually on the principle that what was massive was beautiful. An attempt was made to provide help for the South and 57 per cent of revenue was spent in that area.

The advent of the Ethiopian war cut unemployment and stimulated the economy in the short run, but intervention in the Spanish Civil War and Albania strained Italy. By 1936 the budget was badly in deficit and the government was forced to devalue the lira and increase taxes. An inflation rate of 20 per cent was reached in 1937, and the programme of autarchy was proved to be an absurd one, given Italy's limited resources. Genuine economic growth in the fascist years was small, and real incomes fell generally between 1925 and 1938.

(g) The Church and the Jews

In his youth Mussolini had been violently anti-clerical but even before the March on Rome he had moved towards friendlier relations with the Church, which, as we have seen, materially helped him to establish his power. The Duce fastened on the deeply rooted sentiments of many Italians who were disturbed that the Church was not yet formally reconciled with the government, and he tried for even closer relations with the Vatican. The crucifix was restored to schools and courtrooms and masses were scheduled for public functions. Negotiations went ahead for a full solution to the problems of relations between Church and State, despite disputes over youth organisations, which led to the virtual disbanding of the Catholic Boy Scouts in 1928.

In 1929 a concordat was at last signed. The Pope's temporal power over the Vatican City and St Peter's was restored in return for papal recognition of the Kingdom of Italy and a renunciation of papal claims to former papal estates. The government agreed to compensate the Church for ecclesiastical property which had been confiscated during the unification of Italy, and the Pope was given the right to appoint all bishops in Italy after consulting the Italian government. The State was to continue to pay the salaries of churchmen and was not to molest Catholic societies. The agreement was fascism's most enduring legacy, and devout Italians were overjoyed that, after half a century of hostility between Church and State, peace was now achieved. Mussolini reached a new peak of popularity in Italy and his reputation soared throughout the Catholic world.

The peace was, however, an uneasy one. Indeed, as Daniel Binchy has pointed out, the experience with fascist Italy and Nazi Germany in the 1930s eventually 'led Pius XI although by temperament inclined to sympathise with authoritarian government, to recognise in modern dictatorships the most formidable danger to Christianity in our time'. The issue which most divided the fascists and the Church in the early 1930s was the status of the Catholic lay organisation, Catholic Action. It had grown when the Popular Party disintegrated and by 1929 possessed 4,000 adult centres and 5,000 youth clubs. Mussolini was jealous of its influence, for in many rural areas it was stronger than the PNF. Therefore, despite recognition of its independence in the Concordat, Mussolini sought to destroy it and began by accusing it in 1931 of harbouring leaders of the outlawed Popular Party. He then closed down the university branch of Catholic Action, a move for which he was vigorously denounced by the Pope. The Fascists then declared that participation in Catholic Action was incompatible with party membership, but this merely led to mass resignations from both the party and Catholic Action. To the relief of both sides a shaky compromise was reached whereby Catholic Action fell more under the control of the bishops, who were not to select lay officers in any way hostile to the regime.

Up to 1938, despite such difficulties, the Church had not been opposed to fascism, and in 1929 Pius had even referred to Mussolini as the Man of Destiny. Unfortunately Mussolini, who had in earlier years expressed disgust at Hitler's racial ideas, proclaimed a racialist manifesto in 1938, setting out reasons for an Aryan racial policy in Italy. It was this new racialism that provoked the great breach between Church and State. The Pope had already expressed sorrow in 1937 over Hitler's racial programme, and now he condemned anti-Semitism as a denial of the brotherhood of man. He infuriated Mussolini by taunting him for imitating the Nazis and in September he remarked to some Belgian pilgrims, 'Spiritually we are Jews.' Unwisely Mussolini brought in a law for the 'Defence of the Italian race', which prohibited marriage between 'Aryan' Italians and 'Jewish' Italians and insisted on public registration of Jews. Jews were forbidden to own important industry and were banned from a number of occupations, including education and the armed forces. But in comparison to their brothers in Germany, Jews in Italy were not greatly affected until 1943, thanks to the attitude of most Italians and discreet help from the Church. When the Nazis seized Northern Italy in 1943, about 9,000 Jews were murdered.

In 1939 Piux XI died and Cardinal Pacelli, an aristocrat who had seen service in Germany, was elected Pius XII. He was more suave and cautious than Pius XI or his successor John XXIII, and he made it clear that he intended to follow a more conciliatory policy towards Germany and Italy than had Pius XI. When the Pope quickly ended lay direction of Catholic Action, Ciano wrote in his diary, 'I believe that we can get along with this Pope.' As C. F. Delzell explains, 'Pacelli's cautious diplomatic behaviour and training were to prevent him from being a first rate moral leader of the Church during a time of unprecedented violence and destruction.'

The Pope, it is true, did try to prevent war breaking out in 1939 and then threw his influence on the side of Italian neutrality. It is his silence over Nazi atrocities which has been criticised. In the book *Into That Darkness* Gitta Sereny has claimed that the Vatican knew of Nazi genocide programmes from an early point in the war, and only in 1943 made any clear protest about them. Sereny gives four possible reasons for the papal attitude. He feared Bolshevism above all else as the arch-enemy of the Church, and for this reason did not condemn the murder of Russian civilians. He also feared that if he did attack the Nazis, they might wipe out Catholicism in Europe. Perhaps he did not believe the stories of German atrocities, despite their thorough documentation, because he had spent his happiest years in Germany, Finally, claims Sereny, the Pope was instinctively anti-Semitic himself, and kept silent when a firm stand from the beginning might have rallied European Catholic opinion sufficiently to force the Nazis to change their policies.

Sereny's views are conjectural and one-sided. It is natural that the Pope should feel concerned to act in a way that did not increase the risk of Nazi mass murder of Catholics. By following a cautious policy he would retain some chance of mediating in the war, whereas had a clear denunciation of the Axis powers been made, Mussolini could have cut him off completely from the outside world. Futhermore the Pope did at times act courageously. The German invasion of Scandinavia in 1940 was condemned, and when Pius learned of the impending German attack on the Low Countries, he informed representatives of the states concerned. Pius also saved the lives of some thousands of Jews in Italy by hiding some in the Ardeatine Caves in 1944 and by instructing monasteries to give refuge to Jews in flight.

Only scrutiny of the Papal archives can reveal the full truth on this vexed question, but it may well be that the Church has been particularly criticised on the issue because of its pretensions. If over the centuries it had claimed less for its wisdom, less might have been expected of it in a difficult position. The Roman Catholic Church claimed the highest standards and was therefore judged by them. It was in fact no worse and no better than the other appeasers of fascism. As Kedward has remarked, 'Fascism revealed the insecurity and fallibility of many well-established historic institutions.'

(h) The nature of the fascist regime

Fascists claimed to have created a totalitarian one-party state in Italy, but it is clear that in comparison with Nazi Germany or Soviet Russia the power of the regime was very limited. Gentile, in an article in the *Italian Encyclopaedia*, gave the chief criterion of totalitarianism: 'No individuals or groups outside the State'. But in Italy the Church and the monarchy retained a large measure of real independence, and Italy was as much dynastic and Catholic as totalitarian. Other important groups, such as the industrialists and the armed forces, kept much of their autonomy.

Nor did the Fascists convert the masses so as to win their allegiance. Italians viewed Fascism with the same scepticism as they had viewed earlier regimes. One reason for this was the lack of a clear-cut Fascist ideology. The Fascists claimed to worship action, and Ernst Nolte emphasises 'the priority of action over doctrine' in fascist Italy, but in practice this merely meant opportunistic and inefficient government. We must agree with Hannah Arendt's verdict on Mussolini's regime as 'not totalitarian, but just an ordinary nationalist dictatorship'.

The limits of the fascist dictatorship can be seen in the relative freedom which was allowed the liberal philosopher Benedetto Croce. When his former friend Gentile proclaimed the 'Manifesto of the Fascist intellectuals' in 1925, Croce made a scathing attack on fascist ideas as 'an incoherent and bizarre ragbag', and he was backed by many of Italy's leading intellectuals. Though irritated, Mussolini did not dare to arrest Croce, partly out of fear of foreign criticism, and the philosopher continued to publish freely in his review *La Critica*.

When Italy entered the Second World War in 1940, the pretensions of the regime were brutally exposed. Fascism had been very much the creation of one man, whom Denis Mack Smith describes as a 'stupendous poseur'. Mussolini lacked real administrative ability and was too concerned with womanising or in projecting an image of himself as a superman. He held nine ministries and claimed to work a 14-hour day, though his personal secretary has revealed that he slept at his desk during office hours and was in bed by 10 o'clock. Mussolini's one talent lay in propaganda, which prevented the sheer inefficiency of fascism from being appreciated and remedied. His warlike pretences deceived foreign statesmen into an exaggerated view of Italian power because Mussolini spoke of his capacity to mobilise 8 million bayonets in a few hours and how his aircraft would blot out the sun. The press was used to showing Mussolini's prowess at fencing, riding, driving and playing the violin, but he was far from being a dynamic man of action in 1940. By then he was myopic and his ulcer necessitated a milk diet. Unfortunately he had begun to believe his own propaganda and his one genuine skill contributed to his ruin.

(i) Fascist foreign policy and the road to disaster

'Better to live one day as a lion than a thousand years as a lamb,' Mussolini told his Blackshirts in 1935. By then an aggressive militarism and active foreign policy had become the most obvious features of fascism. In contrast, one might view the first decade of fascism as one of good behaviour, but this would be a half-truth. In the early years Mussolini was still feeling his way and did not have a coherent foreign policy. He had a mania for signing pacts with foreign countries, and eight such pacts were signed between 1926 and 1930. This supports the contention of Stuart Hughes that Mussolini was striking out in all directions in the hope of scoring points on the cheap; it was a policy of improvisations without a definite aim.

Mussolini knew that he had to improve Italy's international status, for in the last resort this was the criterion by which his regime would stand or fall. Therefore, despite his domestic concerns, he did indulge in a number of diplomatic adventures in the early years. In August 1923 at a conference delimiting the frontier between Albania and Greece, the Italian representatives were murdered by a terrorist. This atrocity gave Mussolini the opportunity to display the fascist spirit. He dispatched an ultimatum to the Greek government and, despite a conciliatory reply, occupied Corfu. A conference of ambassadors arranged compensation for Italy, which Mussolini was forced to accept. He had wished to annex Corfu, but a veiled British threat to use the Mediterranean fleet made him withdraw from the island.

Italy was more successful in a second escapade. Two weeks after the Corfu incident Mussolini sent a military commandant to govern Fiume on the pretext that negotiations beteen Italy and Yugoslavia to found an independent Fiume had reached deadlock and that the town was falling into anarchy. The Yugoslav government accepted this high-handed action, as France, Yugoslavia's protector, was engaged in the Ruhr and also because King Alexander of Yugoslavia admired Mussolini. Italy therefore won a certain prestige, but it was a pyrrhic victory, as it aggravated the rivalry of the two countries in the Balkans.

Mussolini worked with some success to win the approval of British statesmen. He assisted the British in putting pressure on Turkey to cede the Mosul area to Iraq, and in return Britain gave Jubaland to Italy in 1924. But Mussolini's patience declined as the 1920s went by without any major Italian successes. He was irritated by the failure to gain a guarantee of the Brenner frontier at Locarno in 1925, and became, as Elizabeth Wiskemann terms it, 'the chief anti-democratic conspirator of Europe' by 1927. He quarrelled with France and Yugoslavia and gave military assistance to such revisionist powers as Hungary and Austria.

A new phase of Italian foreign policy began in 1930, when Mussolini declared that the struggle had moved beyond Italy to a world arena, and he called for rearmament, revision of treaties and expansion towards the Danubian basin. Soon he was talking about 'fascism for export', declaring that in another decade all Europe would be fascist. In 1932 he took over the foreign ministry himself, and moderates such as Grandi were sacked. By 1936 he had taken command of all the service ministries, and allowed his son-in-law Count Ciano to become foreign minister.

For a brief period Mussolini acted as the principal champion of Austrian independence in the face of the threat from Nazi Germany. Since 1928 he had tried to make Austria an Italian satellite, first backing Prince Stahremberg's Heimwehr movement and later the dictatorship of Dollfuss. In March 1934 the Rome Protocols to promote trade were agreed between Austria, Hungary and Italy, but this was more than offset by Mussolini's fatal error of encouraging Dollfuss to crush the Austrian Socialists. A 4-day civil war occurred in February in Austria, which resulted in the destruction of the socialist movement. Many Austrian workers joined the Nazis in desperation against the Dollfuss government. In July the Nazis murdered Dollfuss and tried to take over Austria, but they called off their 'putsch' when Mussolini ordered Italian troops to the Brenner Pass.

With such an obvious threat to Austrian independence, Mussolini should have avoided any wild imperial adventures, yet it was at this precise juncture that he chose to involve himself in Abyssinia. His motives are not hard to fathom. The years of depression and the failure of the corporate state had sapped his popularity in Italy. He now wished to employ the classical device of dictators to draw public attention away from domestic troubles – a successful war abroad. Italian nationalists still nurtured a desire to revenge the Italian humiliation at Adowa in 1896 and the war could be justified with arguments that Abyssinia would provide Italy with raw materials and markets and furnish the base for a new Roman Empire.

To initiate the war Mussolini required both a pretext and an assurance of French neutrality. A clash at the oasis of Walwal near the border of Italian Somaliland gave him the first requirement. In January 1935 Pierre Laval came to Italy, and in return for Italian renunciation of privileges in Tunisia, he gave tacit French approval of undefined Italian action in Abyssinia. The stage was now set and in October 1935 war was declared.

It can truly be seen as a turning point in the interwar years. At the League of Nations, a sanctions policy was adopted mainly at Britain's prompting, and the long friendship between Italy and Britain was ended. In December Hoare, the British foreign secretary, and Laval concluded a deal which would have given Mussolini two-thirds of Abyssinia. When news of the deal leaked out, it inflicted a lethal blow at the League and caused the fall of Laval's government. The war had for once diverted attention away from Europe and encouraged Hitler to occupy the Rhineland in March 1936. Meanwhile Emperor Haile Selassie had been driven out of his country, and in May Mussolini was able to proclaim victory and grant his king a new title, Emperor of Ethiopia. For a short period the Duce was again popular in Italy.

Mussolini's victory went to his head and he became over-confident, but perhaps the most fatal consequence of the war was its effect on German–Italian relations. Hitler was the only major leader not to have criticised Italian aggression, and the two countries drew closer together through joint aid to General Franco during the Spanish Civil War. Mussolini supported Franco in order to spread fascism, to encircle France and increase Italian influence in the western Mediterranean.

In November 1937 Mussolini made his first visit to Nazi Germany, and it was a great success, despite a torrential rainstorm reducing his text to a sodden rag as he tried to read it faster and faster, to the great confusion of the crowd! He was most impressed at the spectacle of German efficiency, and from this point fell more and more under Hitler's influence. Italy joined Germany and Japan in the Anti-Comintern Pact and in March 1938 made no move to prevent Hitler's annexation of Austria. This passivity, combined with the rapprochement with Germany, ruined Mussolini's prestige at home and abroad, yet he remained blind to his real interests. His last triumph, his part in the Munich settlement, should have demonstrated to him the means by which he would win and retain public support in Italy. There was great relief in Italy that Mussolini had helped to save the world from war, but he failed to learn the right lesson.

After Hitler had absorbed the rest of Czechoslovakia in March 1939 without informing Italy, Mussolini responded by invading Albania in April. The war was quite unnecessary, for Albania was already an Italian vassal and the war, though successful, further dissipated Italy's resources. In May Ribbentrop came to Italy to conclude a full alliance. By the terms of the 'Pact of Steel' Italy found herself pledged to support Germany even in a war of aggression. Ribbentrop promised that Hitler would not go to war for at least 3 years, but when the Germans signed a non-aggression pact with Stalin in August, both Ciano and Mussolini realised the imminence of war. They sent to Berlin a long list of reasons why Italy could not go to war at this juncture and requested huge amounts of aid. 'It's enough to kill a bull, if a bull could read,' Ciano wrote in his diary.

When the Second World War broke out, Mussolini announced that Italy would be a non-belligerent, but when Hitler's armies began to overrun France, Mussolini was desperately afraid that he would lose his share of the booty and declared war. It was his most fatal error and led to the fall of his regime. The war was most unpopular in Italy and, in Chabod's words, enlarged 'the profound abyss that had opened up between the country and Mussolini'. In any case Italy was patently unprepared for a major war. The army, nearly one-third of which was serving overseas, was still equipped with rifles of 1891 vintage and First World War artillery. The airforce had over 3,000 planes on paper but only 980 of them were ready for service. The best prepared of the services was the navy, but it did not possess any aircraft carriers, so vital in modern warfare at sea. In 1943 Mussolini belatedly confessed that Italy had been better equipped for war in 1915 than in 1939.

The sham of fascism was now cruelly exposed. Mussolini's hope of obtaining territory from a defeated France was treated with contempt by Hitler and Italian armies were utterly defeated in Greece and Africa. By 1942 Mussolini was physically spent and his authority shattered. Most Italians had come to hate what F. W. Deakin has called the brutal friendship; the German alliance had reduced Italy to the status of a vassal. By early in 1943 three interlocking conspiracies against Mussolini were developing. Army leaders plotted to replace him with Marshal Badoglio, while certain fascists wished to put government in the hands of Ciano and Bottai. Anti-fascists were still hoping that the king would act to end Mussolini's rule and restore liberal government, but, as ever, he was indecisive. In July at a meeting of the Fascist Grand Council Mussolini faced a determined party revolt, led by Ciano and Grandi, which gave the king the opportunity to arrest him and replace him with Badoglio.

The German response was an invasion of Italy which forced the government to flee from Rome and conclude an armistice with the Allies. In October Italy re-entered the war on the side of the Allies. Meanwhile Mussolini had been liberated in July by German paratroopers and flown to Germany, where in humiliation he confronted Hitler. In September he was sent back to Northern Italy to organise the 'Italian Social Republic', with its capital at Salo. Supported by the most fanatical fascists, he tried to win support by new socialist measures, but both the workers and middle class were rightly sceptical of this transformation. The neo-Fascist regime had a new brutality, which was made evident in January 1944 when several of the rebel fascists, including Ciano, were shot. A genuine resistance movement now grew up, and in April it was able to launch an insurrection in Milan as the Allies moved north from Bologna. Mussolini, with his faithful mistress, Clara Petacci, headed for Switzerland but they were stopped by partisans and shot. Their bodies were hung upside down in Milan for the infuriated mob to kick and spit upon.

Italian fascism was now formally defunct, but in truth it had been moribund since 1941. Little of the regime's works remained by the end of the war – the agreement with the Church, a few public works and some social welfare. The only remnants of the vaunted corporate state in modern Italy are a few such practices as state intervention in labour disputes and industry. But though to later observers Mussolini may appear a mere windbag, he was the founder of a formidable political movement which was imitated in other countries, and but for him history would have been very different. Hitler always admired Mussolini and said that but for his example he would not have had the courage to seek power himself.

FURTHER READING

Cassels, A., *Fascism*, Davidson, London, 1981

Cassels, A., *Fascist Italy*, Routledge, London, 1969

Chabod, F., *A History of Fascism*, Cedric Chivers, Bath, 1974

Clark, M., *Modern Italy 1971–1982*, Longmans, London, 1985

Kedward, H. R. D., *Fascism 1900–1945*, Blackie, London, 1973

Laqueur, W., *Fascism: A Reader's Guide*, Penguin, Harmondsworth, 1976

Lyttelton, A., *The Seizure of Power*, Weidenfeld and Nicolson, London, 1973

Smith, D. Mack, *Mussolini*, Weidenfeld and Nicolson, London, 1982.

QUESTIONS

1. What did the European fascist movements have in common?
2. 'Liberal Italy sealed its fate when it permitted itself to be dragged into war in 1915 by a wilful minority' (C. F. Delzell). Discuss this statement.
3. Why was Mussolini able to seize power in 1922?
4. Account for Mussolini's success in consolidating his dictatorship between 1922 and 1929.
5. To what extent was the Fascist regime in Italy totalitarian?

5
The Germany tragedy, 1918–39

(a) The revolution of 1918 and the founding of the Weimar Republic

With the failure of Ludendorff's spring offensive in 1918 Germany began to crack under the strain of war and blockade. The public wanted more say in the affairs of a nation run more and more by a military clique, and opinion turned against the Kaiser, who was regarded as an obstacle to peace. Discipline began to break down, a phenomenon which for Germany was novel and horrifying. In October mutiny broke out at the Kiel naval base when it was rumoured that the German High Seas Fleet was to be ordered to sea to make a last stand against the British. A. J. Ryder notes the special irony that the revolt began in the navy, 'which more than anything else had symbolised the pride and ambition of the Hohenzollern regime'. A workers' council on the Russian model was founded in Kiel and the example was imitated in other German towns. In Bavaria Kurt Eisner's action in proclaiming an independent communist republic in November seemed to foreshadow the dissolution of Germany itself.

With Germany's allies in even worse straits, it had become clear to Hindenburg and Ludendorff in late September that the war must be ended. They suggested the setting up of a new parliamentary regime which would bear the responsibility for a peace settlement. The German parliament and public had been kept in the dark about the true seriousness of Germany's position and, when the Reichstag was so informed, the Conservative leader Heydebrand expressed the general bitterness: 'We have been lied to and cheated.'

Germany's first full parliamentary government was a compromise. It was headed by Prince Max of Baden, but most of his colleagues were from the Centre, Progressive and Social Democratic Parties. It began negotiations for an armistice in October, and when Ludendorff opposed the armistice terms, Prince Max obtained his dismissal. Later in the month William himself had to abdicate and go into exile, as did the other crowned heads of Germany. There was really no alternative; the Allies were insisting on this course of action and in any case many Germans hoped for a more lenient peace if a republic were set up. At first William refused to go, and the socialists in Prince Max's cabinet resigned in protest. This in turn forced the prince to hand in his resignation, and the socialist leader Ebert became chancellor.

Unfortunately the parties of the Left contained divisions which were to prevent the consolidation of a really sound democracy in Germany. The revisionist socialists under Ebert wanted a moderate parliamentary regime while the Independent Socialists sought the immediate socialisation of the economy and radical changes in the army and civil service. The most extreme group, led by Karl Liebnecht, were the Spartacists, who wanted a soviet regime on the Russian model, and they rejected Ebert's offer to join his government, hoping that he would fall as Kerensky had in Russia. The new government therefore needed the support of the army, and it was forthcoming. On 10 November General Groener, in a historic telephone call, offered the army's help in maintaining Ebert in office in return for the preservation of the officers' authority in the army. Ebert accepted and also authorised his colleague Gustav Noske to recruit volunteer forces to keep order should an emergency arise. These volunteer bands came to be known as the Free Corps, and were made up of ex-soldiers whose political convictions were anti-Bolshevik and anti-democratic. Ebert's reliance on the army and the Free Corps was to be a serious handicap for the new democracy.

Ebert's fear of the Spartacists was well founded. They had now constituted themselves the German Communist Party (KPD) and in January 1919 they attempted an armed revolution in Berlin. Ebert's government was saved only by the aid of the Free Corps, which brutally murdered the Spartacist leaders Liebknecht and Rosa Luxemburg. Other cities where communist resistance had broken out were purged, and in June Eisner's regime in Bavaria was ended and the leader himself murdered. Though now supported by the Independent Socialists, the KPD lacked mass support, and in the white terror that followed their defeat the Communists lost most of their leaders.

(b) The problems of the new republic

Order was now restored, but, as Hannah Vogt has stressed, 'the men who were to pick up the reins of government faced a tremendous, thankless task'. The consequences of the war were grim. Germany had lost 2 million dead, the people were half-starved and with the demobilisation of the army fears of unemployment and inflation grew. A legend that the army had been defeated not by the Allies but by the treachery of the government at home was already spreading. This was the 'stab in the back' or *dolchstoss* myth. When the same government signed the Versailles treaty, the German people, who had been led to expect a lenient treaty, condemned it as a robber peace.

From the beginning the Weimar Republic was attacked by inveterate enemies on both ends of the political spectrum. The Communists never forgave the moderate socialists for the thorough repression of the Spartacist revolt and the gulf between the two parties widened. On the radical right the German National People's Party (DNVP) and the National Socialist German Workers Party (NSDAP), led by Adolf Hitler, depicted Weimar politicians as betrayers of their country. It was vital therefore that the republic be able to rely upon such fundamental institutions as the judiciary, the civil service and the army – but such was not the case. The revolution of 1918 had left intact the pillars of the former regime – the junkers, the army, the bureaucracy, the great industrialists and the judges. These were more often in opposition to than behind the infant republic.

Few changes had been made in the judiciary, and the judges were anti-democratic in spirit. They abused their discretionary powers, condoning crimes committed by the Right while dealing severely with the excesses of the Left. Of 354 political assassinations by the Right between 1918 and 1922, 326 went unpunished, whereas only 4 of 22 assassins of the Left went unpunished. This degree of bias was an incitement to the radical right to indulge in further acts of violence. The Weimar system of justice prepared the way for the total breakdown of legal standards which was to follow Hitler's accession to power, and Franz Neumann is right to describe political justice as 'the blackest page in the life of the German republic'.

The civil service was also taken over without any drastic changes and the bureaucratic machine continued to function smoothly. However, officials educated by an authoritarian state were not democratic in outlook and blocked the implementation of any progressive decree. The contempt felt for the Weimar regime was serious, as it pervaded education. Many teachers resented the disappearance of the Empire and heaped abuse on the republic. History and other textbooks propagated the 'stab in the back' legend and beliefs in Germany's racial superiority.

The most crucial institution was the army. In view of the nation's experience with generals like Ludendorff during the war, it was essential that the army should be firmly under political control. With a reduced army, a corps of officers upon whom the republic could rely might have been selected. The opportunity was missed because, as we have seen, the new government relied on the army to suppress the menace from the Left. Thus the army remained a state within a state and, though it could be relied upon to crush Communist subversion with alacrity, it was most reluctant to act against right-wing movements. The intrigues of army leaders were to become a major factor in the paralysis of the Weimar democracy in the 1930s, when, as F. L. Carsten has shown, loyal support by the army might have enabled democracy to survive. 'If the republic after 1930 had possessed an army entirely loyal to it, the great crisis would have taken a different course. A Reichswehr which in the hour of peril would have cooperated with the Prussian police and the republican organisations instead of intriguing against them, could have been the rock on which the waves broke.'

The attitude of the army towards the republic was soon demonstrated in the affair known as the Kapp Putsch. Passions had been revived in the army and the Free Corps by the military clauses of the Versailles Treaty. In March 1920 a plot was hatched by a rabid nationalist, Dr Kapp, and certain army officers who wished to set up a military dictatorship. When the government requested help in crushing the rebellion, the army leaders refused. General von Seeckt, shortly to be commander-in-chief, exclaimed tersely, 'Reichswehr does not fire on Reichswehr.' The government was forced to abandon Berlin, and only a general strike by the unions paralysed the putsch and saved the republic. Little was done to punish the Kapp rebels or those in the army like von Seeckt who had been less than loyal to the republic. Of 755 officers implicated in the affair, a mere 48 were relieved of their duties. The army continued to operate as a state within a state, and under von Seeckt's intelligent direction a nucleus of a future German army was created in the 1920s – one stressed the need for mobility and evaded the restrictions of the Versailles Treaty where possible.

Another unfortunate feature of the Weimar years was the introduction of a totally new level of violence in national life. Political murder had been rare in Germany before the war, but 376 political murders were committed between 1918 and 1922. Free Corps officers murdered the Communist leaders; and Matthias Erzberger, the Centre party leader, and Walther Rathenau, the industrialist, were both assassinated. The larger parties had their private armies, formed initially to recruit members and guard party meetings. The largest was the Stahlhelm (Steel helmet), founded as an army veterans' organisation and very right wing. The parties with republican sympathies countered with the Reichsbanner, the Communists formed a Red Veterans League, and the Nazis formed the Sturm Abteilung (SA) or Storm Troops. In the last years of the republic election campaigns became veritable battles in the halls and streets as argument gave way to brutal terrorism.

(c) The new constitution and the parties

In 1919 the National Assembly approved a new constitution which its author, Hugo Preuss, a professor of consitutional law, hoped would embody liberal ideals. Germany remained a federal state, but central government was given more power than before in its control of foreign affairs and finance. Prussia lost its old predominance, as the upper house was subordinate to the Reichstag, and inside Prussia the junkers lost their monopoly of power with the abolition of the three class franchise. Power rested with the Reichstag, elected by citizens by both sexes over the age of 20. The president was to be elected by the nation, not by parliament. He did not lead the executive but was to command the armed forces and had the power to dissolve the Reichstag. In a state of emergency he possessed the authority under Article 48 of the constitution to suspend civil rights and use the armed forces.

It seemed a genuinely democratic system, but certain weaknesses were revealed in its working. Candidates for the Reichstag were elected by proportional representation, a method which encouraged the growth of small parties. In 1932 twenty-seven parties contested the election, and fifteen gained seats in the Reichstag. It was therefore necessary to form coalition governments, which were often weak and short-lived, and between 1919 and 1933 there were twenty-one different cabinets. Even more serious were the special powers given to the president under Article 48. The first president, Ebert, acted constitutionally, but when Hindenburg became president in 1925, he began to exploit these powers in an undemocratic way. Whether any constitution could have worked effectively in the dark period after 1930 is, however, questionable.

The four chief democratic parties were the Social Democratic Party, the Catholic Centre, the German Democratic Party and the German People's Party. The socialists, as we have seen, were weakened by divisions, and the most stable party was the Catholic Centre; it drew votes from all strata of society and therefore, having to compromise between the various interests within the party, was moderate. It played an important part in Weimar politics, since its position in the middle of the political spectrum meant that no government could be formed without its participation. The German Democratic Party was liberal and boasted such outstanding individuals as Rathenau and Max Weber. The German People's Party, with Stresemann as its outstanding personality, was more moderately liberal. These four parties entered into various coalitions with each other and formed seventeen governments, but from 1930 they all lost seats to the more extreme parties on the left and the right. In 1920 the democratic parties had gained 82 per cent of votes cast but by 1932 the figure had fallen to only 39 per cent.

(d) The inflation of 1923

Germany's recovery from the war was a slow process made more difficult by Allied efforts to extract reparations from her. Living standards remained low and inflation was rampant. By July 1922 the mark was worth less than one-hundredth of its 1914 value. The Allied attitude to Germany stiffened after Germany signed the Treaty of

Rapallo with Russia in 1922. The French obsession for security was revived, and in January 1923 Poincaré, convinced that Germany could pay reparations if she wanted to, seized the opportunity to send troops into the Ruhr when Germany defaulted on her deliveries of timber. The ostensible reason for this action was the extraction of reparations, but the French also hoped to weaken the German economy and detach the Rhineland from Germany by supporting a separatist movement there. The German government replied with passive resistance, and clashes between French soldiers and German civilians resulted in the death of 132 people.

The affair paralysed the German economy, causing more shortages and runaway inflation. The inflation was fuelled by the German government, which, in trying to balance its budget, printed vast quantities of notes and allowed easy credit. The result was a crazy world in which the value of money fell by the hour. The dollar had been worth 14 marks in July 1918; by November 1923 it was worth 4,200,000 marks. A typical story of the period is of a woman who left a basket full of notes outside a shop; when she returned, the notes were still there but the basket had been stolen! William Guttman recalls how at this time he went into a café for a cup of coffee, which cost 5,000 marks. By the time he had finished his coffee, the price had risen to 8,000 marks. In a period of collective insanity people insisted on being paid by the day, and then rushed off to convert their paper money into goods. As no one wanted to accept the worthless paper, a barter economy developed. The fabric of German life appeared to be crumbling away.

It was at this point that Gustav Stresemann, leader of the German People's Party, became chancellor, the first genuine liberal to do so. This courageous realist took a number of steps to end the crisis. The policy of passive resistance was ended and a new bank was set up to issue controlled amounts of a new currency, the Rentenmark, said to have the backing of farmland. The 'miracle of the Rentenmark' now occurred; the German people believed in its stability and it gradually replaced the old mark. It was, in the words of Stolper, 'a psychological device', as there was no way in which the land backing the new currency could be converted into cash. Anyway, confidence was restored, especially as government expenditure was drastically cut and the budget balanced.

The consequences of 'the death of money' in 1923 were, however, grave for the regime, which faced a fresh wave of disorder. In November the Nazis under Hitler staged their Beerhall Putsch in Munich, a move checked by the loyalty of the Bavarian police. The inflation was a traumatic experience for the German people, already demoralised by war and disunion. The poverty caused by the inflation was extreme, and those on fixed incomes were hit incredibly harshly. Unlike wages, salaries were not revised upwards twice a week, and pensions and insurances became worthless. It was therefore the middle classes who were dealt the hardest blow, and their confidence in the republic was shattered. They had become proletarianised and therefore 1923 was a more genuine revolution than the political collapse of 1918. 'From the ranks of the disinherited bourgeoisie', comments Ryder, 'much future support for Hitler was to come.'

Some groups of course gained from the tragedy. It was galling for Germans who were forced to beg and were suffering poor health that foreigners could live in the best hotels for next to nothing. Speculators and businessmen took advantage of cheap credit to invest in industry and amass gigantic fortunes rapidly. Hugo Stinnes, the iron and coal magnate, was the chief example of this phenomenon. Finally government circles could not easily forget the events of 1923, and their fear of inflation explains the timid reaction to the problems of mass unemployment after 1929.

(e) Recovery and collapse

With the conclusion of the Dawes Agreement in 1924 came a loan of 800 million dollars, mostly from America, which enabled Germany to re-equip her industries and initiate a general economic recovery, helped by the introduction of scientific management and mass production methods. 'It is not merely a figure of speech', asserts Stolper, 'to say that in these fat years a new Germany was building up.' Real wages rose above prewar levels, hours were shortened and social insurance was improved. The inflow of foreign capital enabled local authorities to build new schools and hospitals, while the extension of public ownership to gas and electricity reflected the socialist influences in the republic. The concentration in big business continued. In 1925 the giant chemical combine I. G. Farben came into existence, followed in 1926 by a similar combine of steel firms, Vereinigte Stahlwerke.

The extent of the economic recovery should not be exaggerated; even in the peak year of 1928 unemployment stood at 1.8 million, and Germany was dangerously reliant on short-term foreign loans. Stresemann uttered a prophetic warning in 1928. 'Germany is dancing on a volcano. If the short-term credits are called in a large section of our economy would collapse.' His advice was ignored and easy borrowing from abroad ended with the Wall Street Crash of October 1929. Stresemann's worst fears were now justified, as an appalling depression gripped the German economy. At the trough of the depression in 1932, when over 6 million people were out of work, the unemployment rate was almost one in three of the male working population. The depression discredited parliamentary government, which seemed unable to take any effective action against the problem. Businessmen came to believe that only an authoritarian regime could help them, while hunger and despair drove millions of voters to support the Nazis and the Communists.

Meanwhile the republic had suffered irreparable losses with the deaths of Ebert in 1925 and Stresemann in 1929. The German liberal historian Erich Eyck has asserted that Germany should be proud of Ebert, because 'a man who excelled in political commonsense, mature judgement and moral integrity had risen from the lower ranks'. He was succeeded as president by Hindenburg, now 78, a man who had fought in the campaigns of 1866 and 1870, more a myth than a man, with an undeserved reputation for patriotism that the next few years were to belie. At the time it appeared that he was providing a focus of loyalty which the German people had lacked since 1918. As Stresemann had commented, 'the truth is that the German people want no President in a top hat. He must wear a military uniform and plenty of decorations'. But Hindenburg was a monarchist who disliked the republic, and he was to depend totally on his military clique for advice, with disastrous results for Germany.

The death of Stresemann in October 1929 from a heart attack brought on by years of overwork and abuse was truly tragic. His death, affirms Ryder, was a turning point in the life of the republic, because he had no successor. No later foreign minister 'combined his unflagging pursuit of national aims with the diplomatic skill that won foreign confidence'. His realism had contributed to the one period of real peace in the interwar years, and if he had lived to guide Germany though the approaching world depression, Hitler might never have become chancellor.

The last truly democratic cabinet in the Weimar Republic was that of the Social Democrat Hermann Müller. It was formed in 1928, with Stresemann as foreign minister until his death and General Groener as defence minister, as he had the confidence of Hindenburg. The government was bitterly attacked by the Left and the Right for accepting the Young Plan on reparations in June 1929, despite the fact that it reduced Germany's payments. Unemployment was, however, a much more acute problem, as the winter of 1928–9 saw unemployment rise to 2.6 million, and in the following winter the 3 million mark was passed. Unemployment insurance was hopelessly inadequate as it was designed only to build up a fund sufficient to sustain 600,000 unemployed for 3 months. The unemployed had to rely more on the hand-outs provided by municipal welfare agencies, though there was another choice: membership in the private army of one of the extremist parties.

The unemployment question finally cracked the Müller cabinet. It was composed mainly of Social Democrats and members of the German People's Party, and had therefore always been an uneasy coalition, because the latter group represented the interests of the propertied classes. In March 1930 the government parties split over a proposal to cover the budget deficit by increasing unemployment insurance contributions, a move which the German People's Party opposed. When the socialists refused to consider a compromise suggested by the Centre Party leader Brüning, the Müller cabinet resigned. It was a grave moment in the history of the republic, for after this no party combination that commanded a majority in the Reichstag existed. The way now lay open for Hindenburg to use, or rather abuse, his emergency powers.

Hindenburg, who liked the Centre Party leader Brüning, as he had a good war record and was an austere Catholic, nominated him as the next chancellor. Brüning formed a government made up of members from the Centre and Conservative Parties, but it relied on the confidence of the President, who listened increasingly to the advice of Generals Groener and von Schleicher. Kurt von Schleicher was a shrewd manipulator and urged Hindenburg to make use of his presidential powers under Article 48 from this point, with Brüning as merely a front man. Thus in a very real sense parliamentary government ended in March 1930. Brüning's reliance on Hindenburg increased after the general election in September, which increased greatly the strength of the extremist parties. The Communists added 23 to their existing 54 deputies, but the most astonishing phenomenon in the elections was the rise of the National Socialists: they increased their seats from 12 to 107, and now comprised the largest party after the Social Democrats. Hitler at this point demanded a place in the cabinet, but Hindenburg refused, declaring that the best position that he would give Hitler was postmaster-general so that he could lick stamps!

Brüning's position as chancellor was now even more hopeless. The economic situation grew worse as both unemployment and the balance of payments deficit grew. The chancellor was not helped by issues in foreign affairs. When he suggested an Austro-German Customs Union in 1931, the French forced the scheme to be dropped on the grounds that the customs union might foreshadow closer political ties. This latest revelation that Germany was still under the tutelage of the Allies further inflamed national passions. Brüning also tried to persuade the powers to put an end to reparations. All he gained while in office was President Hoover's declaration in June 1931 of a year's moratorium on all international debts. He did in fact negotiate an end to reparations, but by the time this was ratified at the Lausanne Conference of July 1932, he had already fallen from office. At home Brüning was forced to use deflationary policies, which Stolper condemns as 'one of the strongest contributing factors in the downfall of the Republic'. Yet if Brüning had used reflationary policies, the balance of payment deficit would have worsened and caused a loss of confidence in the mark. The fear of a repetition of 1923 cast a long shadow over the government's fiscal attitudes.

Brüning's policies made the majority of the Reichstag more hostile, and the Chancellor ever more dependent on Hindenburg, who was re-elected president in 1932 in preference to Hitler, who nevertheless won nearly 37 per cent of the votes cast.

In the state elections of April 1932 the Nazis became the leading party in the Prussian state parliament, and this latest success convinced the military clique behind Hindenburg that it would be advisable to do a deal with Hitler. In May Schleicher persuaded Hindenburg to dismiss Brüning, a move that the President was only too willing to make, as Brüning had recently suggested settling the unemployed on estates in East Prussia, a plan which smacked too much of Bolshevism for the old man. Hindenburg's brutal dismissal of Brüning demonstrated his own ingratitude and his toleration of Schleicher's intrigues. German liberal historians condemn Hindenburg's 'stab in the back' of the man who had served him well. With this act, says Erick Eyck, Hindenburg 'killed not only the German Republic but the peace of Europe'.

Schleicher now suggested as the next chancellor Franz von Papen, an aristocratic member of the Centre party and a political lightweight. Schleicher himself was defence minister in a new government dubbed 'the cabinet of barons', which had even less support in the Reichstag, as the Centre Party was furious at the way Brüning had been dismissed. The choice of such a government at a time when the unemployed numbered over 6 millions was utterly irresponsible. Schleicher had nominated Papen, as he seemed the right man to do a deal with the Nazis, and one of the chancellor's first measures was to lift the ban imposed by Groener during the life of the previous government on Hitler's private armies, the SA and the SS.

The consequences were only too predictable. The Nazis increased their violence and in July they clashed with the Communists at Altona in Prussia. Papen seized on the incident as a pretext for dismissing the Prussian socialist government under Otto Braun on the grounds that it was incapable of keeping order. When the socialists indicated their determination to resist what was after all an illegal move by Papen, the army was brought in to settle the question and the socialists had no other course but resignation. Prussia had been a stronghold of republicanism and socialism since 1919, and Papen's action dealt a heavy blow at what remained of the Weimar regime.

Despite his attempt to pose as the champion of order, Papen still could not handle the Reichstag, and had to ask Hindenburg to dissolve it. The elections in July merely made his position worse, as the Nazis, who became the largest party, won 220 seats and the Communists 89 seats. Hitler's bargaining position was now great; he demanded that he be appointed chancellor, but Hindenburg was not yet willing to accept an Austrian corporal as chancellor and Hitler would accept no other position. At the first meeting of the new parliament, a vote of no confidence was passed by 512 votes to 42, and the humiliated Papen was forced to request another dissolution. In the next elections, held in November, the Nazis lost ground quite significantly, the number of their seats falling from 220 to 196. Nevertheless Hitler remained as stubborn as before on the issue of the chancellorship.

The atmosphere of rumour and intrigue now thickened. As Papen had failed to gain Hitler's support and faced the opposition of nine-tenths of the Reichstag, Schleicher now engineered his dismissal and became chancellor himself in December. He hoped to split the Nazis by winning over the support of such genuine socialists in the party as the Strasser brothers, as well as the trade unions. These rather amateurish moves merely aroused the suspicion of the Left. Meanwhile in early January Hitler and Papen, eager for revenge on Schleicher, had begun to negotiate for a joint government. Schleicher, unable to gain the cooperation of the Reichstag, asked Hindenburg to dissolve it and give him special powers to govern without it. Hindenburg refused, as he feared that civil war might result, and Schleicher, having lost the president's confidence, resigned on 28 January. Papen and other advisers at last persuaded the president that the next government would have to include Hitler and on Hitler's terms.

On 30th January a new government was formed with Hitler as Chancellor in a cabinet comprising three Nazis and ten conservatives. Hugenberg was minister of economics, General von Blomberg war minister and Papen vice-chancellor. The army clique was convinced that only a regime founded on mass support could govern Germany, and only the Nazis possessed such support. At the time there seemed no alternative to admitting the Nazis into power. On the evening of 30 January the Nazi storm troopers held a 7-hour torch parade in Berlin in celebration of Hitler's triumph. The hour of National Socialism had arrived.

(f) Why did Hilter gain power?

Many reasons have been put forward for a development which was to have such disastrous consequences. The Versailles Treaty, the weakness of the party system and the economic catastrophes of the period all gave Hitler opportunities which he readily accepted. His success marked the failure of the Left, on whom considerable blame can be placed. The Soviet government forbade German Communists to cooperate with the Social Democrats, underrating the danger which Hitler presented. The result was a failure of the Left to combine against him. The Social Democrats themselves are far from blameless. Their policies were in fact moderate but they still shouted revolution, and Hitler was able to pose as the saviour of Germany against Communist subversion. The Socialists never mustered the courage to drop either their Marxism or their gradualism. To have dropped Marxism would have meant losing votes to the Communists, while the abandonment of gradualism would have meant cutting the party's links with the existing state. By 1933 the SPD was dispirited by recent election failures.

But if the Left was guilty of a sin of omission, the failure to unite against Hitler, the Right by actively inviting Hitler into high office was guilty of a far greater sin of commission. Hitler in fact never won a majority at the polls. According to Alan Bullock:

> Despite the mass support he had won, Hitler came to office in 1933 as the result, not of any irresistible revolutionary or national movement sweeping him into power, nor even of a popular victory at the polls, but as part of a shoddy political deal with the 'Old Gang' whom he had been attacking for months past. Hitler did not seize power; he was jobbed into office by a backstairs intrigue . . . the heaviest responsibility of all rests on the German Right who not only failed to combine with the other parties in defence of the Republic but made Hitler their partner in a coalition government.

For Hitler this success came in the nick of time for in the previous November his party had lost 2 million votes, was short of funds, and was exhausted.

Perhaps the conservative politicians like Papen assumed that Hitler in power could be tamed. Hitler would be the front man; real power would be exercised by Papen and Hindenburg. 'In two months we'll have pushed Hitler so far into the corner that he'll be squeaking,' Papen told a friend. Yet Hitler had proclaimed often enough his determination to destroy the constitution once in power, and his followers had demonstrated by their brutal murders what the nature of a Nazi regime would be. Bearing this in mind, one can only say that the 'Old Gang' was guilty of not only gross dereliction of duty but of gross political blindness as well in underestimating Hitler's talents.

In 6 months Hitler had set up a dictatorship which was a total denial of all the traditional values of European civilisation. It was to transform Germany, and its destructive urge to wage war ended most of Europe's remaining power in the outside world.

(g) Hitler's rise to power

Hitler was born the son of a civil servant at Braunau in Austria in 1889. Though he later claimed that he lived in poverty and was beaten by his drunkard father, it would appear that the family was comfortably placed and his father quite progressive. Hitler was lazy, and went to the Realschule (Secondary Modern School) rather than to the Gymnasium (Grammar School). His record was poor and he failed to learn Latin or gain the customary school-leaving certificate, which for most Austrian boys was the passport for a career. By the time he had reached the age of 18 both his parents were dead and his attempts to become an architect in Vienna had failed.

Hitler lived in Vienna in obscurity for 4 years, from 1909 to 1913. They were the formative years, believes Alan Bullock, in which his character and opinions were given definite shape. He soon ran through his inheritance and mixed with the flotsam and jetsam of Vienna. Here he learned the need to be brutal and unscrupulous, to feel contempt for the masses, and to hate the Jewish race and Socialism. By the time he left Vienna he was a convinced pan-German, living in a fantasy world all of his own.

It was the outbreak of war in 1914 that rescued Hitler from a life of frustration. He joined the Bavarian army and spent four years on the western front, winning the Iron Cross, First Class, a distinction rare for a corporal.

Like many other servicemen he was profoundly shaken by Germany's surrender. He returned to Munich, where he had lived just before the war, now interested in politics, and in 1919 he joined the German Workers' Party, which soon adopted a new name, the National Socialist German Workers' Party. Hitler's personality made him its leader, despite the socialism of much of its programme, which appealed to many of the early Nazis, such as Gregor Strasser. As far as Hitler was concerned, he was the Nazi programme, and his aims were the overthrow of the Republic, an end to the Versailles Treaty, the union of all Germans, living space for Germany's surplus population and the elimination of the Jews. The times favoured such extremism, and Hitler's audiences grew in size. As Alan Bullock has shown, 'Nazism was a phenomenon which throve only in conditions of disorder and insecurity.' Many ex-soldiers who could not adjust to civilian life joined the military wing of the party, the SA led by Ernst Röhm.

The catastrophic events of 1923 highlighted the fragility of the Republic, and in November Hitler attempted to overthrow the Bavarian government with the help of Ludendorff. The abortive putsch was a fiasco, but so unfortunately was Hitler's trial, where his eloquence won him a light 5-year sentence, of which he only served 9 months. During his term in prison he wrote *Mein Kampf*, in which he expressed his most deeply felt convictions.

Hitler now perceived the need to adopt parliamentary tactics, and between 1925 and 1929 the party grew slowly, despite these being the 'fat' years of the Republic. The socialist element in the party lost influence as new men came to the fore. Three men may be singled out here, as they each represented one of the chief Nazi 'types'. The able but malevolent Goebbels, a dwarfish individual with a club foot, found his *métier* in propaganda, persuading Hitler to use the new techniques available in the mass media. The unscrupulous Göring was a manipulator of power, and led the Nazis in the Reichstag from 1928, as Hitler, still an Austrian citizen, was debarred. Unlike the first two, Himmler had a doctrinaire belief in Nazi racial theories and organised the SS as a military élite.

In 1929 the Nazis gained considerably from a tactical alliance with the conservative and respectable German Nationalist Party led by Hugenberg. W. S. Allen, in his book *The Nazi Seizure of Power*, looks at Thalburg, a fictitious name for a real German town and points out that the alliance with the Nationalists helped the Nazis in two ways: (1) as all the 'best' people belonged to the Nationalist party, the Nazis gained in respectability while still appearing revolutionary, and (2) the Nationalists provided much needed cash for the Nazi propaganda machine.

Hugenberg, like many others, believed that he could exploit the Nazis, but he was sadly disappointed in the elections of September 1930 when the Nazi seats leapt from 12 to 107. The chief reason for this success has been well emphasised by Alan Bullock. Hitler's speeches in 1930 had 'a psychological perception of the mood of a large section of the German people which was wholly lacking from the campaigns of the other parties'. He believed that a political leader needed to be able to move the masses, and Hitler knew how to move them. In *Mein Kampf* he had outlined the method. Effective propaganda must be confined to a few bare necessities, lies should be big lies, all points should be painted in black and white and hammered home with passionate and violent rhetoric. Hitler followed this method only too well, and he was unsurpassed in modern times in his ability to win over mass audiences. He played on their fears and told them what they wanted to hear. Rarely has a political leader promised so much to so many. To the unemployed among the embittered middle and working classes he offered jobs, to the peasantry he offered more land, to big business he offered government contracts and a free hand for private enterprise, to the army he offered rearmament, to the nationalists he offered the recovery of German greatness, to youth he offered action and commitment, and to all he offered strong leadership, economic recovery and the re-establishment of law and order.

The verbal impact was buttressed by the visual. At Nazi meetings the posters, the swastika emblem, the flags, the salutes, the uniforms all combined to create a sense of power, a sense of belonging to a movement whose success was irresistible. Hitler, affirms Bullock, hit on a psychological fact of the greatest importance – 'that violence and terror have their own propaganda value and that the display of physical force attracts as many as it repels'.

Hitler of course craved for power, but this craving was allied to a sense of mission, which was perhaps the greatest source of his strength. He had a fanatical belief that he had been selected by destiny to lead Germany to a new and secure greatness. Such faith in himself gave him a hold over his followers and the confidence to take risks.

(h) Revolution after power

Hitler had come to high office in January 1933 with a veneer of legality, and the odds on his acquisition of dictatorial power seemed unfavourable, as only three of the eleven man cabinet were Nazis – Hitler himself, Frick as minister of the interior and Göring as minister without portfolio. Also ranged against Hitler were the powers of the president and the majority of the Reichstag.

Despite this situation, Hitler was to concentrate dictatorial powers in his own hands in 6 months, continually taking his opponents by surprise in his use of force as the first, not the last, resort. He persuaded Hindenburg that new elections were necessary, and during the campaign the Nazis besieged the electorate through their control of the police, press and radio. Opposition party meetings were banned and 400,000 SA and SS men were drafted into the Prussian police so that Nazi terror could be used legally.

Hitler claimed that such terror was necessary if he were to fulfil his task of saving Germany from Communism. His lie was made to appear truth when in February a young Dutchman, van der Lubbe, was accused of setting fire to the Reichstag. Whether he was the guilty party is a question that still intrigues historians. Research by German historians like Bracher and Hofer indicates that it was impossible for Lubbe, who was half-witted and almost totally blind, to have started a fire of such magnitude in so short a space of time. As he was known to associate with SA men, it seems likely that the Nazis started the fire. They of course claimed that Lubbe was a Communist, and used the incident as a pretext to outlaw the Communist Party and arrest 4,000 of its leading members.

Despite their frenzied propaganda, the Nazis polled only 43.9 per cent of the votes, which, with the Nationalist Party vote, gave them a bare majority. In practice this turned out to be a good working majority, as the 81 Communist deputies were debarred from sitting. At the opening of the new Reichstag in March, the Third Reich replaced the unlamented Weimar Republic in a ceremony brilliantly stage-managed by Goebbels.

Wishing to be free of the president's emergency powers, Hitler now presented the Reichstag with an Enabling Bill which would authorise the government to pass laws without consulting the Reichstag. To their eternal credit, the Social Democrats, led by Otto Wels, voted against the bill, despite the fact that the Reichstag was surrounded by baying SA and SS men. No other party displayed similar courage, the Centre Party approving the bill after it had received vague promises from Hitler about the rights of the Roman Catholic Church. Had the Centre opposed the bill, Hitler would have lacked the two-thirds majority required for constitutional changes, though it seems almost inevitable that he would have forced the bill through by one means or another.

The Reichstag was now a rubber stamp, and the parties who had approved the Enabling Law had signed their own death warrant. Hitler was now independent of the Reichstag and the president. As Bullock remarks, the gutter had come to power. Nazi governments were appointed in all the states, and opposition parties were liquidated. Socialist leaders were arrested, the Party's funds seized and its press banned. The Centre and Nationalist Parties were not spared either, in spite of their cooperation with the Nazis. By the end of 1933 Germany was a one-party state. The unions too were simply dissolved, and in May in their place was set up the Labour Front, to which all people engaged in industry or trade, including employers, would belong.

There was little opposition to these developments. Hindenburg was so old and lethargic that he did not appreciate the trend of events, nor was there any public reaction to Nazi brutality. This was no doubt due partly to self-deception or fear, but an important factor must have been a willingness to respond to the appeal of a magnetic leader. By identifying National Socialism with Germany, Hitler, in calling for a national revival, touched on people's deepest loyalties at a time of national crisis.

Hitler's chief worry by 1934 was growing unrest in his own party. Some members were disappointed at their failure to gain the rewards of office, and many storm-troopers who took the socialist ideas of the movement seriously were chagrined at how little of the socialist programme had been implemented. Hitler clashed with the SA leader, Ernst Röhm, on this question and also on Röhm's proposal that the SA and the army should be united, presumably under his leadership. This also alarmed the army, on whose benevolent neutrality Hitler still relied. When he heard from Himmler and Göring that Röhm was planning a *coup d'état*, Hitler acted swiftly. On 30 June the Nazis murdered about 400 people, including members of the SA, such as Röhm, socialists in the party, such as Gregor Strasser, several leaders of the Centre Party and Generals von Schleicher and von Kahr.

The 'Night of the Long Knives' revealed the true nature of the Nazi regime, but Hitler's power was consolidated when Hindenburg died in August 1934. Hitler simply merged the office of president and chancellor and made civil servants and army personnel swear an oath of allegiance to him personally.

(i) The nature of Hitler's rule

Hannah Vogt has remarked on the contrast between the present image of life in the Third Reich and what many people who lived through it report about the good features of the period. Even discounting the claims of Nazi propaganda, the regime became popular. The skill of the propaganda itself was one reason for this. Goebbels controlled the mass media and was able to kill most criticism in Germany stone dead in 2 years. Of more importance was the capacity of the regime to live up to its promises. Germany was given strong leadership, unemployment vanished, big business received contracts, Germany rearmed and moved from triumph to triumph in foreign affairs. Hitler seemed indeed the national saviour that he claimed to be.

The outstanding feature of Nazi rule was Hitler's own unquestioned authority. Other Nazis fought each other for influence, but there was never any question of challenging Hitler, and indeed conflicts were taken to him for arbitration. Not that the power he wielded was used efficiently. Delow describes Hitler as the 'antithesis of an effective bureaucrat', because he disliked administration and shirked difficult decisions. He preferred public speaking or leisure in company with friends from his Munich days and his mistress Eva Braun.

The administrative confusion already existing in Germany, owing to the overlapping institutions of the central and state governments, was made worse by the Nazis when they created a third competing authority, their own party machine. Nor did Hitler's practice of deliberately causing quarrels among subordinates help efficiency. Those who came to the top built up their own administrative empires, so that Germany became a veritable administrative maze. It would be fair to say that German government in the period was less efficient than before 1933, was less totalitarian than Soviet Russia and is best described as 'authoritarian anarchy'.

Hitler's supreme authority was exercised through the Nazi Party Central Office, while in the regions Germany was divided into *Gaus* headed by a Gauleiter responsible for ensuring the authority of the party in his district. In addition to this territorial organisation, the party maintained many functional organisations, such as the Hitler Youth and the party militia, through which most aspects of the German life could be controlled. It was the task of Central Office to supervise these organisations. In the early years the Central Office came under Hitler's deputy, Rudolf Hess, who had the right to initiate legislation, select personnel and settle differences between party members. When Hess flew to Scotland in 1941 in a vain attempt to persuade Britain to make peace with Germany, he was replaced by Martin Bormann, an efficient fanatic who served Hitler with devotion and whose easy access to Hitler gave him an immense amount of power.

The most important of the functional organisations in the early years were the Sturm Abteilung (SA) or storm-troopers, and the Schutz Staffel (SS) or Elite Guard. After the Night of the Long Knives, the SS, under Himmler, was the more influential, and it now kept watch on all political life. Himmler built it up as an élite force within the party and the state. Members were selected with great care for their physical fitness and racial pedigree, but above all for their fanatical devotion to the person of Hitler. The SS motto was 'My honour is true', which meant absolute loyalty to Hitler and Himmler. At the beginning of the war entire units of the SS were introduced into the army under the name of Waffen SS.

As Prussian Minister of the Interior, Göring rapidly purged the Prussian police and established reliable Nazis in key positions. It was this control of the police that enabled the Nazi revolution to retain its sham appearance of legality. Göring also reorganised the political police, better known as the Gestapo. Himmler was soon its commander, and he appointed SS men to the key positions in all the police organisations. In his seizure of this power Himmler was helped by the head of SS intelligence, Reinhard Heydrich. A gifted and handsome individual, Heydrich was one of the few Nazi leaders who matched up to the Nazi ideal of German youth. He saw the advantage of compiling files on all the prominent figures in government. When the Nazis moved into other countries after 1938, Himmler and Heydrich organised special task forces to accompany the army into occupied areas to round up Jews and potential opponents.

A number of agencies were set up for racial questions, including the Ancestral Heritage Office to investigate the racial credentials of Germans, and the Well of Life (*Lebensborn*), which were orphanages for racially valuable children. In 1939 Himmler set up a supreme supervisory office for all racial questions – the Reich Commission for the Consolidation of the German People. It was designed to carry out the Nazis' racial programme, which meant the provision of land for Germans in newly acquired areas, the seizure of Polish and Jewish property, and the mass execution of the Jews. The implementing of this programme did much to disrupt the economy, as it used vast resources, but Himmler was moved by ideological considerations only.

The judicial system was twisted so as to serve the regime's perverted ends. Sentences became more severe, and forty-three offences carried the death penalty by 1945. Special courts were established and staffed only by judges of proven loyalty to Nazism. The onus was now on the accused to prove his innocence, a difficult task against a bullying judge. At their worst, trials were conducted in the spirit of the trial of the generals who attempted to murder Hitler in July 1944, at which Roland Freisler, the President of the People's court, screamed abuse at the defendants.

The regime increasingly used torture, execution without trial and the concentration camp. The full extent of the horror was hidden from most people, but the existence of such camps was common knowledge. As Hitler himself said, 'Terrorism is an effective political tool . . . people will think twice before opposing us, if they know what awaits them in the camps.' In the camps the power of the guards was limitless and brutal torture common. A number of methods were used for killing the inmates, including injections, drowning and electrocution, and it is small wonder that prisoners on average only survived for 9 months in the camps. It was a system that attracted sadists, who were positively encouraged by the chief authorities, such as Freisler, to indulge in more cruelty.

(j) The economy

Hitler's most urgent task was a reduction in the number of unemployed, with rearmament as a second, longer-term, aim. He expanded the work of previous governments in the provision of public works programmes and financial incentives to businessmen to invest and therefore employ more labour. Motorways, airfields and frontier defences were built by cheap labour provided by the National Labour Service, which was compulsory for all men between 18 and 25 after 1935. Rearmament added to the demand for labour, as did conscription, which came in in 1935. Hitler was also supremely fortunate that by the time he came to power the trade cycle had reached the trough of the depression and recovery had already started. Unemployment fell in the first year from over 6 million to under 4 million, and by 1938 only 400,000 people were unemployed. By this time industrial output had nearly doubled and national income had risen by 87 per cent. Ironically there was now a labour shortage, which caused an influx of foreign workers and renewed fears of inflation. The minister of economics, Schacht, quarrelled with Hitler over the inflation question, and resigned in 1937 when he found that his authority was being diminished by Göring, who was controller of a 4-year plan launched in 1936.

With unemployment solved, Hitler, remembering the effects of the Allied blockade in the First World War, made German self-sufficiency in food and essential raw materials his next objective. Autarchy was to some extent achieved, as Germany's dependence on agricultural imports fell from 35 to 25 per cent and German scientists struggled with varying success to produce synthetic rubber, wool and oil. Steel output rose impressively from 7 million to 19 millon tons between 1932 and 1937.

The German economy was helped by a number of windfalls. World trade revived in 1937, and when Austria and Czechoslovakia were absorbed into the Third Reich, their assets were seized. The plunder of the Jews, which increased dramatically from 1938, also swelled the coffers of the Reichsbank. Yet when war broke out in 1939, German reserves of essential oil, copper and rubber were still inadequate. Autarchy demonstrates the reason for Hitler's ultimate failure, his refusal to face realities.

The main feature of Nazi policy towards the economy was *Gleichschaltung* (regimentation). Trade unions were dissolved and workers now joined the German Labour Front, led by Robert Ley. Factory owners were given complete authority over their workers, though party officials were also appointed to keep a watch on economic enterprises. From 1935 on all workers were to possess a labour book with their job record and racial background.

One of the most important activities of the Labour Front was the organisation for welfare and leisure known as Strength through Joy, a name that gave rise to not a little mockery. The organisation enabled more Germans than ever before to enjoy subsidised foreign holidays, sport and concerts.

In the drive for autarchy the consumer came off second best. The diet of the German people deteriorated, though the housing and consumer durables sectors improved. Taxation remained high, as only 63 per cent of Germany's net national product was spent on personal consumption, compared with 79 per cent in Britain. Real incomes still rose before the war, for Hitler was aware of the need for popularity. Thus expenditure on armaments, though it was considerable and reached 27 per cent of the gross national product in 1938, was not as thorough as Germany's enemies feared. The real difference lay in the quality and modernity of her weapons. Only late in the war was consumption really held down as Germany began to rearm in depth.

The unity imposed on the economy was more apparent than real. The different agencies competed for influence and scarce resources and issued such a flood of orders that by 1939 confusion reigned supreme. Hitler shut his eyes to the need for long-term planning, and even in 1945 Germany was still not making maximum use of her resources.

(k) Cultural straitjackets

The Nazis aimed at full control of all aspects of cultural life, and a Reich Chamber of Culture with authority over all the arts, the press and the radio was created. Goebbels presided over this organisation, and tried to crush the artistic developments that had been Weimar's chief achievement. Those intellectuals of independent mind rapidly found that they faced two choices – emigration or the concentration camp – especially if they were Jewish. The few, such as the poet Stefan George, who attempted to cooperate with the regime were rapidly disillusioned. That thinkers of the quality of Thomas Mann, Gropius and Einstein had to emigrate was Germany's loss and the gain of the outside world. An inevitable decline of intellectual standards occurred.

In the view of the Nazis the task of the intellectual was service to the state. Scientific objectivity or art for art's sake were regarded as hangovers from discredited liberalism. German art was to be functional and should highlight Nazi ideals. Artists like Adolf Ziegler and Johannes Beutner contributed work on the Aryan figure, and typical paintings featured chaste nudes and peasant girls stripped to the waist working in the fields. Hitler's particular interest was architecture, and he employed Albert Speer to design plans for the rebuilding of Berlin and other cities on a monumental and classical scale. The culture was reflected in the gigantic columns of the Nuremberg stadium and the Chancellory.

The new art of film-making was also twisted to serve the regime. Leni Riefenstahl produced a memorable film, *Triumph of the Will*, a study of the Nazi rally at Nuremberg in 1934. Goebbels appreciated the importance of the cinema as a means of indoctrination, and many films glorifying the German race and heaping scorn on Jews and Slavs were produced.

The attitude of the Third Reich to creative thought was made evident in May 1933 when students took part in a ceremonial burning of 'un-German' books in Berlin. Jewish or left-wing lecturers were dismissed from the universities, and the number of students fell from 116,000 in 1933 to 67,000 in 1937, mainly as a result of Nazi pressure. A grotesque perversion of the curriculum resulted, as each subject was used merely as a tool for propagating Nazi ideals. The academic world failed to protest at this development.

A similar concern for indoctrination was demonstrated in the schools. Teachers had to belong to the Nazi Teachers' Association and many Jewish teachers were arrested, often as a result of being exposed by their pupils. The new emphasis in the curriculum was on physical traning. New schools were built for children chosen for their leadership potential and racial purity. For older pupils destined for high position in the party the Nazis set up residential schools called *Ordensburg*, a name which recalled the castles built by the Teutonic Knights in the Middle Ages.

For the indoctrination of the mass of German youth the main instrument was the Hitler Youth, to which boys were admitted at the age of 10. The movement was led by Baldur von Schirach and reached a membership of 6 million by 1936. Military training was a cardinal feature of its activity, and by 1938 over 300,000 young Germans were organised in units serving the needs of the armed forces.

(l) The Nazis and the Churches

National Socialism was a substitute religion. Hitler's genius lay in his ability to strike responsive chords among the German people, appealing to their idealism as well as their greed and hatred. In Nazi ceremonies 'Heil Hitler', and 'Sieg Heil' gave staccato fury to the rituals of obedience, while the use of the swastika emblem and special uniforms gave the Nazis the appearance of a special order set apart. Given this factor and also Hitler's contempt for Christianity, with its 'effeminate pity-ethics', relations between the Nazis and the Churches were inevitably uneasy.

Both Protestants and Catholics were slow to grasp the full threat posed by the Nazis, and indeed there was much initial goodwill towards Hitler, who was regarded as a bulwark against Communism. Not until the war was the full horror of the regime revealed, and by then the churches had made fatal compromises. Hitler acted shrewdly in not provoking them; indeed in his original programme 'Positive Christianity' was proclaimed as a Nazi aim, and as a result the two Churches failed to unite against him.

In 1933 Hitler won some acceptance from German Catholics by promising a Concordat with the Pope, and he managed to persuade the Centre Catholic party to vote for the vital Enabling Bill. When the Concordat was signed in July, the Roman Catholic Church was promised freedom of activity in Germany. The Catholic hierarchy now intended cooperation with the regime despite its violence and its dissolution of the Centre Party. It is clear that many German Catholic leaders had disliked the Weimar democracy, and were more concerned about the rights of the Roman Catholic Church than civil liberties.

The Protestant or Evangelical Churches were already weakened by 300 years of cooperation with government. Neither was there organisational unity; there were twenty-eight Protestant Churches, some Lutheran, a few Calvinist, and the largest, the Old Prussian Union, was a combination of the two. The Protestant Churches were nationalistic in outlook, believed in obeying the secular power and were taken in by Hitler's promises. The Lutheran Church produced a group called the German Christians, who proclaimed that Jesus Christ was not Jewish but Aryan. Hitler in his desire for control and uniformity appointed a German Christian, Müller, as Reichsbishop for all the Protestant Churches.

This move did arouse opposition from some Protestants, led by Martin Niemöller, who formed a new body, the Confessional Church. It resisted successfully a proposal to exclude Christians of Jewish origin from the Church, and in 1935 issued a clear warning of the dangers that the Nazi regime posed for the Church. Hitler retaliated by arresting 800 leading churchmen, including Niemöller, who was eventually sent to Dachau concentration camp. The Protestant youth movement was merged with the Hitler Youth, church property was taken over and clergy dismissed. Most of the clergy tried to take up a middle position, rejecting the German Christian but unwilling to join the Niemöller group.

In one year alone over 100,000 people left the Roman Catholic Church as the Nazis mounted an attack on Catholic charities, schools, monasteries and press. In 1937 Pius XI gave voice to Catholic disillusionment when he denounced the evils of the Nazi state in an encyclical *With Burning Anxiety*. Nevertheless there existed a fatal ambivalence in Catholic attitudes, despite the arrest of several hundred priests. Both Churches failed to react vigorously to the agonising moral problems facing them. With a few exceptions, such as Niemöller, Bonhoeffer and von Galen, the Catholic Bishop of Munster, the Church leaders allowed Nazi atrocities to go unchallenged. In the greatest crisis which they had ever faced the German Churches had been tested and found wanting.

(m) The army

The greatest single obstacle to full Nazi dictatorship within the German state was the army, but it failed to move against Hitler in the early years when it had both the opportunity and good reason to do so. In the 'Night of the Long Knives' two generals were killed, but despite their anger, the army leaders failed to act. General Beck typified their attitude when he said, 'Mutiny and Revolution are words that do not occur in the vocabulary of a German soldier.' In any case these gentlemen of the old school shared many of Hitler's aims, even if they despised the man himself as proletarian and crude.

As time went on, the chances of an effective army revolt receded rapidly. In March 1935 universal military service was reintroduced. Now Nazified youth filled the army, making any moves by the army leaders against Hitler's regime extremely risky, as they could not trust their soldiers to carry out orders.

Hitler for his part did not trust the generals, who challenged his plans for war at an important conference in November 1937. Therefore he contrived to remove both von Blomberg, the War Minister, and von Fritsch, the commander-in-chief of the army, within a few months. Blomberg was disgraced following allegations that his wife had in the past been a prostitute. Fritsch was accused of being a homosexual, and was forced to retire into private life, despite the chief witness against him confessing in court that the Gestapo had made him incriminate Fritsch. Hitler became his own war minister, appointing to his own military staff obsequious officers like Wilhelm Keitel. In all sixteen generals were dismissed, and Göring became head of the Luftwaffe. The army's indignation at these moves might have crystallised into actual revolt had Hitler suffered a setback in his foreign policy, but in 1938 he was able to absorb both Austria and the Sudetenland. With the army subservient to his wishes, there was now no effective check to Hitler's dictatorship.

FURTHER READING

Bracher, K. D., *The German Dictatorship*, Penguin, Harmondsworth, 1973

Bullock, A., *Hitler: a Study in Tyranny*, Penguin, Harmondsworth, 1962

Carr, W., *A History of Germany 1815–1985*, Edward Arnold, Third Edition, London, 1987

Craig, G., *Germany 1866 – 1945*, Oxford University Press, Oxford, 1981

Fest, J., *Hitler*, Penguin, Harmonsworth, 1977

Kershaw, I., *The Nazi Dictatorship*, Edward Arnold, London, 1985

Nicholls, A. G., *Weimar and the Rise of Hitler*, Macmillan, London, 1979

Noakes, J. and Pridham, G. (eds), *Nazism 1919–1945*, University of Exeter, 1984

Stone, N., *Hitler*, Hodder and Stoughton, London, 1980

QUESTIONS

1. To what extent was the Weimar Republic doomed to failure from the start?
2. How far was the rise of German National Socialism caused by the fear of Bolshevism?
3. 'Jobbed into office by a backstairs intrigue.' Critically examine Bullock's view of Hitler's accession to power in January 1933.
4. Why was Hitler able to consolidate his dictatorship so much more quickly than Mussolini a decade earlier?
5. How truly totalitarian was the Nazi regime by 1939?

6
The Third Republic in decline, 1919–39

(a) France in 1919

'If Spain became the classical case of open civil war, it was France which offered the most striking example of the wider tendency to incipient civil war,' writes David Thomson. The interwar period was one in which parliamentary institutions were discredited in France as short-lived governments failed to stem the rising tide of violence, especially in 1934 and 1936. National unity was destroyed by class warfare, and France entered the Second World War psychologically and materially unprepared for another major struggle with the Germans.

It is tempting to ascribe the root cause of France's malaise to the terrible cost of the First World War. As Clemenceau himself lamented, 'the élite of her youth was at rest in a shroud of glory' – 1,390,000 men (10 per cent of the active male population) were dead or missing; 740,000 were maimed. These losses hit France particularly severely, for she was already a country suffering, in Kemp's phrase, 'demographic anaemia'. Her population was increasing very slowly before 1914; as a result of the war her total population in 1921, excluding the lost provinces of Alsace-Lorraine, was lower than in 1891, and contained the lowest proportion of young and the highest proportion of the elderly of all European countries. Germany still retained her demographic superiority, with a population of over 60 millions to France's 39 millions. With the collapse of Russia and the French failure to obtain the Anglo-American guarantee, Germany's potential international strength was greater than in 1914.

It is small wonder that security obsessed the French. 'This is not peace,' Marshal Foch said of the Versailles Settlement. 'It is an armistice for 20 years.' In a similar vein Clemenceau remarked that France was condemned to eternal vigilance. The determination with which French governments pursued reparations is explained by the underlying feeling of weakness. France was to receive 52 per cent of any sum extracted from Germany, and it was hoped that this would finance the costs of repairing the devastated provinces; time was to show that such hope was vain.

The war had been a traumatic experience for Frenchmen in other ways. It had led to the loss of investments in Russia, necessitated huge governments loans and put the nation in debt to the United States. It ended currency stability, which had lasted for over a century, and, by accelerating the increase in the proletariat, raised the spectre of socialist revolution. Even the peasantry was now an embittered and discontented force.

(b) The elections of 1919 and the 'Bloc National'

Rather like Lloyd George's 'Coupon' election in England in 1918, the French elections of 1919 smacked of declining national standards. The right-wing parties formed a 'Bloc National', supported by the cartels of big business, the most famous of which was the steel cartel, the Comité des Forges. The menace of Communism was denounced, and a brilliant election poster depicted a savage Bolshevik with a bloody knife between his teeth. This, combined with a strange version of proportional representation, gave the Right a specious election victory. According to this system, each department returned a group of deputies in proportion to the votes cast, but if any list of candidates gained a majority of votes, it gained all the seats in that department. As the 'Bloc National' was more united than the Left, it won a landslide victory.

The results were most disappointing to the French labour movement, which during the war had seen the membership of the UGT rise to over 2 millions. The Left was as usual divided between the revolutionary and gradualist elements; the revolutionaries aimed at close links with the Soviet government and the overthrow of the Republic, policies which were anathema to the moderates led by Leon Blum. After a conference at Tours in December 1920, the two wings went their separate ways. The extremists set up a Communist party, with its own trade union organisation, the Confédération Générale du Travail Unitaire (CGTU). 'The significance of the schism', remarks Cobban, 'was that it created two left-wing parties in bitter rivalry with one another. Henceforth the presence of the Communists on their left prevented the Socialists from cooperating whole-heartedly with the Radicals for fear of losing their own clientele to the former.'

Yet the 'Bloc National' was also doomed to weakness through division. Its cohesion was weak because it was made up of men of all parties, including moderate Socialists and Radicals. Many were Catholic and political amateurs, who made a number of serious errors in financial and foreign affairs.

Relations with Britain deteriorated over the Middle East and also as a result of the Washington Conference of 1922, which gave Britain the right to a battleship tonnage twice that of the next two greatest European naval powers, France and Italy, combined. This acquisition of British security only served to throw light on the relative flimsiness of French security, and relations between the two countries became acrimonious over the German reparations question. The British protest at the French invasion of the Ruhr in January 1923 seemed hypocritical to the French; it appeared that the British were only interested in a revival of business with Germany at the expense of justice for France. The invasion of the Ruhr was, however, an error. The French troops resented having to serve in peacetime, and the public resented the higher taxation that resulted from Poincaré's move. In the future French governments were to be reluctant to use the military supremacy gained at Versailles. As Denis Brogan says, 'Germany was still open to French invasion but the will to invade was dead.'

(c) The Cartel des Gauches

Even before the invasion of the Ruhr the 'Bloc National' had become unpopular because of its moves to prevent civil service employees having the right to strike and its attempts to extend the Church's influence in education. Therefore the elections of 1924 saw a decided swing to the Radical–Socialist coalition, the 'Cartel des Gauches', which won 270 seats against 210 to the 'Bloc National'. The results demonstrated the desire of the French public to return to the easier days before the war. Irritation with rising taxes made inevitable by the Ruhr invasion combined with a genuine horror of war. The inflexible Poincaré was now unpopular and Herriot became premier; in sharp contrast to his predecessor, he was a warm, friendly individual with a genuine desire for the well-being of the ordinary Frenchman. Unfortunately the Cartel's troubles only began with victory, as it faced several difficult problems.

The alliance between the Socialists and the Radicals, though a natural combination at election times, did not operate easily in office. The two elements clashed over the question of the economic role of the State. To the Radicals the State was a dangerous machine whose use was to be kept to a minimum, a view that won Socialist contempt. Matters came to a head over finance, which Herriot had assumed France could 'muddle through'.

The French had steeled themselves during the ordeal of war by the thought that, when victory was won, Germany would pay the cost of the war. By 1924 it was clear that she could not do this. With inflation rampant, something urgent was required to restore solvency to French finances. The Herriot government attempted to impose a capital levy, a tax on property-holders, which appealed to the Socialists but not to the Radicals. The government fell on the issue and was succeeded by another short-lived ministry in 1925 at a time when the franc was falling rapidly in value and the cost of living rising rapidly. Only in 1926 was confidence restored, when Poincaré became premier again. His firmness rather than any actual measure impressed the French public and helped stabilise the franc. As the extra taxes he imposed fell on the poor, the Socialists were displeased and the unity of the Cartel des Gauches undermined.

The Cartel also had to contend with the delicate question of Alsace, which Dennis Brogan describes as 'in some ways the greatest cause of French disillusionment with victory'. Under German rule the province had become accustomed to far more local freedom than the French system permitted. The Radicals disliked the continuation of the Concordat in Alsace and the existence there of clerical education. In 1924 Herriot denounced the Concordat and prepared to laicize education in Alsace. These moves antagonised not only Catholics but the Alsatian public in general, and the proposals were dropped.

A linguistic division still prevented good relations between the central government and the people of Alsace. The government wanted all instruction to be in French, while the Alsatians, including the clergy, wanted at least part of the instruction in German. As German was the mother tongue of the population, the French should have perceived the deep emotional attachment to it in Alsace instead of enforcing linguistic uniformity. This lack of tact by the French government caused the growth of an Autonomist movement in the province which was to some extent stimulated by the recovery of Germany after 1924. In 1928 came the unedifying spectacle of the trial and pardon of several Autonomist leaders.

The problem of empire also taxed the French government in this period. Interest in the empire had been increased by the war, which had illustrated dramatically the numerical inferiority of the French population to the German. The empire had provided men and supplies on a considerable scale, but promises of political change had been made to the colonies and in the postwar years the growth of colonial nationalism became a serious issue. Therefore in Indo-China, North Africa and Syria the French faced the necessity of suppressing armed uprisings.

(d) Reconstruction

A more pleasing feature of the 1920s was the rapid recovery of the French economy. The zones of France over which the war had pursued its course had been terribly devastated, and in the ten Northern departments the population had been nearly halved. But 80,000 million francs were spent on reconstructing the devastated areas by 1925, a feat which Brogan calls 'the greatest economic achievement of post-war Europe'. The recovered areas again became the richest producers of crops in Europe, particularly in wheat and beetroot. Against this, the drift to the towns continued and some land went out of cultivation, because 673,000 peasants had been killed in the war. The shortage of labour did, however, begin to encourage improved farming methods, and France, despite a falling rural population, became more nearly self-sufficient than other West European nations.

The damage caused by the war had a more lasting effect on French industry, as the areas destroyed by the war contained France's chief industrial zones, but by 1925 much rebuilding had been completed. Starting from scratch, French industry was able to benefit from new capital equipment. The war had encouraged the expansion of industry elsewhere in France, and the recovery of Alsace-Lorraine gave her new sources of iron ore and potash. The French motor industry expanded rapidly, with new names like Renault, Citroen and Peugeot coming to the fore. An annual production of 200,000 cars was attained, and France for a time was a leader in the cheap car as well as the luxury car market.

France's role as the playground of Europe was of considerable benefit to the balance of payments, though it led to a growth of American influence on French culture. Unemployment was low in the 1920s and wages by French standards were good, with the workers now receiving a larger share of the national income than ever before. Increasingly France imported labour from North Africa and other parts of Europe, including 800,000 workers from Italy alone in 1931.

Thus the 1920s was a comparatively brilliant decade for the French economy. Government help had accelerated modernisation in the metallurgical, engineering and chemicals industries, though backward areas remained. A shift had taken place towards heavy industry, but, as much of the new growth depended on export markets, the French economy became more sensitive to changes in the level of world trade.

(e) The depression

By 1926 serious divisions had opened up in the Cartel des Gauches, while at the same time its achievements in foreign affairs – the Locarno and Kellogg Pacts – were neglected. Therefore in the elections of 1928 the parties of the Right won 330 out of 610 seats. Another feature was the steady growth in the strength of the Communists, who won significant support from many of the 3 million immigrants in France. The Right was fortunate in that for a time France seemed immune from the world slump. The Left, however, was singularly unfortunate in this respect. By the 1932 elections the

Socialists and Radicals had reunited and won 334 seats against 257 for the Right and only 12 for the communists. Once again, as in 1924, the Left inherited difficult economic problems from the Right which it could not tackle.

Though France suffered a less profound shock than the United States after the Wall Street Crash of 1929, the depression was causing serious distress by 1932, and the stagnation of the economy provided a grim contrast with the brilliant performance of the previous decade. French exports, which were largely luxuries could not be afforded by foreign customers, especially after the sterling crisis of 1931 resulted in the overvaluation of the franc and the pricing of French goods out of world markets. Cheap imports from other countries desperate to sell at any price hit the home market. With the decline in tourism, the balance of payments grew more unfavourable and unemployment figures rose. By 1932 the number of registered unemployed was 433,000, but to this figure should be added the 600,000 foreign workers who left France.

Attempts to combat the depression were hampered by the economic sacred cow – sound money. The franc should have been devalued, but opposition to this course was general in government and the capitalist classes, an opposition which Kemp condemns as exceeding all rational limits. Sound money was considered one of the foundations of the social order; to lose it would result in social revolution. Therefore to save the franc the governments of the early 1930s added to the deflationary spiral by cutting government expenditure at a time when they should have increased it.

Such policies were fatal to the unity of the Left coalition. When Daladier's government in 1932 cut the salaries of civil servants, the Socialists were furious and were not appeased by Daladier's promise of socialist measures in the future, for example the nationalisation of the armaments industry and insurance companies. The depression which had been the major reason for the Left's electoral victory was now proving a liability. Left-wing disunity resulted in rapid changes of government, six different cabinets taking office between May 1932 and February 1934. This game of musical chairs, as Brogan calls it, was highly discrediting to parliamentary institutions, and gave the opportunity to several right-wing leagues to mount a vicious campaign against democracy.

(f) The Leagues, the Stavisky Affair and the riots of February 1934

The interwar period saw the development of a number of Fascist groups in France. The earliest of these, the Action Française, aimed at the restoration of royalist authority and national greatness. Though its policies did contain elements of socialism, Action Française, as Eugen Weber has stressed, remained a group rather than a political party seeking power, and with its traditionalism it came to seem rather old-fashioned. In the 1920s many monarchists and Catholics rejected its violence, and in the 1930s it was out-distanced by newer authoritarian groups.

Georges Valois, who had been a member of Action Française, left the movement in 1925 to found Le Faisceau, a French copy of Mussolini's fascist party. Into his organisation flocked war veterans disillusioned by a world unfit for heroes to live in. After Poincaré restored confidence in 1926, the movement lapsed into insignificance and other groups moved into the limelight. Marcel Bucard's Fran-cistes claimed to be Fascist but had only a very small membership. Larger leagues were the Jeunesses Patriotes, the Solidarité Française and the Croix de Feu. Jeunesses Patriotes was founded by a Paris deputy, Pierre Taittinger, in 1924; it was anti-communist and tried to copy the Italian Fascists. By the early 1930s it claimed to have a membership of 90,000, including 6,000 in Paris. Solidarité Français, which was founded in 1933 by talcum powder tycoon François Coty, was violently anti-Semitic.

The most important of the leagues was the Croix de Feu, an organisation for ex-servicemen who had been cited for gallantry in battle. It was founded in 1927 and was led by Colonel de la Rocque. Its success was due to three causes: its discipline, the vague nature of its programme, which gave it a wider appeal than other right-wing groups, and its position as a number one target for the Left. Though its rallies and use of cars and planes were impressive, the Croix de Feu was not truly Fascist. It lacked mass support, and Weber is right to call its members 'patriotic conservatives'. After 1936 the move-ment was to go into a decline, and Jacques Doriot's genuinely Fascist Parti Populaire Français became prominent.

Membership in one of the Leagues offered to the men of the Right what Communism offered to those of the Left – an opportunity for action, entry into the élite and the charismatic attraction of the leader. The appeal to youth was particularly strong in a country where the political leaders like Herriot and Blum were in their 60s, whereas Fascist leaders like Doriot were in their 30s.

Anti-democratic as these movements were, their threat to the Republic should not be overestimated. They never gained a mass following, as in Italy or Germany, because the different groups failed to unite and also because France escaped the worst consequences of the depression. What they did have in common was a righteous indignation at national decadence, which they believed was caused by democracy. Right-wing papers, such as *Le Matin*, *Candide* and *Je suis partout*, whipped up public opinion with indecent invective against republican government. Their campaign might have fizzled out but for the Stavisky Affair, which seemed to prove, in their eyes anyway, that their diagnosis of French democracy was only too correct.

Serge Alexandre Stavisky was a professional swindler whose activities had come to the notice of the police as early as 1927, when he had been arrested and released pending trial. In 1933 he was still at liberty, having been granted nineteen 'provisional' releases, probably through the aid of influential friends. Now, however, he overreached himself by floating a loan of 200 million francs' worth of bonds, allegedly to finance a small municipal pawnshop at Bayonne. In December the scheme collapsed, and, after a warrant had been issued for his arrest, Stavisky disappeared. In January 1934 he was found dead, apparently having committed suicide. The parties of the Right now claimed that Stavisky had been murdered to prevent him disclosing the names of his influential protectors. The prime minister at the time, Chautemps, tried to hush the matter up, an unwise policy, as his brother-in-law was head of the judicial department responsible for Stavisky's provisional releases. When the premier refused a committee of enquiry into the affair, the leagues organised large demonstrations as a protest against Republican corruption.

On 27 January Chautemps was forced to resign and Daladier became prime minister. To please the Socialists, he dismissed the rabidly right-wing prefect of the Paris police, Chiappe, who had persistently made life difficult for the Left. It was the dismissal of Chiappe that sparked off serious trouble on 6 February. When the new government made its first parliamentary appearance, there was utter disorder in the Chamber, caused by the Right and the Communists. Across the river from the Chamber great riots organised by the Leagues broke out, and the police only contained them with difficulty. As a result of the riots, fifteen people were killed and 328 seriously injured. Daladier was forced to resign, and further demonstrations took place in the next few days.

The riots intensified the bitter struggle between the Left and the Right in France. The Left believed that the Leagues had organised the trouble to overthrow the Republic, but the riots were so uncoordinated that this explanation is unlikely. The events of 6 February were merely an explosion of latent anti-parliamentary feeling in Paris sparked off by a succession of weak governments and the revelations of the Stavisky Affair. Probably the only real political objective was the overthrow of Daladier's cabinet.

The affair was slow to peter out. Doumergue's government initiated enquiries into Stavisky's activities, and put much of the blame on the real sinners, the detective police and judiciary. Stavisky had worked as a spy for the Sûreté, which had given him some immunity, while his links with the Radical deputy and lawyer Bonnaure had made the judiciary reluctant to move against him. Public interest in the affair was kept at fever pitch by the death of Albert Prince on 21 February. This important legal official was found fastened to a railway line and horribly mutilated. Again there was speculation about criminal activities in high places, but though the mystery was never solved, it may well be that Prince committed suicide.

(g) The Popular Front

'The most important consequence of the 6th of February', asserts Cobban, 'was the traumatic effect it had on the French Left.' The threat which the Right seemed to pose to the parliamentary system angered the Radicals and Socialists and sobered the Communists, who had begun to appreciate the lesson to be learned from the triumph of the Nazis in Germany. In any case they were now under instructions from Moscow to collaborate with socialists and liberal groups against fascism. The Communists now became belligerently nationalistic, a pose that did not entirely convince the Socialists, who for so long had been the target of Communist slander. Nevertheless the Croix de Feu did appear such a threat to parliamentary government that an alliance on the Left seemed essential.

Therefore in July 1934 Socialists and Communists agreed on common political action, and in July 1935 a common front was formed between the Radicals, Socialists and Communists, with Daladier and Blum addressing a great combined meeting of the three parties on 14 July. By January 1936 a Popular Front programme had been constructed. It called for a return to a system of collective security, the consolidation of the Franco-Soviet pact, the dissolution of the Fascist leagues, and extensive measures of economic and social reform. The slogan of the Popular Front was 'bread, peace, and liberty', and it particularly attacked the 'two hundred families' – the Regents of the Bank of France who embodied the power of organised wealth.

The programme was ideally suited for a country which after years of depression was prepared to consider real political change. By 1935 the slump had bitten hard in the agricultural as well as the industrial sector, and a catastrophic fall had taken place in farm prices. Another factor was swinging opinion towards the Left. Ordinary people were becoming increasingly alarmed by the appeal of the Right to violence. Shortly before the elections in 1936 Leon Blum, happening by chance to meet the funeral procession of the Action Française historian Jacques Bainville, was beaten up and nearly lynched by the mourners. He became a martyr figure, and the Right was discredited by such an ignoble attack on an elderly and defenceless victim. A third factor made victory for the Left certain; while its parties had gained some cohesion, the right had not, for the Croix de Feu refused to run candidates. Thus the elections resulted in a shift of seats to the Left which gave the Popular Front about 380 deputies against their opponents' 237. The Communists gained 62 seats and the Socialists

39, but the Radicals lost 43 seats and their loyalty to the Popular Front became a matter of some doubt.

The new government was headed by Leon Blum. With a shrill voice he was not a great orator, but he deserved his position by virtue of his integrity and considerable intellect. His period in office was to see important measures passed, but the early optimism aroused by the sweeping electoral victory was soon to cool. The Communists refused to take office, despite playing a large part in the election victory, and were therefore in a position to profit from any errors made by the government.

The government was immediately embarrassed by a rash of strikes in May and June at a time when it wished to reassure the employers that they would not be expropriated. The victory of the Popular Front had aroused hopes of better conditions among the workers, the more militant of whom believed that the factories were to be handed over to them to run. Starting in the aircraft factories, sit-down strikes spread from industry to industry, paralysing the economic life of the country. It was therefore Blum's first task to restore industrial peace.

A conference of employers and union leaders was held at the Hotel Matignon in June, at which Blum won a great personal success by persuading the employers to make far-reaching concessions. He saw that the economic stagnation might be solved by increasing the purchasing power of the masses. Accordingly the Matignon agreements awarded an average pay rise of 12 per cent in wages and civil service salaries, and brought in compulsory collective bargaining (a development which encouraged a rise in the membership of the CGT), holidays with pay and a 40-hour week. To help the peasantry, a Wheat Board was to be set up to fix a fair price for the producer. The government also stated its intention to nationalise the armaments industry and implement closer control over the Bank of France. These policies were to leave a permanent mark on France, and, as Tom Kemp says, 'they broke with the deflationary policies of the previous five years and established the foundations of a welfare state'.

Blum's government also brought in some rationalisation of the executive machinery, and in October proceeded to devalue the franc by 25 per cent. This necessary step brought in a more realistic exchange rate and increased the possibilities of economic recovery by cheapening French exports and encouraging tourism. But there were unfortunate results as well. Devaluation, allied with a high level of government expenditure, was inflationary. Retail prices in December were 17 per cent higher than in May. Nor did devaluation stimulate French industry as much as had been hoped. Blum was still distrusted by the employers, who remained reluctant to carry out new investment. The level of unemployment remained high, and in 1939, even with an armaments drive, industrial production was only 86 per cent of what it had been before the slump, and at the same time capital equipment was becoming increasingly obsolescent. France's economic decline relative to other countries was even greater.

The Right, baulked at the polls, was still a threat to stability, because it turned to more ruthless measures. Soon after the 1936 elections members of Action Française and the Croix de Feu set up the CSAR (Comité Secret d'Action Révolutionnaire). Its members, who became known as the Cagoulards or Hoods from their cult of secrecy, were led by an ex-member of Action Française, Eugène Deloncle. The Cagoule was a secret military society whose objective was the establishment of a dictatorship in France to forestall the imminent threat of a communist revolution. It received large sums of money from big businesses such as Michelin, and committed a number of acts of terrorism, but at the end of 1937, after an abortive 'coup', seventy-one Cagoulards were arrested, though they were still awaiting trial when war broke out.

The activities of the Right were only of nuisance value; the worst problems facing the Popular Front lay in foreign affairs. The outbreak of the Spanish Civil War in 1936 posed a thorny question of whether the French should actively support the Republicans. The French government, though sympathetic to the Republican cause, decided against intervention because such a policy would alienate Britain. Blum was able to gain some measure of public support for the government line by playing on the general horror felt in France at the prospect of war; but the Spanish Civil War continued, deepening the divisions in French society. While the Left sympathised with the Spanish Republicans, the Right, which approved of Franco, condemned its attitude and tried to depict its members as the dupes of the Russians. The course of the Spanish war also made French Radicals ponder over the advisability of any association with the Communists.

By February 1937 the Popular Front government was suffering increasing pressure from its enemies on the extreme Left and Right. Despite the Matignon agreements, industrial peace was not maintained, while the Right was antagonised by the government's nationalisation policy and by its decision to dissolve the leagues. Blum came to feel that the only way to restore confidence was to call a temporary halt to reform, with a cut in government expenditure. This merely encouraged the government's enemies to fresh acts of violence. When a Leftist mob attacked a Croix de Feu meeting at Clichy, the police were forced to open fire on the mob and six people were killed. The CGT response to this 'massacre' was to call a general strike. In June Blum was forced to resign when his proposals for foreign exchange control to protect the franc were defeated in the Senate.

The optimism of 1935 and 1936 was now dead and France experienced more rapid changes of government; the instability of French politics was dramatically demonstrated by the absence of any French government at all when Hitler marched into Austria in March 1938. Only in April, when Daladier became prime minister in a Government of National Defence, was some semblance of stability restored. By this point foreign affairs were absorbing most of the government's attention. Daladier and his foreign minister, Bonnet, were content to follow Britain's lead in the attempt to win back Italian support and appease Hitler. Only the Communists attacked appeasement with any vigour; the French public sincerely feared another holocaust and doubts about the effectiveness of the armed forces grew each year.

When the Second World War broke out in September 1939, France was unprepared for a fresh struggle. The downfall of the Third Republic in the summer of 1940 startled the world, but it cannot be explained solely by reference to military factors. Rather the French collapse represented the culmination of a long process of inner decline, which was partly economic, partly political, partly psychological. 'It can hardly be contested that the economic decline of the interwar period prepared the way for, if it did not make inevitable, the military defeat which ended the life of the Third Republic,' asserts Tom Kemp. But to this factor must be added the acute divisions in French society between the Left and the Right. Afraid of socialist measures, the Right for years before 1939 had been spreading the slogan 'better Hitler than Blum', while the workers were in no mood to support a government which had allowed the gains of the Matignon agreements to be eroded by inflation. Finally a psychological dimension is required to explain the paralysis of will which seized France on the outbreak of war. A universal pessimism at the prospects of success gripped both the political and military leaders. The real test of any regime is how well it can face up to crisis; in 1939–40 the Third Republic was tested and found wanting.

FURTHER READING

Adamthwaite, A., *France and the Coming of the Second World War*, CUP, Cambridge, 1970

Brogan, D. W., *The Development of Modern France 1870–1939*, Hamish Hamilton, London, 1967

Cobban, A., *A History of France, Volume 3, 1871–1962*, Penguin, Harmondsworth, 1970

Colton, G., *Leon Blum*, Duke University Press, 1987

Kemp, T., *The French Economy*, Longmans, London, 1972

McMillan, J. F., *Dreyfus to de Gaulle, Politics and Society in France 1898–1969*, Edward Arnold, London, 1985

QUESTIONS

1. Account for the feeling of insecurity in France after 1919.
2. Did the events of February 1934 in France threaten the over-throw of the Republic?
3. What were the chief successes of the Popular Front government?
4. 'A nation at war with itself, torn by social strife.' Critically examine Adamthwaite's view of France in the 1930s.

7
Britain, 1906–39

(1) Political developments to 1939

(a) The final era of Liberal supremacy, 1906–22

After virtually 20 years out of office, the Liberal Party, led by Sir Henry Campbell-Bannerman, won the 1906 election. This victory signified a Liberal recovery from the split over Home Rule for Ireland in 1886, while in contrast the Conservatives themselves were now divided over the policy of tariff reform, vigorously campaigned for by their colonial secretary, Joseph Chamberlain, as a means of protecting industry and jobs.

The new Liberal government has become legendary for its talent, its members including Asquith, Lloyd George and Churchill. Its record on reform was commendable, and embraced reorganisation of the armed forces, changes in trade union law and the introduction of old age pensions and national insurance. Members of parliament were paid a salary from 1911 on, and poorer members of society could now enter politics more easily. In 1909 the government was forced into a battle with the House of Lords which resulted in the upper house losing its power to reject money bills, a development which T. O. Lloyd calls 'a heavy blow to the old British upper classes'.

In 1908 Campbell-Bannerman retired and was replaced by Asquith, a fine debater with the ability to discern the long-term implications of a policy. He was not original in his thinking, but gave opportunities to the more imaginative minds in the cabinet to make important changes. However, he was not a vigorous war leader and by 1915 the inadequacy of the British preparation for war was made clear by the scandal of a shortage of shells on the Western front and by the failure of the Gallipoli expedition. The Conservatives now became prepared to oppose government policy openly, a reality that forced Asquith to invite them into a coalition government in the interests of national unity. Liberal members of the coalition contrived to hold on to all the important posts, so that the Conservatives felt little loyalty to the new arrangement. Meanwhile Lloyd George, first as minister of munitions and then as secretary of war, increased his reputation and influence. Asquith's methods of running the war through ministerial committees whose work was coordinated through the cabinet proved to be too slow. Consequently Lloyd George ousted Asquith as premier in November 1916, his coalition having the support of some Conservatives, most of the Labour Party and half of the Liberals.

The new premier imparted a unique drive to the war effort. He set up a War Cabinet of five which could meet every day to speed up decision-making. His energy and new ideas, and also his willingness to listen to other people's ideas, led to much more effective prosecution of the war, for example in the creation of essential new ministries and the imposition of the convoy system on a reluctant Admiralty. His government tried to show the people that the country was fighting for democracy by passing an important electoral reform act in 1918. By giving the vote to all men over 21 and to all women over 30, it trebled the electorate. One-third of the male population now gained the vote and for the first time women were enfranchised.

A deep split had opened up in the Liberal party. Asquith refused to serve under Lloyd George in 1916, and when a general election was held in 1918, he again rejected an invitation to join the government. Therefore Lloyd George and the Conservative leader, Bonar Law, decided to fight the election under the Coalition banner, a strategy which, by exploiting Lloyd George's prestige as war leader, ensured a huge majority. Liberal candidates in the election had little hope of winning unless they had a guarantee of respectability from Lloyd George and Bonar Law. This guarantee was a letter signed by the two leaders saying that the candidate was a loyal member of the Coalition. Asquith dubbed this 'the coupon', after the ration coupon, and the election has been called 'the coupon election' ever since.

Lloyd George's conduct in the election is not to his credit in other ways. He did not do enough to check the demands of the electorate for vengeful policies on Germany or warn the people of the difficulties to come. Yet the tactics worked. The Coalition parties won 478 seats, while the Asquithian Liberals were reduced to 28. Significantly the Irish electorate returned 73 Sinn Fein members, who declared themselves to be the Irish parliament and refused to come to Westminster.

Conservative back-benchers now made up a majority in the Commons, unlike the earlier years of the Coalition, and they were able to force the hands of the government on certain issues, for example the return of the coalmines to private hands. Nevertheless the government did achieve some reforms. A 7-hour day was brought in for miners, the Fisher Education Act of 1918 raised the school-leaving age to 14 and a Ministry of Health was set up under Christopher Addison in 1919 to tackle housing. Unemployment insurance was extended to all industrial workers.

Yet in truth the government faced a host of problems. The war had seen a growth in trade union power and the war years saw a rash of strikes. In particular the miners resented the return of the mines to private control and attempts by the owners to reduce their wages. They wished to rebuild their prewar alliance with two other large unions, the railwaymen and transport workers. However, when they went on strike in 1921, they were not joined by the other unions, a lack of support which the miners regarded as desertion.

Economic affairs became critical as unemployment rose to 2 million in 1920. Britain had lost many of her overseas markets during the war, and so many overseas investments had been sold off that there was no longer a favourable balance of payments to finance new investment. Government policy may have aggravated the situation. As the pound had slipped in value on the foreign exchange markets, Bank Rate was raised to 7 per cent in 1920, not only increasing the cost of borrowing to businessmen, but, by making the pound stronger, also increasing the price of British exports abroad. A further deflationary influence came from government spending cuts organised by Sir Eric Geddes.

Lloyd George also lost popularity through the lavish granting of honours to businessmen who were willing to pay for them. Honours had been sold by previous premiers and this was hardly a secret, but the scale of Lloyd George's operations and the sort of people to whom he sold the honours angered the Establishment, especially as he set up his own political treasure chest, which reached at least £1 million in value.

The government's chief problem was Ireland. The war years had further alienated Irish opinion. The willingness of most Irishmen to support the war was not shared by the extreme nationalists, and at Easter 1916 Patrick Pearse and James Connolly led a rebellion in Dublin. It received little support but its defeat was followed by the execution of most of the leaders, thus giving the cause its martyrs. Eamonn de Valera, one of the leaders, was only saved from execution because he was an American citizen.

Only in 1920 did the Coalition government finally pass the long-delayed Home Rule Bill of 1912. The bill gave special treatment to Ulster, whose counties would be allowed plebiscites on whether to opt out of the new Ireland ruled from Dublin. This angered Irish Nationalists, and the fighting which began in 1919 had reached new levels of brutality by 1921. The Irish Republican Army (IRA) could not fight pitched battles against the British army, but it mounted effective guerrilla warfare in the streets. It regarded all Irish people who cooperated with the British as traitors.

The British government also resorted to extreme measures. To strengthen the police, it raised special forces, the Black and Tans, recruited from demobilised soldiers. Their practice of exacting reprisals for any Nationalist outrage led to the destruction of farmhouses and the murder of innocent Irish people. Only in December 1921 was a compromise settlement reached. Ireland, except for the Six Northern counties, would become the Irish Free State, with the same dominion status as Canada. The Irish negotiators accepted these terms without referring the issue back to the Irish leader de Valera. Ireland now disintegrated into a new civil war between pro-Treaty and anti-Treaty parties.

Events in India further divided the Coalition. Agitation for independence led to the massacre of Amritsar in 1919, when General Dyer dispersed a crowd with machine-gun fire, killing 379 people (see Chapter 16). The Conservatives blamed the Liberal secretary of state for India, Montagu, for giving way to Indian demands for independence.

Events in the Middle East finally precipitated the break-up of the Coalition. The Turks had repudiated the Treaty of Sèvres and had driven out the Greeks from Smyrna (see Chapter 2). They now came face to face with British forces stationed at Chanak to guard the area of the Dardanelles Straits, neutralised under the Sèvres Treaty. War seemed near and indeed desired by Churchill and Lloyd George, alarming the Conservatives, who no longer regarded Lloyd George as an electoral asset. At a meeting of the Carlton Club in October 1922 they decided to end their participation in the Coalition. Behind the mobilisation of support for ending the Coalition lay the influence of Stanley Baldwin, a politician unwisely underrated by Lloyd George.

(b) The Conservative Government, 1922–3

The end of the Coalition led to the Conservatives' victory in the ensuing general election. They realised that the turmoil of the last decade had left voters desiring tranquillity above all, and this was exactly what Bonar Law promised them. It was this policy of stability or safety first that in part explains the Conservative domination of British politics in the interwar period. The October election in 1922 saw the Conservatives win 345 seats, but the other significant result in the election was the Labour advance from 62 seats in 1918 to 142 seats in 1922.

Bonar Law retired in May 1923, a victim of cancer, and he was replaced by Baldwin, who had made himself a reputation for honesty, caution and geniality. Lord Curzon, the more able but arrogant foreign secretary, described him as a man of the utmost insignificance, but the more perceptive Churchill pointed to his skill as 'the greatest party manager the Conservatives ever had'. He cultivated a reassuring public image; the public liked to see him smoking one of his many pipes. Perhaps at times he seemed indolent, especially in the field of foreign affairs.

In 1923 unemployment running at 12 per cent of the work-force was his main concern. He became convinced that tariff reform would help certain industries, such as steel and agriculture, face foreign competition, and as this policy had not been part of the 1922 election manifesto, another election became necessary. Unfortunately for Baldwin this challenge to free trade principles was one of the few factors that could have reunited the Asquith and Lloyd George Liberal groups. The election of December 1923 left the Conservatives with 258, the Liberals 159 and Labour 191 seats. The Liberals could now decide which of the two larger parties should govern, and opted for Labour. Behind Asquith's thinking was the belief that the Liberal Party could expect to survive an alliance with Labour, but alliance with the Conservatives might easily turn into fusion.

(c) The first Labour Government, 1924

The immediate origins of the Labour Party lie in the formation of the Independent Labour Party by a small group of socialists led by Keir Hardie, a Scottish miner who was elected to parliament in 1892. Hardie was a good leader for the early years of the movement, because he was devoted and energetic, but he did not possess the organising ability to lead a large party. A key necessity for the new movement was the attraction of trade union support, and in 1900 the Labour Representation Committee was set up to increase the number of Labour members of parliament. After the 1900 Taff Vale case (see Chapter 1) many trade unions determined to support the LRC, which after 1906 called itself the Labour Party. As the century progressed, the new party began to build up strongholds in certain working-class areas, usually at the expense of the Liberals but in Lancashire at the expense of the Conservatives. The party benefited from collaboration with the Liberals in some elections, such as that of 1906, and it gradually increased its number of seats.

Another factor in its rise was the regaining of the leadership by Ramsay MacDonald in 1922. The illegitimate son of a crofter, he had tried to become a Liberal member of parliament in the 1880s and in a sense became a socialist as second best. He became a rich man through his marriage to Margaret Gladstone in 1896, but her death in 1911 left a void in his life. He became party secretary and then in 1911 leader of the Labour Party, but had to resign the leadership in 1914 because he courageously opposed British entry into the war despite being offered a cabinet post. He was vilified as a traitor and experienced 8 years in the political wilderness, losing his seat in 1918. As he had suffered for his beliefs, he was assumed by many of the new Labour members to be more strongly socialist than he was; but he made little effort to develop close relations with the unions and his diaries show a contempt for the working classes. Nevertheless, as Ross McKibbin has shown, he was probably the best man the party could have chosen to get a Labour government elected quickly, because he possessed organising abilities, was a fine orator and clearly wanted some social reform, even if he was unclear at times on how to implement it.

The first Labour government lasted only 9 months; dependent on Liberal support, it could not implement its cherished policies on nationalisation and welfare. What it was able to do was to prove its competence to govern and further displace the Liberal Party as the chief party of the left. It is clear from his diaries that MacDonald had this latter aim clearly in mind.

The government also passed some useful measures. The McKenna duties (imposed on luxury goods in 1915) were abolished, and there were three main achievements in social policy. Firstly, the Wheatley Housing Act provided a most positive initiative to increase the housing stock by granting subsidies for the building of local authority houses. Secondly, Trevelyan, an aristocratic Liberal turned socialist, restored the cuts in education made in the early 1920s, and finally there was a slight increase in unemployment benefits, which were made easier to obtain.

A trivial incident ended the first Labour government. It was voted out of office by its opponents when it decided to withdraw a prosecution for sedition against Campbell, the editor of the *Worker's Weekly*, who had published an article calling on soldiers not to shoot their working-class comrades during military or industrial warfare.

The general election of October 1924 is remembered for the publication of the Zinoviev letter. The Foreign Office published a letter, apparently from the Comintern and signed by the Soviet leader Zinoviev, calling on British Communists to undertake armed revolution. Debate still continues over its authenticity, but its publication may have led some voters to believe that the Labour government had been unwise in recognising the Soviet government and negotiating a trade treaty with it. Whether the letter was influential or not, the Conservatives won a landslide victory, winning 419 seats to Labour's 151 and the Liberals' 40. The Liberal representation to parliament fell to a level where they ceased to be taken very seriously. The Labour Party felt that it had been defeated by a trick, and was not consoled by a rise in its votes of 1 million.

(d) The Baldwin years, 1924–9

Baldwin's government was to demonstrate some competence in a number of areas, but it did little to cure unemployment. Indeed the return to the gold standard in 1925 pegged the exchange rate at $4.86 to the pound, and this increase in the value of sterling made British exports dearer.

The revaluation of sterling particularly hit coalmining. As labour was so large a part of the costs of production, it was very hard to cut prices to remain competitive. The industry was also plagued by bad industrial relations, Lord Birkenhead commenting, 'I should have thought that the miners' leaders were the stupidest men in the kingdom if I had not met the owners.'

Baldwin appreciated the dangerous situation and tried to avoid strife, but all to no avail. The miners believed that nationalisation would make coal cheap and saleable and enable wages to remain high if all coal from good and bad pits was pooled and sold at a price which meant that good pits subsidised the bad. The Samuel Commission, which reported in 1926, had some sympathy with this view and advocated the nationalisation of mining royalties, amalgamation of mines and a national wages agreement. At the same time it suggested that wage cuts were needed.

The response of the miners was predictably inflexible. Their leader, A. J. Cook, coined the phrase, 'Not a minute on the day, not a penny off the pay'. The owners were similarly stubborn; they wanted both longer hours and lower wages, and announced new scales in April 1926. The two sides held aloof from attempts by the government and the TUC to reach a solution. In May the government ended negotiations and the General Council of the TUC called for a general stike in support of the miners. It was not revolutionary in intention but merely a device to put pressure on the government. Baldwin remained calm during the dispute; he felt that the opposition would crack and his chief concern was to sidetrack Churchill (who had wanted armed soldiers to escort food convoys) into editing a government emergency newspaper, *The British Gazette*.

The General Strike only lasted 9 days. It was not a general strike in the true sense, many groups of workers continuing work. In addition, the union leaders were cautious men, afraid that a long strike would be expensive and lead to anti-union legislation. The miners stayed out for months but eventually had to surrender. In 1927 a Trade Disputes Act made general strikes illegal and banned civil servants from belonging to unions. Union members wishing to contribute to Labour Party funds now had to 'contract in', a clause which resulted in a fall in the proportion of union members subscribing to the political fund. As the TUC was unlikely to indulge in any more general strikes, the Act was at least in part unnecessary. It was resented by the trade union movement and repealed by the Labour government in 1946.

The government was more creative in other spheres and enacted six useful reforms. Neville Chamberlain used the Ministry of Health to extend the social services, and in 1925 he brought in pensions for widows and orphans and the granting of the old age pension at 65 instead of 70.

In 1929 Chamberlain produced a comprehensive reform of local government which increased the responsibility of the county and borough councils for poor relief and road-making. The Board of Guardians for poor relief disappeared and parish councils were relieved of their road-making duties, which were becoming harder with the advent of motor transport.

An Unemployment Insurance Act in 1927 lowered benefits and contributions but brought in a standard benefit for an indefinite period, provided that workers had paid contributions for 30 weeks in the previous 2 years and were genuinely searching for work.

In 1928 the Representation of the People Act gave the vote to women at 21 instead of 30, but it did not deal with the question of plural voting, by which a man could vote both in the constituency where he resided and in that in which he owned business premises.

The high cost of electricity, the many generating stations and the variety of frequencies were a handicap to industry. Therefore in 1926 the Central Electricity Board was set up to buy electricity at cost from selected power stations and distribute it. A national grid, standardisation of frequencies and larger generating stations resulted from this early experiment in nationalisation.

Finally, broadcasting came of age. The Post Office had set up the British Broadcasting Company in 1922 to take over the function of wireless broadcasting. In 1926 it was made into a public corporation with a royal charter – the British Broadcasting Corporation (BBC). Its first Director General was the formidable John Reith, who insisted on the BBC's high moral function. 'Our responsibility is to carry into the greatest possible number of homes everything that is best in every human department of knowledge, endeavour and achievement and to avoid the things which are, or may be, hurtful.'

As C. L. Mowat suggests, 'the government's record of useful social legislation was greater than that of any other inter-war government save that of Lloyd George's Coalition government'. With Austen Chamberlain's efforts at Locarno, the government also had its successes in foreign policy (see Chapter 2). Nevertheless the Conservatives had not conquered unemployment, though it had fallen by 600,000. Its slogan of 'Safety First' for the 1929 election was unexciting and it seemed to lack energy, Lloyd George deriding it as sleepy, torpid and barren. With the Labour Party also unwilling to offer radical ideas, the 1929 election produced another hung parliament, the Conservatives winning 260 seats, the Liberals 59 and Labour 288.

(e) The second Labour Government and the 1931 crisis

As the Labour and Liberal parties could agree on foreign and imperial issues and the great domestic question of Free Trade, MacDonald was able to form the second Labour government. He would have liked to concentrate on foreign and imperial issues but he and his party were unfortunate in coming to office in 1929.

In October the Wall Street Crash signalled the start of a world depression, and unemployment in Britain started to rise. Philip Snowden, Chancellor of the Exchequer, insisted on balanced budgets and declined to provide money for public works as a means of relieving unemployment. MacDonald knew little about economics and refused to consider alternative economic policies, for example the deficit financing ideas of Mosley, who, lacking the patience to wait upon events, left the party in 1931.

With the slowing down of exports, owing to the world depression, the government felt pressurised on three interlinked questions – the reduction of unemployment, the wish to balance the budget and the pound's international value. But the pursuit of the first objective would tend to exacerbate difficulties over the other two objectives. Thus public works programmes which might have alleviated unemployment were ruled out in the interest of a balanced budget. Nevertheless growing unemployment meant less revenue for the government through taxation. It also led to a loss of confidence in the pound; fearing that it might be devalued, foreign investors began to take their money out of London. In May 1931 a series of bank collapses in central Europe resulted in further withdrawals of funds from London and a loss of British assets deposited in central Europe.

On the insistence of the Liberals, a committee under the direction of Sir George May was appointed to investigate ways of pruning government expenditure so as to build up foreign confidence in Britain. When it reported in July 1931, it forecast a budget deficit of £120 millions and suggested ways of cutting expenditure, mainly through cuts in public servant salaries and in unemployment relief. Such a gloomy report accelerated the outflow of funds, and had this trend continued, it would have led to the devaluation of the pound and the abandonment of the Gold Standard, both of which, it was believed, would undermine London's position as an international financial centre. The collapse of London as an international money market would then result in a loss of invisible earnings from banking and insurance, and Britain's balance of payments would then go into deficit.

MacDonald, in an attempt to restore confidence, entered into discussions with the opposition leaders over the measures needed to balance the budget. The move angered the unions and Labour left-wingers, who disliked what they regarded as a fatal compromising stance. Remorselessly, however, a financial crisis resulted, because the Bank of England was paying out gold to meet the stream of withdrawals and was coming to the end of its resources. It was forced into attempts to raise loans from American and French banks, but on 23 August it became known that the Federal Reserve Bank in New

York would only grant a loan if the government proved its resolution to prune government expenditure by a 10 per cent cut in unemployment benefits.

The recommendation of the bankers was distasteful to about eight of the Labour cabinet, and Macdonald was obliged to inform George V that his government was about to break up. The King then asked him to lead a National government (in effect a coalition), and after some hesitation MacDonald accepted, prior promise of support having been gained from the Conservatives and Liberals. MacDonald returned to his Labour cabinet, informed that they were now out of office, and asked Snowden, Thomas and Sankey to join his new cabinet. The remainder of the Labour cabinet and most of the Labour party went into opposition against the new government led by a former Labour prime minister.

The Labour party claimed at the time and has ever since that MacDonald plotted with the King and the bankers to turn Labour out of office just to prolong his premiership. But the King had a constitutional duty to name the strongest government available, while New York bankers were entitled to demand measures that would make their loans to Britain a safer proposition. As for MacDonald, David Marquand has shown that he intended to resign but was persuaded to help form a coalition government because such a move would obviate the need for a general election, and such a swift resolution of the political crisis would impress opinion abroad. In particular, suggests Marquand, the King's appeal turned the scales. MacDonald attached great value to George V's good opinion, and without a wife or close confidant the prime minister needed someone to talk to at a time of great strain. Moreover the King's appeal was couched in terms to which MacDonald was likely to respond – patriotism, duty and self-respect. The decision to form the coalition was to cost him dear. He had spent 40 years in the Labour movement. Now he was savagely attacked from the Labour back benches, and soon after he was expelled from the party. 'If I die soon', he told George Strauss, 'I shall die of a broken heart.' He remained premier until 1935 and died at sea in 1937, but by then he was an exhausted old man. In Marquand's words, 'Politically he had died six years before.'

(f) The National Government, 1931–9

Despite its apparent seriousness at the time, the 1931 crisis was solved remarkably quickly, the ease with which the National Government was created with members from all parties pointing to Britain's deep political stability. MacDonald was the most convenient leader for the new government. In September Snowden brought in a deflationary budget, which raised income tax and surtax and reduced government spending by cutting unemployment benefit and the salaries of teachers and the armed forces. The formation of the government reassured foreign lenders somewhat, but a strike by sailors of the Royal Navy at Invergordon over pay reductions accelerated Bank of England gold payments as foreign money continued to leave Britain. Finally the Bank had to suspend its sales of gold and Britain was forced off the Gold Standard. No crisis resulted; indeed, as the pound floated down, British exporters enjoyed an improved competitive position.

The British people as a whole trusted the new government and accepted the budget as necessary retrenchment. In October the Conservatives held an election on the platform of Protection while Labour countered this with Free Trade, planning and extra spending. Snowden was able to protray Labour policies as irresponsible and likely to undermine the value of savings, as in Germany in 1923. The National Government won 554 seats to Labour's 54 seats. The Labour Party naturally blamed this disaster on MacDonald's betrayal, but, as C. L. Mowat has stressed, Labour's hopes of winning the election would have been slim anyway, because it had followed the half-measures of its predecessors. By 1931 it had forfeited the confidence of the nation, suggests Mowat. 'It was weakened from within by resignations and by criticism from the Left. It fell a victim of its own shortcomings as much as of some strange political manoeuvres.' Yet Labour's defeat was not a complete rout; it polled more votes in 1931 than in any other election save 1929. Worse hit was the Liberal Party, which polled 3 million fewer votes in 1931 than in 1929, most of these votes accruing to the Conservatives.

With such a decisive mandate, Neville Chamberlain was able to bring in Protection. In 1930 over 80 per cent of imports entered Britain duty-free but between 1932 and 1934 a general system of tariffs was evolved. In 1932 at the Ottawa Conference the government worked out a system of Imperial Preference with Commonwealth leaders. All colonial imports were exempt from tariffs, while Dominion imports would be given preference over foreign imports through a system of quotas. In return the Dominions, who to British surprise had bargained keenly, agreed to raise their tariffs on foreign imports to a higher level than on British goods. Hopes of a vast increase in intra-Commonwealth trade were disappointed, though some increases did take place. The general level of tariffs increased as the 1930s progressed, a steel tariff in 1935 being as high as 50 per cent.

Valuable steps were taken to stimulate agriculture. Tariffs and quotas restricted imports, and subsidies were paid on the production of cereals, milk and cattle. Marketing boards were created to regulate the terms and conditions of sale.

Chamberlain, as chancellor of the exchequer, followed orthodox policies to stimulate investment. Bank rate, which had reached 6 per cent in 1931, was brought down to 2 per cent. In 1934 Chamberlain brought in an Unemployment Insurance Act which made central government fully responsible for looking after the unemployed by taking welfare services out of the hands of the local authorities. The centrally financed Unemployment Assistance Board was the core of the system, but certain provisions created resentment. When a man had used up all the unemployment benefit to which he was entitled, he had to apply for additional benefit under a means test. This meant that his financial resources were examined to make sure that he did not have savings which he could draw on instead of receiving public assistance.

In June 1935 MacDonald retired from the premiership, in which he had become a figurehead, and was succeeded by Baldwin. Foreign and imperial concerns absorbed much of his attention (see Chapters 9 and 16) but the government's position remained secure. In the 1935 election the Conservatives won 432 seats to Labour's 154 seats.

Baldwin's position weakened when he admitted in November 1936 that the government had been convinced of the need for rearmament since 1933 but had delayed acting until 1935 because such a policy would be electorally damaging. In fact, as Middlemas and Barnes have demonstrated, Baldwin edged the country towards more rearmament from 1934 while MacDonald was ill and against the opposition of Chamberlain. Nevertheless his admission was held against him and unfairly clouded his reputation after 1939.

In 1936 Baldwin quickly redeemed his popularity by his handling of the Abdication Crisis. The new king, Edward VIII, was in love with Wallis Simpson, who was American and married. She could obtain a divorce easily but marriage to a divorced American commoner was thought improper by the British Establishment. Baldwin himself opposed the marriage because he believed that it would damage the reputation of the monarchy and therefore its value as a focus of national and imperial unity. In December he made it clear that he would not serve Edward if the marriage took place. Edward for his part would not be separated from Mrs Simpson and abdicated, an event which led to the schoolboy refrain

> 'Hark the herald angels sing
> Mrs Simpson's pinched our King.'

Baldwin was generally regarded as behaving well in the crisis, while those who supported Edward, especially Churchill, were seen as irresponsible. In May 1937 Baldwin retired from politics. He had shown real gifts in picking sound cabinets and leaving the members free to do their work, while he was adroit in moments of crisis at waiting for the right time to act, as he showed in the General Strike and Abdication Crisis. Churchill called him 'the most formidable politician I have ever known in public life', while T. O. Lloyd suggests that he was the most successful of all British politicians this century in achieving the objectives he set himself: standards of integrity in politics, the absorption of the Labour Party into political life and the warding off of class war.

Baldwin was succeeded by Chamberlain, a man of a very different stamp. Though as honest as Baldwin, he was more able, more dictatorial and impatient of the opinion of colleagues and opponents. His foreign secretary, Halifax, said, 'Chamberlain's great fault was that he sneered at people; he sneered at Labour members and they never forgave him.' More and more of the new premier's time was absorbed by the threat of Nazism as he became a missionary in the cause of European peace (see Chapter 9).

The National governments of the 1930s were increasingly dominated by the Conservatives, their electoral strength increased by the eclipse of the Liberals. Liberal decline can partly be explained by the 1916 split between Asquith and Lloyd George, for which both men must bear a share of the responsibility. However, more fundamental factors undermined the Liberals. The Labour Party demonstrated its capacity in the interwar years to govern, and though it was not in any sense full-bloodedly socialist, its policies were more left-wing than those of the Liberals and enticed working-class voters away from the Liberals. The rise of the Labour Party hit the Liberal vote in another way; it frightened right-wing Liberals into voting Conservative as the surest way of keeping Labour out of power, while left-wing Liberals voted Labour in the hope of keeping the Conservatives out of office. The Liberals in time lacked support from any interest group large enough to keep them in power.

The Liberals were also at a disadvantage as a result of the British electoral system. With three parties contesting most seats, a high proportion of candidates were returned on a minority vote. Often the Liberal candidate came second, and consequently the Liberal votes were not reflected by the number of seats won.

Finally the impact of the First World War undermined the credibility of the Liberal creed. The war led to a vast extension of state intervention, and after 1918 it continued to extend its spheres of influence. Increasingly therefore the Liberal adhesion to *laissez-faire* principles appeared more and more old-fashioned. Had Lloyd George been able to re-unite the party under a programme of Keynesian-style expansion, the Liberal decline might have been temporarily arrested, but by the 1920s he was not trusted by large sections of the party.

British political life remained orderly, despite the threats to stability posed by the high unemployment. Extremist parties failed to flourish as they did on the continent. The Communist Party of Great Britain remained small, though its membership rose from about 3,000 in 1924 to 56,000 in 1942. Its operations had no appeal to the mass of

British people, its clique of leaders following the Moscow line. It alienated supporters when it severed connections with the Labour Party and the TUC.

The failure of the Communists stemmed in part from Britain's constitutional and non-revolutionary traditions. In addition, the emergence of the unions and the Labour Party provided a focus of allegiance for the groups which in other countries became Marxist; Communism was also considered an alien philosophy and British intellectuals on the whole remained wedded to parliamentary politics. Therefore, in the words of Stevenson and Cook, the Communists remained 'a small coterie influential in one or two areas but largely outside the mainstream of British politics'. When they sought a united front against Fascism after 1933, they were regarded with suspicion by the TUC and the Labour Party. Their sole electoral success was that of Willie Gallacher at West Fife in 1935.

On the face of it, many of the ingredients which brought Hitler to power in Germany (high unemployment and an insecure middle class) existed in Britain, yet British Fascism failed to attract mass support. The British Union of Fascists was founded by Sir Oswald Mosley in 1932. He had been Chancellor of the Duchy of Lancaster in the second Labour government and had wanted Keynesian methods to tackle unemployment. When the leadership of the party turned down his ideas, he resigned from the government and, with the help of William Morris (later Lord Nuffield), he formed a New Party in 1930. Its lack of success pushed Mosley towards fascism, but he also appears to have believed that the liberal economic system was doomed and that only fascism could prevent chaos and the rise of Communism. The BUF was thus unashamedly modelled on German and Italian examples, but Mosley brought his own drive, oratory and intelligence to the movement.

Two aspects of the movement alienated British opinion – its violence and its anti-Semitism. The Olympia meeting in 1934 led to much violence on hecklers by fascist thugs, and the adverse publicity marked a turning point in public opinion. From 1934 Mosley turned to a more open anti-Semitism and tried to provoke the large Jewish communities in the East End of London. In October 1937 a fascist march through the East End led to the so-called battle of Cable Street between fascists and their opponents.

Consequently the movement declined, its membership falling from about 35,000 in 1935 to under 5,000 in 1937. Most members were young people from the middle classes, and there was a strong military element. Yet Mosley failed to win over the working class or lower middle class, for Conservative domination of politics, the rout of Labour and the insignificance of the Communists meant that the middle classes were much more secure than in Germany. The return of more prosperity after 1932 and Mosley's own impatience condemned the BUF in the words of Stevenson and Cook to being 'almost a non-starter'.

(2) Economic and social developments

The interwar years in Britain have had a bad press. Mass unemployment more than anything else gave the period its image of 'the wasted years'. By the end of the 1930s a 'dole' literature had grown up, as seen in such books as George Orwell's *The Road to Wigan Pier*. The hunger marches, especially the Jarrow Crusade of 1936, seemed to symbolise the human consequences of mass unemployment.

Yet to call the period the 'black' years is harsh, and in 1965 A. J. P. Taylor warned against such a sweeping view, pointing out that most English people were enjoying a richer life than ever before. The revision of the old view was carried further by Stevenson and Cook in 1977. While rightly admitting that much hardship still existed, they gave firm evidence which pointed to rising living standards.

The interwar years saw the creation of new industries, producing consumer goods such as motor vehicles, processed foods, electrical appliances and construction. Some sectors enjoyed boom conditions and laid the foundations for postwar economic expansion. The completion of the national grid by 1933 gave Britain one of the most advanced systems of electricity supply in the world, and by 1939 two houses in three were wired up for electricity. Industries were able to move away from the old centres of production near coalfields to greenfield sites in the South. Motor vehicle production increased from 95,000 in 1923 to over 500,000 in 1937. Mass production methods led to a fall in car prices. Aircraft production and the chemicals industry also did well, and even the traditional industries attained some recovery.

These developments contributed to a rise in living standards for the great majority of the population. The interwar years witnessed an increase in national income per head by a third. Only part of this increase was caused by wage rises. The main reason, according to Stevenson and Cook, was the fall in the prices of food and manufactures after 1920. The trend to smaller families meant that there was a higher proportion of income per head available in each family, and this extra income could be spent on more food, entertainment and consumer durables.

The period saw real advances in health. Life expectancy increased from 45 years in 1900 to 60 years in 1932, mainly as a result of the control of infectious diseases. Infant mortality fell dramatically. A clear indication of the improvement in general health was shown in the classification of men called up for military service in 1914 and 1939. In 1939 under one-third of the men were unfit for military service, compared to nearer two-thirds in 1914. In addition to better medical care, the improvement of health was helped by better housing, the introduction of old age pensions and especially the better diet which higher incomes and cheaper food prices made possible. Improved housing conditions were one of the major advances of the 1930s, when nearly 3 million homes were built. Houses became relatively cheap; a typical 'semi' could be bought for £450, about twice the annual salary for an average professional man. Mortgage interest was low at around 4½ per cent.

Another significant development was the motoring revolution. Private motoring came within the reach of many people and altered their way of life. It gave them a new dimension of freedom; it also had its adverse side, with road accidents higher in the late 1930s than in the early 1970s.

The quality of life improved. More people could enjoy real holidays with the spread of the paid holiday, and British seaside towns reached a peak of popularity. The 1930s offered a wider range of entertainment than any previous decade, with the cinema and the advent of the wireless.

Advances were made in the social services, despite the image of the means test and the dole. Spending on welfare increased £100 millions in the period; by 1939 Britain had a more comprehensive set of welfare services than almost any other country, and the foundations were laid for the advances of the 1940s.

These improvements provide one crucial reason why Britain did not fall a prey to political extremism in the interwar years. The British people were on average better paid, better fed, better clothed and housed and healthier than in 1918. Yet the tragedy of the unemployed cannot be ignored. From 1921 to 1939 there were never less than 1 million people out of work, and in 1932 the figure reached nearly 3 million. As certain categories of workers, such as the self-employed, were excluded from the official figures, the real total of unemployed was even higher than the official figures suggested.

The problem of unemployment was caused mainly by the decline of Britain's major export industries. Before 1914 coal, textiles, iron and steel and shipbuilding had provided almost three-quarters of the country's exports. After 1918 these industries suffered severe contraction. The war resulted in a loss of overseas markets to such industrial rivals as Japan and the USA. Foreign competition was not the only reason. A declining level of world trade, an over-valued pound, poor labour relations and inadequate investment also contributed to the decline of Britain's staple industries.

The social tragedy was the concentration of high unemployment in particular depressed areas overly dependent on these industries – South Wales, Tyneside, industrial Scotland, Northern Ireland and West Cumberland. In 1929, for example, one shipbuilder in three was out of work, and the number of long-term unemployed rose through-out the depression. Jarrow, a town dependent on shipbuilding, experienced an unemployment rate of nearly 80 per cent when the town's largest employer, Palmer's shipyard, closed.

Despite such suffering, no revolutionary attitudes developed among the unemployed. The most common reaction to unemploy-ment was apathy. The feelings of boredom, impotence and despair robbed men of the desire to be politically active. Perhaps too the concentration of unemployment helped to check violent reactions, because whole communities were affected and there was less resent-ment at a commonly shared fate than if the unemployed had felt themselves to be starving in the midst of plenty. The dole too provided a living, however basic or humiliating its receipt might be. Indeed many unemployed were better off on the dole than they had been on low or irregular wages. The geographical isolation of the unemployed, hidden away in closed communities in the Welsh valleys or the pit villages of the north-east, also militated against the unem-ployed becoming a political force. As Cole and Postgate commented, 'What was the use of rioting in South Wales or of making orderly demonstrations? Who would take notice of them?'

The 1930s nevertheless left an important legacy. The Conservatives were discredited in two ways – as the party of appeasement and as the party which had allowed unacceptable levels of unemployment. This legacy of bitterness led to a feeling of 'Never Again', and accounts in part for the Labour landslide victory in the 1945 general election.

FURTHER READING

Adelman, P., *The Rise of the Labour Party*, Longmans, London, 1972

Lloyd, T. O., *Empire to Welfare State: English History 1906–1976*, OUP, Oxford, 1984

Marquand, D., *Ramsey MacDonald*, Cape, London, 1977

Middlemas, K. and Barnes, J., *Baldwin*, Weidenfeld and Nicolson, London, 1969

Mowat, C. L., *Britain between the Wars*, Methuen, London, 1968

Skidelsky, R., *Oswald Mosley*, Macmillan, London, 1975

Stevenson, J. and Cook, C., *The Slump*, Jonathan Cape, London, 1977

Taylor, A. J. P., *English History 1914–1945*, OUP, Oxford, 1965

QUESTIONS

1. 'It was the First World War which blasted the ground from under the feet of the Liberals' (Marwick). Discuss this statement.

2. Why was there no revolution in Britain in the interwar years?
3. Critically examine the achievements of Baldwin as statesman and party leader.
4. Why did Britain suffer a political and financial crisis in 1931 and what were its consequences?
5. Assess the services of Ramsay MacDonald to his country and to his party.
6. What was the political legacy of the 1930s?

8
The United States of America, 1914–41

(a) American intervention in the First World War

The increased participation in world affairs that had marked Theodore Roosevelt's presidency ebbed under his more placid successor, Taft, incumbent of the White House from 1909 to 1912. The trend towards a renewal of American isolationism was at first continued by the next Democratic president, Woodrow Wilson, who adopted a strong moral tone in international affairs, asserting, 'It is a very perilous thing to determine the foreign policy of a nation in terms of material interest.'

Yet gradually and inexorably the war dragged the USA into its vortex. The country's sympathies were divided; many Americans of British descent hoped for an Allied victory, while those of German, Irish or Jewish extraction supported the Central Powers. Wilson himself was profoundly suspicious of German autocracy, but had no great love of Britain and hated war. His initial stance was strict neutrality, but in practice this proved a difficult policy to sustain. Britain and her allies desperately needed American manufactures and raw materials for the conduct of the war, and a vast expansion of American trade with the Allies compensated for the German trade lost to the USA as a result of the Allied blockade. Indeed the quadrupling of her trade with Europe was a major factor in pulling the USA out of a depression from which the country was suffering when war broke out. At the same time the British imposition of a blockade on American trade with Germany soured Anglo-American relations. In 1916 Wilson declared to the House, 'I am, I must admit, about at the end of my patience with Great Britain and the Allies,' and he considered blocking loans and exports to the Allies.

Yet despite infringements on her freedom of trade, the USA was too closely bound to Britain by her growing economic and financial stake in Allied victory ever to oppose the Allies. Of more significance in actually bringing America into the war was the submarine campaign waged by Germany (see Chapter 2). It united American opinion as nothing else could, swamping American irritation with the blockade and traditional feelings of Anglophobia. As Senator Henry Cabot Lodge phrased it, his heart was more moved by the thought of a drowned baby than an unsold bale of cotton.

The announcment by the Germans of unrestricted U-boat warfare in February 1917, and the extraordinary blunder of the Zimmermann telegram in March (see Chapter 2), finally forced an American declaration of war in April, but it was with a heavy heart that the President called upon Congress to accept the status of belligerent. The USA now showed for the first time the enormous strength that she could generate. Wilson was a vigorous war leader and used his presidential powers to set up boards under a Council for National Defence. These boards had wide powers to requisition supplies, fix prices and commandeer essential equipment. In May conscription was introduced, while in 1918 the Sedition Act led to censorship of the press, which H. C. Allen considers pointed forward to the McCarthyism of the 1950s (see Chapter 17). American mobilisation was highly effective. It was financed by heavy taxation, which helped to prevent the excessive inflation experienced in Europe. Armed forces of over 4 millions were raised, and by October 1918 nearly 2 million Americans had reached Europe and played a vital part in the defeat of Germany.

The increased output had a fundamental effect on the international economic position of the USA. In 1917 the government in response to the appeal of the Allies, whose dollar reserves were almost exhausted as a result of buying American goods, began to make direct loans to European governments. The huge total of $10 billions lent symbolised American economic domination. The USA was not merely for the first time a creditor nation but the world's largest one. American economic power gave Wilson great influence in the closing stages of the war and the peacemaking process at Versailles. Moved by the plight of broken European countries, he began to see himself in the role of a world saviour who would dictate a new world order, under a League of Nations pledged to universal peace, in which all countries would have rights to self-government. As he sailed for France in December 1918, this Virginian Presbyterian declared, 'We are to be an instrument in the hands of God to see that liberty is made secure for mankind.'

Unfortunately for Wilson, American opinion turned against aspects of the peace settlement, especially the Anglo-American guarantee and the question of American membership of the League. His forceful use of his powers had alienated Congress, and after the 1918 elections he faced a Republican majority in both the House of Representatives and the Senate. He alienated Republicans by omitting them completely from the American delegation which went to Europe. By going to Paris in person he cut himself off from public opinion at home and did not appreciate the objection to long-term

American involvement in world affairs. Many Americans, especially Republicans, regarded the League as unrealistic and over-idealistic. Only belatedly did Wilson attempt to conciliate the opposition at home by waging a strenuous campaign in September 1919 to win acceptance of the Versailles Treaty and the League, but he was taken ill with a stroke in the middle of his tour and this effectively ended any real hope of acceptance of the League. Perhaps if Wilson had agreed to certain amendments, such as Congressional approval of any American obligations to other American states in the League, he would have gained the support not only of his own Democrats but also of the Republican Reservationists led by Lodge, who were not opposed to some American obligations, to gain the necessary two-thirds majority in Congress. But compromise was foreign to his nature, and he lost the support of some Democrats, the Republican Reservationists and those Republicans totally opposed to the Treaty (the Irreconcilables led by William E. Borah) when the issue was voted on in March 1920.

There seems little doubt that the decision reflected the feelings of the American public. Many Americans had by 1920 come to believe that intervention had been a mistake, costly in blood and treasure, and that the Versailles Treaty was unjust not only to Germany but to Italy. America never entered the League and no American president ever seriously contemplated such a step, not even Roosevelt. It was a sad end to Wilson's career; despite his irritating virtue and pride, he was in a sense a prophet warning that if America fell back into isolation she would surely be caught up in another and more terrible war.

(b) Republican ascendancy: boom and bust, 1921–33

The period 1921–33 saw three Republican presidents, Harding, Coolidge and Hoover. The presidential elections of 1921 gave the Republican Warren G. Harding a large majority over the unknown Democratic candidate, Governor James Cox of Ohio, Wilson's illness ruling out his nomination. Harding gauged the public temper correctly when he announced, 'America's present need is not heroics but healing; not nostrums but normalcy; not revolution but restoration, not surgery but serenity.' Harding's victory was explained by Walter Lippmann as the backwash of the excitement and sacrifice when the people were war-weary and angry at the disappointing peace which followed the war. There was resentment at so much government intervention in the form of rationing and conscription, and dislike of the Versailles Treaty itself, especially by German and Italian Americans.

The first two presidents were fortunate men in that their period of office saw a real and dramatic growth in the American economy, with an increase in labour productivity of 35 per cent between 1922 and 1925. There was increased public expenditure on roads and social services, but in general government intervention was kept to a minimum, with the Republicans in their quest for normalcy displaying an attitude of cooperation if not reverence for business interests. As Coolidge, president from 1923, remarked, 'The Business of America is Business.'

This intimate association of business with government led to more corruption in politics at both a state and city level. The prime example of such corruption was the Teapot Dome Scandal. The genial Harding had been picked as Republican candidate mainly because, with his good looks, he possessed a certain presence; he looked like a president! Unfortunately he took with him to the White House several of his old cronies from Ohio, and the White House came to have the atmosphere of a bar-room. In addition, Harding was out of his depth, particularly in financial matters; as he touchingly admitted, 'I was a small-town editor; I could not grasp I was President of the United States.' It was fortunate for him that much of the scandal broke after his death in August 1923. One of his Ohio gang, Albert B. Ball, secretary of the interior, did a corrupt deal with the Doheny and Sinclair oil interests to allow them to gain control of valuable oil deposits, including the Teapot Dome oil reserve in Wyoming; Ball's rake-off for these favours was around $400,000.

Harding's successor was Calvin Coolidge, a mean, taciturn mediocrity. 'Cool Cal' followed policies of high tariffs, tax reductions and government support for industry. He was a relatively inactive president who distrusted progressive legislation. He blocked measures to help farmers in 1927, despite a collapse in farm prices, and did nothing to check the wild speculation in shares. In the spring of 1928 he announced that he was not going to run again for the presidency, and Herbert Hoover became the Republican candidate and victor over the Democrat candidate, Alfred E. Smith. Coolidge was lucky; as H. L. Mencken wrote, 'There was a volcano boiling under him but he did not know it and was not singed. When it burst forth at last, it was Hoover who got its blast and was fried, boiled, roasted and fricaseed.'

On the face of it Hoover appeared to be the right man for modern America. A mining engineer by profession, he had earned a reputation as a humanitarian by his administration of food distribution in the war and also by famine relief in Russia. He had been secretary of commerce and seemed to be a new type of political leader – a socially minded efficiency expert. But compared to his successor, Roosevelt, Hoover was a pessimistic individual who exuded gloom and lacked rapport with the American public. As the sculptor Gutzon Borglum remarked, 'If you put a rose in Hoover's hand, it would wilt.'

It was Hoover's ill-luck to come to high office on the eve of the great Wall Street Crash of October 1929. American prosperity, Germany's recovery after 1924 and the growth of world trade all justified a rise in share values, but they began to rise much more than was warranted as the American people indulged in a mania of share-buying in the 1920s. In fact there were weaknesses in both the procedures of the American stock exchanges and in the real economy. The stock market was manipulated by investment trusts, and a host of bad practices, such as insider trading, obtained. The worst weakness was the right of speculators to buy on margin, i.e. to purchase stock for as little as 10 per cent down. This produced a phenomenon called leverage, by which investment trusts, owing to constantly rising prices, could buy another set of shares using the shares as yet unpaid for. As share prices rose over the years, this device seemed a safe one, but it helped to increase demand for shares and led to their overvaluation. The government should have done more to regulate the stock market and reduce the unwarranted optimism of the public, but failed to do so.

The rot set in in October 1929; the worst day, Black Thursday, 24 October, saw the boom in shares burst and in panic shareholders, large and small, attempted to unload their stock, thus precipitating a steep decline in share prices which continued until the summer of 1932. The Dow Jones Industrial Index, which had stood at 350 in 1929, had dropped to 58 by July 1932. General Motors' stock plummeted from 73 to 8 in that same period.

Underlying the stock-market collapse were fundamental weaknesses in the economy. By 1929 a period of boom was ending because over-production meant that too many goods were chasing too few buyers. Wholesale prices dropped by two-thirds and over 3,500 banks failed. Industrial production declined by nearly a half and exports by 70 per cent in value. Unemployment rose from 2 million in 1929 to 13 million by 1933. The agricultural depression, which had begun earlier, deepened with the worldwide depression, contraction of foreign trade and a generally steeper decline in the price of primary products than for industrial goods.

America's Economic Blizzard affected the whole world economy. The USA had emerged from the war as the greatest creditor nation, but the only way her debtors could repay the huge debts was by earning foreign exchange, particularly by exporting to the USA. But now American trade policy, protectionist even before October 1929, became ever more so, the Smoot-Hawley Act of 1930 imposing duties of over 60 per cent on a number of imports.

Such policy aggravated the position of American agriculture, which could only be revived by greater exports, and these the Europeans could not buy if they could not export manufactures to the USA. As for American industry, the rest of the world was too poor to buy

American products to compensate for the declining domestic market.

The economist J. K. Galbraith has pointed to certain basic causes of the crisis. First, American income was very unevenly divided, with about 5 per cent of the population having a third of all income, much of which was spent on luxuries and capital investment. As a consequence, there was a failure to maintain consumer demand in basic areas like house-building, while over-expansion occurred in the construction of industrial plant and a saturation of that market. Second, corporate structure was weak, particularly as regards the activities of investment trusts. Third, banking practices were faulty, and the many bank failures had a grave psychological effect on business confidence. Too many banks had made unwise loans, and rumours led to runs even on sound banks, forcing them to close their doors. Fourth, the stock exchange had attracted a higher than usual proportion of swindlers; even the President of the Exchange in the 1930s, Richard Whitney, was arrested for larceny in 1938.

Government policy in the face of the crisis was unimaginative. Hoover had a warm heart, which responded to suffering, but he was restrained from taking any bold steps by wrong estimates of the situation, which for years promised a recovery that did not materialise. He was also restrained by his *laissez-faire* philosophy, which taught him that recovery would be held back by government intervention. He remained deaf to pleas for a programme of public works, though some of his measures foreshadowed the New Deal, e.g. the Reconstruction Finance Company, whose loans saved many American businesses. In general the government believed in balanced budgets, and positive action via deficit financing was ruled out.

(c) Roosevelt and the New Deal

It was virtually inevitable that Hoover would lose the presidential election of 1932. His failure to tackle the slump was allied to an apparent insensitivity, as illustrated in June 1932, when he ordered the forcible expulsion from Washington of an army of veteran ex-soldiers who were now unemployed. His Democrat opponent was Franklin Delano Roosevelt, whose reputation as yet was hardly great. Even the shrewd political commentator Walter Lippmann described him as lacking any real qualifications for high office, though the great jurist Oliver Wendell Holmes was nearer the mark when he opined that Roosevelt had a second-class intellect but a first-class temperament. After a vigorous election campaign, in which he set forth his New Deal reforms, Roosevelt won control of both Houses.

Roosevelt was born to a patrician family in 1882 and went to Harvard and law school. In 1905 he made a successful marriage with Eleanor Roosevelt, niece of his remote cousin Theodore, whom he greatly admired. After work in the Navy Department under Wilson, his career seemed finished when he suffered a severe attack of polio in 1921. Despite being left a cripple, he fought his way back to health and won the governorship of New York in 1928. He was a complex character, who at times acted with great courage and at other times with great caution. Therefore, in the view of his biographer Burns, Roosevelt was following Machiavelli's advice that a leader should be as brave as the lion and as shrewd as the fox, but the way he moved from lion to fox and back again baffled colleagues. The reason for this was that he was not wedded to any particular programme but was a subtle pragmatist ready to try any course of action which might bring results.

Roosevelt's hold over the American people came from his immense charm and from a magnetism which he first fully displayed in 1932 when he accepted the Democratic nomination and declared, 'I pledge you, I pledge myself, to a new deal for the American people.' He seemed to feel a concern for the predicament of ordinary people, his perceptions sharpened by his own sufferings.

In his dramatic inaugural speech as president in March 1933, on a day when nearly all the banks had closed, Roosevelt put into practice his belief that the presidency was a place for moral leadership. He asserted that 'the only thing we have to fear is fear itself – nameless, unreasoning, unjustified terror', and he demanded from Congress powers to wage war against the economic crisis.

The first 100 days of his presidency saw hectic activity, with Roosevelt gaining the approval of both Houses for emergency powers over banking and government spending. A number of important measures were passed. The Agricultural Adjustment Act (AAA) aimed at raising farm prices and agricultural spending power. Farmers could obtain a subsidy from the government by limiting their production of staple crops, and farm income rose from $5.6 billion to $8.7 billion by 1935. A Civilian Conservation Corps was created to put 250,000 young men to work by the early summer. A Federal Emergency Relief Act (FERA) was passed to allow the federal government to give grants to states for direct unemployment relief. For every $3 spent by a state for such purposes, Washington would add a further dollar to stimulate the states to action. Congress also made available $500 millions to the Reconstruction Finance Corporation created by Hoover.

Most far-reaching of the early measures was the creation of the National Recovery Administration (NRA). It was envisaged that this body would spend over $3 billion on public works and set up machinery for 'a great cooperative movement' throughout all industry in order to boost employment, shorten the working week, set decent wage levels, prevent unfair competition and avoid overproduction. However, more important in the long term was the creation of the Tennessee Valley Authority. It was authorised to plan the whole river watershed, 'a revolutionary concept' in the view of H. C. Allen. The TVA was able to promote the well-being of the valley in a number of ways – by bringing in flood controls, by use of locks to increase navigation, by development of hydro-electricity, by reafforesting millions of acres of the valley and by the creation of parks for public enjoyment. Though no similar scheme was brought in for other river valleys, the Roosevelt administration did plan and complete a number of multi-purpose dams in the West and other national parks. It also set up, in 1936 the Rural Electrification Administration, a body which lent money to rural co-operative power plants so successfully that the number of farms provided with electricity trebled in 5 years.

The 100 Days was an extraordinary legislative achievement and commanded wide public support. It indicated Roosevelt's dynamic leadership and his capacity for forcing different groups to work together for the national good. Further measures to stimulate economic recovery included the USA coming off the Gold Standard and the devaluation of the dollar by 40 per cent, which made American exports cheaper abroad. In June 1933 the Glass–Steagall Banking Act gave the Federal Reserve Board power to check speculative credit expansion by banks and created the Federal Deposit Insurance Corporation to insure the deposits of small banks. Stock exchanges became regulated by the Security and Exchange Commission under Joseph P. Kennedy. One change was the raising of the required margin for stock from 10 per cent to 45 per cent. FERA was replaced by a new Works Progress Administration (WPA) under Harry L. Hopkins in 1935. The WPA employed some 2 million Americans annually until the war on a wide variety of jobs.

The New Deal did not move forward smoothly all the time. It was not popular with business interests, and created too many new agencies, which were not always efficient. For example, the NRA, which strove to develop codes of fair practice for 500 industries, became bogged down in the details of adminstration and was believed by the unions to be harming the interests of labour which it was supposed to protect. Allen goes so far as to call it a white elephant.

The second factor holding back the New Deal was the power of the Supreme Court, in which the majority of its members were conservative. In May 1935 it declared the work of the NRA unconstitutional, which was no great loss, but the invalidation of the AAA in January 1936 was a serious blow. In response a more carefully worded AAA was brought in in 1938.

Despite the opposition of the Court and business interests, which regarded his empiricism as dangerous socialism, Roosevelt swept to a great victory in the 1936 presidential election, soundly defeating his Republican opponent, Governor Alfred M. Landon, by winning 60 per cent of the popular vote. He now attempted to weaken the power of the Supreme Court by a bill proposing that if Supreme Court justices failed to retire after the age of 70, the president should be empowered to appoint new members to the Court up to a total of six additional justices. For once Roosevelt had miscalculated; the Court was venerated as an integral part of the American Constitution and a necessary check on government power. Thus, despite huge Democrat majorities in both Houses, Roosevelt failed to find support for the measure. His only consolation was that the Supreme Court brought in its own voluntary retirement and took a more liberal line, but the incident demonstrated that governments with large majorities can find life more difficult than those with small majorities, where party discipline is necessary. Roosevelt now found that Southern right-wing Democrats began to align themselves with the Republicans to oppose his more radical measures.

The need for such measures was still pressing, because, after years of steady recovery, 1937 saw a renewed slump and a rise in unemployment from 7.7 millions to 10.3 millions in 1938, a blow to national morale. Therefore Roosevelt launched what was termed the second New Deal, but this was only partially successful in curing the depression. Unemployment stood at around 7 million even in 1941, and only the coming of war stimulated full recovery. Some measures had insufficient time to develop and insufficient funds, for example the Social Security system set up by WPA.

One stimulant to recovery was the growth in the power of the unions and a rise in wage levels which increased effective demand. To an extent the government could take some credit, as, under the National Industrial Recovery Act which had set up NRA, the unions had gained the right of collective bargaining, and after NRA was declared unconstitutional, the Roosevelt administration passed the National Labour Act in 1935, sometimes known as the Wagner Act. This established the principle of collective bargaining, guaranteed workers the right to join a union of their own choosing and outlawed such unfair employer practices as discrimination against union members in hiring and firing. A National Labour Relations Board was established to enforce the provisions and hear complaints from unions.

Many employers refused to recognise the law, but in 1937 the Supreme Court upheld its constitutionality. In a case brought against the Jones and Laughlin Steel Corporation Chief Justice Charles Evans Hughes asserted, 'Employees have as clear a right to organise and select their representatives for lawful purposes as a corporation has to organise its business and select its own officers and agents.' The more favourable attitude to unions shown by government contributed to a rise in union membership from 2.9 millions in 1933 to 7.7 millions in 1939. Another union development was the rise of the Congress of Industrial Organisations (CIO), a radical secession from the American Federation of Labour. Under John L. Lewis, the mineworkers' leader, the CIO unionised industries which had hitherto resisted, e.g. steel and cars, and by 1937 it had gained 4 million members.

Roosevelt followed no master plan in these years and indeed boasted of playing by ear. Yet the New Deal, along with such other factors as the recovery of international trade, contributed to American economic recovery. It also gave hope to the American people and restored their faith in democracy. As Burns emphasises, 'a remarkable aspect of the New Deal was the sweep and variety of the groups it helped'. It gave support not only to millions of blue-collar workers and farmers, but, through the WPA artists, teachers and actors found jobs which salvaged their self-respect. A National Youth Administration helped thousands of college students to continue their education. Businessmen gained from government contracts and freer lending policies. Burns says, 'The impact of Roosevelt and his New Deal had been to arouse the energies and aspirations of a people chilled by the bleak hand of depression.'

The New Deal made more acceptable the thesis that federal government was ultimately responsible through planning for the nation's welfare, and that by humane measures it should protect the disadvantaged groups from the worst evils of the industrial system. The new levels of government intervention in economic life were illustrated not only by the many new agencies but by the increase in the number of civil servants, from 500,000 in 1933 to 850,000 in 1938.

Despite its element of expediency, the New Deal achieved much of permanent benefit, such as the TVA, the regulation of the stock market, the rural electrification programme and the enhanced status of unions. Much was still left to private enterprise, with the government merely purging American capitalism of some of its worst abuses, and in that sense Roosevelt may be seen as an effective Conservative.

Roosevelt, in the words of Leuchtenburg, recreated the modern presidency. He took an office which had lost much of its prestige and power in the previous 12 years and gave it a new importance. He was the first president to master the technique of reaching people directly through radio. In his 'fireside chats' he talked like a father discussing public affairs with his own family in a warm reassuring voice, making difficult issues like banking comprehensible to ordinary Americans.

More than ever before, the presidency became the focus of all government, as Roosevelt expanded the president's legislative functions. In some ways he was a poor administrator in his reluctance to sack the incompetent, and in the creation of too many new agencies, but this was more than compensated for by the creative ideas of his government and by his attracting thousands of able men whose ingenuity helped to implement the new ideas. Such innovations generated a new excitement about the potential of government. 'Once again', Roosevelt told young Democrats in 1936, 'the very air of America is exhilarating.'

(d) Economic and social life

Throughout the interwar years the American people were undergoing profound changes in their environment and their moral climate. Rural America was moving to the city in a period which saw some emancipation of women and more liberal morals.

Fundamental to these changes was the development of the car. Henry Ford's invention of the assembly line method of production led to his Model T 'tin lizzie' becoming the first mass production car. By 1927 he had sold 15 million of this model, which helped to revolutionise American life by its use for farmers and urban workers, who could live miles from their work. Spin-off effects were the creation of service garages, country restaurants and better roads. Earlier types of transport, such as trams, horse and steamboat, were eliminated, while the railways became less profitable.

Ford had plenty of competition from such other car firms as Chrysler and General Motors, which overtook Ford in 1927, but a process of consolidation eliminated most other rivals. Fierce competition increased a relatively new business – high-powered salesmanship and advertising. Before 1910 advertisements were relatively few and simple, like cures for physical ills, but the Motor Age changed advertising to a series of urges to spend and buy. Such advertising promoted the revolution of rising expectations among the working classes by making the luxuries of yesterday the necessities of today.

Two postwar policies that helped to create a revolution in American life were immigration restriction and the prohibition of alcoholic beverages. Unlimited immigration except for Orientals, paupers, imbeciles and prostitutes had been national policy up to 1914, but the fear of union leaders that immigration held down wages led to demands for new restrictions. Some intellectuals also feared that the number of immigrants from south and east Europe, with different traditions to those of northern Europe, would undermine true American society. Acts passed in 1921, 1924 and 1929 virtually eliminated immigration from south-east Europe and Asia. The introduction of a visa system, with national quotas, was so surrounded by documentation and red tape as to discourage all but the most persistent.

The legislation did not apply to immigrants from countries in the New World, and those from Canada, Mexico and the West Indies increased. The social effects were considerable; old ghettoes gradually faded out but new ones were created by the migration of Southern negroes and Puerto Ricans to Northern cities. Absence of cheap immigrant labour allowed a big rise in real wage in the 1920s.

The new laws eliminated the chief source of domestic servants, whose scarcity stimulated the production of labour-saving devices and convenience food.

In 1919 the Volstead Act prohibited the manufacture, sale or transportation of intoxicating liquors (defined as those containing over one half of 1 per cent of alcohol) in the USA. This extraordinary move resulted from a number of factors. It had its roots in fundamentalist Protestantism, but the Act was only passed through the coincidence of two related facts – the call for efficiency in the First World War and the coming of votes for women, who constituted the true heart of the prohibition movement. Many businessmen favoured it, hoping that it would eliminate 'blue Monday' absenteeism.

The Volstead Act was a disaster because it was unenforceable. A new occupation, bootlegging, sprang up to supply the public with illegal alcohol, and between 1919 and 1929 300,000 convictions were secured. The bootlegging nevertheless increased by sea from surrounding countries, with much production in homes. Every city became studded with 'speakeasies', which replaced the saloon. As G. K. Chesterton put it, 'the Americans may go mad when they make laws but they recover their reason when they disobey them'.

Bootlegging may have become 'the respectable crime', but prohibition encouraged lawbreaking and the building up of a criminal class that turned to gambling, drugs and the unions when Roosevelt repealed the Volstead Act in 1933. Bootlegging fed gang warfare, the high point of which was the St Valentine's Day Massacre of 1929 in Chicago, when Al Capone gunned down six of the Moran gang in a garage where they were waiting to buy a truckload of liquor from hijackers. H. C. Allen rightly calls prohibition a veritable cancer on the body politic, because it increased through the rise of organised crime the American tradition of violence, both in crime and law enforcement, while it brought all law into disrepute and increased corruption in the legal system and politics.

Despite the severities of the slump, the interwar years saw remarkable economic developments in the USA. In many ways a second Industrial Revolution occurred as science was applied more to industrial processes, for example in the petrochemical industries. The scientific study of petroleum led to fresh innovation, with the development of major new end products, such as synthetic rubber, and synthetic fibres, such as nylon and plastics. In this field the leaders were Du Pont, Union Carbide and Carbon, and Monsanto. A feature of the chemicals industry was the close relations forged with the universities and their research staff. Another area of rapid development was the metal industry, with new metals such as aluminium and alloy steels which could withstand high temperatures.

There was a revolution in energy. At the beginning of the twentieth century coal was king, but was bulkier and less energy efficient than natural gas or oil, consumption of the latter increasing twelvefold between 1910 and 1957.

The process of concentration leading to domination of markets by a few firms continued, with a wave of mergers in the 1920s. In 1933 57 per cent of corporate wealth was held by 200 firms, with a consequent danger of cartels being formed against the public interest. Fortunately the American consumer became better off, because, as Galbraith pointed out, giant sellers were met by giant buyers.

The classic example of concentration was the car industry where the Big Three – Ford, General Motors and Chrysler – soon accounted for 97 per cent of American cars. Such concentration occurred because large companies could integrate both horizontally and vertically, especially Ford, with its own coal and iron mines, steel plants and glass and tyre factories. Large companies alone could enjoy the economies of scale which would allow them to bring in improvements and offer a variety of models much more easily than small companies could. Their advertising costs were proportionately lighter, and they had more outlets through which to sell and repair their cars.

The car industry was the archetypal example of America's success in being the first country to bring in mass-production methods – the process whereby great quantities of a standardised commodity are produced. Scarcity of labour peculiar to the USA helped the early use of mass-production techniques. Because labour was relatively dear, American manufacturers mechanised during the nineteenth century and brought in standardisation earlier than other countries, such as Britain, where labour was relatively cheap.

The new methods would only be worth implementing if, in Ford's words, they were linked with 'the capacity, latent or developed, of mass consumption, the ability to absorb large production'. The American market was ideally suited to absorb mass production because of its sheer size and purchasing power. The USA's population, only 76 millions in 1900, had reached 150 millions by 1950. A mass market grew up with internal free trade, heavy tariff protection and an excellent transport system, a great contrast to Europe with its fragmented markets. The average per capita income of the American people increased threefold between 1869 and 1929, and with the increase in leisure provided further opportunities for a broadened pattern of consumption. In 1928 the total national income of the USA was one-third greater than the combined incomes of twenty European states with three times the population. Even in the richest European states, income levels were not high enough to give the stimulus of demand for mass-produced goods on a really large scale.

To implement the mass-production methods, the requisite technology had to be available. Americans were born engineers and very adaptable. They first developed high speed carbon steel through the work of F. W. Taylor and J. Mansel White, and led in the practical application of electricity after Edison built the first generating station in 1882. By 1914 over one-third of industrial power in the USA was derived from electricity. The innovative streak in American economic life can be seen in the rise in the number of patents taken out from 4,400 in 1860 to 40,000 in 1914.

FURTHER READING

Adams, D. K., 'Franklin Delano Roosevelt and the New Deal', Historical Association Pamphlet, 1979

Allen, H. C., *A Concise History of the U.S.A.*, Ernest Benn, London, 1976

Burns, J. M., *Roosevelt: the Lion and the Fox*, Harcourt, New York, 1956

Fearon, P., *The Origins and Nature of the Great Slump 1929–32*, Macmillan, London, 1979

Galbraith, K., *The Great Crash*, Penguin, Harmondsworth, 1969

Leuchtenburg, W. L., *Franklin D. Roosevelt and the New Deal*, Harper Torchbooks, New York, 1963

Morison, S. E., *et al.*, *The Growth of the American Republic*, Seventh Edition, OUP, Oxford, 1980

QUESTIONS

1. Why did the USA enter the First World War in 1917?
2. Account for the period of Republican ascendancy in the 1920s.
3. Examine the origins and consequences of the Wall Street Crash.
4. 'In eight years. Roosevelt and the New Dealers had almost revolutionised the agenda of American politics' (Leuchtenburg). Discuss this statement.
5. Critically examine the causes and consequences of Prohibition on American life.
6. In what ways, and why, did the USA lead the world in mass-production techniques by 1939?

9
International relations between the two world wars

(1) The League of Nations

(a) Origins and formation of the League

The League of Nations was born out of the futility and waste of the First World War. Its name was reputedly first coined in 1914 by the writer H. Lowes Dickinson, one of a number of idealists who were determined that out of evil must come good in the sense that the war had created, in their view, an opportunity to form a new kind of international organisation of democratic states. Many politicians and academics formulated schemes embodying their ideas on postwar international reconstruction, notably Sir Robert Cecil, the younger son of Lord Salisbury and Under-Secretary of State for Foreign Affairs during the war.

When a Commission to draft the rules of the League (the League Covenant) was set up in Paris in 1919, the driving force was Woodrow Wilson, the American President, who had also advocated the establishment of an international organisation throughout the war years but had no very clear-cut ideas on how it should be organised. The scheme which fired his imagination was Smuts' 'The League of Nations: A Practical Suggestion'. America's principal allies did not share Wilson's enthusiasm for the new venture but went along with the proposal out of fears of a separate American peace with Germany, and out of a desire to win the President's approval for their territorial and political designs during the peace conference.

The Commission eventually succeeded in drafting the League Covenant, and, to French chagrin, it reflected Anglo-American thinking on the subject. The League had two main aims, the first being to maintain peace through collective security. If one state attacked another, the member states of the League would act together to restrain the aggressor by economic and military measures. The second aim was international cooperation to tackle economic and social problems.

The number of member states grew to fifty-five by 1926, and several main organs developed. The General Assembly of all member states decided general policy and required unanimity in decision-making. The Council contained four permanent members – Britain, France, Italy and Japan – and other states elected for 3 years; its role was to deal with specific political disputes, and again decisions had to be unanimous. The Permanent Court of International Justice based at the Hague dealt with legal disputes between states.

(b) Underlying problems of the League

From the outset the League was expected to play many roles, as Ruth Henig has emphasised. It was cast as an international conference pledged to settle disputes, it was a body guaranteeing the political and territorial status quo and recommending changes where necessary, and it was an agency for promoting disarmament. It was also given the task of overseeing the Versailles settlement over Danzig, the Saar and Upper Silesia, protecting minority groups in the new East European states and administering the mandate system. The League was to be the coordinating agency for the numerous international scientific and technical bodies which had mushroomed since 1900, and it was to be the financier for the International Labour Organisation (ILO), a body set up after the war to improve working conditions throughout the world.

Clearly too much was expected of the League, especially given the defection of the USA. The reception of the draft League Covenant in the USA was mixed. Personal hostility to Wilson, resentment at the growing power of the presidential office and widespread reluctance to assume onerous worldwide obligations at the end of the war were exploited by Wilson's opponents in the Senate. Wilson would not accept any of the compromises proposed by the Senate on League issues, and, in addition, in March 1920 the necessary two-thirds majority was not obtained for the Versailles Settlement in the Senate (see Chapter 8).

The American refusal to join was an early bodyblow to the League. It undermined the idealism and drive in the new organisation, and made it seem even more too Euro-centred. It weakened the ability of the League to apply sanctions, and confirmed the French in their view that the League could not in its present form provide security.

British leaders and advisers considered that membership of the League was useless without the presence of the USA. 'Britain stayed in the League', asserts Henig, 'not out of conviction but out of cowardice.' The public believed in it and to disavow it might be to court electoral disaster, as Baldwin admitted when he included Lord Robert Cecil in his 1923–4 cabinet as a sign to League supporters that Britain fully supported the League. Unfortunately governments, including Britain's, did not educate their publics as to the real limitations of the League. Thus at times of crisis, such as the Manchurian incident of 1931, the public expected powerful reprisals by the League and were disappointed. They did not appreciate that the effective functioning of the League in the Pacific area depended on American support.

The withdrawal of the USA from the League left as its leading members Britain, France, Italy and from 1926 Germany, all of whom had different views about the League's role in international affairs. This was the case even as regards Britain and France, the two mature democracies whose close collaboration was essential if the League were to function effectively. France, deprived of the Anglo-American guarantee of the Versailles Treaty, saw the League as a source of extra security and wanted its machinery tightened so that more economic and military sanctions would be available against any aggressor. The British, already unhappy about the fairness of the Versailles Treaty, resisted French attempts to strengthen the League machinery, preferring to limit League activities to regulation of international crises by enforcement of a statutory period of delay to allow for impartial investigations to take place and for tempers to cool down.

The wording of the League Covenant gave nations the legal right to go to war if, after a League enquiry into a dispute, the League Council could come to no unanimous decision on the rights and wrongs of the case. Even in cases of flagrant abuse of the provisions of the Covenant, the League Council could only advise members on what military measures to undertake against an aggressor. The French wanted such loopholes closed, and refused to consider disarmament until League security provisions were improved.

While France sought to strengthen the Covenant provisions, other powers, notably Germany, Italy and Japan, were determined to minimise its coercive powers so as to prevent the League from interfering with their expansionist aims. In Japan the military gained more influence as the 1920s proceeded (see Chapter 13), Mussolini's government in Italy evinced from 1922 on an attitude of hostility towards the League, and even such 'good' Weimar politicians as Stresemann valued League membership only in so far as it might help modification of the Versailles clauses on Germany's eastern frontiers.

The aloofness of both the Soviet Union and the USA limited the League's scope for action during the 1920s. The Soviet government was then very hostile to the League, regarding it as a club for the victorious capitalist powers, though it toned down its bellicosity after Hitler's accession to power in Germany, and was drawn into League activities, especially on disarmament. The USA refused throughout the entire interwar period to be drawn into close contact with the League, and emphasised its independent position by pursuing a parallel course to that of the League through other mechanisms. For example, it pursued the maintenance of peace through the 1928 Kellogg–Briand Pact, which bound its signatories to renounce war as an instrument of policy.

One of the major roles expected of the League was the promotion of disarmament by providing a framework within which member nations could conclude agreements about arms limitation. It was felt in 1919 that the high levels of armaments were wasteful and had contributed to the outbreak of war in 1914. Therefore a reduction in armaments levels would reduce the likelihood of a major war in the future and save states from having to spend money on a costly arms race. As the stringent conditions on German armaments in the Versailles Treaty were prefaced by the observation that these measures were to prepare for a general limitation of armaments, many statesmen, particularly such British politicans as Cecil, felt a moral obligation to pursue vigorous disarmament policies through the League.

Yet equally there were those who were opposed to the ideal of disarmament as unrealisable, given human nature and the technical difficulties of ensuring that devious states were actually disarming. The British were not prepared to accept naval disarmament below a certain level, while European states bordered by revisionist powers were reluctant to accept any arms limitation at all. The Poles and Rumanians feared Russia, while French and Belgian governments were alarmed at German evasion of the Versailles restrictions through military and industrial collaboration with Russia after 1922. Therefore only in 1926 was a Preparatory Commission for Disarmament set up to draw up a programme for a League Disarmament Conference, a process which took 5 tedious years to negotiate. When the General Disarmament Conference did finally take place in 1932, both Russia and Germany voted against the proposals as a gesture of disapproval at their limited scope. The conference took place against the background of the slump, and countries bordering on Germany demanded more effective security before adopting deep cuts in armaments. Germany retorted by demanding equality of treatment in armaments, since her neighbours were not displaying any serious intention of disarming. The French for their part suggested at least 8 years' postponement of Germany's right to equality in armaments, insisting that their large forces were needed to police their empire as well as for security.

In this atmosphere proposals such as those put forward by Hoover to cut offensive weapons such as tanks and bombers by a third fell on stony ground and led to disillusionment about the possibilities of real disarmament by the major powers. The final blow to the hopes of the League disarmament conference was Hitler's accession to power in January 1933, two of his early moves being to withdraw Grmany from the conference and from the League itself. The implications of the German moves were not lost on Stalin, who realigned his foreign policy and applied for Russian membership of the League in October 1933.

(c) The League exposed: the Manchurian and Abyssinian crises

The first major challenge to the League was Japan's attack on Mukden in Manchuria in September 1931 (see Chapter 13). From the start it was a difficult issue, owing to the geographical location of the disputed area, the near-anarchic conditions in that part of China, and the general international situation. The repercussions of the slump were dominating the attention of world leaders and had just caused a change of government in Britain. In the USA a presidential election was pending, while in Europe France was obsessed by the rise of German Fascism. As Henig has commented, 'The timing could not have been more unpropitious for a major League initiative.'

The obscurity of the facts clouded the reality of Japanese aggression for European statesmen. Manchuria was known to be a lawless area only nominally under the control of the Chinese Nationalist government, and Japan had treaty rights dating back to the 1905 Treaty of Portsmouth, allowing her the use of troops to guard concession areas and railways. The Europeans gave the crisis low priority, as the diary of Maurice Hankey, secretary to the British cabinet at the time, reveals. He referred to the Manchurian crisis as 'an interesting minor development . . . We will poke our noses into everyone's business at the League'. Many Europeans believed that Japanese troops had been provoked by marauding Chinese warlord forces and had acted in self-defence. Later when it became clear that the Japanese army in Manchuria had acted on its own initiative, agreements reached between the League Council and the Japanese government could not be enforced because the Kwantung Army refused to obey civilian commands. The leading members of the League and the USA were thus concerned to do nothing which would further weaken the Japanese government and strengthen the position of the military faction.

A further difficulty was the attitude of the world's leading non-member states, the USA and the USSR, which could have applied more pressure on Japan than any League member. Neither government was prepared to cooperate with the League in settling the dispute. The USA would not participate in League meetings, refused to consider economic or military sanctions and would only agree to a policy of concerted international protest. The US Secretary of State, Stimson, told the British Foreign Secretary, Simon, in April 1932 that 'nothing beyond protest could be done' but 'if suitable occasions were chosen, the accumulated effect on public opinion was considerable and this would in the end influence Japan'. The Russians feared a strong Japanese presence in Manchuria, but, as Russia was not yet a member of the League, they merely derided the League's weak response in sending out a commission under Lord Lytton to investigate the situation in the disputed area.

As Japanese action in Manchuria increased, the Chinese government appealed in vain for League action. The Lytton Commission duly investigated and reported the facts of the dispute by the end of 1932. Meanwhile the Japanese had taken control of Manchuria, and the Japanese miltary had gained more influence in central government. When the League proposed Sino-Japanese discussions over Manchuria, and stressed the need to change Manchuria's new status as a Japanese puppet state (Manchukuo), Japan refused to accept the recommendations and left the League in March 1933.

The League's failure was even clearer over the Abyssinian affair, for when fascist Italy attacked Abyssinia in October 1935, it indulged in the most patent act of aggression in the entire interwar period (see Chapter 4). The League's handling of the crisis was complicated by the different views of its members on the issue. Britain and France wanted to come to terms with Mussolini, whereas the smaller powers were eager to enforce the coercive provisions of the Covenant. The French, obsessed by the growing Nazi threat, wished to maintain Italy as an ally against German expansionist aims in Europe. The British government was aware that France would not support a strong League stand against Italy, and also wished to conciliate Mussolini in the interests of an anti-German front. However, a general election was pending and the Prime Minister, Baldwin, knew that a strong British stand on the principle of collective League action against Mussolini would command strong electoral support. Caught on the horns of a dilemma, the British attempted a dual policy – conciliation of Italy's aspirations and coercive action through the League.

The results were predictably disastrous. At British prompting the League adopted a policy of mild economic sanctions on Italy, with the intention of making them more stringent if necessary. This policy foundered from the start, as non-members such as Japan and Germany would not participate in such sanctions; neither would Austria and Hungary. In addition, neither Britain nor France would risk imposing sanctions on such vital war commodities as oil in case this brought war with Italy uncomfortably close.

While economic sanctions were being put into operation, the French premier, Laval, tried to effect a settlement of the dispute which would placate Mussolini. The British were similarly anxious, and in December 1935 Laval and Hoare, the British Foreign Secretary, cobbled together a proposal which would have given Italy two-thirds of Abyssinia, with the rump of Abyssinia being given a new outlet to the sea. While Mussolini might have accepted this, it was not acceptable to Haile Selassie, the Emperor of Abyssinia, and when its details were revealed to the British public, it caused such an outcry that the British government was forced to disavow it, to the anger of both France and Italy. Hoare had to resign but no more stringent sanctions were imposed on Italy. By May 1936 Mussolini had annexed Abyssinia and declared it to be part of the Italian Empire.

As Ruth Henig rightly declares, 'The credibility of the League as a coercive organisation was completely destroyed and even more importantly the will of its members to work together was greatly weakened.' Anglo-French relations became even frostier, and they failed to work together effectively against the far greater menace of Nazi Germany. In the late 1930s the major issues of world peace were tackled by individual nations working largely outside the League. The Abyssinian crisis had shattered the League as a peacekeeping body and paved the way for Hitler's domination of Europe.

Thus, as a guarantee scheme for members' territorial integrity and political independence, the League was a complete failure. It was not equipped with its own forces, as the French had wished, nor was it empowered to call upon members' forces to carry out its suggestions. Though Article 16 expected member states to supply troops if necessary, a 1923 resolution allowed each member to decide for itself whether or not to fight in a crisis. When its more powerful members disagreed, as Britain and France often did, the League was paralysed. Its idealistic supporters had placed too much faith in the power of international public opinion, when in fact such opinion proved to be a broken reed when international crises occurred.

The League's failure may be explained by many factors, especially the absence of such major states as the USA and the uniquely difficult years of the depression. But for all member states there was a built-in tension between their sovereignty (which implied a reluctance to permit outside interference in their domestic affairs) and the corporate purposes of the international organisation. Such tensions still face nations which are members of the United Nations or the European Community. In addition, while the League was created to preserve peace, it was also committed to retaining a status quo which was not supported by many of its members. Therefore a paradox arose: the only way that the League, created to preserve peace, could preserve the existing world was by the threat of the use of force. Committed to the idea of the just war against the aggressor when its leading members would not support it, the League's paralysis in major crises was ensured.

(d) The successes of the League

Despite its limitations, the League had its successes both in the political and social fields. In the 1920s it was at the centre of international activity and administered two potential trouble-spots – the Saar until 1935 and Danzig until 1939. It undertook the division of Upper Silesia in 1921 after the French and British had failed to find a solution. It supervised the mandates over the territories taken from Germany and Turkey, and created a new kind of international secretariat drawn from many nations.

The League was successful in the field of preventive action in the 1920s. Its members were empowered to bring any issues which were felt to be endangering peace before the League for investigation. Britain used this to bring about a settlement of the Aaland Islands dispute between Sweden and Finland in 1920 (in favour of Finland), and it was also used to decide that the Mosul area claimed by both Turkey and Iraq should go to the latter country. Briand brought before the League the invasion of Greece by Bulgarian troops in 1925, a crisis which the League resolved speedily. In the Corfu dispute of 1923 the force of League Assembly opposition to Mussolini's occupation of Corfu helped to induce Italian evacuation of the island, even though the Greeks had to pay an indemnity.

The League's greatest successes lay in its humanitarian activities. It coordinated the work of many ad hoc organisations which had sprung up around the turn of the century to deal with new scientific advances. Its efforts in the fields of health, international labour legislation and refugee settlement were promising developments for the future. The International Labour Organisation aimed to improve working conditions all over the world by persuading governments to fix maximum working hours, minimum wages and adequate welfare provisions. The Refugee Organisation under Fridtjof Nansen, the explorer, helped refugees from both Soviet Russia and Nazi Germany. The Health Organisation carried out useful research into the causes of epidemics and helped to combat a typhus epidemic in Russia. The League tried to combat drug-smuggling, and gave important economic aid to Austria and Hungary in 1922.

The determination of the Allies during the Second World War to establish a successor to the League is proof that they felt it to be a valuable experiment in international affairs. Indeed the League experience was most useful in the forming of the more durable United Nations in 1945 (see Chapter 11). The UNO was able to expand on the League's social and economic activities and to learn from the League's shortcomings in its organisation. In the final session of the League Assembly in April 1946 Lord Cecil was still able to call it 'a great advance in the international organisation of peace'. But for the great experiment of the League, the United Nations could never have come into existence.

(2) The international impact of the Spanish Civil War

Twentieth-century Spain was beset by a number of fundamental problems which conspired by July 1936 to precipitate the country into a savage civil war. The loss of empire in the nineteenth century, the lack of natural resources, the strength of regional feeling and above all the unending struggle between the forces of reform and reaction resulted in acute political instablity. In the 1920s the relatively benevolent dictatorship of Primo de Rivera replaced the bankrupt parliamentary system, but in 1931 Primo and the king, Alfonso XIII, came under increasing criticism and the king abdicated.

From 1931 to 1936 Spain was governed by a republican regime, but the period saw a further polarisation of politics. From 1931 to 1933 a moderate republican government under Azana attempted to tackle Spain's most pressing problems – the land, the Church, regionalism, and the army, which had for over a century displayed an unfortunate tendency to interfere in politics. The government succeeded in offending the Spanish Establishment, especially the Church, land-owners and army, and lost the elections of November 1933. From then until February 1936 a right-wing government under Lerroux governed Spain, but such events as the savage repression of an Anarchist revolt in October 1934 meant that political tensions continued to grow. Extremist parties – the Spanish Fascists (Falange) and the Communists – grew in importance.

The elections of February 1936 led to a left-wing regime, which goaded the Right into armed revolt. Right-wing politicians, such as Sotelo, were murdered and the last straw was the posting of top generals to positions outside mainland Spain. As Raymond Carr notes, 'discontent was tightened into a plan of revolt by the government's defensive action against the military malcontents'. On 18 July General Franco flew to Morocco to lead the Army of Africa in revolt.

Both the Republicans and the rebels (Nationalists) perpetrated blunders that forfeited the chances of either side winning the war quickly. Gradually, however, the tide of war began to move in favour of the rebels for four reasons – the leadership of Franco, his possession of the best trained Spanish troops (the Army of Africa), the divisions among the Republicans (a motley collection of liberals, socialists, communists, anarchists, and Trotskyites) and the superior quality of foreign aid given to the rebels. By March 1939 the Civil War was over and Franco consolidated a harsh right-wing regime, which Gabriel Jackson has described as 'awe-inspiring in its lack of pity and lack of imagination'. Franco ruled Spain until his death in November 1975, since when the country has enjoyed steady progress towards being a modern constitutional monarchy under King Juan

Carlos. A significant step in this transition was Spanish accession to the European Community in January 1986.

The Spanish Civil War itself was of immense significance in European history. For Spain itself it was a tragedy; over 600,000 people were killed, the majority by summary execution. Rapidly the war became an international issue. Within a few months Germany and Italy were supplying men and arms to the rebels and the Soviet Union was assisting the Republican government. For a time it looked as if Spain would spark off a general conflagration.

The significance of the war, as Anthony Adamthwaite has shown, was ideological, economic and strategic. It was seen as a battleground between the forces of the Left and Right, between Communism and Fascism. The Spanish economy was important, for it supplied a large share of the world's requirements of quicksilver and iron pyrites. Spain's strategic importance lay in her control of the entrance to the West Mediterranean and Atlantic approaches.

The aid that Franco gained from Germany and Italy made a crucial contribution to his victory. Lacking aircraft, he could not transport his crack troops of the Army of Africa from Morocco to mainland Spain. It was the Germans who quickly provided twenty Junker JU-52 transport planes to ferry Franco's troops to Spain. Italian help soon followed, and by October 1937 there were 60,000 Italian 'volunteers' in Spain, together with 6,000 men of the German Condor Legion (eleven aircraft squadrons). The Italian ground forces were inefficient, as their defeat at the hands of the pro-Republican International Brigade at Guadalajara in 1937 demonstrated. However, the Italians also contributed 414 planes to Germany's 282, and, contrary to popular belief, these planes were of good quality, as were Italian submarines which attacked ships attempting to bring supplies to the Republicans. The Salazar regime in Portugal also sent 20,000 troops to assist Franco. In the long run it was the continuity of German and Italian aid that tipped the scales in Franco's favour, for only the Soviet Union gave the Republicans much assistance, and this was not only restricted but Soviet arms had to be paid for by the Republicans sending over half their gold reserves to Russia.

What were the motives of the three chief states which intervened in the Spanish Civil War? In Adamthwaite's view Hitler's main reason for intervening in Spain was ideological – the desire to prevent the emergence of a Bolshevik regime in Spain which might combine with Blum's socialist government in France to form an anti-German bloc. For Hitler's right-hand man, Göring, who was in charge of both Germany's Four Year Plan and the Luftwaffe, intervention in Spain would give Germany valuable raw materials and blood her young airmen in real battle experience. The Germans also limited their aid to Franco with the aim of prolonging the war so that it would distract attention away from Hitler's machinations in Central Europe.

Italy's motives for intervention were ideological and military. Mussolini wanted a regime in Spain which was friendly to fascism, and hoped that his help might win Italy rewards such as the Balearic Islands as military bases.

The Soviet Union's motives are harder to fathom. Ostensibly Stalin wished to support the Republicans for ideological reasons, but he also hoped that limited Soviet aid would prolong the war so as to occupy international attention. This would leave his country free to implement its Five Year Plans with less risk of immediate invasion from the West.

Only speedy and substantial French aid could have saved the Spanish Republic, but for two reasons the French government adopted a policy of non-intervention. Some British pressure was applied on French ministers but the decisive factor that led the French premier Blum to adopt non-intervention was domestic – the risk of a civil war in France. The outbreak of war in Spain further polarised French politics, and in Blum's view French help to Republican Spain would provoke the French Right into a rebellion which might topple his government and destroy his socialist reforms.

The international significance of the war is immense. It led to a complete paralysis of French foreign policy in the late 1930s. The French now had to face the reality that in the event of a Franco victory France would be encircled by a triple alliance of Germany, Italy and Nationalist Spain. This would pose a threat to France across the Pyrenees and cut her off from her North African colonies, where one-third of her army was stationed. The nightmare of encirclement made France cede initiatives in foreign policy to Britain, and give up all hope of maintaining her commitments to allies such as Czechoslovakia in Eastern Europe.

Stalin's intervention increased British and French suspicion of his intentions, but likewise the inactivity of the two major Western democracies made Stalin doubt his policy of collective security, and here may be seen the genesis of his pact with Hitler in August 1939. Franco-British inactivity also convinced Hitler and Mussolini that the two democracies would not oppose their ambitions in Central Europe and the Mediterranean.

Three general conclusions were drawn from the war. The bombing of the Basque town of Guernica by German planes in 1937 seemed to demonstrate the destructive potential of air power, while the relative ineffectiveness of the tank led to its underestimation in Britain and France. The length of the Spanish war indicated that a European war would be a long one.

The obsession with Spain diverted attention from Hitler and contributed to the bloodless successes of his foreign policy between 1937 and 1939. Lastly Spain created a climate of war; the Spanish Civil War, it was widely believed, was merely a dress rehearsal for a full international war in the near future. The French ambassador to Germany, François-Poncet, commented in September 1937, 'The present state of affairs is in reality no longer peace but undeclared war.'

(3) The foreign policy of the Third Reich, 1933–9

(a) The area of debate

A. J. P. Taylor's book *The Origins of the Second World War* (1961) aroused fresh argument on why war broke out in 1939. Taylor maintained that Hitler was in many ways an ordinary German statesman in the tradition of Brüning or Stresemann, differing from them primarily in the skill with which he took advantage of diplomatic situations. Like them, he wished, as any German leader would, to restore Germany's position in Europe. Opportunities, however, were presented to him by other leading figures, such as Neville Chamberlain, and it was these opportunities, not Hitler's aggression, that allowed him to gain complete control of Austria and Czechoslovakia. Hitler, argued Taylor, did not want a general war in 1939 when he attacked Poland; the incomplete state of German rearmament is decisive proof of this. The Nazi–Soviet Pact of August 1939 convinced Hitler that the Western powers would not dare to stand by Poland, and it was a surprise to him that they did. Thus to Taylor, the war broke out by accident.

Taylor also repudiates the importance of the Hossbach Conference of November 1937, when Hitler declared his intention to solve Germany's need for territory in Eastern Europe quickly, the initial steps required being the absorption of Austria and Czechoslovakia and confrontation with the Western powers. In Taylor's view, Hitler's aim at the conference was merely to overcome the resistance of Schacht, the economics minister, to rearmament. Taylor also praises the Munich settlement of 1938 as 'a triumph for all that was best and most enlightened in British life' and believes that Chamberlain should have completed his task of eliminating German grievances, instead of supporting Poland against Germany in 1939. Even Hitler's wartime conquests are played down by Taylor. Agreeing with the views of Fritz Fischer, he asserts that Hitler was only aiming at the same conquests as German leaders during the First World War.

The Taylor thesis provoked spirited comment from a number of historians, including Hugh Trevor-Roper, Tim Mason and Christopher Thorne. Their criticisms may be summarised in three main points.

First, they accuse Taylor of underestimating Germany's expansionist drive because he relied on the German Foreign Office documents, which do not reveal Nazi disruption in Austria and Czechoslovakia. It was this disruption that forced other statesmen into actions which provided Hitler with his chief opportunities. As Christopher Thorne put it, 'the tension which caused others to act sprang from the expansionist aims – however uncoordinated – of the Third Reich, and from the nature of Nazism'.

Second, unlike Taylor, they believe that Hitler's remarks at the Hossbach Conference mark a step forward in positive aggression. As Mason says, the conference was 'the point at which the latent expansionism of the Third Reich ceased to be latent and became explicit'.

Third, for his figures on German rearmament before the war, Taylor relied on the work of B. H. Klein. In fact, asserts Mason, German rearmament was much greater than Taylor has stated; the Third Reich spent half as much again on armaments between 1933 and 1939 as Britain and France put together. Other economic factors point to the Nazi planning for war, particularly the drive for autarchy and the emphasis on heavy industry. Finally the regime saw war as a way out of its domestic difficulties. Public spending had increased fourfold and inflation and labour shortages were increasing. The Nazi leaders, afraid to hold down wages severely, saw the solution in immediate foreign conquest.

(b) What were Hitler's aims?

From his earliest days with the Nazi party, Hitler was always passionately interested in foreign affairs. In *Mein Kampf* much space is devoted to them, and it seems probable that the views expressed were sincerely held and reveal Hitler's true intentions. Hitler had three major objectives: (1) he wished to overturn the shameful Versailles Treaty which meant winning Germany's right to rearm and the recovery of the lands lost in 1919 – the Saar, Alsace-Lorraine, German colonies and above all the areas lost to Poland; (2) he wished to extend the frontiers of Germany to include all people of German race, especially the Germans of Austria and Czechoslovakia; and (3) the first two objectives were in a sense only steps on the road towards the real goal, which was to make the Germans the dominant race in Europe at the expense of the racially 'inferior' peoples in the east.

Hitler, in Norman Rich's phrase, was a thoroughgoing Malthusian, and feared the time when Germany could no longer feed her growing population. Therefore Germany must expand for survival, as she was surrounded by inferior races who might combine to destroy her. This was the justification of the doctrine of *Lebensraum* or living-space, at the expense mainly of the Poles and the Russians. 'History proves', wrote Hitler, 'that the German people owes its existence solely to its determination to fight in the East and to obtain land by military conquest. Land in Europe is only to be obtained at the expense of Russia. The German Reich must therefore follow in the footsteps of the Teutonic Knights in order to guarantee the nation its daily bread through occupation of Russian territory.' Of course there would be no incorporation of non-Germans in this larger Germany; that had been the error of the British and Spanish in their empires. The inferior inhabitants were to be made useful or removed.

The struggle would also be turned against the Jews. As William Carr has shown, Hitler lived in a nightmare world of his own making where sinister Jewish wire-pullers lurked behind every movement of which he disapproved, from Freemasonry to Marxism. He saw the Jew as a member of a lower race which lived like a parasite on higher races, spreading such doctrines as democracy or Bolshevism. This made Hitler even more decided on attacking Russia, and explains why he assumed that Russia was 'ripe for dissolution' when in fact she was on the road to becoming a great industrial power.

Hitler believed that struggle was inevitable and humanity mere weakness. His ideas can be described as a kind of crude Social Darwinism, and had been picked up in the gutters of Vienna; but his foreign policy can only be understood as an expression of his racialist philosophy. The work of Fritz Fischer has revived the old argument about the continuity of German foreign policy from William II to Hitler. Similarities obviously exist, if one bears in mind Hitler's first and second objectives, but the differences are as striking as the similarities. The aims of Imperial Germany pale into insignificance compared to the appalling ruthlessness of the Nazis, with their emphasis on race and aim to enslave the peoples of Eastern Europe. 'In this very real sense', as William Carr asserts, 'one can still maintain that Hitler's policy was uniquely different from that of preceding regimes.'

Hitler believed that Imperial Germany had committed a grave error in alienating Britain by chasing colonies and building a large navy. Underestimating Britain's concern for Europe, he believed that he could win her friendship by waiving colonial and naval ambitions, and he hoped also to gain Italian cooperation. France would then be helpless and Germany would be free to strike at Russia in the East. Of course these ideas did not represent a blueprint for aggression. Hitler was at the mercy of events, like other statesmen, and had to alter course from time to time as events unfolded, but he was the supreme opportunist who exploited to the full the opportunities that were now to occur.

(c) The years of caution, 1933–5

Germany's diplomatic position on Hitler's accession was superficially unpromising. She was disarmed, lacked allies and was still surrounded by members of the French alliance system – Belgium, Czechoslovakia, Poland and France herself. The hostility of Soviet Russia could be assumed on ideological grounds, while Mussolini's Italy was concerned about the German threat to Austrian independence.

The Versailles Treaty had limited Germany's armed forces to 100,000 men, and, despite von Seeckt's secret rearmament, the army consisted of only ten divisions when Hitler came to power. It was his first task to resurrect the army, but such a policy might lead to French intervention while it was being accomplished. Therefore a cautious and pacific foreign policy was absolutely necessary so that rearmament could continue without hindrance.

This situation explains the surprising moderation which Hitler displayed in the early years. He was always talking peace, and his speeches were masterpieces in the art of propaganda. The Germans attended the Disarmament Conference and accepted British proposals for a general reduction in armaments, knowing full well that the French would refuse to agree. The French refusal gave Hitler the pretext which he needed to leave the conference on grounds of inequality of treatment, and in October Germany also left the League of Nations, a move justified by a plebiscite.

In January 1934 Hitler was able to demonstrate his 'peaceful' intentions by concluding a 10-year non-aggression pact with Poland. This was a complete break with Weimar foreign policy and seemed to have three advantages: (1) it was a breach in the French alliance system, (2) Hitler saw Poland as a potential ally against Russia, and (3) the pact was also a temporary expedient to forestall any Polish attack on Germany. What Hitler failed to realise was that the pact would accelerate a rapprochement between France and Russia, and in fact these two countries signed a non-aggression pact in February.

Despite this, rearmament was well under way by the end of 1934. In December 1933 the army put forward plans for a peacetime army of twenty-one divisions by 1937, and a period of service reduced from 12 years to 1 year, so that reserves could be built up. Over 50,000 men were recruited in April 1934, but Hitler was not satisfied, and in October another 70,000 men were recruited, bringing the total strength of the army to 240,000; to this figure could be added 200,000 policemen trained as infantrymen. By the end of 1934 Germany had created an airforce of 2,000 planes.

That Germany's diplomatic position was still one of insecure isolation was demonstrated by events in Austria in 1934. Hitler had a special affection for Austria and assumed that with the help of the Austrian Nazis he would soon assimilate his native country into Germany. The Austrian chancellor Dollfuss countered Nazi violence in 1933 by banning the Austrian Nazis, and he solicited the support of France, Britain and Italy. Hitler lost interest but in July 1934 the

Austrian Nazis provoked an uprising which, though it was suppressed, led to the death of Dollfuss. The powers reacted strongly, especially the Italian government, which sent four divisions to the Brenner Pass as a gesture of support for Austria. Hitler was forced to repudiate all connection with the conspiracy, and realised that the union of Austria and Germany was out of the question until Germany was stronger.

Nevertheless the year 1935 saw a radical improvement in Germany's diplomatic position. In January a plebiscite was held in the Saar, as agreed at Versailles, and it resulted in a 90 per cent vote in favour of return to Germany. Next came Hitler's first major gamble in international affairs. After the Austrian fiasco he was anxious to introduce conscription and expand the army to thirty-six divisions. Despite the protest of the army leaders at the pace of the expansion, he announced the reintroduction of conscription in March. Foreign reaction was what he expected. Britain, France and Italy protested at this unilateral breach of the Versailles Treaty but took no action to prevent it.

True, European opinion seemed to harden against Hitler. In April the foreign secretaries of Britain, France and Italy met at Stresa, condemned the German action, reaffirmed their loyalty to the Locarno treaties and repeated their declaration on the need for Austrian independence. To this Stresa 'front' was added in May a pact between France and Russia pledging mutual assistance against unprovoked aggression. Russia also concluded a similar pact with Czechoslovakia, promising support against aggression on condition that France honoured her pledges first. Hitler was not, however, overawed by these developments. He intuitively perceived that this apparent unity of opinion against him was flimsy. He realised the mutual suspicion between Russia and the Western powers, the longing of the democracies for peace, and the feelings of sympathy that existed in Britain over the German position. The unity, he felt, would not last long, and he was soon proved correct in his analysis.

In June came a major German success when the signing of an Anglo-German naval agreement limited German tonnage to 35 per cent of that of Britain and her Commonwealth. The limitation was no hardship for Germany because it would take her some time to reach the 35 per cent ceiling anyway. The treaty itself is evidence that a rapprochement with Britain was one of Hitler's long-term aims, and only in 1937 did he conclude that a full alliance with her could not be secured.

Britain's failure to consult her partners, France and Italy, about the naval agreement gave a disastrous impression of bad faith and gravely sabotaged the Stresa Front. It was, writes Norman Rich, 'a horrendous diplomatic blunder for in effect it recognised Germany's right to rearm and consequently its right to break international treaties forbidding such rearmament'. Worse was to follow, for the Stresa Front collapsed completely in the autumn when Britain and France imposed sanctions on Italy following her attack on Abyssinia. The Western democracies succeeded in getting the worst of both worlds; their imposition of sanctions alienated Italy but their failure to take any really effective action against Mussolini dealt their prestige, and that of the League of Nations, a fatal blow. Hitler noted the passivity of the Western powers, and all he was required to do to strengthen Germany's diplomatic position was to remain neutral in the dispute. Attention was drawn away from Europe to African affairs, and the Italians, offended by Britain and France, began to draw nearer to Germany. The fragile unity was shattered and the way lay open for further German advances.

(d) New opportunities, 1936–7

At the beginning of 1936 Hitler could survey the European scene with great satisfaction. The Stresa Front had collapsed and in France a weak caretaker government was in office. Convinced that no state would oppose him, Hitler felt that the time was ripe for the remilitarisation of the Rhineland, especially as enthusiasm for the Nazi regime was on the decline in Germany. Therefore in February a plan was drawn up for contingents of the German army to reoccupy the Rhineland with orders to make a fighting withdrawal if the French intervened. Hitler used the ratification of the Franco-Soviet agreement by the French Chamber of Deputies in late February as a pretext for his troops to enter the Rhineland in March, asserting that the pact was incompatible with the Locarno agreements. As usual he played on his opponents' desire for peace by immediately offering a non-aggression pact to Belgium and France.

   The move was a huge gamble, for France and Poland could launch ninety divisions against Germany, as his generals pointed out; yet the gamble succeeded. The British government under Baldwin was more concerned at checking any action that the French might take than in condemning this latest German breach of the Versailles Settlement. In *The Times* a leader article saw the crisis as 'A chance to rebuild'. Lord Lothian expressed the British view when he commented, 'After all they are only going into their own back garden.' The French government was most reluctant to act on its own, and in any case was informed by the defeatist French military that an offensive operation against the German troops in the Rhineland was impossible. 'The Rhineland crisis', says Donald Watt, 'showed weakness to be embedded in the national will of France.' By her failure to act, she virtually admitted that she was no longer willing to defend the security system which she had been at pains to build since 1918. Sunk deep in a

Maginot mentality, French governments from this point on tended more and more to follow British policies.

The League of Nations had achieved much in the 1920s, but was shaken already by the Japanese invasion of Manchuria in 1931 and the Italian aggression in Africa in 1935. It now was further undermined by Hitler's illegal action. The smaller powers lost faith in the League, and sought security either in neutrality or by attempting to court Germany. Belgium, for example, though still a member of the League of Nations, refused any longer to be a guarantor of the Locarno Treaties. Most significant of all, the remilitarisation of the Rhineland opened the way for all Hitler's later outrages. In his prophecy that the powers would not move against him, he was proved right and his generals were proved wrong. His confidence increased greatly and he felt able to tell the German people, 'I go with the assurance of a sleepwalker on the path providence dictates.' For the next 2 years he would still need to exercise caution while Germany constructed her Rhineland defences. Then, in the event of another conflict, German forces would be poised directly on the French border, while, conversely, the French would be deprived of their former advantage of being able to strike at Germany through a demilitarised zone which was also Germany's industrial heartland.

The year 1936 continued to bring success to the Germans. In July an Austro-German agreement was signed. The German government recognised Austria's sovereignty but in return Austria promised to maintain a foreign policy based on the principle that she was a German state and also to give Austrian Nazis a share of political responsibility. In the next year and a half the Germans used the agreement as a lever by which pressure could be applied on the Austrian government. In August the Nazis won considerable prestige by the way in which they organised the Olympic Games held in Berlin. In November Ribbentrop, who, like Mussolini, had a mania for pacts, signed the anti-Comintern Pact with Japan, in which the partners pledged themselves to defeat the Communist world conspiracy. Italy joined the pact in the following year.

The most important German move after the Rhineland escapade in 1936 was the promise to help General Franco when the Spanish Civil War broke out in July. Germany stood to gain in several directions from such action. In the next 3 years she sent military supplies and men, including the famous Condor Air Legion, thus gaining useful experience in the training of men and the value of equipment such as tanks in battle conditions. Intervention in the war also gave Germany access to Spanish mineral resources, and would counter the threat of a Communist success in Spain. Franco's victory would be a 'Fascist' victory and would give France another frontier to defend in time of war. As the Italians sent large numbers of troops, they were more embroiled in the Spanish Civil War than the Germans, and therefore were less likely to oppose German aims in Austria. At the same time the two 'Fascist' powers were now clearly on the same side, and in November Mussolini referred to their two countries as the 'axis' powers. Hitler hoped that Germany and Italy would form such a powerful front that Britain would be forced to come to terms with the dictators. With this end in view, he sent Ribbentrop to Britain as ambassador in August. 'Arrogant, vain, humourless and spiteful, Ribbentrop was one of the worst choices Hitler ever made for high office,' writes Alan Bullock. It is hardly surprising that the British government did not respond to his overtures for mutual support against Communism.

(e) Gathering momentum, 1937–9

The adoption of the Four Year Plan in 1936 is highly significant as a mark of Hitler's determination to prepare Germany for war. It was appropriate that his choice as supervisor of the plan was Göring, who was regarded as the party's strong man. The Plan itself fell short of its objectives. There was no total mobilisation of the economy and inefficient small units of production were not eliminated, but this does not invalidate the thesis that Hitler saw autarchy as assisting the rapid expansion of the armed forces for short campaigns with limited objectives. When Schacht protested that arms cuts were necessary, Hitler and Göring brushed his advice aside. When they faced opposition from the steel bosses, the Nazi leaders set up a state-owned steel corporation, later known as the Hermann Göring Works.

In November 1937 the military implications of the new policy were spelt out by Hitler at the Hossbach Conference. Five others were present besides Hitler himself and Colonel Hossbach, whose minutes provide us with our information. They were the war minister, von Blomberg, the commander-in-chief of the army, von Fritsch, the commander-in-chief of the navy, Raedar, the airforce chief, Göring, and the foreign minister, Neurath. Hitler declared that Germany needed 'living-space' but would have to reckon with the opposition of two 'hate-inspired' antagonists, Britain and France. Germany's military superiority would last until 1943–5, after which her enemies would begin to catch up with her, and therefore he was resolved to solve Germany's problem by that period at the latest. If France was torn by internal strife or clashed with Italy in the Mediterranean, the opportunity must be taken to overrun Czechoslovakia and Austria. Hitler did not believe that the Western powers would oppose this.

The significance of the meeting, as we have seen, has caused controversy among historians. Its importance may be gauged by the fact that Hitler wished it to be regarded as his last will and testament in the event of his death. 'In its explicitness and its anti-Western rather than anti-Bolshevik framework here was a significant moment in the development of Nazi expansionism,' writes Christopher Thorne. It is no accident that those who protested at Hitler's plans – Neurath, Blomberg and Fritsch – were soon dismissed and replaced by more pliable servants. Strategic plans for war, formerly defensive in character, now aimed at a pre-emptive strike at Czechoslovakia to forestall any effective action by that power in the event of a war in the west. Thus the harangue of November 1937, in the words of E. M. Robertson, marked 'a real turning-point in Hitler's pre-war policy'.

With the Rhineland fortified, Hitler felt that he could adopt a more violent foreign policy, and, as he said at the conference, he wished to strike down his opponents before Germany's military advantage disappeared. But other factors probably played a large part in his thinking. The international situation was now favourable as closer relations with Italy developed, as France appeared to drift towards civil war, and as the purges in the Red Army appeared to make Russia a negligible factor. The conference also reveals Hitler's disillusionment with Britain, as hopes of an alliance with her faded. His own hypochondria is important; he was always preoccupied with his own mortality and wished to accelerate events while he still enjoyed good health. Finally, he was concerned that the German people appeared to be more interested in social and economic matters, and what interest they had in foreign affairs was waning. Committed to rearmament, Hitler knew that he could not satisfy the hopes of the people for higher living standards. Therefore the only way in which unity could be preserved and the weakening of the regime prevented was by an active foreign policy. As Mason has shown, 'the Third Reich had either to set itself new tasks by expanding or . . . cease from being totalitarian'.

(f) Appeasement

One of the reasons for the Nazi commitment to a more violent foreign policy in 1937 was the assumption of British hostility. It is therefore most ironic that in May of that year the statesman most associated with appeasement of Hitler, Neville Chamberlain, became prime minister, replacing the indolent Baldwin, who had evinced little interest in foreign affairs. Appeasement is still a term of abuse, signifying to many people a policy born of cowardice and stupidity. The writer deplores such a facile view while recognising that Chamberlain did possess faults. He was certainly arrogant. Comparing him to Baldwin, Taylor says that he was 'a harder, more practical man, impatient with drift in foreign affairs and confident that he could stop it'. He was also intolerant of opposition and refused to listen to the advice of such colleagues as Eden, who advised caution in his attempts to deal with Hitler. He became blinded to reality by regarding appeasement of Hitler as a mission. He therefore ignored unpalatable facts, such as the sufferings of the Czechs. So desirous was he of peace that he convinced himself that Hitler could be trusted, and as a result the Munich settlement in Christopher Thorne's phrase became 'a study in self-delusion'. Finally, it may be said that Conservatives like Chamberlain had a blind spot about Soviet Russia, whose power they underrated and whose ideology they detested. Chamberlain wrote in his diary in March 1939, 'I must confess to the most profound mistrust of Russia. I have no belief whatever in her ability to maintain an effective offensive, even if she wanted to.'

Yet what moved the British prime minister was a horror of war and the feeling that in any future conflict the devastation would be greater than ever before. The potential of the bomber had been dramatically demonstrated at Guernica in the Spanish Civil War. Therefore war, the ultimate evil, must be avoided at all costs by the peaceful elimination of German grievances. F. N. Northedge writes:

> To this enterprise Chamberlain brought great assets and vices which were the reverse of the assets. He was courageous, energetic, dedicated, austere. No one could doubt that his hatred of war was deeply felt or that he would exert himself to the utmost to avert it. His mind was lucid, logical, tenacious, capable of seeing the drift of an argument or the implication of a proposal with lightning speed.

Chamberlain then was a humane individual; he was also following a rational policy. Britain in the 1930s lacked the power to rule her global empire, which in the Far East was threatened by Japan. Only by concessions in Europe which would secure peace could the reality of British weakness be hidden. With most German governments, such a policy could have borne fruit, but the novel extremism of the Nazi state made its foreign policy incompatible with that of Britain's. Thus the ultimate failure of Chamberlain's policies was inevitable, for it is most doubtful whether any British government could for long have remained at peace with the Third Reich. Perhaps Chamberlain should have realised how unscrupulous Hitler was earlier than he did, but the German leader, who possessed great charm and magnetism when he wished, fooled many intelligent people in his time.

(g) The Anschluss

Perhaps the most un-Wilsonian article in the Versailles Settlement was that forbidding the union of Austrian Germans with Germany. All shades of political opinion in Austria resented the clause, and the difficult postwar years only aggravated this feeling. Only after Hitler came to power did pan-German sentiment lose ground. The Austrian government should at this point have combined with the socialists to crush the Austrian Nazis, but in fact one of the last acts of Dollfuss was to crush the socialists in the civil war of February 1934, a policy that could only strengthen the Austrian Nazi position. After the Austro-German agreement of 1936, Austrian Nazis like Seyss-Inquart entered the government, thus further undermining its real independence.

At the same time a decline in Austria's external protection was taking place. In the abortive Nazi coup of 1934 Mussolini had stood firmly behind Austria; by 1937 Italy and Germany were drawing together, and it was clear to the Nazis after Mussolini's visit to Germany in September that the Italian leader would not again oppose German aims in Austria. In Britain and France feeling was widespread that Germany could not be prevented from swallowing Austria in the near future. In November Lord Halifax visited Germany as Chamberlain's emissary, and told the Nazis that the British government desired a peaceful correction of German grievances; specific mention was made of Austria as well as Czechoslovakia and Danzig. Such well-intentioned naivety was of course an invitation to Hitler to indulge in diplomatic blackmail.

It now appeared to the German leader that the passage of time would bring Austria into Germany, and he told Göring in September 1937 that Germany should avoid any explosion of the Austrian problem in the foreseeable future, but should continue to seek an evolutionary solution. That he did not rule out a swift stroke if the opportunity occurred was then made clear at the Hossbach conference in November, and by early 1938 both Göring and Ribbentrop were urging him to seek an early solution to the Austrian problem.

An opportunity now arose for Hitler in the subversive activities of the Austrian Nazis. In January 1938 Austrian police raided Nazi headquarters in Vienna and discovered plans for an uprising, the repression of which would provide the pretext for intervention by the German army. Realising the threat to his country's independence, the Austrian chancellor, Schuschnigg, decided to seek a meeting with Hitler in an attempt to check the unrest and gain time until the international situation improved in Austria's favour. When he visited Hitler at Berchtesgaden on 12 February he received a rude awakening. Displaying himself as the gangster he was, Hitler subjected the chancellor to a torrent of abuse in which he condemned the high treason of Austrian history. Before he left, Schuschnigg was forced to sign an agreement which provided for the alignment of the foreign policies of Austria and Germany, complete freedom for the Nazis in Austria and the appointment of Seyss-Inquart as minister of the interior and another Nazi, Glaise-Horstenau, as war minister.

Schuschnigg's behaviour on his return home was initially acquiescent. He did nothing to mobilise foreign support for Austria in case such action might enrage Hitler, 'a madman with a mission', as Schuschnigg described him. He also complied with the terms of the agreement, bringing Seyss-Inquart into the cabinet as minister of the interior with authority over the police. Hitler for his part believed that more concessions could be wrung out of the Austrian government and still wished to follow an evolutionary absorption of Austria.

Then in March Schuschnigg decided belatedly on an act of defiance, with an intensity born of despair. Realising that time would mean more Nazi control, he called on his countrymen on 9 March to vote on the following Sunday for 'a free and German, independent and social, Christian and united Austria'. This plebiscite was an attempt to destroy Hitler's argument that the majority of the Austrian people wanted union with Germany. Hitler was taken by surprise and furious at Schuschnigg's temerity, especially as the chancellor's announcement was greeted with enthusiasm in Austria. It seemed likely that the plebiscite would result in a vote of confidence for Schuschnigg, and Hitler was determined to prevent it. The German army was ordered to prepare an improvised invasion of Austria, and when Austrian Nazis managed to force Schuschnigg into resigning, Hitler acted. On 12 March German troops moved into Austria to be greeted with applause. Hitler decided that instead of a union of states under common leadership, Austria would be a province of the Third Reich.

The European powers acquiesced in the aggression. France was without a government during this vital period, while Chamberlain was more interested in dealing with future questions. The British government did protest at the use of force against an independent state, but Neville Henderson, the British Ambassador to Germany, took away any impact that this might have had by agreeing that Schuschnigg had acted with precipitate folly. Hitler's main anxiety was over the possibility of Italian action. He need not have worried; Mussolini had not forgotten the Western disapproval of his Abyssinian adventure and refused to contemplate the idea of any cooperation with the Western powers against Hitler. Hitler's gratitude to Mussolini for his non-intervention was genuine and long-lasting.

As a result of the Anschluss, the balance of power in South Eastern Europe moved sharply in Germany's favour. Control of Austria gave the Germans domination of the Balkans, and the strategic position of Czechoslovakia became grave, for Germany could now threaten her from three directions. Germany also gained 100,000 men for her armed forces, and useful economic resources, mainly in steel capacity, iron ore mines and Austria's foreign exchange reserves. Hitler was elated by the ease of his victory and turned next to the Czechs.

(h) Munich

Of the new states created after the First World War, Czechoslovakia alone had been successful. The country possessed an advanced economy and the constitution, which gave universal suffrage, created a genuine parliamentary regime in which the rights of the minority nationalities were safeguarded. The new republic was fortunate in its presidents, Thomas Masaryk and, from 1935, Eduard Benes.

On the other hand the racial problems of the new state remained serious. The rural Slovaks wished for more autonomy within Czechoslovakia, and their relations with the urban Czechs were uneasy. More vociferous than the Slovaks were the 3 million Sudeten Germans, who continually complained of injustices inflicted on them by the Czechs. In 1933 Konrad Henlein founded the Sudeten German Party, which came to be a fifth column; it was in all essentials a Nazi party and began to demand more independence for Germans as a prelude to incorporation into the Third Reich. Hitler encouraged the activities of the Sudeten German Party, subsidising its efforts at the rate of 15,000 marks a month. He had an intense hatred of the Czechs, a legacy of his Vienna days, when Czech rivalry seemed to threaten German dominance in the Habsburg Empire. Postwar Czechoslovakia was doubly obnoxious to Hitler because it was democratic and a part of the Versailles Treaty. It was also the key to Eastern Europe and must be destroyed.

The Anschluss inflamed the situation. The Czech government felt that its defences were now outflanked, and that it would be more susceptible to economic pressure. For his part Henlein felt bold enough to spell out his demands at Karlsbad in April 1938. He still demanded autonomy rather than complete independence, but he wanted a revision of Czech foreign policy and freedom for the Sudeten Germans to adhere to German ideology. He was under orders from Hitler to step up his demands periodically, so that no negotiated settlement could be arrived at with the Czech government.

The German menace was underrated by Benes. He felt that if Czechoslovakia were threatened, the Western powers in their own interests would be bound to stand by her. 'As a supposition', remarks Christopher Thorne, 'it was entirely reasonable and entirely erroneous.' To be sure, Czechoslovakia seemed secure; all parties had a high regard for her army and fortifications, while France was pledged to assist her if she were attacked.

Yet Czech security was illusory. In France Daladier was now premier and Bonnet was foreign secretary. Both were appeasers who felt that Czechoslovakia could not be saved, and they were glad to see the British take the initiative in the events that were now to unfold. Chamberlain's government was eager to thrust Benes towards agreement with the Sudeten Germans as part of a comprehensive programme of appeasement, after which a new Concert of Europe of the four great powers – Britain, Germany, Italy and France – could be reestablished. It was widely felt in British government circles that in the interests of European peace the Czechs must be coerced or abandoned. As for Russia, her treaty of 1935 bound her to help Czechoslovakia only if France acted first, and in any case the Polish and Rumanian governments made it clear that they would refuse the necessary passage to Russian troops through their countries. The Soviet government did wish to help Czechoslovakia, but when Litvinov, the commissar for foreign affairs, approached the Western powers on the question he found them most unresponsive. Chamberlain still hoped to draw Mussolini away from Hitler rather than cooperate with a Communist regime whose army was of doubtful value after the recent purges. The British and the French held talks in April and agreed to give strong advice to Benes to make all necessary concessions to the Sudeten Germans. At the same time the German government was given private assurance that it would with a little patience gain all that it desired in the Czech question.

In May came an unexpected rebuff for Hitler. Two Sudeten Germans were shot by the Czech police, and as rumours spread of German troop movements, the Czechs mobilised. Both Western powers warned Germany against making any aggressive move against Czechoslovakia, which infuriated Hitler, as in fact no German troop movements had taken place and the foreign press crowed over what they regarded as a German defeat. Now Hitler's desire to crush the Czechs became something of a personal vendetta. At the end of May he confirmed 'his unalterable intention to smash Czechoslovakia by military force in the near future'. Operation Green, which provided for the seizure of Bohemia and Moravia, had already been worked out in detail. It was now envisaged that it would take place in September, and twelve German divisions were stationed on the Czech frontier.

During the summer negotiations between the Czech government and the Sudeten German Party dragged on without result. This impasse, together with the May scare, made Chamberlain all the more anxious to see a speedy agreement reached. He sent Lord Runciman as mediator in the dispute, a high-handed move which shocked the Czechs. Despite favouring the Sudeten Germans, Runciman was unable to solve the deadlock, even though Benes made concessions in August that met all the Karlsbad demands. With Hitler preparing Operation Green and the Hungarian and Polish governments claiming Slovakia and Teschen respectively, the threat to Czechoslovakia was mounting. In early September the crisis seemed near breaking point. Hitler ordered Henlein to break off negotiations with the Czech government, and on 12 September made an inflammatory speech at Nuremberg in which he referred to the Sudeten Germans as 'neither defenceless nor deserted'. This was a direct incitement to the Sudeten Germans to instigate riots, which led to a proclamation of martial law by the Czechs and Henlein's flight to Germany, where he now openly proclaimed the desire of his people to return to the Reich.

The crisis impelled Neville Chamberlain to make the dramatic move of offering to fly to Germany to see Hitler. When the two men met at Berchtesgaden, Hitler insisted that the Sudeten Germans must be incorporated into the Reich but promised to stay his hand until Chamberlain, who agreed in principle to the move, had consulted his colleagues and the French. The British premier received the impression that Hitler 'was a man who could be relied on when he had given his word'. By 21 September the Western powers had 'persuaded' Benes to promise the cession to Germany of those areas of Czechoslovakia with more than 50 per cent Germans.

Chamberlain then met Hitler again at Godesberg on 22 September, and was stunned to learn that the German leader was unwilling to accept the Czech concessions on the pretext that Czech brutality made an immediate German invasion necessary. At their previous meeting it had been understood that any German occupation would only take place after due negotiations with the Czechs and other interested powers. Hitler demanded that the problem must be settled by 1 October. War was now near, for Hitler wanted a military triumph and he kept the tension screwed up by a speech on 26 September full of burning invective against Benes. However, on the 28th he agreed to accept a conference on the matter. On the 27th an armoured division had passed through Berlin before silent crowds, and the apathy displayed by the German public, combined with Italian representations, probably made Hitler change his mind. In any case it was apparent that he would make considerable gains at any conference.

In Britain Chamberlain had broadcast to the nation on the 27th and referred to the Czech crisis as 'a quarrel in a far away country between people of whom we know nothing'. Nevertheless the forces were put on a war footing. The news that Hitler had agreed to a conference reached the prime minister as he was speaking to the Commons. His announcement of Hitler's concession made virtually the whole House of Commons cheer in hysterical relief.

The conference to which the Czechs and the Russians were not invited was duly held at Munich, between Germany, Britain, Italy and France. Agreement was reached by 30 September. The Sudetenland was to be occupied by the Germans by 10 October up to a line determined by an international commission. After Polish and Hungarian claims were settled, the four powers would guarantee the remainder of the Czech state. Before he left, Chamberlain persuaded

Hitler to sign a declaration affirming the intention of Britain and Germany never to go to war with each other again, and on his arrival home he told an enthusiastic crowd, 'I believe it is peace for our time.'

The consequences of Munich were immense. Czechoslovakia lost Teschen to Poland and South Ruthenia to Hungary. Germany gained virtually all the Czech fortifications, and territory which included 800,000 Czechs. Czechoslovakia lost 11,000 square miles of territory and 70 per cent of her iron and steel capacity, including the Skoda arms factory at Pilsen. She was now helpless, and her army of thirty-five divisions was removed from the scales of European power, which moved decisively in Germany's favour.

The Western capitulation to Hitler had serious consequences in other ways. The Soviet government now believed that France and Britain would always be weak and unreliable, and it began to entertain seriously the idea of doing a deal with Germany. As Hildebrand says, 'the foundations of the Nazi-Soviet Pact of the 23rd August, 1939 were laid in Munich'. Western inactivity was also noted by the Japanese government, and it was soon to announce plans for a New Order in East Asia. Hitler's prestige rose to new heights in Germany, though he was angry at being robbed of his military triumph. 'That fellow Chamberlain has spoiled my entry into Prague,' he muttered. However, he now felt sure that the democracies would never oppose him, and aimed to absorb the rest of Czechoslovakia in the near future. Finally, Hitler's success at Munich disheartened the German opposition to his rule, led by Beck, Halder and Canaris.

(i) The final disillusionment

Munich had demonstrated how stubbornly Chamberlain was prepared to pursue his mission of peace, but his faith in Hitler was soon to be shattered. Germany repeatedly procrastinated over signing the guarantee of the remainder of the Czech state. Chamberlain and Halifax hoped to moderate Hitler by persuading Mussolini to counsel caution. With this end in view they visited Rome in January 1939, but they merely won Mussolini's contempt and further inclined him towards a full military alliance with Germany.

Meanwhile the rump state of Czechoslovakia found that its real freedom of action was negligible. The Slovaks were now demanding more autonomy, and in March their leaders, Tiso and Durcansky, went to Hitler for help in the matter. Seeing a further opportunity for undermining the Czech state, Hitler bullied the Slovak leaders into drawing up a draft declaration of independence and an appeal for German help. With the situation deteriorating, the aged President Hacha of Czechoslovakia visited Hitler on 15 March to see what could be preserved. He was so violently upbraided by Hitler that he fainted. When he recovered he was made to sign an agreement putting Czechoslovakia in Hitler's hands to preserve order.

German troops now moved into Bohemia and Moravia while Hungarian troops moved into Ruthenia. On the 16th Tiso requested Germany to assume a protectorate over Slovakia. Again Hitler was able to claim to have acted within the bounds of legality, as he merely 'complied' with the requests of the Czechs and Slovaks. There was no question of Western intervention, despite the guarantees made at Munich. Yet Hitler's latest act had at last aroused not only the British government but the Commons and the public as well.

That the dictators would only understand force seemed fully proved by two further aggressions. In late March Germany seized the Lithuanian port of Memel and Hitler visited it on the battleship *Deutschland*; it was to be his last bloodless territorial gain. The recent German successes had incensed Mussolini, who remarked querulously that 'every time Hitler occupies a country he sends me a message'. In the words of Christopher Thorne, 'it remained only for the jackal to ape its master'. Mussolini, eager to win back the approval of the Italian public by a new success, sent troops into Albania in April on the pretext of restoring order.

(j) Danzig and war

The next German target was only too clearly Poland. The loss to Poland of Danzig, the Polish Corridor and part of Silesia was more resented by Germans than any other part of the Versailles Treaty. Ribbentrop raised the Danzig and Polish Corridor questions in October 1938. As the Poles refused to concede anything, his tone, at first friendly, became threatening, and in early 1939 tension between the two countries increased. Therefore in April the British proposed an unconditional defence pact with Poland, followed by similar pledges to Rumania and Greece. Chamberlain's promise to Poland was striking in that for the first time Britain was guaranteeing a state in Eastern Europe. Hitler was enraged but still regarded the British guarantee as bluff, and indeed the irony of the situation was considerable, for the British were guaranteeing the country they were least able to help effectively. Hitler now allowed the tension to relax so that the British and French might scale down their obligations to Poland.

What was really required for an effective guarantee of Poland was alliance with Soviet Russia, which was now courted by both sides. Negotiations between the Western powers and Russia began in April but were carried on with a lack of sincerity by both parties. Stalin suspected the West of trying to engineer a Russo-German war and kept alive the possiblity of an agreement with Hitler. The Western powers wanted a superficial rather than a real agreement with Russia merely to impress Hitler, as they still disliked the whole concept of a Communist alliance. Thus it was that the British showed no sense of urgency in the negotiations, even sending a mission to Russia by sea in August. The Russian foreign minister was now Molotov, who wanted a firm British commitment or nothing. Negotiations finally broke down on 21 August over the Polish refusal to allow the Red Army into Poland in the event of a German attack. The Polish hatred of Russia was intense. 'With the Germans we risk losing our liberty,' said Beck, the Polish foreign minister, 'with the Russians we lose our souls.' Learning the wrong lesson from the mistakes of the Czechs, he was resolved to refuse any concessions to either Germany or Russia.

Faced with Polish intransigence, Hitler decided in April to smash Poland in the near future, and Operation White, the plan for the invasion of Poland, was prepared to take effect on 1 September. His confidence grew in May with the conclusion of a firm alliance with Italy, the Pact of Steel. Based on the German draft, the pact pledged the two nations to support each other if one 'became involved in hostilities with another Power or Powers'. It was in effect an offensive alliance, though Ribbentrop assured the nervous Italians that there would be no war for 4 or 5 years. In fact the day after the pact was signed Hitler harangued his generals on the need to smash Poland at the first suitable opportunity. By August it was clear to Mussolini and Ciano how far they had been duped by the Germans. Ciano wrote in his diary of a meeting with Ribbentrop at which the German foreign secretary declared that even the cession by Poland of Danzig and the Polish Corridor would not suffice. ' "We want war," he said, gazing at me with his cold metallic eyes.'

War was made virtually certain by an event that astonished the world – the conclusion of the Nazi-Soviet Pact in August. The West had assumed that such a pact was impossible in view of Hitler's long-standing hatred of Bolshevism. 'The factor they overlooked', explains Alan Bullock, 'was Hitler's utter lack of scruple and his skill as a power politician.' He did not relinquish his long-term aim of attacking Russia, but he saw that a temporary alliance would assist in the destruction of Poland. The two countries had begun to move closer together after Munich, on Soviet initiative, and by May 1939 serious negotiations were under way. By August the Russians were offering a non-aggression pact, though they wished for a careful discussion of details first. This did not suit the Germans who, in view of the September deadline for their invasion of Poland, were in a fever of impatience to settle the matter fully. Ribbentrop persuaded Hitler on 20 August to send a telegram to Stalin requesting permission for the German foreign secretary to go to Russia to sign the pact. The Russians agreed and the pact was signed on 23 August. Hitler's need for a rapid conclusion of the pact and his fear that Russia might come to an agreement with the West enabled Stalin to drive a hard bargain. Finland, Esthonia, Latvia and Eastern Poland were to fall in the Russian sphere of influence, while Lithuania and Western and Central Poland would be in the German sphere of influence.

Hitler declared that the pact was his masterstroke, which would enable him to eliminate Poland without the intervention of the Western powers, who would now, he assumed, realise that the Polish position was beyond help. The Russians in fact were gambling on the opposite, and Stalin warned Ribbentrop that 'Britain would wage war craftily and stubbornly'. The Russian leader hoped that the pact would prevent the old Soviet nightmare – a combined European attack on Russia. Thus Ulam believes that 'the agreement and the steps leading to it represent the quintessence of Stalin's diplomacy'. Some historians, however, condemn the Russian move as appeasement of Hitler, and point to the way it made war inevitable. 'Stalin gave the green light to aggression in 1939,' asserts Snell, who argues that the pact not only sealed Poland's fate but brought nearer a German attack on Russia.

Hitler's determination to attack Poland was now firm, and 26 August was the date fixed for the invasion. Two disappointments in fact made him delay for a few days. Against his expectations the British ratified the Anglo-Polish treaty, and Neville Chamberlain reiterated his determination to stand by the Poles. Then the Italians, realising the implications of the Nazi-Soviet Pact, told Hitler that they could only support Germany in a general war if they received huge stocks of war materials. Hitler's nerve was shaken but not broken; he postponed the attack until 1 September in a final attempt to undermine British support for Poland by offering supposedly more moderate terms to the Poles.

This guile failed to work, and on 1 September German troops invaded Poland on the pretext of Polish frontier violations, which were in fact rigged by the Nazis themselves. The French and British governments after some hesitation demanded the evacuation of Polish territory. As no German reply was received, the two Western powers declared war on 3 September.

Germany was quite well prepared for war by the autumn of 1939. The peacetime strength of the army had reached fifty-two divisions, which on general mobilisation could be expanded to 103 divisions. She now possessed a considerable navy and 3,000 aircraft. After Hitler's diplomatic successes, the morale of the German armed forces was now high. Yet Hitler would have been wiser to slow down his triumphal progress. By 1938 he had transformed Germany's international position and could have consolidated his gains. Instead he pressed on and drove other European powers into a reluctant coalition against him. It was this inability to stop that was to destroy him, but, as Alan Bullock says, he was 'already on the way to that assumption of his own infallibility which marked the deterioration of his judgment'.

(4) The coming of the Great Pacific War, 1937–41

Tensions between the USA and Japan led to the fatal denouement at Pearl Harbor, the main American naval base in the Pacific, on 7 December 1941. The root cause was the desire of Japan to secure economic independence and a greater degree of authority in Asia and the Pacific. Yet it would be wrong to view Japan as from the first determined on the use of aggressive means to achieve these objectives. Japanese ministers would have preferred to avoid war with the USA and Britain, but were prepared to face it if in their judgement it became unavoidable. The emperor, Hirohito, was more sceptical about the wisdom of such a war than his ministers, but even the army leaders, while more eager for war than the civilians, were racked by doubts. They believed that if they did not go to war in 1941, their position would deteriorate and they would fall slowly but irretrievably under the economic control of the USA. As Irye explains, 'Japan had the choice of doing nothing which would lead to its collapse in a few years or going to war while there was at least a 70 or 80 per cent chance of initial victory.' In choosing the latter course Japan forged a coalition of powers against herself and ensured ultimate defeat.

Japan had not been such a disturber of international peace before. In the 1920s Japanese leaders sought to establish their country as a respected member of the great powers. Japan signed the treaties arising from the Washington Conference of 1921–2. In the naval disarmament treaty, the Japanese navy was limited to three-fifths of the size of the American and British navies, but the treaty did recognise Japan as one of the three foremost naval powers. Another treaty signed by the three states plus France provided for joint consultation whenever international stability was threatened. Most importantly, the Nine Power treaty, signed by the USA, Britain, Japan, France, Italy, Belgium, the Netherlands, Portugal and China, established the principle of international cooperation in China to maintain that country's independence.

The Washington Conference system worked for a few years in the sense of bringing stability to the Asia–Pacific region. However, as China began to modernise with the help of Western capital, groups in Japan were driven to desperation by an international system that made concessions to China while leaving Japan at the mercy of fluctuations in world trade. Their solution was to seize Manchuria in 1931, the first serious challenge to the postwar international system in the Asia–Pacific region (see Chapter 13). The Japanese were successful in incorporating Manchuria into their empire, but, as Irye has pointed out, the action was 'the first of a series of miscalculations that were to bring about its steady isolation in world affairs'. China's leaders were able to point to their country as a wronged member of the international community. In 1931 and for years afterwards the powers were too obsessed with their own domestic problems, mainly unemployment, to go beyond verbal criticism of Japan in the League of Nations. Such criticism was sufficient to provoke Japan into leaving the League in 1933, and Tokyo also abrogated the Washington naval treaty in 1934. Japan further alienated the Western powers by signing the anti-Comintern Pact with Germany in 1936.

Occasionally in the 1930s the Japanese government attempted to follow more conciliatory policies. In January 1937 the new Hayashi government appointed Sato Naotake as foreign minister. Sato believed strongly in an open international system from which Japan would benefit by increased industrialisation and exports (as was to occur after the war). But the Hayashi government was weak and resigned in June, to be replaced by a government under Prince Konoe Fuminuro, who wholeheartedly supported control of Manchuria as a means of making available its rich resources to Japan. In any case Sato, even had he survived in office, would have faced the intractable opposition of the army.

Japan's more aggressive stance had led to her isolation by the time the European war broke out. In July 1937 came the Marco Polo bridge incident in Peking (a clash between Japanese and Chinese soldiers). It was an isolated incident which could have been contained if the Japanese and Chinese Nationalist governments had wished, but the Konoe government gave way in the face of clamour for action by officials, politicians, businessmen and the press, and sent fresh divisions to the area. Similarly Chiang Kai-shek, the Chinese Nationalist leader, took a hard line over the incident, feeling that China was in better shape than before to resist Japan and might even obtain help from Germany or Russia. Chiang in fact miscalculated, Japanese troops soon took control of the Peking–Tientsin region and in August fighting spread to Shanghai.

The renewal of war caused the Japanese government real problems. It threatened to drain resources away from military preparedness against other countries, and raised the question of what precise objectives the Japanese were fighting for in China, for the country was too huge and populous to swallow in its entirety. In addition, certain incidents increased tensions with the USA. In December 1937 Nanking fell to Japanese forces and many Chinese people were murdered. The day before Nanking fell, an American navy gunboat, the *Panay*, busy evacuating Americans from Nanking, was fired on by Japanese planes and sunk. A rapid Japanese apology hardly repaired the damage to American–Japanese relations. Roosevelt now instigated Anglo-American staff talks with the idea of a joint blockade of Japan.

The appointment of Ribbentrop as German foreign minister in February 1938 brought some temporary relief from isolation for Japan. German policy had been previously pro-China, but now became supportive of Japan as a fellow Fascist state fighting communism. Yet in other respects 1938 was a frustrating year for Japan. The war in China spread and became more costly, and the Konoe government feared that it might cause a war with Russia and the Anglo-Americans. Therefore attempts were made to negotiate peace terms with the Chinese Nationalists, but no compromise could be reached. In August a clash between Russia and Japan on the border of Russian Manchuria and Japanese Korea seemed to indicate a serious danger of Russian intervention.

The Western powers were unwilling to appease Japan, as they had Germany, because Japan was more transparently aggressive and had no ethnic claim to Chinese territory as Germany did to Austria and the Sudetenland. They believed that European problems were more likely to cause a world war than the Asian situation. The USA was also more prepared to take action in Asia than in Europe. Opinion polls indicated that the American people were far more willing to take a stand on the Sino-Japanese war than on any European issue, with three-quarters of the people polled expressing sympathy for China. The Roosevelt regime could not therefore come to any agreement with Japan, short of the latter's withdrawal from China, an unrealistic goal. Moreover there was a growth of opposition in the USA to the increasing American trade with Japan. Japan's dependence on American scrap iron and steel was particularly noticeable, and such deliveries were pictured as being turned into Japanese weapons for use in China. This revelation began a movement to stop the shipment of raw materials and arms to Japan. Former secretary of state Henry L. Stimson became head of the American Committee for Non-Participation in Japanese Aggression, and called for an embargo of war materials.

The Japanese government, faced with the option of continuing the war in China or making major concessions, retained a provocative stance. In November 1938 Konoe formally renounced the Washington treaty structure by defining Japan's objective as the construction of a new order in East Asia. The USA, which supported the Open Door principle in China, interpreted this as a sign that Japan was bent on permanent control of China, and the American government made a small loan to the Nationalists as an indication of American support.

Japan's relations with the Soviet Union became more acrimonious as a result of a more serious clash at Nomonhan on the Russian–Manchuria border, which led to heavy fighting from July to September. The Soviet forces acquitted themselves well, as Stalin deployed his best troops in the hope that a strong stance would deter the Japanese from making a full alliance with Germany. The Soviet troops inflicted heavy casualties on the Japanese in August, and in the same month the announcement of the Nazi–Soviet Pact meant that a double blow to Japanese strategy had occurred.

At the same time American pressure on Japan increased. In June the US government abrogated its 1911 treaty of commerce with Japan, the abrogation to take effect in 6 months after notification. The American move could not be brushed off as of no consequence, because the USA was the biggest supplier to Japan outside Asia of scrap iron, steel, oil and other essential commodities. Thus by the outbreak of the European war Japan's position had deteriorated seriously. Japanese policy had been based on obtaining a German alliance against Russia; the Nazi–Soviet Pact had taken Japanese officials by surprise and no alternative policy was available.

Accordingly from September 1939 Japan was forced to pursue a diplomatic revolution. With the German victories in Europe in 1939–40, aided and abetted by the Soviet Union, Tokyo made a conscious decision to conclude an alliance with Germany and Italy and effect a rapprochement with the Soviet Union. A coalition against the Western democracies would be established, and if a deal with the Soviets was reached, Russian aid to China might be curtailed and the Chinese forced to make peace on terms favourable to Japan. Such Japanese thinking underestimated the resistance by the Chinese themselves as the real cause of the long war. They preferred to blame Soviet aid for continuing Chinese resistance. As a first step towards a rapprochement with Russia a ceasefire was signed in Moscow in September.

Irye criticises Japan's leaders for failing to think through all the implications of their grand design. Even in 1939, Japan's economic and political systems had much in common with those of the Western powers, in that political parties and an independent press still existed. Furthermore, despite dreams of autarchy, Japan was still very dependent on imported oil, copper, scrap iron and machine tools from the USA, especially after September 1939, when supplies from Germany were cut off. However, the defeats suffered by Britain, France and the Netherlands encouraged Japanese leaders to believe that Japan should move south against the vulnerable Western colonies in Asia.

Such views were not universally held. In late 1939 Admiral Nomura Kichisaburo attempted to effect a rapprochement with the USA, fearful that if Japan was seen to join an anti-democratic coalition, the USA would continue to tighten its economic restrictions on Japan and increase its aid to China. But Nomura could only offer modest concessions, such as the opening of the Yangtze river to foreign shipping, when what the Americans wanted was Japanese evacuation of China. Therefore the American government responded coolly to Nomura's overtures, talks broke down in December and the abrogation of the existing trade treaty went into effect in January 1940.

Meanwhile fierce fighting in China from December 1939 on led to more Japanese troops being sent to China. Once again the hopes of a knockout blow proved illusory, as the Japanese found themselves facing much larger numbers of Chinese soldiers. By early 1940 850,000 Japanese troops were stationed in China in a war which seemed likely to drag on now that more American aid was reaching the Chinese Nationalists.

American determination to check Japan was obvious in two other ways in 1940. The Roosevelt government was determined to help Britain for a number of reasons. If Britain was defeated, the USA would be a lone island in a world dominated by force. But British collapse would mean Japanese acquisition of British possessions in the Far East – Burma, Hong-Kong, Singapore and Malaya, with their resources of tin and rubber. Accordingly American aid to Britain increased in 1940.

The second signal sent by the USA was its decision in the spring of 1940 to station the bulk of its fleet at Pearl Harbor in Hawaii. But Japan was not deterred from putting pressure on the Dutch authorities in the East Indies in May to guarantee supplies of tin, rubber and oil to Japan, so that Japanese dependence on the USA would be reduced. Similar Japanese pressure forced Vichy France and Britain to stop their supplies to China. Such Japanese actions hardened rather than decreased American determination to help Britain.

Increased American help to Britain was taken by the Japanese as a clear sign that the USA would oppose their domination of South East Asia, and accordingly opinion hardened in Japan as well as in the USA. In July 1940 Prince Konoe became premier again, determined to create an Asian bloc against the Western powers and win a German alliance and a rapprochement with Russia. He appointed as foreign minister Matsuoka Yosuke, a keen pro-German revisionist who believed that a clash between Japan and the USA was inevitable. In addition, General Tojo Hideki and Admiral Yoshida Zengo became war and navy ministers respectively. They believed that Japan should incorporate the Western colonies in Asia with Japan's new order. The American response to the appointment of such a hard-line cabinet was to put an embargo on aviation fuel, lubricating oil and some scrap iron.

The Japanese did succeed in joining a tripartite pact with Italy and Germany in September 1940, but it failed to weaken American or British morale. However, the Japanese signing of the pact showed that Japanese leaders saw a war against the USA as more and more likely. They believed that the choice was between succumbing to American pressures and accepting Western domination of the Pacific, or resisting them and establishing a new regional order. To the

Americans, the signing of the Axis pact by Japan confirmed their perceptions of Japanese ambitions to dominate South East Asia. When Japan occupied Northern Indo-China to try to cut off supplies to China, Washington immediately embargoed the export of all types of scrap iron to Japan in October. In November Roosevelt won a third term in office and explicitly supported more aid to Britain in the form of lend-lease and all aid short of war. In December he declared that the USA must become the great arsenal of democracy. Extra loans were given to China and an American volunteer air force, the Flying Tigers, was set up for service in China.

In Japan the support for a southern strategy gained strength, because navy leaders like Admiral Yamamoto Isoruku favoured it, as it would allow the navy to play a larger role. Yamamoto argued that Japan needed the resources of the Dutch East Indies, and if they could be obtained peacefully, so much the better. However, the Dutch might resist if they knew that they could count on Anglo-American support. If a Pacific War then resulted, Japan should then first strike at the Philippines.

In March 1941 Matsuoka visited Europe in a further attempt to create a revisionist bloc of Italy, Japan, Russia and Germany against the Anglo-Americans. He hoped to repair the growing rift between Germany and Russia, unaware that Hitler had already decided to attack the Soviet Union in the spring. Matsuoka gained nothing from his visit to Berlin but he did conclude a 5-year neutrality treaty with the Soviet Union in April. The bankruptcy of Matsuoka's grand strategy of a bloc of four powers was laid bare in June when Germany attacked Russia, and once again the Japanese leadership was forced to consider alternatives. One option – a rapprochement with the USA – would have called for concessions which Matsuoka and the military would not accept. Matsuoka's solution was to stay in the Axis camp and declare war on Russia, and he abrogated the recently signed neutrality pact. Hoping to keep its options open, the Japanese government decided to try again to end the China war and prepare for either a war against Russia or expansion south.

As far as the USA was concerned, Japanese moves north or south were undesirable. The Americans were angered by Japanese occupation of Southern Indo-China in July and were not mollified by Konoe's dismissal of Matsuoka. In retaliation for the latest Japanese transgression, the USA and Britain froze Japanese assets and increased aid to China, while, by the device of processing export licences slowly, the Americans instituted a de facto embargo on oil. The USA opposed any Japanese attack on Russia, because this could lead to a Nazi victory in Europe.

By August Japan accepted that it would be unwise to attack the Soviet Union, given the strong Russian resistance to the German attack and Japan's inadequate military resources. Japanese strategy now focused on a conflict with the ABCD powers (America, Britain, China and the Dutch). At an important meeting on 9 August, described by Irye as 'the point of no return' as far as Japanese–American relations were concerned, both civilian and military leaders reasoned that after a year of the oil embargo Japan would have to find alternative sources of supply in South East Asia. Military action would be needed, and this would inevitably draw in the Dutch and Anglo-Americans. For Japan to act effectively, her navy would have to move before its oil reserve was used up in 4 months' time.

Precisely what plan of attack should be used now divided army and navy leaders. The army wished to attack Malaya and the East Indies, while the navy, whose primary worry was the USA, preferred to attack the Philippines first. As a way out of the impasse, the navy broached another possibility – an air attack on the US fleet at Pearl Harbor. Admiral Yamamoto, commander-in-chief of the combined fleet, and his colleagues believed that Japan had no chance of winning a prolonged conflict against the USA and its allies, but the elimination of the American fleet at Hawaii would give Japan a temporary tactical advantage and enable her to build up a defensible empire.

The Japanese still hoped to avoid war with the USA, but the enunciation of the Atlantic Charter by Churchill and Roosevelt after their meeting off Newfoundland between 9 and 14 August was a further blow to Japanese hopes, because it contained a specific warning against further military action by Japan. On 6 September a joint meeting of civilian and military leaders decided that Japan was to be ready for war by late October, and if no diplomatic settlement had been arrived at with the ABCD powers by then, war would be the only option. This decision was virtually a declaration of war by Japan, as a diplomatic settlement acceptable to her leaders would have included an end to Western aid to China and military preparations in the Pacific, as well as a restoration of full trading relations with Japan in terms of renewed supplies of steel and oil. The Japanese leaders appreciated that the war was a gamble, but to do nothing would result in further Anglo-American control of Japan, while war gave a 70 per cent chance of initial victory, which might constitute total British defeat against the Axis powers, a break-up of the American alliance and possible American withdrawal from a war with a strengthened Japan.

The meeting did sanction one last diplomatic effort, but the military leaders, including the war minister Tojo, were sceptical of its chances of success and prepared plans for a simultaneous attack on Hong-Kong, Malaya, the Philippines, Guam, the Dutch East Indies and the American fleet at Hawaii. Meanwhile Japanese-American conversations between Nomura and Hull continued to founder over the issue of Japan's presence in China, which Tojo and the army would not give up. To Tojo Japanese possession of China lay at the very core of the new order, or Co-Prosperity Sphere, which Japan hoped to develop, and he overrode doubts expressed by navy leaders, who suggested concessions in China to avoid war with the USA. The premier Konoe was thus left isolated in his attempts to avoid war, and resigned on 16 October.

A new cabinet was formed under Tojo, a development that for the ABCD powers confirmed the ascendancy of the military in Japanese politics. Tojo was an efficient military man who had loyally represented the interests of the army. He now tried to show a wider vision, and appointed as foreign minister the veteran Togo Shigenori, a man genuinely in favour of a rapprochement with the USA. Nevertheless the military planning continued, and on 1 November the military leaders gave the politicians until 30 November to find a diplomatic solution.

But American policy was similarly rigid and necessarily so. Through 'Magic', their code-breaking device, top American officials understood Japanese desperation, but could not make concessions which would weaken support for China, for such concessions would alarm the British and the Dutch as well as the Chinese Nationalists, all of whom wished to see continued firm American opposition to Japanese expansion. On 26 November Cordell Hull, the American secretary of state, laid down the basic conditions for an agreement with Japan. As these included Japanese evacuation of both China and Indo-China, the Japanese government mistakenly regarded Hull's declaration as an ultimatum. On 30 November Hirohito formally endorsed the decision for war, which was adopted at a meeting of war leaders on 1 December.

Already on 26 November the Japanese naval task force had left on its long journey to Hawaii. Convinced that only a surprise attack would bring success, the Japanese did not want to give any inkling of ending negotiations until the very last moment. Through 'Magic', the American government knew that war was imminent, and warned American commanders on Hawaii and the Philippines that war must be expected. On 7 December Japanese planes attacked Pearl Harbor. Unfortunately for Japanese honour, the telegram declaring war on the USA was delayed, and reached Hull 50 minutes after the attack on Pearl Harbor took place, and equally unfortunately for American military prestige, the attack took the Americans by surprise. The question whether this was wilful neglect has been much debated. Proponents of a conspiracy theory have blamed the Roosevelt government for keeping officials on Hawaii ignorant of crucial information, so as to ensure that Japan fired the first shots, which would then allow an American declaration of war backed by a united public. In fact an American destroyer sank a Japanese submarine in Hawaii hours before the aerial attack took place, so that the authorities there had sufficient information on which to make the necessary inferences.

As Liddell Hart has shown, the Pearl Harbor coup did bring advantages to Japan. It put the US Pacific Fleet out of action, thus enabling Japan's operations in the South West Pacific to be implemented successfully. In the next 6 months a defensive ring was established. But the Japanese planes had missed the American aircraft carriers and oil tanks, and the surprise attack aroused fury in the USA and united public opinion behind Roosevelt's declaration of war. Japanese strategy generally was to be proved too optimistic. It underestimated the capacity and determination of the USA and Britain to launch speedy counter-attacks despite initial disasters. Secondly, it overestimated German power to immobilise Britain in Europe, and exaggerated Japan's own ability to fight a multi-national war, which required a comprehensive strategy quite beyond the ability of the service chiefs to implement.

FURTHER READING

Bell, P. M. H., *The Origins of the Second World War in Europe*, Longmans, London, 1986

Carr, R., *Modern Spain*, OUP, Oxford, 1981

Carr, W., *Arms, Autarky and Aggression*, Edward Arnold, London, 1972

Dallek, R., *Franklin D. Roosevelt and American Foreign Policy*, OUP, Oxford, 1979

Fuchser, L., *Neville Chamberlain and Appeasement*, W.W. Norton, 1982

Henig, R., *The League of Nations*, Oliver and Boyd, Edinburgh, 1973

Irye, A., *The Origins of the Second World War in Asia and the Pacific*, Longmans, London, 1987

Middlemas, K., *The Diplomacy of Illusion*, Weidenfeld and Nicolson, London, 1972

Robertson, E. M. (ed.), *The Origins of the Second World War*, Macmillan, London, 1971

Taylor, A. J. P., *The Origins of the Second World War*, Penguin, Harmondsworth, 1963

Taylor, T., *Munich: The Price of Peace*, Hodder and Stoughton, London, 1979

Walters, F. P., *A History of the League of Nations*, OUP, London, 1952

Weinberg, G. L., *The Foreign Policy of Hitler's Germany*, 2 volumes, Chicago University Press, Chicago, 1980

QUESTIONS

1. Why did the League of Nations prove ineffectual in preventing war?

2. 'The Abyssinian crisis shattered the League as a peacekeeping body and paved the way for Hitler's domination of Europe' (Ruth Henig). Discuss.

3. Critically analyse the international importance of the Spanish Civil War.

4. According to A. J. P. Taylor, the Second World War was implicit since the moment when the First World War ended. Do you agree?

5. Was Germany's path to war in 1939 guided more by opportunism than a master plan?

6. What were the attractions to Britain of Appeasement in the 1930s?

7. What pressures led Japan to implement a more aggressive foreign policy by 1931?

8. Why did Japan attack the USA at Pearl Harbor in December 1941?

10
The Second World War

(a) The early German victories, 1939–40

On the outbreak of war Germany was stronger than any other belligerent power, for, as A. S. Milward has pointed out, 'no nation had ever previously spent so vast a sum in peacetime on preparation for war'. Hitler could mobilise approximately 5 million men, though he did not enjoy numerical superiority. Against his 105 divisions, the French could muster 94, the Poles 40 and the British 4. Germany's advantage lay in her more modern equipment, particularly the six armoured (panzer) divisions, in which were incorporated most of her 3,200 tanks. The French and the British had the same strength in tanks on paper, but their tanks were inferior to those of Germany.

The two sides had similar numbers of planes, but the German Luftwaffe was organised to support advancing ground forces and its light bombers and fighters were of high quality. The British fighters – the Spitfire and the Hurricane – were good, but their bombers lacked sufficient range, while the French airforce in general was out of date. Only on the sea did the Western powers enjoy real superiority over Germany.

Germany's opponents made a cardinal error in assuming that the new war would resemble the First World War, in that the Germans could be ground down by a war of attrition. They were soon to see the error of this assumption. In 10 days the German armies had reached Warsaw after the Luftwaffe had prepared the way by destroying the Polish airforce and disrupting communications. The fate of the Poles was sealed when, on 17 September, the Russian armies struck from the east, and by the end of the month all Poland had been overrun. Giving another sign that peace with Britain was a long-held desire, Hitler called on the Western powers to accept the situation and come to terms, but his peace offer was ignored.

There now occurred a period of inactivity on the Western front which has won the contemptuous description of the 'phony war'. Instead of launching an offensive, the Western powers stood on the defensive behind the fortifications of the Maginot Line, and Hitler was given time to shift his troops from the east to the Western front, which had previously been lightly fortified. He had envisaged a

German offensive in the West in November, but it was to be rescheduled twenty-nine times, a vivid example of Hitler's incapacity for making a firm decision.

The centre of interest now shifted east to the Baltic. In November Russia attacked Finland and by March 1940 had imposed harsh terms on the Finns, who had to cede Karelia, territory to the south and west of Lake Ladoga, and islands in the Gulf of Finland; yet the Finns fought with courage and inflicted heavy casualties on the Russian troops, an achievement which made Hitler even more disdainful of Russian fighting capacity.

Meanwhile Germany and her opponents had been attempting to persuade the Scandinavian states to take a more active interest in the war, but they stuck resolutely to neutrality. The British First Lord of the Admiralty, Winston Churchill, wanted the Norwegian coast mined to prevent supplies of iron ore going to Germany. By the time the Cabinet approved the plan, it was too late. Germany derived 51 per cent of her iron ore from Sweden and Norway, and in April 1940 German troops invaded Denmark and Norway to safeguard these supplies. Again Hitler refused to listen to the objections of his generals, who opposed the dispersion of German troops. Denmark was forced to surrender within hours, but the Norwegians resisted with Allied help. The British took Narvik in June and sank three German cruisers and ten destroyers, but the larger objective – the interruption of supplies of iron ore to Germany – was not gained. With Hitler's offensive in the West in June, the British had to abandon Narvik, and Norway fell under Nazi control.

By May Germany had massed 134 divisions on the Western front against 94 French and 10 British divisions, to which were added, when the Low Countries were invaded, 22 Belgian and 8 Dutch divisions. The German advantages in armour and planes were to prove decisive. Franco-British relations were far from harmonious, with continual French demands for more British troops and planes in France. On 10 May the German offensive in the west began with a drive into the Netherlands, and the Dutch surrendered in 5 days after the bombing of Rotterdam had killed 900 civilians. German troops also moved into Belgium and in a surprise move German armour crossed the Meuse to strike through the Ardennes. By 20 May Guderian's mechanised columns had smashed through the French lines at Sedan and reached the Channel. The Allied armies were now in chaos and in June the British government had to authorise its commander, General Gort, to evacuate his troops from Dunkirk. In an operation lasting 8 days 200,000 British and 130,000 French soldiers were rescued from the Dunkirk beaches by a motley collection of craft. Hitler neglected an opportunity to send in German tanks to finish off the Allied troops, because he assumed that the task could be left to the Luftwaffe. As Gordon Wright has noted, his error 'enabled a salvage operation of inestimable military and psychological importance to be carried out'. After it a new mood of national unity prevailed in Britain.

But nothing could save France. On 16 June the French government, now under Marshal Pétain, asked Germany for armistice terms, which were signed a week later at Compiègne in the same railway car used for the German capitulation in November 1918. Hitler literally danced for joy. His terms were deliberately moderate, for he hoped to keep a French government nominally in control of much of France. Therefore the Germans only occupied the north-west of France, leaving the Vichy regime in control of the remaining three-fifths of the country.

To an extent the astonishing collapse of France is to be explained by prewar developments. The decline of the French economy in the 1930s meant that attempts to modernise the armed forces were constrained by lack of finance, while the polarisation of politics meant that France entered the war a deeply divided society. Divisions were made worse by the Nazi–Soviet Pact, which meant that all French Communists were automatically suspect. Many were interned, and acts of sabotage occurred in armaments factories.

The weakness in the Anglo-French alliance also contributed to the French capitulation. The two governments never developed a truly coordinated system of cooperation. Symbolic of the lack of liaison was Churchill's horror on 16 May when he learned for the first time on a visit to Paris that there was no French strategic reserve to counter the German advance. The alliance broke down under the strain of defeat; the evacuation of British troops at Dunkirk and the British refusal to send more fighter squadrons to France led the French to believe that they owed their ally nothing.

Nevertheless military factors were fundamental. French thinking was conditioned by victory in the First World War, but one bought at enormous cost in lives. This bred a belief that defensive methods would not only ensure victory but minimise casualties. The French therefore put their faith in a line of forts (the Maginot Line). Other methods were decried by an increasingly conservative military. In the main planning body, the Army Council, generals became life members. Thus by 1940 the chief military men were well stricken in years. Pétain was 80, Gamelin 67, Weygand 72 and Georges 65 years of age.

Thus the French failed to develop the new offensive methods of warfare made possible by the tank and the plane. Tanks remained merely as support for the infantry, and defensive methods ruled. When the war broke out, the French Commander-in-Chief, Gamelin, was content, in his own words, to shelter under the Maginot Line and wait.

In contrast the Germans had learned the right lesson from the First World War – that to follow defensive methods could lead to a war of attrition and ultimate defeat. Therefore from the 1920s they were eager converts to the new ideas on offensive warfare pioneered by two British generals, Fuller and Liddell Hart. General von Seeckt, Commander-in-Chief of the German army, concluded as early as 1921, 'The whole future of warfare appears to me to be in the employment of mobile armies, relatively small but of high quality, and rendered distinctly more effective by the addition of aircraft.'

His successors built on his work after his retirement in 1926. Heinz Guderian, in his book *Achtung Panzer*, noted the fault in the way tanks had been used by the Allies in the First World War and developed the concept of fully mechanised Panzer divisions of tanks as the spearhead of an offensive. Tanks would break through enemy lines in large numbers for concentrated fire-power. Close behind would come motorised infantry to mop up enemy units, with mobile anti-tank guns to hold the vulnerable flanks of the Panzer salient against any counter-attack by enemy tanks. In place of preliminary artillery barrages (which only warned the enemy of where an attack was due to take place) the Stuka dive-bomber, with its screaming siren, would help to demoralise the enemy.

It is to Hitler's credit that he saw the possibilities of such warfare. By 1939 he had ordered the construction of ten such Panzer divisions and a Luftwaffe geared for offensive action in support of the army. In addition to the Stuka, the Messerschmitt Me-109 and the standard Junkers Ju-88 bomber had been developed, and they were superior to their French counterparts. France's best fighter, the Morane 406, was 50 mph slower than the Me-109.

(b) The Battle of Britain

Hitler confidently expected that the British would be forced to sue for peace now that their situation appeared hopeless. In this he was to be disappointed, for the British now possessed a charismatic war leader in Winston Churchill. It has perhaps become all too fashionable to write off Churchill's achievements but they were considerable. He became prime minister in May after the failure of the Norwegian campaign had led to the fall of Chamberlain. Churchill brought a new urgency to government, and after the evacuation at Dunkirk his resolution was clear to all. 'We shall fight on the beaches, we shall fight on the landing-grounds, we shall fight in the hills; we shall never surrender.'

Churchill soon won an astonishing personal popularity with the British public through his broadcasts, which succeeded because they were both rhetorical and cheeky. With his speeches, his cigar and his unconventional dress, his appeal to the man in the street was tremendous. As Henry Pelling has said in his biography, 'Churchill's most endearing quality was his evident humanity. This reflected or seemed to reflect the mood of the people in the country; there was nothing of the remote intellectual about him.'

As supreme director of the war, Churchill possessed great power, a situation that eliminated the emasculating quarrel between soldiers and civilians of the First World War. The task of supervising the conduct of the war imposed a heavy burden on the British premier. As A. J. P. Taylor has noted, 'in this turmoil of activity he made some great mistakes and many small ones. The wonder is that he did not make more. No other man could have done what he did, and with a zest that rarely flagged'.

When the British failed to oblige him by a prompt capitulation, Hitler reluctantly began to prepare a plan for the invasion of Britain. For such a plan to succeed, control of the air was essential. The Luftwaffe commander, Göring, cockily promised that the RAF would soon be destroyed and that an invasion of Britain would be simple. In August the greatest battle in air history, the Battle of Britain, began, with thirteen German divisions at French Channel ports ready for Operation Sea Lion. The Luftwaffe had stationed in France 1,200 bombers and about 1,000 fighters against a British fighter strength of 900, but the Spitfires and Hurricanes were faster and more heavily armed than any German plane except the Messerschmitt 109, which lacked their range. The RAF's radar provided an early warning of German attacks and its radio ground-control system permitted the best use of British planes.

Göring's blunders also improved Britain's position. Instead of concentrating on fighter bases and radar stations, he ordered the Luftwaffe to bomb inessential targets like London. Thus though the British lost 650 planes, German losses were even heavier, at about 1,100 planes, and on 17 September Hitler postponed Operation Sea Lion indefinitely. The Battle of Britain was a triumph of foresight and organisation over improvisation and sloppy thinking. It saved Britain from invasion and, as Churchill said of the RAF, 'Never in the field of human conflict was so much owed by so many to so few.'

(c) The invasion of Russia

In July 1940 Hitler told his generals that he had decided to make war on Russia as soon as the strategic position allowed it. He originally envisaged an offensive in the autumn, but realised that the date would have to be postponed until a proper plan had been worked out. His staff tried to persuade him to invest German forces in the Mediterranean, where Mussolini, having massed troops in Libya, was planning to attack the British in Egypt. As Alan Bullock comments, Hitler 'declined to look at the Mediterranean as anything more than a sideshow which could be left to the Italians with a stiffening of German troops. It was to prove one of the supreme blunders of his strategy'. By May 1941 the plans for the invasion of Russia, Operation Barbarossa, were near completion.

Several reasons impelled Hitler towards a campaign in Russia. First, he believed that the British had stayed in the war only because of the hope of Russian aid at some time in the future. Therefore, he told his generals, Russia must be smashed in order to obtain security in the West. Second, another advantage would arise out of a Russian defeat; by increasing the power of Japan in the Far East it would effectively neutralise Britain's other hope, the United States. Hitler did in fact nurse hopes of a simultaneous attack by Japan and Germany on Russia, but the Japanese government was now more interested in southern Asia and was in any case too wily to do Germany's dirty work for her! Third, another reason for Hitler's desire to attack Russia was his belief that the Russians would never tolerate a definitive German victory in the West. He had no confidence in Stalin's good faith, and Russian actions since September 1939 convinced him that Russia would try to obstruct a full German victory. Not only had the Russians invaded Finland, but, by their diplomatic pressure on Rumania, Bulgaria and Turkey, they had become the bitter rivals of the Germans in the Balkans. In June 1940, Rumania had been forced to cede Bessarabia and Northern Bukovina to Russia, and these gains meant that Russia became an even greater threat to the Rumanian oilfields. True, the Russians were fulfilling their obligations in supplying Germany with stocks of raw materials, but in Hitler's view the arrangement had two flaws. The Russians might well cut off deliveries to Germany at any time that suited them, and they demanded prompt payment in the form of armour and munitions, which one day would almost certainly be used against German troops.

Overriding all other factors was Hitler's obsession with *Lebensraum*. The Nazi–Soviet Pact had always been a temporary expedient as far as he was concerned, just as total control of all western Russia had been his ultimate objective. 'Hitler invaded Russia', asserts Alan Bullock, 'for the simple and sufficient reason that he had always meant to establish the foundations of his thousand year Reich by the annexation of the territory lying between the Vistula and the Urals.'

Operation Barbarossa was planned for May 1941, but a serious delay occurred, partly caused by the attempts of the Italians to gain some of the glory. In September 1940 the Italian army in Libya drove back the British forces 60 miles into Egypt, and Mussolini was so elated by his success that he was rash enough to attack Greece in October as a counter to growing German influence in the Balkans. From this point on the Italians experienced only disaster. They were sharply checked in Greece and lost most of their fleet at the hands of the British at the battles of Taranto and Cape Matapan. In December

Italian forces in North Africa were routed by a British counter-attack led by Wavell, and 130,000 Italians were taken prisoner. Mussolini was forced to accept German help in Africa, and German forces, led by Erwin Rommel, beat the British back into Egypt in April 1941.

Before Barbarossa could be launched, Hitler believed that it was necessary to remove the threat to the German flank caused by Mussolini's failure to crush the Greeks, who were now receiving British aid. Pressure was put on the Bulgarian and Yugoslavian governments to permit the transit of German troops through their respective countries for deployment against the Greeks. Both finally acquiesced, but in Yugoslavia the surrender to German bullying provoked a palace revolution and a repudiation of the agreement with Germany. In rage Hitler ordered the invasion of Yugoslavia in April, and German forces destroyed organised resistance in 11 days. A week later Greece surrendered and British forces there had to be evacuated. The two operations have often been held responsible for the 6-week delay in the invasion of Russia, but in fact German preparations for the offensive were not complete by May.

Hitler assumed that the German blitzkrieg would work as success-fully in Russia as it had in the West. He did not bother to lay plans for a winter campaign, or even lay up stores of winter equipment or clothing. By June 1941 about 4 million men, 3,300 tanks and 5,000 aircraft were ready to invade Russia. When Operation Barbarossa commenced on 22 June, the Russian forces were taken by surprise. By mid-July the Germans were two-thirds of the way to Moscow, having captured more than a million prisoners. In the north Lenin-grad came under siege, and in the Kiev region a Russian army of 600,000 was surrounded. When Kiev fell in September, the drive towards Moscow was continued.

For many of these disasters Stalin must be held responsible. He refused to believe Allied and Russian reports that Hitler was about to strike because he assumed that a German attack would only come when Britain was defeated. No plans had been made for a strategic withdrawal to take advantage of Russia's greatest resource, space. In fact Stalin ordered his troops on to the offensive, so that they were more easily encircled by the invaders. Russia seemed near collapse: 1,200 planes had been destroyed within hours of the German attack, and within a few months 2.5 million men had been lost out of a total force of 4.5 millions. Stalin's nerve appeared to go and, in Ulam's words, in the early period of the war 'he left the country rudderless'.

The situation was saved by the flow of Russian troops from the Far East and by the rain, mud and ice of the Russian winter, which brought German armour to a standstill. When Hitler ordered a final effort to take Moscow in 1941, the Russians counter-attacked magni-ficently in December with 100 divisions skilfully led by Zhukov, probably the best general in the war. The Führer had fallen into the trap of allowing the Russians to retreat and draw his armies further and further into their vast hinterland. Now he ordered that the German forces should not retreat but stand fast regardless of losses. On this score he was undoubtedly correct, for a retreat in winter conditions would have degenerated into a rout. His order caused conflicts with the generals, and with the resignation of Brauchitsch and the dismissal of Guderian and Runstedt, the army lost its top professional commanders.

Meanwhile the European war had become a truly global war. On 7 December Japan made a surprise attack on the American naval base of Pearl Harbor and precipitated a Pacific war. Hitler without hesitation declared war on the United States, an act that calls for some explanation, as up to this point Hitler had shown caution in his dealings with the Americans, despite their increasing aid to Britain. It is sometimes argued that he had no conception of the economic and military potential of the United States. More plausibly he realised that Roosevelt was only waiting for the right opportunity to intervene in the European war, and that in the near future some incident would give the president a suitable pretext. Hitler had also promised the Japanese in November to join in a war against the United States; he kept his promise in the vain hope that the Japanese would not only help him against Russia but tie down the Americans in the Pacific as well. Finally he saw that an early declaration of war would allow German aircraft and submarines to strike at American shipping before America's defences had been properly organised.

But whatever the reasons, historians for once concur in condemning the enormity of Hitler's error in declaring war on the United States. Bullock describes it as 'the greatest single mistake of his career', while Rich asserts that Hitler had now 'created a situation which virtually guaranteed Germany's ultimate defeat'.

For a season the consequences of Hitler's errors were hidden by new victories. In the Far East Japanese forces seemed invincible as they took the Philippines, Malaya and many Pacific islands. Hitler believed that the Japanese entry into the war would dry up the flow of American aid to Britain and Russia, so that he could finally destroy Russia in 1942. Despite his failure to concentrate on the Moscow region, where the strongest Russian forces were encamped – he also struck at Leningrad and the Caucasus in an effort to seize the oilfields – his forces gained huge successes. Two Russian armies were encircled and German forces advanced deep into southern Russia. In North Africa Rommel, having suffered reverses in the winter, renewed his offensive in Libya, and by taking Tobruk in June threatened Cairo and the Suez Canal. In the autumn of 1942 the Axis powers seemed close to victory on all fronts, but appearances were deceptive.

(d) The sinews of war

Imperceptibly the fortunes of war were already turning against Germany through Hitler's failure to achieve the efficient mobilisation of all Germany's resources for the war effort. This was in stark contrast to Britain, where after Dunkirk the ground was prepared for the most thoroughly coordinated war economy of any warring nation. The British were regimented in a way that the Axis leaders never dared ask of their own people – in the direction of labour, in the rationing of food, through the imposition of high taxation. The American historian Gordon Wright asserts that 'operating by consent rather than compulsion, utilizing a partially antiquated industrial complex and working with limited resources, the British government managed to convert a loosely articulated peacetime economy into a fully mobilised economy for total war'. One statistic vividly illustrates this achievement; from 1940 to 1942 British production of tanks and aircraft surpassed that of Germany, where the highest level of war production was not reached until 1944.

The Soviet efforts to mobilise for total war were equally impressive. The third Five Year Plan had resulted in new industries in the Urals and Western Siberia, and by June 1941 the eastern regions of Russia were producing 39 per cent of her steel and 35 per cent of her coal. But for this powerful new industrial base, secure from enemy attack, the German attack might well have succeeded.

Russia still faced an appalling situation, for the German troops overran the older industrial regions, and war production was cut by over half by December 1941. The crisis was surmounted by titanic efforts: 1,560 factories were transferred from the threatened areas in the west to the Volga and the Urals, and 2,250 completely new plants were built between 1942 and 1944 so that the output of tanks rose to 2,000 a month and aircraft production from 1,000 to 3,000 a month. The contribution of British and American aid was also important, mainly in the form of vehicles, foodstuffs and clothing.

The Soviet regime made great efforts to mobilise its manpower by the direction of labour to the east. Improved management and the high morale of a nation fighting for survival resulted in greater productivity after 1942. The greatest flaw in the economy continued to be agriculture, where, despite the use of young people and women to fill the gaps in the labour force, the Soviets relied heavily on imported foodstuffs from their Western allies. Like the British, the Russians held down consumption by rationing and high taxation. By the later stages of the war the Russians could deploy on the eastern front twice as many soldiers as the Germans and possessed 8,000 tanks to Germany's 2,300, despite the concentration of two-thirds of all German forces in the east.

Only slowly did Hitler consent to full mobilisation of the German economy for war. After the successful Russian resistance in late 1941 he ordered vast increases in arms and the size of the army in January 1942. His Minister of Armaments and Munitions, Albert Speer, was talented and managed to treble arms production in the next 2 years – despite the rivalry of competing agencies, chiefly the army's War Economy Branch, Göring's Four Year Plan Office, and Himmler's SS, which was a particular hindrance in its barbarous and wasteful use of labour. Speer also clashed with the Nazi gauleiter Fritz Sauckel, who headed the manpower agency, and the labour shortage was never really solved. Speer believed that foreign workers could best be used in their own countries, but Sauckel insisted on transporting them to Germany. Speer's reliance on the industrialists met sharp criticism from many Nazis, who wanted stricter party control of the economy, and they also resisted his attempts to hold down consumption.

Considering these obstacles, Speer's achievement in trebling arms production was impressive. His authority over aircraft production remained limited, and bombers continued to be built instead of the more necessary fighters. When he did gain a measure of control in 1943, he raised the production of planes from 2,300 to 3,538 in little over a year, despite Allied bombing and shortage of materials. In the end even Speer could not work a miracle in the face of harsh economic realities. Germany was facing a coalition vastly superior in manpower, industrial potential and scientific knowledge.

(e) Hitler's New Order

By 1942 the Nazi empire covered most of Europe, which would enjoy, boasted Hitler, a new order for 1,000 years. He now had a unique opportunity to implement his long-harboured objectives to make the German race absolutely supreme in Europe. The conquered areas were to be colonised by Germans and the indigenous population cleared out. Responsibility for this task lay with Himmler's SS, and early in the war a million Jews and Poles were removed from Poland to make room for German settlers. After the invasion of Russia vast new possibilities were opened up. Some Slavs would be kept as a source of cheap labour; most would be expelled to Siberia and central Asia. Fortunately there was time only for a few scattered colonial experiments before the tide of war turned in 1943. One practice was selecting 'racially valuable' members from the Slav races with the intention of making them good Germans.

To counterbalance the superiority of the Allied economies, the Germans resorted to the simple process of commandeering all the raw materials, food and manpower in the conquered areas. As Göring remarked with refreshing honesty, 'I intend to plunder and plunder copiously.' That the conquered races might starve was a matter of complete indifference to Himmler and Hitler. German rule was worst in the east, where mass confiscation was practised by the SS, whereas in the West some veneer of legality was preserved.

One of the most acute problems which Germany faced was the labour shortage, exacerbated by the failure to use female labour on any large scale. Foreign workers were shipped into Germany to meet the shortage. At the peak of this exploitation, over 7 million were stationed in Germany, while another 7 million foreign workers were working for the German war effort in their native countries. Yet the Nazi inefficiency and tyranny made poor use of potentially enormous economic assets, and shattered the myth that totalitarian states organise for war more effectively than do the democracies. It seems incredible that, despite the acute labour shortage, 3 million out of 4 million Russian prisoners-of-war died of ill-treatment in German camps.

There was indeed a striking contradiction in Nazi policies. While striving for economic growth, they could not free themselves from their heinous racial doctrines, which, when implemented, robbed Germany of its necessary labour force. When Poland was purged of its political élite by execution, gaol or deportation, one German field-marshal protested at such methods. 'Wars are not won with the methods of the Sally Army,' Hitler retorted.

Nazi behaviour was particularly atrocious in Russia. 'This is a war of extermination,' Hitler told his military advisers in 1941, and Himmler instructed his SS on the necessity of destroying 30 million Slavs to make room for German colonists in the east. 'The Russians', Goebbels noted in his diary, 'are not people but a conglomeration of animals.' The Nazi atrocities in Russia were both criminal and stupid. More generous behaviour might have induced many Russians, especially in the Ukraine, to welcome the German invaders and support them against the detested Soviet regime. Nazi barbarism made the Russian people fight with heroic zeal, as exemplified at Leningrad, which withstood a German seige of 890 days.

If any resistance was met in any occupied country, the Germans did not hesitate to impose collective punishments, as at Oradour in France, where the entire population of the village was murdered for an act of sabotage committed elsewhere. When the SS chief Heydrich was assassinated in Czechoslovakia in 1941, the Nazis killed 15,000 Czechs, and the villages of Lidice and Lezaky were destroyed.

The nadir of Nazi genocide was seen in the treatment of the Jews. From 1933 pressure on them had mounted in Germany as Hitler's Brownshirts organised a boycott of Jewish shops and daubed Jewish stars on the shop windows. In 1935 enaction of the Nuremburg Laws reduced Jews to the status of second-class citizens. In November 1938 the Brownshirts burned down 267 synagogues and 815 Jewish stores in an affair known as the 'Crystal night'. Thirty-six Jews were killed and the Jewish race was heavily fined for causing trouble. Gradually

Jews were excluded from education, the civil service and businesses. Those Jews who could now left the country.

Persecution grew worse with the outbreak of war, and in September 1941 Jews were ordered to wear a hexagonal star made of yellow material and bordered in black, inscribed with the word 'Jude'. The use of the Star of David as a stigma was typical of Nazi vindictiveness, but worse was to come. Göring instructed Heydrich to submit plans for a final solution to the Jewish problem. The Reichsmarshal meant only evacuation to the east but the doctrinaires around Himmler worked out plans for the extermination of the whole Jewish race. The SS combed Europe for Jews, took them to a remote place, made them dig their own graves and strip naked. Then they were mown down by machine-gun fire and buried in a mass grave.

This was too slow for the zealous Himmler, and mass extermination camps were set up, notably at Auschwitz and Buchenwald. Here the Jews were given poison gas in chambers disguised as shower rooms. The SS administrators kept copious records of all these foul murders. An office was founded to collect and package all the possessions of the dead – their clothing, gold teeth and hair. Thus the Jews were not only exterminated as if they were vermin, they were used as raw material for the war effort. Gerald Reitlinger puts the cost of the Final Solution in human lives at between 4,200,000 and 4,600,000 Jews, and to this figure should be added about 3 million people of other races who became victims of Nazi savagery in the camps.

It must not be assumed, however, that the Nazis had a monopoly in atrocities. The Soviet regime was as barbarous as the Nazis in Poland, and deported 1 million Poles to Siberia and Central Asia. In 1943 the Germans made some political capital out of the discovery in Katyn Forest of a mass grave containing the bodies of some 12,000 Polish officers captured by the Russians and almost certainly murdered by them.

(f) The German resistance to Hitler

The German resistance, in the words of A. J. Ryder, was 'a tragedy within a tragedy'. Those Germans who felt obliged to oppose Hitler faced an agonising crisis of conscience, because their actions could so easily be interpreted as treason. Such a moral dilemma meant that German resistance remained divided and ineffective, and in any case many potential anti-Nazis had been imprisoned before the war started.

Opposition to Hitler in Germany came from five directions (1) On the Left, Socialists and Communists began underground groups, the most successful of which was 'Rote Kapelle', a Communist spying organization. (2) Members of the General Staff such as Halder and

Beck grew increasingly uneasy under Hitler's rule and were supported by a number of civilians, chiefly the ex-Lord Mayor of Leipzig, Gördeler. (3) A similar group developed inside the Military Intelligence Department of the OKW (Combined Services), and included Admiral Canaris and General Oster. (4) Among the students the most notable group was the White Rose in Munich led by Hans and Sophie Scholl, who both paid with their lives for their courage. (5) Finally a group grew up around Count von Moltke called the Kreisau circle. It included Bonhoeffer and many gifted men from diverse backgrounds. A member of the group, Count Claus von Stauffenberg, was finally chosen to assassinate Hitler, and after several near misses, an attempt was made in July 1944, but Hitler by a lucky accident escaped death. His vengeance was barbaric. Several of the instigators of the plot, including Stauffenberg, were summarily shot; others were given a slow hanging with cords suspended from meat-hooks after torture and trial before Freisler in the People's Court. Over 4,000 people lost their lives as a result of the July plot, including Rommel, who was given the choice of trial or suicide and opted for the latter.

(g) The collapse of Hitler's empire

(i) The American contribution
By the end of 1941 the entry of the United States into the European war had become imminent, as the American government had stepped up its aid to Britain on a massive scale in the previous 2 years. Her European allies were thankful that, despite Pearl Harbor, Roosevelt insisted on giving priority to the European theatre of the global conflict, for America's huge production potential was always likely to ensure the defeat of the Axis. Her economy when fully mobilised for war was to produce 75,000 tanks, 10 million tons of merchant shipping and 120,000 aircraft a year; and 15 million American men and women were enlisted in the war effort. Yet the American entry into the war had another major consequence; it marked another stage in the decline of Europe, which became more and more dependent on decisions made in Washington.

(ii) The war at sea
It was fortunate that Hitler had shown little concern or comprehension of naval warfare, and as a result had constructed only a small submarine fleet of 56 craft. These alone began to inflict alarming casualties on the Allies and between June 1940 and December 1941 Britain lost more than one-third of her merchant tonnage. The Allied need to help the Russians by the Arctic sea route to Murmansk gave the Germans new opportunities for destruction, and a shortage of merchant ships threatened because most of the American mercantile

marine had to be assigned to Pacific duties. In 1942 Hitler, now converted to the idea of submarine warfare, had over 300 U-boats built and they inflicted appalling casualties on Allied shipping. In 1942 over 6 million tons of shipping were lost, and in March 1943 new record losses were experienced, with 97 ships lost in 20 days.

The Battle of the Atlantic was, however, already turning in the favour of the Allies through the tenacity of British merchant seamen and improved use of the convoy system. American yards were producing ships faster than the U-boats could sink them, and new techniques were developed to combat the submarines, including the use of long-range aircraft (the Liberator), aircraft carriers and centrimetric radar. In April 1943 Allied losses halved and in May the Germans lost 41 U-boats, a blow from which their naval effort never really recovered.

In comparison to the U-boats, German surface raiders achieved little and in time were hunted down by the Royal Navy. In September 1939 the pocket battleship *Admiral Graf Spee* was damaged by British warships and her commander scuttled her in the River Plate. In May 1941 the mighty *Bismarck*, having sunk Britain's most famous battleship, the *Hood*, was herself destroyed by the combined efforts of British planes and ships. In December 1943 the *Scharnhorst* was sunk by torpedoes and in April 1944 the *Tirpitz*, having been immobilised by British midget submarines, was destroyed by aircraft in a Norwegian fjord.

(iii) The war in the air

One of the most controversial issues in the Second World War was the strategic bombing of Germany. After German air raids on British cities in 1940, the RAF retaliated in kind by area bombing at night in the hope of undermining German civilian morale. Churchill and the head of Bomber Command, Sir Arthur Harris, felt that attempts to destroy vital German resources like synthetic oil plants by precision bombing were impracticable. From 1942 Lancaster heavy bombers began to pound German cities, the climax being the raids on Hamburg, which caused firestorms and made a million people homeless. German civilian morale did not crumble, however, as in time airraids became accepted as a matter of course.

The American attempts to make day-time raids on precise targets led to alarming casualties. In the raid on the ballbearing plants at Schweinfurt in October 1943, 148 bombers were lost. The situation was to some extent transformed by the use of the P-51 Mustang fighter. Powered by an Anglo-American Rolls Royce Packard engine, it was not only the best single-seat fighter in the war, but could be equipped with long-range fuel tanks, so that it could escort bombers all the way to Berlin. German fighters were eliminated from the skies and American bombers disrupted Germany's supplies of synthetic oil.

The extent of the damage done to Germany's war effort has been a matter of debate. German war production continued to rise until late in the war (1944), but Germany did become starved of petrol and many newly constructed planes lay idle for this reason. One and a half million people were required to repair the damage to communications and Ruhr industry in general. Perhaps Albert Speer should have the last word on the subject; he was of the opinion that American attacks on key industrial targets were a serious cause of the breakdown of the German arms industry in the final stages of the war.

(iv) The war on land

In November 1942 three clear signs showed that the war was moving into a new phase. After a period of efficient preparation General Montgomery's Eighth Army shattered the Axis forces at El Alamein in Egypt, after Rommel's supply lines across the Mediterranean had become overstretched and increasingly harassed by the British. This battle has always been remembered with pride in Britain and the Commonwealth, and was a great tonic after years of defeat. It made secure Montgomery's reputation as the best British field-commander since Wellington.

The Russians meanwhile had become restless at what they regarded as Western sloth and clamoured for a second front in Europe. The British refused an American suggestion for a small cross-Channel operation of 6 divisions on the grounds that it would hardly draw German troops away from the Russian front, as there were 33 German divisions in the West anyway. Still, a diversionary action to help the Russians was required, and Churchill proposed a surprise descent on Morocco and Algeria. In November an Anglo-American armada landed in North Africa, and, with Montgomery's forces pressing from the east, moved on Tunis. By May 1943 the fighting in North Africa was over, though the campaign has its critics, who condemn it for delaying the cross-Channel invasion by its consumption of time, men and materials. On the other hand, Italy was not within easy reach, and the Desert War cost Germany and Italy about 1 million soldiers killed or taken prisoner.

A third triumph marked Allied progress in November 1942. The German armies in Russia had driven far towards the Caucasus oilfields, but in the way lay Stalingrad on the lower Volga. Obsessed by its name and strategic importance Hitler did not choose to bypass it, and in September his troops entered the city. They found themselves facing ferocious resistance from the Russian forces, who were being regularly reinforced. Hitler refused to allow his army commander, von Paulus, to withdraw, and as a consequence, when three Russian armies counter-attacked in November, they were able to trap 330,000 axis troops in a pincer movement. After fierce fighting for 10 weeks, the remnants of the German army, about 100,000 men, were forced to surrender. Like El Alamein, Stalingrad proved that the German armies were far from invincible, and as Michael Howard has remarked, if ever there was a decisive battle in history, it was Stalingrad. It demonstrated the extent to which Hitler's daring and determination had degenerated into blind overconfidence and belief in his own infallibility. As Alan Bullock explains, 'This was the reverse side of the strength which he derived from his own belief in himself – and it was the weakness which was to destroy him, for in the end it destroyed all power of self-criticism and cut him off from all contact with reality.'

By May 1943 the British and American leaders, to Stalin's chagrin, decided that a cross-Channel invasion would have to wait until 1944. As an alternative Churchill proposed an immediate attack on Italy, where Mussolini's power was now patently crumbling. The British argued that such a campaign would knock Italy out of the war, clear the Mediterranean for Allied shipping and provide bases for aerial bombardment of Germany and the Rumanian oilfields. In July the Allies landed successfully in Sicily, a development that paved the way for the fall of Mussolini. His successor Badoglio wasted little time in bringing Italy on to the side of the Allies.

The German response was to seize control of nearly all the Italian peninsula, and the Allies, who had landed on the Italian mainland in September, faced a long and bloody campaign to dislodge an enemy who for some time enjoyed numerical superiority. Only in June 1944 was Rome taken, and it was April 1945 before the German hold on Northern Italy was broken. Nevertheless the costly campaign contributed to ultimate victory in three ways. It eliminated Italy from the war and provided aerodromes from which the Allies could bomb the Balkans, central Europe and southern France, but most important of all it pinned down 25 German divisions in Italy and a similar number of troops in the Balkans against a possible Allied attack there, including forces that would otherwise have been used in Russia.

On the Russian front the early months of 1943 saw German troops on the retreat, but they were still strong enough to launch their third summer offensive in July. This offensive was routed at Kursk, the scene of the greatest tank battle in history until the Middle East War of 1973. The heavy Stalin and medium T34 tanks were more than a match for the German Tiger tanks, a sign that the Russian armaments industry had overtaken that of Germany. By the end of 1943 two-thirds of Russian territory occupied by the Nazis had been liberated. In 1944 Russian forces swept into Poland, Warsaw was taken and by the end of the year Germany itself was threatened. Russian forces had also rolled through Rumania and Bulgaria, though their advance was checked in Hungary.

At Teheran in November 1943 the three major Allies had at last fixed the date of the cross-Channel invasion of Normandy, which would be supported by an attack on the south coast of France. The preparation for the D-Day invasion was enormous; it was hoped to land 200,000 men with their equipment in the first 2 days, with the landing of another 440,000 men in the next 9 days. On 6 June 1944 five seaborne and three airborne divisions were landed in Normandy and four beachheads established without any serious hitches. By the end of July the Allies had broken out from these beachheads and by the end of August Paris had been liberated. The landing on France's southern coast was also successful in August, so that for a time it was hoped that the war would end in 1944.

General Montgomery at this point pressed hard for a powerful dash to Berlin across the Rhine, but an attempt to outflank Germany's Siegfried Line by dropping airborne troops at Arnhem in September failed. This convinced the commander-in-chief of the Allied forces, Eisenhower, that a broad front advance was safer than Montgomery's plan. In any case he believed that the offensive would have to pause so that his forces could be reinforced.

In December 1944 came the last desperate German fling of the war, a thrust through the Ardennes spearheaded by a powerful tank force which it was hoped would split the Allied forces and take Antwerp, the main Allied supply port. This 'Battle of the Bulge' led to the temporary rout of the 6 American divisions which lay in the way of the German attack, but in the end the Germans lost 600 tanks. The Allied advance continued on all fronts in February 1945. To the disgust of the British, Eisenhower would not make the capture of Berlin a top priority, and the honour of taking the German capital fell to the Russians, when in April they launched a great final assault with 1½ million troops. Hitler and Goebbels committed suicide and early in May the German forces surrendered unconditionally. Victory over Japan was not long delayed; in August, after President Truman authorised the dropping of atomic bombs on Hiroshima and Nagasaki, the Japanese government surrendered and the global war was over.

(h) The war in the Far East

At the news of the American entry into the war, Winston Churchill openly rejoiced. For him the fate of the European dictators was sealed, and 'as for the Japanese, they would be ground into powder. All the rest was merely the proper application of overwhelming force'. For a time his confidence appeared wildly misplaced in both the main theatres. For 6 months after Pearl Harbor, Japanese forces were rampant in the Pacific and South East Asia, overwhelming the European colonial empires, encircling China from the south and threatening India, Australia and Hawaii.

Japan's victories in a few weeks shocked the West. In Malaya Britain had constructed the Singapore naval base, and in an attempt to deter the Japanese from declaring war Churchill had insisted on sending two battleships to the area, the *Prince of Wales* and the *Repulse*. But air defence was inadequate, and on the outbreak of war Japanese planes sank both battleships. In February 1942 a Japanese army took Malaya and forced the surrender of Singapore. Some 88,000 British and Commonwealth troops surrendered. As Grenville has commented, the fall of Singapore was a great psychological blow, which undermined the faith of Asian peoples in 'white' superiority.

In the Philippines the Americans had to surrender by April 1942, despite MacArthur's skilful defence. In December the Japanese took Hong-Kong and by April had driven the British out of most of Burma. The Dutch East Indies had been captured the previous month. The Japanese even bombed Colombo in Ceylon and Darwin in Australia, and their submarines penetrated Sydney Harbour. The whole of South East Asia was now dominated by Japan.

The fundamental causes of this Allied catastrophe were American unpreparedness and Western commitments in Europe. For example, as Paul Kennedy has pointed out, it was Britain's strategical juggling act which led to the loss of Singapore, because the British had concentrated aircraft and troops in the Mediterranean theatre. The Allied performance was not helped by quarrels within the American high command and between the Allies over the allocation of resources. In January 1943 Roosevelt urged Churchill to launch an offensive in Burma to help the Chinese Nationalists, who were tying down 50 Japanese divisions. Massive American aid helped the survival of Chiang Kai-shek's forces, but, as he retained a large percentage of troops and equipment for his future confrontation with the Chinese Communists, much of the aid was wasted. Thus even in 1944 the Japanese were capable of launching an offensive which nearly doubled their area of Chinese territory.

As Basil Liddell Hart has demonstrated, while the two sides were closely balanced in most respects on the outbreak of war, the Japanese had a great advantage in aircraft carriers. Qualitatively Japanese forces were superior to those of the Allies. The Japanese force was well trained, especially in night-fighting. It did not suffer command or language difficulties, as did the Allied side, with its mixture of Western and Asian elements. There were 6,000 miles of ocean between the two main bases of the Allies, Pearl Harbor and Singapore. Materially the Japanese navy was superior. It had many newer ships, and most of them were better armed and faster. Of the capital ships, only the *Prince of Wales* was a match for the better Japanese battleships. Air superiority was also on the side of the Japanese in the early months. Over 1,500 aircraft were available for attacks on Allied positions, and the Zero fighter, with a total range of nearly 1,000 miles, outclassed Allied fighters. Many Allied planes were patently obsolete.

Nevertheless Churchill's basic assumption was correct, and the balance of advantage swung to the Allies as the USA was properly mobilised. The further the Japanese extended their conquests, the less capable they were of meeting the counter-offensives which the Allies steadily prepared. As early as May 1942 the tide of the Pacific War began to turn when in the battle of the Coral Sea Japan's thrust towards Australia was checked. The key turning point, however, was the battle of Midway in June. This naval battle was dominated by aircraft carriers, and when the Japanese lost four aircraft carriers while the USA lost only one, they broke off the battle and at the same time surrendered the initiative in the Pacific. With the loss of their carriers and 330 aircraft, the preponderance of the Japanese in battleships and cruisers counted for little, and Midway spelt the ultimate doom of Japan.

The American counter-offensive began in August 1942, when American forces attacked Guadalcanal, one of the Solomon Islands. The ferocious fighting between the American marines and the defending Japanese set the pattern for the rest of the Pacific War. The American troops under the command of Admiral Nimitz pushed the Japanese back from one tropical island to another, only after crushing fanatical defensive resistance by the Japanese. By 1943 the Americans were able to apply overwhelming force for each operation; when they attacked the Gilbert Islands in November, the invasion was covered by two powerful fleets protected by twelve aircraft carriers. By 1944 American forces were closing in on Japan itself, capturing Saipan, Tinian and Guam.

Meanwhile British and Dominion troops had halted a Japanese offensive from Burma into India, and under Mountbatten's command they beat the Japanese out of Burma between December 1944 and May 1945. In October 1944 MacArthur began an attack on the Philippines. In an attempt to destroy his supply lines, the Japanese committed large naval contingents in Leyte Gulf. The ensuing clash was the last great naval battle of the Second World War. It was also the greatest naval battle of all time, and cost Japan four carriers, three battleships, six heavy cruisers, three light cruisers and eight destroyers. Japan now possessed no more carriers, and thus her remaining battleships were rendered helpless. Despite the bravery of her Kamikaze pilots, who volunteered to carry out the suicide mission of crash-diving their planes on to enemy shipping, Japan had lost command of the sea to the Americans in her home waters.

With the capture of the islands of Iwo Jima and Okinawa by June

1945, the USA was poised to attack Japan itself. Japan's cities were being reduced to rubble by constant air attacks, and the Japanese military knew that the war could not be won. Yet they hoped that the Allies would be deterred from invading Japan itself, where for the first time they would have to face large Japanese armies. In the hope of obtaining reasonable peace terms the Japanese government approached the Soviet Union in July to act as mediator. Stalin refused because he hoped that Russia might soon enter the war and make gains in Manchuria. Nevertheless he did inform the USA and Britain about the Japanese overtures at the Potsdam conference. Accordingly, on 26 July, Britain and the USA set out their peace terms for Japan. They called for the unconditional surrender of Japanese forces, the removal of military influences in Japanese life, the punishment of war criminals, the surrender of all imperial conquests and Allied occupation of Japan. At the same time the declaration also promised the rebuilding of the Japanese economy, the restoration of democracy and the removal of occupation forces as soon as feasible. Unfortunately the declaration was unclear on the future of Emperor Hirohito, and was therefore unacceptable to the Japanese.

Japan's 80-year-old prime minister, Admiral Suzuki, responded to the declaration in a noncommital way, because he was forced to temporise in the face of military opposition to the peace terms. Translation of his reply made it appear offensive and Truman decided to use the atomic bomb in the interest of saving American lives. On 6 and 9 August respectively atomic bombs devastated Hiroshima and Nagasaki. Only after this terrible havoc did Hirohito assert himself by overruling the military, many of whom were still inclined to continue the war. The Soviet declaration of war and Russian invasion of Manchuria on 8 and 9 August added to the pressure on the Japanese government to make peace and on 13 August the Allied promise that the emperor would not be removed from his throne finally made surrender acceptable. On 14 August Hirohito broadcast Japan's surrender, told his people that they must endure the unendurable and in so doing brought the Second World War to a close.

While never making the same number of major errors as their German allies, the Japanese nonetheless made some serious strategic mistakes. Because Japan was carrying out a 'continental' strategy, in which the army's influence predominated, its operations in the Pacific and South East Asia were supported by too few troops – only 11 divisions compared to 13 in Manchuria and 22 in China. Even when the Americans counter-attacked in the central Pacific in 1943, Japanese troop and aerial reinforcements were too few and too late, especially when they are compared with the divisions allocated for the massive offensives in China in 1943–4. Consequently an absurd position developed by 1945. With Japan threatened by Nimitz's forces and its cities pulverised from the air, there were still a million Japanese soldiers in China and 780,000 in Manchuria. They were now incapable of being withdrawn because of the effectiveness of the American submarine campaign.

Yet the Imperial Japanese navy also made errors. The operational handling of key battles like Midway was riddled with mistakes, for example the failure to fly sufficient search planes to spot the American carriers and the error of striking with the planes of all four carriers at once, which meant that they had to rearm their aircraft at the same time, so that there was a period when their carrier force had no striking power. Even more serious, when the aircraft carriers were proving themselves supreme in Pacific warfare, many Japanese admirals remained wedded to the battleship, as the Battle of Leyte Gulf demonstrated. Precious resources continued to be devoted to building obsolete giant battleships, while no destroyer escorts at all were built between 1941 and 1943. Japanese submarines, with their formidable torpedoes, were misused as scouts for the battle fleet or even in running supplies to beleaguered island garrisons rather than sinking Allied shipping. The navy also failed to protect its own merchant marine, and was slow to develop a convoy system or anti-submarine techniques, although Japan was even more dependent than Britain on imported materials. Japan also lost the battle of intelligence and secret codes.

Resistance against Japan was increased by Japanese treatment of prisoners-of-war and conquered Asian peoples. Japanese troops behaved brutally towards Allied POW's because to them becoming a POW was a disgrace. Many prisoners died on forced labour projects, 16,000 Europeans on the construction of the Burma–Siam railway alone. But many more Asians were killed, despite Japan's claim to be fulfilling a mission of liberating Asia from Western imperialism. In its place Japan would build a 'Greater East Asia Co-Prosperity Sphere', symbolising the solidarity of Eastern Asia against the West. The reality was very different. The needs of captured territories were subordinated to Japan's war effort, and local economies were made to produce raw materials for Japan's requirements. Japanese propaganda emphasised the superiority of the Japanese and alienated local populations. Japanese colonialism was far more repressive than the Western rule which it replaced. Independence movements were crushed, and such autonomy as was granted, as in Indonesia, was a thin veneer for Japanese imperial exploitation.

No coherent plan for the future of East Asia was ever worked out, and brutal government meant that Japan's attempts to win over the mass of Asian peoples to support the war against their former colonial masters was a failure. Of all the peoples under Japanese rule, the Chinese suffered most, both in China and wherever Chinese communities existed in South East Asia, for example Singapore and

Malaya. Japanese barbarism drove the Malay Chinese into armed resistance. Thus while no policy of planned extermination was carried out, as it was in Eastern Europe, the Japanese failed to exploit a potential source of support in the European colonies they conquered.

Yet even if Japan had avoided such errors, her defeat would merely have been postponed. Even if the Japanese had inflicted a crushing defeat on Nimitz's forces at Midway, the Americans in 1942 would still have been able to field 21 new aircraft carriers and by 1944 at least 44 new aircraft carriers.

The most telling statistics relate to aircraft production. Command of the air enabled the Americans to achieve both campaign victories and the inflicting of heavy blows at the foe's economy. Disregarding the superior quality of Allied planes as the war continued, comparative production figures are striking. Japanese aircraft production rose from 4,467 in 1939 to a peak of 28,180 in 1944, before falling to 11,066 in 1945. American aircraft production dwarfed such achievements, rising from 5,856 in 1939 to a peak of 96,318 in 1944, and sustaining a figure of 49,761 in 1945. Such air supremacy swung key battles, for example Slim's Burma Army reinforcement of Imphal and the American conquest of Japanese bases in the Pacific, such as Guadalcanal. Reinforcing air supremacy of course was the greater number of trained pilots available to the Americans. When Japan lost her best pilots, they were irreplaceable.

Even after the expansion of the Japanese and German empires, the economic forces ranged on each side were much more disproportionate than in the First World War. By 1943 the USA alone was producing a ship every day and an aircraft every 5 minutes. Moreover the Allies were producing many newer types of weapons, such as the American fighter, the Mustang, and light fleet aircraft carriers. The eightfold rise in American arms production between 1941 and 1943 meant that by the latter year total Allied armaments' production was over three times that of its enemies. The supremacy was also demographic: by 1945 American military personnel numbered 12.5 millions with 7.5 millions serving overseas.

Thus by 1945 the USA had a number of military tools by which it could compel Japanese surrender. The successful American submarine campaign threatened Japan with starvation. The B29 bombers were reducing Japan's cities to ashes, the raid on Tokyo on 9 March 1945 causing a firestorm which resulted in 185,000 casualties. A third option was a massive invasion of Japan itself. The decision to use the atomic bombs on Hiroshima and Nagasaki was reached for a number of reasons – the wish to save Allied casualties, the desire to send a warning to Stalin and even the need to justify the vast expense of the atomic project. Only the USA had the resources to wage two large-scale conventional wars and also to invest about $2 billions in a new weapon which might or might not have worked.

(i) The consequences of the war

Despite all the suffering, the Second World War was worth fighting if only because it led to the destruction of a regime that could perpetrate the horrors of Belsen and Auschwitz, a regime indeed that was the greatest threat to European civilisation so far encountered. For this reason A. J. P. Taylor believes that the Second World War was that rarity, a just war. 'Despite all the killing and destruction that accompanied it, the Second World War was a good war.'

The conflict also brought certain indirect benefits, for the requirements of total war necessitated great advances in science and in state planning. In Britain, for example, the Beveridge Report of 1942 laid down the guidelines for the creation of the Welfare State, and state socialism, allied with American aid, was to be a major factor in Europe's rapid material recovery after the war. Even the invention of nuclear weapons, with all their potential for evil, has benefited mankind. By multiplying man's power to destroy his own kind, they have made the consequences of another war so horrifying that they have so far been an effective deterrent and contributed to peace.

Against these benefits must be set the evil results of the most destructive war in all history, which, in Gordon Wright's phrase, 'speeded the downward spiral of European power and influence'. Over 30 million people were killed in the carnage; over half were Russians but it was the Poles who suffered the highest casualty rate of all. They lost nearly 6 million of their people, 15 per cent of the entire population. The slaughter was accompanied by an uprooting of peoples unprecedented in European history. Between 1939 and 1947, 16 million Europeans were forced to leave their homes and move to other regions.

The destruction of material assets was enormous, and Europe seemed destined for some years to endure poverty and starvation. In contrast the extra-European powers appeared immensely strong. The United States had suffered relatively few casualties, and the war had stimulated her true revival from the depression years of the 1930s. Russia too had demonstrated her immense military might, and it was clear even by 1945 that these two superpowers would now enjoy a preponderant influence in world affairs. Their rivalry, which was to become the most important feature of the postwar decades, was soon to split Europe into two ideological camps.

The war also transformed the relations of European states with their colonies. Japanese victories in Asia over European armies fatally undermined the prestige of such colonial powers as France, Britain and Holland. Colonial nationalism in Asia and Africa was stronger than ever before, and the peoples of these continents would no longer tolerate a position of subjection.

Finally the atrocities of the war provoked doubt and despair about the very nature of the human race. The Final Solution was not the work of Germans alone. The Danes, Norwegians and Hungarians tried to protect their Jews, but in Rumania, France and Russia locally recruited collaborators astonished the Germans by the virulence of their anti-Semitic sentiments. The guilt was appallingly widespread. 'In the end', says Norman Rich, 'one of the saddest features of the Nazi experience is that out of all the suffering, the bloodshed and the destruction which Nazism inflicted on the world, the Nazi movement contributed nothing to human culture and civilisation. Nothing except a terrible lesson about how fragile and vulnerable human civilisation is.'

FURTHER READING

Calvocoressi, P. and Wint, S., *Total War*, Penguin, Harmondsworth, 1972

Dawidowicz, L., *The War Against The Jews*, Penguin, Harmondsworth, 1977

Deighton, L., *Blitzkrieg*, Cape, London, 1979

Horne, A., *To Lose a Battle*, Penguin, Harmondsworth, 1979

Kennedy, P., *The Rise and Fall of the Great Powers*, Unwin Hyman, London, 1988

Liddell Hart, B., *The History of the Second World War*, Cassell, London, 1970

Rich, N., *Hitler's War Aims: the Establishment of the New Order*, Andre Deutsch, London, 1974

Wright, G., *The Ordeal of Total War*, Harper Torchbooks, New York, 1968

QUESTIONS

1. Account for the rapid German victories between 1939 and 1941.
2. Why did Hitler attack Russia in June 1941?
3. Critically examine the main features of Hitler's New Order.
4. 'The proper application of overwhelming force.' How far does Churchill's comment explain American victory in the Pacific war?
5. Do you agree with A. J. P. Taylor's view that the Second World War was 'a good war'?

11

The aftermath of the Second World War

(1) The creation of the United Nations Organisation (UNO)

(a) Origins and formation

The stimulus for the creation of a new world organisation came paradoxically from war, for it grew out of the anti-axis coalition. When Churchill and Roosevelt met in August 1941, they formulated the Atlantic Charter, which spoke of the need for 'a wider and permanent system of security', and in 1942 twenty-six Allied nations fighting Germany affirmed the United Nations Declaration. A new organisation was preferred to a revived League of Nations, because, as H. G. Nicholas comments, 'the League reeked with the odour of failure'. Russia had been offended by the League at the time of the Russo-Finnish war in 1939, and in the United States the public was more likely to support a new body than the League. Further declarations of intent to create a new international organisation based on the sovereign equality of all peaceloving states for the maintenance of international peace and security were made at the Moscow and Teheran conferences in 1943.

The basic structure of the new system was hammered out at the conference at Dumbarton Oaks in August 1944. The general atmosphere at the conference was cordial, and agreement on the main points was reached. There would be a large legislative assembly (the General Assembly) in which all member states would be represented, and a small executive body (the Security Council), which, with a nucleus of Great Powers, would carry the main responsibility for peace and security. Some crucial issues were not settled at Dumbarton Oaks, notably on voting arrangements in the Security Council, where the Russians wanted a comprehensive Great Power veto. As Snell remarks, 'Soviet intent was clear; the new organisation should have no power to curb one of the Great Powers, specifically the USSR.' The Russians also proposed that the sixteen constituent republics of the USSR should be treated as individual states eligible for membership. This was a ruse to counter the votes of the states in the British Empire and Western Europe, and was naturally opposed by the Western powers.

At the Yalta conference of 1945 the outstanding issues on the structure had to be completed. Stalin dropped the demand that all sixteen republics of the Soviet Union should have seats in the General Assembly and instead accepted just two additional seats for the Ukraine and White Russia. He also agreed that the permanent members of the Security Council (France, China and the Big Three) could not veto discussion of any matter affecting themselves, though of course they would be able to veto action affecting themselves.

The conference drafting the United Nations Charter took place in San Francisco in April 1945 in the full glare of publicity, an attempt to win the interest of the American public. Again the crucial issue was over the veto. It emerged that the Russians were still aiming at a complete veto in the Security Council, and only after much wrangling was Stalin persuaded to adhere to the Yalta formula. After much labour, a United Nations Charter was agreed on, and representatives from fifty countries signed the necessary documents in June. That Truman then managed to persuade the American Senate to approve the Charter was a crucial step forward, for it was a sign that the United States would accept the obligations proportionate to its new superpower status in the world. It was perhaps a sign of this new status that New York was chosen as the home of the United Nations in 1946.

(b) The League of Nations and the United Nations

No mention of the League had been made in these early activities of the United Nations, yet a profound tribute was paid to the earlier organisation by the way in which the new creation copied it. There was a basic identity of objectives, methods and structure. Both world organisations have aimed at peace and security, with voluntary association being the accepted method of procedure. The sovereign state is still the unit of membership. In both organisations four organs discharged similar functions: (1) the assembly which included all members, (2) a council built around the Great Powers, (3) a permanent, international secretariat under an elected secretary-general, and (4) a court – in the case of the League the Permanent Court of Justice and in the case of UNO the International Court of Justice.

The powers of the United Nations Assembly and the League Assembly were similar in practice, but the United Nations did make one important change. It abandoned the League's principle of unanimity, the Assembly being empowered to make decisions by majority vote, with a two-thirds majority necessary on important decisions.

In structure the Security Council was similar to its League predecessor, with its core of Great Power members and its elected non-permanent members. The major differences was the attempt to make the Security Council more powerful. It had the right to decide on behalf of the whole UNO whether peace was threatened, and in a crisis could decide on the necessary measures, which were binding on all members even if this necessitated the use of armed force. Here the UNO went further than the League, its objective being to make the Security Council, in the words of H. G. Nicholas, 'the permanent policeman of the world'.

Two final differences between the two organisations may be noted. Though the work of the League in economic and social matters had expanded greatly by 1939, the UNO was to go much further in these fields through the work of its specialised agencies. Secondly the UNO has a much wider membership and is a more genuine world organisation than the Euro-centred League, which had as a maximum 50 member states compared to the 1980 UNO membership of over 150 states.

(c) The United Nations in action

The creators of both the League and the United Nations had realised that harmonious Great Power relationships would be required if their world organisations were to be successful. The hope that such a Concert of the Great Powers might survive after 1945 was soon shattered when the first General Assembly of the United Nations met in January 1946. By then the Cold War was already developing, and soon the United Nations became a battleground between the East and West. In January Iran complained of the Russian refusal to move troops from Iranian soil, which the Russians countered by complaining of British interference in Greece. Soon the Russians began to use the veto so persistently that the work of the Security Council was frustrated. Between 1945 and 1963 the Soviet Union used the veto 100 times. The United Nations merely reflected the gulf between East and West as the Cold War intensified. 'Though the parents had not actually applied for a divorce', comments H. G. Nicholas, 'the marriage was now an open failure.'

In 1950 the organisation faced its first major crisis. After China had become Communist in 1949, the Russians proposed the removal of the Nationalist China representative from his seat in the Security Council on the grounds that Communist China really represented the Chinese people. When this proposal was defeated, the Russians boycotted the Security Council and other UN organisations. Then in June 1950 the Communist state of North Korea invaded South Korea. In the absence of the Russian representative, the Security Council accepted an American resolution recommending members to help South Korea against aggression. Twenty-one states sent contingents to swell the United Nations forces, which were put under the command of the American general Douglas MacArthur in July. The Security Council had acted promptly to counter a clear case of aggression. The Russians realised that they had made a tactical error in boycotting the United Nations. Their representative, Jacob Malik, returned to his duties in August and again succeeded in obstructing the work of the Security Council.

To deal with the problem raised by Soviet abuse of the veto, the United States put forward the Acheson Plan, which the Assembly passed in November 1950. The Plan empowered the Assembly to meet within 24 hours to deal with an emergency if the Security Council was paralysed by the veto and could not exercise its responsibility to maintain peace and security.

Meanwhile the war in Korea became a stalemate that lasted 3 years. Critics of the United Nations complained that its action in Korea became virtually an American operation, but it was surely inevitable that the world's strongest power would play a dominant part in the war. In July 1953 an armistice ended the Korean War and the UNO could take some satisfaction at the containment of North Korean aggression.

The first secretary general of the United Nations had been Trygve Lie of Norway. His support for collective security had earned him the hostility of the Soviet camp, and in 1952 he retired, being succeeded by the Swede Dag Hammarskjold, who was fortunate that it was not until 1956 that the United Nations was faced with another major crisis. After Colonel Nasser had seized the Suez Canal Company in July, Britain, France and Israel launched an attack on Egypt. After Britain used her veto for the first time in the Security Council, the Assembly was called into emergency session on 2 November and adopted an American resolution urging an immediate ceasefire and the withdrawal of the attacking forces. The British and French governments agreed to withdraw their forces, provided that a United Nations force could take over. It was at this point that the Secretary-General demonstrated great diplomatic skill. He not only played a major part in fashioning such a force (the United Nations Emergency Force) but persuaded the Nasser government to allow its entry into Egypt. UNEF kept Israeli and Egyptian forces apart and deprived Russia of any excuse for military intervention. By April 1957 hostile forces had been withdrawn from the area and the Suez Canal cleared by a United Nations salvage team.

The experiment of UNEF was the most important legacy of the Suez affair for the United Nations. It operated successfully as a buffer force, inserting itself, in the words of H. G. Nicholas, 'non-violently but yet physically, visibly, tangibly into a situation which mere diplomacy could not solve'. The value of the experiment was to be proved anew in the next three decades, notably in the Congo and again in the Arab–Israeli wars of 1967 and 1973.

No such adequate solution could be found for the second area of crisis in 1956. In October the Hungarian uprising (see Chapter 18) was brutally suppressed by Russian troops, and the General Assembly called in vain for their withdrawal. United Nations action was confined to condemnation of the Russian and Hungarian regimes, and the organisation's failure made a strong impression on contemporary observers. It was clear that the proper enforcement of the Charter was impossible where a Great Power was determined to defy it. The Russians, in refusing to change their policy over Hungary, had demonstrated the limited powers of the United Nations and its basically voluntary character.

By 1960 a new focus for United Nations activities lay in Africa, where, with the rapid decolonisation of that continent, seventeen new states had joined the organisation. The new states needed United Nations aid, particularly the huge Congo, which in June 1960 arrived at an independence for which its previous ruler, Belgium, had not properly prepared it. The internal anarchy of the Congo grew as a breakaway regime was set up in Katanga province, where the West had an economic interest in the copper mines. The whole affair became one of the most complex and controversial that the United Nations has ever faced.

Hammarskjold faced the problem with his usual acumen. Appreciating that a catastrophe in the Congo could lead to a power scramble in Africa, he recommended the use of a United Nations force drawn mainly from African states to restore order in the Congo and supervise the withdrawal of Belgian troops. By the end of August a force of 15,000 had achieved this, but as it had to control an area four times the size of France, the restoration of order was a protracted process.

By July 1961 a Congolese parliament had been established under United Nations protection, but Katanga refused to be integrated in the new state and employed white mercenaries to attack the United Nations forces, which were forced to take over Katanga and remove the foreign troops, an action causing heavy casualties. Hammarskjold was killed on a flight to see Tshombe, the Katangan president, in September 1961, and it was the next Secretary-General, U Thant, who supervised the final stages of the Congo crisis. In 1963 Tshombe announced the end of Katangan secession and accepted a United Nations federal plan for the Congo.

The Congo affair had two consequences for the United Nations. Kruschev led a campaign in 1960 to curb the powers of the Secretary-General, putting forward a scheme for three chief executives instead of one, but it found no favour with the Afro-Asian bloc. Secondly, the cost of the prolonged Congo operation increased the financial problems of the organisation. It was already short of funds, as a number of countries, especially the states of the Soviet bloc, Latin America and the Middle East, defaulted on their membership dues. Attempts to extract payment by threatening defaulting countries with the loss of their vote in the General Assembly failed completely.

The election of U Thant of Burma as Secretary-General was a reflection of the added prominence of the new Afro-Asian membership of the United Nations. In 1970, out of a total membership of 126, 40 were African and 26 were Asian states. This shift in membership was clear in 1961 when India invaded the Portuguese colony of Goa. The three Afro-Asian members of the Security Council refused to vote for a ceasefire, because in their view any form of colonialism was permanent aggression.

The decade of the 1960s was a bad period for the United Nations. It still carried out peacekeeping operations, as in Cyprus in 1964, where United Nations troops replaced British forces in an attempt to prevent Greek–Turkish hostilities on the island. In the gravest crises, however, the United Nations was virtually ignored. In the Cuban Affair of 1962 (see Chapter 17), the most direct confrontation that had ever taken place between Russia and the United States, the role of the United Nations was marginal. The Russian occupation of Czechoslovakia in 1968 was an even more serious blow to the credibility of the organisation. It paralleled the Hungarian tragedy of 1956 as a demonstration of the impotence of the United Nations in the face of criminal action by a Great Power. The fact of this impotence was driven home in the 1970s and 1980s. The United Nations has had only a small amount of influence on the course of events in the Middle East, and none at all in the Far East at a time when Cambodia and South Vietnam have fallen under Communist rule. It seems likely that the chief role of the United Nations will now lie in the areas of aid and development.

(d) Welfare work in the United Nations

From early days the United Nations has aimed at the creation of a network of organisations which would avoid controversial political issues and deal with the economic, social and financial needs of its members, particularly the poorer countries. Such organisations, it was argued, would prove the value of international cooperation and gradually eliminate national rivalries.

The United Nations took over one of the later plans of the League to create a new organisation, the Economic and Social Council (ECOSOC), which coordinates all the economic and social work of the specialised agencies. Thus it concerns itself with a wide range of activities, from the status of women to the problem of narcotics. The specialised agencies emanating from ECOSOC are better known and have taken shape in response to specific needs. The United Nations Educational, Scientific and Cultural Organisation (UNESCO), established in 1946, has suffered from a confusion of aims but has some genuine achievements to its credit in attacking illiteracy and providing educational facilities. The World Health Organisation (WHO), created in 1948, has tried to combat epidemic diseases and improve living standards. The Food and Agricultural Organisation (FAO) has striven to mount a world campaign against hunger by furnishing technical knowledge. The United Nations International Children's Emergency Fund (UNICEF) has raised funds from governments and public appeals to feed starving children. The General Agreement on Tariffs and Trade (GATT) was a multilateral tariff treaty negotiated in Geneva in 1947, to which was grafted a permanent body to supervise the liberalising of world trade. Its culmination was the signing of the Kennedy Round agreements (in honour of the American president) in 1967, which have provided for more substantial tariff reductions in the last few years, despite facing a growing climate of protectionism since 1973.

Two financial institutions have developed under the auspices of the United Nations. The International Bank for Reconstruction (known as the World Bank) is a lending agency whose objective is to encourage productive investment. The International Monetary Fund (IMF) is devoted to the promotion of exchange stability and international trade by making needed currencies available to members. In the first decade of its existence the IMF was too small for the demands made on it, but since 1956, with larger holdings than before, it has improved its performance.

Useful as these agencies have been, their limitations are considerable. Their work has not initiated peaceful coexistence nor have they been able to make significant inroads into the problem of world poverty. Nevertheless the World Bank and the IMF could still prove to be the best instruments to help Third World countries escape from poverty.

(e) The United Nations in the 1980s

The UNO has continued to play a useful role in world crises during the last two decades where second-class powers were at odds, as during the Falklands war in 1982. The organisation is a forum for even the smallest nations, and the current Secretary-General, Perez de Cuellar, is a persistent and a skilful diplomat.

Nevertheless the organisation's weaknesses have become more rather than less evident over time. Where the superpowers are fundamentally involved, it is powerless. Its motion condemning Russian aggression in Afghanistan in 1979 was vetoed by the Soviet

Union in the Security Council, and although a similar motion passed the General Assembly by a large majority, Russian troops remained in Afghanistan until 1988 and only evacuated then for reasons other than UN pressure. Increasingly the UN has seemed irrelevant on really large issues, where, not unlike the 1930s, the major conferences have taken place outside the international organisation. The best example of the relegation of the UN to the status of a sideshow was the succession of Gorbachev–Reagan summits carried out without any reference to the organisation.

The prestige of the UN has not been helped in the late 1980s by revelations that Kurt Waldheim, Secretary-General from 1971 to 1981, had lied about his wartime career and was far more involved in Nazi activities in the Balkans than he was prepared to admit. The preponderance of Third World members has led to other blocs facing difficulty in having their resolutions passed, and cases are not voted on on their merits. With even the USA joining other states in reducing contributions to the UN, the organisation's welfare work has been severely constrained.

(2) The demise of colonialism

Nothing in the history of the colonial empires was more remarkable than the speed with which they disappeared. In 1939 500 million people in Asia and Africa were ruled by Europeans. By 1970 the number had fallen to 21 millions, and with the 1974 revolution in Portugal leading to the independence of Angola and Mozambique, old-style colonialism has practically ceased to exist. The rapid loss of their colonial empires threw into sharper relief the changed position of European states in the world. They had become second- or even third-rank powers, a fact of life driven home by the Suez Affair (see Chapter 19).

In Asia the British rapidly granted independence to India, Pakistan, Burma and Malaya after the war. The Dutch were in no position to reoccupy their Far Eastern possessions, and the Dutch East Indies became Indonesia in 1945. It was, however, France which suffered the most disastrous retreat in Asia. An attempt was made to create a Federation of Indo-China to include Laos, Cambodia and Vietnam. The resulting struggle with Ho Chi Minh's Communists led to the calamitous French defeat at Dien Bien Phu in 1954.

The defeat of France in Indo-China made the retention of her African empire infinitely more difficult. In fact, as far as Africa was concerned, the retreat from empire, in Fieldhouse's phrase, changed from a measured crawl to an uncontrolled gallop. Tunis, Morocco, Algeria, French West Africa and French Equatorial Africa had all gained their independence from France by 1962. Meanwhile the

British had pushed their more advanced African colonies towards self-rule. Ghana (the former Gold Coast) became independent in 1957, followed by Nigeria in 1960. As the 1960s progressed, all Britain's former African possessions gained self-government, including Kenya, Uganda and Zambia (the former Northern Rhodesia).

It is still difficult to account for this rapid pace of decolonisation, because the events are too recent and no one explanation fits all cases. Certainly both the United States and Russia were hostile in sentiment and policy towards colonialism, and obstructed the attempts by Europeans to re-establish colonial control after 1945. American policy was negatively hostile, as seen in the reluctance of the United States to answer French appeals for help in Indo-China. Material help was given, but Eisenhower was unwilling to intervene directly by using American troops. The Russians were positively hostile to Western imperialism, and through the Cominform a coordinated Soviet offensive was launched in Asia. Soviet aid was a significant factor in Ho Chi Minh's success in Indo-China.

Of more importance than the hostility of the superpowers was the change in the influence and attitudes of the colonial powers themselves. The coercive power of European states had declined, owing to the ravages of two world wars. In 1945 they were so exhausted and bankrupt that their priority was domestic reconstruction. If empire was to be retained only at the cost of further imperial wars, then for most European governments the price was too high. Again the case of Indo-China furnishes the most vivid example of this mood. This apparently unending war, in which the average Frenchman had little interest, imposed an intolerable psychological strain on France. The sense of relief once total withdrawal had been decided upon in 1954 was reflected in the vote of the French Assembly, which approved the Indo-China settlement by 471 votes to 14.

In any case European opinion had become more responsive to the principle that colonial peoples should be encouraged to seek independence. Before 1939 imperial rule still seemed morally justifiable, provided that its methods were benevolent. The war changed this self-confidence, as German imperialism within Europe aroused horror. Yet even before the war it had been appreciated in British government circles that India would have to become independent. The Labour prime minister between 1945 and 1951, Clement Attlee, had served on the Simon Commission of 1928, which investigated Indian affairs, and he had become convinced that the British must leave India. His views were paralleled in other West European countries, and as a result Europe emancipated many of her colonies long before she was forced to do so.

Japanese victories in Asia over the white races during the war had profound implications for the future of Western colonialism. At the height of her power, Imperial Japan controlled Indo-China, Malaya,

Burma, the Philippines, the East Indies and Thailand. A Greater East Asia ministry was created to exploit the conquered territories, and the harsh rule implemented by the Japanese did much to arouse East Asian nationalism. At the same time the Japanese paid lip-service to the principle of independence, and a number of concessions were given to their new possessions after the tide of war had turned in favour of the Allies. As Richard Storry explains in *The History of Modern Japan*:

> The granting of even sham independence to the occupied countries of Asia . . . meant that it would be normally impossible for the Western colonial nations to refuse them real independence once Japan was defeated . . . Thus Japanese victories, by destroying the mystique of White supremacy, and Japanese policies, by according to the occupied territories at least the outward form of independence, greatly hastened the birth after the war of the new nations in South and South-east Asia.

Finally the new strength of colonial nationalism made a rapid end to the European empires likely once the war had ended. D. K. Fieldhouse suggests that this colonial nationalism had three roots. First, it existed continuously from the moment of occupation in areas like Hindu India and Moslem North Africa, where non-Christian and non-European cultures survived. Second, it was stimulated by an infusion of European ideas and practices. European ideals of liberty, equality and independence were incompatible with colonial rule and made the colonial peoples resent their subordination. Third, European rule affected most aspects of colonial society and many of the fundamental changes that occurred were resented. For example, large-scale industry and mining produced shanty towns and with them a new rootless proletariat.

Where two or more of these influences coincided, as in India and Indonesia, strong national movements arose. India, by extracting concessions before 1939 and by gaining independence in 1947, proved colonial nationalism to be a force which could no longer be ignored. By the time that he visited Africa in 1960, Harold Macmillan, the British prime minister, felt it necessary to comment on the new power of African nationalism. 'The most striking of all the impressions I have formed since I left London a month ago is the strength of this African national consciousness. In different places it may take different forms. But it is happening everywhere. The wind of change is blowing through the continent.'

It is still too early to draw up a final balance sheet for the period of European imperialism. In defence of the imperial experiment it may be suggested that living standards in many colonies have risen through European rule higher than otherwise they would have done. Secondly, the peoples of Asia and Africa were introduced to the

European ideals of equality and independence. Finally, the European empires provided for many years a framework of political stability over much of the globe.

There were two chief drawbacks to imperial rule. It destroyed the old social and political institutions in many colonies and left a dangerous vacuum in colonial societies. Secondly, it failed to give the colonies adequate education for independence, and the history of many former colonies since independence has been one of political chaos and economic decline rather than progress. Particularly saddening has been the failure of parliamentary government in the former colonies, as many African countries have succumbed to dictatorship.

(3) The onset of the Cold War

(a) The Grand Alliance

When the Nazis attacked Russia in June 1941 both Churchill and Roosevelt arranged to send aid to the Russians. Churchill remarked to his secretary, 'If Hitler invaded Hell I would make at least a favourable reference to the Devil in the House of Commons.' In the course of the war the decisions of the Grand Alliance – the United States, Russia and Britain – determined the territorial and political structure of postwar Europe.

Western relations with Russia were never really cordial, and were clouded by mutual suspicion. The two Western powers nevertheless sent massive aid to Russia, and, according to Snell, 4,400 tanks and 3,100 planes had reached Russia by mid-1942. Stalin demanded more Western action, in particular the opening of a second front. The Russian leader was most suspicious that the West was deliberately delaying this move in the hope of seeing Russia permanently weakened by the German attack. To reassure the Russians, Churchill offered a formal alliance, and at the Casablanca conference in January 1943 the two Western leaders insisted that Germany would have to surrender unconditionally. Stalin was not noticeably appeased by their declaration, and when he was informed that the Normandy operations would be delayed until 1944 he hinted that Russia might be forced to make a separate peace with Germany. There seems little doubt that his confidence in his Allies was severely strained.

At the Teheran conference in November 1943 relations between the allies improved. The Western leaders made a definite promise that the Normandy invasion would take place in May 1944, and in return Stalin promised to make war on Japan once Germany was defeated.

As the war went on, the meetings of the Big Three revealed a growing discrepancy between Stalin's aims and those of the Western statesmen. Churchill and Roosevelt had met off the coast of Newfoundland in August 1941 to draft the Atlantic Charter, a general statement of principles on which a postwar settlement might be based. Both powers disavowed any national gain or the implementing of any territorial changes contrary to the wishes of the inhabitants. All peoples would have the right to choose their own forms of government in a new world of economic cooperation. The aggressive nations would be disarmed and a general system of security created. In January 1942 these principles were embodied in a Declaration of the United Nations, which all governments at war with Germany signed.

With the advantage of hindsight we can appreciate that Stalin could never be persuaded to subscribe to the principles of the Atlantic Charter, though he subscribed to them on paper. His objective was Russian control of all Eastern Europe, and to his diplomacy he brought his greatest gifts of patience, tenacity and shrewd appreciation of the strength and weaknesses of his partners in the Grand Alliance. He was assisted by the attitude of Roosevelt. Unlike Churchill the American trusted Stalin and hoped to play the mediator between the British and the Russians. He was deeply convinced that the most serious problem for the postwar world was not Soviet strength but British imperialism. He told Milolajczk, 'Of one thing I am certain, Stalin is not an Imperialist.' While he was president, the Americans showed relatively little concern for Poland or, in the military sphere, the need for the West to gain Berlin.

As the war continued, Stalin's diplomatic position improved, and by 1945 the Red Army was in occupation of most of Eastern Europe. The differences between the allies now became acute. At Teheran a cordial atmosphere had reigned, but at the next two important meetings of the Big Three – at Yalta in February and at Potsdam in July – the cracks in the Grand Alliance could not be papered over.

(b) The major areas of disagreement

Many issues divided the Western powers from Russia. They quarrelled with the Soviets over the structure of the new United Nations Organisation, in which Russia was to repeatedly abuse her right of veto in the Security Council. They rebuffed Stalin's suggestion that Russia should join in the occupation of Japan after Japan's surrender in August 1945. The growth of Russia's influence in the Balkans broke agreements with the Western powers, provoked furious rows at Potsdam and led to British intervention in Greece in 1944 and 1947. But the problems that divided the West and Soviet Russia above all others were Poland and Germany.

Poland was the first issue that revealed the inability of the Allies to compromise, and it became, in Snell's phrase, 'a touch-stone of Great Power relationships'. The West and the Soviets disagreed sharply on the question of Poland's postwar frontiers and government. Britain had officially gone to war to defend Polish independence and wished Poland to recover her lost territories and have an independent government. The Russians were not prepared to return their gains made at Poland's expense, but would allow Poland to receive compensation at Germany's expense. Stalin was inflexibly opposed to the creation of any anti-Soviet government in Poland.

At Teheran in 1943 an agreement on the Polish boundaries was reached. Russia would retain her gains, with Poland gaining much of East Germany up to the Oder and East Neisse rivers. No agreement was reached on the nature of the postwar Polish government. Britain and the United States favoured the London-based Polish government in exile. As the London Poles were opposed to giving up any territory to Russia, Stalin refused to recognise them, and set up another Polish group, the Union of Polish Patriots.

The hostility of the London Poles towards Russia had increased after the discovery by the Germans in 1943 of a mass grave in Katyn Forest in which were buried the bodies of several thousand Polish officers captured by the Russians in 1939. Relations between the London Poles and Russia deteriorated even more after the Warsaw Rising in 1944. The Russians refused to help the rising, and even prevented the Western allies from using Russian airfields to drop supplies to the Poles.

The attitude of the London Poles to Russia was understandable but hardly politic, as it was always likely to encourage Stalin to take a harder line. In December 1944 the Union of Polish Patriots, now the Lublin Committee, proclaimed itself the provisional government, and in January 1945 Stalin recognised it, much to the anger of the West. At Yalta a new agreement was reached. The Lublin Committee was to form the nucleus of a Polish government, with Russia guaranteeing free elections and the inclusion of the London Poles in the new government. These guarantees were never implemented.

Germany was an even more serious problem than Poland, because the issues at stake were much greater. The power that controlled Germany would control the whole continent of Europe. At Yalta it was agreed that Germany and Berlin would be divided into four Allied zones, controlled by Britain, Russia, the United States and France. As Berlin was surrounded by the Soviet zone, it was to be the source of several crises in the next few years.

The Soviets and the Western powers were soon at loggerheads over the treatment Germany was to receive. The Russians wanted Germany permanently crippled, while the West wanted her domination broken without leaving the continent under Russian sway. The Russians demanded huge reparations, and ravaged their own zone when the West suggested more modest payments. The amount of German territory that should go to Poland was still in dispute. At Potsdam the Russians insisted that the Polish–German border should now run along the Oder–West Neisse line, an arrangement giving more territory to Poland than had the Teheran agreement.

What Stalin really desired was a partition of Germany, with the Rhineland and Bavaria being separated from the rest of the country. The Western powers had themselves considered such schemes earlier in the war but were unwilling to implement them in 1945. At Potsdam the Big Three agreed to treat Germany as a unit with the frontiers of 1937. Ironically Stalin still achieved his objective. In time a de facto partition of Germany into two states was accomplished by Russia's refusal to merge her zone of occupation with the Western zones to form a united Germany.

(c) Europe in two blocs

In March 1946 Churchill in a speech at Fulton, Missouri, commented, 'From Stettin in the Baltic to Trieste in the Adriatic, an iron curtain has descended across the continent.' At the time many in the West thought that he was exaggerating the Russian menace, but later events appeared to prove the accuracy of Churchill's opinion. The Soviets consolidated their hold over nearly all Eastern Europe, and fears that Greece and Turkey were in danger led to the enunciation of the Truman Doctrine in 1947. President Truman declared that the security of Greece and Turkey was vital to American national interests and began a substantial programme of aid. Soon both blocs had formed alliance systems, NATO and the Warsaw Pact. In 1950 the Cold War 'hotted up', with the invasion of South Korea by Communist North Korea. Only after Stalin's death in 1953 were the first hesitant steps towards better relations taken.

By the very completeness of its victory the decline of the Grand Alliance became inevitable. Only mutual fear of Germany had kept such contrasting partners together for so long, and once the German threat receded, then so the unity of the Allies dissolved as well. Indeed it is remarkable that the coalition was maintained until the end of the war.

The main reason for conflict must be sought in the character of the state system. Suspicion of the West was built into the Soviet system, and it was inherent in the character of Stalin. He remarked to one of Tito's colleagues, Djilas, 'Churchill is the kind who, if you don't watch him, will slip a kopek out of your pocket. Roosevelt is not like that. He dips in his hands only for bigger coins.' Collaboration with the West after 1945 would have meant Russia being opened to Western influences, which would have eroded the strength of Stalin's totalitarian regime. It was a risk Stalin was not prepared to take. He even rejected Marshall Aid, after which step, as Ulam says, 'both sides became frozen in mutual unfriendliness'.

A clash with the West was likely for a second reason. As Feis and Ulam have emphasised, Stalin was a Great Russian nationalist. One of the supreme motives behind his war aims and peace plans was a Russian domination of Europe more complete than that achieved by the tsars. No demonstration of Western goodwill could have overcome this blend of suspicion and ambition in Stalin. Nor would a tougher Western policy towards Russia have been possible in 1945. The publics in the West would not have tolerated a new confrontation with an ally, nor could the Western powers have negotiated from a position of strength. Territories in dispute were occupied by Russian troops and the use of the atom bomb was unthinkable.

No doubt the Soviet threat was exaggerated in the West. Russia emerged from the war gravely weakened, and the Russian army was reduced to under 3 million by 1948 from over 11 million during the war. Though Stalin was determined to expand his influence, he did not wish to incur the risk of war. The reality of Russian weakness was not appreciated in the West, where it was widely believed that massive Soviet armies were ready to march to the English Channel. Yet Western apprehension was understandable. The war had eliminated Germany and left Russia as the only great power on the continent. George Kennan was in essence correct when he stated in 1947 that the main aim of Soviet policy was to 'make sure that it has filled every nook and cranny available to it in the basin of world power'. He advocated that the West carry out a long-term policy of containing Communism in the hope that in time the Soviet regime would either mellow or break up.

Kennan's policy of containment still makes sense in a European context. The Cold War is still being waged but it is now no longer a two-sided but a triangular phenomenon. The split between Moscow and Peking has created a new Cold War. As the West and the Soviets moved closer in the 1950s, Russia and China moved further apart, and since 1964 Sino-Soviet relations have been bitter (see Chapter 18).

(4)   The North Atlantic Treaty Organisation and the Warsaw Pact

The menace which West European countries believed lay behind the Iron Curtain accelerated moves to strengthen their defences. The French proposed a predominantly European scheme, but the United States, Britain and the Commonwealth pressed for a form of Atlantic Union. This was surely more realistic. The time had passed when Europe could defend itself, and the United States was needed to play the leading role in a new defence force.

The groundwork for this new force was laid in Brussels in 1948, and in 1949 a treaty setting up the North Atlantic Treaty Organisation (NATO) was signed. It was primarily a treaty of collective self-defence in which it was understood that if any NATO member was the object of an armed attack, the other members would afford it all military and other such aid. Within a few years the United States, Britain, Canada, the Benelux countris, Norway, Iceland, Denmark, Greece, Turkey, Italy, West Germany, France and Portugal had all joined the organisation. The decision to join in NATO marked a revolutionary step forward in American foreign policy. The United States since the days of George Washington had avoided entangling alliances; by signing the NATO treaty the American government made a definite commitment to safeguard European security.

Two important developments in NATO were provoked by the outbreak of the Korean War, which drew attention to the danger of war in Europe and the inadequate state of the West European defences. The Americans, who had been bearing the burden of re-equipping European armies, now pressed for the integration of NATO forces under a centralised command, with the inclusion of West German units. The first phase of this development went smoothly enough. In 1950 General Eisenhower was appointed as supreme Allied Commander of all NATO forces, and established his military headquarters, known as SHAPE (Supreme Headquarters Allied Powers Europe) near Paris. Under this central direction, regional commands were later established for Northern, Central and Southern Europe. The evolution of this rather complex structure was a remarkable example of the new spirit of cooperation.

The question of German rearmament was a much thornier problem. Understandably the French were deeply apprehensive at the dangers of reviving German militarism, but in October 1954 they accepted a British proposal for West German membership of NATO, combined with certain assurances for France. Both Britain and the United States promised to keep their forces on the continent for an unlimited period.

By 1957 NATO was able to claim that its forces for the defence of Europe had increased fourfold, and that these forces had become more effective in fire-power, planning and standardisation of equipment. Yet in many respects the organisation fell short of expectations and faced many difficulties. Its original aim was to provide a force of 96 divisions to combat any Soviet attack on Western Europe, and this was never achieved. More seriously, after the relaxation of tension after Stalin's death in 1953, the whole cohesion of the organisation deteriorated. Member states were variously engaged in areas of the world other than Europe – the United States in Korea, Britain in the Middle East and France in Algeria and Indo-China. At times, as in the Suez crisis of 1956, NATO members were in open disagreement with each other, the Anglo-French attack on Egypt coming under direct American condemnation.

A fundamental long-term strain on the NATO alliance lay in the area of nuclear strategy. It was only natural that the European members resented American nuclear supremacy, which, though it was a valuable deterrent, meant that NATO was dominated by the United States. In any crisis the Americans would decide whether or not to use nuclear weapons to help Europe, and the European states were bound to question the extent to which the Americans were really committed to Europe. The American government in its turn was reluctant to let European countries have control over nuclear weapons, because of the risk that they might be used in relatively unimportant local conflicts which would yet trigger off a nuclear war. With Britain and France already developing their own nuclear weaponry, the American fears of a proliferation of nuclear arsenals were realistic.

The British and American governments managed to reach some agreement on this vexed question. At Nassau in December 1962 Macmillan and Kennedy hammered out an arrangement by which the British abandoned their plan for Skybolt missiles in return for American Polaris missiles to be used in British nuclear submarines. The United States went further in 1964 in proposing the creation of a multilateral nuclear force (MLF), consisting of 25 surface vessels, each equipped with eight Polaris missiles and manned by crews of mixed nationalities, so that her partners in NATO could enjoy some participation in the operation of a nuclear force. The plan seemed to cause more division than unity in the NATO alliance and was dropped. The French president, de Gaulle, opposed the MLF on the ground that it would in fact reinforce the American domination of NATO. He refused to accept Polaris missiles or participate in the formation of a multilateral fleet, affirming his belief in the effectiveness of national nuclear deterrents.

De Gaulle disliked the whole structure of the organisation, with its American leadership and the placing of French forces under a Supreme Allied Commander who was not French. In 1966 he withdrew French forces from NATO, and the headquarters of the organisation had to be transferred at great expense from Paris to Brussels.

Other NATO difficulties have led Western alarmists in recent years to question the organisation's effectiveness. They have pointed to its 300 committees and byzantine bureaucracy. They have contrasted its ineffectiveness with the Soviet bloc's equivalent of NATO, the Warsaw Pact, to which belong Russia, East Germany, Poland, Czechoslovakia, Rumania, Bulgaria and Hungary. According to such critics, NATO is relatively disunited when such members as Greece and Turkey quarrel, e.g. over Cyprus, and is patently inferior in conventional weapons to the Warsaw Pact.

The Warsaw Pact, it is alleged, has the advantage of standardised weaponry, which NATO has failed to implement because it is an explosive political issue. In 1975 the French government waxed furious at a decision by Belgium and other NATO allies to buy American F16 planes in preference to the French Mirage fighter in what was called the arms deal of the century. In the Warsaw Pact countries standardisation is complete, but NATO countries compete with each other to supply arms, and this leads to much waste of research resources, while the use of national weapons systems hampers the efficiency of the fighting units themselves. As a 1975 American report stressed, NATO is not getting enough 'bang for its buck'.

Perhaps the most serious question mark hanging over NATO is the strength of the American commitment. The value of NATO to the USA has been questioned since the late 1960s, and particularly in the 1980s, when the nation's resources have been strained by global commitments (see Chapter 17). The number of American troops has been reduced (though they still number 250,000) and the American government has repeatedly stressed that the European members of NATO should assume a greater share of the burden of European defence. In January 1984 *The Economist* published an article in which it showed that an image of the 'Useless European' was taking shape in the American mind. The accusations were of European tightfisted-ness in defence spending and of always asking what America could do for Europe rather than what Europe could do for America. Such a perception, *The Economist* suggested, would cause Europe to be pushed another notch downwards in America's priorities, below the Pacific basin, south-west Asia and central America. Certainly, after Vietnam in the 1970s and her economic problems of the 1980s, the danger that the USA might return to her old isolationism cannot be dismissed lightly.

Nevertheless it may well be that the Western observers have been too alarmist. Western superiority in nuclear weapons is profoundly disturbing to Russian military planners, who are also worried at recent developments in conventional weapons. European countries now provide 90 per cent of the manpower and most of the weaponry for NATO forces in Europe, while the Warsaw Pact is heavily dependent on Russia.

Recent studies show that the Warsaw Pact has only a slight edge in manpower (14 million as against NATO's 12 million). Many of Russia's 52,000 battle tanks are the obsolescent T-54s, which would find it difficult to conduct a fast offensive in the crowded terrain of North Germany. In addition, Moscow is worried about the reliability of its Polish contingents at a time when Solidarity is so popular, of its East German contingents when East Germany wishes to improve relations with West Germany, and of most of its partners' effective-ness. Indeed the Polish armed forces may not be an addition of strength but the reverse, since they and important Polish road and rail links would require Red Army supervision in wartime.

Russian military planners have also had to bear in mind since the 1960s the horrifying scenario whereby they might be engaged in large-scale conflict with NATO and China simultaneously. Accordingly the USSR is compelled to keep about 50 divisions and 13,000 tanks ready for the eventuality of a Sino-Soviet clash.

Despite its impressive expansion in the last 25 years, the Soviet navy is still inferior to the USA's fifteen carrier task-forces. When the fleets of the two alliances are compared, the Western allies have twice as many surface ships and three times as much naval air power as the Warsaw Pact, with near parity in submarines. Nor are such imbalances likely to be easily corrected by the Soviet Union, given its host of economic problems (see Chapter 18).

FURTHER READING

Ambrose, S. E., *Rise to Globalism: American foreign policy since 1938*, Penguin, Harmondsworth, 1983
Calvocoressi, P., *World Politics since 1945*, Longmans, London, 1971
Feis, H., *From Trust to Terror: The Onset of the Cold War*, Anthony Blond, London, 1970
Fieldhouse, D. K., *The Colonial Empires*, Weidenfeld and Nicolson, London, 1966
Jenks, C. W., *The World Beyond the Charter*, Allen and Unwin, London, 1969
Luard, E., *A History of the United Nations*, Macmillan, London, 1982
Nicholas, H. G., *The United Nations as a Political Institution*, OUP, New York, 1987
Siracusa, J. M., *The American Diplomatic Revolution*, Open University Press, Milton Keynes, 1976

QUESTIONS

1. To what extent was the United Nations modelled on the League of Nations?
2. What factors have constrained the activities of the United Nations since 1945?
3. Was the rapid demise of colonialism after 1945 the consequence of European weakness or colonial nationalism?
4. How far do you agree with Schlesinger's view that the Cold War was 'the brave and essential response of free men to Communist aggression'?
5. Have Western critics exaggerated NATO's weaknesses and Soviet strengths in the last two decades?

12
Western Europe since 1945

(1) The development of the European Economic Community (EEC)

(a) The origins of the EEC

The First World War, with its totally new scale of senseless slaughter, led to renewed consideration of the idea of European unity. The outstanding figure in the interwar years was Count Coudenhove-Kalergi. His international outlook is understandable when it is recalled that his father, who was of Greek and Dutch extraction, was an Austro-Hungarian diplomat, and that his mother was Japanese. The Count started a Pan-European Union, which had the support of several famous politicians, notably Aristide Briand. Briand, who was the first to coin the phrase 'Common Market', was French foreign minister in the 1920s, and in 1929 he put forward a scheme for a European Union to the League of Nations. It was, however, too long and vague. It was received with considerable reservation by most countries, including England; the onset of the Great Depression, the rise of Nazism and the death of Briand himself in 1932 ensured its complete failure.

It was the impact of the Second World War which really stimulated genuine moves towards European integration. The war had impoverished Europe, destroyed Europe's political system and had produced such a collapse of all civilised standards that bold new solutions were considered essential. It was now widely believed that Europe could only be rebuilt by a cooperative effort in an age when the nation-state was no longer a viable unit.

The creation of new institutions was accelerated not only by the natural fear of a future revived Germany but also by the prevalent apprehension about the intentions of Russian Communism under Stalin. The West feared both the sheer military might of Russia and the kind of subversion seen in the communist takeover of Czechoslovakia in 1948. The presence of large communist parties in both Italy and France made the communist threat appear only too real. Integration was also encouraged by United States pressure in favour of a united Europe, as the Americans believed that such a Europe would be prosperous, thus providing both a barrier to Communism and a field for American exports and investment.

After 1945 solid support for European initiatives came from a group of dedicated European-minded politicians, whose experience and background made them loathe the internecine warfare in Europe since 1914. Three of the men in the vanguard of the movement were devout Catholics – Konrad Adenauer, the anti-Prussian mayor of Cologne, who became chancellor of West Germany; Alcide de Gasperi, a deputy in the Vienna Diet while Austria-Hungary was fighting Italy in the First World War, then prime minister of Italy after 1945; and Robert Schuman, a German national during the First World War and then prime minister of France after the return of Alsace-Lorraine.

Special mention should also be made of Jean Monnet, who died as recently as 1979 at the age of 90. He was more responsible than any other man for bringing the nations of Europe together in the Common Market, and his ultimate aim was a truly united Europe. Though he was one of the most remarkable Frenchmen of his time, he was a prophet with little honour in his own country, because much of his work and influence was exercised behind the scenes. He served in the Franco-British Economic Coordination Committees in both world wars and was responsible for the adoption of the 'dirigiste' approach in French economic planning after 1945. It was Monnet who conceived the idea of Franco-German cooperation in economic matters, which finally bore fruit in the Schuman Plan and the European Coal and Steel Community of 1951. Next Monnet founded the Action Committee for the United States of Europe, a body which played an important role in the negotiations leading up to the ratification of the EEC in 1957.

(b) The creation of new European institutions

(i) The organisation for European Economic Cooperation

With the proclamation of Marshall Aid in 1947, the Organisation for European Economic Cooperation (OEEC) was established. Its first task was the delicate one of dividing American aid among the member states. This objective was successfully achieved over a 3-year period. The second principal activity was the liberalisation of trade, the free flow of which had been severely limited by many restrictions in the postwar period. As tariff reductions were the concern of GATT, the OEEC concentrated on other barriers to free trade, principally quantitative restrictions. Within 6 years trade between European nations doubled. A third area of activity lay in finance. To improve the system of payments between member states, a European Payments Union was created in 1950 to institute a general multilateral system of payments.

Some members wished to push ahead and develop a European customs union, a move opposed by Britain because of her close ties with the Commonwealth. Despite this disappointment, the OEEC flourished. By 1959 it had eighteen members, including Spain, and since then the United States, Canada, Japan and Australia have joined to convert the organisation into a more global institution. The word 'Europe' has been dropped and it has become the Organisation for Economic Cooperation and Development (OECD), reflecting one of the major problems of our time – the economic development of underdeveloped countries.

(ii) The Council of Europe

Economic institutions have played the most important part in the moves towards European integration since the war, but they have tended to concentrate on specialised functions. A more comprehensive attempt to unite Europe has been attempted under the Council of Europe, established in 1949 by ten West European states. Again the British attitude at the time profoundly disappointed other European states. Though Britain became a founder member, Attlee's Labour government regarded the Council of Europe with the utmost reserve. The British were not attracted by the abstract idea of European unity, a concept they distrusted as a potential infringement of sovereignty. At this stage, too, it was felt that Britain's true interests lay more with the Commonwealth and the United States than with Europe.

Nevertheless the Council had expanded its membership to seventeen countries by 1971. With its headquarters in Strasbourg, it had two central organs, a Committee of Ministers composed of the foreign ministers of the member states, and an Assembly, whose members are elected by the parliaments of the member states. The assembly is not a parliament as such, for it has no authority to legislate for the member states. If a two-thirds majority of the Assembly is in favour, it can make recommendations to the Council of Ministers, which in turn can make recommendations to the member states. Real power has therefore so far eluded the Council of Europe, as individual states guard their sovereignty.

The Council has failed to achieve its original aim – the political unity of Europe – but it has been useful as a policy-formulating body, sponsoring some important treaties, such as the European Convention for the Protection of Human Rights and Fundamental Freedom, which came into force in 1953.

(iii) The European Economic Community

The first success for the apostles of economic union was the economic integration of the Low Countries, with Belgium, Holland and Luxembourg forming the Benelux Union in 1948. At the same time French statesmen, notably Jean Monnet and Robert Schuman, were active in promoting European integration. In 1951 the heavy industries such as coal and iron came under the control of a European Coal, Iron and Steel Community, which established a common market in these products and a common programme of expansion. In the 1950s supranational machinery was set up to supervise the work of this organisation. Again, while many European countries expressed an interest in joining, the British preferred to stay aloof.

The evolution of a common market in coal and steel was of profound importance in preparing the way for more fundamental attempts to establish a European Community. In 1955 delegates representing Belgium, West Germany, France, Holland, Italy and Luxembourg met at Messina and agreed to form the European Economic Community. The constitution and programme were worked out in the next 18 months and in March 1957 the Treaty of Rome, setting up the EEC, was ready for signature. It established a customs union of the six countries concerned, and pledged to reduce and by 1969 abolish all tariffs on their mutual trade. However, this was only the initial objective of the EEC, for the preamble to the Treaty of Rome expressed the intention to establish the foundations of an ever closer union among the European peoples. Therefore from the start the political concept of European union underlies the whole endeavour. The aim is to end historic rivalries in a fusion of essential interests, and therefore the title 'Community' is a more appropriate one than 'Common Market'. The aim of the Community is not merely the establishment of free trade in a common market but the harmonious development of all economic activities, a rising standard of living and closer relations between member states. Obstacles to the free movement of persons, services and capital were to be abolished, and a common agricultural policy was to be inaugurated. Other aims were the improvement of working conditions, the use of a European Investment Bank and the expansion of trade with overseas countries.

The European treaties were soon negotiated, because the Six agreed on goals and principles but did not even try to resolve most of the problems inherent in an economic community. The Treaty of Rome only established a framework within which policies were to be devised at a later date. In other words, the Six adopted the notion of 'agreeing to agree', leaving the details to be worked out later. Perhaps the British made an error in not following such tactics in their first attempt to join the Community. Instead they sought detailed arrangements, a course which gave de Gaulle an opportunity to block British membership. By 1970 the British had evidently learnt the lesson. Heath's government then made it clear that the priority was British accession to the Community rather than working out the fine details of entry.

(c) British attitudes to European unity

Britain had cooperated with her West European neighbours after 1945 on matters of economic recovery and defence, for example in the distribution of Marshall Aid, the work of the OEEC and the creation of the North Atlantic Treaty Organisation. But British governments had remained convinced that cooperation in Europe must not advance to a point at which there was a risk of the loss of British independence. Therefore in 1957 Britain was unwilling to sign the Treaty of Rome which set up the EEC, and her rather disdainful diplomacy seemed designed to minimise the importance of the new institution. In 1957, for example, the British suggested to the OEEC that all non-EEC countries in the OEEC should join in a free trade area. For Britain this would mean that she could keep her preferential links with the Commonwealth and her system of agricultural protection (an advantage that she would have to forfeit in the EEC, with its common external tariff). The six countries of the EEC opposed the British proposal and as a result Britain's only option was to set up a small free-trade area centred on herself. In 1959 the European Free Trade Association (EFTA) was created, comprising Britain, Sweden, Norway, Denmark, Austria, Switzerland and Portugal.

Thus the idea of European unity was one from which British governments, whether Labour or Conservative, shrank. It was traditional British policy to avoid firm commitments in peacetime, and also the British feared that European unity might turn into unity against them. Even if this were not the case, the process of attaining unity in Europe presented Britain with an awkward choice – to join or not to join. If she chose the former course, she might endanger her position as a world power, while if she chose to stand aside, she might lose much of her European influence.

An understanding of psychological factors in essential if we are to understand British attitudes in the immediate postwar years. F. N. Northedge refers to 'the notorious emotional detachment of the British people from mainland Europe', a detachment which perhaps prevented a proper appreciation of national interests. Europeans were foreigners who ran their affairs badly (like the Frenchmen of the unstable Fourth Republic) and who dragged honest Englishmen into costly or risky wars. British survival during the Second World War heightened what has been termed 'the Channel Complex'. In her finest hour Britain had stood alone. She had been undefeated, she had escaped occupation and she emerged from the war with renewed pride in her national virtues and institutions. The countries of Western Europe, on the other hand, had just passed through the worst ordeal in their history, and the common experience of Nazi occupation made it imperative for them to develop some form of European unity from the ruins.

In government circles the belief that Britain could still maintain a world role died hard. As Winston Churchill phrased it in 1950, Britain stood at the intersection of three overlapping circles – the English-speaking world, the Commonwealth and Europe. It was by her unique position within all three that she might still play a unique world role. Therefore, as Uwe Kitzinger emphasises, 'none of these three bonds, and certainly not that with Europe could afford to be tightened to the extent that they might damage the other two'.

To put it bluntly, Europe was by far the least important of the three overlapping circles to Britain in the immediate postwar years. There was still considerable belief in the idea of the Commonwealth and in the 'special relationship' with the United States of America. It should also be remembered that the British standard of living in the late 1940s and early 1950s was far superior to that of the Continent, and therefore there seemed little to be gained from integration with nations suffering economic difficulties and political instability.

Nevertheless a thorough re-examination of Britain's relationship with Europe was taking place by the 1950s, and it led to a considerable if reluctant change of attitudes. Again psychological factors were important. The movement of the Six towards unity, in the words of Northedge, 'left Britain stranded and increasingly cut off from one of the most notable forms of political change in the twentieth century'. As the Community progressed towards harmonised economies and political integration, Britain would be shut out of a new union of 200 million people.

Economic factors also influenced British thinking. By 1961 the EEC was proving itself in economic terms, with EEC countries forging ahead while Britain stagnated. Enjoying internal tariff cuts of 30 per cent by 1960, the EEC countries succeeded in raising industrial output by more than 50 per cent between 1954 and 1960, while Britain's industrial output rose by only 20 per cent in the same period. This EEC economic performance appeared to be attracting American investment which had previously gone to Britain. Before the EEC came into existence, over half of American investment in Europe was in Britain; by 1960 this percentage had fallen to 41 per cent.

However, arguments over the economic merits of joining the EEC have always been evenly balanced, as the 1975 debate was to demonstrate. In the late 1950s, as Miriam Camps reminds us, 'to most people the political reasons for joining were more important than the economic reasons and as time went on, the political case seemed to most people to grow stronger and the economic case rather weaker. It is clear in the British government's decision, political considerations were the controlling ones'. As Edward Heath put it, 'We now see opposite us on the mainland of Europe a large group comparable in size only to the United States and the Soviet Union, and as its economic power increases, so will its political influence.' It seemed clear that the EEC could become a third superpower, and that British non-membership would lead to political insignificance.

The decline of the so-called 'special relationship' with the United States reinforced such thinking. The limitations of this relationship had been cruelly demonstrated by the Suez disaster of 1956, when Britain, in collusion with France and Israel, invaded Egypt in an attempt to retain control over the Suez Canal, only to be forced primarily by American pressure to call for a ceasefire after 1 day's fighting. This humiliation was one of many incidents which showed that the greatest issue in Anglo-American relations in this period was not so much similar interests (as the British had optimistically assumed before 1956) but the conflict between Britain's desire to retain a measure of global influence and the American desire to inherit that influence, a desire which sometimes masqueraded as support for self-determination for colonial peoples.

The Americans tended to regard Britain as an ageing prima donna, and her stand outside Europe tended to confirm this opinion. The relation in any case ran counter to reality. As British power and influence plummeted, the United States became ever more the superior partner. 'All notion of equality on which the special relationship seemed to rest was visibly eroded,' remarks F. N. Northedge. The old role of Britain as a mediator between East and West no longer existed, even as a theory, after Russo-American détente followed the 1962 Cuba crisis. The cancellation of Blue Streak in 1960 meant that the British would in future have to accept dependence on the United States for her nuclear armoury. In the future it appeared that the United States would be more likely to forge new special relationships with the EEC. Therefore if Britain wished to retain any vestige of the old special relationship, then she should join the EEC.

The second of Churchill's overlapping circles was also declining in importance by the early 1960s. Strong forces made for a rapid disintegration of the Commonwealth and Empire after 1945. The hostility of the two superpowers towards traditional colonialism, Britain's lack of coercive power after 1945, the growing strength of colonial nationalism and the growing belief in British government circles that colonial peoples should be encouraged to seek independence – all these factors contributed to the rapid demise of Britain's imperial legacy. For a time the disintegration proceeded slowly, but by the late 1950s and early 1960s it had become, in D. K. Fieldhouse's phrase, 'an uncontrolled gallop'. For example, Cyprus, Malta, Ghana, Malaya, Singapore, Nigeria and Uganda all received their independence between 1957 and 1962. Nor was this regretted by the

British, who felt, as Northedge explains, 'a perceptible feeling of grievance at the anxieties and burdens of empire, a desire to be rid of the imperial mantle and to begin a quieter life at home'.

The idea of the Commonwealth forming any kind of unity around Britain was in any case a fiction. The growth of colonial nationalism excluded any scheme of political unification, and strategically the Commonwealth had lost whatever unity it had, with Britain's inability after 1945 to offer any protection to Commonwealth countries against external attack. Economic ties were also becoming less important. Britain was too poor herself to give much aid to the Commonwealth, and her trade with the Commonwealth suffered relative decline, as the new countries were too poor to buy British exports. While Britain's exports to Western Europe rose, her exports to the Commonwealth fell from 45 per cent of total exports in 1945 to 25 per cent in 1960.

The rapid pace of decolonisation forced a change in attitudes to the Commonwealth within the Conservative Party. Conservative devotion to the Commonwealth idea was reduced by the transformation of the 'Family of Nations' from a white man's club into a mainly Afro-Asian grouping of self-governing countries. The British prime minister Harold Macmillan, in his 'Wind of Change' speech in 1960, did his best to convert the old guard in the party to the idea of the new Commonwealth, but it is likely that more important than his efforts was the enforced withdrawal of South Africa from the Commonwealth in 1961, a withdrawal provoked by former colonies against the wishes of Britain and the old dominions. 'From then on for many Tories', suggests Nora Beloff, 'the Commonwealth remained an object of hope and charity but was no longer an article of faith.'

Thus by the late 1950s the Churchillian notion of Britain as the overlapping area in three international circles was plainly in need of revision. So unconvincing had the other two circles become as homes of last resort that there was nowhere else for Britain to go but into the Europe of the Six.

In addition to the broad issues outlined above, there were a number of short-term reasons which help to explain the precise moment of Britain's conversion to the idea of joining Europe. Firstly, a considerable shift in public opinion had taken place in 1960, by which time the Common Market debate was well under way. Apart from the Beaverbrook press and the *Daily Worker*, the British press was united in the feeling that Britain should work for the closest possible relationship with Europe, and several advocated joining the Common Market. The government's decision to abandon Blue Streak was seen by several commentators as a turning point which proved that Britain needed to join the EEC; this was the view of the *Financial Times*, *The Guardian*, *The Economist* and the *Observer*, and it was a view shared by many in the business community.

Pressure on the government came from a number of members of parliament from all three major parties. Major debates took place in the Commons in the summer of 1960, with motions on the need for political and economic unity in Europe passed overwhelmingly.

Nora Beloff gives three reasons for the government's conversion. The year 1960 was for Macmillan disillusioning. After the 1959 'hat trick', when the Conservatives won their third election in a row, an autumn budget was necessary in 1960 to check a run on the pound. As Beloff puts it, 'the stop-go policy seemed to be more stop than go, and only accentuated the contrast between Britain's stagnant economy and the continuing boom across the Channel'. Even more important was the evident failure of Macmillan's visit to Moscow in 1959 to prepare the way for a new Summit meeting. In 1960 the U2 spy plane incident gave the Soviets a convenient excuse to explode the Summit meeting scheduled to take place in Paris. 'The Prime Minister was badly shaken,' asserts Beloff. 'Those who worked most closely with him believe that it was this experience which launched him on his European course.'

But Beloff adds a third factor. After 9 years in office the party needed a new policy, and the Conservative Central Office had come to believe that a bold bid for Europe might give the party the new look which it needed to win another election. This motive appears a valid one, especially when one recalls the political capital the Labour Party was making out of the government's European policy. In the summer of 1960, after the failure of the government to throw a bridge between the EEC and EFTA, the Labour leader, Wilson, declared, 'The free trade area is dead and damned. Europe is looking to Britain for leadership and the Government seems to be in a rut.' So was the Labour Party on this issue, but the Conservatives were the party in office and knew that too static a policy would play into their opponents' hands.

Finally there were two hopeful developments on the international scene which seemed to augur well for the new policy. Macmillan visited the new American President, John Kennedy, in April 1961 and was left in no doubt that the United States government would welcome British entry into the EEC. As Miriam Camps suggests, 'the reflection that the shortest and perhaps the only way to a real Atlantic partnership lay through Britain's joining the Common Market seems to have been a very important – perhaps the controlling – element in Mr. Macmillan's decision that the right course for the United Kingdom was to apply for membership'. The other hopeful sign was a partial reconciliation with West Germany. The West German Chancellor, Konrad Adenauer, had no reason to like the British, who had dismissed him as Mayor of Cologne after the war; he was also on very good terms with the French President, de Gaulle. However, by August 1960, when Macmillan visited him, the German Chancellor was under pressure from the German business interests and appeared more favourable to the idea of British entry. In fact he still had reservations on the matter and these were to become apparent, but at the time his attitude encouraged Macmillan to seek full membership of the EEC.

In July 1960 Macmillan gave his government an overhaul which marked the advance of the pro-Europeans. Lord Home became foreign secretary, Edward Heath was given special responsibility for European Affairs and Christopher Soames became minister for agriculture. In August 1961 negotiations were initiated with the Six.

(d) The decade of British frustration

The French President, Charles de Gaulle, had been born in 1890, midway in the period between the Franco-Prussian War and the First World War. What moved de Gaulle was the fallen greatness of France and the absolute necessity of restoring it. He was sceptical of such postwar developments as the EEC and believed in close ties with Adenauer's West Germany. He was profoundly opposed to any Anglo-Saxon influence in Europe and believed that Britain in the Common Market would be a kind of American Trojan horse. When in December 1962 Macmillan and Kennedy came to a rapid agreement on Polaris missiles, de Gaulle commented sourly on the contrast between Britain's 16-month haggling over the terms of her Common Market entry and her nuclear settlement with the United States in 48 hours. He saw in this yet more proof that Britain was more concerned for the American connection than for links with Europe.

His attitude to British membership was in any case inflexible. There is no doubt that British interest in the EEC was genuine as links with the Commonwealth loosened. Perhaps the British negotiators made an error in insisting on certain conditions before entry, primarily the safeguarding of agriculture, trade with the Commonwealth and the future of Britain's partners in EFTA. This led to lengthy negotiations and gave de Gaulle an opportunity to assert his will. In January 1963 he announced at a press conference that Britain was not yet ready to join the Community, but his real motive was his fear that Britain would become a serious rival to France inside the Community. France's partners favoured British entry, but were not consulted by the General before he applied his veto.

When the Wilson government applied for membership in 1966, it was no more successful than the Conservatives. Again the British overtures were rejected, largely because of de Gaulle's attitude. To demonstrate France's independence of the United States was the keynote of his foreign policy, and he disliked Britain's 'special relationship' with the Americans and Anglo-American cooperation in the field of nuclear research.

However, in 1967 the General used new arguments to reject British entry, asserting that Britain was not yet sufficiently strong economically to enter the Community. But his real reasons were political, as Guy de Carmoy has stressed. 'Britain's presence would alter the balance of power within the enlarged Community. France would no longer have the freedom of action she enjoyed in an institution where she held the political reins and Germany was content to follow her lead.' By now three other countries were also applying for Community membership, and de Gaulle was concerned to retain French dominance. In 1966 he remarked to George Brown, Deputy Leader of the Labour Party, on the impossibility of two cocks (France and Britain) living in one farmyard with ten hens. Brown records de Gaulle as saying that 'he had had a lot of trouble getting the five hens to do what France wanted, and he wasn't going to have Britain coming in and creating trouble all over again, this time with ten'.

The General's second attack on European unity was aimed at the structure of the EEC itself. The two main decision-making organs of the Community were the Council of Ministers and the Commission, the former composed of the foreign ministers of the Common Market countries, with a voting system giving more votes to large countries than to small ones. In the Commission a more supranational approach was adopted, the Eurocrats of the Commission representing the common interests of the organisation. The national governments had already begun to view the work of the Eurocrats in Brussels with suspicion. They feared that this supranational authority, already possessing 3,000 personnel by 1962, was becoming too powerful, and were apprehensive that a new technocratic élite whose first loyalty was to the EEC, not to their own country, was being created.

De Gaulle was particularly hostile to the attempts of the Commission to increase its power. In 1965 he took a dislike to the Commission's proposals on agricultural policy, which called not only for increases in farm prices (which France wanted) but also independent financing of the Community out of its own resources (which the Commission wanted). He threatened to withdraw France from the Community unless a solution acceptable to France was adopted. His real aim was to weaken the Commission and forestall any possibility of France being outvoted by their partners. Even the Germans were angered at the General's outrageously high-handed approach, and in the end the French made some concessions on agricultural policy. But de Gaulle's real objective was achieved. All important decisions were in future to be decided by the foreign ministers and the Commission's authority was weakened. The General's vanity may have temporarily strengthened French prestige but it weakened Europe. The process of European unity was delayed by a decade, and only after de Gaulle's retirement could it again move forward.

(e) New horizons – and new problems

With the accession to the French presidency of Pompidou in 1969, the European climate changed. Politically the mood was suited to a more favourable consideration of British membership. West Germany's Chancellor, Willi Brandt, was a good European but his Ostpolitik (an attempt to reach better relations with East Europe) and the growing political and economic strength of West Germany made other EEC members wish to see Britain in the Community as a counter-balance to West Germany. French attitudes to British entry certainly changed, but the reasons for this are still a matter of historical debate. It has been asserted that de Gaulle's attitude to Britain mellowed in the final year of his presidency. If this is the case, then Pompidou merely followed a policy already laid down by his illustrious predecessor. An alternative view is that the main pressure on Pompidou was exerted by the other five Community members, anxious not to see Britain rebuffed for a third time. Pompidou himself was not hostile to Britain, though, coming as he did from peasant and banking stock, he had a keen eye for French interests.

The new British prime minister in 1970 was Edward Heath, a man with genuine and fervent European attitudes. He had in fact made his maiden parliamentary speech in 1950, attacking the failure of the then Labour government even to consider joining the Schuman Plan. His travels in Europe in his youth and his experiences as a lieutenant-colonel in the Second World War helped to form his commitment to Europe, and in the 1950s he had taken a far more European line than his party leaders. Heath's European sentiments were not merely negative in the sense that he saw integration as a means of avoiding war; as Uwe Kitzinger has explained, there was a more positive side. Heath believed that European countries did some things better than Britain, and he anticipated that if Britain joined Europe, she would gain economically and culturally. The British prime minister was also a most stubborn individual in pursuit of what was his major political objective – British membership.

Accordingly, the Community opened negotiations in 1970 with Britain, Ireland, Denmark and Norway. At one point discussions with Britain seemed to be reaching an impasse, but this was solved by private Anglo-French talks on six contentious issues – Britain's budget contribution, her application of Community preference, New Zealand dairy produce, cane sugar, sterling and fish. Eventually the Treaty of Accession was signed and came into effect on 1 January 1973. Ireland and Denmark joined Britain as new members of the Community, but the Norwegian people rejected membership in a referendum.

For various reasons the year 1975 proved to be crucial for the survival of the Community. The British elections of 1974 had returned to office a Labour government pledged to fundamental re-negotiation of Britain's terms of entry to the Community and the putting of the results to the whole British people. This hurdle was eventually overcome in June 1975, when the Labour government, having renegotiated the terms, put the issue in the hands of the British people through a referendum. The result was a massive Yes to staying in by 17 million votes to 8 million, and Wilson hailed the vote as 'the end of 14 years of national argument'. On this point he was emphatically wrong; the arguments over British membership have continued into the 1980s with considerable opposition to membership within the Labour Party.

The year 1975 was also critical in purely economic terms. The startling rise in oil prices in 1974 pushed the Community towards recession, and in 1975 it suffered its first negative rate of growth, which resulted in a decline in living standards in some countries and dealt a brutal blow to Community confidence. By 1977 over 5 million people were out of work, and by 1982 this figure had risen to 10 million.

Community leaders put a brave face on it, asserting that the unemployment and inflation would have been much worse but for the existence of the Community. As Walter Scheel, President of West Germany, emphasised in 1977, 'Individually we would not have withstood the storms of world economic development – that is, the crisis that began in 1973 – at all. Each country would have been sucked into catastrophe. So we must agree that it was indeed well that twenty years ago we founded the European Community.' Yet as the 1980s arrived, the Community faced a formidable array of problems, of which rising unemployment, budgetary issues and agriculture were only the most obvious. Such problems were exacerbated by the enlargement of the Community. Greece raised the number of countries in the Community to ten in 1981, and both Spain and Portugal joined the Community in 1986. By then unemployment in the twelve member states reached 17 million.

Against this grim statistic, the Community had at last begun to grasp the nettle of reform of the Common Agricultural Policy, as well as making promising initiatives on European technological cooperation and the completion of the internal market by 1992.

(2) Politics in Western Europe since 1945

(a) West Germany

(i) *Germany in 1945*
May 1945 was the darkest hour in German history. The state that had dominated Europe lay in ruins, divided into four main occupation

zones. Such was the destruction that it seemed inconceivable that the country would ever revive. In addition, the Russians aimed at a punitive squeezing of Germany and stripped their zone of its industrial equipment. The Western powers saw the ultimate folly of such a policy in a situation made even more difficult by the refugee problem. From the territories lost to Poland and Czechoslovakia about 13 million Germans were expelled, and two-thirds of whom settled in the Western zones. Their conditions were appallingly hard and the process of assimilation necessarily prolonged.

In this grim situation the immediate task of the occupying powers was to keep the basic necessities of life going. A shortage of healthy Germans hampered this work, for 3 million Germans had been killed in the war, 2 million were disabled and millions more lingered in hospitals and POW camps.

In the Western zones democratic parties again emerged. The Christian Democratic Union (CDU) replaced the Centre Party, which had lost prestige by its failure to oppose Hitler. The CDU was a more inter-denominational party than the Centre Party had been, and stood firmly for denominational schools, religious education and general conservative principles. Its leader was the ex-lord mayor of Cologne, Konrad Adenauer. The Social Democrat Party (SPD) was led by Kurt Schumacher, and, as before 1933, was divided into hard-line Marxists and gradualists. The third important party, a long way behind the other two, was the liberal Free Democratic Party (FDP), an alliance of business and the intelligentsia. The Communist Party (KPD) failed to make headway in Western Germany, as it was seen to be the tool of the Russians.

In the summer of 1946 the British accepted an American proposal for the economic merger of their two zones, which became effective in January 1947. In retrospect this came to be interpreted as a move towards dividing Germany permanently. In fact the Russians and French were invited to join the scheme and refused. Yet the need for cooperation between the zones was essential because of Germany's desperate economic situation. Output in 1946 was one-third of the 1936 total, with acute food shortages, especially in the urbanised British zone, where there were 260,000 cases of tuberculosis.

One of the most delicate tasks of the military government was the rooting out of Nazism. The occupying powers agreed on the objective but the process itself was difficult. Eight million people had belonged to the Nazi party and it was often impossible to determine the extent of an individual's devotion to the Nazi doctrines. In the American zone 800,000 people received penalties of varying severity, in the British zone 156,000 were removed from office, and in the Russian zone nearly 500,000 people were dismissed, according to official figures.

The trial of twenty-four top Nazis was conducted at a special international court which sat at Nuremberg from November 1945 to August 1946. Twelve Nazis received the death sentence, though Ley and Göring committed suicide. Many other Germans who had served the Nazi regime, e.g. generals such as Manstein and industrialists such as Krupp, were tried for crimes against humanity. In the end 600 people were executed and over 4,000 imprisoned. Though a witch-hunt was avoided, this justice could not be exact. As time passed and with the onset of the Cold War, a more tolerant attitude began to prevail.

A. J. Ryder reminds us that with all its flaws the process of denazification was essential. 'It was both a moral imperative and a matter of commonsense that the new regime should depend on civil servants, teachers, judges, policemen and journalists who had not actively supported Hitler's ideology.' The process was in fact incomplete: two-thirds of the judges and nearly all the staff in the Foreign Office in the Federal Republic in 1950 had held office during the third Reich. Yet denazification was a substitute for the revolution Germany never had.

(ii) The German phoenix

By 1947 the harsh realities of the Cold War were forcing the Western powers to reappraise their German policies. It was seen that Germany must be helped to pay its way and contribute to the reconstruction of Western Europe. In September 1946 James F. Byrnes, the American Secretary of State, told an audience at Stuttgart that the British and American zones would merge to help the recovery of the German economy and that the German people would be given more self-government.

Gradually the West German economy revived after 1947, and the announcement of Marshall Aid in June provided it with the essential injection of capital. A new bank was created, later to become the Deutsche Bundesbank, but the key move was a drastic currency reform in June 1948, 10 old marks being exchanged for 1 new mark. The reform led to an immediate economic revival, as the German people now had confidence in the currency. The Christian Democrats believed in competition and freedom for industry from economic controls. Their economics expert, Professor Ludwig Erhard, described his policy as a social market economy, because public resources were used for social purposes, while industrial output left in private hands would, he believed, expand to meet the demand. He made sure that Marshall Aid was used for industrial investment, and the foundations for Germany's future prosperity were laid. Between June 1948 and December 1949 industrial production rose 125 per cent. The West German economic miracle was under way, and by 1953 living standards were higher than in 1938.

It was this economic revival that provoked the Russians into bringing pressure on the West at its weakest point – Berlin. In June 1948 all land traffic from the West to Berlin was stopped, the purpose being to starve the city into surrender. The Western reply to this Soviet coercion was to supply Berlin by an air-lift, and in the course of 200,000 flights, West Berlin was supplied with 1½ million tons of goods. The Soviet government had two alternatives – it could either attack the West's planes or end the blockade. As the former alternative could have led to war, Stalin lifted the blockade in May 1949. The uneasy joint government of Berlin was ended, and in 1950 West Berlin became a semi-autonomous city state, sharing in the prosperity of Western Germany. In practice it has been part of the Federal Republic and has become a symbol of freedom for refugees fleeing from Russian tyranny.

(iii) The creation of the Federal Republic

The failure to reach an agreement with the Russians over uniting Germany led the three Western powers to promote the creation of a democratic West German state, which, it was hoped, would strengthen Europe economically and militarily. In June 1948 the three military governors called on the West German state governments to convene a constituent assembly. In September a committee chosen from the state parliaments drew up the Basic Law, which laid the foundations of a constitution. A major issue was the degree of central government power and the rights of the individual states. In the end, after hard bargaining, the Social Democrats gained the financial supremacy of the central government while cultural policy remained the preserve of the state governments. The main legislative body was to be the Bundestag, with nearly 500 members elected by universal suffrage for 4 years. The upper house, the Bundesrat, was to number 45 members, composed of representatives of the state governments.

The creators of the Basic Law worked sensibly to avoid the weaknesses of the Weimar constitution. The powers of the president were limited; unlike Hindenburg, he was not to be the commander-in-chief of the armed forces nor was he to possess any emergency powers. One of his principal functions was to appoint the chancellor, who must have the confidence of the Bundestag. An attempt was made to combine the advantages of the British system of voting for known candidates in single member constituencies with those of proportional representation, whereby each party receives exactly as many seats as its total of voters entitles it to. Under the postwar German system each voter has two votes, one for a specific candidate and one for a party list, so that half the members of the Bundestag are chosen in one way and half by the other. Any party failing to win three seats directly or at least 5 per cent of the total votes cast forfeits its right to be represented, a move to prevent the proliferation of small parties which had been a feature of the Weimar period.

Important powers were given to a Federal Constitutional Court, which could pronounce on the legality of political parties and condemn any threat to the rule of law. In 1956 it declared the German Communist Party to be unconstitutional, and it has been a pillar of the new state. The new constitution has worked well through the commonsense of its creators, the ability of political leaders and the consensus of opinion which the Federal Republic has enjoyed and which was conspicuously lacking in the Weimar Republic.

In August 1949 Germany's first general election was held, with no one party gaining an overall majority. The Christian Democrats gained 139 seats, the Social Democrats 131 and the Free Democrats 52, with the extremist parties winning very few seats. Adenauer became the chancellor of a coalition government with the Free Democrats. Erhard was given the post of economics minister, while the Free Democrat Theodor Heuss became the Federal Republic's first president. The election results were a grave disappointment to Schumacher's SPD, but though a man of immense courage, the socialist leader had been too uncompromising and very difficult to work with. Another reason for the SPD defeat was the loss of the Protestant East, which meant that nearly half the population were Catholics.

Now began the Adenauer era. Born in 1876, the new chancellor was deeply rooted in the Catholic faith and had been dismissed as lord mayor of Cologne by the Nazis in 1933. Serious, resolute and astute, he stood for much of what most Germans wanted – liberal economic policies after years of state interference, Christian standards after years of Nazi barbarism and international cooperation after a period of fanatical nationalism. He did not believe in full parliamentary democracy, as in his view it had contributed to the destruction of the Weimar Republic. As Laqueur remarks, 'Adenauer's style of work was paternalistic, if not authoritarian.'

Adenauer's stable government and his obvious desire for a rapprochement with Germany's hereditary enemy, France, soon led to an improvement in his country's international status, with Germany joining the Council of Europe and the Schuman Plan. The chancellor gained the confidence of the Allies in general because he refused to negotiate with the Russians over German reunification. Therefore by 1952 the Allies ended the occupation regime entirely, and the Federal Republic was recognised as a completely sovereign state. A more contentious issue was German rearmament. In 1950 NATO decided that, for the sake of West European security, the rearmament of West Germany was essential. The decision caused an uproar in France and Britain as well as in West Germany, but nevertheless the Federal Republic joined NATO and contributed contingents of troops. Special care has been taken to avoid the creation of any military élite. The Bundestag's Defence Committee has kept a careful watch over the army, though, as it has never reached its original target of 500,000 men, it would appear that young Germans are not attracted by the ethos of the barrack square.

During the 1950s Adenauer steadily pursued his two major objectives in foreign policy – reconciliation with France and close cooperation with the United States. The Federal Republic's entry into the EEC by the Treaty of Rome fulfilled his dream, especially as a close colleague, Professor Hallstein, was the first president of the EEC Commission. The burning question of the Saar, which had divided France and Germany since the First World War, was settled in 1957 by the return of this territory to the Federal Republic after France had again tried to absorb it.

The Federal Republic's relations with the United States became extremely cordial. Both countries loathed Communism, and the Federal government refused to recognise either Poland's right to Germany's eastern lands or the legality of the East German government on the grounds that it was a puppet regime imposed by the Russians. Even if the West Germans had adopted a more flexible approach to the Communist bloc, it is unlikely that the two parts of Germany could have been united. The Russian attitude to German unity hardened in the 1950s, and in November 1958 Kruschev created a crisis by demanding that the Western occupation of Berlin must be ended in 6 months. Though this crisis fizzled out, the East German government built the Berlin Wall in 1961 to prevent refugees escaping from East to West Berlin. The Wall was a terrible symbol of East Germany's tyranny, and many who attempted to escape were shot down.

The new parliamentary democracy was soon proved to be a most stable regime. The number of effective parties had fallen to three by 1961, with only the FDP preventing the formation of a complete two-party system. Adenauer's CDU again formed a coalition government in 1953, but in 1957 it gained a clear majority. In 1961 the CDU suffered reverses, but was still able to hold on to power in another coalition with the Free Democrats.

In his last 2 years of power, between 1961 and 1963, Adenauer's reputation suffered a decline. His decision to run again for the chancellorship in 1961 at the age of 85 was resented even by some of his own party, because it was felt that he was trying to keep out Erhard, whose talents he rather despised. A second reason for Adenauer's decline was a grave political crisis in October 1962. The weekly news magazine *Der Spiegel* criticised the West German army's reliance on America's nuclear deterrent and its lack of good conventional weapons. In high-handed fashion the government arrested the proprietor and defence editor of the magazine on a charge of high treason, and broke into the magazine's offices at the instigation of the minister of defence, Franz Josef Strauss. When the charges against *Der Spiegel* could not be substantiated, the government appeared ridiculous. At the behest of the Free Democrats Adenauer had to dismiss Strauss and promise to retire in 1963.

This anticlimax to his career should not blind us to Adenauer's place in German history. He was, asserts A. J. Ryder, the greatest German statesman since Bismarck. Both were strong personalities who loved power and could be unscrupulous, yet both demonstrated high skill as diplomats. Like Bismarck, Adenauer was no democrat; he treated his colleagues as subordinates and showed little respect for the Bundestag, from which he withheld information. At times his conservative policies seemed negative, for too little attention was paid to education and his foreign policy can be criticised as rigid because he refused to make any move towards reconciliation with East Germany. But it may be argued with equal force that Adenauer's authoritarian brand of democracy was the right form of transitional government for Germany in this period. If at times he was inflexible, he was also at other times subtle and sensitive, for example in the way his government paid compensation of £3,450 million to the Jews for their sufferings under the Nazis. Adenauer was a master in the exercise of legitimate power, and if his government was dull, it gave many Germans a security and contentment they had never before experienced.

(iv) The economic miracle

The term 'economic miracle' has become a cliché, but when applied to West Germany it still retains some validity. From 1950 to 1964 the country's Gross National Product rose threefold, faster than any other European state. After 1950 over half a million new dwelling units were built every year, and by 1960 West Germany was producing 50 per cent more steel than united Germany had before the war. The symbol of German recovery was the Volkswagen car, and by 1961 over a million German cars had been exported. The standard of living was transformed, with consumption per head trebling between 1950 and 1964. The boom was export-led, and in the early years domestic consumption was kept down to enable a high percentage of the gross national product to be spent on capital formation.

An important reason for West Germany's success was relatively harmonious labour relations. The inflation of 1923 was still not forgotten, and organised labour was willing to practise wage restraint in the interest of controlling inflation. German unions also numbered only sixteen, which has contributed to an absence of demarcation disputes. Worker participation too has contributed to stable labour relations. Hans Böckler, chairman of the General Trades Union, favoured worker participation in industry, and Adenauer, with whom Böckler was on good terms, was willing to concede to the unions on the matter. In 1951 and 1952 new laws laid down that half the supervisory council in each firm was to consist of workers. In practice the workers have a considerable say in conditions of work and still leave management to the managers, but their new status has helped morale.

The relative backwardness of German agriculture was solved by the consolidation of small units and mechanisation. As a result, less than one person in ten now works on the land, compared to one person in five in 1950. In 1964 a much smaller number of farm workers produced 50 per cent more food than before the war. 'It is not too much to describe these changes as an agrarian revolution,' asserts A. J. Ryder.

The stream of farm workers to the towns was one reason for the absence of inflation. So was the huge influx of refugees, who were continually increased by people fleeing from the Russian zone; between 1949 and 1962 over 3 million entered West Germany from the East. A third source of fresh labour has been the guest worker; over 2 million workers from the poorer parts of Europe, e.g. Italy, Yugoslavia and Turkey, flocked to West Germany to enjoy the higher wages of that thriving economy.

(v) Brandt and détente

Adenauer's resignation in 1963 ushered in an unsettled period in German politics. Erhard, Adenauer's successor as chancellor, faced a number of problems and showed a lack of decisiveness in coping with them. He was pulled both ways by the French show of independence from the United States, and by 1966 faced growing unemployment. The Free Democrats disliked the tax increases in the 1966 budget, lost confidence in Erhard and withdrew from the coalition, a move that forced Erhard's resignation in November. The two main parties now formed a Grand Coalition, with the Christian Democrat Kiesinger as chancellor and Willi Brandt, the socialist Mayor of West Berlin as foreign minister.

The decision of the Social Democrats to join in such a coalition was a turning point in their history. Since the creation of the Federal Republic, they had endured a long period in the political wilderness, and had lost their best leaders, Schumacher and Reuter. The new leaders of the party, such as Brandt, believed that Schumacher's hard-line approach was out of date, and in 1959 the SPD adopted the new Godesberg programme, declaring itself to be a people's, not a class, party. It accepted the economic formula of as much competition as possible, as much planning as necessary. It ended its old hostility to the Churches and its opposition to rearmament. The SPD was now only slightly left of centre, and the gap between itself and the CDU was much smaller. Nevertheless the Grand Coalition was an uneasy combination, and by its very nature was bound to be a temporary expedient. In the 1969 elections the SPD for the first time gained more votes than the CDU, and joined in a coalition with the FDP, with Brandt as the new chancellor.

Brandt was a firm believer in the need for reconciliation with the Communist countries of Eastern Europe, a policy known as 'Ostpolitik'. Erhard's government had first moved towards more cordial relations with Eastern Europe in 1966, and when Brandt became foreign minister in December of that year, he continued to seek a rapprochement. The Russian invasion of Czechoslovakia in 1968 delayed reconciliation, but Brandt persevered, and when he became chancellor in 1969, he defined his aims as better relations with all the East European states, including East Germany. A man of sincerity with an impeccable record as an opponent of Nazism, Brandt was helped by the election of a fellow Social Democrat, Gustav Heinemann, as president. Heinemann's courage and integrity as minister of justice had won respect, and he was more tolerant of Communism than many of his colleagues.

Now 'Ostpolitik' made some headway. In 1970 the Federal Republic concluded treaties with Russia and Poland in which the signatories renounced the use of force and confirmed the Oder-Neisse line as the de facto frontier between Poland and East Germany. In 1971 a compromise agreement on Berlin was reached. Russia acknowledged that access to Berlin was still a four-power responsibility and relaxed the rules so that West Berliners could visit their relations on the other side of the Wall. In seeking this new relationship with Eastern Europe Brandt showed considerable courage. His real objectives were long term; ultimately he hoped that 'Ostpolitik' would result in a united Germany. In the short term this was out of the question, bearing in mind East Germany's strategic importance to Russia.

That 'Ostpolitik' was also a risky policy became evident in May 1974, when a tired and discouraged Brandt suddenly resigned after the scandal that followed the arrest in April of Günter Guillaume, a close personal aide, who confessed to being an East German spy.

(vi) Contemporary West Germany

Brandt's successor was the abrasive, blunt and dynamic Helmut Schmidt, who won the nickname Schmidt the Lip! He represented the technocratic element in the SPD, and gave little priority to social reform. He claimed, 'I'm not a visionary and I'm sceptical of all visionaries.' He concentrated on resolving the economic problems caused by the recession which followed the 1973 oil crisis. Germany overcame trade deficits arising from the high cost of imported oil by cutting its use by 20 per cent. Government help boosted the export industries.

By 1982 Schmidt faced growing political problems, which led to his fall from power. His own party became increasingly divided, and after the 1976 elections had only a small majority even in alliance with the Free Democrats, who pressurised the government to reduce spending as a way of controlling inflation. With unemployment rising, the left wing of the SPD objected to such monetarist policies. When Schmidt refused a Free Democrat demand to reduce welfare benefits, the Free Democrats left the coalition and joined with Helmut Köhl's CDU.

The ensuing elections in 1983 saw the CDU increase its number of seats, with both the SPD and FDP losing ground. A new phenomenon was the success of the environmental party, the Greens, in winning 27 seats and threatening the position of the FDP as the third party.

The rise in unemployment to 2.5 million and the invasion of the home market by Japanese products were worrying developments in the late 1980s. Nevertheless the West German economy remained strong. Strict control of the money supply and wages kept inflation at only 2 per cent a year, and West Germany's export industries did so well in the European and American markets that a huge trade surplus was earned. West Germany continued to be powerful in the important sectors of motor vehicles, mechanical engineering, aerospace and chemicals. The South, particularly Bavaria, has become the heartland of the country's microelectronics development.

(b) Britain

(i) *The legacy of the war*

The early months of the Second World War saw a continuation of the Chamberlain government, but the period of the 'phony war' and the failure to prevent the German occupation of Norway led to sharp attacks on the government. Leo Amery, who had been a Cabinet minister under Baldwin, applied to the government the words with which Cromwell had dismissed the Rump Parliament – 'You have sat here too long for any good you have been doing . . . in the name of God, go.' With support from his own party dwindling and with Labour refusing to serve in his government, Chamberlain resigned in May 1940 and Churchill became prime minister. A new coalition now ran the war with much more vigour; Labour members joined it because they respected Churchill's opposition to dictatorship and support of the League of Nations in the 1930s. Chamberlain won over many Conservatives, so that they also supported the coalition, and he himself served Churchill loyally until cancer forced his retirement in October.

Under Churchill's dynamic leadership the British contribution to Allied success was considerable (see Chapter 10), but it was bought at a heavy cost. Nearly all overseas assets had been sold off to pay for imports and Britain was deeply in debt to the USA. The merchant fleet had been reduced by a third and exports were under half the

1938 figure. Five million houses had been destroyed, and 303,000 members of the armed forces, 60,000 civilians and 30,000 seamen had been killed. The two superpowers now dominated world affairs and Britain was reduced to a second rank power whose links with its empire had been further loosened by war.

Compared to those suffered by Russia, Germany and Japan, such losses were small. In addition the national spirit was high; Britain was the only country to fight Nazi Germany through the whole war, and she continued to be a place for hope in the occupied countries in their darkest hours. British prestige was therefore high at the end of the war; the British had not made peace with Germany like Vichy France, nor had they executed political somersaults of the kind performed by Stalin. In the long run such prestige had its disadvantages. In *The Price of Victory* Michael Charlton has shown that victory tempted her political leaders into believing that Britain could still play a global role after the war, and that consequently they both overestimated British power and underestimated the importance to Britain of the movement for European integration.

In other ways the war had a more constructive impact on Britain. The experience of rationing and conscription shared by all classes perhaps did something to soften class barriers. British society was certainly made more egalitarian by the government's punitive taxes, the tax on the highest incomes reaching 97½ pence in the pound.

One of the most admirable traits of the wartime coalition was the way in which, despite all the strains of war, it continued to look forward to the postwar world. In 1942 Sir William Beveridge produced a plan for a comprehensive system of welfare which would include longer-term unemployment benefits, a national health service, pensions for old people, widows and orphans and family allowances for children. The report was received with tremendous enthusiasm and was the foundation of the later reforms under Labour.

The 1944 Education Act, usually known as the Butler Act, was the one really large piece of legislation passed during the war. It gave the education minister power to raise the school-leaving age to 15 and then to 16 for all children when this was considered feasible. In place of schools which had educated children of all ages, children would now change schools at 11; those who passed the scholarship examination would go to grammar schools and those who did not would go to secondary modern schools. Such a sharp and early division was later criticised and by the 1950s a new system of comprehensive schools was being created.

A third major concern was the issue of unemployment. In 1944 the government published a White Paper which committed it to maintaining a high and stable level of employment. Beveridge in his book *Full Employment in a Free Society* also stressed the need for budget deficits as a means of creating jobs, and to an extent the White Paper endorsed Keynesian-style public works. In time all postwar governments were to adopt the practice of deficit spending in the economy.

In May 1945 the Labour Party indicated that it did not wish to continue the coalition, and in July a general election was held. To an extent, as T. O. Lloyd has pointed out, the election was about prewar Conservative policy. Most people now regarded Chamberlain's appeasement as ill-advised and Conservative economic policy as responsible for the high unemployment of the 1930s. Admittedly the Conservatives now had Churchill, who was immensely popular, but he was in error in believing that the people's gratitude meant the security of their vote. He did not seem to have a clear idea of what to do in the future, and some of his electoral rhetoric was foolish, in particular his remark that Labour in power would set up a Gestapo to run the country. Labour leaders such as Attlee and Bevin had after all served in his coalition and had a good record in opposing the dictators.

Churchill did not appreciate that the electorate was in a serious mood after the privations of war, and were looking for specific commitments on issues like welfare and employment. It was Labour which made the clearer promises on these issues; government planning would tackle problems like the housing shortage, while nationalisation (which the Conservatives clearly opposed) would revivify the economy. Consequently Labour won a landslide victory, gaining 393 seats to the Conservatives' 213. Conservative failure to adapt to a changed world had been severely punished.

(ii) Labour in power, 1945–51

The Britain which Labour inherited was a much weakened country. Heavy external debt meant that it no longer had a surplus on invisible trade (trade in services like shipping), and consequently needed to increase exports to 175 per cent of the prewar volume to maintain the balance of payments. British exporters were in fact able to achieve such a rise because primary producing countries were doing well and could afford British exports while old trading rivals like Germany were too shattered by war to compete. Britain also benefited from the Marshall Plan to the tune of £700 millions, though, despite such help, the pound was devalued in 1949 from \$4.03 to \$2.80.

Despite economic pressures, both major parties believed that Britain could still play a decisive role in the world, and under Labour a larger proportion of national income was spent on armaments than in any country in Europe. In 1947 a National Service Act imposed a year's military service and Labour also began the quest for a British atomic bomb. In Imperial affairs, the government was more realistic, quitting both India and Palestine (see Chapters 16 and 19).

The new Labour cabinet was composed of men of widely differing backgrounds. The prime minister, Clement Attlee, was of public school and university education. He seemed an insignificant individual – in Churchill's unkind phrase 'a modest little man with much to be modest about' – but he was a man of integrity and a good party manager who held together a difficult team. The ebullient Ernest Bevin, son of an agricultural worker, had been secretary of the Transport and General Workers' Union and minister of labour in the wartime coalition; he now became foreign secretary. The austere, intellectual Stafford Cripps was president of the board of Trade and then chancellor of the exchequer. Aneurin Bevan, the fiery Welsh orator, became minister of health. The mass of legislation to be tackled kept the party too busy for serious quarrels.

Whether such legislation amounted to a social revolution is open to question, but it was a great achievement to effect it. The most controversial area was the nationalisation programme, but even here the Conservatives only put up mild resistance, fearful that strenuous opposition would make them more unpopular. The Bank of England and airlines were nationalised without any trouble in 1946. In 1947 two rundown industries – coal and the railways – were nationalised. Unfortunately the winter of 1946–7 was the coldest for 60 years, and when coal could not be moved from the pithead, shortages were severe. Such disappointments reduced public enthusiasm for nationalisation, though gas and electricity were nationalised in 1948 and 1949. The only intense struggle arose over the steel industry. As the industry was profitable, the Conservatives believed that its nationalisation was unjustified, and opposed the nationalisation bill fiercely.

The government's social reform was a great achievement. In 1946 Bevan introduced the National Health Service Act, one of the most important foundations of the welfare state. It laid down that there would be free medical treatment for everyone, with doctors and dentists paid by the state. The serious resistance to the change came from the doctors, especially the general practitioners. Despite receiving higher incomes through a basic fee and a payment for each patient, the doctors were afraid that the system might be converted to a salaried one and that they might lose their right to remain in private practice. Assurances were given on the latter point and the health service started in 1948.

The measure was supported by the 1946 National Insurance Act and the 1948 National Assistance Act. The former Act insured all working people from the time they left school until their retirement, with both employer and employee contributing to the scheme. The latter Act was a safety net for the particularly disadvantaged; people with small incomes and large families or those disabled could claim extra help.

Despite real achievements, the government began to lose popularity by 1950. Under Cripps taxes were increased in the 1948 budget, and the continuation of food rationing was a tiresome restriction. Sometimes the strident language of government members alarmed the middle classes, as when Bevan said that the Tory Party which imposed the means test was lower than vermin. The same middle classes also resented the discovery that skilled manual workers were earning more than they were.

Despite a faster expansion of the British economy than for any peacetime period since 1873, the government was criticised in business circles for holding back economic growth through its controls on steel, building licences and imported raw materials. As Lloyd succinctly phrases it, 'People had had enough of Whitehall; they wanted to be free to manage, or even mismanage, their own affairs.' Perhaps, too, Labour had attempted too much too quickly, and the public had become suspicious of innovation. As for Labour leaders like Attlee, they had been in office for 10 years and were feeling the strain.

For its part, the Conservative party, badly shaken by the 1945 election defeat, applied itself to its own reorganisation. It raised money successfully and accepted the welfare state. Its press found plenty on which to attack the government, for example the large losses made by the failure of the groundnuts scheme in East Africa.

Consequently the general election of February 1950 saw Labour's majority reduced to six. The government's plans to end restrictions were then thrown off course by the outbreak of the Korean War, which led to increases in the cost of imported raw materials, owing to stockpiling by the American government. The economy was further taxed by the government's large rearmament programme, which aimed at raising the proportion of national income spent on armaments from 7 per cent to 14 per cent. The strain led to the illness of both Cripps and Bevin, and to new divisions in the government. When the new chancellor of the exchequer, Hugh Gaitskell, imposed charges on prescriptions, spectacles and false teeth, both Bevan and Wilson resigned. The government was also humiliated by events abroad; for instance, in April 1951 the government of Iran nationalised the Anglo-Iranian Oil Company, most of whose shares were owned by the British government. In that month Bevin died and confidence in the government further declined.

By November the Labour government was exhausted and the majority of six made control of the Commons difficult, especially given the Conservative tactic of forcing extended late night sittings. Attlee decided to hold an election to clear the air, rebuild the Labour majority and even perhaps repair the divisions in the party. The Conservatives' programme of ending restrictions, including food rationing, the building of 300,000 houses a year and the retention of the Welfare State had more appeal; they won 321 seats to Labour's 295, though Labour polled more votes.

(iii) The era of Conservative supremacy, 1951–64
The Conservatives were to govern the country for the next 13 years.
Their grasp of office is only partly to be explained by the success of
their own exertions. They were fortunate to govern Britain in a
period of world economic expansion, and they were helped too by the
acute divisions within Labour. Out of office, it failed to develop new
policies, and divisions developed between the left and right wings
over such issues as nationalisation and rearmament.

Churchill now headed his first peacetime government at the age of
76. Until recently most historians have asserted that he was a sick and
virtually senile man by 1951, but Martin Gilbert in his official
biography of Churchill has refuted such suggestions. What is indis-
putable is that Churchill showed most interest in foreign affairs and
defence, leaving economic affairs to the chancellor of the exchequer,
R. A. Butler.

Butler fulfilled Conservative election promises to set the economy
free. He reduced income tax and the licensing system and ended
rationing and restrictions on hire-purchase. An improvement in the
terms of trade for manufactures led to a surplus on the balance of
payments. Average incomes improved and Harold Macmillan, the
housing minister, achieved the Conservative target of 300,000 houses
a year in 1953, an impressive development which was sustained in
1954. The proportion of income spent on defence declined slightly,
and much of the previous government's reforms was left untouched,
only steel and parts of road haulage being returned to the private
sector. Where the government did show a pronounced trend to a free
market system was over the question of independent television. On
taking office the government had little interest in the question, but
pressure-group activity led to the creation of an alternative to the
BBC, the Independent Television Authority.

In April 1955 Churchill retired and his heir apparent for so many
years, Anthony Eden, was able to lead his party to a convincing win
in the general election, the Conservatives winning 344 seats to
Labour's 277. Unfortunately the inevitable comparisons made with
his illustrious predecessor was not to Eden's advantage, and a
campaign in Conservative newspapers intimated that he was not
firmly in command of the situation. The more traditionally minded
Conservatives had not dared to criticise the leadership when Churchill was premier; now they wanted policies to restore their economic
position and Britain's imperial position. Such traditional groups had
not enjoyed the rising salaries of new middle-class groups such as
TV producers and market research consultants, and they also disliked what they regarded as the government's retreat in the Middle
East. A famous *Daily Telegraph* editorial exhorted the prime minister to show 'the smack of firm government'.

It was this criticism from the ranks of his own supporters that in part explains Eden's actions during the Suez Crisis of July 1956 (see Chapter 19). After agreeing to the Anglo-French attack on Egypt on 31 October he came under violent criticism from the Opposition, and tempers became so frayed that one sitting of the House had to be suspended. United Nations pressure and dissatisfaction within his own Cabinet (notably from Macleod, Monckton and Nutting) further weakened Eden's position. The crucial influence was the weakness of sterling and the need for American cooperation to obtain IMF (International Monetary Fund) money to support it. In addition, oil was in short supply and again only the Americans could provide it. Consequently the British, to French chagrin, obeyed the American demand to call for a ceasefire. British stock in the world fell further when the government claimed that it had not known of the Israeli plan to attack Egypt, and that it had intervened merely to separate the combatants. Thus Britain contrived to seem both dishonest and imperialist.

At home party politics became more bitter. Some Conservatives felt a particular animus against the Labour leader, Gaitskell, asserting that the operation might have succeeded but for Labour opposition. For Labour the crisis seemed to indicate that the Conservative Party had not changed as much as its moderation in the early 1950s had led them to hope. For Eden personally the Suez fiasco was a tragic end to an honourable career. His health never recovered from the strain of the crisis and he resigned in 1957.

Eden's successor was Harold Macmillan, who had more support in the party than Eden's deputy, Butler. In the past Macmillan had criticised his party for failing to tackle unemployment, but by 1957 such views were orthodox. His Edwardian charm and service in the First World War won over Conservative back-benchers. He showed great skill in overcoming several problems in his first 18 months in office, and soon won the title 'Supermac'. Good relations were restored with the USA, and defence spending was cut in real terms by following the option of developing a British nuclear force instead of conventional weapons. Consequently the government was able to end National Service. The government also demonstrated its talents over the issue of decolonisation, as a number of colonies, e.g. Cyprus, Ghana and Malaya, moved towards independence. On a tour of Africa in 1960 Macmillan warned the South African parliament that a wind of change was sweeping over Africa and that Britain would not resist it. Determined to play a role on the world stage, the prime minister also worked hard to create the right conditions for a summit conference.

A particular feature of the late 1950s was growing economic expansion. In 1957 Macmillan had commented (in a phrase he was later to regret) that the people had never had it so good, but it was in

1958 that expansion was particularly rapid, helped by easier credit, buoyant consumer demand, tax cuts, increased government spending and a world boom. Such prosperity, combined with a wonderful summer in 1959, encouraged Macmillan to hold a general election in the autumn. Predictably the Conservatives gained an easy victory, winning 365 seats to Labour's 258.

However, from 1959 on the government began to experience failure on a number of fronts. Macmillan's dream of a successful summit conference was ruined in May 1960 when the shooting down of an American U-2 spy plane gave the Russians an excuse to boycott the conference. The prime minister was unable to prevent Commonwealth pressure on South Africa over apartheid, and in 1961 that country withdrew from the Commonwealth. In 1960 the rapid growth in the economy led to growing trade deficits, and deflationary budgets were brought in; consequently unemployment rose and the government lost popularity. The difficult issue of whether to apply for membership of the EEC exercised the prime minister in 1960 and 1961, and when negotiations for entry began, they were of extraordinary complexity, even though they were conducted by Edward Heath with great skill.

The twelve months from October 1962 saw a string of unlucky reverses. British prestige suffered when the Cuban crisis was settled without any American consultation with Britain whatsoever. All hopes of an independent British nuclear deterrent had to be abandoned with the cancellation of the Blue Streak and Skybolt projects, and Britain was forced to acquire American Polaris submarines. A severe winter in 1962-3 contributed to the unemployment figures reaching 878,000. As the government had claimed the credit for the 1959 boom, so it now had to take the blame for economic reverses. It became the butt of a new kind of TV satire, the most celebrated programme being 'That Was The Week That Was' (TW3). The country seemed to be losing a sense of national purpose, a point touched on by Dean Acheson, the former American Secretary of State, when he commented, 'Britain has lost an Empire and has not yet found a role.'

Macmillan's own reputation declined for two reasons – the rejection of Britain's application to join the EEC by de Gaulle in January 1963 and his handling of the Profumo case. The minister of war, John Profumo, was discovered to have had an affair with Christine Keeler, a call-girl who was also associating with a Russian diplomat called Ivanov. Macmillan was judged to have taken the affair too lightly. In September 1963 illness finally forced his resignation, and Sir Alec Douglas-Home replaced him. In October 1964 the period of Conservative supremacy ended when Labour gained a tiny majority, winning 317 seats to the Conservatives' 303.

(iv) Growing problems, 1964–79

The new Labour government was led by Harold Wilson, Hugh Gaitskell having died in 1963. Conservative efforts to expand the economy had led to a severe balance of payments deficit, and the new administration was forced to consider devaluation of the pound as a corrective measure. It avoided such a step in the short run because such a course was considered an admission of British weakness, but the alternative of tax increases was hardly a pleasant one.

The government's plans for economic change rested on a prices and incomes policy and a National Plan similar to the French system. The other main issue which absorbed Labour's attention was the Rhodesian problem (see Chapter 20). Nevertheless Wilson and his cabinet had appeared to demonstrate some competence and Wilson was also able to score points against the new Conservative leader, Edward Heath. Accordingly in the elections of March 1966, Labour increased its seats to 363 while the Conservative number was reduced to 253.

After this victory the Wilson government was faced by a number of unpleasant realities. The National Plan's ambitious target of 4 per cent per annum growth was given up, as was most of the Plan itself, but the steel industry was renationalised. A second attempt to join the EEC was again thwarted by de Gaulle's intransigence. In October 1967, after repeatedly stressing the desirability of avoiding devaluation of the pound, the government did exactly that. Another sign of British weakness was the withdrawal of troops from responsibilities 'East of Suez'.

The final years of the 1960s were troubled ones for the government. The 1968 budget, formulated by Roy Jenkins, included real cuts in government spending. Such a budget controlled inflation, but unemployment by 1970 was double that of 1965, to the anger of Labour's left wing. The cabinet itself was weakened by division, the deputy leader, George Brown, resigning in 1968. Attempts to bring some of the worst trade union practices under control, a plan called *In Place of Strife*, met with fierce opposition from the unions and union-sponsored Labour MPs and had to be given up. Violence flared in Northern Ireland between the Protestant majority and Catholic minority, and British troops were sent in to protect the Catholics. Thus began the troubles which were to plague Ulster for the next two decades. Despite such problems a Labour victory was still predicted in the election of June 1970, but Heath's Conservatives gained 330 seats to Labour's 287. The Wilson years had seen only a little progress, in welfare, housing and the creation of the Open University.

Of all British premiers, the new leader, Edward Heath, was the most committed to Europe and he successfully negotiated Britain's entry into the EEC. Elsewhere his government was less successful. After a conference at Selsdon Park, Conservative economic policy was wedded to the idea of a free market, with less government intervention. However, a sharp rise in unemployment forced the government to make a U-turn. Despite its intention not to bail out 'lame-duck' industries, it was deemed necessary to rescue Rolls-Royce when the engineering firm faced bankruptcy in 1971.

The rise in unemployment strengthened resistance to the government's Industrial Relations Act of 1971, which attempted to impose controls on strike action. In 1973 a miner's strike, combined with the effects of the oil crisis following the Yom Kippur War (see Chapter 19), forced Britain into a 3-day week. Heath regarded the strike as raising the fundamental question of who governed the country, and held a general election on the issue in February 1974. Labour gained more seats than the Conservatives (301 to 296), but not an overall majority. A second general election in October led to a Labour overall majority of 3. The two elections saw significant gains for the two nationalist parties – Plaid Cymru and the Scottish Nationalists. The loss of two elections in a year and dislike of his interventionist approach by Conservatives led to Heath losing his position as party leader to Mrs Margaret Thatcher.

The new Labour chancellor of the exchequer, Dennis Healey, tried to reflate the economy, but this, combined with large pay settlements, led to inflation of 26 per cent by 1975. Government expenditure rose remorselessly on lame ducks like British Leyland. In 1976 Wilson retired, but James Callaghan, his successor, faced similar difficulties. Britain's low growth, high inflation and rising unemployment led to a new reputation, that of the Sick Man of Europe. A renewed burst of strikes in the public sector led to 1978–9 being called 'the winter of discontent' and contributed to Conservative victory in the elections of May 1979.

(v) The Thatcher years: Britain in the 1980s

The new Conservative government was of a very different stamp to previous Conservative administrations. Its philosophy was that of the radical right, and Mrs Thatcher soon demonstrated that she was also a conviction politician; compromise was foreign to her nature and, as she told a party conference, 'This lady's not for turning.' She and her supporters believed that the economic problems faced since the war had pushed government into too interventionist an approach, and they also had a healthy fear of excessive union power. The new government was determined to implement the monetarist ideas of Milton Friedman and the Chicago School of Economists, who taught that the chief economic enemy was inflation, and that the chief cause of inflation was excessive government spending. What was therefore required was (a) more control of government spending so as to reduce inflation, (b) a rolling back of the frontiers of the state by a programme of privatisation, and (c) the encouragement of initiative and hard work in the private sector by the creation of the right enterprise culture through moves like tax cuts and control of the unions.

Such policies were followed vigorously after 1979, and had disastrous effects in the short run. The withdrawal of support from lame-duck industries, the policy of high interest rates when the pound was already strong, owing to its new status as a petro-currency, combined with a world recession and led to a collapse in industrial employment. Unemployment rose from 1.3 million in 1979 to 3.3 million by 1982. The government insisted that this was evidence of the policies actually working.

Such a track record would normally have lost any government the next election. However, in 1982 the Argentinian government of General Galtieri occupied the British South Atlantic possession of the Falkland Islands. The British responded by sending a task force to the area to expel Argentinian forces. The episode aroused national pride and thus the 'Falklands factor' contributed to the Conservative victory in the 1983 general election. The other major factor explaining the victory was the split in the Labour ranks. In 1981 several right-wing Labour notables, such as Dr David Owen, left the party to form a new party, the Social Democrats. Throughout the 1980s Labour struggled to restore both its unity and its credibility.

After 1983 the economic policies appeared to be more successful. Unemployment stopped rising and by 1988 had fallen to just over 2 million. For most people in work, there was a rise in living standards as the 1980s progressed. Inflation, which had again risen to over 20 per cent in 1980, fell to 4 per cent in 1987. Some of the revenues of North Sea oil were invested in new industry, and Britain, once derided as the Sick Man of Europe, began to enjoy higher growth rates than most of her competitors.

The 1980s also saw a reduction in union militancy, caused partly by the recession and partly by government legislation. Trade Union Acts in 1980, 1982 and 1984 implemented such reforms as the secret ballot on strike action and the outlawing of secondary picketing.

Such developments enabled the Conservatives to win the election of 1987, but whether the changes may be termed a revolution is open to doubt. The government enjoyed some good luck in the 1980s through the Falklands factor, the revenues from North Sea oil and privatisation, and a revival in the world economy. However, it failed to control its own expenditure, which doubled in the 1980s and its control of inflation was unsure and necessitated cripplingly high interest rates and an overvalued pound. Nevertheless British industry was more enterprising than in 1979, though a skills shortage and high interest rates threatened to choke back the growth of the British economy.

(c) France

(i) The Fourth Republic

With the fall of France in June 1940 there came to the fore a little known brigadier-general, Charles de Gaulle. Born in 1890, he had fought in the First World War, being taken prisoner at Verdun. Arrogant and unorthodox, his relations with his superiors were normally bad and he only became a colonel in 1938. Having fought well during the Battle of France, he became the leader of the Free French and returned to Paris in triumph in 1944. He restored order and constituted a new government composed of members from thirteen different parties.

It is difficult to be neutral about de Gaulle. Walter Laqueur rightly refers to his 'colossal egocentricity and his dictatorial and capricious style even when he was at his best'. Possessed by overweening self-confidence, he was convinced that his historical mission was to restore France's prestige and great power status. His experience during the war, when the Allies refused to regard him as the legal head of the French government in exile, offended his self-esteem and made him a difficult colleague for Roosevelt and Churchill to work with.

France herself faced grave problems. She was expected to make a real contribution to the peace effort when in fact she was on the brink of anarchy. A difficult issue was that of the punishment to be meted out to collaborators. They were more severely purged than in most other countries. Almost 2,000 death sentences were carried out, but to this figure should be added 4,500 collaborators killed by partisans. With the prewar leaders discredited, the Communists led by Thorez were now the strongest party, with nearly a million members. De Gaulle disliked them because of their links with Russia, and refused to grant them any key positions in his cabinet.

In October 1945 elections were held for a new Constituent Assembly whose chief task was to write a constitution for the Fourth Republic. Three parties – the Communists, the Socialists and the MRP (Mouvement Republicain Populaire) – won 75 per cent of the vote and wanted to adopt measures depriving future presidents of the Republic of all authority. De Gaulle, who had advocated a strong presidency, resigned in protest in January 1946. He felt sure that his hour would come again when the political parties had discredited themselves. If he hoped for an early return to power, he was disappointed. The French people showed profound indifference to his departure, an intolerable affront to his proud spirit. He returned to the family home at Colombey and in vain attempted to prevent the adoption of the new constitution, but in October 1946 the French people voted in favour of virtually the same political system as before the war. They did so with some apathy, for 9 million abstained from casting their vote.

(ii) Economic recovery
In the early postwar years the French economy appeared to reflect the paralysis of political life. It suffered more than most countries from price inflation, which was the product of disordered state finances and high government spending on social services, wage settlements in the public sector and costly military operations in Indo-China and Algeria. France's balance of payments difficulties were grave, and left her with a large foreign debt. Gradually, however, the economy revived, with substantial increases in output in both the industrial and agricultural sectors. From being the museum of Europe, France began to gain a more progressive outlook. Even the population figures, for so long static, took an upward turn; between 1938 and 1967 France's population grew by 9 million.

The French economy benefited from Marshall Aid and from the creation of an office for overall planning. A number of able directors, including Jean Monnet, who headed the office between 1941 and 1952, exercised considerable influence on the economy through the development of nationalised industries and the direction of investment credit. By 1954 industrial production was 50 per cent higher than in 1939, with modernisation in steel, electricity, car manufacture and the railways.

When de Gaulle came to power in 1958, the government carried out stiff measures to halt inflation, but the chief stimulus to the economy accrued from the development of the Common Market. France's exports to her fellow EEC partners grew from 22 per cent of her total foreign sales in 1958 to 41 per cent in 1968. Another reason for advance was an influx of American capital. Abundant supplies of labour contributed to the revival, for, as Postan has shown, the French economy always possessed large untapped reserves of productive capacity. Labour flowed from agriculture at the rate of 90,000 a year, but an even larger supply of labour came from the 2½ million immigrants who had entered France by 1963. After the Algerian war, nearly a million expatriates returned to France, adding 300,000 to the labour force. Finally, France was helped by her greater self-sufficiency in foodstuffs and her increasing exports of agricultural produce in the 1960s. These exports, coupled with the discovery of oil and gas in her territories, helped to sustain the balance of payments. By the early 1960s a new spirit of optimism had replaced the gloom of previous decades, as France's GNP grew between 4 and 7 per cent a year.

(iii) Political instability

France's economic progress during the years of the Fourth Republic was not matched by any similar development in her political institutions. With parties on the left and right that were enemies of the regime – the Communists and de Gaulle's Rassemblement du Peuple Francais (RPF) respectively – government relied on frail coalitions of Socialists, Radicals and members of the Mouvement Republicain Populaire (MRP). Between 1946 and 1958 there were twenty-five different governments, and, as Denis Brogan has written, such a system 'made for an amiable form of parliamentary life but destroyed the voter's sense that he was voting for anything or anybody in particular, or that his formal representatives, once they were elected, were responsible to him or to anybody'. Gradually public confidence in the regime was eroded.

The only new party proper was the MRP, led by Georges Bidault and Maurice Schumann. Throughout the Fourth Republic it played an important role in politics and was represented in most of the cabinets. Bidault was prime minister in 1946 and in 1949–50, while Schumann held that office in 1947 and 1948. The MRP was a party of the left in favour of nationalisation, and it tried to act as a bridge between the Communists and their enemies. However, the unremitting hostilitiy of the Communists prevented any real cooperation.

It was in Indo-China that France's worst trauma occurred. In 1946 the Communist and Nationalist leader Ho Chi Minh and his military commander, Vo Nguyen Giap, started their long-planned campaign for Vietnamese independence, using the Communist organisation, the Vietminh. Ho Chi Minh was to fight first the French and then the Americans until his death in 1969, his dream of a Communist Indo-China finally being realised in 1975.

The French stuck doggedly to their objective of holding Indo-China until 1954. Then a disastrous decision by General Henri Navarre led to complete collapse. Navarre tried to draw the Vietminh into battle at Dien Bien Phu, but as it lay in a hollow surrounded by hills, the French found themselves surrounded by Vietminh artillery and could only be supplied by air. After a long siege Dien Bien Phu fell in May, and France's will to continue the war was broken. Pierre Mendes-France became prime minister with liquidation of the war as his principal objective. By July an armistice was arranged, and the French withdrew from Indo-China, which was divided into North and South Vietnam. The war, which lasted 7½ years, had cost France 92,000 dead and 114,000 wounded. The defeat in the Far East had a profound impact on France's hold over her North African empire, and by 1956 Morocco and Tunisia had been granted virtual independence.

(iv) The Fifth Republic

The Fourth Republic never won the respect of the majority of Frenchmen, because it patently failed to provide political stability, yet it took another great colonial crisis to undermine it. In 1954 a revolt broke out in Algeria, and soon 350,000 French troops were fighting in the colony against 150,000 members of the Algerian Liberation Movement (FLN). The war itself split French society deeply. Many Frenchmen opposed any retreat from Algeria, for it was not only part of metropolitan France but the home of 1 million French people. By the fourth year of the war it was becoming clearer that a negotiated peace would have to come. The French Right and the Algerian French were determined to resist this, and set up the OAS (Organisation de l'Armée Secrète), which, like the FLN, indulged in acts of terrorism in France and Algeria. When in May 1958 it was rumoured that the Pflimlin government was considering a settlement with the Algerian rebels, the French army in Algeria, determined that there should be no second Dien Bien Phu, came out in open revolt and demanded that de Gaulle be called to head the government.

De Gaulle, who had himself almost despaired of ever returning to power, suddenly became the central figure in the crisis. As the Algerian situation worsened, his leadership alone seemed essential if civil war were to be avoided. The general was now a more cunning and subtle politician than in 1947; instead of trying to add to the Fourth Republic's problems, he was shrewd enough to wait until power was offered to him. He merely issued the statement that he held himself ready to take over the powers of the Republic if needed. The Pflimlin government, unable to deal with the army rebels, resigned on 28 May, and President Coty called on de Gaulle to avert civil war. The general accepted on condition that he was given a free hand to draft a new constitution for approval by popular referendum. In early June the Assembly accepted his terms, and by its surrender assisted him in destroying the Fourth Republic by a bloodless revolution.

The new Constitution incorporated de Gaulle's own political theories, as the president was to be vested with wide powers. He was to have the right to appoint the prime minister and dissolve parliament. Effective control over defence and foreign policy lay in his hands. He was to be elected by the people for 7 years and could make use of the popular referendum, thus further reducing the importance of parliament. In September, after de Gaulle had made shrewd use of the television network, nearly 80 per cent of metropolitan France approved the new constitution.

In the winter months of 1958–9 a reorganised two-house parliament (National Assembly and Senate) was elected, and de Gaulle was chosen as president by an electoral college of 80,000 delegates from local councils. For the parliamentary elections dedicated Gaullists regrouped to form a new party, the Union for the New Republic (UNR), which became the ruling party of the Fifth Republic until 1981.

(v) Algeria

The new president's overriding initial task was to find a solution to the Algerian question. The war in Algeria had a peculiarly vicious character about it. As Alfred Cobban writes, 'the Algerian nationalists intensified their campaign of largely indiscriminate murder, while the army organised underground counter-terrorist services. Terrorism was met by counter-terrorism and torture by torture'. The cost in lives and resources sickened the French people, who were weary of decades of futile colonial wars.

The Algerian war then was the supreme test of de Gaulle's political ability. The army and settlers in Algeria had supported his return to power for the specific purpose of keeping Algeria French. De Gaulle, who had not committed himself on the question, would have liked a victory by the French army there, but was realistic enough to see that it was impossible. His thinking on the issue evolved until he was determined to give independence to Algeria. Brian Crozier sees another motive in the president's mind. He was so possessed by a burning ambition to restore French greatness and break the American leadership in Western international affairs that he wished for the most speedy end to the Algerian problem, which had become a tiresome distraction for him.

In September 1959 de Gaulle publicly grasped the nettle by offering Algeria self-determination within 4 years of the restoration of peace. The declaration accelerated the process of polarisation in Algerian politics. In January 1960 the French settlers and army in Algeria attempted a second revolt, after de Gaulle had recalled General Massu for declaring that the French army would never leave Algeria. This rebellion collapsed quickly, but in April 1961 more serious trouble occurred when the OAS, led by four generals, Salan, Challe, Jouhaud and Zeller, seized power in Algeria. De Gaulle did not flinch in the face of this daunting challenge; in the words of Crozier, he met it 'by an inflexible display of personal authority'. He appeared on television in his general's uniform and, condemning the rebels for their stupid adventure, forbade all Frenchmen to carry out their orders. The rebellion lost impetus, and by the end of the month most of its leaders had been arrested.

The OAS now went underground and devised new murderous tactics, hoping to kill the president and keep Algeria French. At least four attempts were made on de Gaulle's life between September 1961 and August 1962. A bloody campaign of urban terrorism led to many deaths, but it did not prevent a 90 per cent vote in favour of Algerian independence when a referendum was held on the issue in 1962. Agreement with the FLN was finally reached and Algeria became independent, but only at heavy human cost: 800,000 of the 900,000 European Algerians felt it expedient to seek refuge in France and 10,000 Moslems who had served in the French army were massacred by the new Algerian government. De Gaulle must take part of the blame for these excesses, because, in his haste to be rid of the Algerian burden, he virtually gave the country away.

Nevertheless, as Brian Crozier has admitted, 'that he was able to part with Algeria without a civil war in France was a great though negative achievement which in all probability would have been beyond the capacity of any other leader France possessed'. The general was now at the height of his power and prestige. France for the first time since the war seemed to have effective leadership, which was welcome after the chaotic politics of the Fourth Republic. De Gaulle reaped the benefits of the work of predecessors as the economy improved; yet even in 1962 a slow erosion of the Gaullist regime was beginning. The general's main interests lay in defence and foreign policy, and his actions in those fields had no relevance to the needs of ordinary Frenchmen. Support drained from the Gaullists, and in the Presidential elections of 1965 de Gaulle was elected by only 54 per cent to the socialist Mitterrand's 46 per cent.

(vi) De Gaulle's foreign policy

It was soon clear when he came to power for a second time that de Gaulle's views on Europe were rigid and uncompromising. His desire to restore French greatness and break American influence in Europe amounted to an obsession. He nursed a bitter resentment against Britain and the United States, because, in his view, they had treated him with a lack of due regard. 'Yalta', asserts Crozier, 'was the intolerable lump that stuck in de Gaulle's throat.' He could never forgive the Anglo-Saxons for keeping him out of the conference that was to determine the shape of the postwar world. In any case he stood uncompromisingly for French self-interest, and believed that his country had few common interests with Britain and the United States. It was, as Walter Laqueur reminds us, an essentially eighteenth-century concept of international politics, with ideology playing little if any part in it. He dismissed as imaginary the Soviet threat to Western Europe, and his attitude to NATO and the EEC proves that he saw no necessity for Atlantic or European unity.

A conflict of views with the Americans was therefore almost inevitable. In the general's mind, France was a world power, whereas the Americans regarded France as merely one of the great European powers. Therefore he determined to demonstrate France's capacity to be independent of the United States. In March 1959 he withdrew French naval units from NATO Mediterranean Command, and established a pattern which was to be repeated in the next few years. He was in fact touching on a real issue – the extent of America's commitment to the defence of Europe, which is still concerning West European states in 1989. The general believed that only a strong European power could assure European security, and he insisted that France should have her own nuclear deterrent, the 'force de frappe'. Yet he was ignoring the realities of power; the French nuclear deterrent, though it cost $1 billion a year, was of little military value, and only a concerted effort by several European powers together could really strengthen the continent. De Gaulle sabotaged such efforts.

The general's European policy was based on friendship with West Germany. In return for his support of the Germans against the Soviet bloc, he expected West German cooperation with his own plans for French domination of the Common Market and independence of the United States. Other European states were not consulted.

After the solution of the Algerian question, de Gaulle felt sufficiently confident to make more grand gestures. In 1965 France left SEATO, the South East Asian equivalent of NATO, and ceased to participate in any NATO manoeuvres. In 1966 France partly withdrew from NATO, with the general attempting to forge new links with Russia. In 1964 he visited Russia, and Kosygin returned the visit. De Gaulle referred to the new alliance between the countries, but the prestige he gained was largely spurious. The Russians certainly did not regard France as a superpower, and in any emergency she would have to be defended by the Western Alliance. The practical limits of French power were well illustrated by the loss of influence in Algeria, which came more and more under Russian rather than French control after independence.

The events of 1968 in France not only revealed the brittleness of de Gaulle's rule there but the absurdity of his foreign policy as well. With unrest undermining the franc, France needed massive foreign help, especially from West Germany and the United States. Perhaps the general began to realise the unreality of his own policies, for his actions became those of an embittered and frustrated man, as seen in his brutal rejection of Britain's membership of the Common Market and his exclamation of 'Vive le Quebec Libre' to encourage French separatists during a visit to Canada in 1967. In trying to carry out a foreign policy based on 'grandeur', as Crozier comments, de Gaulle was 'never to acquire the means commensurate with his ambitions'.

(vii) The French Revolution of 1968

The period of the 1950s and early 1960s was a relatively quiet one in Western Europe. The various regimes seemed stable, as unions and students appeared to have little interest in politics. Thus the wave of student revolts which affected the whole of Europe in 1968 asto-

nished the continent. Perhaps it should not have done; a new generation had grown up discontented with the sterility of modern society.

The unrest was most serious in France, where the student population had arisen from 122,000 in 1939 to 643,000 in 1969, with
consequent problems over accommodation and the relevance of
academic courses. The government did little for the students, and for
many of the student fraternity the president seemed to be an
anachronism. The first notable event was a strike by students and
teachers at Nanterre in November 1967. In February 1968 the Paris
students went on strike, and use was made of Molotov cocktails. The
French students' union was now in the hands of a militant group,
including Cohn-Bendit, and in May really serious trouble occurred,
with huge demonstrations leading to clashes between police and
students as the latter attempted to take over the university buildings.

The violence of the police swung public opinion behind the students. Unemployment, too, contributed to the unrest. Though the
number of unemployed was only 450,000, it was rising sharply and
causing alarm. On 13 May hundreds of thousands of Parisians
demonstrated against the regime, and all over France action committees were created as workers joined the movement. The Sorbonne
was occupied, and on 17 May a million workers went on strike. De
Gaulle, who was on a state visit to Rumania, had to interrupt his
grand foreign policy tour and return home.

France was not, however, in the throes of a revolution, though the
troubles revealed the profound discontent of many French people at
the authoritarian pretentiousness of de Gaulle's government and its
failure to deal with social and academic problems. The regime
seemed in danger as the parties of the Left joined the movement, and
the CGT won substantial pay awards at the end of May, which the
rank and file turned down.

Yet the movement lacked any real unity; the radical slogans of
Cohn-Bendit and his associates antagonised wide sections of the
French public. Fervent assertions through irritating chants took the
place of rational discussion and the search for truth. There was much
talk about destroying the regime, but a palpable lack of constructive
thinking about what to put in its place. In the end the great majority
of the population in France and elsewhere were bound to repudiate
extremists like Cohn-Bendit, Tariq Ali or Rudi Dutschke. Most
people, including the workers, had a stake in the maintenance of law
and order, and disliked the student predilection for violence and
destruction.

An opportunity therefore for de Gaulle to reassert his authority
still existed. Having assured himself of the loyalty of the French
army, he announced on 30 May that he would not resign, and called
for the defence of the Republic against the threat of Communist
dictatorship. The general's verbal magic was again effective. A

million of his supporters now demonstrated in his favour, and gradually the occupied factories and universities were evacuated by workers and students.

Though he survived the events of May 1968, de Gaulle's prestige was destroyed. That he was taken by surprise is an indictment of his rule; he was too remote from real life and had no interest in the conditions under which ordinary French people lived. Problems like inadequate housing and social services had been ignored. His overbearing paternalism, especially in his use of the judicial machine and the constitution, was intensely irritating, as was his increasingly theatrical and eccentric handling of foreign affairs.

The general sought to restore his prestige by implementing changes in the Senate and by the creation of regional councils. However, by deciding to hold a referendum on these reforms and by announcing that he would regard the referendum as a vote of confidence, he took an unnecessary risk. In April 1969, while nearly 11 million French people supported the reforms, over 12 million voted against them. True to his word, the general resigned. In exposing hmself to public rejection, he had again demonstrated his taste for the theatrical. The French nation greeted the news of his departure with some relief, for there was a feeling that he had outlived his usefulness. De Gaulle settled down to writing. He died in November 1970 and was buried at Colombey-les-Deux-Eglises.

Brian Crozier is right when he states that 'the fame of de Gaulle outstrips his achievements'. Between 1940 and 1945 he launched the Resistance and restored the Republic. In his second period in power he can be credited with two undeniable achievements – the constitution of the Fifth Republic and the solution of the Algerian question. The constitution has proved itself a durable instrument under de Gaulle's successors and France has been given generally effective government. That the Algerian settlement was achieved without a civil war was a masterly performance, though the general's impatient shedding of the problem increased the price in human terms that had to be paid.

Against these achievements must be set the neglect of social problems and the absurdity of his foreign policy, which was divisive and weakened NATO and the Common Market. Perhaps he hung on to power for too long; he should have retired in 1965 when he was still popular, having rid France of the Algerian burden, but though he possessed charisma and intelligence, he behaved as if he were living in a previous century. In the end he wasted his talents; he could have contributed to a more united Europe in full partnership with the United States. Instead, as Crozier reminds us, he chose to make repeated gestures of petulance and defiance that weakened the West without compensating advantages to France.

(viii) French politics after de Gaulle

De Gaulle had changed the system whereby the president was elected by an electoral college, replacing it with election by direct popular vote. It was this system of election by universal suffrage which brought to the presidency the affable and shrewd Georges Pompidou. He had been a teacher and banker for much of his life, but he became de Gaulle's second prime minister in 1962, holding the premiership until 1968, when he became the scapegoat for the 1968 Revolution. He was popular with the UDR, because he paid attention to the wishes of members of parliament. Though less abrasive than the general, he was no figurehead president.

Pompidou was more favourable than de Gaulle to British entry to the Common Market, and in 1972 held a referendum in France on the question of Britain's entry, which was approved by a decisive majority. Unlike de Gaulle, he was interested in domestic issues, and tried to implement a new social policy – almost a new 'social contract'. He was less autocratic than the general, playing a steering role on many issues affecting the nation's welfare. Therefore it tended to be on financial matters that he intervened most. De Gaulle in 1968 had refused to devalue the franc on grounds of prestige. Pompidou less than a year later reversed this decision.

Pompidou did not strive for the grand manner in foreign affairs, as had de Gaulle. While he followed the main tenets of de Gaulle's foreign policy, he worked towards warmer relations with the United States. At the same time his government retained the desire to maintain France's and Europe's independence of the United States, so that Europe under French leadership might appear as an alternative to the two power blocs. Thus Pompidou retained France's nuclear deterrent and tried to create a special position in the Middle East by selling arms to the Arab states in return for secure supplies of oil.

In April 1974 this skilful and patient politician died of a rare kind of leukemia. He was succeeded by Valery Giscard d'Estaing who narrowly beat the socialist François Mitterrand in the presidential elections. Giscard d'Estaing's achievement in becoming president without a mass party (he was not a Gaullist) was proof of his political talents and personal magnetism. His record as finance minister from 1962, when he helped to control inflation, particularly contributed to his success. Only 48 when elected, Giscard became the youngest French president in 80 years, which gave him something of a Kennedyesque image. Though a member of the French aristocracy, he adopted a more relaxed, informal style of presidency than de Gaulle's, believing it important to establish direct links with the man in the street. Whether the man in the street was convinced by such a style is doubtful.

Giscard's popularity had declined by the late 1970s. The effects of the oil price shocks, the world slump and the attempt to nationalise France's older industries led to a doubling of inflation to 13 per cent by 1980, combined with a halving of growth rates to 2.6 per cent. Unemployment rose from 700,000 in 1974 to 1.6 million by 1981. Thus economic factors largely explain his defeat in the 1981 presidential elections.

In an atmosphere of euphoria the socialist François Mitterrand became president, with an ambitious programme of economic and social reforms. His government hoped to reduce unemployment, reindustrialise France and reconquer the domestic market (invaded by too many imports) by making French business more competitive. It was hoped that heavy investment would make France the Japan of Western Europe.

The chief policy instruments used were a programme of nationalisation, a new national plan and an expansionary budget. Quickly in 1981–2 twelve major industrial firms, e.g. St Gobain, and thirty-six banks were nationalised and a big programme of state spending implemented in a dash for growth. Unfortunately such policies sucked in imports and led to high inflation, high interest rates and huge trade deficits. By 1983 the government was forced to do a U-turn and follow policies akin to those of the Thatcher government in Britain. Public spending became more controlled and lame-duck industries, such as steel, were severely rationalised.

In 1986 further complications arose for the president. Parliamentary elections led to a conservative majority, and France now experienced for the first time the uneasy phenomenon of 'co-habitation' between a socialist president, Mitterrand, and a conservative prime minister, Jacques Chirac. Chirac's cabinet implemented some privatisation and tax cuts before new presidential and parliamentary elections in 1988 saw Mitterrand returned for a second term as president with the moderate socialist Michel Rocard as the new prime minister.

The outlook for the current government was not bright. There was rising criticism of Mitterrand himself for his adoption of a Napoleonic style. In addition Rocard did not have a majority in the French parliament, and was therefore constrained in his attempts to reduce the figure of 2.5 million unemployed. A rash of strikes by unions normally regarded as the government's natural supporters ended 1988 on an unpropitious note.

FURTHER READING

Addison, P., *The Road to 1945: British Politics and the Second World War*, Cape, London, 1975

Crozier, B., *De Gaulle. The Statesman*, Methuen, London, 1974

Landes, D., *The Unbound Prometheus*, CUP, Cambridge, 1970

Laqueur, W., *The Rebirth of Europe*, Penguin, Harmondsworth, 1982

MacInnes, J., *Thatcherism at Work*, Open University Press, Milton Keynes, 1987

McMillan, J. F., *Dreyfus to de Gaulle*, Edward Arnold, London, 1985

Morgan, K. O., *Labour in Power 1945–1951*, OUP, Oxford, 1984

Prittie, T. F., *The Velvet Chancellors: A History of Post-War Germany*, Frederick Muller, London, 1979

Robbins, K., *The Eclipse of a Great Power: Modern Britain 1870–1945*, Longmans, London, 1983

Vaughan, R., *Twentieth Century Europe: Paths to Unity*, Croom Helm, 1979

Wegs, J. R., *Europe Since 1945*, Second Edition, Macmillan, London, 1984

QUESTIONS

1. Why did political and economic integration take place in Western Europe after 1945?
2. Critically analyse the changes in Britain's attitude to the EEC between 1957 and 1973.
3. Which postwar British government most fully achieved its key objectives?
4. Why has the Bonn Federal Republic enjoyed so much more stability than its Weimar predecessor?
5. What did the Fifth Republic in France owe to the achievements of the Fourth Republic?

13
The Far East in the twentieth century: Japan

(a) The rise of the new Japan, 1868–1918

Japanese history in modern times has been interesting as a response to intrusion by the Western world. As Richard Storry explains, 'This response was a highly nervous, vivid compound of love and hate. Japan was the first country in Asia to be industrialised and therefore the first in Asia to use the weapons of the West against the West.'

The national religion was Shinto, a form of nature worship, with the Emperors tracing their origins to the Sun Goddess. The appeal of this religion was aesthetic and emotional rather than moral. A stronger cultural influence came from China; through the Japanese connection with Korea came the introduction of Chinese script and Buddhism. Japanese people usually were believers in both Buddhism and Shintoism, and the two religions existed side by side. Buddhism provided the philosophical speculation, Zen Buddhism in the fourteenth century, for example, giving a warrior creed with an emphasis on self-discipline and meditation.

Unlike South and South East Asia, which were partitioned by the Western powers, and East Asia, which remained only partly independent of the West, Japan in the nineteenth century retained its autonomy and indeed had begun to rise to great power status by 1914. By then the foundations of a modern state had been laid, the speed of the transformation being unequalled until South Korea's development in recent years. The modernisation of Japan was partly a matter of geography. It was a group of compact islands with a population of about 30 million in 1850, compared with China's huge population of over 400 million, so that the imposition of coherent policies aroused a sense of national consciousness more easily than in the vast expanses of China.

Two reasons explain why the West did not attempt to carve out spheres of interest or colonies in Japan, as had occurred in China. Firstly, Europeans were impressed by Japanese progress in adopting Western ways and by the consequent growing strength of Japan. Secondly, China appeared to have much more potential as a commercial market than Japan, and thus became the main target in Asia for Western aggression. As J. A. S. Grenville says, 'The West's image of China protected Japan and contributed to the very different development of the two nations after the incursion of the West into east Asia.'

Yet before the middle of the nineteenth century Japan was a feudal society. Different clans clashed with each other, the strongest being able to dictate to the emperor, who was thus a puppet. Though never displaced from his position, he was forced to invest the most successful of the feudal chiefs (or *daimyo*) with the office of shogun (barbarian-quelling generalissimo). This domination by feudal lords gave a military character to Japanese government.

In 1603 Iyeyasu became shogun, the first of a long line of Tokugawa shoguns who ruled Japan until the restoration of the Emperor in 1867. It was Iyeyasu and other seventeenth-century shoguns who evolved the administrative system that Europeans found in 1853. Though the emperor was maintained as the theoretical temporal and spiritual ruler, he reigned without governing, living in seclusion at Kyoto. Actual power lay with the shogun. The Tokugawa, when they came to power in 1603, divided Japan among their own supporters, with opponents being dispossessed. Even the power of the shogun was limited by his councils. By 1853 much administration had passed into the hands of the retainers of the *daimyo* (the *karo*) while the old warrior class (the samurai) remained a privileged group who still glorified the warrior code (*bushido*). When not called upon to fight, they were supported in idleness by the rest of the inhabitants. Yet, as Storry reminds us, the samurai mentality pervaded Japanese society at large, the ethic of loyalty achieving a semi-religious status.

Though in many respects Japan remained heavily dependent on the cultivation of rice, town life developed from the seventeenth century on, and a new class of merchants arose in towns like Yedo (Tokyo) and Nagasaki, advancing its social status by marriage into samurai families. The period saw little contact with the West, the Japanese remaining most suspicious of Western motives after the activities of Portuguese and Spanish missionaries in the sixteenth century. For 200 years Japan was undisturbed by foreign wars and enjoyed a great degree of internal peace.

Yet by 1853 the spread of education had led to more criticism of the shogun and a demand for the restoration of the emperor's original powers. By this time too some opening of the country became almost inevitable, as Western powers began to develop commercial links with China and needed coaling stations or ports of call en route. Several attempts were made by the West to extract concessions before 1853, but these were all resolutely resisted by the Japanese. However, in that year the Americans, who particularly needed coaling facilities, sent an expedition under Commodore Perry to

Yokohama Bay. Peremptorily, in a style that anticipated Douglas MacArthur later, Perry disregarded all signals to stop, and, after anchoring, he demanded and obtained proper treatment of American sailors wrecked on Japan's shore and the opening of three ports to foreign vessels for purposes of coaling and provisioning. Other Western powers negotiated similar treaties in the following years.

Such events acted as a catalyst for profound internal changes in Japan. The Western presence led to several acts of violence against foreigners and subsequent Western reprisals, for example the British bombardment of Kagoshima in 1862. The inability of the shogun either to resist the foreigner or prevent acts of violence by Japanese undermined his remaining authority. In 1867 the accession of a new emperor, Mutsuhito, who took as his title Meiji (enlightened rule), provided the occasion for the most powerful clans to unite and demand the end of the shogunate and the restoration of the authority of the emperor. Their motives were probably mixed. While they wished to see more effective government in Japan, they also hoped to replace the shogun as advisers to the Emperor, so as to break the Tokugawa monopoly of appointments to office.

The restoration of the emperor to power did not in itself mark a sharp break with the past, because the feudal regime was left intact. A great break had, however, been made by the shogun when he gave up the policy of isolation and admitted foreigners. Western influences now grew in Japan, and after 1868 it became a country undergoing uniquely rapid transition.

In 1871 feudalism was formally abolished, with the important clan leaders accepting pensions in place of their feudal privileges. They did so because they were under pressure from the samurai, but they also appreciated that Japan must modernise and concentrate authority in the face of the foreign challenge. In 1889 a new constitution was devised through the influence of a member of the oligarchy, Okuma, who had been influenced by visits to Germany. The emperor was restored to a position of real power; he was sacred and inviolable and could issue ordinances with the force of law. He would be advised by a small group of elders (*genro*), who wielded great influence. If his *genro* disagreed among themselves, the emperor could use his prerogative as final arbiter. A Western structure of government, with a prime minister, cabinet and elected parliament, was set up, but real power remained in the hands of the emperor and his chief oligarchs, mainly members of the Choshu and Satsuma clans. The franchise was limited to wealthy property owners and was a right enjoyed by less than 1 per cent of the population.

It was the oligarchs who transformed Japan in the final three decades of the nineteenth century by introducing widespread economic, military and educational reform. 'In no field of activity was the spirit of the new Japan more clearly revealed than education,' comments Vinacke. Students became free to study abroad, and compulsory education was introduced as early as 1872, with a German-style emphasis on vocational education. At the same time an authoritarian element in educational reform boded ill for the future. The 1890 Rescript on Education exhorted the young to observe the Confucian obligations of filial piety and obedience, and to offer themselves courageously to the State if the need arose. This law was an early sign of some reaction against the growth of Western liberal influences in Japan.

The new rulers also undertook military reorganisation with the introduction of national service replacing the samurai system. French and German assistance was used to improve weaponry and organisation in the army, while for naval development British advice was gleaned and ships bought from Britain.

Yet it was Japan's economic development before 1914 which was most astonishing. As Lockwood stresses, 'The speed with which Japan emerged from quasi-feudalism to become a modern state with a large sector of its economy organised along industrial capitalistic lines is in striking contrast to the centuries of evolutionary growth characterising the process in the West.' The prime reason for this speed was the vision of the new rulers, not only in appreciating the need for radical economic development but in providing the resources for the most important initiatives. G. C. Allen is right to comment that there was scarcely any important Japanese industry of the Western type during the latter decades of the nineteenth century which did not owe its establishment to State initiative.

From the 1870s road, rail and steamship development proceeded apace, and improved transport was a most important factor in unifying the nation. The first railway was built from Tokyo to Yokohama in 1872, and by 1893 some 2,000 miles of railway line had been constructed. The first National Bank was started in 1873, and by 1879 there were 151 National Banks; and in 1882, a central bank, the Bank of Japan, was founded.

The government fostered the growth of foreign trade, and Lockwood attaches particular importance to the export of silk. 'Throughout the modern history of Japan', he writes, 'this single raw material played a unique role. Until as late as 1930 it continued to be the chief source of foreign exchange to finance Japan's industrialisation as well as the chief source of rural income supplementing the proceeds of rice cultivation.' Its value lay in the fact that it required no imported raw materials (unlike the cotton industry) and it was thus able to finance 40 per cent of Japan's imports of machinery and raw materials. Nevertheless the cotton industry too rose rapidly to prominence. Modern factory methods were introduced, so that not only did home producers capture the domestic market but by 1914 Japan already contributed one-quarter of the world exports of cotton yarn.

The government intervened more in industry than in agriculture to set up a wide range of industries. These new sectors, once under way, were then, with the important exception of armaments, sold off to private companies. Such a policy gave rise to the rapid growth of large combines (*zaibatsus*), such as Mitsui and Mitsubishi. On the land the Meiji years saw the spread of peasant ownership, though heavy taxation imposed to provide the capital for industrial modernisation forced many peasants to become tenants.

(b) Japan enters the world stage, 1894–1905

Relations with the West remained tense, with the Japanese constantly attempting to revise the treaties of the 1850s, which had humiliatingly placed Westerners in Japan beyond the jurisdiction of Japanese courts on the grounds that the Japanese lacked the civilisation to be entrusted with applying their laws to foreigners. (The slight also spurred the evolution of a new judicial system on Western lines.) Japan was also denied the right to impose her own customs duties. By the 1890s several major Western states, including Britain and the USA, had agreed to revise the original treaties.

Sino-Japanese relations became strained by rivalry over Korea, a country nominally ruled by China, but which in modern times had been by far the most secluded of the Far Eastern nations. This Hermit Kingdom, as it was called, was so badly governed by the Yi dynasty, and so regularly was violence perpetrated against foreigners, that Japanese and Western intervention became almost inevitable. To Japanese leaders, Korea was a dagger pointed at the heart of Japan; it was essential that it should not fall into the hands of China, much less Russia, which had revealed an interest in Korea in 1884 by helping the reform of the Korean army. Another factor in Japan's interest in Korea was economic, as the kingdom produced a considerable amount of rice, the export of which was forbidden, while Japanese business had a large stake in shipping and commerce in Korea.

In 1894 Japan declared war on China on the pretext that the Chinese had refused to urge reform on the Korean government. To the surprise of Western observers, Japanese troops proved to be more disciplined and better armed than the Chinese. Korea was soon occupied, Japanese forces moved into Manchuria, and Formosa and China itself was threatened. By the Treaty of Shimonoseki (1895), which ended the war, China acknowledged the independence of Korea and ceded Formosa, the Pescadores and Manchuria east of the Liaotung to Japan. An indemnity was to be paid and four new ports opened to foreign trade.

The cession of the Liaotung Peninsula, with its proximity to Peking, alarmed the Western powers, especially Russia. Russia,

France and Germany now demanded that the Liaotung territory be restored to China, and Japan was forced to give way in the face of such a superior combination. Despite this, there were still consolations for Japan. The friendly British attitude had been pleasing, and the war had demonstrated the weakness of China and the growing strength of the Japanese, who had gained more from the war in the shape of Formosa and the Pescadores than they had originally expected.

Nevertheless the need to bow to pressure from the Western powers was a national humiliation, Meiji saying that the Japanese had to bear the unbearable. It was galling, too, for the Japanese to observe growing Russian influence in Korea after 1895, and Russo-Japanese rivalry now became intense in both Korea and Manchuria, as Russia extracted concessions from both the Korean and Chinese governments. Manchuria produced large amounts of cereals, pulses and minerals, and Russia needed control of North Manchuria to facilitate the completion of the Trans-Siberian railway to Vladivostock. The right to run the railway across Northern Manchuria was conceded by the Chinese in 1896, but Russian policy aimed at the incorporation of all Manchuria into the Russian empire. As part of this strategy Russia acquired Port Arthur in 1898, with the aim of making it the strongest naval base in the Far East and through it exercising control of the whole Liaotung Peninsula.

Russian penetration of Manchuria was resented by Japanese leaders, who saw the economic potential of Manchuria as a stimulus for Japanese industrialisation and the growth of Japan's political power. It was now logical for Japan to draw nearer the other power which most feared Russian expansion in the Far East – Britain – and an alliance was signed in 1902, an event which Vinacke calls 'a milestone in the development of Japan as an Asiatic power'. It was the first treaty of alliance in modern times between a Western and an Oriental state in which the two were equal parties. For Japan the protection afforded by British support now allowed a firmer line against Russia, because if in the event of a Russo-Japanese war, Russia gained the support of another power, Britain would immediately come to the aid of Japan. Russia did have the alliance with France, but France began to make it clear that she would only support Russia in the event of a war in Europe.

Attempts to negotiate a compromise on Manchurian and Korean issues were made between 1902 and 1904, but these proved fruitless, and in February 1904 Japan launched a surprise attack on the Russian naval base of Port Arthur. The Russo-Japanese War of 1904–5 proved to be a series of uninterrupted successes for Japan, as she took Port Arthur after a long siege, defeated Russian armies on the Yalu River and at Mukden and destroyed Russian fleets at Port Arthur and Tsushima. Yet the war also caused heavy loss of life and a drain on the national treasury. The Japanese government became anxious to end the war if key objectives could be gained, and, with Theodore Roosevelt's mediation, the Treaty of Portsmouth was concluded in September 1905. Russia ceded the southern half of Sakhalin and transferred to Japan the lease of Liaotung. Both powers agreed to withdraw from Manchuria, and Russia agreed to a Japanese protectorate over Korea. In 1910 Japan annexed that country outright, with Russian acquiescence.

The Russo-Japanese war was of the utmost significance for a number of reasons. It established Japan as the great power of the Far East for the next 40 years. Her recognition as an equal by the other powers was enhanced by a new and closer alliance with Britain, concluded in August 1905. Though the Japanese public was angry at the absence of an indemnity on the Russians, this concession, plus the British alliance, opened the way for a Russo-Japanese rapprochement, and Russian eyes turned back to South East Europe. The only unfortunate consequence of the war for Japan was that the USA, which had acquired the Philippines and Guam as a result of the 1898 Spanish-American war, now came to regard Japan as a formidable rival. Japan-American relations also deteriorated as a result of increasing American controls on Japanese emigration to California. By the 1924 American Immigration Act Japanese were completely excluded, as aliens ineligible to become American citizens.

(c) Tensions in Japanese society: the growth of militarism after 1918

Richard Storry has called the first decades of the twentieth century in Japan 'the golden years', but the period did see growing divisions within Japan. Firstly, there was growing pressure from merchants, landowners and educated élites for a share in power, and resentment that an entrenched oligarchy monopolised the best positions in the state. Top military men, such as Field-Marshal Prince Yamagata, their prestige raised by recent successes against China and Russia, won growing influence over the Emperor, so bypassing civilian government, especially on such issues as military expenditure. With unity even in the old oligarchs waning, Japanese government began to lose its former coherence, especially after the death of Emperor Mutsuhito in 1912. His successor, Yoshihito (1912–26), was feeble-minded, and a regency was set up under his heir apparent, who became Emperor Hirohito in 1926 (and reigned until his death in 1989). By then the tradition that all was done in the monarch's name but practically nothing by him personally had again become firmly rooted.

Industrialisation imposed more strains on Japanese society. It caused a deterioration of labour relations, though the growth of the *zaibatsu* prevented the development of a democratic labour movement. In addition, the process of industrialisation highlighted two problems for Japan – its lack of raw materials and its need for constantly expanding markets for Japanese goods. When both markets and resources are outside the control of the state, the livelihood of the people dependent on industry becomes precarious. Certainly Japanese leaders came to fear such insecurity, and out of industrialisation came an economic redirection of, and a more aggressive edge to, Japanese foreign policy.

The new aggressiveness soon became evident at the beginning of the First World War. Japan entered the war as Britain's ally, the German action in 1895 in supporting France and Russia against Japan still recalled with bitterness by the Japanese. The war presented Japan with political and economic opportunities. As European states could not supply their export markets, Japanese industry was able to step in to fill the vacuum. In addition, with Germany unable to defend its colonies, Japan was able to capture German possessions at Shantung.

Unfortunately the foreign minister, Kato, overplayed his hand in 1915 by presenting China with the infamous twenty-one demands, which included the transfer to Japan of the German leaseholds in Shantung, the extension of Japanese rights in Southern Manchuria, the employment by the Chinese government of Japanese advisers and of Japanese policemen in certain important Chinese cities, and the purchase from Japan of over half of China's war needs. Storry rightly calls Kato's move 'an opportunist and maladroit attempt by Japan to bring China under her supervision if not control'. Though Japan dropped the worst of the demands in ensuing negotiations, virulent anti-Japanese feeling had been aroused in China, and the affair caused a further deterioration in American-Japanese relations. Henceforward Japan was viewed by American governments as aggressive, even when Japanese policy was relatively conciliatory, as in the 1920s. To be sure Japan made some important gains at the Versailles Conference in 1919 – the German rights in Shantung and the mandated former German islands in the Pacific, such as the Marianas, as well as a permanent seat on the League Council. But Western opinion had hardened against Japan; American and dominion pressure was put on Britain to drop the Anglo-Japanese alliance in favour of a four-power pact between the British Empire, the USA, France and Japan in 1923.

Meanwhile the influence of the military continued to grow within Japan. After 1920 new officers came from the families of farmers and the lower middle classes in urban areas. Their background led these young officers to oppose the effects of monopoly capitalism, while their personal interests led them to challenge the positions in the army held by the older conservative clan generals. The conscript system was constantly bringing young men into the army and navy from social strata most seriously affected by economic conditions. They were consequently ripe for the propaganda, which began to be circulated, attacking the alliance between government and business and emphasising the corruption in politics which had grown out of this relationship.

Unfortunately there was enough truth in the propaganda for it to be effective. Elections were characterised by both bribery and violence, and so were proceedings in the parliament. Such brawls were deeply shocking to many Japanese who loved decorum. There was also a real concern for the welfare of the state, young patriots being angered by the implication of high placed officials in scandals. Young officers also disliked cuts in military and naval expenditure in the mid-1920s and also in the depression years. The virtues of liberal government, for example Kato's extension of the suffrage in 1925 and a more conciliatory policy towards China, were therefore overlooked. Japanese began to feel that the army, as the only uncorrupt force in Japan, should resume control of political life. Large sections of Japanese public opinion came to regard party politics with disgust, as the parties continued to be cliques or factions which continually split and which had no answer to economic problems.

Thus a new form of ultra-nationalism grew up in Japan. Patriotic societies which espoused traditional ways at home and expansion abroad had always exerted considerable backstairs influence – one example was the Black Dragon. But in the 1920s newer societies of a more radical character appeared. All believed in a more equal distribution of wealth at home and in Japanese expansion abroad against such possessor nations as the USA, Britain, France and the Soviet Union. Such a programme could only be accomplished by the army. The leaders of these societies, such men as Ikki Kita and Seikyo Gondo, did not think in terms of a mass totalitarian party like Mussolini's Fascists or Hitler's Nazis. They hoped for action by the army, which, acting in the emperor's name, would overthrow the power of big business and the political party bosses. Then under a more disciplined militarist regime their programme could be carried out.

Such ideas found a ready acceptance among many army and navy officers. Ultra-nationalist associations therefore grew up in the armed forces, the most famous being Colonel Hashimoto's Cherry Blossom or *Sahurakai*, which was so-called because the short-lived cherry blossom symbolised the precarious life of the warrior. Younger field officers were inclined to the ideas of Gondo, who wanted big business destroyed and a reversion to a more agrarian economy. As F. C. Jones explains, they were loosely associated in what became known as the Imperial Way or *Kodoha* faction, and were connected with civilian terrorist groups. In contrast, many officers of the General Staff did not want industry destroyed. Their Control Group or

Toseiha aimed at the control of industry so that it could serve military ends, as in the Soviet Union.

Underpinning all the discontent was the world slump, which hit Japan hard. Japanese exports in general faced higher and higher tariffs as the recession deepened, while the collapse of over 50 per cent in the price of primary products undermined the profits from particular Japanese exports like silk, the price of which was by 1931 only one-quarter of that of 1925. Farmers' costs did not fall in proportion, and rural discontent was a principal factor in the growing political unrest. In addition, the depression led to the collapse of thirty-six Japanese banks and further domination of the banking system by a few large banks, such as the Bank of Japan. These were in turn dominated by the *zaibatsu*, which grew rapidly in the 1920s as smaller concerns collapsed. Their greater unpopularity reflected also upon the parliamentary system, owing to the unhealthily close links between politicians and big business. Faith in Japanese liberalism declined, and a growth in military influence culminated in the invasion of Manchuria in 1931. By then to many Japanese, including newly graduated students with no employment prospects, territorial expansion seemed to be the only answer. Japan would then gain the raw materials and markets she needed, and there would be jobs available in the administration of the newly won regions. As the leader of a Greater East Asia Japan would fulfil her imperial destiny and be secure and prosperous.

For this destiny and even for Japan's continued existence, Manchuria with its coal, iron and other resources was deemed indispensable. Japan had control of the Kwantung leased zone and the South Manchurian railways, gained from Russia in 1905, and had since then made great investments in Manchuria in port, railway facilities and in the coal, iron-ore and soya bean trade. She maintained a garrison there, the Kwantung Army. Yet by 1931, with the Chinese population increasing through immigration (ironically helped by Japanese-built railways), Japan's hold over the region seemed tenuous. The continued Russian threat and the growing power of the Kuomintang, which clearly wished to force Japan to relinquish the Kwantung leased zone, worried officers of the Kwantung Army, who determined to solve the problem by force of arms. They had the backing of senior officers at home, and by 1931 the time was judged ripe. The divided Minseito government was unpopular, anti-Japanese incidents in Manchuria had inflamed public opinion and the Western powers, absorbed by their own economic problems, were in no position to intervene.

In September 1931 Japanese soldiers investigating a bomb explosion on the South Manchuria Railway near Mukden came into collision with Chinese troops. At once, by a prearranged plan, the Kwantung Army went into action and quickly took control of the

whole of Manchuria. Wakatsuki, the Japanese premier, would probably have liked to obey a League of Nations call for a ceasefire, but
was unable to control the military, as indeed were subsequent
governments. In Manchuria the Kwantung Army proceeded to establish a new state independent of China called Manchukuo. In March
1932 the deposed Emperor of China, Henry P'u-yi, accepted its
leadership, but he was a Japanese puppet. Such a step offended not
only China and the League of Nations but also Russia, which now
faced Japan over a common frontier and consequently built up its
border defences.

Manchuria was in several ways a disappointing gain for Japan.
Japanese emigration there was limited, and banditry held back economic development. Nevertheless the Manchurian adventure had
profound consequences for Japan. The success of its army in defying
world opinion increased its prestige and influence at home. When the
Minseito government attempted to cooperate with the League, it
came under army criticism and fell in December 1932. This was,
however, merely the beginning of a renewed assault on the party
system by hotheads in the army, and 1932 saw the assassination of
key politicians, for example Baron Dan, head of Mitsui interests, and
Premier Inukai. Though the Army disowned such acts officially, the
offenders were given light sentences. After a period of calm, a mutiny
led by *Kodoha* officers occurred in 1936. This time the Emperor and
the Army High Command took the matter more seriously, especially
as the main figures murdered were Admiral Saito and Generals
Watanabe and Nagata, members of the *Toseiha* group, whose moderation had enraged younger officers. Yet though the mutiny was
crushed, Japanese government became more dominated by the
military.

The years 1933 to 1936 saw military expenditure double and a
boom in industry occur, helped by a general rise in exports to
Manchukuo and in textiles to such markets as British India. The trade
boom was helped by the low wages paid to Japanese workers, by
increasing mechanisation of industry, by the depreciation of the yen,
which made Japanese exports more competitive, and by renewed
government aid to industry. The invasion of British markets by Japan
naturally caused friction in Anglo-Japanese relations. Western states
increasingly brought in trade restrictions on Japanese products, as did
China, but this in turn stimulated the use by Japan of political and
military means to safeguard her overseas economic interests.

As four-fifths of her overseas investments were in China, this
meant that Japan had to maintain her economic empire there and if
possible dominate east and south-east Asia. The Japanese resented
Western criticism of their actions in China as two-faced. The Japanese foreign minister in the late 1930s, Matsuoka, looked at earlier
Western imperialism and its later support for League of Nations'

principles, and claimed that the West had changed the rules of international law to suit its own selfish interests. 'The Western powers had taught the Japanese the game of poker but then after acquiring most of the chips they pronounced the game immoral and took up contract bridge.'

Unfortunately the growing strength of militant nationalism in Japan was not immediately appreciated in the West. As Christopher Thorne suggests, 'In the West there was a widespread failure to grasp its nature and the extent of its hold in the 1930's.' The reason for such a failure of perception was because there was no striking coup, as in Germany, but a gradual consolidation of power by groups already influential. This Japanese militancy was also backed by formidable modern armed forces. By the 1930s the Japanese navy boasted 10 battleships, 8 heavy cruisers, 19 light cruisers, 110 destroyers, 67 submarines and 4 aircraft carriers. The navy was jealous of the army's success in Manchuria, and had its quota of restless young officers who favoured expansion to the East Indies. All navy officers resented the inferior fleet ratio imposed by the Washington and London treaties of 1922 and 1930 respectively. Japan therefore demanded a common upper limit of naval tonnage in 1934, and when Britain and the USA refused, the Japanese government declined to continue the naval limitation treaties.

Japan's other armed forces were also developing: there were 250,000 men in the army and the air force numbered 1,250 planes. In contrast, severe economies had been carried out by Western governments in their armed forces; the British for example had 112 planes to protect India and Singapore. Western weakness was appreciated by the Japanese, and the prestige of Western nations in Japanese eyes fell accordingly.

By 1937, when renewed Sino-Japanese fighting occurred, the seeds of a Pacific war were truly sown. Japanese government circles believed that for real autonomy the Manchuria–Korea bloc of territory was insufficient. Japan must not only dominate China but move south as well. As Thorne emphasises, 'The virtually inescapable logic of the quest for autonomy lay in an extension of Japanese power and dominion southwards towards the tin, rubber and above all the oil of the Dutch East Indies and Malaya.' Such logic inevitably set Japan on a collision course with the Western powers, especially the USA (see Chapters 9 and 10 for Japanese history, 1937–45).

(d) The impact of the Second World War and Japan's postwar reconstruction

Japan surrendered to General MacArthur, Supreme Commander of the Allied Powers, on the battleship *Missouri* on 2 September, 1945. Her war performance had been impressive, and, as Lockwood stresses, 'she lost the struggle less from engineering backwardness than because of the limited scale of her material resources'. During the war direct military rule of captured Western colonies under the Greater East Asia Co-Prosperity Scheme (see Chapter 10) had enabled the Japanese to seize stocks of tin, petroleum, and rubber, but further supply depended on the ability of the Japanese to take over the products of the mines, wells and fields, and move them from the captured territories to Japan. Successful allied submarine and air attacks on Japanese shipping were, however, launched with greater rapidity than had been anticipated, and Japan's production from the Greater East Asia storehouse was undermined. Consequently, in the final stages of the war Japan was forced to meet her needs almost exclusively out of rapidly diminishing domestic stockpiles.

In many ways the war was a bigger strain on Japan than on Germany, because she had been engaged in continuous fighting since 1931. Destruction from bombing was particularly severe, most of the merchant marine and one-quarter of all buildings being wiped out; and 1½ million men were lost in action and 8 million civilians killed or wounded. Defeat in the Pacific war reduced Japan's territory to its original core. The Kuriles and South Sakhalin were taken by the Soviet Union, whose entry into the Pacific war in August 1945 led to the defeat of the Kwantung Army in Manchuria. Korea was divided between the USSR and the USA, with a view to future independence. Formosa was reclaimed by China, and the Pacific islands mandated to Japan after the First World War were transferred to the USA as a trusteeship under the United Nations. The loss of these colonies meant also the liquidation of Japan's prewar investments.

Thus Japan was reduced to the four original islands of 1867, but on those islands by 1958 were living 90 million Japanese, compared to only 30 million in 1867. This was the result of the natural increase in the population over the century, together with the repatriation of Japanese from the lost territories of the Empire. The consequent serious problem of livelihood for the Japanese people could be solved only through the re-establishment of prewar levels of foreign trade, by which raw materials could be imported to be processed for sale on the world market. But Japan's expansionist policies had created the conditions and attitudes which meant that the desirable recovery of foreign trade would be a slow process. The immediate objectives of the victors lay in the opposite direction, and they controlled Japan's destinies.

Other factors militated against rapid economic recovery. Unlike Germany, Japan was not surrounded by countries recovering quickly, while the occupying power carried out policies which adversely affected production. For example, the American policy of attempting to break up the *zaibatsu* was a heavy additional burden. The dismemberment of Japan's powerful trading organisations struck a heavy blow at her commercial efficiency, as Japanese manufacturing had relied almost exclusively on these firms for foreign sales. The carrying out of land reform and the promotion of democracy and trade unionism might also have affected economic recovery. Certainly restrictive European trade policies hit Japanese exports in the early postwar years, with Japan only being admitted to GATT in 1955. As a result of several factors, Japan's postwar recovery took longer than any other industrial country. Whereas Germany regained prewar levels of output in 1950, Japan failed to do so until 1954, and prewar output per capita was not reached until 1957.

Under the surrender terms Japan was allowed to keep the Imperial family, but was to be occupied by Allied forces. Her forces were to be completely demobilised and the country demilitarised and democratised. With MacArthur as Supreme Commander Allied Powers (SCAP), the Allied occupation came to have an exclusively American character, the main advantage being that, unlike Germany or Korea, Japan was not partitioned. Under MacArthur's aegis an International Tribunal was set up to punish war criminals such as General Tojo, and Japanese forces were rapidly demobilised. A new constitution became effective in 1947; the Diet became the highest organ of state power and the Emperor was reduced to the role of a symbolic head of state. Along with full parliamentary government, an independent judiciary was created.

F. C. Jones praises the new constitution. Although it contained much that was alien to Japanese tradition, 'it made for a more unified and effective cabinet and got rid of the old disharmony between executive and legislative which had been the baleful heritage of the Meiji Constitution'. It also ensured, so far as constitutional arrangements could, the supremacy of the civilian government over any future armed forces.

Of equal importance were the economic and educational reforms instituted by SCAP. The Land Law of 1946 ushered in more peasant proprietorship by virtual confiscation of land from absentee landlords and to an extent from resident landlords as well. The land secured by the government was sold mostly to former tenants on easy terms. The reform did not solve the problems of rural overpopulation and small farm units, but it did make for a more contented peasantry and checked the growth of communist influence, because many farmers supported the conservative Liberal Democratic Party (LDP).

Educational reforms led to a restructuring of the school curriculum so as to develop the individual rather than to promote the ends of the state. Trade unions were organised along American lines into two major organisations, a Japanese Federation of Labour and a Congress of Industrial Unions. It was clear from 1947 on, when MacArthur bluntly banned a large strike, that unions in Japan would have to act circumspectly.

From 1948 American policy shifted its emphasis. Recent policies, e.g. the enforced dissolution of the *zaibatsu*, had created some economic chaos, and the USA had the prospect of having to provide large sums of money for imports of raw materials and food into Japan for some time to come – unless policy changes were made. Accordingly in 1949 the USA decreed the end of reparations and gave up all ideas on limiting Japan's industrial capacity. The Korean War in 1950 accelerated this change of direction. Japan benefited greatly from American orders for military equipment needed in Korea, and also from the spending by UN troops on leave in Japan. By the mid-1950s Japan was again becoming the workshop of Asia, and in 1951, through the Treaty of San Francisco, she made a formal peace with forty-eight former enemies. In 1956 Russia also ended the state of war with Japan, though disputes have continued over Russian control of the four most southerly of the Kurile Islands.

The two chief political parties which emerged during the occupation were the Liberal Democrats and the Socialists. The former party was rather conservative and dominated Japanese politics in the postwar period. It benefited from the Socialist Party's internal divisions and the Communist Party's advocacy of violent revolution. All the parties to an extent exhibited the same defects as had marred those of the interwar period. They were aggregates of cliques, each headed by a prominent politician, and subject to the same phenomena of divisions, breakaways and reunions. Proceedings in the Diet were frequently beset by brawls and riots. However, though Japan again developed her armed forces, there was no military threat to civilian rule, because the armed forces were voluntary and subject to civilian direction.

The LDP enjoyed two decades of uninterrupted rule but lost prestige in 1976 as a result of the Lockheed bribery case. A former prime minister, Kakuei Tanaka, was accused of accepting a bribe while in office of $1.6 million from Lockheed to help sell its planes in Japan. In many ways Lockheed was to Japan what Watergate was to the USA. It revealed the close ties between corporate business and conservative politicans, and put a spotlight on the extent of corruption and manipulation.

Yet to Western observers it is her economic miracle that has been the most startling of Japan's postwar characteristics. Like West Germany, Japan rose phoenix-like from the ashes, and as early as 1963 her industrial production was four times what it had been in 1936. She underwent two medium-term investment cycles after 1945, and was in the middle of a third cycle by the early 1980s. The first of these concentrated on the expansion of basic and heavy industries. The second concentrated on improvements in the production of such consumer durables as cars. The third cycle aimed at the development of the high technology sectors, such as computers. During Japan's immediate postwar reconstruction, government intervention was universal throughout industry. In the 1950s the implementation of a series of national plans showed that government, especially the Ministry for International Trade and Development (MITI), still retained an important role in devising policy. Through an emphasis on technical innovation, penetration of well-defined target markets and a combination of value in terms of price and quality of product, Japanese industry became extremely competitive.

The success of the Japanese economy was striking. Between 1948 and 1958 Japan increased its share of world exports sixfold, from 0.5 per cent to 3 per cent, and by 1970 it had more than doubled it again to 7.2 per cent. Between 1970 and 1980 this share of world exports remained at over 7 per cent, despite the greater part taken in that trade by oil. Japan's GDP was only one-third of Britain's in 1950; by 1969 it had overtaken Britain's, France's and West Germany's, and its present GDP is equal to West Germany's and Italy's combined.

Japan is now responsible for one-tenth of world output. Despite or because of rapid moves towards the development of a high technology service economy, its unemployment rate was only 2.7 per cent in 1985. Its population is now 120 million, and it is a healthy population; life expectancy for women is now on average 80 years and for men 75 years, both the longest in the world.

Ironically these very successes have created problems for Japan's relations with her industrial rivals in the West, especially the USA and the European Community. Three major factors have been at work. Firstly, Japan has exported much more to the EC and the USA than she has imported from them. In 1984 her trade surplus with the USA was $36.8 billion, and the trend was upward. Secondly, Japanese exports have concentrated on the most sensitive sectors in rival countries. Critical markets – cars, motor-bikes, consumer electronics and numerically controlled machine tools – have been given Japan's 'laser-beam' approach, so that often domestic producers have been wiped out. If other advanced industrial countries could counter such trends by increasing exports to Japan, the trade problems would be reduced, but unfortunately the third factor – Japanese protectionism – has obviated such a possibility. Exporters to Japan have faced innumerable technical barriers to trade or non-tariff barriers (NTBs). Such practices threaten a revival of world trade protectionism in the last decade of the twentieth century, a development which would hurt Japan more than most countries.

FURTHER READING

Jones, F. C., *The Far East: A Concise History*, Pergamon Press, London, 1968

Lockwood, W. L., *The Economic Development of Japan*, Princeton University Press, Princeton, 1968

Nish, I., *Japanese Foreign Policy 1869–1942*, Routledge, London, 1977

Storry, R., *A History of Modern Japan*, Penguin, Harmondsworth, 1975

Storry, R., *Japan and the Decline of the West in Asia*, Macmillan, London, 1979

Thorne, C., *The Limits of Foreign Policy*, Macmillan, London, 1973

Vinacke, H. M., *A History of the Far East in Modern Times* (Sixth Edition), Allen and Unwin, London, 1971

QUESTIONS

1. Compare and contrast the reactions of China and Japan to Western intrusion in the period before 1914.
2. Critically examine the significance of the Russo-Japanese War of 1904–5.
3. Account for the growth of the influence of the military in interwar Japan and discuss the consequences.
4. To what extent did Japan become a fascist state in the interwar period?
5. What difficulties lay in the path of Japan's postwar recovery and how were they overcome?

14
The Far East in the twentieth century: China

(a) The fall of the Manchu Dynasty

Since 1800 the Chinese people have experienced violent change, partly prompted by foreign incursions beginning with the Anglo-Chinese Opium Wars of 1839–42 and ending with the 8 years of Japanese invasion 1937–45. Yet these foreign attacks (except the Japanese) were largely superficial compared to the five revolutionary civil wars within China during the same period: the Taiping Rebellion of 1850–64, the Republican Revolution of 1911, the Nationalist Revolution of 1925–8 against foreign imperialism, the Kuomintang–Communist civil war of 1945–9 and finally the 10 years of Mao Tse-Tung's Cultural Revolution, from 1966 to 1976.

To understand China it must be borne in mind that it is a country roughly the same size as the USA but with four times the population. The cultivable land is only about half the area exploitable by Americans, and poverty has therefore been a permanent feature of China's history. A second key feature has been China's backwardness in technology in modern times. The new technology of the nineteenth century in transport and industry emanated from the West, but was resented by conservative Chinese as a foreign import.

Unlike European peoples who became seafarers, the Chinese were largely landlocked, and developed a rice culture which was labour-intensive and produced a larger crop than the dry farming of wheat. A rural society in which farming was done by families dominated by patriarchs was the consequence. The essence of China's traditional culture, dating from the age of Confucius in the sixth century BC, was to emphasise the goal of harmony which would be attained by the individual's virtue and by the right ordering of the family, where the old enjoyed seniority over the young and men over women (the practice of foot-binding symbolised women's permanent state of subservience). The theory of the state was based on the family, with the emperor's role that of a virtuous head of his family of all the Chinese people.

This Chinese society developed distinct institutions, creating bureaucratic government run by a literate élite as early as the seventh century, when Europe was in the Dark Ages. The arts and technology flowered in China from the seventh to the twelfth centuries. As Francis Bacon remarked, the three technical feats that moulded modern European history were printing, the compass for sea navigation and gunpowder. All first appeared in China, which was culturally superior to the West until modern times. However, this superiority bred an arrogance in the Chinese people and made it harder for them to come to terms with their later technological backwardness.

From 1644 to 1912 the Manchu or Ch'ing dynasty ruled China, but its prestige and the cohesion of China itself were threatened in the nineteenth century by two factors. The first fundamental cause of unrest was that population growth was no longer matched by an increase in the land under cultivation. General distress led to the Taiping Rebellion of 1850–64, which caused huge destruction and the loss of 20 million lives. The peasant rebellion was led by Hung Hsiu-ch'uan, who developed his own version of Old Testament Protestant Christianity. The rebellion was only mastered by gentry-led regional armies, and led to a weakening of the emperor's central authority.

The second great blow to central authority was the intrusion of the West, which used force to create trading opportunities in China. From 1839 to 1842 the British fought the Opium Wars and China ceded Hong-Kong. British success encouraged other Western powers to demand and obtain trading rights. Later Christian missionary activity was resented by local élites, to whom foreign missionaries were subversives backed up by gunboats.

In 1895 war with Japan led to China ceding Taiwan and Southern Manchuria. The defeat was shocking to the Chinese élite, who now had to face the reality of China's technological backwardness. The humiliation led to the inescapable conclusion that China must make great changes. Attempts at reform, however, caused a reaction in 1900 in the Boxer movement, a revolt against both the foreign presence and government-inspired changes. The revolt was crushed by a Western international army joined by the Japanese.

Despite the rebellion, China after 1900 was a different country. There was a rising tide of change, sparked by a new nationalism, which was anti-imperialist, favoured the creation of a centralised nation-state and wished to expel the Manchu dynasty. This new nationalism stemmed partly from the long Chinese tradition of book production, which combined with the growth of journalism in Shanghai and other cities to produce more political awareness. After 1901, too, renewed Christian missionary activity spread Western medicine and knowledge. However, in all the South East Asian ports Chinese communities had grown up through the development of commerce, and these were politically aware. Discontent with the regime was felt even among conservative administrators, many of whom had received part of their education in Japan or the West, and who contrasted Japan's success in maintaining national independence and in inflicting defeat on Russia with China's weakness. The more radical students wanted more than mere reform of the dynasty. They wanted its expulsion, and identified with the Western-educated Sun Yat-sen (1866–1925).

A farmer's son, Sun Yat-sen had emigrated abroad, joining his brothers in Hawaii. Despite graduating in medicine, he became a revolutionary, seeing his task to be the removal of the Manchu dynasty and the development of China as a modern nation–state. In Japan he founded the revolutionary League of Common Alliance, a group which joined with others in 1912 to form the Kuomintang or Nationalist Party (KMT).

Sun Yat-sen had three main political aims: (a) the removal of the 'foreign' Manchu dynasty and foreign imperialism, for which the creation of a real national spirit was essential; (b) China to develop as a real democracy, with a strong executive and an electoral process; and (c) more socialism, with more land ownership by the peasantry and control of big business. Unfortunately, since the Kuomintang drew support from landowners and big business, this principle was blurred.

The Kuomintang did not play a major role in the revolution of 1911. Its importance was to come after Sun Yat-sen's death in 1925. In 1911 its membership was only a few thousand and in October its leader was in Denver in the USA.

Nevertheless by 1911 the ruling regime was bankrupt. Until 1908 the formidable Empress Dowager Tz'u-hsi, who was intent on preserving Manchu rule at all costs, had exerted real authority by the device of playing off reformers against conservatives, so that she could hold the balance. Westernisation was thus left to the efforts of a few provincial officials, in contrast to Japan, where the Meiji emperor gave innovators consistent backing. When the Empress Dowager died in 1908, she left, in the words of Fairbank, a thoroughly unmemorable leadership consisting of a child emperor and a venal regent. Such was the murderous nature of her rule that it led to a permanent suspicion of rule by women, as Madame Chiang Kai-shek and Mao's wife Chiang Ch'ing were later to find.

It now needed only a weak revolt to expel the dynasty. Most influential were provincial merchants and gentry, who took the opportunity of constitutional reform to assert the independence of the provinces in newly elected assemblies. The revolution was started by a small group of rebel soldiers in Wuchang in central China in October 1911, and so weak was the central authority that many other provinces declared their independence from the central government.

The court turned for help to Yuan Shih-kai, who had been governor-general in Northern China and had built up a modern army.

However, Yuan had been dismissed in 1909 by the central government and he was determined to be his own master. He came to an agreement with the revolutionaries whereby he became the first president of China, and the boy emperor P'u-yi was forced to abdicate in March 1912. Yuan was the man most acceptable to the conservative gentry and merchants, and there was no social reform. From 1912 to 1916, despite the existence of frail parliamentary institutions, he ruled as a military dictator. He showed no vision of the need for a new system, closed down parliamentary and provincial assemblies and dissolved the KMT as a public body.

When Yuan died in 1916, China further disintegrated, the years from 1916 to 1928 marking the warlord era in modern Chinese history. The central government in Peking had nominal authority, but in reality it was merely one of hundreds of governments, each headed by a warlord with a private army in control of a particular area. The worst type of such warlords was personified by the governor of Shantung (Chang Tsung-ch'ang), who murdered the peasants and hung their heads on telegraph poles. He was known as the Dog Meat general for a betting game he enjoyed. Not all warlords were such men of violence. Some tried to bring in reform, but were too absorbed in the power struggle to achieve much.

As central power declined, foreign influence grew to fill the vacuum. With the Western powers engaged in the European war, Japan occupied the German sphere in Shantung province in 1914 and the next year presented the twenty-one demands, in practice a claim for a Japanese protectorate and for the employment of Japanese advisers in the affairs of the Chinese government. The Japanese demands provoked impotent fury in China, and even greater anger was occasioned by the Paris Peace Conference in 1919. Though China was an ally of the Big Three, Japan's right to Shantung was acknowledged, the warlord government in Peking which represented China at the conference accepting this transfer of Chinese territory. News of this decision triggered a demonstration on 4 May 1919 by 3,000 Peking students. The nationwide campaign which ensued was joined not only by students but the merchant class and the labour unions. The date of 4 May 1919 marked an important moment in the history of modern China, because it represented the moment when Chinese nationalism reasserted itself. A boycott of Japanese goods took place, and students arrested by the Peking warlords were released as a result of widespread public pressure.

(b) The growth of Kuomintang–Communist rivalry

The period of the warlords saw the revival of the Kuomintang from its low point under Yuan Shih-kai and also the creation of a new party, the Chinese Communist Party (CCP). The two parties began by cooperating, but by the 1930s they were rivals engaged in a triangular struggle against the Japanese and against each other. After the defeat of the Japanese in 1945, civil war divided China, and only in 1949, with the victory of the communists, was China at last set on a course of national unity. In this struggle between the two parties, a continual background influence was exercised by the Soviet Union, which helped found the CCP in 1921.

Another key influence in its foundation was that of Li Ta-chao, China's pioneer Marxist. A professor at Peking University, he was the guiding light of a university study group which included a young man named Mao Tse-tung. The founding generation of the CCP were mainly intellectuals, with very few members from the working classes, but in time, in the words of Fairbank, the party's historic role was to bring the common man into politics. Its disciplined central organisation, the Politburo, was helped by the Comintern. Unfortunately for the CCP, Russian policy ran on two tracks, and the Comintern also helped the KMT. The Russians believed that the KMT as a bourgeois nationalist movement could be helped to gain power, whereupon the CCP would take over from it. This Russian error was to let the KMT develop its Whampoa Military Academy when the CCP was developing no armed force at all.

Both parties claimed to stand for a nationalist revolution in which both the influence of the warlords and foreigners would be ended. Nationalist fervour continued to mount, fanned by the events of 1925, when British-officered police killed thirteen demonstrators in Shanghai in May and Anglo-French marines killed fifty-two demonstrators at Canton in June. Yet the KMT was by far the stronger of the two parties in the 1920s. Sun Yat-sen reorganised his party in 1923 to be a Soviet-style party dictatorship with the aim of unifying China, but the rising man in the party was Chiang Kai-shek, who was to be the principal figure in Chinese politics from 1927 to 1949. A military man, Chiang had 'the qualities of patriotic determination to unify China plus qualities of personal leadership, decisiveness, foresight and chicanery' (Fairbank). Such qualities were needed if the influence of the warlords was to be liquidated and a central government re-established. However, he had no vision of a social revolution through the incorporation of the masses into politics. Here was a major limitation in KMT policy compared to that of the CCP.

Chiang believed China could be saved from imperialism only by military strength. He was the son of a salt merchant, and, after his military training in Tokyo, he had risen in the KMT in Shanghai and helped Sun Yat-sen in Canton in 1922. After a KMT mission to the USSR in 1923, he returned to China, impressed with the Soviet dictatorship and, following his appointment as head of the Whampoa Military Academy and top commander in Canton, he worked with the Soviet military mission in China and in the KMT–CCP united front. On Sun's death in 1925 Chiang was able to claim the leadership of the KMT.

The Soviet investment in the Nationalist regime at Canton followed Lenin's strategy of allying with nationalistic–bourgeois–democratic revolutions in Asia against the common enemy – capitalist imperialism. However, it completely misfired, because Chiang Kai-shek, who hitherto had considered himself essentially a military man, became conscious of CCP infiltration of the KMT. At the second KMT congress in 1926 more than one-third of the delegates were also members of the CCP.

In dealing with this communist threat, Chiang showed a combination of force and guile. In March 1926 he ousted some CCP leaders and Soviet advisers, at the same time reaffirming his devotion to the Canton–Moscow alliance. In 1927 he used his contacts with the Shanghai underworld gangs (particularly the Green Gang – *Ch'ing pang*) to terrorise the Communist-led labour unions. Many left-wing members defected from the KMT–Soviet alliance when they realised that the Soviet strategy was to use them for a Communist take-over. Soon the CCP leadership was left as a small minority with no military defence, and its members had to go underground to avoid being destroyed by the KMT terror tactics in 1927–8. The Chinese communists learned from bitter experience that their only hope of seizing power was by securing a territorial base in which food and manpower could support a military effort. Such a base was gained only in 1934–5.

Until then the KMT enjoyed further successes. In 1926–7 Chiang's Northern Expedition from Canton to the Yangtze saw the six main Nationalist armies defeat thirty-four warlord forces in Southern China. Nanking and Shanghai, owing to their wealth, became the centre of Nationalist power. By 1928 China's future seemed to lie with the KMT, the CCP apparently defeated. Yet 20 years later the verdict was reversed, since the Nationalist government had become burdened with the problems of the old establishment, while the CCP made itself the leader of a long overdue social revolution.

In some respects the Nationalist government at Nanking seemed a modernising force, setting up the rudiments of a national administration. Reforms such as new ministries for education created an initial atmosphere of hope. Too soon, however, the government began to act in the manner of earlier regimes. For example, it intimidated the business class through its underworld allies, to extract large donations to use for military purposes. It showed little interest in rural problems, leaving land taxes to be collected by the provinces and generally leaving landlords in power. Indeed central government army officers often became landowners.

In addition, the Nanking government's area of authority was limited. It was presiding over 400 million people still embedded in the traditions of manpower agriculture, widespread illiteracy and a family system that kept youth and women subservient. In attempting to foster modern agricultural methods, better transport and a more liberal society, the government thus faced an overwhelming task. Influential in the seaport cities, it found great difficulty in reaching the mass of the peasantry, especially as at first, given the continuing battle with the warlords, it only controlled the Lower Yangtze provinces.

Another factor which militated against the development of KMT power was the menace of Japan. After the Japanese invasion of Manchuria in 1931, important revenues were lost, and the Chinese government had to concentrate on military preparation, especially after the renewal of hostilities with Japan in 1937. Consequently other aspects of government were neglected and plans for agricultural improvement remained paper proposals.

The Nationalist government was plagued from the start with certain internal weaknesses. Much of its revenue continued to come from its rake-off from the Shanghai underworld, while the slaughter of communists had expunged much youthful idealism. Many remaining KMT members came from the ranks of the old bureaucracy and warlord regimes. Not enough careful selection of members was undertaken, and, once in power, what revolutionary idealism the KMT possessed was, in the words of Fairbank, 'watered down by the admission of corrupt and time-serving officials and the accumulation of opportunists generally lacking in principle'. Officials brought before the courts for malpractice were seldom punished. In addition the regime used terror against other parties than the CCP and also against the professions and the press.

This inner corruption put a heavy burden on Chiang, who remained an austere and dedicated leader, fervently desiring his country's unity. By 1932 he was so disillusioned with his party that he organised a fascist body known as the Blueshirts, a select group of a few thousand army officers who would secretly devote themselves to building up Chiang as a leader in the fashion of Mussolini or Hitler. His position was indeed powerful and one key to his domination was that, rather like Franco in Spain, he committed himself to no one faction. The disadvantage of such a tactic was that the urban capitalists, the big landlords, the students, the unions and particularly the peasants felt little benefit from KMT government, as Chiang seemed more concerned in building up a military dictatorship with German help.

Meanwhile the CCP struggled to survive in the villages. In 1927 its 60,000 membership had been decimated by the KMT terror, and the dedicated remaining members sought safety in the remote vastnesses in the countryside, especially in the Kiangsi region. It was in these bases that the CCP found a new way of mobilising the peasantry.

Communist cells in the cities continued to be destroyed by the KMT.

It was in Kiangsi that Mao Tse-tung became a central figure in the CCP. Educated at Hunan and at Peking University, he began as a disciple of the 4 May movement, believing in gradual reform, despite joining the CCP in 1921. Only later, after a period of frustration, did he conclude that violent revolution was the only feasible course. For a time he worked in the united front under the KMT in Shanghai, but he was perceptive enough to see that the Comintern stress on the mobilisation of the proletariat was unrealistic, and that the future for the CCP lay in mobilising the peasantry in a class struggle against their oppressors.

After the KMT–CCP split in 1927, the Kiangsi Soviet Republic carried out guerrilla warfare to resist Chiang's spearheads, which became more vulnerable the further they advanced. However, by 1934 the Nationalist government, helped by German advisers, devised a system of blockhouses on the hillsides along the invasion routes, so placed that gunfire from one could help defend the next. This string of strongpoints supplied by truck could not be dislodged, and Chiang's armies gained the upper hand. The CCP patently required a more secure territorial base, and in late 1934 there began the Long March to Shensi in North West China. About 100,000 people started the march, but when it ended a year later, only about 40,000 remained.

The objective of the Long March was to find a new territorial base which would be on the periphery of Nationalist power, a haven where the CCP could expand. It has seemed almost like a miracle, with 6,000 miles travelled at a daily average of 17 miles. The inhospitable mountainous terrain meant that everything was carried on foot. For a time Mao himself was downgraded by the Soviet-trained clique in the CCP, but he regained the leadership in 1935 and Chou En-lai, his former superior, became his chief supporter. Losses were extremely heavy, especially at river crossings. The need to move speedily led to the jettisoning of much equipment.

Those who survived the Long March became the aristocracy of the CCP and it helped the emergence of Mao as undisputed leader. Even on the march itself he was distancing himself from the rest of the leadership. Another consequence of the march was that Mao found his closest working colleague and future prime minister in Chou En-lai. From a family which had done well in the Chinese civil service, Chou spent time in Japan and France, where he showed qualities of leadership before joining the staff of the Whampoa Military Academy in 1924. Later he shared in the development of the CCP, becoming devoted to the service of the party and the leader. His contribution as a mediator, diplomat and administrator was crucial to Mao's success. Though a charismatic figure himself, he had the wit to appreciate that he lacked Mao's capacity to adapt CCP policy to

Chinese conditions, and had the good sense never to become a rival for the top post.

One of the strengths of the CCP leadership was its unity and continuity. As Fairbanks comments, 'the leadership that survived the Long March was indeed closely knit. In addition to having a common faith and ideology, and accepting party discipline as the basis of their work, they were a group of long-time comrades'.

In 1936 a Comintern directive ordered Mao to join in a united front with Chiang, and, after Chou's negotiations with the Nationalists, a second united front was agreed in April 1937. In practice, however, Mao now had much greater power in the CCP than the Russian-trained members. Thus while the CCP worked for the national revolution to expel the Japanese, Mao also planned the social revolution on the land in areas under CCP control. In this way the party would develop its own bases and popular support for combating the Nationalists as well as the Japanese.

(c) The War of Resistance and Civil War, 1937–49

The disasters which befell the Nationalist government in this period may be attributed to three factors: (1) the brutally destructive Japanese armies, (2) the actions of the Nationalist leadership, and (3) the growth of CCP power.

The Japanese invasion caused the Nanking government to remove itself to Wuhan in 1938 and then to Chungking in the province of Szechwan. This change in location had several unfortunate consequences. Firstly, there was a loss of revenue from customs duties and from the Shanghai opium trade. Secondly, in the refugee government the modern trained administrators lost influence to provincial militarists and landlords, who were against mobilising the peasantry as Mao would have done. Thus, in Fairbank's phrase, the regime remained as 'unimaginatively conservative' as it had been in Nanking. The peasantry were conscripted and taxed but otherwise ignored, while strong-arm methods against students and publishers widened the split between the government and intellectuals.

Except for a fertile rice area around the capital, Chengtu, Szechwan province was mountainous and did not produce enough food. Inflation was the inevitable result. Heavy taxation eroded any gains which farmers derived from higher prices for their crops. They were in fact subject to hundreds of taxes imposed by ingenious local administrators, e.g. a 'contribute straw-sandals to recruits' tax. The government also authorised the army commanders to live off the country by enforcing grain requisitions, a policy that resulted in famine in 1942–3. By the end of the war peasant rebellions were incipient in several provinces of Free China.

Meanwhile the united front agreement of August 1937 between the

KMT and CCP remained a paper agreement only. The CCP built up its base areas, with party membership growing from 40,000 in 1937 to 910,000 in 1945. The party possessed disciplined and enthusiastic members, who went into the villages to maintain order, encourage mutual aid and recruit poor peasant activists who would eventually get the upper hand of rich peasants. In the CCP's capital, Yenan, an infectious revolutionary enthusiasm abounded, as Edgar Snow, the American journalist, pointed out in his book *Red Star over China*.

A key factor in the growth of CCP power was its mobilisation of the peasantry. The Japanese made excellent targets to mobilise against, but CCP control was essentially based on three principles. First, the principle of party control was based on indoctrination of cadres and enforcement of party discipline. Second came finding out what the peasants wanted and giving it to them. Thus the CCP gave the peasants local peace and order, provided a friendly army which helped with the crops when necessary, encouraged the recruitment of poor peasants as activists and stimulated the local economy through agricultural cooperation in the form of mutual aid, better transport, improved crops and the production of consumer goods in cooperatives. Third, as such developments occurred, they became the basis for the principle of class struggle, a principle which had to be approached in a discreet fashion until local CCP members had won popular esteem over local landlords and could begin land reform, i.e. the redistribution of land on a more equitable basis.

Given their success in mobilising the peasantry, the CCP had a new power base by 1945, based not in the cities but in the villages, and could lead an organised populace to support its armed forces against the superior fire-power of the KMT in its city fortresses.

During the war itself the CCP succeeded in expanding across North China despite opposition from the Japanese. The Japanese, like the Americans in Vietnam and the Russians in Afghanistan, faced the problem of how to control an alien population, but a big Japanese offensive in 1940 was successful. The CCP also faced the hostility of the KMT and a force of Communist troops was ambushed in 1941 by Nationalist forces. Fortunately efforts to attain self-sufficiency offset attempts by the KMT and the Japanese to blockade Communist-held areas.

In the early 1940s, too, Mao finally established his ascendancy over the CCP. His reading of realities after 1936 led him to put forward his ideas on the sinification of Marxism in China, i.e. that Marxism might be fundamentally altered when adapted to Chinese uses. These ideas were enshrined in his most important works, *The Chinese Revolution* (1939) and *On New Democracy* (1940). Mao argued that as China's proletariat was really the peasantry, this meant that the Chinese revolution would necessarily have a more rural character than that in the Soviet Union, with the peasantry being the chief revolutionaries.

In addition, given the strong sentiment of Chinese nationalism, the Chinese people could accept only a Chinese Marxism – that proposed by Mao himself. The CCP's adoption in 1945 of *The Thoughts of Mao Tse-tung* as the party's guide marked the triumph of this nationalist principle.

In contrast, the KMT came to appear the less truly patriotic of the two main parties, as it became very dependent on American help during the war. Roosevelt believed that the Nationalist government would move into the vacuum created by the fall of Japan, but a late Japanese offensive in 1944 rolled down from Honan, south of the Yangtze, and destroyed much of the Nationalists' best armies. The Americans were motivated by a fear of a Soviet take-over of China after the war, and tried to push the CCP and KMT into accepting the idea of a coalition government in 1945. Though both sides accepted the idea in principle, full civil war broke out, and efforts to mediate by General George C. Marshall failed.

The KMT continued to receive massive supplies of American equipment after 1945, and much of the American contribution to the United Nations Relief and Rehabilitation Administration (UNRRA). Nationalist forces were also at least twice the size of the CCP's and held all of China's major cities and most of its territory. In these circumstances for Chiang and the Nationalists to lose the civil war was a remarkable achievement, caused by errors both on the battlefield and behind the lines.

Firstly, the Nationalists mismanaged the economy, failing to stimulate any recovery of industrial production in the cities taken back from the Japanese. Heavy unemployment and inflation became the urban norm, while in the countryside heavy taxation and requisitioning of food made the Nationalists unpopular.

The Nationalists lost more popularity for a second reason. They used Japanese troops and their puppet Chinese soldiers to fight the Communists at a time when most Chinese hoped for peace. Thus the Nationalists seemed to be the instigators of civil war even more than the Communists. Pro-government elements began to lose faith in the KMT, the moneyed classes being appalled by the 850-fold rise in prices in 6 months in 1948.

In contrast, the CCP accelerated its land reform, which had been slowed down since 1937. This reform meant the dispossession of landlords, with a corresponding advancement of the activists among the poor peasants, who under CCP leadership could dominate the villages. Consequently the villages all across Northern China supported the Communist armies.

On the battlefield itself, the CCP armies faced Nationalist armies which held all the major cities and railways and were far superior in fire-power. However, the CCP forces under General Lin Piao withdrew and forced the Nationalists into overextending their lines. Their surprise raids cut up Nationalist forces, isolating Nationalist field armies in their own cities. Rural areas once captured by the CCP were quickly mobilised for the war effort in a way which the Nationalist forces, not trained to fraternise with the populace, were quite unable to match.

Chiang made a major error in refusing to evacuate garrisons in major cities while there was still opportunity to do so. The result was that his best troops, after being besieged and isolated, surrendered with their equipment (supplied originally by the Americans). When Mao entered Peking, his troops were riding in American trucks led by American tanks. Chiang's mistake was to accept American military hardware but not American military advice, which had warned him against overextension of his forces and against hoarding of his tanks and planes. He had also refused to let local commanders on the spot make tactical decisions, insisting instead on sending orders to the division level even though he lacked the intelligence facilities to mastermind the battlefield.

By 1949, the CCP had conquered mainland China, the defeated Nationalists seeking refuge on the island of Taiwan (Formosa). There the effects of efficient Japanese colonialism, American economic and military aid, the pool of refugee talent from the mainland, the reform of the KMT by Chiang and its cooperation with Taiwanese Chinese in business and government led to Taiwan's success in industrialisation. It is now one of the leading Newly Industrialising Countries (NICs), its growth being export-led.

(d) Creating the new communist state

The period after 1949 has been marked by two great cycles or spasms, Mao's Great Leap Forward (GLF) of 1958 to 1960 and his Great Proletarian Cultural Revolution (GPCR) of 1966 to 1976. In each case he mobilised popular support in the hopes of effecting revolutionary changes in Chinese society by the use of people from outside the government and the CCP. Each spasm was followed by a swing back to more systematic economic development, respectively in 1961 to 1965 and 1976 on into the late 1980s.

The CCP's takeover after 1949 and the establishment of a new government was, in Fairbank's view, 'a great creative achievement'. Under Mao as undisputed leader, the party leadership worked as a team, debating policy issues in the Politburo and adapting central directives to local conditions. The party was helped by the willingness of the majority of the people to accept them, such was the craving for peace once the KMT armies were defeated. KMT officials could even be left largely in place for the first 2 years.

The economy recovered quickly, with a reduction in inflation achieved by control of credit and the creation of national trading associations for key products. With regular supplies of goods coming on stream, inflation fell to 15 per cent a year. Urban support was increased, because the new government restored services in the cities, liberated women and mounted an attack on prostitution and corruption.

The totalitarian tendencies of the regime were seen in the charges brought against employers and the gradual replacement of non-CCP personnel in government. Mass organisations were set up for labour, women, youth and the professions, and from these organisations came activists who were recruited into the CCP. Accordingly party membership rose from 2.7 millions in 1947 to 6.1 millions in 1953. By the latter date the CCP was ready to begin economic planning and a systematic transition to socialism, a state constitution formulated in 1954 being very similar to the Soviet constitution of 1936, except that Mao became state chairman.

In the newly conquered areas south of the Yangtze, the use of terror and executions eliminated the rich peasants as a class. Nevertheless the collectivisation of agriculture was achieved in a less destructive way than in the Soviet Union in the 1930s. As a rural organisation, the CCP knew how to take gradual steps, and organised peasants into mutual aid teams and cooperatives before moving on to full collectivisation, thus sidestepping any danger of opposition from rich peasants, as had occurred in Russia in the 1930s. Mao's intense interest and the considerable willingness of most Chinese to accept a collective system were factors in the rapid success of collectivisation.

Control over the countryside produced revenues that could be used for industrialisation. State monopoly of industry was soon achieved, though unrealistic targets were set by the party cadres, whose agricultural background made them less aware of the problems of industry. Over-regimentation was probably counter-productive, despite the first Five Year Plan from 1953 to 1957 achieving an average growth in national income of 8.9 per cent a year. Nevertheless it is doubtful whether concentration on large-scale heavy industry (following the Soviet model) in the first plan was wise, because China was at a less advanced industrial stage than Russia had been in 1929. Greater growth would have been achieved by more small-scale developments in agriculture and light industry.

This was in fact the intention of the second Five Year Plan, but it was superseded by the Great Leap Forward in 1958. By then Mao had shifted his ground on important issues, not least the relationship of the intellectuals to the CCP. Originally Mao encouraged their criticism as constructive, believing that they were essentially Communist in outlook. This was the period of the Hundred Flowers of 1956–7, so named for the phrase 'Let a hundred flowers bloom, let a hundred schools of thought contend.' But in 1957 Mao lost his trust in the intellectuals and instigated a campaign against them. About half a million were removed from their posts, skilled personnel that China could ill afford to lose. The atmosphere was set for the Great Leap Forward.

(e) Two catastrophes: the Great Leap Forward and the Great Proletarian Cultural Revolution

The national tragedy of the GLF was directly due to Mao, and probably caused the loss of 20 to 30 million lives through famine. The unsuitability of China for heavy industry and the slow growth rates in agricultural production under the first Five Year Plan had angered the Chinese leader, who persuaded his colleagues that the country-side could be made more productive by a massive reorganisation of the peasantry. The material incentives for an individual's work would be reduced, appeal being made instead to his ideological ardour and spirit of self-sacrifice. The Chinese peasants were now formed into communes, huge organisations which were as big as central market-ing areas. Villages were now called production teams, and a group of teams became a brigade, which formed part of the commune. However, the result was a shambles. Unlike the 1958 harvest, the 1959 harvest was poor, the results of chaotic organisation being exacerbated by bad weather. Many peasants starved in 1959–60, despite real self-sacrifice, because requisitioning of grain from the villages was increased when communes erroneously reported in-creases in production.

Mao himself lost face as a result of the GLF, and a split developed in the CCP leadership. Mao became head of a faction, and, though he remained as party leader, he was replaced for a time as head of state by Liu Shao-chi, who advocated a more gradual road to a planned economy. It may well be that Mao's motives were partly good ones. He wished to liberate the peasants from their burdens, including possible exploitation by the powerful new class of officials. He was much influenced by what he saw as revisionism in Russia, where in his view a ruling élite of urban educated people, uninterested in equality, had developed.

From 1962 Mao was concerned to restore his prestige, until in 1965 he judged that the time was right to make another great effort to mould the Chinese people – the Great Proletarian Cultural Revolu-tion. It was one of the most bizarre events in modern history, marked by the participation of 100 million people and with one weird happen-ing following another – Chairman Mao swimming the Yangtze and teenage Red Guards rampaging through the cities, perpetrating much brutality.

Fairbank divides the GPCR into four phases. (1) In 1966 Mao attacked his revisionist opponents in the party, army and government and secured their dismissal. (2) At the end of 1966 he decided to mount a full attack on revisionism wherever it could be found, and his group mobilised the Red Guards, who mounted vicious attacks on intellectuals and on party leaders, such as former head of state Liu and the secretary-general of the party, Deng Hsiao-p'ing. The Guards were fond of brandishing the little red book of quotations from Chairman Mao. (3) In 1967–8 the Red Guards took over much of the establishment, but they then broke into factions, between which open warfare occurred. Mao had to demobilise the Red Guards and call in the People's Liberation Army (PLA) to restore order. (4) From 1968 to 1976 an attempt was made to rebuild the party and government, though some violence still occurred, and Mao's faction (later called the Gang of Four) remained in power until his death in 1976.

Mao had become a cult figure, venerated almost as a monarch. The CCP was mainly his creation and if he wished to reform it, that was his privilege in the opinion of the rest of the party leadership, which acquiesced in his attacks on them. This power Mao wished to use against the emergence of élites in order to make China more democratic. Going against Chinese tradition, he hoped to end exploitation of the peasantry by the new bureaucracy. Thus though he had helped to create it, Mao launched a full assault on the new establishment, his weapons being young urban students, who became the Red Guards, and the PLA itself, which was fully politicised, especially in its regional wing. Also supporting Mao was Lin Piao, the able army general, and Mao's wife, Chiang Ch'ing, an ex-movie actress and competent politician despite a disposition to nurse grudges. Mao himself was a great showman in this period, the Chinese being electrified in July 1966 to learn that Mao had swum across the Yangtze. As most Chinese could not swin, Mao seemed to them a paragon of athleticism!

Yet the whole bizarre event got out of control. Not only was the purge rate of officials about 60 per cent but about 400,000 people died as a result of maltreatment. When the Gang of Four were tried in 1977, they were charged with the persecution of 700,000 people.

There were several other consequences of the GPCR. Military men became more prominent in China's leadership, and the quality of the bureaucracy declined, new appointees not comparing with their predecessors. As the mindless zealotry of the time was turned against foreign influences, China's foreign relations suffered, and diplomatic relations were broken off with several countries, for example Burma and Cambodia. The British and Indonesian embassies were burned to the ground. Clashes occurred with Soviet and Indian troops on their respective borders, a serious battle being provoked by the Chinese in 1969 when Chinese troops attacked a Russian border patrol.

From 1969 on, a power struggle to secure the succession to Mao developed. Lin Piao's influence faded as he came under attack as a consequence of Mao's wish to reduce the recently increased role of the military in the political system. When Lin and his wife tried to escape by air from China in 1971, his plane was destroyed. From 1973 the Shanghai faction (the Gang of Four) acquired much influence over Mao. With Mao increasingly infirm, the Gang of Four launched an attack on Chou En-lai, who died of cancer in January 1976.

The GPCR may be viewed as 10 lost years in China's development. There was massive public humiliation of innocent people and much mindless destruction of China's artistic heritage. Furthermore the GPCR created disillusionment with socialist government, as agriculture failed to make progress. Mao by the time of his own death in September 1976 had killed his own revolution. In Fairbank's shrewd judgement, he was 'a peasant hero who lacked the knowledge, humility and patience to build up the modern institutions that China needed'. Like other dynastic founders, he tried to go too far too quickly.

(f) China after Mao: the reforms of Deng Hsiao-p'ing

The death of Mao led to a more naked power struggle, but in the end the Gang of Four (Mao's wife Chiang Ch'ing and three others) were arrested and put on trial in 1977. By 1978 Deng Hsiao-p'ing had won control, a control he retained for the next decade, until his voluntary renunciation of power in 1987. As Fairbank rightly stresses, 'China now turned a corner. The era of revolution and violent struggle was followed by an era of reform and consolidation.' Deng was a skilful and dynamic politician. He was helped by his military contacts but he had the good sense to make his leadership less obvious, in the sense that he remained only a vice-premier and used his seniority informally by working through others. The Chinese people, relieved perhaps to be rid of Mao's cantankerous unpredictability, accepted the new approach to reform.

Deng and Mao had the same objective – to speed up China's economic growth and power – but Deng tried to advance by the different and more realistic route of fostering initiative and rebuilding the party and government. He realised that China's growth had to be engineered through a trained bureaucracy, not through trying to go around it. Therefore he rehabilitated several hundred thousand 'rightists' who had been expelled from the party since 1957. Mao's errors since the GLF were acknowledged, while his early career was still praised. Attempts were made to recruit intellectuals and technicians into the party to upgrade the quality of the membership. Some older party members were pensioned off, and the size of the army reduced, along with its influence in government.

Essential reform took place in China's foreign affairs, with China normalising relations with a number of countries, including the USA; many Chinese now studied abroad. Deng realised that China needed more technology and capital, which could only be obtained from abroad, and contracts were made with many foreign firms for the installation of new machinery, factories, hotels and mines.

With the population rising from 586 million in 1953 to over 1 billion in the early 1980s, reform of agriculture was essential. The amount of agricultural land had declined and the rural population was still in need of technical training. Mao's attempts to increase productivity through motivating the rural population had failed, as had his attempts to equalise farm incomes, because farmers in poor areas were condemned to poverty.

After 1976 China's planners encouraged side-line or by-product production, as well as more grain production. By-products could be sold on free markets locally to increase farm incomes. Another important change was the contract system, whereby an individual household would contribute only a certain amount to the village and keep the rest for itself – previously all that was produced had been pooled. The new incentives made a real contribution to increased production.

For industrial development Deng turned his back on the Soviet model of industrial advance, which had used domestic capital only to develop heavy industry. Before 1976 the Chinese had invested 30 per cent of their national income and had refused to countenance foreign assistance. But attempts at autarchy had failed, especially as much investment had been diverted to defence. The use of old equipment and over-rigid central planning had also held back progress.

Now new officials were brought in, and, instead of a concentration on heavy industry, there occurred a shift to agriculture and consumer goods. Individual enterprises were given more autonomy and were able to keep part of their profits for reinvestment in machinery or for the improvement of worker amenities. To assist the financing of new projects, the People's Bank of China expanded its credit, but, by making loans on which interest was payable, not grants, it encouraged cost efficiency.

Other reforms have included efforts to implement a more modern legal system and contain the remorseless rise in the population by campaigns for one child per couple, the latter being most urgent given estimates of a Chinese population of 1.5 billion by 2050.

Thus, by the end of the 1980s, China appeared to be heading for peaceful economic modernisation. However, political reform did not keep pace with economic reform and in June 1989 demonstrations by Chinese students in Peking in favour of more liberal structures were brutally suppressed by units of the Chinese army. A power struggle among the top politicians, combined with growing divisions within the army, created a most confused situation in China. Both the permanence of Deng's reforms and the very unity of China itself were now put in doubt.

FURTHER READING

Bailey, P., *China in the Twentieth Century*, Basil Blackwell, London, 1988

Fairbank, J. K., *The Great Chinese Revolution 1800–1985*, Harper Row, New York, 1985

Jones, F. C., *The Far East: A Concise History*, Pergamon Press, Oxford, 1968

Schram, S., *Mao Zedong: A Preliminary Reassessment*, CUP, Cambridge, 1983

Sheridan, J. E., *China in Disintegration*, Collier, London, 1977

Vinacke, H. M., *A History of the Far East in Modern Times*, Allen and Unwin, London, 1971

QUESTIONS

1. To what extent was the fall of the Manchu dynasty in 1912 the result of the new Chinese nationalism?
2. Why was the KMT able to dominate Chinese politics in the 1920s and 1930s?
3. Account for the victory of the CCP in China's civil war by 1949.
4. Critically examine the causes and consequences of the Great Leap Forwad and the Great Proletarian Cultural Revolution.
5. Compare and contrast the policies and achievements of Mao Tse-tung and Deng H'siao-ping.

15
Postwar Asian wars: Korea and Vietnam

(1) The Korean War

(a) The origins of the War

Until the Sino-Japanese war of 1894–5, Korea had come under Chinese influence. With the defeat of China by Japan, Korea had become an integral part of the Japanese empire by 1910, and the Korean monarchy was terminated. Japanese administrators governed Korea competently if at times harshly, the country being regarded as crucial for the Japanese economy. There was rapid industrial growth in the 1930s which laid the base for South Korea's development as a Newly Industrialising Country (NIC) in the 1970s.

Opposition to Japanese rule came from both sides of the political spectrum, ironically stimulated by Japanese provision of educational opportunities. The most famous of the conservative nationalists was Dr Syngman Rhee, a subtle and ruthless politician who built up important contacts during his years in the USA between 1912 and 1945. His sojourn there also meant that he had not compromised his principles by working with the Japanese (unlike many on the right) and he had a record of consistently condemning Japanese rule. On the left the Korean Communist Party, started in 1925, was riddled with division, but draconian methods used by the Japanese brought in more members. Gradually Kim Il Sung became more prominent, although he was not a major personality until after 1945. Unlike Kim, most communists were loyal to Moscow.

At the 1945 Yalta Conference no precise arrangements were made for Korea beyond a decision that it should become independent at some future date. American interest in Korea's future intensified after Truman became president. General Marshall, among others, believed that the USA should occupy part of Korea in order to increase American power in the postwar balance between Russia and the USA in the Far East. In August 1945 the two superpowers agreed on the 38th parallel as the most satisfactory dividing line between the Soviet and American spheres. Though this made economic nonsense, it gave enough territory to please the Russians while keeping the capital Seoul and most of the population in the American sphere. Russo-American talks were to take place over Korea's future independence.

It had been assumed that the Korean people would accept Russian and American trusteeship docilely, but by September 1945 Korea was, in the words of Peter Lowe 'in a ferment of revolutionary upheaval'. Colonial servitude had been cast off, and Koreans of all political persuasions longed for unity and independence. In the south (the American sphere) many local committees sprang up spontaneously. They were radical and anti-Japanese. The new American administrators under General John Reed Hodge misunderstood their objectives and believed their activities had been fomented by communists. The Americans also made the error of keeping Japanese officials in office for longer than was advisable. Hodge further affronted centre and left-wing Koreans by his preference for right-wing Koreans.

From May 1946 Rhee began to campaign for a separate government for South Korea, much to American embarrassment, as this further polarised the political parties. Elections held in October 1946 for an interim legislature were riddled with corrupt practices but led to a right-wing-dominated assembly. Russo-American talks over the future of Korea broke down finally in August 1947, and in November the Americans persuaded the United Nations to establish a commission on Korea.

The West believed that North Korea was simply Stalin's creature, but Kim Il Sung was no Soviet stooge. Lowe describes him as 'a passionate nationalist imbued with determination to restore self-respect to Korea and to unify the peninsula, to liquidate feudalism and to remove foreign dominance – American or Russian – from Korea'. While Russian forces were present in North Korea from 1945 to 1948, Kim had to tread warily, but he defeated political rivals, built up a North Korean Interim People's Committee and developed a North Korean army. Collectivisation of farming took place. By 1948 North Korea possessed much more cohesion than the South, while the two leaders, Rhee and Kim, were adamantly opposed to each other. Both were nationalistic, ruthless, confident and driven by a sense of destiny over the future unity of Korea.

The United Nations was drawn into Korean affairs in 1948, when the General Assembly accepted an American proposal that elections be held in both parts of Korea to achieve one national assembly and one state. The US government hoped to disengage from Korea and free the troops stationed there for service elsewhere. But the Russians soon made it clear that the UN resolution on free elections would not be fulfilled in North Korea, which they were determined to keep communist. This left the Americans in a dilemma; if they pulled out of Korea as they wished, the peninsula would surely fall under Soviet domination. The alternative was to provide considerable support for a South Korean state. However, as South Korea was not deemed a priority area of American strategy against the Soviet Union, Truman ordered American forces to withdraw. In July Rhee was elected president of the new state, the Republic of Korea.

In the north the Democratic People's Republic of Korea was established as a communist state, with Kim Il Sung as president. Soviet help had improved its armed forces, especially its airforce, by 1950. Kim continued to enjoy a stronger position than his rival. Rhee possessed considerable power, but his autocratic style, high inflation and the corruption in the system all combined to make him unpopular. There was also great unease over South Korea's security once American forces were withdrawn by mid-1949. A major rebellion on Cheju island in April 1948 led to 30,000 deaths, while the Yosu rebellion in 1949 proved that some communist infiltration had occurred in the police force. Young communist infiltrators from North Korea also carried out guerrilla raids, the main victims being ordinary farmers.

To compensate South Korea for the withdrawal of their forces, the Americans gave much economic and military aid, with the aim of building up an efficient South Korean army of 65,000 troops. Yet while such forces were sufficient to maintain internal order, they were insufficient to repel a North Korean invasion. The US government feared, however, to create a larger South Korean army, lest Rhee, a wild old man in a hurry (he was 75 in 1950), might use a larger army to attack North Korea. The Americans in any case disliked the idea of the greater expense in developing a larger force.

American reactions infuriated Rhee. Given the collapse of Nationalist power in China and reduced American support for Chiang Kaishek, Rhee feared that the US government regarded South Korea as expendable, and complained bitterly. The Americans responded by advising him to tackle inflation and prevent the growth of a police state. American reservations in helping South Korea meant that on the eve of the Korean War the South Korean army lacked the range and quality of the equipment possessed by North Korea. Neither did its officers have the fanaticism of their North Korean counterparts. South Korea had no airforce or navy, and air power was one of the main reasons for North Korea's early success in the Korean War.

Meanwhile Sino-American relations had deteriorated sharply between 1945 and 1950. The new Chinese communist regime was viewed with suspicion by the American government as representing an alien ideology and being a puppet of the Soviet Union. For their part the Chinese communists felt bitter at the amount of aid the USA had given Chiang Kai-shek, and duly noted that the American Seventh Fleet was protecting the Nationalist island of Taiwan. The Chinese resented American sympathy and help for the South Korean regime, and saw the rebuilding of Japan under SCAP as a future danger for China. In addition, the Chinese were angered by the American refusal to recognise the communist government (unlike Britain) or to allow China to become a member of the UN Security Council.

The continuation of the Cold War in Europe also cast its shadow over Korea, especially after the fall of Czechoslovakia to Communism in 1948 and the Berlin Airlift of 1948–9. It led to a belief in the West that Stalin must be resisted wherever he probed. Therefore when North Korea attacked South Korea on 25 June 1950, the West assumed that Stalin, not Kim, had devised the aggression and must be resisted in Korea as a warning against attempting any adventures in Europe.

(b) The outbreak of the War

Both sides blamed each other for provoking the outbreak of war in June 1950. Certainly the North Korean forces were more prepared and advanced on a wide front, but Rhee's regime had been provocative on a number of occasions in the year preceding hostilities. At the time it was believed that the Soviet Union, with Chinese communist assistance, had masterminded the North Korean attack, but most probably North Korea was the vital agent; Kim Il Sung wished to attack South Korea to fulfil his dream of a united Korea. Stalin may have given grudging assent, but in any case Kim was impatient of opposition, and his secondary objective was to end political dependence upon the Soviet Union and China.

To the cautious Stalin Korea was not a priority, and he soon pulled out Russian pilots and military advisers to minimise the risk of Soviet involvement. Furnished with information from spies such as Guy Burgess, Donald Maclean and Kim Philby, he would have been aware that the USA would react firmly to an attack on an American-supported regime. China too had little reason to provoke a new war, given the country's task of rebuilding after the civil war, and also given that Kim was more sympathetic to Russia than to China. Only after UN forces approached China's borders with North Korea (the Yalu river) did the Chinese feel constrained to intervene.

American reaction to the news of the North Korean attack was speedy and decisive. Taking advantage of the Soviet Union's absence from the UN Security Council (ostensibly on the grounds that China was represented there by the Nationalists rather than by Communist China), the USA persuaded the Security Council to adopt a resolution on 25 June deploring the North Korean aggression. On 29 June

Truman instructed MacArthur to use American forces in the Far East Command to support the South Koreans as they fell back before the better armed North Koreans. Behind the thinking of such top American politicians as Truman and Secretary of State Dean Acheson was the fear that if North Korean aggression was not blocked, then other communist targets in the Far East – Taiwan, Indo-China and Japan – would fall like dominoes. Such a sweeping assessment of communist aims in the Far East was not held by the British, and the Korean War strained Anglo-American relations because the British believed that American policy-making tended to over-react. Yet Truman was a courageous man who lived up to his slogan of 'the buck stops here'. He was a straightforward individual who saw the North Korean attack as a flagrant piece of Soviet aggression which must be resisted if a Far East Munich was to be avoided.

It was important to Truman that the USA should not act alone in Korea, but merely be the main agent in an operation under UN authority. On 7 July the UN Security Council passed a resolution recommending all members to supply military forces and requested that the US government appoint the commander-in-chief of such forces. Truman at once announced MacArthur's appointment. MacArthur was one of America's greatest soldiers, with vast experience of the Far East. Privately the president knew that MacArthur would be difficult to control; the general was averse to taking orders and had presidential ambitions himself, with hopes of becoming the Republican candidate in 1952.

(c) The course of the war

The development of the war between July and November 1950 was largely dominated by MacArthur. He restored confidence to the UN forces in the early period of retreat, helped to stabilise a defence line in the Pusan redoubt, and promoted the drive north which culminated in China's entry into the war. His actions to October were courageous and vigorous, but he squandered his achievements by miscalculating the effect on China of the UN advance towards the Yalu river.

The North Korean forces advanced relentlessly during July until the UN forces were pinned back in a narrow bridgehead at Pusan in the south-east part of the peninsula. The first American troops were thrust from a life of comparative luxury in Japan and were unprepared for the rigours of a new campaign. MacArthur's experience of a much worse situation (the Japanese onslaught of 1942) enabled him to restore discipline, hold on to the Pusan redoubt and prepare the ground for counter-attack. On 15 September came his brilliantly conceived and implemented landing at Inchon, halfway up the peninsula, which sapped the morale of the North Koreans and enabled the

UN forces to relieve Seoul and push north of the 38th parallel in October. By then fifteen other nations had contributed troops and five more supplied medical units, but this was a veneer on the overwhelming American contribution.

In other respects MacArthur proved a source of growing anxiety to Washington by his addiction to interference in political issues. His promise of support for the Nationalist regime on Taiwan (which the American government detested) if the Chinese Communists attacked ran counter to American policy, which aimed at neutralising Taiwan so that it would not become another area of American responsibility.

The most vital question between July and September 1950 was whether UN forces should cross the 38th parallel and what North Korea's future should be. The UN was committed to a united Korea, but advance north risked the intervention of either the Soviet Union or/and China, and such a risk should not have been taken. The issue of the advance north divided the State Department. Hawks like Dean Rusk felt that the opportunity to unite Korea should be taken, but George Kennan urged caution in the interests of better relations with Moscow. The military chiefs believed that action should be taken north of the parallel, and the success of the Inchon landings induced a mood of euphoria in Washington which led the US government to support advance north. The decision immediately complicated Truman's relations with MacArthur, for the president became worried that the general would not limit his operations to North Korea (despite orders to that effect) but carry out air strikes on Chinese territory, thus increasing the risk of Chinese entry into the war.

UN forces moved forward in North Korea, reaching its capital Pyongyang on 19 October, but in the west progress was more rapid and by 26 October UN troops were approaching the Yalu river. The Chinese government warned that it would not tolerate this growing threat to its security, and October did see a gradual increase in the number of Chinese soldiers on the North Korean side. MacArthur ignored the warning signs and several of his actions, for example the bombing of the Yalu river bridges, were provocative and led to criticism from Britain. The general dismissed the possibility of large-scale Chinese intervention and derided British attitudes as redolent of appeasement. He continued to thwart the efforts of Washington to curb him and, let down by his own intelligence service, felt sure that the Chinese would only intervene in a limited way. Therefore he refused to halt the offensive and hoped for a speedy conclusion to the war, so that American troops could return home and the two Koreas unite.

MacArthur estimated that between 40,000 and 70,000 Chinese had entered North Korea by November. In fact about 300,000 Chinese had moved in to North Korea in previous weeks without being detected by American intelligence. On 25 November the Chinese launched an offensive against Macarthur's exposed forces, making a mockery of his disregard of China. The general had to admit, 'We face an entirely new war.' China's participation might well have been avoided if Washington had controlled MacArthur's offensive and recognised the Chinese communist government, but no one in Truman's administration wished to be accused of appeasing communism.

The Chinese offensive surprised the UN forces, which were driven out of North Korea in a month of headlong humiliating retreat. On 1 January 1951 Chinese forces crossed into South Korea and soon captured Seoul. Only in February did UN troops regroup sufficiently to mount a counter-attack. A slow Allied advance under Ridgeway led to the UN forces crossing the 38th parallel again in April. The advance now met a second Chinese offensive, which was suicidal in its intensity, as it used weight of numbers alone to overrun UN positions.

By April MacArthur exhausted the patience of the long suffering Truman when the general sent a letter to a Republican Joseph Martin which became public. In it he conveyed his distaste for the president's foreign policy in the Far East. Truman dismissed MacArthur who, despite a magnificent ovation on his return home, like the old soldiers in his own phrase did not die but just faded away.

In June 1951 Jacob Malik, the Soviet delegate to the UN, indicated that the Communists were now willing to discuss peace terms. Truce talks began in a most chilling atmosphere in July but it was to take exactly two years before the war ended because there were difficult issues to overcome especially the thorny question of repatriation of POWs. Meanwhile fighting of a sporadic nature continued. When Eisenhower became president in January 1953 he threatened the use of the atomic bomb but a more flexible approach came from the Communists after the death of Stalin. In July 1953 the Korean War ended with agreement on demarcation lines between the two Korean states and on the return of POWs.

There was also a clause to the effect that the two Koreas should reunite, but this hope was not fulfilled and the two countries remained hostile. In North Korea Kim Il Sung consolidated his power and eliminated rivals. He ruled supreme and prepared for his son, Kim Jong Il, to succeed him. He remained independent of both China and Russia, and the cult of personality flourished as his thoughts were elevated to the same status as Stalin's and Mao's.

South Korea became a successful newly industrialising country by the 1970s, to a point where she has rivalled Japan in shipbuilding, cars and electrical goods. Syngman Rhee remained in power until 1960, and, after a military coup in 1961, Chung Hee Park became president from 1961 to 1979. Though some fragile parliamentary life developed, the regime was generally repressive. After Park was murdered by his own security chief, the South Korean government became more obviously a right-wing military dictatorship in the 1980s. The regime has continued to receive American military support, with about 60,000 American troops stationed in South Korea.

A bitter futile war had been caused by the murderous animosities within Korea and by the mutual suspicion of the superpowers. UN casualties (mainly South Korean) numbered about 1.5 millions, while Communist casualties (mainly Chinese) approached 2 millions.

With all the major powers participating directly or by proxy, the Korean War was a significant event in the evolution of the Cold War. In the USA it gave an impetus to the Red Scare and led to the banning of the Communist Party. It stimulated a massive American defence programme and increased American military support for Western Europe. The new NATO was strengthened and West Germany admitted as a member in 1955, though at times Anglo-American relations were strained over differing attitudes towards China.

The Korean War drew a reluctant USA inexorably into Far Eastern problems. In 1951 the US government was pushed into giving military aid to the Taiwan regime, and eventually considerable aid was given to the French in Vietnam as well. Treaties with Japan in 1952 and Taiwan and South Korea in 1954 meant heavy American commitment in the area, a commitment that along with others was in time to strain the resources even of the richest superpower. The state that gained most from the Korean War was Japan, which received added military guarantees and whose economy was boosted by the demand for equipment and services required by the American armed forces.

The two Koreas faded into the background of world politics until 1988, when South Korea gained prestige for its efficient organisation of the Olympic Games. However the regime's repressive nature was evident, as were increased public demands for the two Koreas to reunite.

(2) War in Vietnam

(a) The origins of modern Vietnam

The geographical area called Vietnam has been much affected by Chinese civilisation. The Vietnamese language is related to Chinese, the literary culture of the country is largely of Chinese origin and the land was for long periods under Chinese rule. Despite such influences, 'the Vietnamese since the tenth century have remained politically distinct from China, even while assiduously copying Chinese models' (Fairbank, Reischauer and Craig).

Until the nineteenth century Vietnam's relations with Europeans were slight, but in 1789 Nguyen Anh, whose family had been ousted from power in 1777, used French help to recover control and his dynasty was to survive in Vietnam until 1945. Nguyen westernised Vietnam to some extent, with the help of the French, but he was shrewd in maintaining Chinese institutions and Confucianism. His successors were not so able; gradually French control increased as the nineteenth century progressed, the excuse for intervention coming from Vietnamese persecution of the Roman Catholic Church. By 1885, after a short war with China, the French had established rule over four regions – Cochin China, Cambodia, Annam (central Vietnam) and Tongking (Northern Vietnam), and by the 1890s were moving into Laos.

French administrators believed that French culture was of universal value and superiority, and trained the Vietnamese in French ways, incorporating them into the bureaucracy. Native agencies of government were created so that French rule would be indirect and therefore more acceptable. Thus the emperor of Vietnam and the kings of Cambodia and Laos still maintained courts, councils and consultative asemblies in an imposing façade while real power lay with the French administrators. The general effect of French rule was to weaken traditional institutions of law, ethics, family and the village community. It helped the growth of a more powerful class of landlords, and the rice-farming economy suffered. In Vietnam therefore the Nguyen dynasty was discredited, as it was clearly maintained as a puppet regime.

Inspired by Western ideals and Chinese models, a nationalist movement had begun to protest against French rule by the early years of the twentieth century. Phan Boi Chau (died 1940) wrote *A History of the Destruction of the Vietnamese State* and formed an association which aimed at Vietnamese independence under a constitutional monarchy. For his pains he was imprisoned by the French in 1913.

Vietnamese reformers who tried to cooperate with the French were frustrated by the disconcerting oscillations of French policy; conservative administrators would often crack down on reforms which more liberal predecessors had permitted. A discontented group of young Vietnamese scholars grew up hoping to be the future ruling class and natural saviours of their oppressed country. They resented the fact that French personnel not only monopolised top posts but staffed much of the civil service at lower levels. Indigenous political activity was smothered by French police control, and suspects were summarily shipped to the island of Pulo Condore. Education for the people as a whole remained minimal, and, among the South East Asian colonies of the West, only the Dutch East Indies had a poorer record. Nevertheless coteries of writers imbued with programmes of social reform did emerge, the most famous being the Self-Reliance Literary Group, formed in 1933.

French rule did create attractive new cities, such as Saigon, and improvements in public health were implemented, but unfortunately the population increased faster than the food supply, especially in the crowded delta around Hanoi in the north. In the south much land was expropriated and granted to French colonists or Vietnamese collaborators, who created large plantations to produce such cash crops as rubber for export, thus aggravating the food shortage.

Therefore many Vietnamese came to believe that revolution rather than reform was the answer to economic exploitation, political repression and cultural stagnation. The First World War increased the strength of such feelings; many of the 100,000 Vietnamese soldiers and labourers sent to France during the war returned with renewed beliefs in national self-determination and revolutionary class struggle, especially when such ideas flourished in China in the 1920s.

(b) The communist movement in Vietnam

The Vietnam Nationalist Party, founded in 1927, was indebted to the Kuomintang in China for much of its ideology and practices. Denied any chance of participating in elections, it turned to terrorism. Meanwhile a more highly trained professional revolutionary movement was set up by Ho Chi Minh (1892–1967). He began as a nationalist but turned to communism, helping to set up the French Communist Party in 1920. He studied in Soviet Russia and worked in China, recruiting Vietnamese into his Vietnam Revolutionary Youth League as the first step towards forming a Vietnam Communist Party. Secret communist cells were established in French Indo-China.

The first phase of the Vietnam Revolution began in 1930. Indo-China had been severely hit by the world slump in primary produce prices, and the Vietnam Nationalist Party attempted an armed uprising which the French crushed with such severity that the party was all but destroyed. Members from this party now joined the communist network, which succeeded in stirring up strikes and peasant uprisings. The French used their Foreign Legion to quell the agitation, and Ho Chi Minh was jailed.

Nevertheless the Communists were now firmly the leaders of the national revolution in Vietnam. To a nation whose élite had a long tradition of cultural borrowing, international communism offered an intelligible system of political ideas and organisational methods that could be adopted by Vietnamese revolutionaries in the same way as Vietnam's rulers had adopted Chinese bureaucratic blueprints a century before. Contacts were maintained with the Chinese communists, one senior Vietnamese Communist even adopting as his pseudonym the Vietnamese version of the Chinese term for 'Long March'.

The Vietnamese communists could mobilise support easily because their target was an obvious one, the French imperialists who bore direct responsibility for domestic affairs. Yet on the practical level French control was so complete that external aid was essential. This came during the Second World War, when Nationalist China gave Ho Chi Minh and his followers active support against Vichy France, and a staging area across the border in China, where in the spring of 1941 the Vietnamese communists created a united front, the League for the Independence of Vietnam, or Viet Minh, with Ho Chi Minh as general secretary. By 1945 the Viet Minh's forces were led by a very able general, Vo Nguyen Giap, a young Vietnamese teacher who had been trained by the Chinese communsits in the art of guerrilla warfare.

By 1945 the Japanese had taken over control of French Indo-China from Vichy, while allowing nominal control to remain with Emperor Bao-dai, who had come to the throne in 1925. The Viet Minh established a liberated zone on the Chinese border, and from this base they infiltrated the Red river delta. On Japan's surrender in August the Viet Minh found themselves the only effective power in Vietnam. Emperor Bao-dai was forced to abdicate and Ho Chi Minh proclaimed the independence of the Democratic Republic of Vietnam in September.

The struggle was, however, only just beginning. Opposition to the communists came from armed religious sects, including the syncretic Cao Dai sect and the Hoa Hao Buddhist revival society in Cochin China. British and Free French forces arrived, and by January 1946 had regained control of Cochin China. The Viet Minh were well-entrenched in Tongking, but were handicapped by lack of government experience and by attempting a dual revolution – the expulsion of the French and the class struggle against the propertied minority.

In March 1946 both sides agreed to negotiations, but these broke down by November and full-scale war ensued, with the Viet Minh organising national resistance against 115,000 French troops. As fighting continued throughout 1947 and 1948, the communist core of the Viet Minh became more overt, and this helped the French to set up a Vietnamese regime at Saigon under ex-Emperor Bao-dai as a rallying point for nationalist anti-communists. American arms were soon flowing in great quantity to the French, while Chinese economic aid, arms and training bolstered the Viet Minh forces. French forces totalled 420,000 (nearly half of them Vietnamese), but Viet Minh forces were formidable because they were entrenched in mountain bases and among the populace. When the communist group which was pledged to free Laos, the Pathet Lao, invaded Laos to the West, the French decided to block the main route by an airborne build-up of the mountain-ringed base, Dien Bien Phu. In April–May 1954 Giap, to French surprise, transported artillery to the area and forced the surrender of the French forces there. The defeat broke France's will to continue the war; an armistice was arranged in July and the French withdrew from Indo-China, which was divided into North and South Vietnam. An international conference at Geneva, however, recognised that the partition was explicitly temporary.

The communists now ruled North Vietnam from Hanoi while in the South the Bao-dai government was in control, with Ngo Dinh Diem as premier. In 1955 Diem ousted Bao-dai and made himself president. With American support he refused to join in the nationwide elections promised at the Geneva conference. By 1960 a campaign of rural unrest and terrorism was under way in South Vietnam, aided by the North. In March 1960 a full-scale revolt against Diem's regime began. Diem labelled his opponents the Viet Cong (Vietnamese communists), though his opponents included many anti-communists. Ho Chi Minh after some hesitation gave the revolt his blessing.

(c) American intervention

The Truman administration had approved $60 million for support of the French effort against the Viet Minh in 1952. Both Truman and Eisenhower labelled Ho a communist agent of Peking and Moscow, and saw the war in Vietnam as another example of communist aggression. But American attitudes in this period were ambivalent, because the Americans disliked French imperialism and recognised that the French were unpopular in Vietnam. Therefore, while aiding France, the American government confined its aid to material assistance and did not send in its own troops; furthermore the French were pressurised to state unequivocally that they would give complete independence to Vietnam on the conclusion of hostilities.

However, when the French faced defeat in 1954, Eisenhower and Dulles saw the impending communist victory as a defeat for containment. Therefore, as early as April 1954, Dulles sought Congressional support to authorise American entry into the war, but Congressmen remembered all too well the American embroilment in Korea. Both Eisenhower and Dulles remained worried about what would happen if the French lost. In April 1954 the president introduced a new political use for an old word when he explained that all South East Asia was like a row of dominoes. If you knocked the first one over what would happen to the last one was 'the certainty that it would go over very quickly'. Therefore in the closing stages of the French defeat at Dien Bien Phu the Americans considered air strikes on the Viet Minh, an invasion at Haiphong and even the use of small atomic bombs.

After the Geneva arrangements (July 1954) Dulles wished to shore up the government of South Vietnam. In so doing, affirms Stephen Ambrose, he revealed much about American attitudes to revolution in the Third World. It was an issue where American military might was almost useless in the struggle, and where Russia had a tremendous initial advantage, as the Third World countries did not regard the Russians as white exploiters and colonists. Indeed Soviet Russia's example as a command economy had great appeal to the emerging nations, whose revolutions aimed at changing the entire political, economic and social order. Such radicalism was disliked by Dulles and his cohorts. While they demanded great changes behind the Iron Curtain, they wanted to prevent them elsewhere.

Accordingly in South Vietnam American military advisers began training a South Vietnamese army, while Eisenhower also promised economic aid to Ngo Dinh Diem, whose regime drew its support from landlords and French plantation owners. No pressure to hold the Geneva promised elections for the whole of Vietnam was put on Diem by the Americans, because they were afraid that Ho would win 80 per cent of the votes.

By 1961, with the Diem regime facing more unrest, the new Kennedy administration determined on direct military intervention. Kennedy built up an élite force – the Green Berets – which, equipped with the latest military technology, would, he hoped, resist communist aggression while avoiding direct confrontation with the Soviet Union. Vietnam would be an ideal battleground for the Green Berets. Small unit actions in the jungle or paddy-fields would suit them, while technical and medical aid would win the hearts of the Vietnamese. The American Secretary of State, Dean Rusk, saw the revolt in South Vietnam as North Vietnamese aggression sponsored by communist China. If the USA allowed the Viet Cong to win in South Vietnam, the Chinese would gobble up the rest of Asia. Rusk, as Ambrose emphasises, 'warned his countrymen of a Far Eastern Munich, thereby equating Ho Chi Minh with Hitler and raising the dreaded spectre of appeasement'. Most of the Kennedy government agreed that more military equipment and training should be given to South Vietnam, and between October 1961 and November 1963 the number of American advisers in South Vietnam rose from 1,360 to 15,000. Diem's refusal to bring in reforms led to CIA plots to overthrow him, and in November 1963 the South Vietnamese army, with covert American support, overthrew and killed Diem.

Under President Johnson the number of American advisers in Vietnam rose to 21,000, but the American government failed to see that North Vietnam could match American escalation step by step. The Americans were also confounded by old myths, especially the notion that Asians could not stand up to Western military techniques and that communism could never inspire genuine support. In fact the Viet Cong fought with fanatical courage, and when they liberated a village, they told the peasants that the land was theirs; when the South Vietnamese army took a village, the landlords returned.

In the 1964 presidential election the Republican candidate, Barry

Goldwater, condemned Johnson for not doing enough to help South Vietnam. However, in August an alleged attack on American destroyers by North Vietnam torpedo boats took place in the Gulf of Tonkin. Johnson ordered air attacks on North Vietnam's ports to destroy the torpedo boats, and, more importantly, he gained Senate approval to widen the war as he saw fit without consulting Congress (the Gulf of Tonkin Resolution).

(d) The course of the war

The South Vietnam army continued to make little progress against the Viet Cong. Its officer corps had little connection with the troops, corruption was rife and desertion widespread. It was trained to fight a conventional war, not one against guerrillas. Clearly the policy of material support and Green Beret advisers had failed. Johnson was therefore faced with a dilemma – either to negotiate with Ho or introduce American combat troops to prevent the collapse of the Saigon regime.

Johnson rejected negotiation because he felt that Vietnam was a testing ground for the American policy of containing communist China. He still hoped that American air strikes would reduce North Vietnam's morale and reduce the flow of men and equipment from North to South Vietnam. However, in February 1965 the Viet Cong's raid on the American air base at Pleiku in South Vietnam provoked the Americans into a retaliatory raid, an escalation of American action. Simultaneously American airmen stepped up their bombing, not only over North Vietnam but in the South as well. By 1970 they had dropped more bombs than in the whole of human history, including napalm and defoliating weedkillers.

The air campaign failed to break Hanoi or revive the morale of the South Vietnam government. In April Johnson sent 15,000 additional troops to Vietnam and in June authorised American forces, formerly confined to patrolling, to seek out the enemy. In July 50,000 more American troops were sent to Vietnam, bringing the total commitment to 125,000. It was now clear that American forces would actively engage in ground combat. Swayed by views of international communism which had not changed in 20 years, the Americans had contrived to trap themselves in a land war in Asia.

Vietnam provided the setting for the agony of the president and the whole American nation. The price of containment proved to be far higher than anyone had expected in both financial and human terms. The cost of American commitment rose from $10 billion to $30 billion a year, while the number of US troops rose to over 500,000. As bombing raids over Vietnam increased, opposition at home mounted, especially from students, and prompted questions as to what kind of society could support such a war. Older critics, such as

Walter Lippman and senator Fulbright, stressed the need for the USA to set a moral example and cease acting like an empire.

Most Americans and certainly most of Johnson's advisers, such as Rusk, supported the war on the grounds that communism must be stopped in Vietnam, for otherwise Americans would soon have to fight communism in the Western hemisphere. Yet American thinking was muddled; the only way of defeating the Viet Cong was by cutting off their supplies from China, and the American government did not dare to take the risk of war with China. Consequently, whenever the Viet Cong wished to gain a breathing space after heavy losses, they could withdraw into the jungle or cross the Cambodian or Laotion borders and wait for Chinese equipment. Johnson's predictions of imminent victory from 1965 on proved illusory, and in February 1968 a Viet Cong offensive drove the American forces and the South Vietnam army out of the countryside and into the cities. The Americans retaliated by destroying the ancient cultural capital of Hue, which had been captured by the Viet Cong, an act which in Ambrose's opinion highlighted the racist attitudes of the Americans, who did not understand or respect Asian culture. The point blank shooting of hundreds of women and children at My Lai in March 1968 by an American company under Lieutenant William Calley demonstrated little respect for Asian people either. Such actions increased the tide of domestic opposition to the war and hid the reality of North Vietnam's atrocities.

American failure in Vietnam was caused by many factors. The South Vietnam government, from June 1965 under Generals Nguyen Cao Ky and Van Thieu, was unpopular and inefficient; its army, which numbered 750,000 on paper, was incompetent and underequipped. It resisted Americans attempts to impose reforms. The USA also lost the support of its allies during the war. Initially some 72,000 Allied troops went to Vietnam from Australia, New Zealand, South Korea and Thailand, but France and Britain disassociated themselves from the American position. The American army itself, recruited by the draft system, had too many malcontents. Desertion, drug abuse and insubordination became widespread. American radical opinion highlighted the odd statistic that over half the American casualties were black.

When Nixon became president in November 1968, his initial policy was to strengthen the South Vietnamese government and army so that American forces could play a reduced role, and considerable American troop withdrawals did occur in 1969. Nixon and his Secretary of State, Henry Kissinger, wanted to end the war quickly, but with an honourable American withdrawal that would leave a secure independent South Vietnam. In an attempt to force North Vietnam to the conference table the president ordered the bombing of Viet Cong sanctuaries in neutral Cambodia, but North Vietnam, aware that American public opinion would force Nixon to withdraw his troops in time, was prepared to continue resistance.

Nixon's next step was to send American troops into Cambodia, where the neutralist Prince Sihanouk had been overthrown by a pro-American clique headed by Lon Nol in March 1970. He defended the extension of a war which he had promised to wind down on the grounds that a friendly ally should be defended. However, the move was a grave error; it aroused opposition at home which exceeded Nixon's fears. Demonstrations on campuses were nationwide and Congress terminated the Gulf of Tonkin Resolution. The move extended American commitments, and Lon Nol faced increasing opposition from the Communist Khmer Rouge.

American forces were soon withdrawn from Cambodia, but in 1971 the American's stepped up air activity and sent troops into Laos to disrupt enemy supply lines. This Laotion adventure gave Giap an opportunity to inflict heavy defeats on South Vietnamese units engaged in the operation. Then in March 1972 North Vietnam launched a massive conventional invasion of the South timed to coincide with the American presidential campaign. With most of the South Vietnamese army engaged in resisting this offensive, the way was clear for the Viet Cong to mount extensive operations around Saigon. Nixon responded with massive bombing attacks and a naval blockade of North Vietnam.

By now, however, both sides were inching towards a settlement. North Vietnam had suffered terribly in the war, and was finding aid harder to obtain from China and Russia. The North Vietnamese also believed that they could gain better terms from Nixon before the presidential elections due to be held in November 1973. Therefore in September 1972 Kissinger and Le Duc Tho began serious negotiations, and a ceasefire was agreed in January 1973, despite the objections of Thieu's South Vietnam government. A settlement was arrived at whereby American forces would be withdrawn within 60 days of the ceasefire, and North Vietnam would return American POWs. But peace with honour was not obtained. North Vietnamese troops remained in the South and the political wing of the Viet Cong – the People's Revolutionary government or National Liberation Front – was to be given formal recognition and a say in South Vietnam's internal settlement.

(e) The consequences of the war

The war had resulted in over 55,000 American deaths and over 107,000 South Vietnamese battle casualties, while North Vietnam and Viet Cong losses were over 500,000. Untold devastation had been wreaked on Vietnam. Neither did the January 1973 settlement last long. The North Vietnamese built up their forces, which steadily infiltrated the South. In March 1975 they mounted a major offensive and South Vietnam collapsed with stunning rapidity. Nixon, distracted by the Watergate scandal and facing a defiant Congress, had not given the military and economic support to South Vietnam which he had promised, and had resigned in August 1974. This was a massive blow to the morale of South Vietnam. By May 1975 the North Vietnamese were able to capture Saigon, which was renamed Ho Chi Minh City. The two Vietnams were now united in the Socialist Republic of Vietnam. President Ford could gain Congress approval for the evacuation of American citizens from Vietnam and nothing else. About 250,000 refugees fled from Vietnam – the Vietnamese boat people, many of whom settled in Western countries.

The consequences for American and global politics were immense. As Paul Kennedy emphasises in his blockbuster work, *The Rise and Fall of the Great Powers*, 'In so many ways, symbolic as well as practical, it would be difficult to exaggerate the impact of the lengthy American campaign in Vietnam upon the international power system – or upon the national psyche of the American people themselves.' The fact that the war was fought by an open society and was well covered by the media drove home the carnage and the apparent futility. It was the first war that the USA had unequivocally lost, it destroyed many political and military reputations and eliminated the consensus in American society. As it was attended by inflation, student protests and soon after by the Watergate crisis, the war seemed to contradict everything that the Founding Fathers had taught and made the USA unpopular in the world. Despite attempts at the time to indulge in a sort of collective amnesia, the shabby treatment of the GI's who returned from Vietnam surfaced a decade later in such films as *The Deer Hunter* and Philip Caputo's *A Rumor of War*, and ensured that the conflict continued to prey upon the public consciousness.

The war was a sobering reminder that military superiority could not be automatically translated into military effectiveness. Public and world opinion ruled out the use of American nuclear weapons, while domestic opinion ruled out the full use of conventional weapons. Although Johnson did send more troops to Vietnam, the number peaked at 542,00 in 1969, never enough to meet General Westmoreland's demands.

The vast boom in spending on the war at the same time as Johnson's administration was increasing domestic spending on the Great Society badly affected the American economy. It also enabled the Russians to close the nuclear gap and improve their navy. The war itself obscured for a decade Washington's recognition of the extent of the Sino-Soviet split, and only with Nixon was advantage taken of it. Finally the Vietnam experience led to a reluctance at government and public level for the USA to act as the world's leading gendarme unless American interests were directly concerned.

In some ways the defeat in Vietnam was not as disastrous as American policy-makers had feared. The domino theory was proved only partly correct. True, Cambodia fell to the Khmer Rouge in March 1975 and Laos in the following May, but elsewhere the dominoes did not fall. Ironically one effect of the Vietnam war was to heighten tensions among the various communist nations in Asia, especially between Vietnam and China and between Vietnam and Cambodia, and it is in this sense that North Vietnam's victory became a destabilising force in South East Asia. Vietnam was now the strongest military power in the region, and as such was now feared by China, with the result that Vietnam soon turned to the Soviet Union as an ally in preference to China.

Vietnam regarded Cambodia as rightfully hers, and waited for an opportunity for invasion to present itself. Lon Nol's government was overthrown by opposition from pro-Sihanouk forces and the Khmer Rouge backed by China in March 1974 and Cambodia was renamed Kampuchea. Sihanouk never re-established his power, and his flight left Kampuchea at the mercy of Pol Pot's Khmer Rouge. The country now entered a new dark age, as the regime systematically slaughtered any Cambodians suspected of being Vietnamese or pro-Russian. In this episode, known as the killing fields, the best of the professional classes were eliminated and the populations fell from 8 million to 6 million.

Meanwhile Van Dong's government in Vietnam developed close relations with Russia, which was keen to encircle China. In 1979 a Vietnamese army rolled into Kampuchea to expel the Khmer Rouge and install a pro-Vietnam government. Ironically Kampuchea became Vietnam's Vietnam, as an occupation army of 100,000 had to be stationed there to maintain a friendly government against the guerrilla activites of the Khmer Rouge and pro-Sihanouk elements. By 1988 Vietnam began withdrawing its troops to ease the strain on its resources and because the presence of its army was unpopular with ordinary Cambodians. In addition, Vietnam came under pressure from Gorbachev, who saw the evacuation of Vietnamese troops from Kampuchea as furthering better Sino-Soviet relations.

Such developments will still leave the region unstable. If Pol Pot's Khmer Rouge were able to regain power in Kampuchea, the killing fields could begin again and world opinion would not prevent it. In fact during the Khmer Rouge's first spell in power, there were no human rights demonstrations against the regime's atrocities in Europe or America, and unbelievably and disgracefully the United Nations recognised Pol Pot as the rightful ruler in September 1979 after his expulsion from Kampuchea.

FURTHER READING

Ambrose, S. E., *Rise to Globalism: American Foreign Policy Since 1938*, Penguin, Harmondsworth, 1983

Hastings, M., *The Korean War*, Michael Joseph, London, 1987

Karnow, S., *Vietnam: A History*, Penguin, Harmondsworth, 1986

Kolko, G., *Vietnam: Anatomy of a War 1940–1975*, Unwin, London, 1986

Lewy, G., *America in Vietnam*, OUP, New York, 1978

Lowe, P., *The Origins of the Korean War*, Longmans, London, 1986

QUESTIONS

1. To what extent was the outbreak of the Korean War caused by the ambitions of Kim Il Sung?
2. Comment on the view that Truman's policy of limited war in Korea was the logical extension of his policy of containment in Europe.
3. Account for the failure of the French to maintain their control of Indo-China.
4. Critically examine the reasons for American involvement in Vietnam.
5. 'The United States tried to win a political war by military means.' How acceptable is this explanation of American defeat in Vietnam.
6. What were the international consequences of the Vietnam war?

16
The Indian subcontinent in the twentieth century

(a) The rise of Indian nationalism

Modern India is the result of the impact of the West on Indian traditions. No other Asian or African country that has gained freedom since 1945 bears so markedly the influence of European, and particularly British, thought and way of life. The first European to reach the shores of India with any strength was Vasco da Gama in 1498, but the decisive European impact came after the British expelled the French from India in the Seven Years War (1756–63). The British East India Company now controlled Bengal, and its authority fanned out from the three centres of Calcutta, Madras and Bombay. By the middle of the nineteenth century the Company had been extended to cover the whole of India, often through political arrangements with Indian princes.

To Indian historians the period represented exploitation and nothing else, but the administrative and political unification of the country paved the way for a development of national consciousness. Another step in this direction was the decision to introduce Western teaching in the English language. The administration required a supply of clerks and officials whom it would be too expensive to bring out from Britain, and therefore higher education colleges were established from 1817 on.

Attempts were made to reform the quality of British rule after the Indian Mutiny of 1857, which, as Spear emphasises, came as a profound shock to the British, shaking their complacency if not their self-confidence. The rule of the Company was replaced by direct British government control. The army was reformed, with greater inclusion of Gurkhas, Sikhs and Punjabis, and a new camaradie established between Indians and their European officers. The British became less prone to bring in reforms which would challenge traditional Indian customs, and instead concentrated on material projects which would, they hoped, more peacefully modernise India. Their record of public works was patchy, though railway and irrigation development was impressive. India gained the best railway system in

Asia, and by 1947 one-fifth of the cultivable area was under irrigation. A famine control scheme, brought in by Lord Lytton in the
1870s, saved India from famine down to 1943.

The Indian Civil Service was run by about 1,000 British officials
who were often able and efficient. At the same time their disbelief in
Indian capacity was pronounced, and they opposed the entry of
Indians into the higher echelons of the service. Unfortunately this led
to the neglect of the new rising westernised Indian middle class. This
English-speaking group of clerks, lawyers, teachers and officials had
loyally supported the government during the Mutiny and were not
rewarded.

It was this disaffected group of westernised Indians that most
readily embraced the new Indian nationalism of the late nineteenth
century, which was a mingling of old and new ideas. One of its
elements was a traditional dislike of the foreigner; another was tribal
or regional loyalty. To these emotions were added the beliefs of
Hindu Brahmins such as Ram Mohan Roy (1772–1833), who wished
to apply Western ideals of civil liberty and equality to Indian society.
Adherents to such reforming attitudes were therefore opposed not
only to the British but also to the old aristocratic classes.

The grievances of the new educated stratum of Indians took
concrete shape with the formation of the Indian National Congress.
The cohesion of this class, remarks Spear, had been promoted by the
joint stimuli of encouragement and irritation. The encouragement
had come from the government's liberal measures, such as the
beginnings of municipal self-government. It came also from the
works of oriental scholars, who presented India as a great civilisation.
The irritation was caused by the racial and cultural contempt of
Europeans and the exclusion of Indians from high office. The catalyst
came in 1880, when Europeans campaigned to block legal reforms
which would have meant Indian judges trying Europeans in Bengal.
Such agitation was resented by Indians as racialist, and the result was
the Indian National Congress, which first met at Bombay in 1885.

The Congress soon gained a national organisation, and was the
natural mouthpiece for middle-class aspirations, receiving support
from the professional groups, with a sprinkling of businessmen and
landlords. As it developed, two main tendencies began to reveal
themselves. One group, the Moderates, under Gopal Krishna
Gopale, admired Western liberalism and believed in cooperation
with the British, while the Extremists, led by Bal Gangadhar Tilak,
admired the Indian past and believed concessions should be demanded from the British. The two groups agreed on many issues, such as
the unfairness of the competition from Lancashire cotton, the slow
advance towards representative government and the lack of promotion for Indians in the civil service.

While the Congress was a clique of India's westernised classes, it was a movement rather than a force, made up of smartly dressed individuals such as Jawaharlal Nehru, who had been trained as a lawyer, like 40 per cent of the members. However, when the Congress gained popular backing, as it did in 1904, when the division of Bengal into two provinces was widely disliked, the British were forced to take notice and accept the need to win the goodwill of India's political class.

Accordingly the Liberal government produced the Indian Councils Act of 1909, the fruits of the labours of John Morley, Secretary of State for India, and the Viceroy, Lord Minto. Indians had already been appointed to the Viceroy's Imperial Council; now the way was opened for Indian membership of the provincial executive councils as well. Some seats were elective and some reserved for Muslims. The Act was, states Spear, 'a clear step towards representative and responsible government' and as such it satisfied moderate Congressmen. The new responsiveness of the government was further evidenced by the reuniting of the two Bengals in 1911 as a consolation for Delhi replacing Calcutta as the capital.

This Congress–government honeymoon lasted until 1914, when the First World War provoked a revolution in Indian national consciousness. Until then it had seemed that self-government would come gradually through lordly British concessions to suitably grateful Indians! The war, however, demonstrated that British power was limited, and that Europeans who engaged in such a fratricidal struggle need not be put on a pedestal by Indians. The Russian Revolution causing the fall of the world's leading repressive regime, and Wilson's fourteen points, which included a declaration on self-determination, transformed Indian thinking. Modest concessions were no longer sufficient, especially as India had made a large contribution to the British war effort, mobilising 800,000 troops. It was only reasonable to expect real recognition for such effort and sacrifice, and the mood of the political class changed from loyalty to expectation of change.

The new Secretary of State for India, Edwin Montagu, recognised such feelings, and in August 1917 promised India self-government of the kind enjoyed by the white dominions. With the Viceroy, Lord Chelmsford, he then put forward measures in 1919 to implement the new policy in the Government of India Act. It proposed a national bicameral parliament, with about 5 million wealthy Indians having the vote. In provincial governments certain ministries, such as health and education, would be headed by Indians. In 10 years a commission would decide on further measures.

The reforms marked a real departure from merely consultative government towards mass politics, with the promise of further changes in the future. Such measures might have worked well in the India of 1910; they fell far short of Indian aspirations in 1919, because the British kept control of central government and still reserved key provincial ministries, such as law and order and taxation.

(b) Enter Gandhi: India, 1919–47

The new indignation found a new leader in Congress, Mahandas Gandhi, a lawyer who had recently returned to India after leading a passive resistance movement against the South African government. Gokhale had died in 1915 and all eyes were on Tilak, but Gandhi's policy of non-violence soon captured public support. Gandhi's method of opposition was the traditional Indian protest, *hartal*, the cessation of all activity for a day. But *hartals* staged in the big cities led to riots and a government fear of open rebellion. In April 1919 riots in Amritsar led to General Dyer breaking up a prohibited meeting by firing on a crowd without warning. The official casualty list was 379 killed. Dyer was retired, but India was shocked when the House of Lords voted in his favour. In 1920 Gandhi launched a non-cooperation movement in which his supporters withdrew from government offices and schools and boycotted elections to councils. This lasted until 1922, and was further evidence that Congress was now a mass movement able to treat with the government on equal terms.

Gandhi became known as the Mahatma or great soul. Born in 1869 into a Hindu merchant family, he had qualified as a barrister in London, coming in touch both with liberal, Christian ideas and British aloofness. A second formative experience was his work in South Africa helping the Indian community there. He came to believe that Western society was corrupt, and he abhorred violence as a canker in society. He regarded Gokhale as his teacher or guru. On his return to India the poverty of the masses burned into his soul, and, as he felt that a true leader must identify with those whom he aspired to lead, he gave up European clothes for the peasant's humble loincloth and shawl, and adhered to a strict vegetarian diet. It was such gestures that won the hearts of people and marked him in their eyes as a great soul.

Though Hindu, Gandhi opposed Hindu caste distinctions as much as British repression. He emphasised the equality of the untouchables or outcasts and on occasions ordered the mercy killing of a suffering calf. Not surprisingly, it was a Brahmin who eventually murdered him.

At the heart of his ideas lay the doctrine of non-violence. To Gandhi violence was an expression of hate which must be met by reason and entreaty. With non-violence went severe self-discipline, which included fasts of purification. Such practices were needed to work towards truth or right living. In time, Gandhi hoped, India would be freed from foreign domination and Hindu society freed from the barriers of caste. He envisaged a peasant society of self-supporting workers, with the state composed of a loose federation of village republics. He rejected Western industrial methods and preached the necessity of hand spinning and weaving.

Gandhi was an artful politician, able to dramatise issues in a way which appealed to ordinary people, as, for example, when he walked to the sea at Dandi to make illicit salt. In this lay his greatest achievement – the drawing in of the masses into the nationalist movement. The more established groups accepted his ideas, because they knew that he won them the essential mass support and could surpass them all in tactics which made the British uncomfortable.

Arrested for his activities in 1922, Gandhi was released in 1924 after a serious operation. In the next few years his support continued to grow. In 1927 the British, under the terms of the 1919 Act, appointed a commission of enquiry under Sir John Simon, but Indians were angered by its all-British membership. The Congress now declared for complete independence, led by its young radicals, Nehru and Subash Bose. The Viceroy, Lord Irwin (later Lord Halifax), gained the Labour Government's approval to declare, ahead of the Simon Commission's report, that British policy aimed at dominion status for India, with a round-table conference immediately to consider the next step.

Congress, whose radicals wanted a showdown, rejected the offer, and Gandhi, whose first instinct had been to accept, now insisted that the proposed conference should discuss not the next step forward but the actual implementation of dominion status. His next step to embarrass the British was his announcement of his intention to make illicit salt from seawater by a 60-mile walk to the sea at Dandi. The masses followed him and about 100,000 were arrested. Hindu women joined him, and their participation gave a boost to women's rights.

Irwin and Gandhi came to an understanding after Gandhi had again been arrested. Two round-table conferences were held in London, in 1930 and 1931, and Gandhi was persuaded to attend the second one. At the time little progress seemed to have been made, because the National Government was less favourable to Indian aspirations than Labour, and within the Conservative party itself diehards like Churchill opposed any concessions. However, the Baldwin government passed the Government of India Act in 1935. It was a blueprint for Indian independence, and many sections of its text were absorbed into the 1950 Constitution. It gave the eleven provinces full self-government, while at central government level responsibility for some affairs would be given to elected representatives, with the viceroy retaining defence and foreign affairs in his own hands.

The Act did not solve all issues by any means. The Congress was determined that India should run its own foreign policy, as the dominions had since 1918, and its left-wingers called for direct action. In addition, mutual suspicion between Muslims and Hindus increased as independence became a real possibility. As Congress was overwhelmingly Hindu, Muslims demanded British protection, while British sympathy for the minority led Indians to accuse Britain of a 'divide and rule' policy. A third problem was that the federal central government would only come into existence when half the princes agreed, and they were allowed to nominate one-third of the representatives in the lower house and one-fifth in the upper house, with considerable power therefore to block measures. Thus the 1935 Act had a conservative, even a reactionary element, and the voluntary aspect allowed the princes to play for time after 1935, and in 1939 they had not yet been incorporated into the arrangements for the new India.

The British policy-makers, with their commitment to a single state and rule by majorities, did not appreciate that there were areas in life and conduct that no Muslim could take from a Hindu or Hindu from a Muslim. This was in the words of Spear, 'an ill wind which was to reap the whirlwind of the post-partition massacres'. Nevertheless the final years before the Second World War were a period of hope as provincial elections, which went ahead in 1937, resulted in Congress securing clear majorities in five provinces and winning power in two others with the help of allies.

The Second World War, however, soon provoked a mood of suspicion, when Britain postponed all steps towards dominion status until after the war. Though India was more affected by the war after Japan's entry in 1941, the country was far more detached in attitude than in 1914. Bose even fled from India and raised the Indian National Army from Indian prisoners in Japanese hands, with the hope of invading British India. Nevertheless the Indian war record was impressive in both the European and Asian theatres. Two million men and women were mobilised and came under westernising influences. But the war also saw the tragedy of the 1943 famine, which claimed 2 million lives.

Politics entered a deadlock from which they did not emerge until 1947, as the British stuck to their line of no wartime changes until 1942. Then Sir Stafford Cripps made a radical offer of a constituent assembly elected by the provincial legislatures to draw up a dominion constitution immediately at the end of the war. The Indian leaders wanted a new council to replace that of the viceroy, and, with Gandhi also opposing the new proposal, discussions broke down. The Congress believed that the British would be forced to make more concessions as the Japanese threat to India increased. Gandhi, with his usual skill, invented a new slogan 'Quit India', and a new campaign of civil disobedience cost 1,000 lives. Congress had made an error; it could have gained power before the Muslim League became too strong to be crushed. The price of error was partition.

(c) The Pakistan movement

Muslim traders had first appeared in India soon after the death of Muhammad in AD 632. By the fourteenth century Islamic domination had spread over much of India, as Turkish invaders followed the traders. Conversion of the population, though sometimes forcible, was usually voluntary, through the preaching of Muslim sufis or devotees. Therefore by the twentieth century a quarter of the Indian population was Muslim, and in some areas, such as Sind, the Punjab and East Bengal, they were in the majority. The heyday of the Muslim community was the Mughal empire of the sixteenth and seventeenth centuries, when Muslims were the ruling race in India, but their influence declined in the eighteenth century. Under British rule they failed to learn English, so that Hindus monopolised subordinate offices. Between the two religious groups there was no possiblity of cooperation, because the Muslims detested Hindu cowworship and caste and such Hindu beliefs as reincarnation.

These factors combined with the threat of Christian missionary activity and Western scepticism to provoke an Indian Islamic revival in the nineteenth century. The lead came from Sayyid Ahmad Khan of Delhi, who stressed that Indian Islam must make terms with the West as well as remaining distinct from Hinduism if it was to avoid remaining a political backwater. He pointed to the common roots of Islam and Christianity, and believed that young Muslims should take up Western education to resume their rightful place in the public life of their country.

From the first this Islamic movement held aloof from the Indian National Congress, because it feared that majority rule in India would mean Hindu rule. In 1906 the Muslim League was founded to demand separate constituencies for Muslims in elections. For a time Tilak won over Muslim support, because Muslims disliked the war against the Turkish Sultan, who was recognised as Caliph in India. However, in 1930 young Muslims took readily to the idea of the poet Sir Muhammad Iqbal for a separate Muslim homeland in north west India. Iqbal portrayed Islam as a dynamic religion which need have no truck with the decadent West. At the same time the visionary Chaudhuri Rahmat Ali coined the word Pakistan – P for Punjab, A for Afghans (Pathans), K for Kashmir, S for Sind and *stan*, the Persian suffix meaning country.

As independence drew nearer, the Muslims found the political leader they needed – a westernised lawyer, Muhammad Ali Jinnah

(1876–1948). Jinnah originally hoped to work in a coalition with Congress, and revived the Muslim League with this intention. When the Congress rejected his approaches, he lost his trust in their leaders and preached that Indian Islam was a separate nation which could never accept Hindu rule. In March 1940 the Muslim League proclaimed that its goal was now a separate independent Pakistan.

(d) Independence for India and Pakistan

In 1945 the Labour government won power in Britain and decided to test the strength of the parties in India by holding provincial and central elections. These elections demonstrated that, while Congress was the strongest party in Hindu India, the Muslim League had an almost equal hold over the Muslim electorate and could block solutions acceptable to the Congress Party. A third element in the situation was the clear wish of Britain to give India independence as soon as possible. By 1946 British military units had returned home and the government no longer had much physical force at its disposal.

The British government sent a mission to India in April 1946 with the aim of preserving a united India while calming Muslim fears. The Congress, including Gandhi and Nehru, still underestimated the Muslim League and opposed partition, while Jinnah, a man of iron will, would agree to nothing else. Compromise plans, based on a series of federal government bodies and an interim government to draft proposals, were rejected by both sides, and, even if they had been accepted, their implementation would have left central government weak.

The 1946 mission was the point of no return after which partition was inevitable. India now slid into a frightful civil war, in which communal killings were carried out by both Hindus and Muslims. To concentrate the minds of the two sides, the British government announced in February 1947 that power would be handed over no later than June 1948, and that Lord Louis Mountbatten would succeed the previous viceroy, the able but taciturn Wavell, to prepare a plan for the handover. Both sides realised that if no settlement was reached, full-scale civil war would result, and Congress broke with Gandhi in accepting that partition was inevitable. In June 1947 Mountbatten produced a plan for the creation of two states, India and Pakistan, with the handover to take place in August. In the Punjab and Bengal, where communal numbers were nearly equal, there would be division decided on by a boundary commission. Both sides reluctantly agreed to the plan, and Mountbatten, a master of rush tactics, pushed through the final arrangements with great speed, helped by the unaffected concern of his wife, Edwina, for the Indian people. On 14 August India and Pakistan became independent.

From the British point of view, the story ended happily, because

Britain remained on relatively good terms with both new states (to the puzzlement of Russian and American observers). Mountbatten, the last viceroy, stayed on as the first governor-general of independent India, with Nehru as prime minister.

The new government soon faced great strains arising from the boundary divisions. The divisions in the Punjab divided the Sikh community into two almost equal groups, and many Sikhs resented the division. Both Sikhs and Hindus attacked the Muslims in East Punjab and Muslims attacked the Sikhs in the West. Many atrocities were carried out, and a huge exchange of populations occurred. About 5½ million people travelled each way across the new India-Pakistan border in the Punjab. In addition, about 400,000 Hindus migrated from Sind and over half a million moved from East Pakistan to West Bengal.

The communal strife cost Gandhi his life. Having originally opposed partition, he now used his influence to persuade his followers to give up violence against Muslims, and in January 1948 he was shot by a young Hindu fanatic. His death helped to discredit Hindu extremists and strengthened Nehru's position. He was able to tackle the two basic problems of the integration of the Indian states and the drawing up of a constitution. The main flashpoint was Kashmir, a state adjacent to both India and Pakistan, with a Hindu ruler and a Muslim majority. In October 1947 Pathan tribesmen from Pakistan attempted to seize Kashmir. In panic the ruler, who had been prevaricating, now acceded to India, whose airborne troops maintained Indian control of the state, to the permanent embittering of Indian-Pakistan relations.

A new constitution was drawn up and implemented in India from 1950. Though a federal state, central government had many real powers, as it controlled defence and foreign affairs. In addition, the president had powers to override the states' decisions, and it was this strong centre that was to allow Nehru to carry out his development programmes. The constitution had a Western flavour in that it abolished caste distinctions.

(e) India after independence: the era of Nehru

Both new countries were to face difficulties in the transition to independence. India was a mixture of different peoples divided in language and united only in part by religion. The problem of language plagued Indian governments. In 1950 equal status was given to India's fourteen major languages, and English guaranteed as an official language after attempts to impose Hindi produced adverse reactions from the 70 per cent of Indians who could not speak it, especially in the Madras area, where the Tamil language had strong roots. The country, already desperately poor, faced the ever-increasing pressure of population increase on a limited and primitive agriculture. India's population, already 389 millions in 1947, had risen to 751 millions by 1985. The 500 princes were also a barrier to progress.

The years from 1947 to 1964 have a clear unity in Indian history through the premiership of Nehru. Born in a select Hindu Brahmin family, he had been first the disciple and subsequently the favoured lieutenant of Gandhi, so that much of the veneration bestowed on the Mahatma descended on him. Imprisoned by the British, he was the idol of left-wing congressmen and was able to dominate the Congress Party after 1950, becoming regarded as indispensable. His position was supported by a magnetic energetic personality, and his eloquence could move the masses. Even opponents respected his integrity.

Nehru's outlook was that of a democratic socialist. A secular man, he opposed Hindu orthodoxy where it transgressed personal rights, and he wished to make war on poverty and privilege. In foreign affairs he believed in self-governing nationalities and he remained suspicious of European imperialism. Yet one must question how far Nehru really changed India, because his interests were so varied, and his unwillingness to delegate authority so pronounced, that at times conservative interests could undermine his decisions on one subject while his attention was occupied by another. Thus, for example, primary education for the masses expanded slowly, and on Nehru's death in 1970 70 per cent of the population were still illiterate. Nevertheless Nehru did lead India into being Asia's most successful democracy, where universal suffrage to an extent undermined high caste monopoly of office, because no Brahmin could gain election without low caste votes. The attack on privilege extended to the princes.

Nehru's economic policy held back India's development. His socialism, combined with his suspicion of Western firms as representing a new kind of imperialism, led to the construction of a mass of controls which restricted Indian firms and put off foreign firms from investing in India. The absurd situation developed, whereby Indian firms, in a country short of capital investment, preferred to locate new plants in other Asian countries rather than in India.

The programmes nearest Nehru's heart were those relating to welfare and individual rights. To implement India's modernisation and to raise the standard of living, he set up the National Planning Commission in 1950. Its first plan in 1951, which placed emphasis on agricultural production to free India from dependence on overseas suppliers, increased production by 25 per cent in 5 years. A second, more ambitious, plan was launched in 1956 to accelerate Indian industrialisation through development of basic industries. A grave error was committed in neglecting agriculture, for, after a series of poor harvests, India became even more dependent on imported grain, which in turn led to higher taxation, foreign loans and exchange controls.

In his social programme Nehru wished to give his people legal rights. Such aims clashed with traditional Hindu law, in which the group mattered more than the individual. In 1955 a Hindu Succession Act gave women equal rights with men in holding and in succession to property, while the 1956 Hindu Marriage Act gave monogamy a legal basis and provided for divorce, with alimony and maintenance.

Nehru had a free hand over Indian foreign policy and wanted his country to play a real role in international relations. He insisted on India's full independence and was angered by continued Portuguese control of Goa, and in 1961 Indian forces ejected the Portuguese. Nehru remained suspicious of the former imperial powers, and in 1956 he seemed to condemn the British escapade at Suez more severely than the Russian invasion of Hungary.

Three issues preoccupied Nehru in his foreign policy – Pakistan, relations with the great powers and his position in Asia. Relations with Pakistan remained icy, owing to the dispute over Kashmir. Despite Anglo-American pressure to find a compromise, Nehru was adamant that Kashmir should stay part of India. His motives were mixed – the area was a buffer against China and his own prestige was bound up with the affair. Perhaps too he hoped that Muslim Kashmir as part of mainly Hindu India would be in Spear's phrase 'a living witness to secular democracy'. He might also have been afraid that cession of Kashmir to Pakistan would provoke renewed Hindu outrages against the remaining Muslims in India.

In the world at large Nehru's policy was one of non-alignment with great power blocs. He believed that the more states were uncommitted, the more the two power blocs would be careful before going to war. However, his prestige declined in his final years, especially as India's alleged non-alignment was tested by a border quarrel with China in which Indian troops were routed. Despite China's occupation of Tibet in 1949, Nehru attempted to maintain friendly relations, but he failed to follow a consistent policy over the issue of the Sino-Indian border, which had never been clarified in the days of British rule. Tension rose when the Dalai Lama fled to India in 1959. A border dispute flared over the frontier regions of Aksai Chin and Longju on India's north-east border, and Nehru, having previously failed to tackle the problem, was now compelled by Indian public opinion to take the rigid line that India's frontiers were not negotiable. This meant evicting Chinese forces which had occupied the disputed areas, but the Indian armed forces had been starved of funds and could only be supplied by air. Nehru was provocative, and in October 1962 Chinese patience ran out; Chinese troops attacked Indian positions and swept back Indian forces before assuming a ceasefire. Besides tarnishing Nehru's image, the episode ended India's non-alignment, as India asked for and received Western material aid.

Thus Nehru's achievements must be seen as limited. Conservative forces dominated the actual performance of his government, so that his biographer, Michael Edwardes, characterises Congress rule as 'the permanent non-revolution', especially as Nehru was not an efficient administrator and would not delegate. The new Indian democracy too had its limitations. The Congress Party dominated elections, and though other parties such as the Socialists and Communists existed, there was no really credible alternative to Congress. Within the Congress Party itself special interest groups proliferated, and the old spirit of sacrifice vanished as nepotism and corruption increased. In foreign affairs Nehru's adoption of a high moral tone in his lectures to the West was allied with a tendency to give Soviet Russia the benefit of the doubt. At the same time he alleged that Indian foreign policy was non-violent, when in fact his period in office saw clashes with Pakistan, Portugal and China. The net result of his foreign policy was India's growing isolation by the 1960s, especially after the occupation of Goa in 1961, an act which seemed strangely at odds with Nehru's lectures on the righteousness of non-violence.

(e) Contemporary India

Nehru's successor was a very different individual, Lai Bahadur Shastri, a diminutive and conciliatory individual. His short period in office saw two crises – disturbances in Madras when Hindi was proclaimed as the national language, and clashes with Pakistan in the disputed areas of the Rann of Cutch and Kashmir in 1965. Shastri died in January 1966 and the next premier was the formidable Mrs Indira Gandhi, Nehru's daughter, who was born in 1917. Nehru may have deliberatley groomed her as his successor. Certainly he gave her considerable talents full scope by making her a member of the Congress Working Committee in 1955, and by allowing her to accompany him on foreign and domestic tours. In 1958 she was elected president of the Congress, though Nehru hotly denied that he was trying to found a dynasty.

Mrs Gandhi's career as premier was controversial, and some commentators, such as David Selbourne, have seen her actions as nothing short of tyrannical. After winning the 1967 elections, she drove her main rival, Morarji Desai, out of office. Some of the old guard of the party – known as the Syndicate – tried to expel her from the party in 1969, and Congress was split into two parties. The prime minister commanded vast popular support, especially from disadvantaged groups, and in 1971 won an overwhelming victory in the general election.

Mrs Gandhi's position further improved as a result of the Pakistan invasion of East Bengal in March 1971. Ten million refugees poured from East Pakistan into India, creating a situation that for India was unacceptable. Only India's military intervention could ensure that the refugees could or would return home. Therefore in December 1971 the Indian army moved into East Bengal, routed Pakistan forces, and enabled the new state of Bangladesh to come into being. Mrs Gandhi's popularity was now great, and she appeared to have a unique opportunity to implement economic and social reform; but perhaps expectations were now too high and her dictatorial tendencies too pronounced. She did not have a comprehensive economic programme, and the costs of refugee relief and the war were compounded by a severe drought in 1977 and the difficulties caused by the 1973 world energy crisis.

Therefore the years from 1972 to 1975 saw a rise in the tempo of political unrest, with unions and students particular active. In 1975 Mrs Gandhi suffered two major blows: she was found guilty by the High Court of Allahabad of corrupt electoral practices and then her Congress Party lost the Gujarat state elections to her old opponent Desai. In 1975, when opposition leaders mounted a campaign to unseat her, Mrs Gandhi proclaimed a state of emergency, and over 600 political opponents were arrested, including Desai. Rigid press censorship was introduced and various organisations banned. The power of the courts to make judgements on parliamentary issues was reduced and strikes were outlawed.

In trying to cast herself as India's saviour Mrs Gandhi invoked her childhood heroine, Joan of Arc, claiming that she had acted in order to save Indian democracy. A new twenty-point programme promised new reforms, while her son Sanjay brought in a family planning policy through vasectomy as he gained influence in the government as Indira's heir-apparent. Forced sterilisation provoked riots.

In 1977, confident of victory, Mrs Gandhi held a general election in March. A new united Janata front had, however, built up against her. The front was formed out of four parties – the Congress (O), led by Desai; the Jana Sangh, a Hindu nationalist party; the Socialist Party; and the Bharatiya Lok Dal (BLD), whose support came from the prosperous agricultural classes of Northern India. The elections saw a stunning defeat for Mrs Gandhi, and the austere, puritanical Desai became prime minister at the age of 81.

Janata was from the beginning badly divided and lacking in any coherent policy. The premier's obsession with the prohibition of alcohol was unpopular, and his government made errors in its treatment of Mrs Gandhi. The Congress Party in opposition had split in January 1978 and the Congress (I) Party was formed (I for Indira). She now faced charges of misconduct and abuse of authority, and for these she was jailed. She now assumed a mantle of martyrdom, and by January 1980 the Janita government had fallen apart as a result of internal quarrels. The consequent elections led to the Congress (I) Party winning 351 out of 535 seats, as Mrs Gandhi exploited the lack of law and order in the two previous years.

Mrs Gandhi suffered a bad personal blow later in the year when her son Sanjay was killed in an air crash, but it was no loss politically, as he had gained a reputation for high-handedness. Mrs Gandhi continued to rule supreme until 1984, when traditional religious problems led to her death.

Under the 1968 Official Languages Amendment Act the proposed replacement of English by Hindi had been postponed. English remained as the language of parliamentary debates and had equal status with Hindi in official business. Secondary schools were encouraged to teach three languages, two of which were to be Hindi and English, but this clause was rejected by Tamil and Urdu speakers and others.

This linguistic nationalism was connected with religion, for it was Muslims who rallied behind the defence of Urdu. A second religious group, the Sikh nationalist movement, developed, largely in the Punjab, where Sikhs formed 60 per cent of the population. The Sikhs asserted that the Punjab should become an independent state – Khalistan or Land of the Pure. In October 1984, after violence in Amritsar had led to the storming of the Sikhs' holiest shrine, the Golden Temple, by government forces, Mrs Gandhi was assassinated by Sikh members of her bodyguard, and her son Rajiv took over power.

Mrs Gandhi's achievements are debatable, and her highly personalised autocratic style hindered the development of Indian democracy. Internal debate even within the Congress (I) Party itself had been stifled. Since her death, Rajiv has continued to face a host of problems, including the Tamil problem in Sri Lanka. Sikh unrest has continued and Hindu–Muslim riots in 1987 showed that old antagonisms die hard. So do old traditions; in 1987 an 18-year-old girl committee suttee, and the government ran into much opposition when it prevented her suicide being celebrated.

Yet all has not been gloom. India has achieved a 'green revolution' in recent years, improving agriculture so successfully that she is now almost self-sufficient. Since 1984 Rajiv has removed many of the stifling central government controls over industry in order to give it freedom to restructure and become more competitive.

(g) Pakistan since 1947

The state of Pakistan began with many disadvantages. It seemed an artificial creation – two large areas of land separated by an even larger area of India – and made even less plausible by ethnic and linguistic differences between the inhabitants of east and west. Visionary leadership was needed for this desperately poor country, but the man most likely to have given it, Jinnah, died in 1948.

From the first, linguistic tensions were severe. Jinnah had advocated that Urdu should be the official language. Though in West Pakistan only 4 per cent spoke Urdu compared to 66 per cent Punjabi, Urdu was the language of the army of the Moghul Empire and was the second language of the educated élite. The suggestion angered the people of East Bengal, where more than half of Pakistan's population lived and where the predominant language was Bengali. When Bengali was recognised as an official language in 1954, the issue provoked demonstrations in the West Pakistan city of Karachi. Thus from the early days the unity of the two Pakistans was in doubt.

Stable constitutional government was also difficult to attain. A constitution was adopted in 1956, but in 1958 Field Marshal Ayub Khan carried out a coup d'état and remained in power until 1969.

Two factors now split Pakistan. Ali Bhutto led the People's Party, which wanted a more democratic socialist state, but by far the greater problem was Pakistan's physical division. East Pakistan, with its Bengali population, had suffered from the 1947 partition through the loss of much of its former élite and industry. Its population was even by Asian standards impoverished. It was West Pakistan which provided the political élite and had benefited from recent industrialisation. Thus the gap in per capita incomes between East and West widened in the 1960s.

As a reaction to this political and economic inferiority, the Awami League was founded in 1949 as the main opposition party in East Bengal. In 1966 its leader, Mujib-ur-Rahman, demanded that East Pakistan should be independent on internal matters, with central government controlling only defence and foreign affairs. When Ayub's successor, Yahya Khan, restored real elections in December 1970, the Awami League won all but two seats in the East and had a majority in the whole of Pakistan.

Civil war now broke out. Yahya postponed the meeting of the National Assembly, a move that provoked guerrilla activity by the East Pakistan guerrilla group the Mukti Bahim. Yahya's decision to send in troops to East Pakistan to restore order led to a flood of refugees and the intervention of the Indian army. By December 1971 Pakistan's force had been defeated and a new sovereign state, Bangladesh, came into being under Mujib. The new state was plagued with civil war and famine. Mujib's attempts to create a strict Muslim state led to his murder by the army in 1975, and in 1977 Zia-ur Rahman established a military dictatorship.

Pakistan's problems continued. Ali Bhutto asserted that he was going to drag Pakistan into the twentieth century by its beard, and he brought in a number of socialist reforms, including nationalisation of banks, transport and industry. Unfortunately he offended two important élites – the mullahs, and the army, which resented his purge of over 1,000 right-wing officers. After winning the 1977 elections, Bhutto was accused of corruption and replaced by General Zia ul-Haq in a bloodless coup. Bhutto had been Zia's patron, but, despite this, the former premier was hanged in 1979. Behind an almost Terry-Thomas exterior Zia was a ruthless leader determined to make Pakistan a fully theocratic state in which Muslim practices would reign supreme. Alcohol was banned and Islamic punishments restored.

Opposition to Zia was focused on Benazir Bhutto, daughter of the hanged premier, and the People's Party. However, the Soviet invasion of Afghanistan in 1981 rehabilitated Zia, and he now gained American friendship and aid as his country became a base for Afghan opponents of the Russian-backed Kabul regime. Zia himself showed some flexibility in agreeing to restore elections, a concession that won over Benazir Bhutto to working within the system for the next elections. In August 1988 Zia was killed in an air crash, and Pakistan entered on a new period of uncertainty when Benazir Bhutto gained power in the subsequent elections.

FURTHER READING

Copley, A., *Gandhi*, Basil Blackwell, London, 1987

Edwardes, M., *Nehru*, Penguin, Harmondsworth, 1971

Hardgrave, R. L., *India: Government and Politics in a Developing Nation*, Harcourt, New York, 1980

Kulke, H. and Rothermund, D., *A History of India*, Routledge, London, 1986

Seal, A., *The Emergence of Indian Nationalism*, CUP, Cambridge, 1968

Selbourne, D., *An Eye to India: The Unmasking of a Tyranny*, Penguin, Harmondsworth, 1977

Spear, P., *A History of India*, Volume 2, Penguin, Harmondsworth, 1975

QUESTIONS

1. Why did a strong nationalist movement develop in India by 1919?
2. Critically analyse the ideas and political methods of Gandhi.
3. Examine the reasons for the growth of the Pakistan movement by 1940.

4. Compare and contrast the contributions of Nehru and Indira Gandhi to the consolidation of post-independence India.
5. In what ways does the experience of India and Pakistan illustrate the problems facing Third World countries moving to independence?

17
The United States of America since 1945

(a) Harry S. Truman and recovery

The death of Roosevelt in April 1945 was a shock to the world. American soldiers wept like children and the American poor lamented his passing. His services in peace and war had been gigantic. He had given his country a modern governmental structure, taught it to face up to its international responsibilities and led it to victory. If he had his faults and committed blunders in diplomacy, his achievements far outweighed his limitations.

His vice-president, Harry S. Truman, now took the oath of office as president. He was experienced in Missouri politics and had enjoyed two terms in the Senate. If at first, in the words of Morison, Commager and Leuchtenburg, he seemed 'the very epitome of the average small-town American', he grew in office. Though at times he was over-impulsive, he possessed virtues of decisiveness and courage. His domestic record was not as impressive as Roosevelt's, but more so than Eisenhower's, and no president did so much to shape American foreign policy. He had to lead his country in the final months of war and guide it through the difficult transition years of the Cold War.

Truman's good fortune lay in the continuation of the wartime prosperity. Unlike the aftermath of the First World War, full employment was maintained, with an impressive rise in real wages. Even the farmers enjoyed unprecedented prosperity as a result of increased foreign and domestic demand and government subsidies. The renewed economic growth was caused by the vast domestic demand for consumer and durable goods, by demand from abroad for American products, especially from Europe, funded by Marshall Aid, and by Federal government spending, which reached $40 billions in 1950 compared to $9 billions in 1932. Truman did, however, fail to control inflation, and this factor contributed to Republican victory in the 1946 Congressional elections. New Republican faces included Joseph McCarthy and Richard Nixon.

The Republicans now had an opportunity to demonstrate that they were moderates, not reactionaries, but the new Congress cut funds for public works projects, and its only significant piece of legislation was the 1947 Taft–Hartley Act, which severely regulated trade unions in outlawing the closed shop and secondary picketing. Truman tried to veto the bill but Congress reenacted it. The defeat was beneficial for the president, as the new legislation drove back organised labour into supporting the Democrats more vigorously.

The Republicans made another error in blocking civil rights reform. A number of racial murders in the South persuaded Truman to appoint a Committee of Civil Rights. Its report suggested that there should be a permanent Civil Rights Commission, a Federal Fair Employment Practices Act and laws to prevent lynching and to protect the negro's right to vote. Truman faced vehement opposition to such proposals, both from the Republican majority and many of his own Southern Democrats.

Truman's prospects in the 1948 presidential and congressional elections seemed poor indeed. Democratic support fell away, as did supporters of Henry Wallace, who disliked what he regarded as Truman's hard-line attitude to the Soviet Union. But the Republican candidate, Thomas E. Dewey, ran a bland campaign, while Truman showed vigour in condemning the sterile performance of the Republican Congress. Consequently he scored the biggest political upset of the century, winning the votes of workers, negroes and farmers. The Democrats recaptured control of both Houses of Congress.

Truman, inaugurated in January 1949 for his first full term, promised a Fair Deal for the American people. The Fair Deal had its successes, with the new Congress enacting more liberal legislation than any since 1938. It increased social security benefits and extended their coverage to 10 million more people. Public works programmes, especially soil conservation and public housing, were increased. Most of this legislation represented only extensions of the New Deal, and Truman had less success when he tried to break new ground. For example, Congress blocked his proposals for national health insurance, federal aid to education and extensions of the TVA approach to the Columbia and Missouri rivers.

The reasons for this failure were several. The obsession with the dangers of communism distracted attention away from reform, and the president faced powerful opposition in Congress. But to some extent Truman himself must carry some of the blame. Although genuinely interested in achieving change, he never could arouse the kind of popular enthusiasm for his reforms that Roosevelt had. Nor had he the patience to cultivate support in Congress.

Truman's final period in office was dogged by the perversion of McCarthyism. American public opinion is on occasions prone to bursts of hysterical emotion. As de Tocqueville saw in the nineteenth century, the tyranny of the majority was to be one of the great problems of democracy when that majority seeks to impose a set of views on those who are less conformist, be they members of ethnic minorities or communists. Genuine individualism has been more difficult to maintain in America than in Britain in view of what Allen calls 'the American pack instinct'. Even before the coming of the Cold War, there was suspicion that communists had infiltrated American public life and aimed at destroying freedom. As early as 1938 the House had established the House Un-American Activities Committee (HUAC), and though its powers were never defined, it sought to root out radical and communist subversion. Then in 1949 the Soviet Union exploded its first atomic bomb and the Chinese communists drove the Nationalists out of China. The end of the American atomic monopoly and the loss of American influence in China were assumed by many average Americans to be the result of treachery in the State Department.

The Republicans saw a heaven-sent opportunity to embarrass the Truman administration when the Hiss case seemed to support this fantastic conclusion. In August 1948 *Time* magazine accused Alger Hiss, a State Department official, of having been a communist and in December asserted that he was a spy as well. Hiss was convicted in January 1950 for perjury, the Court alleging that he had denied under oath before HUAC that he had once been a Russian agent. Unfortunately his presence in a minor capacity at Yalta seemed to confirm his guilt.

Hiss was a severe embarrassment to the Democrats, as he had been close to Dean Acheson, who was now Secretary of State and to his credit would not disavow him. The situation was made for demagogues, and in February 1950 Senator Joseph McCarthy announced that he had a list of 205 communists known to the Secretary of State who were still working in the State Department. Mainstream American politics had always had its element of the demagogic, but McCarthy was a particularly able scoundrel whose instinctive cunning told him how to win influence by manipulating the worst prejudices of his fellow countrymen. His constitutional power came from his use of congressional committees, which have powers of subpoena and interrogation while not being subject to the same strict rules of evidence or codes of procedure as a law court. While this can on occasions help incisive probes into matters of public concern, in the wrong hands such committees can abuse the rights of individuals. McCarthy was a liar on a truly awesome scale who was supported in his wild charges by Republican colleagues.

Out of the panic aroused by McCarthy came the McCarran–Nixon Internal Security Act of 1950, which required all communist organisations to register with the attorney-general, excluded communists from employment in defence plants and prevented communists from holding passports.

In calling the episode as squalid as any in American history, Hugh Brogan asserts that it bred a threefold evil. It certainly affected foreign opinion in that such witchhunts were a gift to Soviet propaganda and offended public opinion in Europe. Secondly it created what David Caute has called 'the great fear' in the minds of American citizens, many of whom were investigated by HUAC, especially journalists, academics and members of Hollywood. Such people were publicly bullied, their right to hold nonconformist opinions condemned, and their own associates questioned by a permanent government committee which ignored their actual conduct.

The worst, because longest-lasting, consequence of McCarthyism was its impact on government. The anti-communist frenzy discredited all moderate progressive influences in government, especially in the State Department. The advice of professional diplomats was ignored, policy was more and more made under the influence of lobbyists and by the end of the 1950s the USA was committed to propping up weak and worthless regimes in Latin America, Asia and the Middle East simply because they were anti-communist. A great reservoir of opposition to liberal reforms, from negro rights to federal-aided education, was created.

By 1952 Americans were ready to listen to the Republican contention that it was time for a change after 20 years of Democratic administration whose only recent success was the creation of NATO. Against this the Korean War had reached a stalemate, and Truman himself incurred unpopularity by his dismissal of MacArthur in 1951. He decided not to run for re-election, and Adlai Stevenson, a liberal of charm and eloquence, became the Democratic candidate. The Republicans had as their trump card General Dwight D. Eisenhower, Supreme Commander of NATO, who was much admired by Americans, especially when he promised to go to Korea personally to end the war. The elections of November 1952 saw him win 55 per cent of the popular vote and capture thirty-nine states to Stevenson's nine.

(b) The Eisenhower years, 1952–60

Eisenhower was 62 years old in 1952, a self-made man who had risen in army service since 1915 before becoming Supreme Commander of Allied Forces in Europe during the war. He had qualitites of honesty, a talent for mediation and the ability to inspire loyalty among associates. He believed that government had become too pervasive, and hoped to check its growing activity. Until recently it was believed that he was impatient of detail and left much to such subordinates as his special assistant, Sherman Adams. Those who hoped that he would lead the nation in new ventures, such as Walter Lippmann were to be disappointed, but probably most Americans wanted him to give the country a respite from political stress after a generation of unrelieved crisis.

Eisenhower's two favourite phrases were 'middle of the road' and 'dynamic conservatism', but to his critics his administration was more conservative than dynamic. Six of his first cabinet were businessmen, including secretary of defence Charles E. Wilson, who, as head of General Motors, achieved a kind of immortality when he stated that 'what was good for our country was good for General Motors and vice-versa'. Private enterprise was favoured by the new administration. Federal control of underseas oil reserves were turned over to seaboard states, and new atomic energy plants were farmed out to private corporations. The resources of the TVA, which Eisenhower cited as creeping socialism, were cut from $185 millions to $12 millions between 1952 and 1960. However, the administration increased spending on farm subsidies sixfold in these years, carried out a $33 billion road-building programme and made some improvements in social security and education, sufficient to merit the term 'middle of the road'.

The administration's record over McCarthy was inglorious. Eisenhower avoided criticising him before the election, nor did he act boldly against him once in power, explaining privately that 'I just will not – I refuse – to get into the gutter with that guy.' McCarthy was left free to intensify his persecution of the State Department, and even dared to launch a new campaign against the army. Luckily for Eisenhower, McCarthy had now overreached himself, and in December 1954 the senate censured him for improper conduct after he had been seen on television bullying army officers and officials. His power was now broken and he died in obscurity in 1957.

Though the Eisenhower years seemed ones of comfortable lethargy in one area, a revolution – that of civil rights – was beginning to take place. Negroes were second-class citizens in the South, fobbed off with inferior segregated schools and denied entrance to the state universities, which they helped to support by taxation. Segregation applied to many other areas of life – transport, places of entertainment, restaurants and even some churches. Their right to vote was flouted by various devices, and, with no right to be members of juries, they usually found fair trials impossible to obtain. They were mostly confined to being tenant farmers or farm labourers. In the North urban negroes met discrimination over jobs and were confined to slum dwellings in black ghettoes despite Roosevelt's measures. The experience of segregation in the armed forces during the war antagonised Northern blacks, and Truman ended this by 1950.

Ironically Eisenhower's road-building programme was one of several factors moving negroes from South to North, where their numbers increased from 2.8 million to 7.2 million between 1940 and 1960. Some cities now had black majorities, and negroes became a force to be reckoned with. The issue also disturbed the conscience of many Americans in a period which had witnessed Nazi racism and the liberation of coloured peoples in the European colonies. Therefore, though most white Americans wanted white supremacy, it was embarrassing to maintain a policy that made a dark skin a badge of inferiority.

Slowly the Supreme Court began chipping away at some of the worst features of discrimination. Negroes were allowed on juries and in 1954 Chief Justice Earl Warren of the Supreme Court reversed a Court decision of 1896 which allowed segregated education, holding that 'segregated educational facilities are inherently unequal'. In 1955 the Supreme Court followed up this ruling with another, which required the Southern states to proceed with desegregation 'with all deliberate speed'. In border states progress was rapid but in the Deep South states such as Georgia segregationists sought to prevent implementation of the Court's ruling. When legal obstruction failed, more violent methods were used; the Klu Klux Clan enjoyed a revival and White Citizens' Councils were formed as pressure groups designed to whip up opposition to fever pitch and push state legislatures into throwing up a barricade of new regulations designed to impede integration. Office-holders who did not comply faced the prospect of losing votes in the next election. North Carolina was a typical example of such obstructionism; the state government there withheld school funds from any school district which integrated its public schools. When such methods failed, intimidation was used; in February 1956 Autherine Lucy became the first negro to register at the University of Alabama, but a howling mob drove her from the campus.

In Little Rock, Arkansas, Governor Orval Faubus called out the National Guard in 1957 to deny negro children their right to attend integrated schools, and when the Federal district judge ordered their withdrawal, a mob prevented negro students from attending school. Eisenhower, who had so far chickened out of backing the Supreme Court, had to meet this act of defiance, and he sent Federal troops to protect negro children. In other respects he rather lost the opportunity to use his prestige to educate his people on civil rights. The Deep South states continued to obstruct, and in 1963 only 9 per cent of the South's bi-racial schools had been desegregated, and in the Deep South the percentage was much less.

The real spark for the civil rights revolution came from the negroes themselves. The National Association for the Advancement of Coloured People, a partnership of blacks and whites, developed strategy under the astute leadership of Roy Wilkins. Brave negroes had to face ugly mobs and the taunts of fellow students. The most important development came from the rise to national leadership of a Baptist minister, the Reverend Martin Luther King, who developed a successful Gandhi-like technique of non-violence to end segregation on the buses in Montgomery, Alabama, despite his house being bombed and his suffering arrest thirty times in his career. King was a remarkable prophet, who perceived how to use Gandhi's techniques and dramatise the civil rights doctrine for millions.

The prosperity of the 1950s, combined with Eisenhower's record of ending the Korean War and keeping the peace, ensured his victory in the 1956 presidential elections over Stevenson. His second term in office saw more trouble than the first; unemployment soared to the highest rate since 1941, the civil rights issue became more pressing and his administration was seen to have corrupt elements when Sherman Adams had to resign as a result of his dealings with an industrial promoter. American foreign policy faced reversals on every continent, culminating in 1959 with Castro's victory in Cuba, the first time the Soviet Union had gained an ally in the Western hemisphere.

Eisenhower never risked his personal popularity by intervening on controversial issues, and problems like welfare and civil rights were neglected. Stevenson attacked the lack of public sector spending, protesting that the USA had become a society characterised by 'public squalor and private affluence'. The richest country in the world had neglected its education, hospitals, housing and negroes. Stephen Ambrose, in a recent biography of Eisenhower, asserts that 'on one of the great moral issues of the day, the struggle to eliminate racial segregation from American life, he provided almost no leadership at all'. Yet Ambrose also defends Eisenhower's record seeing him as a hardworking dignified president who was fully in control of American policy. He presided over 8 years of prosperity and refused to dismantle New Deal policies. His greatest success was in foreign policy; he won peace in Korea and refused to spend extra on armaments or extend American commitments in new areas. In managing crises, such as Indo-China or Suez, he put up a magnificent performance, and perhaps, given the record of his successors, historians are now seeing his presidency in a better light.

(c) John F. Kennedy and the New Frontier, 1961–3

All that Republicanism could offer after Eisenhower in the 1960 presidential elections was his vice-president, Richard Nixon, whose one certain talent was a sort of deodorised McCarthyism. He lacked Eisenhower's authority or charm, and a Democrat joke of the period was a picture of Nixon looking shifty, with the caption 'Would you buy a used car from this man?' The Democrats fielded John F. Kennedy, who had much more appeal than Nixon and a good war record. But he was a Roman Catholic (which lost him support in Protestant rural areas) and, unlike Nixon, lacked experience in government. Consequently he needed to run a good campaign and he did. He stressed the themes of sacrifice and boldness, referring to a New Frontier, the frontier of the 1960s and outpointed his Republican rival when Nixon made the error of agreeing to television debates. The result was a Democrat victory, though the closest contest since Harrison's in 1888.

Kennedy set a new style in American government; his administration was notable for its youth and included his 35-year-old brother Robert. The White House now welcomed intellectuals and artists, and dinners there supervised by the president's wife Jacqueline, a member of the Newport aristocracy, were gracious affairs.

Much of the president's short time in office was absorbed by foreign crises. Despite his dislike of the Cold War rhetoric of Eisenhower's Secretary of State, J. F. Dulles, Kennedy sought to advance American interests and on occasions carried brinkmanship further than Dulles had dared, as the Cuban missile crisis demonstrated. The USA had given the Cuban dictator Batista millions of dollars in aid since he had come to power in 1933, but a combination of economic stagnation, the gangsterism of the regime, the loss of American aid and a crumbling support base caused his fall in January 1959. The new Cuban regime was led by Fidel Castro, who radicalised the revolution between 1959 and 1961, bringing in agrarian reform and confiscating the wealth of the Cuban rich and foreigners.

Kennedy, like most Americans, was affronted by what appeared to be a Russian satellite in America's backyard. He gave reluctant approval to a scheme planned from the spring of 1960 by the Central Intelligency Agency (CIA) to arm and train anti-Casto Cuban exiles with the aim of overthrowing the Castro regime, which was seen as a centre of subversion throughout Latin America. In April 1961 the invaders landed at the Bahia de Cochinos (Bay of Pigs) in Cuba, but were quickly overwhelmed by Castro's forces.

The fiasco damaged the prestige of the Kennedy administration and helped to convince Kruschev that the young president was a man who crumpled under pressure. In August 1961 the Berlin Wall was built and in August 1962 came the Cuban missile crisis, which brought the world to the brink of nuclear war. Throughout the summer of 1962 Soviet Russia had been supplying its new Cuban ally with armaments, but while there was no evidence that these shipments included offensive missiles, Kennedy stayed his hand. On 16 October, however, a U2 plane spotted Russian medium-range missiles in place in Cuba, with Russian ships carrying launching pads for the missiles on their way to Cuba.

Kennedy responded with both determination and restraint. On 22 October he imposed a quarantine on arms shipments to Cuba and issued orders to intercept Russian vessels headed for the island. He warned Kruschev that a nuclear attack by Cuba on any nation in the Western hemisphere would require 'a full retaliatory response on the Soviet Union'. Yet at the same time he rejected advice from the military to order an air strike on Cuba lest this might lead to general war. His firm stand prevailed; the Russian ships carrying the launch pads turned back and after a time the Cuban missile bases were dismantled. Kennedy had won the war of nerves with Kruschev.

The worst feature of Kennedy's foreign policy was his increase of American intervention in Vietnam by sending military advisers, the Green Berets, to support the Diem government in South Vietnam. In November 1963 the American contingent there was still small, but, in Morison's words, Kennedy had 'planted the grapes of wrath which the next administration would nurture and harvest'.

Yet there was a much more constructive side to Kennedy's foreign policy. He hoped for a new era of international cooperation and expanded American aid to the Third World. When the Congo operation threatened the UN with bankruptcy, the president persuaded Congress to buy $100 millions of UN bonds. He recognised that the Soviet Union should not be seen as America's permanent enemy and made consistent efforts to implement detente. In July 1963 the USA, Britain and Russia signed a pact banning atmospheric and underwater testing of nuclear devices. It was a small step but was the first time that the powers had reached any agreement on nuclear weapons. The two superpowers also agreed to the installation of a hot line which would connect the Kremlin to the White House by telephone in the event of a crisis threatening nuclear war.

Kennedy's New Frontier hopes were not easy to fulfil. In Congress he faced a conservative coalition of Northern Republicans and Southern Democrats which blocked some of his welfare reforms, such as medical care for the aged. Improvements were made in raising the minimum wage, worker retraining and pollution control. Modest measures, such as easier credit and increased military and road spending, helped lift the economy out of a depression, as did tax cuts.

Kennedy attached no particular urgency to the civil rights question, moving rather cautiously on the issue for fear of antagonising Southern Democrats, who might oppose the rest of his programme. Negroes were appointed to high office, especially by his brother Robert, who was attorney-general. Robert Kennedy also acted vigorously against Alabama mobs who mauled 'freedom riders' travelling through the South to challenge segregation on buses. The attorney general sent hundreds of Federal marshals to Alabama, and ordered the desegregation of interstate buses. The Kennedy administration also acted strongly to enforce the admission of a negro airforce veteran, James H. Meredith, to the University of Mississippi by using troops to oppose a howling mob.

But for civil rights leaders Kennedy was moving too slowly. They wanted action in such other areas of severe discrimination as housing and jobs. King declared, 'We're through with tokenism and gradualism and see-how-far-you've-comeism. We're through with we've-done-more-for-your-people-than-anyone-elseism. We can't wait any longer. Now is the time.' The summer of 1963 witnessed major demonstrations, which won some desegregation in hotels, universities and leisure areas, such as swimming pools. The last state to submit on education was Alabama, under its governor George C. Wallace.

Kennedy was forced to change his priorities, and called for more far-reaching legislation to curb discrimination, but Congress delayed a comprehensive civil rights bill as a rising tide of violence spread across America. Several ugly, racially motivated murders took place, a bomb in a Birmingham church killing four negro girls.

On 22 November 1963 Kennedy visited Dallas, a centre of white opposition to progress on civil rights, and was murdered by Lee Harvey Oswald. His death caused grief and despair throughout the world because he had charmed millions and seemed to be ushering in a new age of development in American life. His actual achievements were relatively small because he was not given the time to fulfil his plans, despite promise of greatness. His admirers, such as Arthur Schlesinger, disagree, stressing that he accomplished much by raising new hopes over nuclear agreements, concern for poverty and emancipation of the negro. Nevertheless, as time has passed, Kennedy's personal faults have come to the fore. Even Macmillan, who developed a deep affection for the young president, excoriated Kennedy for 'spending half his time thinking about adultery, the other half about second-hand ideas passed on by his advisers'.

(d) Lyndon B. Johnson and the Great Society, 1963–8

On Kennedy's death his vice-president, Lyndon B. Johnson, a man of a very different stamp, became president. This self-made Texan was irascible and egocentric, lacked Kennedy's patrician grace but radiated a desire for power. Perhaps this contrast, combined with understandable nostalgia for Kennedy, led to some underestimation of Johnson's achievements; he was in fact an adroit politician who broke up the logjam on Kennedy's legislation and actually implemented it.

Within months he had persuaded Congress to vote money for college construction, which, combined with tax cuts, helped to expand the economy. He urged Congress to enact the civil rights bill as a memorial to Kennedy, and, with the help of Hubert Humphrey and such progressive Republicans as Everett Dirksen, he broke the Southern filibustering in the Senate which had been preventing the passing of the bill. The Civil Rights Act of 1964 prohibited discrimination in places of public accommodation, authorised the Attorney-General to bring suits to speed up desegregation, set up an Equal Opportunity Commission to attack job discrimination and empowered Federal agencies to withhold funds from state-administered programmes that discriminated against negroes.

Johnson brought in ideas of his own, including a war on poverty in the United States. In 1964 he emphasised that he wanted to improve the quality of American life in order to achieve a 'Great Society', which he described as 'a place where the city of man serves not only the needs of the body and the demands of commerce but the desire for beauty and the hunger for community'.

In the 1964 presidential elections the Republican candidate, Barry Goldwater, opposed the Democrat's economic and social policies and the detente with Russia. 'Extremism in the defence of liberty is no vice,' he told the Republican convention, but his militant foreign policy, especially his wish to enlarge the Vietnam war, gave Johnson the chance to pose as the peace candidate, and he won 61 per cent of the vote, the biggest majority in American history, while the Congressional elections gave the Democrats their biggest majority since the 1930s.

Johnson now had a mandate to bring in a succession of measures. Medicare provided medical care for the aged under the social security system. Federal aid for education was brought in, and a Department of Housing and Urban Development created. Aid was found for the arts and medical care for the poor, but the most important step concerned negro voting rights.

The Voting Rights Act of 1965 resulted from demonstrations organised by King against the obstacles to voting faced by negroes. For example, in Dallas County, Alabama, where negroes of voting age outnumbered whites, there were twenty-eight whites registered for every negro. Johnson supported a massive civil rights march from Selma to Montgomery in Alabama, and approved a new law which enacted that in districts where 50 per cent or more of the voting age population was unregistered, Federal examiners would enrol voters. The Act was enforced in the next few years, and 150,000 negroes in the Deep South states were registered. Now more negroes could make successful bids for public office, and in 1967 Thurgood Marshall was appointed to the Supreme Court by Johnson, the first negro elevated to that office.

What checked this impressive advance was Johnson sliding into the quagmire of Vietnam (see Chapter 15), which undermined his whole administration. The confusing and contradictory statements issued by his government created a credibility gap between the president and the nation. His critics ridiculed his analogies with Munich and the domino theory. The corrupt and repressive regime in South Vietnam made a mockery of Washington's claim that it was defending democracy, and Vietnam so obsessed Johnson that relations with Europe and the Third World (which disliked the bombing of non-white populations) were neglected and deteriorated. The administration refused to listen to its critics, who escalated their activity on the campuses and elsewhere. Dr Benjamin Spock and others were convicted of encouraging draft resistance.

The Vietnam war drained money and energy away from domestic issues and halted the most promising reform movement in a generation. By 1966 the government was spending more on Vietnam than on the entire welfare programme. The cost of the war – $30 billions a year – overheated the economy and pushed up taxes and interest rates. Funds for the Great Society projects were cut.

In March 1968 Johnson announced that he would not seek a second term as president. By then the Tet offensive in Vietnam had cruelly exposed the delusions of his policy, and the USA was a more divided nation, in which violence was increasing. Despite the Voting Rights Act bloody race riots became frequent between 1965 and 1968. In August 1965 the worst riot in the nation's history in the Watts Community of Los Angeles left thirty-four dead. A new black militancy evolved in the Black Muslim movement and other black organisations, alienated by the continuation of poor urban conditions and the hostility of the police. Martin Luther King worked hard to maintain non-violence, but in April 1968 he was murdered in Memphis by an escaped white convict, James Earl Ray.

King's death resulted in a wave of riots in a hundred cities, and only Robert Kennedy had the confidence of both races. He was campaigning to be the Democratic candidate in the November 1968 elections and was beginning to win the necessary support when in June he was murdered at the age of 42 by a Jordanian, Sirhan Sirhan, who resented Kennedy's support of Israel. The Democratic candidacy went to Hubert Humphrey, a hard-liner on Vietnam, rather than to the more reform-minded George McGovern or Eugene McCarthy. In the presidential elections the Republican Richard Nixon was able to gain a narrow victory over Humphrey.

(2) Nixon and Watergate

Nixon was a seasoned politician who had an opportunity to end an unpopular war, but he lacked insight and imagination and allowed the Vietnam war to expand. He was an introspective and morally shallow individual. Coming from a poor Quaker family, he brought to his duties as president a festering rancour; he had been poor and never ceased to envy the rich. Beaten by Kennedy in 1960, he was obsessed by the dead hero's memory. He had a reputation as a loser after several electoral defeats, which he blamed on a hostile press, and he was determined to hang on to power now it had at last been won.

In foreign affairs Nixon had his successes, with the help of one of the most intellectual and energetic diplomats of modern times, Henry Kissinger. Unemotional and uninterested in ideology, Kissinger was a believer in the balance of power, and stressed the need for good relations with China to offset the Soviet threat. Accordingly the Americans gave up opposition to China's entry into the United Nations and in 1972 Nixon visited Peking. Peace was reached over Vietnam in January 1973, if not peace with honour as Nixon claimed.

At home too Nixon's first term appeared successful. He followed what his adviser Daniel Moynihan called 'a policy of benign neglect' on the civil rights issue – in effect, indifference. He inherited some of the benefits of the work of previous administrations as schools were desegregated and welfare spending increased. The violence in American cities quietened down and the relative domestic calm, allied to his international successes, ensured Nixon's victory in the 1972 presidential elections over McGovern.

Now Nixon no longer acted like a man of the centre but moved sharply to the right. Obsessed with the notion that most politicians, journalists, civil servants and lawyers were his bitter enemies, he built up a Praetorian Guard of aides who were absolutely loyal to him – men such as Harry R. Haldeman and John Erlichman – and increasingly tried to ignore Congress.

It was a public concern over abuse of power that became the chief theme of Nixon's second administration. The first occasion was in the spring of 1973, when his vice-president, Spiro Agnew, faced with the charge of accepting bribes while Governor of Maryland, had to resign. In his place Nixon appointed the dull but honest Gerald Ford.

This was merely the curtain-raiser for an issue which by 1973 was beginning to monopolise public attention – the Watergate Affair. The starting point of this extraordinary event was the Supreme Court decision of 1971 that the government could not prevent publication of the Pentagon Papers, a detailed and frank examination of Vietnam policy which a Pentagon (Defence Department) expert, Daniel Ellsberg, leaked to the press. The decision confirmed in the mind of Nixon and his advisers the belief that liberals in the Democratic Party were their worst enemies, and might one day make public more secrets of the Nixon administration. Therefore 'plumbers' had to stop such leaks of information and use any manner of dirty tricks to discredit the opposition. Chief of the plumbers were Gordon Liddy and Howard Hunt, who even burgled the office of Ellsberg's psychiatrist in a vain attempt to find incriminating evidence. In June 1972 they broke into the offices of the Democratic National Committee in the Watergate building in Washington, hoping to bug the telephones. They were detected by security guards and later arrested, along with other plumbers.

Nixon denied having any knowledge of these activities, despite the fact that Liddy, Hunt and others were employees of his own Committee to Re-elect the President (CREEP). However, two young *Washington Post* reporters began to investigate the affair, and when the plumbers came up for sentence for burglary in January 1973, the judge indicated that he suspected a cover-up and that unless somebody talked the sentences would be heavy. This cracked the nerves of most defendants, and they began to make confessions sufficient to warrant the Senate setting up a special committee to investigate Watergate. The dirty tricks campaign came to light, as did the revelation that a number of Nixon's closest advisers had been paying 'hush money' to cover up the Watergate scandal.

Nixon began a long rearguard action in which he sought to avoid any culpability, but the Senate investigation ground on remorselessly, and a number of his advisers decided that the game was lost and confessed to having taken part in a conspiracy to bug the Democratic Party headquarters and to cover up the facts. In addition to Ehrlichman and Haldeman, Nixon's counsel, John W. Dean, and the acting director of the FBI, Patrick Gray, were implicated. Equally startling was the discovery that Nixon had been tape-recording the discussions and telephone conversations of his own Cabinet and their advisers.

These tapes spelled Nixon's doom. His reputation had already been tarnished by the discovery that he owed $500,000 in back tax. Now he faced the question that, if he was innocent, he could prove it by handing over the tapes. This in the end Nixon was forced to do, but only after some portions of the tapes had been erased. Even so, the transcripts of the tapes shocked the country by exposing both Nixon's indifference to the best interests of the nation and also his crude language. He was now faced with the threat of impeachment on the grounds that he had betrayed his oath of office in three ways – by lying, by obstructing justice and by manipulating the Internal Revenue Service and other agencies to breach the constitutional rights of citizens. Nixon preferred to resign in August 1974.

(f) Contemporary America, 1974–88

Nixon's replacement, Gerald Ford, won some reservoir of goodwill through his transparent honesty, but his lack of grip over economic issues worried Americans, who thought he was a decent man, but, in the terms of one opinion poll, 'not very smart about the issues the country is facing'. Consequently the 1976 elections saw victory go, though narrowly, to the Democratic candidate James Earl Carter.

As a born-again Christian Jimmy Carter brought a moral earnestness to the White House, and the hope that he would offer more honest government than the Republicans had in fact won him the election. He was a farmer from Plains, Georgia, and he brought in a folksy style of presidency, scrapping much White House ceremonial. He attempted to tackle the energy crisis resulting from the Yom Kippur War (see Chapter 19) by creating a Department of Energy, which aimed to lessen American dependence on imported oil. In line with his civil rights objectives more negroes were appointed to high office, Andrew Young becoming ambassador to the United Nations. On the other hand he did little to lessen the high rates of unemployment among black youth or to improve black slums.

In foreign affairs Carter's performance was more striking. He allowed no extension of American commitments, and in 1979 ended three decades of American refusal to accept the legitimacy of the Chinese communist regime by establishing full diplomatic relations with China. He made a bold attempt to settle the Middle East question by inviting the premiers of Egypt and Israel to the USA in September 1978, an initiative which helped to improve Egypt–Israel relations in the next decade. He was unfairly criticised for taking no effective action against the Russian occupation of Afghanistan in 1979, which destroyed hopes of progress towards detente. Even more frustrating was the failure to free the American hostages seized in Teheran by Iranian students in November 1979 and held for over a year (see Chapter 19).

In November 1980 Carter was defeated in the presidential elections by the Republican candidate, Ronald Reagan. His defeat was due to the failures of his administration, Reagan's personal popularity and the feeling among many American voters that federal government had become too intrusive of state rights. Reagan was to serve two terms as president, retiring at the end of 1988 and being succeeded by his vice-president, George Bush. It is obviously too early to make any firm judgements on his record. In some aspects of government, especially economic issues, he was inept, and it was all too easy to make jokes about his earlier career as a Hollywood actor. In fact he was an experienced politician, with a good record as governor of California, and he remained popular throughout his terms as president despite the scandal of Irangate, when the administration was discovered providing arms for Iran clandestinely, as well as financing the Nicaraguan Contras. More positively Reagan showed flexibility in his dealings with the Soviet Union. Pledged to restore

America's declining position in the world, he initially took a hard line towards Russia, calling it 'the evil empire'. However, in his second term as president he modified such attitudes and moved towards strategic arms limitation treaties with Gorbachev. The summit meetings between the leaders of the two superpowers in 1987 and 1988 gave new hope to the world that a stable peace could yet be fashioned.

At home the Reagan administration showed similar flexibility in its economic policy. The early years saw some attempt to implement the precepts of the Chicago School of economists, notably Milton Friedman, who believed in cutting government spending and taxes and withdrawing government from economic life so that free markets could work effectively. When such policies were followed, unemployment rose to 12 million by 1983, and surreptitiously Reagonomics, as it was termed, was given up. Tax cuts continued, but a boom was fuelled by high government spending and by high interest rates, which attracted much foreign capital into the USA. By 1988 unemployment had fallen to 5 million but at the cost of the USA incurring two massive deficits – on the Federal budget and on the balance of trade.

The 1980s saw the USA, once the world's largest creditor nation, become within a few years the world's largest debtor nation. Such a startling development has driven home the reality of America's relative political and economic decline. In place of American domination of the world economy from the 1940s to the 1960s has come a multipolar distribution of economic power. Consequently, as Paul Kennedy has shown, the Americans have had to face what Spain around 1600 and Britain around 1900 had to face – the problem of too many global commitments, which seem larger than the country's power to defend them simultaneously.

Yet these key commitments appear under threat in many parts of the globe, especially in the Middle East, important for its oil and where a major ally, Israel, faces Arab hostility. Latin America too poses its problems; it is a region plagued by a number of unstable right-wing regimes, a demographic explosion and huge international debt. American relations with neighbouring Mexico are marred by the problems of illegal immigrants and the drug traffic. The USA has massive commitments in the Far East through a number of treaties, for example SEATO, the South East Asia Treaty Organisation, modelled on NATO, which itself has involved a heavy American military presence in Europe. By a rich irony maps showing American military deployment round the world look to historians remarkably similar to the chain of bases possessed by Britain at the height of her strategic overstretch in 1900. In 1985 the USA had 520,000 members of its armed forces abroad, but, despite a trebling of defence budgets in the last decade, this is perceived as being insufficient not merely through the strain on numbers but because beliefs in American efficiency have been eroded as a result of inter-service rivalries, fraud and waste in military procurement and the consequent under-performance of weapons bought at horrendously spiralling costs.

How are the Americans to pay for their superpower status when the economy is facing relative decline? In 1945 the American share of the Gross World Product was over 40 per cent; by 1980 its share had fallen to 21 per cent. Both new and traditional industries were facing increasing foreign competition, while the agricultural sector was producing food surplus to domestic or foreign requirements. The uncompetitiveness of American industrial products abroad and the decline of agricultural exports have produced the huge trade deficits of the 1980s, and this gap can no longer be covered by earnings on such 'invisibles' as shipping and dividends from abroad because the USA has become the world's largest debtor nation; far from receiving dividends from abroad, it will be paying interest and dividends on the foreign capital which it has imported.

For all these factors a growing mood of anxiety has become evident in American governing circles similar to that which pervaded Edwardian England. If military spending continues to absorb 7 per cent of the Gross National Product, other advanced economies, such as Japan and West Germany, will benefit, because they can concentrate their research funds on commercial rather than military projects. Only the reality of the Soviet Union's far greater problems can mitigate American gloom, and the mutual economic problems of the two superpowers may yet prove to be a vital factor forcing through real limitations on nuclear armaments.

FURTHER READING

Ambrose, S. E., *Eisenhower: the President*, Allen and Unwin, London, 1984

Brogan, H., *A History of the United States of America*, Longmans, London, 1985

Caute, D., *The Great Fear*, Secker and Warburg, London, 1978

Kennedy, P., *The Rise and Fall of the Great Powers*, Unwin Hyman, London, 1988

Lewis, D. L., *Martin Luther King*, Allen Lane, London, 1970

Lukas, J. A., *Nightmare: The Underside of the Nixon Years*, Viking, New York, 1976

Morison, S. E. *et al.*, *The Growth of the American Republic*, OUP, Oxford, 1980

Sorensen, T. C., *Kennedy*, Hodder and Stoughton, London, 1965

Thomas, H., *The Cuban Revolution*, Weidenfeld and Nicolson, London, 1986

QUESTIONS

1. Acount for the phenomenon of McCarthyism and critically analyse its impact on American politics.
2. 'He gave the nation 8 years of peace and prosperity.' Do you agree with Ambrose's view of Eisenhower's presidencies?
3. Estimate and explain the successes of the civil rights movement in the USA since 1955.
4. To what extent has J. F. Kennedy enjoyed an unwarrantedly high reputation?
5. 'Johnson's work as a reformer was not spectacular, yet it was firmly in the tradition of the New Deal in which he had served his political apprenticeship.' Do you agree with this assessment of Johnson's domestic achievements between 1963 and 1968?
6. In what ways has the USA's position as the world's leading power been eroded in the last 20 years?

18
The Soviet orbit since 1945

(a) The final years of Stalin, 1945–53

Despite his failure to prepare Russia against the impending German attack in 1941, Stalin emerged from the war with increased stature as a leader. The Russian defeats early in the war were so enormous that he appeared to be the only man capable of saving his country from the Nazi menace. Therefore, as Ulam explains, Stalin was 'outrageously the beneficiary of the magnitude of the disaster'. The Russian people supported him, despite his crimes and errors, as the only barrier against complete collapse.

Stalin in many ways was a mediocre war leader. He was a military dilettante whose choice of such generals as Timoshenko was usually poor, and he interfered with the work of his most able commander, Zhukov. Again he was saved from the consequences of his own shortcomings by the even grosser errors of Hitler. Stalin did score real triumphs in the field of diplomacy, where he displayed patience and tenacity, and also succeeded in creating an image of himself as the patriotic generalissimo of unyielding willpower.

Russia emerged from the war with increased stature as one of the world's two superpowers – deservedly so as she had borne the greatest share of the burden in the European war. Yet the cost was enormous; about 20 million Russians had died and many cities had been reduced to ashes. Agricultural production was only 60 per cent and steel production only 50 per cent of their prewar levels. Soviet citizens had been compelled to undergo more hardship than almost any other country in Europe.

If the Russian people or Stalin's colleagues hoped for a breathing space at the end of the war, they were soon disillusioned. In Ulam's phrase, he strove to rule as ubiquitously as before. He appreciated Russia's real weakness and wanted his country to catch up with the West before the Americans realised their power and used it. Totalitarian terror was again to be imposed. Russians disloyal enough to be taken prisoner were to be treated with exemplary severity. Over 5 million Soviet citizens still lived west of the Soviet borders at the end of the war, and at Yalta the Allies agreed that they should be repatriated. Truly horrible events occurred as a result of this arrangement. Nicholas Bethell, in his book *The Last Secret*, has shown how many Russian soldiers had to be forcibly repatriated because they knew that a hideous fate awaited them in Russia. Many committed suicide after killing their families rather than return; even more were shot out of hand on their arrival in Russia.

It is clear that time had not mellowed Stalin's lust for power; rather it had eroded his patience and made him more eager to humiliate others. He was angry at growing old and distrusted his subordinates, fearing that he might become their prisoner through illness, as had happened to Lenin. Fear of those closest to him is a despot's occupational disease, Alam Ulam reminds us. Stalin hated his colleagues not only as potential rivals but as potential successors. Therefore Zhukov, who had brought him victory, was soon consigned to professional obscurity and his contribution to that victory written off. The faithful Molotov was not only replaced as foreign minister by Vyshinsky in 1949, but had to stand by as his wife Pauline was sent into exile.

During the war Russian citizens had gained greater freedom, and many of them had been abroad and seen the relatively liberal conditions in the West. Stalin feared that foreign political and cultural ideas would make returning Russian soldiers a potential revolutionary force. Russia had also acquired some 22 million new citizens by her gain of the Baltic provinces, Bessarabia, Bukovina, Eastern Poland, South Sakhalin and part of East Prussia. The returning soldiers and new citizens were to be indoctrinated or reindoctrinated, and in the summer of 1946 an ideological campaign, led by Andre Zhdanov started. The campaign was provoked partly by Stalin's personal whim, but also by a hard, serious calculation. Russians had to be taught to despise foreigners, with their dangerous ideas on political and cultural freedom, for otherwise the strength of the totalitarian regime in Russia would be eroded.

The leading figures in Russian cultural life again found themselves under fire, including Anna Akhmatova, one of the greatest Russian poets of her generation. The most important Russian composers, Prokofiev and Shostakovich, were criticised as degenerates, Zhdanov contemptuously comparing Shostakovich's music to the dentist's drill. Even the film director Eisenstein was not safe from attack. Russia's leading economist, Eugeni Varga, was disgraced for suggesting that an imminent economic crisis in the West was not inevitable.

Propaganda became more intense and ideological control much stricter, a great effort being made in education. The number of students in higher education rose from 800,000 before the war to 1,200,000 in 1946. They were taught that Russia was superior to the West in science and indeed all other fields as well. 'The all-pervasive, absurd and mendacious propaganda was an insult to the intelligence and the maturity of Soviet citizens,' comments Laqueur. It was in the atmosphere created by such propaganda that the most famous scientific fraud of modern history was perpetrated. Trafim Lysenko, with the backing of Stalin and Zhdanov, preached that environment not heredity transformed and made man, inducing in one individual in his lifetime changes that could be transmitted to that individual's descendants. Russian scientists who attempted to object to Lysenko's theories were victimised by the loss of their jobs and laboratories. In Stalin's last years anti-Semitism was increasingly practised. Stalin always disliked the Jews because of their cosmopolitan attitudes and they were harried out of intellectual life.

(b) Communist expansion in Eastern Europe and Asia

The Russian successes during the war gave the openings to communist parties loyal to the Soviet Union to increase their influence throughout Europe. The two countries which were exceptions to the rule were Greece, where the communists were checked by British intervention in December 1944, and Yugoslavia, where Tito took a strongly independent line. In the rest of Eastern Europe local communists came to power, backed by the might of the Russian armies. In former Axis satellites, such as Rumania, Bulgaria and Hungary, communist regimes could simply be imposed on the native populations, but in the cases of Poland and Czechoslovakia a more delicate approach was required. Polish communists were particularly dependent on Russian help because of the traditional Polish hostility to Russia, recently increased by the Russian refusal to help the Warsaw rising. In Czechoslovakia the communists moved cautiously, taking part in Benes' People's Front government and gaining control of crucial ministries.

In each of the European countries the communists had to overcome opposition, which was centred in the peasant parties and the Christian Churches. This task was made more difficult by the conduct or rather misconduct of the Russian troops. In Poland Mikolajczyk and the People's party came under increasing pressure, and in fear for his life the leader was forced to escape abroad. In Czechoslovakia free elections were held in 1946 in which the communists gained 38 per cent of the vote; it was only in 1948 that the communists proceeded to more extreme measures. The only non-communist minister, Jan Masaryk, son of the founder of the republic, died after falling from a window in most dubious circumstances, and Benes resigned as president in June. With the political opposition crushed, the new communist regimes felt able to implement a social revolution by collectivising agriculture and nationalising industry.

In Yugoslavia Tito continued his defiant and independent attitude, which angered Stalin. The Russian leader continued to hope that

Yugoslav communists would depose Tito, so that Yugoslavia could be brought into line with other satellites. He made a grave error in failing to appreciate Tito's strong grip on his country. The Yugoslav leader was capable of acting ruthlessly, and had quickly eliminated such non-communists as General Mihaelovic, who was executed in July 1946. But Tito's position in the Yugoslav communist party was unrivalled, because of his part in the epic wartime resistance. Therefore the denunciation of the Yugoslav leader by the Cominform (the revived Comintern) and by *Pravda* that he was guilty of failing to implement communist programmes had no success whatever. The criticism was in any case untrue. Tito collectivised agriculture in Yugoslavia more rapidly than did leaders in other East European countries, and only after his quarrel with Stalin did he become relatively moderate and liberal. In 1951 Tito accepted aid from the West and then tried to institute a decentralised communism with a human face. He ruled Yugoslavia until his death in 1980. He was ruthless in suppressing Croatian nationalism, but followed relatively liberal economic policies. He repeatedly stated his determination that Yugoslavia should be socialist yet non-aligned, a clear warning to Russia against any interference in Yugoslav affairs.

Tito's defiance of Stalin made the Soviet leader more determined to complete his stranglehold over other East European countries, and purges of party members occurred in all the satellites. The Church came in for attack, the most notorious case being the treatment of Cardinal Mindszenty of Hungary, who was arrested and tortured. In East Germany Walther Ulbricht became the key man in Stalin's plans. An energetic organiser, his loyalty to Russia was never in doubt. Having harassed other political parties out of existence, Ulbricht's communists launched a major programme of economic change. The repression of the regime, combined with Russian economic exactions, made it loathed by the people of East Germany. Many voted with their feet by fleeing to the West, and in just over a decade the population of East Germany fell from 19 to 17 million. The drain of manpower, much of it young and skilled, was a further burden on the country's economy. In 1949 East Germany was formally proclaimed the German Democratic Republic. The rulers of East Germany hoped to make their country comparable or indeed superior to the Federal Republic, but they failed in their objective, the building of the Berlin Wall in 1961 being a tacit admission of their failure.

In Asia, as in Europe, the communists had achieved a prominent position in resistance movements during the war. At the end of the war they were able to take power in China, North Vietnam and North Korea, with the important difference that, apart from North Korea, they were not installed by Russian troops. The Chinese communists did, however, receive much aid from Russia at a time when the

United States withheld arms from their Kuomintang rivals. In 1950 the new Chinese leader, Mao Tse-tung, visited Moscow and signed a Sino-Soviet treaty by which the two countries became allies, Russia promising to supply industrial equipment to China. Relations at this point were still cordial, as China depended on Russian aid, but already China had indicated her intention to be treated as the equal of the Soviet Union rather than her satellite. The Cominform now became the spearhead of a Communist offensive in Asia, and it planned several armed risings in that continent from 1948. In India, the Philippines, Burma, Malaya and Indonesia communists risings were checked. In Indo-China Ho Chi Minh's communists defeated the French and won control of Northern Indo-China.

(c) The Soviet economy

The loss of 20 million people and the destruction in West Russia meant a heavy task of reconstruction. Despite these difficulties, economic progress was rapid after 1945, with coal output doubling and steel, oil and electricity output almost trebling in 7 years. By 1950, asserts Alec Nove, the USSR had a stronger industrial structure than before the war. But the Russians failed in their primary objective, that of catching up the United States, which Kruschev said would be achieved by 1970, Russia's GNP being only half that of the United States.

Stalin's economic system after 1945 was a war economy imposed in peacetime, with tight controls and a channelling of resources to heavy industry. Though a welcome improvement in real wages took place after 1947, the standard of living remained among the lowest in Europe, with an intolerable housing shortage caused by disgraceful neglect of the problem. Public affluence was a contrast to private squalor. Enormous power stations were established in Stalingrad, the Volga–Don Canal was built and many targets set down in a new Five Year Plan started in 1946 were reached. At the same time the average Russian family still lived in one room, had little food and very drab clothing.

Agriculture had been neglected to provide labour and capital for heavy industry, and after Stalin's death in 1953 it became a priority, with Kruschev having a special interest in its advance. Virgin lands in Western Siberia were cultivated, higher prices were paid to collective farms, and farmers were given more freedom to work their private plots. After a disastrous grain harvest in 1953 of only 82 million tons, the new policies combined with good weather to produce a record harvest of 170 million tons in 1967. Improvements in livestock were less impressive. Kruschev himself pressed for an increase in the size of collectives by amalgamation of farms. The real purpose for this was political; the formation of even larger units in agriculture would strengthen the Party's control over the peasantry.

The pressures on Soviet leaders were considerable after Stalin's death. They felt obliged to make an attempt to improve living standards, and the construction of new houses doubled between 1955 and 1958; but at the same time they still wished to make a forced march to a mature industrial economy while keeping up with the military and space programmes of the United States. Thus the Soviet government was drawn into attempting to do too much in too many directions at the same time. Defence spending rose by one-third in the years 1959 to 1963, and in consequence the targets of the Seven Year Plan begun in 1959 were not reached in agriculture and some industries, though key industries, such as steel, made considerable progress.

Russia did ease the exploitation of her East European satellites to some extent after 1953, especially after the unrest in East Germany, Hungary and Poland; yet exploitation of satellites still continued in the Council of Mutual Economic Assistance (COMECON), created in 1949. Unlike the EEC, it was not based on a community of economic interests. Russia, with more to gain by collaboration than most of her partners, continued to enjoy advantageous trading arrangements with her satellites. Reluctant partners were kept in line by ideological pressure and the occasional reminder of Soviet military power.

(d) The end of Stalin

The war saw a vast increase in the membership of the Communist Party, from 3.4 million to 6.3 million, and in 1952 Stalin made important changes in its structure. The Central Committee was almost doubled in size and the Politburo was renamed the Praesidium, with twenty-five members. Prominent new members of the Praesidium were Beria, Malenkov, Bulganin, Kosygin and Kruschev. They were Stalin's trusted henchmen, and there is no evidence that they opposed his ruthless measures. In 1952, at the first Party Congress since 1939, it was clear that Malenkov was now the heir apparent.

Stalin's last months were accompanied by strange events that have never been fully explained. In January 1953 *Pravda* announced that nine doctors, six of them Jewish, had been charged with murdering leading Russian politicans through medical mistreatment. Beria and Malenkov were accused of lack of vigilance in failing to detect the plot. New purges were expected, but at this critical juncture Stalin suffered a severe stroke and died on 5 March. He died unmourned, for absolute power had turned him into a monstrous tyrant who built a system of terror and a structure of personal power unprecedented in modern history.

(e) The Kruschev years, 1953-64

On the death of Stalin it appeared for a short while that Malenkov would inherit the dead dictator's position, but a period of collective leadership ensued. Malenkov, Beria and Molotov formed a triumvirate and appearead to hold the reins of power. Criticism of Stalin in this period was implied rather than explicit, but Beria's announcement in April that the doctor's plot was a hoax, and his criticism of harsh police activities, were startling. An impression of confusion had now been created in the Soviet leadership, which encouraged demonstrations in Russia and other countries in the summer. In June 1953 a strike by East Berlin building workers sparked off a revolt which was only crushed by the intervention of Russian troops. Meanwhile the power struggle continued behind the scenes, coming into the open in December when it was announced that Beria and six of his supporters had been executed for being capitalist agents. There need be no tears for Beria; his record as Chief of Police had been particularly vicious.

It was now that Kruschev rose to prominence. He was born in 1894 and joined the Communist party in 1918. Despite being an uneducated coalminer, he showed talent for management, and in 1939 became a member of the Politburo. In 1949 he became secretary of the Central Committee, with a reputation on agricultural matters. His increased influence was demonstrated in 1953 by his condemnation of the record of the collectives and his call for agricultural reform. In 1954 he directed that new areas of Asiatic Russia be used for grain, and by 1956 90 million extra acres were under cultivation.

Apart from this, Kruschev was shrewd enough to remain in the background in the immediate period after Stalin's death. Now First Secretary of the Party, he was able to fill key positions with his own supporters. Thus, when his rivalry with Malenkov came into the open in January 1955, he was able to force Malenkov's resignation as Chairman of the Council of Ministers. Malenkov, after confessing his inexperience and taking the blame for the unsatisfactory state of agriculture, was succeeded by Marshal Bulganin. He and Kruschev were to share power in the next few years, with Kruschev the more dominant personality.

The new Soviet leaders made a number of moves to re-establish Russian power in Eastern Europe. In July 1953 the Hungarian premier, Matyas Rakosi, had been replaced by the more liberal Imre Nagy. In 1955 the Russians forced out Nagy and brought back Rakosi. In May 1956 the signing of the Warsaw Pact strengthened the Russian position in Eastern Europe generally, as satellite armies were placed under Russian command. An attempt was also made to restore relations with Yugoslavia with both 'Mr B. and Mr K.' visiting Belgrade.

The Russian leaders were also prepared to make some moves to the West. In May 1955 Russia signed the Austrian peace treaty and her troops evacuated Austria. In July came a summit meeting at Geneva attended by Britain, France, the USSR and the United States. The main issues discussed were German reunification and European security in general. The cordial relations that were created became known as the 'Geneva spirit', and the more flexible Russian foreign policy strengthened the international prestige of the Russian leaders. In reality the Geneva conference, in Ulam's phrase, 'underlined the new form of impasse in East–West relations'. The more friendly relations made the chances of war appear remote, and therefore there was no need for either side to make concessions. Geneva may have helped to lessen international tension but it could find no solution to the problems of disarmament or the German question.

The most startling breach with the past was Kruschev's secret speech at the Twentieth Party Congress in February 1956, when he revealed many of Stalin's worst crimes. His motives for such a move require some explanation. In Donald Treadgold's view, 'He was trying to exorcise the incubus of his dead master, whom he had loyally served for so long, because of the massive unpopularity of all Stalin stood for among the Soviet people, yet he wished to avoid calling into question the structure of the whole regime or opening the way to public queries about the role of the leaders of 1956 during the commission of the crimes that he detailed.' Kruschev still believed that Stalin had performed great services to Russia, but he called the party to eradicate the cult of personality and restore Leninist principles of 'Soviet socialist democracy'.

His disclosures had a shattering effect on communist governments in other countries. The Italian Communist leader, Togliatti, was prompted to state that communism had now to become polycentric. It had to be tailored to the needs of individual countries rather than to directives emanating from one centre, Russia. These directives, Togliatti believed, should no longer be obligatory. He was not alone in this belief.

(f) Revolution in the Soviet orbit

The year 1956 was a watershed in postwar politics for both the Soviet bloc and the West. For the West the Suez fiasco proved that Britain and France were no longer great powers, whereas in the Soviet orbit trouble flared up in Poland and Hungary. Hopes of a genuine relaxation of Russian rule had been aroused by the Kruschev revelations, and when these hopes were disappointed, protests mounted. In June Polish workers clashed with the police and 100 people were killed. In August Wladyslaw Gomulka, who had been Poland's chief Titoist, was reinstated. In October Russian intervention seemed likely after Kruschev and Gomulka had a stormy interview, at which the Russian threatened the use of Soviet troops. Nevertheless he showed restraint as Gomulka tried to calm the Polish people. Time was to show the wisdom of Kruschev's attitude, for the new Polish regime became a pillar of Soviet orthodoxy, Gomulka only falling from power in 1970 after riots at Gdynia.

Much more serious trouble was encountered in Hungary. In October 1956 a student demonstration was held in Budapest, the students demanding the withdrawal of Russian troops from Hungary, the reinstatement of Imre Nagy and free elections. The Hungarian secret police and Russian troops attacked the students, who were joined by the Hungarian army as fighting spread all over the country. On 27 October a new government which included non-communists was formed, with Nagy at its head. The next day a ceasefire was announced and Russian forces withdrew from Budapest. However, early in November Russian troops returned, and, after bitter fighting, installed a new regime under Janos Kadar. Nagy and his colleagues fled to the Yugoslav embassy for asylum. When they left it under a Kadar pledge of safe conduct, they were imprisoned and executed in 1958. By then 200,000 Hungarians had fled to the West. In time, by a strange irony, Kadar made Hungary a freer country than Gomulka's Poland.

The view is sometimes put forward that the Suez crisis benefited the Russians by distracting attention away from the Hungarian tragedy and preventing help from being sent to the Hungarians, but this is surely erroneous. Neither the United Nations nor the United States would have directly challenged Russia, one of the world's two superpowers. Nor was the force of world opinion likely to deter the Soviet leaders from checking Hungarian deviation. As Walter Laqueur remarks, 'world opinion does not count for much in Moscow's eyes if basic Soviet interests are involved'. Kruschev believed that the passage of time would make the world forget Hungary, and he was right.

The Hungarian tragedy was, however, a blow at Kruschev's own position, and he seemed likely to lose power as his chief rivals – Malenkov, Molotov and Bulganin – tried to force him out of office. They underestimated his tenacity and their failure to oust him meant their dismissal from full membership of the Praesidium. Kruschev's victory was owed partly to the backing of Zhukov and the army, but also to the fact that his supporters had a majority in the Praesidium. In 1958 Bulganin was deposed as premier and Kruschev held the top posts in both the party and government, as Stalin had done. Rivals such as Molotov, who became ambassador to Mongolia, were virtually exiled. No doubt they could console themselves with the thought that in Comrade Stalin's time a harsher fate would have awaited them!

The element of destalinisation in Kruschev's rule should not, however, be exaggerated. His regime was more humane than Stalin's but it was still authoritarian. Artists might have more freedom to express themselves but there were severe limits beyond which they were unwise to transgress. When Boris Pasternak was awarded the Nobel Prize in 1958 for his novel *Dr. Zhivago*, Kruschev compelled him to refuse it. In 1963 the Russian leader denounced abstract art and modern literature as well as carrying out a campaign against religion, which led to the closing of half the churches in Russia. On the other hand, Kruschev allowed Alexander Solzhenitsyn to publish his novel *One Day in the Life of Ivan Denisovich*, a horrifying picture of Stalin's concentration camps.

(g) Relations with China and the United States

Soviet relations with China deteriorated rapidly during the Kruschev years. His denunciation of Stalin angered the Chinese communist leaders, who believed in rigid adherence to the Stalinist type of government. Kruschev's belief in coexistence also alienated the Chinese, for they hoped that, with the Soviet launching of Sputnik in 1957, the Communist world offensive could be intensified. In a sense the two countries were bound to become hostile, because they both desired the leadership of the Communist world. In the words of Walter Laqueur, 'the conflict was not over the correct ideological interpretation of Marx and Lenin but over national interests, autonomy and big power aspirations'.

The Chinese were furious when Kruschev became the first head of any Russian government to visit the United States. The Russian leader visited President Eisenhower at Camp David, with a retinue befitting a tsar. The two statesmen planned another summit meeting for 1960, but it never took place because of the U-2 incident. When this American reconnaissance plane was brought down over Russia, Kruschev demanded an apology which Eisenhower refused. Nevertheless the Russian still condemned the Chinese for their opposition to 'detente', and in July 1960 he cut off Soviet military and economic aid to China.

Relations with the West also remained poor. Kruschev supported Fidel Castro's new Communist regime in Cuba and the question of the Berlin Wall divided the two blocs. In 1962 the Soviet leader brought a severe diplomatic defeat on himself. Misjudging the will of the new American president, John F. Kennedy, Kruschev was tempted into attempting to install Soviet missiles in Cuba. The American met the Soviet move with a firm ultimatum, and the world held its breath as the long-feared clash of the two superpowers appeared imminent. Fortunately Kruschev's good sense finally prevailed; he yielded to the ultimatum and withdrew the missiles. A more peaceful Soviet policy was now pursued. In 1963 the Washington–Moscow 'hot line' was established, and a treaty banning further nuclear tests, except underground, was signed.

The Cuban affair was the perfect opportunity for the Chinese communists to criticise Soviet policy for lack of wisdom and also cowardice in surrendering to American pressure. By 1964 Mao was calling Russia an imperialist state, and China's ally in Eastern Europe, Albania, also heaped abuse on the Russian leader. Clearly the day when Russia directed world communism was gone and polycentrism (a number of different centres of Communism) had come to stay.

(h) The fall of Kruschev

The Cuban affair was a personal disaster from which Kruschev never really recovered, but domestic affairs were also eroding his power. In 1963 the failure of the grain harvest necessitated the import of foreign grain, while Kruschev's cuts in military expenditure offended the powerful military lobby. His attempt to divide the party into an industrial and agricultural branch was unrealistic and was abandoned. General irritation grew with the unpredictable and irrational style of his government. Therefore in October 1964, while Krushchev was on vacation, his enemies proclaimed Brezhnev as first party secretary and Kosygin as head of the Soviet government. It was explained that Kruschev had resigned through old age and poor health. Soon attacks on him began. *Pravda* condemned his 'hare-brained schemes' and his 'bragging and bluster'.

Kruschev was a crude but colourful character. At times his behaviour was absurd, as witness his action at the United Nations in 1960 when he took off his shoe and banged it on the table during Macmillan's speech. Even so his bluster was preferable to Stalin's purges, and in retrospect the Kruschev years seem relatively good ones for Russia, with considerable economic progress and more cultural freedom. He was, in Laqueur's phrase, 'an agent of freedom and progress in Soviet postwar history', yet his period in office also demonstrated the tragic dilemma of Soviet rulers. While wishing to improve the lot of the Soviet people by a more humanitarian communism, he was afraid that excessive concessions would threaten the very survival of the Soviet system.

(i) The era of Brezhnev and Kosygin

Brezhnev and Kosygin proved to be prudent, cautious rulers; they made few important initiatives in domestic affairs, apart from gradually stopping destalinisation and rehabilitating Stalin himself. For a time a more liberal approach was tried in economic policy. individual enterprises were given more power to plan and produce with a view to profit-making. This applied not only to industry but to the collectives, where there was a renewed stress on smaller units. From 1966 attempts to provide for a higher rise in consumer goods than in capital goods were made, and indeed the standard of living has risen in Russia.

The regime attracted an unfavourable press in the West by its intolerance of creative work or of the right of protest. In 1966 Andrei Siniavsky and Uli Daniel were sent to a forced labour camp for having novels and essays published in the West. Andrei Sakharov, one of Russia's greatest nuclear physicists, came under increasing official pressure for protesting at this injustice and other abuses in the Russian system. The case of the ballet dancers Valery and Galina Panov, who had to leave Russia to practise their art, was a vivid illustration of the dead hand of Soviet rule.

The most famous victim of Soviet intolerance has, however, been Alexander Solzhenitzyn. A former army officer interned for 8 years in a forced labour camp, he described his experiences in a powerful autobiographical novel, *One Day in the Life of Ivan Denisovich*. The existence of the camps had never been admitted in print before and the novel caused a sensation. The author was awarded the Nobel Prize in 1970, and, though he was warned off going to Sweden to receive it, he did not refuse it either. He came under increasing official pressure and was expelled from the Union of Soviet Writers.

In 1974 the West was treated to his long-awaited *Gulag Archipelago*, which, unlike earlier works, contains no element of fiction. It is a harrowing account of the horrors of the penal camps and Solzhenitzyn's own fate at the hands of the authorities. As Leonard Schapiro commented, 'it is dynamite so far as the Soviet authorities are concerned since it undermines whatever legitimacy the present regime may have'. There was no place in Russia now for Solzhenitzyn. In 1974 he was exiled to the West.

(j) Brezhnev and Kosygin – the Far East

The new regime's most permanent and urgent problem was the new hostility of China. The day after Kruschev's fall the Chinese leaders were able to announce that they had exploded their first nuclear device, a development that worried the Russians more than the West. Soviet aid to North Vietnam was disliked by the Chinese government, as was Kosygin's mediation in the dispute between India and Pakistan in 1966, which gave Russia great prestige in Asia.

Such Soviet initiatives formed one of the causes of China's Cultural Revolution (see Chapter 14). The Chinese leaders feared a growth of opposition at home, and a number of prominent Chinese were purged with the help of the Red Guards. These puzzling events can be seen as an attempt by Mao to maintain his power and revive the militant spirit of Chinese communism, thus avoiding the revisionism of Soviet Russia. The Cultural Revolution caused a complete end to Sino-Soviet friendship, and, as a number of border incidents ensued, Moscow's attitude became more threatening. Though relations improved temporarily in 1970, they remained tense. The Chinese no longer regard Russia as a communist state at all. In their view Russia is a 'social Fascist' state and a much greater threat to China than Western countries, with whom the Chinese have sought better relations since the 1970s.

(k) Czechoslovakia

The true nature of the Soviet regime was tragically illustrated by the events in Czechoslovakia in 1968. Discontent had grown there with the brutal rule of Antonin Novotny, and in January 1968 he was replaced as first secretary of the Czech Communist party by Alexander Dubcek. Now came the 'Prague Spring', as Dubcek's more liberal regime granted freedom of the press and civil liberties, including the right of other parties to exist. Dubcek and his colleagues were aiming at a more human and democratic socialism, and the new course enjoyed wide popular support.

Despite Dubcek's protestations of loyalty to the Warsaw Pact, the Soviet government was now alarmed, and in July it warned the Czechs not to leave the road to socialism. Meetings between the two governments were held in late July and early August, and it appeared that Russia and other Communist states accepted the Dubcek programme. Then on 20 August Soviet and other Warsaw Pact troops invaded Czechoslovakia and replaced Dubcek with Gustav Husak. In September Brezhnev laid down his views on the Soviet action in Czechoslovakia, and they have become known as the 'Brezhnev Doctrine'. Brezhnev asserted that he was against interference in the affairs of other states except when a threat to socialism arose in a communist country. Then, maintained the Russian leader, it becomes a matter of concern for all socialist countries.

As in the case of Hungary in 1956, a storm of criticism arose abroad, but again, as time passed, the world forgot. Husak humiliated Dubcek by reducing him to the status of a mechanical engineer, and hard-line policies were followed.

The Soviet invasion of Czechoslovakia had a profound effect on European politics. Czechoslovakia was the one East European country with democratic traditions, but its 'Prague Spring' coincided with a hardening of Soviet policies. Albania and Rumania had already demonstrated their independence of Russia, and the

Russians were determined to prevent any more deviation in the Soviet camp. In this they were supported by several of the hard-line leaders in the other satellites, notably Ulbricht and Gomulka. Once again coercion was seen as the real basis of Communist rule, though further disunion was created in the Communist camp as Yugoslavia, Albania and China all condemned the Soviet action.

For the West the crisis showed that true coexistence with Soviet Russia was still far from being realised, and NATO was given a new lease of life. It was clear that the Russians would use force if any of their satellites in Eastern Europe appeared likely to deviate from the Russian view of communism, and therefore the Brezhnev doctrine implied that a communist seizure of power in any country was an irreversible event.

(l) Russia in the early 1980s

In many respects the Soviet government had become tsarism writ large. In its own way it was as expansionist as tsarist Russia ever was, and could not avoid the temptation of indulging in intrigues against the West. As in tsarist days, intellectuals were excluded from participation in their country's government. The leadership still insisted on ideological uniformity, because to grant real cultural freedom would risk opening the floodgates of political liberty. The tension between the intelligentsia and the political leadership worsened in the late 1970s, as the harsh treatment of dissidents like Anatoly Sharansky, the mathematician, and Andrei Sakharov, one of Russia's greatest physicists, demonstrated the ugly side of the Soviet system. Sharansky, for example, having been refused permission to emigrate to Israel, was arrested in 1977 and was imprisoned until 1986.

Soviet society was as class-ridden as Russia in the nineteenth century. The élite was composed of party members, government officials and members of the armed forces. The stultifying hand of the bureaucracy was everywehre, causing inefficient allocation of resources. With independent thought stifled, no way by which these faults could be remedied existed. More than perhaps any other country, Russia was dominated by its secret police, the KGB (Committee of State Security). John Barron, in his book *The K.G.B. The Secret Work of Soviet Agents*, has demonstrated the wide activities of this organisation inside and outside Russia.

The jaundiced Western view of the Soviet system was reinforced by events after 1979. In December 1979 over 60,000 Soviet troops invaded Afghanistan to install a puppet government in Kabul. The invasion was strongly condemned by nearly every country in the world outside the communist bloc, but Russian troops continued to prop up the pro-Soviet Karmal regime in the face of vast popular hostility. By 1984 about one-fifth of the Afghan population had left the country.

Soviet stock also fell sharply as a consequence of events in Poland. In December 1981 General Jaruzelski imposed martial law in Poland as a response to demands for reform led by Lech Walesa's free trade union, Solidarity. An important factor in the survival of Solidarity was the tacit support of the Roman Catholic Church in Poland, led by Archbishop Glemp. The murder of the Solidarity priest Father Jerzy Popieluszko in October 1984 by members of the Polish secret police was deeply shocking.

The Soviet leadership continued to develop its image of consistent gerontocratic leadership. After the death of Brezhnev in November 1982 the former head of the KGB, Yuri Andropov, succeeded as General Secretary of the Soviet Communist Party. He brought new men into government to combat the inertia and corruption within the Soviet system. He also attempted to build better links with Western Europe, but this policy was vitiated by the shooting down of a South Korean airliner by the Soviets in September 1983. Andropov's misfortune was that he succeeded to the leadership when his own health was deteriorating, and he died in February 1984 at the age of 69. He was succeeded by the 73-year-old Konstanin Chernenko, a former Brezhnev man who seemed likely to opt for continuity and tradition. To many Western observers, however, the unyielding nature of Soviet leadership was symbolised by the 75-year-old Andrei Gromyko, who had been Soviet foreign minister for twenty-seven years by 1984.

(m) The Gorbachev phenomenon

The image of stale gerontocratic leadership in the Soviet Union was vividly changed in March 1985, when Mikhail Gorbachev acceded to power at the age of 52 on the death of Chernenko. The son of a farmer, Gorbachev had become a law student at the Moscow State University and was the first intellectual to govern Russia since Lenin. He began to bring a new, pragmatic liberalism into Russian life, not liberalism in the Western sense but rather measures to modernise Russia in the tradition of Alexander II.

Gorbachev knew that, given the level of stagnation, drastic measures were needed if the Soviet Union were to stand a chance in the technological race with the West and emerging Pacific nations. Russia was in danger of becoming an Upper Volta with missiles. The new reform policy was called *perestroika* (reconstruction) and implied a new openness (*glasnost*) in Russian government. Gorbachev attacked central planning and the command economy, urging the need for decentralisation. In 1986 he admitted to the Twenty Seventh Communist Party Congress that Russian economic and social policy had failed since the 1970s, and insisted on the need for honest criticism if the country's development were to be accelerated.

The economic reforms proposed have seemed similar to Lenin's NEP (see Chapter 3), while abroad Gorbachev tried to reduce the Soviet Union's commitments, starting to pull Russian forces out of Afghanistan in 1988 after admitting the futility and bloodshed of a war which had become Russia's Vietnam. The new Russian leader also sought to reduce the expense of the nuclear arms race by coming to an agreement with the USA to reduce intermediate nuclear missiles. He attacked corruption and lethargy in Soviet administration by sacking 100,000 officials. The climate improved for Russian intellectuals; in 1986 Russia's best known dissident, Andrei Sakharov, was released from internal exile, and perhaps Russia's greatest poet since Pasternak, Irina Ratushinskaya, was released from a hard labour camp. Gorbachev's qualities of toughness, courage, wit, charm and intellectual sharpness won him many admirers in the West. On the other hand Western sceptics argued that Gorbachev merely wished for a more efficient, not a more liberal or humane, Russia.

But would his reforms succeed? Despite successes in maintaining a strong army, in achieving nuclear parity with the USA, in developing a large ocean-going navy and in creating a broader based economy, the Soviet Union faced formidable problems by the 1980s. There had been a steady long-term decline in the rate of economic growth since 1959, with consumer demand kept low to preserve national resources for heavy industry and the military. A second worrying symptom was the Soviet Union's relative economic decline. Kruschev's claim that the Marxist mode of production would one day 'bury capitalism' became a risible comment, given the advances made by the EEC, Japan and the USA, and the failure of the Russian standard of living to catch up with that of the West.

The most critical area of weakness in the Russian economy has been agriculture, an amazing situation when it is recalled that a century ago Russia was one of the two largest grain exporters in the world. Yet despite huge investment in agriculture, Russia has been a large net food importer since the 1970s, and its agricultural productivity is one-seventh that of American farming. To an extent certain natural factors – cold winters and frequent droughts – explain the difference but to outside observers the main reason for Soviet agriculture's weakness has been its 'socialisation' – too many subsidies, the waste of investment on large-scale projects rather than on practical peasant needs, the decision-making by bureaucrats and the denial of initiative to the peasants. What could be achieved if the system of collectivisation was changed towards individual peasant farming is indicated by the fact that existing private plots produce 25 per cent of Russia's total crop output, yet occupy a mere 4 per cent of the country's arable land.

But changing the present system of collectivised agriculture will be difficult. The liberalisation of the system by the creation of more private ownership and markets would mean fewer subsidies, and the consequent increase in prices would not be popular with the urban population. More seriously, such change would mean an admission of the failure of the communist system, while the decline in the powers of the bureaucrats and managers who run Soviet agriculture would have implications for the whole Soviet centralised power structure.

Soviet industry has also stagnated. As with agriculture, there has been an excess of bureaucratic planning, with too much concentration on heavy industry, which is unable to respond to consumer choice or new market opportunities. Much of the Soviet output, for example in steel, is therefore wasted, causing the paradox of industrial plenty in the midst of consumer poverty. Since Soviet factories have not gone out of business as in the West, they have lacked the stimulus to produce efficiently.

Three further pressures threaten future industrial efficiency. Firstly, the great expansion in Soviet industry since 1941 depended upon plentiful supplies of coal, oil and natural gas, which were wastefully used. By the 1980s such energy supplies had peaked and begun to decline, and the Russian efforts to build up their nuclear power output were badly hit by the disaster at Chernobyl in 1986.

A second worry for the Russian leadership is the challenge of the new technologies, where the USSR is in danger of falling behind the West. Such Western superiority could neutralise Russia's quantitative advantages in military hardware and increase her economic inferiority. However, the freedom to experiment in the new methods seems difficult to achieve in the intensely secretive and centralised Soviet system. As Paul Kennedy has emphasised, 'the regime's commitment to "modernisation" and its willingness to allocate additional resources of money and manpower are vitiated by an economic substructure and a political ideology which are basic obstacles to change'.

Importing the technology, as Russia did in the 1890s, would be unsatisfactory. The imported technology takes time to set up, is used much less efficiently than in the West and might well be out of date. Its purchase would absorb much hard currency just when Russia's earnings from her exports of oil and other raw materials are shrinking anyway.

The third pressure on Russia's future economic growth lies in demographics. Since the 1970s life-expectancy has declined from 66 to 60 as a result of a decline in the quality of medical care and the fantastic levels of alcoholism. Infant mortality rates have risen to a point where they are over three times the levels in the USA. Yet the Russian population is not only dying faster than before, its birthrates are slowing down as a result of higher female participation in the work-force and poorer housing. The fall in the birthrate has been particularly felt among the Russian ethnic population.

The implications of such trends have worried Russia's leaders. Firstly, more funds will be required for health care, social security and the war against alcoholism. The fall off in the rate of growth of the labour force will affect both Russian industry and the armed forces. Since fertility rates in central Asia republics are three times as large as those among Slav and Baltic peoples, the Russian share of the total Soviet population is expected to decline from 52 per cent in 1980 to 48 per cent in 2000. For the first time in the history of the Soviet Union, Russians will be in a minority.

Given such realities, Gorbachev's fear of falling behind the West is understandable, but two main political obstacles stand in the way of Russia producing a leap forward similar to that achieved by the Chinese. The first is the entrenched position of the party élite (especially in the KGB and Central Committee), and bureaucrats who enjoy both privilege and power. Reform of the Soviet system would threaten their position, and they seem likely to act as a drag against change. There is much corruption in the system, and in 1988 Brezhnev's son-in-law was accused of malpractices.

The second political obstacle lies in the large share of GNP devoted by the USSR to defence. The Soviet armed forces have siphoned off vast stocks of trained manpower and equipment from the civilian economy, and defence expenditure has been rising faster than GNP growth, to the general detriment of the economy. The Russian war machine has been modernised, though Russian leaders are still fearful of Russia's technological backwardness in the face of Reagan's Strategic Defence Initiative (SDI), which could offset Soviet numerical advantage in conventional weapons.

Russia's traditional advantage in quantity is in any case threatened by the decline in the Russian birthrate and the rising share of births in the non-Russian regions. Russia's Asiatic youth are often not well versed in the Russian language, lack technical competence and are strongly influenced by Islam. The Russian general staff regards much of its Asiatic manpower as unreliable, but even in European Russia, national consciousness among Ukrainians, Georgians and others adds to Russia's nationality problem.

Russian military leaders have viewed the acquisition of nuclear capability by three potential enemies in addition to the USA (China, France and Britain) as profoundly disturbing, and this explains the Soviet eagerness that in any Strategic Arms Limitation Treaty with the USA the Anglo-French systems should be taken into account and Russia allowed a margin of nuclear force to take care of China.

Finally, Russian leaders, perhaps with good reason, put little store on the reliability of their partners in the Warsaw Pact. Yet with such a battery of worries, the Russian military leadership will fight tooth and nail to prevent any reduction in the Soviet Union's military budget, and thus will become a further obstacle to reform.

Lastly, a central dilemma for Gorbachev is a perennial one in the Russian context. The gift of a measure of liberty by Russian rulers creates a certain confusion and leads to demands for faster and more fundamental change than the regime wishes to implement. In 1988 the Soviet regime was embarrassed by a wave of national unrest encouraged by the new *glasnost*, especially in Armenia and Azerbaijan. At the same time Soviet dissidents, such as Vladimir Bukovsky, pointed out that many Russians were still political prisoners in the Soviet Union. But for Gorbachev to give in to far-reaching demands for more liberalisation could provoke severe opposition from the Russian establishment.

FURTHER READING

Bialer, S., *Stalin's Successors*, CUP, Cambridge, 1980
Hosking, G., *A History of the Soviet Union*, Fontana, London, 1985
Kennedy, P., *The Rise and Fall of the Great Powers*, Unwin Hyman, London, 1988
McCauley, M., *The Soviet Union since 1917*, Longmans, London, 1981
Medvedev, R., *Gorbachev*, Basil Blackwell, 1987
Okey, R., *Eastern Europe 1740–1985*, Hutchinson, London, 1986
Ulam, A., *Stalin*, Allen Lane, London, 1973

QUESTIONS

1. What can be said for and against Stalin's rule in Russia between 1939 and 1953?
2. In what ways were the Kruschev years beneficial to Russia?
3. Account for the decline in Sino-Soviet relations after 1949.
4. In what ways does the Brezhnev era illustrate the view that Soviet government had become 'tsarism writ large'?
5. Discuss the problems facing Mikhail Gorbachev in his task of modernising Russia.

19
Nationalism in the Middle East and North Africa

(a) Zionism and Arab nationalism

The conviction of Dreyfus, a Jewish army officer, in France in 1894 appalled a young Austro-Hungarian journalist, Theodor Herzl, who reported the trial. Herzl, a Jew himself, was shaken by the hostility to Jews, and in 1895 he began to think that the solution to such anti-Semitism was an end to Jewish dispersal through the creation of a political centre for Jews.

The early nineteenth century had seen some improvement in status for European Jews, and one Jew, Disraeli, even became prime minister of Britain in 1868. However, from around 1860 a new kind of anti-Semitism developed, one based not on religion but on race. In the works of many writers, e.g. Eugen Dühring, it was alleged that Jews had unchangeable racial characteristics and could not be assimilated by other nations. The worst anti-Semitism was experienced in tsarist Russia, where the pogroms led to the flight of 2 million Jews; some of the Jews went to Palestine, then part of the Ottoman Empire and from 1922 a British mandate.

The Dreyfus Affair symbolised the growing inequality faced by Jews in European society, and helped to give birth to the Zionist movement. The word Zionism stands for the movement for the re-establishment of a Jewish nation in Palestine. Zionists emphasise the links between the Jews and Palestine, their historic home in Biblical times before the Diaspora, or dispersal of Jews around the world in the second century AD. Though a number of writers before him had argued for a separate Jewish state, including Disraeli, Herzl is regarded as the father of political Zionism. In his *Der Judenstaat* (The State of the Jews), published in 1896, Herzl argued that the Jews should be granted territory in either Palestine or Argentina, and organise so as to wrest control from the native population, as Rhodes had in Rhodesia. His attempts to gain international backing were frustratingly unproductive, and he died in 1904.

Herzl's successor was Chaim Weizmann, a Russian Jew who had settled in Manchester and founded the Manchester School of

Zionism. He was more practical than Herzl and made useful contacts with such British politicians as Arthur Balfour. He saw that political pressure would not win support from governments but that colonisation might. Accordingly this policy was followed, and between 1882 and 1914 the number of Jews settled in Palestine rose from 24,000 to 85,000.

Palestine was populated by a people commonly known as Arabs. In the second century Arab tribes had moved out of Arabia into Syria and Iraq, but it was only with the rise of Islam in the seventh century that Arab culture and language moved further through Egypt, North Africa and Spain. Thus Arab came to refer to all peoples who spoke the Arabic language or had married Arabs. Most Arabs were Muslim, but the Muslim world became divided between those who accepted the 'orthodox' successors to Muhammad, the Sunis, and those who believed that Ali, Muhammad's son-in-law, was the true successor – the Shias. Jerusalem became a holy place for Muslims as well as for Jews, because a mosque, the Dome of the Rock, was built there in the seventh century. Next to it was the mosque of Aqsa, from which, Muslims believe, Muhammad rode on his magic steed to heaven.

By the late nineteenth century Ottoman control of its empire was crumbling, and Arabs felt increasing antagonism towards Turkish rule. Large areas of Arabia were only loosely controlled by Turkish administrators, with the families of Ibn Saud ruling much of the interior of the Arab lands. From the 1850s a literary revival had stimulated a growth of Arab national consciousness, and with it growing dissatisfaction with Turkish rule. Despite agitation, hopes of more Arab autonomy were frustrated, and the strength of the Arab national movement should not be exaggerated, as most Arabs usually put their tribal loyalties first. In Palestine, though, the Arabs resented the influx of Jews, appreciated the objectives of Zionism and managed to block further Jewish immigration between 1909 and 1914.

(b) The origins of the Arab–Israeli conflict

With the outbreak of the First World War British policy in the Middle East was to encourage Arab activity against Turkish rule. Vague promises were made to the Arabs that after the war the Arabian peninsula and the Muslim holy places would come under the control of an independent Muslim state. Meanwhile Weizmann was making contacts with a number of British politicians, including Lloyd George and Samuel. He made no headway with Asquith, who did not like Jews and believed that the creation of a Jewish homeland composed of European Jews was impractical. In any case the British were more concerned to win Arab support against Turkey, and also had to consider French ambitions in the Middle East. In February 1916 an Anglo-French deal, the Sykes–Picot agreement, was signed. It contained clauses that would win over the Arabs for a war against Turkey, such as the aim of an Arab confederation under the leadership of the Sherif of Mecca. However, great-power control underlay the agreement, as France would have economic priority in the north (Syria) and Britain in the South (Transjordan and Palestine).

In June 1916 Hussein Ibn' Ali, the Sherif of Mecca, raised the Arab revolt and soon captured Mecca and Jedda, but the momentum of the revolt seemed to ebb, and in October T. E. Lawrence was sent by the British to reorganise the Arabs. One of his early decisions was to make one of Hussein's sons, Feisal, leader of the revolt. The Lawrence legend was perpetuated by David Lean's film *Lawrence of Arabia* in 1962. In reality he was a complex character who saw an opportunity to resolve his personal problems through service to the Arab cause (see Chapter 2).

At the end of the war the Arabs were dismayed to learn the full terms of the Sykes–Picot agreement, for, while they liked the British, they did not wish to see the growth of French influence in the Middle East. Even more worrying for the Arabs was the new status of Zionism in British political circles by 1917. Weizmann and his chief colleagues, such as Israel Sieff and Simon Marks, had been busy stressing that not only was Palestine necessary for the security of the British Empire but that a show of sympathy for the Zionist cause would influence opinion in the USA, where 4 million Jews had settled and under the influence of Zionists like Louis Brandeis had become enthusiastic supporters of Zionism. Such factors helped to influence the thinking of the British foreign secretary, Arthur Balfour, who won over the cabinet in November 1917 to espouse the Zionist cause.

The Balfour Declaration stated that Britain viewed with favour the establishment in Palestine of a national home for the Jewish people and promised to help such an objective while at the same time intimating that non-Jews in Palestine should have their civil and religious rights protected. As Colin Cross has shown the Balfour Declaration was a disastrous document because the words 'national home' were not precise. Palestine was already a national home for Jews, and if the phrase meant a Jewish national state, such an objective was incompatible with Arab aspirations.

Both the Sykes–Picot agreement and the Balfour Declaration angered the Arabs, and when in June 1918 Weizmann met Feisal, the Arab leader refused to consider Palestine as a British protectorate or as an area for Jewish colonisation. Arab demands for the complete independence of Arab countries in a federation like the USA were countered by evasive British replies. With the conversion of the British navy to oil and the coming of the internal combustion engine, British policy in the Middle East was increasingly influenced by the need to control oil supplies, and British war aims now included control of Mesopotamia, with its oil wells, and safe passage of oil through the Red Sea, Suez Canal and Mediterranean to Britain. In addition, the British who had used 1.4 million men in the Middle East campaigns, wished to revise the Sykes–Picot agreement to reduce French control of Syria and the Lebanon, arguing that the French had done little fighting in the area. The question caused furious rows between Clemenceau and Lloyd George, who were described by an American observer, Colonel House, as fighting like fishwives. The French, however, stuck to their demand for full control of a large Syria.

Thus at the end of the war both Arab and Jewish aspirations were subordinated to British and French interests. At the Paris Peace conference Feisal and Lawrence pleaded for the independence of all Arab countries, while Weizmann argued in favour of sending 70,000 Jews a year to Palestine, but without any autonomous Jewish government until the Jews formed a large majority of the population. However, a conference of Zionist leaders spelled out the need for many aspects of Jewish control in Palestine, including immigration, water rights, the supervision of education and Hebrew as the main language in all schools. Such wide Jewish aspirations alienated Feisal, who might have accepted a more moderate Zionist programme.

It was the San Remo Conference of April 1920 that decided the future of the Middle East. Mandates for Syria and the Lebanon were allotted to France, and those for Palestine, Transjordan and Mesopotamia to Britain, which was to implement the Balfour Declaration. Feisal was furious and Palestinian Arabs rioted, demanding incorporation of Palestine into Syria. The mandates were now supervised by the British Colonial Office, and when a costly rebellion broke out in Iraq in 1920, the colonial secretary, Churchill, invited Feisal to become King of Iraq. In 1922 Hussein's third son Abdullah was made King of Transjordan, which, though still a mandate, was not to have the Balfour Declaration applied to it. The question of Arabia itself was solved in 1927 when Ibn Saud became King of the Hejaz, after invading it in 1924 with British support; in 1932 he took the title King of Arabia.

As for Palestine, violent clashes between Jews and Arabs occurred in May 1920, and led to a government White Paper in 1922, which formed the basis of British policy for the next decade. It attempted to reassure the Arabs by stating that Palestine as a whole would not be converted into a Jewish national home, merely that such a home would be founded in Palestine. The Zionist organisation would have no share in the administration of Palestine nor would Jewish nationality be imposed on the inhabitants. However, the development of the Jewish community as of right was stressed, and led to Arab rejection of the document. Arab resentment may be understood, given that there were at that time 580,000 Arabs and only

60,000 Jews in Palestine. The terms won for Jews represented a triumph for the effective pressure-group activities by Zionists, who influenced the right British politicians at the right time. Nevertheless the White Paper was a sensible compromise, which attempted to balance the conflicting interests in Palestine by supporting Zionism and seeking to reassure Arabs that Palestine would not constitute *the* national home but only *a* national home for Jews, with no subordination of the Arab population.

In 1922 too formal independence was granted to Egypt under King Faud I, though Britain still had the right to station troops there and in practice retained much influence through the British High Commissioner in Cairo. The Egyptian settlement was the exception to the rule in the Middle East. As Ovendale has trenchantly commented, 'The seeds of the Arab–Israeli conflict were sown at the San Remo Conference. French and British mandates were imposed unceremoniously on reluctant Arab populations and Palestine was specifically excluded from the principle of self-determination. The Western powers carved up an area in their own imperial and domestic interests.'

(c) From the British mandate to the creation of the State of Israel, 1920–48

The 1920 settlement allowed Britain to dominate the Middle East until 1945, and the British ruling élite became fascinated with the Arab world, with its wide empty spaces, and acquired a liking for Arab leaders, who often responded by giving their families a British education. Such attitudes did not exclude some sympathy for Zionism, especially with the rise of Hitler. Preoccupations in Syria and the Lebanon (see Chapter 6) meant that France could not seriously challenge British pre-eminence in the Middle East. British control was greatest in Transjordan, where eight British officials, including General John Glubb, helped the administration of the country, while British influence remained considerable in Egypt and the Sudan. In contrast Iraq was given formal independence in 1930, and after Feisal's death in 1933 a military coup occurred. In 1938 Nuri Said, Feisal's pro-British chief of staff, secured power and protected British interests in Iraq for the next 20 years.

On the whole British policy, though paternalist, was flexible, and ensured comparative stability in the Middle East in the interwar period. Time brought a new generation of Arabs, who resented British domination as oppressive and too favourable to Zionism. When Hitler's persecution led to a flood of Jewish refugees to Palestine, Britain was blamed by the Arabs for the imposition on them of an alien population.

For a few years after 1922 there was comparative calm in Palestine. Few Jews emigrated there, as most preferred to go to the USA. Arab fears of a Zionist take-over lessened. Even so, between 1919 and 1931 the Jewish population in Palestine grew from 60,000 (8 per cent of the total population) to 175,000 (17.5 per cent of the total population). In 1928 religious disputes between Arabs and Jews broke out over the Western Wall in Jerusalem. To Jews it was sacred because it was part of Herod's temple, while to Arabs it was where Muhammad had tethered his horse after his journey from Mecca to Jerusalem. In August 1929 113 Jews and 116 Arabs died in a week of violence, which led to the calling in of British troops and the use of the Jewish army, the Haganah. The tragedy led to a commission of inquiry, which reported in 1930 that Zionist demands on immigration had aroused Arab apprehension about Jewish political domination. A White Paper of 1930 stressed that, as there was insufficient land to provide the Arab population with a decent livelihood, Jewish immigration should be restricted. The document led to an orchestrated Zionist campaign against it throughout the Jewish world, and in 1931 the British, to Arab anger, reaffirmed that they would stand by promises on Jewish immigration. Arab riots occurred in 1933 and a revolt in 1935.

As Jewish purchases of land increased in Palestine, unemployment among Arabs rose. Simultaneously Hitler's accession to power led to the number of Jewish immigrants from Germany rising from 353 in 1932 to a peak of over 61,000 in 1935. A British offer of representative government was rejected by both sides in 1935. In 1936 an Arab general strike provoked violence, which led to 263 deaths and the stationing of more British troops in the mandate. A royal commission under Lord Peel contrived with some difficulty to investigate the problem in 1936 and reported in June 1937. It recommended that Palestine should be divided into three parts – an Arab state, a Jewish state and an area reserved for British control. Zionists were divided over acceptance, while Arabs throughout the Middle East rejected it, Iraq condemning it at the League of Nations. The British Foreign Office also opposed the plan, Eden remarking that the Jewish state would have indefensible frontiers and the Arab state no outlet to the sea.

Behind British attitudes was the fear that the Grand Mufti of Jerusalem, who had fled from Palestine after joining in the recent Arab agitation, would gain support from Nazi Germany, which viewed the prospect of a Jewish state with alarm. Therefore in November 1938 the idea of partition was given up. A further White Paper published in May 1939 recommended that an independent Palestine be created within 10 years, with Arabs and Jews sharing control. Over the next 5 years the number of Jewish immigrants would be restricted to 75,000, and after that immigration would be subject to British consent. Restrictions were placed on the transfer of Arab land to Jews.

The document demonstrated the British wish to win the benevolent neutrality of the Arabs in the coming war. It was, however, too late to placate the Arabs, but it did succeed in angering the American Jewish lobby and turning Zionists in Palestine to more violent tactics, including bombing and illegal immigration through their terrorist organisations, Irgun and Stern. Britain rather than the Arabs now became the Zionists' principal enemy. The other plank of their strategy was to use their influence in the USA, especially at election time (the Jewish vote was important in three key states – New York, Pennsylvania and Illinois) to force the American government into supporting a Jewish state. Consequently by 1945 Palestine had become an area of Anglo-American disagreement, the British resenting the American willingness to sacrifice British strategic interests in the Mediterranean on the altar of American domestic politics.

The style of Zionist leadership changed in May 1942, when Weizmann was replaced by the more activist David Ben-Gurion. Vigorous pressure was put on top American officials, such as Stimson, secretary of war, and Morgenthau, the treasury secretary, to bully Britain to allow more Jewish immigration into Palestine. This policy attracted Americans in two quite different ways; there was sympathy for the Jews, as hints of Nazi genocide began to be known, but the policy would also mean that fewer Jews would enter the USA. However, the Americans were deterred from pushing this policy too strongly by Arab opposition to Zionism; the USA was now less self-sufficient in oil, and Arab opposition could undermine military operations in the Mediterranean. The Americans also feared that Soviet Russia might gain influence in the Middle East by adopting a pro-Arab stance.

The British disliked the prospect of more American interference, and their attitude hardened in November 1944 when Lord Moyne, the Minister Resident in the Middle East, was murdered in Cairo by the underground Zionist terrorist group, the Stern gang. The British government was angered by Zionist agitation in the USA, in which the Zionists gained influence out of all proportion to their numbers. Condemnation of Britain's Palestine policy by Americans seemed hypocritical to the British, a way of easing American consciences over the refusal to admit large numbers of Jews into the USA. With both Russia and the USA seeking to profit from British difficulties in the Middle East, British policy remained one of restricting Jewish immigration into Palestine in the hope of retaining Arab goodwill, while trying to persuade the USA to share or take over responsibility for the mandate. In October 1945 the new Labour foreign secretary, Ernest Bevin, mooted the idea of an Anglo-American commission to investigate the Jewish refugee problem. The commission recommended a bi-national state and the admission of 100,000 refugees, but Truman in an election year was pushed by the American Jewish lobby into commenting favourably on partition.

A clear gap now opened up between Britain and the USA, as British opinion hardened further as a result of Zionist attacks on British troops, especially when the King David Hotel in Jerusalem, a wing of which was used as British army headquarters, was blown up and ninety-one people killed. The atrocity was the work of the Irgun terrorist group led by Menachem Begin, a Polish soldier who arrived in Palestine in 1943. The Haganah was also involved. Begin later claimed that the British were warned of the impending attack, but no real evidence was ever produced.

In February 1947 the British government had more joint meetings with Arabs and Zionists. Both sides remained inflexible. The Arabs opposed partition and asked why Arabs were the only people who were called upon to pay for what Hitler had done to the Jews. They asked the British delegates to say what British reaction would be if a third power were to impose on Britain an alien element whose presence would disrupt her national life and unity. Ben Gurion insisted that the future of the Arabs did not depend on Palestine, but that it was essential for Jewish survival, and he spoke of the need for 1.2 million Jewish immigrants. The British proposed self-government for Palestine after 5 years of trusteeship, with 100,000 Jewish immigrants admitted over the next 2 years. Both Jews and Arabs rejected the plan and the British government decided to submit the problem to the United Nations. By then Anglo-American relations had been further clouded by the traffic in illegal immigrants into Palestine, paid for by American sympathisers and carried out by American crewmen in American ships.

In May following the British move, a UN fact-finding committee was set up – the UN Special Committee on Palestine (UNSCOP). In August it suggested partition into an Arab state, a Jewish state and the city of Jerusalem under international trusteeship. In the interim period Britain should administer the mandate and admit 150,000 refugees.

The period of the UNSCOP enquiry saw the final wearing down of British morale in Palestine through a combination of the expense of the mandate, Zionist activity in the USA, which raised money to arm Irgun and Stern, and the murder of British troops. Two incidents in particular convinced Britain that it had to withdraw from Palestine. One was the arrival in Palestine of the *Exodus* with 4,493 illegal immigrants. When it was sent back to its French port of embarkation, the Irgun hanged two British sergeants and booby-trapped their bodies, justifying this as an act of war. The cold-blooded nature of the murders led to outbreaks of anti-Semitism in Britain and much criticism of the USA. The refugees were shipped back to Germany, but the Zionists exploited the resulting propaganda victory.

In September 1947 the British government decided that it would surrender the Palestine mandate, and planned the withdrawal of British forces by May 1948. It attempted to mollify Arab opinion by promises of continued military equipment and finance to Jordan and Saudi Arabia. In November the General Assembly voted for partition after the American government and the American Jewish lobby exerted pressure on the delegates to secure the necessary majority. Their campaign succeeded because of natural sympathy for the victims of the holocaust and the publicity given to the *Exodus* incident. On a bill to secure the entry of Jewish refugees into the USA, introduced into the House of Representatives in 1947, the American Zionists were strangely inactive, contributing only 11 out of 693 pages of testimony.

In early 1948 the American government became worried at the dangers of alienating the Arabs, moved away from the idea of partition and suggested UN trusteeship for Palestine. The British refused to countenance the scheme, which they believed might prolong their responsibilities in Palestine, and instructed the chiefs of staff to accelerate withdrawal. The British public heartily supported the move to bring British troops home, and American threats that this could damage Anglo-American relations did not make Bevin change his mind.

When British military authorities in the Haifa area of Palestine began withdrawing in April, fighting broke out between Jews and Arabs. The Haganah was well organised and won these exchanges, causing many Arabs to flee from Palestine. At the village of Deir Yassin, Irgun and Stern slaughtered 245 men, women and children. When on 14 May the last British forces left Palestine, Ben Gurion on the same day proclaimed the establishment of a Jewish state in Palestine to be called Israel. The next day Arab armies entered Palestine from Jordan, Egypt and Iraq. The first Arab-Israeli war had begun. The Mufti of Jerusalem had proclaimed a jihad or holy war as soon as the UN partition plan was announced in November 1947. The Arabs refused to accept partition of Palestine, as they felt that such a move went against 1,800 years of Palestine's history. Furthermore the partition plan awarded the Jews over half of Palestine, even though they were less than one-third of the population.

The Israelis were well prepared for the war. Many of their 30,000 troops had experience in the Second World War, and equipment was bought from a number of countries, including communist states, with money received from the USA. The combined Arab forces numbered 40,000, but only Glubb's Arab Legion from Jordan had similar quality of training. Furthermore, though Israeli regular troops clashed on occasions with their Irgun partners, the Israelis were united. In contrast, the Arabs, in Ovendale's words, 'were torn apart by old rivalries'. King Farouk of Egypt only intervened out of fear of his opponents at home, the Muslim Brotherhood, and out of jealousy of any gains that Jordan and Iraq might make. King Abdullah of Jordan infuriated his Arab partners by organising a conference in December in which the delegates called for a union of Palestine and Transjordan. Consequently the Israelis were able to exploit Arab divisions and implement a series of carefully planned offensives, and by the end of 1948 had moved on to Egyptian territory. The UN representative, Count Bernadotte, sent to mediate, was murdered in Jerusalem by the Stern gang, and though Ben Gurion dissolved both Stern and Irgun, those arrested were released without trial.

In February 1949 Israel reached agreement with its enemies by which it gained 21 per cent more land than it had been awarded under the 1947 partition plan. It now covered nearly 80 per cent of Palestine, but in all probability it also acquired more insecure frontiers. The Arab League against Israel split, each member blaming the others for failing to provide enough for the war. Yet surrounding Arab states actually made gains, despite defeat, Egypt acquiring the Gaza Strip and Jordan the West Bank enclave. The real victims were the Palestinian Arabs, who remain a major problem to this day. By 1949 a million Palestinian Arabs were refugees, and by the 1960s this figure had doubled. The population of Israel rose from 1.1 millions to 1.8 millions between 1948 and 1957, as over half a million Jews left Muslim countries in North Africa and the Middle East. Very few American or European Jews who were not refugees settled in Israel.

(d) Change in the Middle East

The first Arab–Israeli war helped to foment a new kind of Arab nationalism, which found a common focal point in hatred of Israel. But it also disliked the reactionary power of the old dynasties and Western imperialism. A number of revolutions therefore occurred after 1948. There was unrest in Syria and Iraq, while in Jordan King Abdullah was murdered in 1951; his successor, Hussein, came to the throne in 1952 and dismissed Glubb in 1956. The most significant change occurred in Egypt, where young officers, appalled by the conduct of the war against Israel, prepared to oust Farouk. In 1952 a bloodless coup led to the exile of the king. General Neguib was president for a year but was replaced by Gamel Abdel Nasser in 1954.

In his book *The Philosophy of the Revolution* Nasser pointed to three key roles for Egypt as leader of the Arab world, of the Muslim world and of Black African nations struggling for independence. Such pan-Arabic and African ambitions were anti-British and anti-French. Whether Nasserism really amounted to very much is a matter of debate. Anthony McDermott has recently commented that it was nothing more than a superb political style without doctrine, and certainly at home Nasser's socialism was merely a series of improvised economic programmes rather than a comprehensive policy.

Meanwhile Israel consolidated its internal and international position. Its introduciton of conscription raised the strength of the army to 200,000, while, in the words of Hugh Thomas, a Franco–Israeli love affair developed; both countries disliked Nasser's Egypt, and France became Israel's principal source of armaments. However, Israel's international reputation was tarnished by its retaliatory raids on neighbouring territory. Though he gave way as premier for a time to the more moderate Moshe Sharett in 1953, Ben Gurion and his cohorts, Shimon Peres and Moshe Dayan, remained influential. They were not afraid to take strong action against the fedayeen – guerrillas who invaded Israel from Egypt.

British power in the Middle East continued to decline. In 1951 Mohammed Mussadeq, the Iranian premier, succeeded in nationalising the Anglo-Iranian Oil Company, and the British share of oil production in the Middle East dropped from 53 per cent to 24 per cent. British relations with Egypt were strained by the British military presence in the Suez Canal Zone, and therefore in 1954 an Anglo-Egyptian treaty arranged that British troops would be withdrawn within 20 months. Nevertheless Nasser instigated wireless broadcasts in Swahili supporting Mau Mau terrorism in Kenya.

Partly to isolate Nasser, Britain took the lead in the formation in 1955 of the Baghdad Pact between Iraq, Turkey, Iran and Pakistan, the more conservative powers in the region. Nasser was also disappointed at rebuffs from Britain and the USA, who refused to provide funds to build the Aswan Dam after initially promising support. Britain was short of resources herself and reluctant to help a man inciting British subjects to rebel in Africa, while the USA was angered by Nasser's request for arms from the Soviet bloc and by his refusal to make peace with Israel.

Tension rose in the Middle East in 1956 as the fedayeen increased their activities from bases in Egypt and Israel prepared for a new confrontation. Ben Gurion had become premier again in November 1955, and he acquired top class military equipment from Britain and France, including the Mystère IV fighters.

(e) The Suez–Sinai War of 1956

Nasser felt slighted by the Anglo-American withdrawal from the Aswan dam venture, and the only alternative means of financing it was by the nationalisation of the Anglo-French Suez Canal Company, a move effected in July. The British premier, Eden, was infuriated and hoped with American support to put economic and military pressure on Nasser. But the British throughout the Suez Crisis failed to appreciate the significance of the American presidential elections due to take place in November. Eisenhower wished to be re-elected president on a platform of maintaining world peace, and therefore he could not be seen to support Britain in what appeared to be an act of imperial aggression. This American view should have been made clear to the British at the outset but was not, the Americans preferring to play for time until November.

Insisting that peaceful measures should be exhausted first, they suggested a conference of maritime nations. At the same time Dulles, the American secretary of state, conceded that Nasser would have to be made to 'disgorge' the Suez Canal Company. This misled the British, who prepared, with the French, an expedition comprising 80,000 troops. The conference of maritime powers met on 16 August and suggested a Suez Canal Board to run the Canal, a proposal rejected by Nasser. Another American device to win time was the creation of Suez Canal Users Association (SCUA), but by the end of September Eisenhower and Dulles were explicitly opposing the use of force.

The strain on Eden became great. Attacked by the Opposition for warlike preparations and by his own party for lack of action, he was a sick man throughout the crisis, dependent on benzadrine. Obsessed by the need to oust Nasser, the British premier began to see in the Egyptian leader as great a threat to peace in the 1950s as the Fascist dictators had been in the 1930's. This view was a wild exaggeration of Nasser's real importance, but it led the British to give consideration on 14 October to a Franco-Israeli plan to attack Egypt. Israel would attack Egypt across the Sinai, and once this was in Israeli control, Britain and France would order Israel and Egypt to withdraw from the Suez Canal zone and occupy it themselves on the pretext of separating the combatants. The Suez Canal could then be restored to Anglo-French control. By 25 October final details were agreed for an Israeli attack on 29 October. The Americans through their intelligence sources knew of the plans, and Eisenhower asked Eden to delay the operation until after the American presidential elections on 6 November. The American request was refused, and on 29 October Dayan's forces mounted an effective attack, occupying most of the Sinai by 3 November. The Anglo-French then presented their ultimatum, which was rejected by Nasser. Bombing raids on Egypt were then carried out by the Anglo-French, and the Israelis reached the Canal by the 5th, on which day the Anglo-French occupied Port Said.

Absurdly after 1 day's preparations the British called for a ceasefire as a result of American pressure. Eisenhower would have liked Nasser disposed of, but he felt that the British had been unreasonable about the timing. The Americans imposed economic measures to force a British withdrawal from Egypt. The sold sterling, held up supplies of oil and blocked Britain's drawing rights from the International Monetary Fund. The American actions forced a collapse of sterling, which, combined with domestic opposition, Russian threats and Commonwealth disapproval, led to a climbdown by Eden, who was not at heart a warmonger. Anglo-French forces were gradually withdrawn and a UN Emergency Force patrolled the Canal, which the Egyptians now regained.

The importance of the Suez Crisis may have been exaggerated at the time, but it did accelerate the decline of Britain's global prestige and its influence in the Middle East, which was already waning. The British withdrawal angered the French, who had wished to push on to Cairo and topple Nasser; they now turned with more conviction to joining the EEC. The real winner in the crisis was Israel. It agreed to evacuate the Sinai, but on condition that the Straits of Tira, which separated the Gulf of Aqaba from the Red Sea, were opened to allow Israel to receive oil through the port of Eilat. In the Gaza strip an Egyptian administration returned but no Egyptian military installations, and Israel was freed from fedayeen attacks for a decade.

Nasser's prestige received a blow as a result of Egypt's military defeat, though he was still able to claim a victory over the two European powers. Superficially his influence increased in the next few years, but a number of his schemes folded, e.g. the union of Syria and Egypt into the United Arab Republic in 1958. The union lasted only 3 years before Syrian army units proclaimed independence. Nasser's ambitions to gain influence in Black Africa were not fulfilled, and his interference in the Yemen from 1962 on tied down 40,000 Egyptian troops. Ovendale rightly calls the Yemen Egypt's Vietnam. Nasser's prestige was also weakened by his reliance on Russian money for armaments and the construction of the Aswan Dam.

(f) The Six-Day and Yom Kippur wars, 1967 and 1973

Nasser's concerns elsewhere meant that the problems of Israel and the Palestinian refugees in Gaza were neglected, much to the disappointment of Yasser Arafat and his militant Fatah resistance group. In 1964 the Palestine Liberation Organisation (PLO) was formed, its aim being to unite all expatriate Palestinians, including those on the West Bank. It did gain equipment and training from Egypt, but a united Arab front against Israel was hard to cement, because Nasser's activities had alienated such conservative Arab leaders as Hussein of Jordan and Feisal of Saudi Arabia. Nasser's propaganda against Britain alienated Western sympathies and hid the plight of the Palestinian refugees. Western audiences were instead spellbound by the 1960 film *Exodus*, starring Paul Newman. By extolling the courage of the Jews and the iniquities of the Arabs, the film created sympathy for Israel in the West.

Israel also won respect on its merits. Its economic achievements, helped by American finance, were considerable. Military preparation was sophisticated. Given Israel's size and geographical position, it was decided that Israeli forces should be ready to make pre-emptive strikes against her enemies through the development of mechanised infantry and the purchase of the most modern planes from the West. By 1967 Israel was therefore in a strong military position, because, though her Arab enemies had been equipped with Russian weapons, they were not sufficiently well trained to handle them.

In early 1967 tension between Israel and her Arab neighbours grew, with clashes on the Syrian–Israeli border in April. The Syrian and Jordanian press taunted Nasser for failing to help fellow Arabs and accused hin of preferring his Yemen ambitions instead. When Israel gave Nasser the impression that it was about to attack Syria, the Egyptian dictator was tempted into sending troops into Sinai and closing the Straits of Tira to Israeli shipping. Levi Eshkol, the Israeli premier, regarded such Egyptian provocation as an act of aggression against Israel.

Under mounting threats from its Arab neighbours, Israel launched the Six-Day War on 5 June before they were ready for full military action. The airforces of Egypt, Jordan and Syria were quickly destroyed, and by 7 June Israeli troops had pushed out the Jordanians from Arab Jerusalem, Jericho and the rest of the West Bank. Syrian troops retreated from the Golan Heights on 10 June and Egyptian troops were swept out of the Sinai. It was a spectacular Israeli victory, the fruit of careful planning.

Ironically the war reduced Israeli security. It created more Palestinian refugees, and after 1967 the question of the Palestinian refugees became a world issue through the terrorist activities of the PLO. Israel's Arab neighbours also hardened their attitude, their objective now more clearly becoming the elimination of Israel. They refused to negotiate or accept peace, and the period from 1967 to 1973 was merely a time of preparation for the next confrontation.

Nasser was helped by the Russians to re-equip his armed forces, and he gave up his wider ambitions to support the PLO against Israel. He attempted to form a united front against Israel in a war of attrition, and many border clashes occurred before his death in 1970. Arab in-fighting still undermined unity. In September 1970 Hussein was nearly murdered by Palestinian fedayeen for trying to reach a settlement with Israel, and he evicted the Palestinians in 1971. Arab tactics also became more extreme after Mummar El Gadaffi overthrew King Idris of Libya in 1969. Terrorism continued to be used against Israelis, the worst example being the murder of the

Israeli Olympic team by Palestinian terrorists in 1972. From 1970 on the Marxist Popular Front for the Liberation of Palestine began hijacking aircraft, because in its view the Western nations were responsible for the Palestinian refugees.

In Syria Hafez el Assad seized power in October 1970, while Anwar el Sadat replaced Nasser. Sadat became disillusioned with the Russian connection, and told the 15,000 Russian advisers to leave Egypt in 1972. He succeeded in increasing Egypt–Syria military cooperation, a united command being achieved in 1973. The two states planned a new offensive against Israel and chose 6 October, Yom Kippur, the Jewish Day of atonement and also Ramadan, the month of the Muslim Fast. The Israelis were almost taken by surprise and were pushed back by a well-executed Arab operation before the tide turned on 18 October. A ceasefire effected on 24 October was gladly accepted by both sides.

The consequences of the war were immense. Sadat emerged as a world statesman, while the improved military performance restored Arab pride somewhat. Israel was induced to negotiate over the occupied territories, especially as the new premier, Golda Meir, had gained a promise from the USA that it would guarantee Israel's survival.

The most astonishing impact of the war was the new appreciation by oil-producing Arab states of the potential hold that they could gain over the West by control of the supply and price of oil. They had formed the Organisation of Petroleum Exporting Countries (OPEC) in 1960, but only in 1973 did they fully exert their power by raising the price of oil steeply.

(g) Oil and the world economy

By the 1970s the advanced industrial countries (AICs) had experienced 25 years of unparalleled sustained growth, in which both inflation and unemployment were kept at low levels. The assumption that such growth would continue during the 1970s was rudely shattered by an outbreak of stagflation (stagnation and inflation) between 1973 and 1975. Economists have pointed to many reasons for this – lower investment, the rising militancy of labour, wasteful government expenditure and increased competition from newly industrialising countries, for example. However, Bruno and Sachs rightly point to 'one clear and central villain of the piece' – the historically unprecedented rise in commodity prices, especially oil. Its price rose steeply at the time of the Yom Kippur War, and again in 1979–80, as a result of the revolution in Iran, which deposed the Shah and disrupted oil supplies. Consequently oil rose from $1.80 a barrel in 1970 to $34 a barrel in 1980, and, even allowing for inflation, was four times as expensive at the end of the decade as at the beginning.

The oil price shocks had five unfortunate results for the world economy:

1. The higher import bill for oil drained money away from non-oil-producing states, and reduced total aggregate demand in those countries.
2. Oil-producing states could not spend all their extra income, saving much of it, and consequently world aggregate demand was reduced. Both these factors caused more unemployment.
3. At the same time the higher price of oil added to the costs of production and therefore increased inflation. A secondary impulse to inflation came from union militancy, as labour demanded wage increases in line with the rise in the cost of living.
4. The extra costs of both oil and labour, combined with declining demand, had an unfortunate result on business confidence as profits were squeezed. Consequently levels of investment fell in the 1970s, further reducing growth and employment.
5. The oil price shocks had direct balance of payments consequences. Countries which needed to import most of their oil now experienced large deficits on their balance of trade. Such deficits caused the value of their currencies to fall, but this meant that all imports rose in price, further increasing inflation.

Thus many countries faced an unpalatable menu of rising unemployment, rising inflation, low growth, large balance of payments deficits and downward pressures on their currencies. No country acting on its own could tackle such thorny problems, and only a large degree of internationally coordinated economic policies would have helped to save the world economy from severe disruption. But such cooperation did not exist in the 1970s. After the second oil price shock of the 1979–80 most industrialised countries saw inflation as the main enemy, and pursued more monetarist and less Keynesian economic policies, one factor causing unemployment to rise to 8.3 per cent in the OECD countries by 1983. The lesson that oil was of vast economic importance had been painfully learned, and accounts for the presence of Western navies in the Persian Gulf to superintend the safe passage of oil tankers through the Gulf during the Iran–Iraqi War in the 1980s.

(h) Egypt and Israel after 9173

Sadat wished to change Nasser's policies by putting Egypt's interests above those of pan-Arabism. He disliked the violence of the Palestinian organisations and such fundamentalist Arab states as Libya. By winning American approval, he hoped for American money to develop the Egyptian economy. Therefore he worked hard for a rapprochement with Israel, meeting Menachem Begin (who had replaced Golda Meir as Israeli premier) twice in 1977. The opportunity for the American president, Jimmy Carter, to act as honest broker had arrived, and in 1978 talks were held at Camp David, the president's retreat in the Maryland hills, between Carter, Begin and Sadat. The resulting Treaty of Washington, signed in March 1979, provided for peaceful relations and Israeli withdrawal from all occupied Egyptian territory, i.e. the Sinai except the Gaza Strip.

The Israeli–Egyptian rapprochement divided the Arab world; extremist Arab states, e.g. Libya and Syria, were infuriated, Gadaffi even offering a reward for Sadat's death. More seriously for Sadat, the opening up of the Egyptian economy to foreign investment widened the gap between rich and poor, and added to the support already being gained by Islamic fundamentalists, who opposed the peace with Israel. In the autumn of 1981 fundamentalist members of his own army murdered Sadat at a military review, but this did not discredit Islamic extremism in Egypt. As McDermott has noted, the number of underground Islamic groups in Egypt has increased in the 1980s, and the main Islamic organisation, the Muslim Brotherhood, won thirty-six seats in the 1987 elections, forming the chief opposition to Sadat's successor, Hosni Mubarak. He has continued Sadat's policies of an open door economic policy, ties with the USA and peace with Israel, but in a much less flamboyant style than Sadat. However, given the level of internal opposition, the future of Egypt as a secular pro-Western state remains uncertain.

For Israel, the new relationship with Egypt was a real gain, and in 1980 Egypt gave Israel diplomatic recognition, the first Arab state to do so. However, only one out of four territorial issues which divided Israel from the Arab world had been settled. The 1967 war had made Israel an occupying power in four territories formerly held by neighbouring Arab states – the Sinai peninsula and the Gaza Strip taken off Egypt, the West Bank of the Jordan river taken off Jordan and the Golan Heights captured from Syria. The restoration of the Sinai to Egypt by Begin in 1979 was a comparatively easy step for Israel to take; it was of little economic value, and, unlike the other territories gained in 1967, was not part of the biblical land of Israel. Many Orthodox Jews in Israel believed – and continue to believe – that the remaining areas should stay Jewish and become a suitable location for Jewish settlement, because they were part of biblical Israel: for example, the West Bank was biblical Judea and Samaria. The disputed territories also had a strategic importance for Israeli security; the Golan Heights in Syrian hands would again become a platform for attacks on Israeli kibbutzim, and in 1980 Begin roundly asserted that Israel would never return the Golan Heights to Syria.

But what of the Palestinians? The PLO leader Yasser Arafat

succeeded in winning some measure of world support for the inclusion of the Palestinians in any peace settlement and for the idea of a Palestinian homeland. Israel opposed any concessions on the Palestinian problem, and in 1978 and 1982 attacked PLO bases in the Lebanon, where a bitter civil war had broken out in 1975 between the Christian government of President Frangie and the Arabs. The 1982 Israeli incursion led to 3 years of Israeli occupation of Southern Lebanon. Initially the local population, despite being Shiite Muslims, welcomed the Israelis as liberators from the PLO, which had infiltrated into the Lebanon from Syria. However, when Israeli occupation persisted, local feeling turned against the foreign presence, and Israeli troops were harassed by guerrilla activity, often of a suicidal nature.

Meanwhile the Palestinian problem continued to be a running sore for Israel within her own borders. The Gaza Strip had housed 100,000 Palestinians before 1948; by the 1980s it was home for 650,000 Palestinians, more than half of whom lived in eight refugee camps, where conditions were appalling. Though conditions among Palestinians in the West Bank were better, the Israeli policy of establishing Jewish settlements on land formerly owned by Palestinians caused much resentment.

Their plight ignored by neighbouring Arab states and their aspirations crushed by a repressive Israeli presence, the only help for the Palestinian Arabs of the West Bank and the Gaza Strip has come from the United Nations Relief and Work Agency (UNRWA) and charitable organisations. Clashes between Palestinian youths and Israeli soldiers became a daily occurrence in 1988, and led to worldwide criticism of Israel; even her major ally, the USA, whose annual aid of \$3 billions has helped to sustain the Israeli economy, has attempted to moderate Israel's policies towards the Palestinians within her borders.

(i) The Iran–Iraq War, 1980–8

Modern Iran (formerly Persia) was dominated by Britain and Russia at the beginning of the twentieth century. Britain's interest in the country arose out of a wish to check Russian expansion, and also out of a need to exploit Persian oil, the Anglo-Persian Oil Company being founded in 1909. The intrusion of foreign influences stimulated the growth of a religious Persian nationalism, fomented by occupations of large parts of Persia by Russian and British troops during the First World War.

From 1941 Mohammad Reza was the Shah of Iran; he combined economic modernisation with an increasingly dictatorial style of government. Great personal extravagance was matched only by large arms purchases, especially from the USA, which backed the Shah because he was anti-communist.

The Shah's pro-Western modernising policies alienated the traditional Shiite Muslim religious leaders, while his repressive measures alienated liberal and left-wing parties, as well as such racial minorities as the Kurds. From 1977 he faced growing opposition from religious leaders, such as Ayatollah Khomeini, and was forced to abdicate in January 1979, fleeing to the USA. Khomeini's theocratic regime restored fundamentalist Islamic rule in Iran, harsh traditional punishments being meted out to opponents among the racial minorities, the Shah's supporters and Sunni Muslims. The regime was rabidly anti-American, and in November 1979 took the occupants of the American embassy in Teheran as hostages, both to humiliate the USA and gain extradition of the Shah. A rescue attempt by American forces failed, and the hostages were only released after the death of the Shah in 1980, with the Americans being forced to hand over Iranian assets in the USA to the new regime.

The Iranian revolution tempted the Iraqi regime under General Sadam Hussein to launch an attack on Iran in April 1980, to gain prestige and the oil-rich area of Khuzestan. Initial Iraqi victories were not sustained, as Iran, which had a much larger population, was able to counter-attack. The war, however, soon became a bloody and futile stalemate which had claimed a million casualties by 1988. By then Iran's army was badly depleted, with many young teenagers drafted in to meet the onslaught of the better armed Iraqis, who were able to launch a new offensive to recapture the Fao Peninsula, lost to Iran in 1983. Iran's cities came under attack by Iraqi missiles and a million of Teheran's population left the city.

The war was much more than a local tragedy. Iran's act in mining the waters of the Persian Gulf threatened oil supplies, and led to increased confrontation between Iran and the West, as Western navies attempted to protect oil tankers in the Gulf. The West as well as the moderate Arab states were further incensed by the visible hand of Iran behind acts of international terrorism.

The war further divided the Arab world. The more conservative states, such as Saudi Arabia under King Fahd, gave support to Iraq, while the more radical states, such as Libya, condemned Iraq for attacking a fellow Muslim state when it should have been concentrating on assisting the destruction of Israel. Saudi–Iran relations deteriorated sharply when Iran tried to undermine Saudi Arabia's position as guardian of Islam's two holiest places – Mecca and Medina. In July 1987 Iranian pilgrims visiting Mecca clashed with Saudi security forces and over 400 people were killed. In May 1988 Saudi Arabia finally broke off diplomatic relations with Iran, and bought Chinese missiles as insurance against acts of Iranian aggression.

By then however Iran's reverses had caused a power struggle within the country between the fundamentalist religious leaders and the moderates led by Hashemi Rafsanjani, nicknamed the Shark. His position as speaker of the Iranian parliament enabled him to put pressure on Khomeini to call for an end to the war in July. In August 1988 a fragile ceasefire brought the futile and costly war to a close. Nevertheless, the Middle East remained a storm centre of world politics despite the death of the Ayatollah Khomeini in June 1989.

FURTHER READING

Bakhash, S., *The Reign of the Ayatollahs*, Unwin, London, 1986

Fraser, T. G., *The Middle East 1914–1979*, Edward Arnold, 1980

Laqueur, W. and Rubin, B. M., *The Israel–Arab Reader*, Penguin, Harmondsworth, 1985

McDermott, A., *Egypt from Nasser to Mubarak*, Croom Helm, Beckenham, 1988

Monroe, E., *Britain's Moment in the Middle East*, Chatto and Windus, London, 1963

Nutting, A., *Nasser*, Constable, London, 1972

Odell, P., *Oil and World Power*, Penguin, Harmondsworth, 1980

Ovendale, R., *The Arab–Israeli Wars*, Longmans, London, 1984

Stewart, D., *T. E. Lawrence*, Paladin, London, 1979

Thomas, H., *The Suez Affair*, Penguin, Harmondsworth, 1970

Vital, D., *Zionism: The Formative Years*, OUP, Oxford, 1982

QUESTIONS

1. Critically examine the importance of the San Remo Conference of April 1920.
2. What can be said for and against British policy in Palestine up to 1948?
3. Discuss the importance of the contribution of the USA to the establishment of the state of Israel.
4. Why did Israel emerge victorious in her wars with Arab states between 1948 and 1973?
5. Why have oil price shocks been of such importance to the world economy since 1973?
6. To what extent have the Arab–Israeli wars since 1948 created more problems than they have solved?

20
Troubled Africa south of the Sahara

(a) The colonial experience

By the end of the nineteenth century the continent of Africa had experienced virtually complete partition by the European powers, though subsequently France was to gain Morocco, and Italy the territories of Tripolitania, Cyrenaica and Ethiopia. The major European colonial powers had usually carried out such partition in Europe itself through major conferences. Often European control was tenuous at the time of the agreement and only later was real power exercised and boundaries drawn. Such a task was not easy, because the areas concerned were enormous and communications non-existent. Thus the infrastructure had to be developed and the endless variety of African communities made amenable, either by agreement with their leaders (who often did not understand the implications of such arrangements) or by military conquest.

J. D. Fage divides the colonial period into three phases. Up to 1914, or even the 1920s, the Europeans had to devote their main efforts to securing a proper hold over the colonies and organising them. As Africa was poor, few Europeans wished to make their careers there, and colonial offices were anxious to avoid too much expense. Apart from missionaries, only one class – the ambitious army officer, exemplified by Kitchener and Joffre – was attracted to service in Africa, given the lack of war in Europe until 1914. The best example of an army officer turned colonial administrator was Frederick Lugard in Nigeria. He implemented the doctrine of indirect rule, whereby Europeans sought to control the traditional African rulers while leaving to them the more difficult task of keeping order over the mass of the people. Therefore the main burden of imposing European rule on Africans was borne by Africans. Colonial armies became much less expensive, as African enlisted troops required less in the way of pensions and pay. Any losses in campaigns needed to complete control of a colony would not lead to so many awkward questions at home.

Once Europeans had imposed their rule over a colony, they continued to rely on Africans to help them govern; but little development took place in many colonies. Before 1939 only colonies with mineral deposits, such as South Africa, or the few colonies climatically suitable for European settlement, such as the Rhodesias, enjoyed significant investment.

To attract capital to Africa large areas of most colonies were leased or granted to private companies. On occasions the governments found it expedient to grant powers of government to companies operating in Africa, such as the Royal Niger Company. However, no private company had sufficient capital to develop an extensive territory, and its commercial interests prevented it from maintaining an impartial administration. Consequently governments were usually forced again to take over direct responsibility for the colonies. Even the richest company – the British South African Company, created in 1889 by Cecil Rhodes to exploit South Africa's gold and diamond resources – was stretched to provide even a flimsy administration in Rhodesia.

Where a company was a governing agency, it was called a chartered company, as opposed to a concession company, which was supposed to operate within a framework of administration provided by the European government's own colonial authorities. It was where such companies were compelled to deliver an assessed quota for products gained in Africa to agents of the state that the worst abuses occurred. In the Belgian Congo some 2,000 white agents of Leopold II of Belgium were sent to organise the rubber trade. As Louis Turner comments in his book *Multinationals in the Third World*, 'Under their leadership an armed headman was installed in each village. Reputable estimates suggest that between five and eight million Congolese were killed in the course of 23 years. Roger Casement's investigations in 1904 showed that the Congolese were expected to produce 20 baskets of rubber from the jungle four times a month for no pay.' Similar scandals occurred in French Equatorial Africa, where eighteen companies were granted concessions and about 20,000 conscripted labourers died between 1921 and 1934 in the construction of a railway.

Thus the results of the first 25 years of active European colonisation in Africa were far from impressive. To an extent, as Fage emphasises, the Europeans were victims of their own propaganda, which had alleged that vast fortunes were there for the making. The continent was not, however, a treasure box waiting to be opened by the key of colonial rule. African societies were not geared to the production of profitable commodities for the world market. Many areas were short of resources, and, even where they existed, considerable expense was incurred in first finding and then developing them. The infrastructure required was beyond the capacity of colonial governments to provide. Colonial administrations were very small in relation to the tasks facing them. In the 1930s there were only 842 European officials controlling 4 million Africans in the Gold

Coast. Therefore it was difficult for even well-motivated colonial administrators to develop their colonies successfully, especially if they were ignorant of African farming needs. Often their activities in sequestrating land for settlers or in the impressment of Africans to serve as soldiers or labourers disrupted African society.

Therefore, even before the First World War, a new phase of colonial rule evolved as colonial governments attempted more positively to embark on schemes to improve health, housing and education. Unfortunately European confidence, already damaged by the carnage of the war, was further undermined by the world slump in the late 1920s. The slump reduced the resources available for African development and weakened the confidence of the administrators in bringing change to Africa.

Nevertheless the slump also proved that if Africa were to be properly developed for the benefit of its own peoples and the world at large, colonial governments would have to play an active role. What was needed to initiate a spiral of development was greater European investment in the colonies, and if private investment was not forthcoming, then government money should be invested. The sense of need for a more active colonial policy was heightened by the experience of the three major colonial powers – Britain, France and Belgium – during the Second World War and in the immediate postwar period, which left them virtually bankrupt.

Therefore from 1945 on the colonial period entered a third phase, in which it became the new orthodoxy for home and colonial administrators to plan and finance comprehensive schemes for social and economic development of African territories. All French and British colonial governments produced 10-year development plans, with the British planning to spend £210 millions in their African colonies by 1955 and the French £277 millions. Therefore by that date the African colonies were participating in the world economy as never before, and economic growth rates were far greater than in the earlier colonial periods.

Yet even this third phase had its limitations. Growth rates were far from uniform, and Africans were still very poor compared to Europeans. Above all, relatively little was done to match the economic and social development with comparable programmes of political training and advancement for the colonies. Such inaction alienated the growing stratum of educated blacks, who increasingly espoused African nationalism, both from a sense of political conviction and from a desire for greater job opportunity.

Nevertheless the period of European rule, though brief, was a fundamental episode in Africa's history. Colonialism incorporated the continent into the world economy and international capitalism. It introduced Africa to modern science and technology, and began the process of African industrialisation. It contributed to African incorporation into the world system of nation-states, former colonies joining the international diplomatic system with boundaries drawn by their European rulers.

European rule in Africa has had a bad press, and undoubtedly a mixed track record. For long, left-wing assertions that colonial rule was complete exploitation held sway. Students were taught to hoot with laughter at Curzon's declamation that the British Empire was 'after Providence the greatest instrument of good the world has ever seen'. Such laughter went along with feelings of guilt. Over the last two decades some revisionism has occurred. As early as 1961, in *The Colonial Reckoning*, the liberal Margery Perham pointed out that no colonial power profited greatly from empire, because colonial possessions were a drain on human, financial and military resources. On the other hand, colonial government gave peace and sound administration, and some increase in prosperity, to formerly anarchic parts of the globe. Colonial officials for the most part sincerely regarded themselves as protectors of their black subjects. Their lives were devoted to their welfare, even though they might often act as stern parents towards wayward children.

Missionaries in Africa also felt themselves to be protectors of their flock, and tended to resist the worst business practices. They were also the pioneers in the creation of schools and hospitals. Their aim was to save souls and lives, but inadvertently their effect was to promote political consciousness among Africans. Many future African leaders received their first education in mission schools, though they did not feel much gratitude to missionaries, as they often resented what they considered to be – and often were – attitudes of cultural and moral superiority. Colonial education was, in truth, very eurocentric. The language was European, and African history and culture were ignored. In both quantity and quality the education left something to be desired, owing to the small budgets available, and in 1960, after 75 years of colonialism, illiteracy in Africa stood at 80 per cent of the population, according to a UNESCO survey.

The major contradiction of colonial education was that while it educated Africans to be subordinate, it stimulated nationalism. A lack of opportunity beyond primary school caused frustration among young people. It also produced a Western-educated black élite, notably such political journalists as Nnamdi Azikiwe in Nigeria and Jomo Kenyatta in Kenya, who played a major role in the struggle for political freedom.

Unfortunately attempts to prepare Africans to usher in Western-style liberal government were doomed to failure. It was inherently unsuited to societies with little tradition of nationhood and no experience of democratic pluralism. The overselling of one-man one-vote democracy, and the failure to redraw boundaries to reflect group identity, meant that the history of the newly independent colonies became one of chaos and division, with bloody conflicts in countries such as Nigeria and Uganda.

(b) Colonies of white settlement: South Africa and Rhodesia

At the climax of the colonial period in the mid-1950s, there were over 5 million settlers of European descent living in Africa. Unlike the colonial administrators, missionaries or businessmen, these Europeans regarded an African country as their home. They were a small minority in a total population of 240 milions, and were concentrated in South Africa (3 millions), Algeria (1 million), Southern Rhodesia (225,000) and Northern Rhodesia (70,000). There were also sizeable numbers of European settlers in the Belgian Congo, Kenya, Angola and Mozambique. The Europeans were not the only immigrant settlers in Africa; south of the Sudan were 1 million resident Asians, mainly from the Indian sub-continent and Arab countries.

The Europeans enjoyed an influence in colonial governments out of all proportion to their numbers. They also possessed a real superiority over most black Africans in military strength, education, wealth, technology and organisation, and naturally wished to maintain their privileged position, since they had committed themselves, their families and fortunes to Africa during the high tide of imperialism. Yet while they continued to maintain a firm belief in their right to rule in Africa, those in power in Europe began to question such assumptions.

In South Africa European settlement was able to take root as a result of an unusual combination of favourable circumstances. Firstly, the strategic interest of the major maritime nations – first the Dutch in 1652 and then the British in 1795 – required some formal establishment of European power at the southernmost tip of Africa, which happened also to be one of the two zones of the continent climatically hospitable to European settlement. Secondly, because this establishment could not supply an adequate livelihood for all the settlers, some began to disperse into the interior (as with the Great Trek 1836–8) and the momentum of this dispersal was maintained owing to clashes of interest between the trekkers – the Boers (farmers) of Dutch descent – and the British authorities based at Cape Town. Thirdly, when this European dispersal began, there were no strongly established African societies in the immediate hinterland of Cape Town, and the Europeans found little difficulty in establishing dominance. Fourthly, the area was found to be exceptionally rich in mineral wealth, which attracted European capital and promoted an industrial revolution. Finally, the external European power responsible for South Africa, Britain, became conscious of the need for eventual self-government for the settler colonies.

What made the South African situation unique, however, was that the South Africans were the only settler group in Africa capable of generating a sense of national identity which was quite independent of their original European connections, and which proclaimed that they were totally committed to an African future for themselves and their children. This Afrikaner nationalism emerged in the late nineteenth century as a movement of resistance by the descendants of the original Dutch settlers against the encroachment of British imperialism. The Boers retained a Calvinist outlook on life and regarded other Africans as inferior. Under Paul Kruger, President of the Transvaal from 1883 to 1900, they developed a 'laager' mentality, seeing themselves as a chosen people surrounded by enemies. The Boers developed their own language – Afrikaans – which replaced Dutch in 1920, a symbolic act to show that they were a separate African white people and not merely European settlers.

After the Boer War of 1899 to 1902 (see Chapter 1) the British colonies and former Boer colonies in the area – Cape Colony, Natal, Transvaal and the Orange Free State – joined together to form the Union of South Africa and in 1910 became self-governing. The interests of the non-European majority were not discussed. The 1,276,000 Europeans, less than one-fifth of the population, owned four-fifths of the land and had a monopoly of political power. As Hugh Seton-Watson has pointed out, what was initially regarded as an act of generosity by the British towards a brave defeated enemy later came to appear as an act of betrayal of the weaker majority peoples abandoned to the mercies of a stronger minority.

But in the constitutional development of South Africa after 1910 the initiative lay with the Afrikaners. Despite immigration from Britain, a high birthrate enabled the Afrikaners to outnumber the English-speaking settlers in a ratio of 3 to 2. Above all, the Afrikaners had a much clearer sense of purpose and were much more adept political animals than their English-speaking counterparts. Consequently all the prime ministers and most government ministers since 1910 in South Africa have been Afrikaners. Some, like Smuts with his South Africa party, in power from 1919 to 1924 and from 1939 to 1948, were more concerned to win the support of the English speakers, but in so doing ran the risk of alienating the majority of voters and lost power to such more overtly nationalist leaders as James Hertzog in 1924 and Daniel Malan in 1948.

Apartheid, the concept that society in South Africa was made up of a number of distinct nations which should live in their own homelands separate from each other, and that non-Europeans might enter the white homeland only as transient wage-earners with no political status, was not enunciated as a formal political doctrine until 1947, as part of Malan's campaign, which led to electoral victory in 1948. But the political climate had been moving steadily in that direction since 1910, when Louis Botha's victory in the first election led immediately to the restricting of Indian and African rights to buy land. Hertzog, who had split from Botha's party to found the Nationalist Party in 1914, won power in 1924 and was premier until 1939. He was the true father of apartheid, his tenure of office seeing in the banning of Indian immigration, the whittling down of the voting rights of non-Europeans and the confining of Africans, 66 per cent of the population, to 13 per cent of the total area of the country. Laws from 1911 on reserved skilled employment for whites, and controlled the manner in which non-Europeans were allowed to enter and work in white areas.

The colony of Southern Rhodesia, between the Limpopo and Zambesi rivers, was deliberately planned by Cecil Rhodes as an extension of South Africa. He was anxious that it should be British and kept out of the hands of the Afrikaner nationalists. His British South Africa Company organised the first white settlements there in 1890, and succeeded in seizing control of the area from Lobengula, King of the Ndebele. The colony was divided into Matabeleland, where the Ndebele lived, and Mashonaland, occupied by Shona tribes. The area did not prove to be as rich in minerals as Rhodes had hoped, and after his company surrendered its charter, Southern Rhodesia became a self-governing colony in 1923, with its own cabinet and legislature. This solution was reached because the whites in Southern Rhodesia did not wish to be part of an Afrikaner-dominated South Africa, while the British Colonial Office did not wish to take on the responsibility for Southern Rhodesia, with its independently minded settlers, especially as it had just taken over from the British South Africa Company the responsibility for the larger and poorer Northern Rhodesia.

There were only 33,000 whites in a population of 1 million in Southern Rhodesia, and they were not to have a monopoly of political power, as in theory blacks had the right to vote. However, by raising the qualifications for the franchise, the whites could in practice monopolise the system; in 1952 only 380 blacks voted out of a total of 45,000 voters. In addition, the whites buttressed their position by discriminatory legislation, which ensured that they owned the best land. The only way the British government had of preventing such developments was by a suspension of the Rhodesian constitution and the imposition of direct rule by the Colonial Office, but only in 1965 was this attempted. Such Colonial Office reluctance to interfere was increased by the difficulties faced by the white settler population in the period of the depression.

After the Second World War conditions improved, with the development of tobacco for export, and by the mid-1950s the European population had risen to 160,000. By then the settlers wanted complete independence, and thought that their best chance of gaining it was by an amalgamation of the two Rhodesias with Nyasaland into a new British Central African Union worthy of dominion status. Union with Northern Rhodesia was now an attractive proposition to Southern Rhodesians, because rich deposits of copper ore in Katanga had been developed from the 1930s to make Northern Rhodesia the richest territory in central Africa. The economies of the two Rhodesias were interdependent, as Northern Rhodesia's copper mines needed Southern Rhodesian coal, and the two Rhodesias were cooperating to develop the hydro-electric potential of the Zambesi river. Northern Rhodesia's economic renaissance had also attracted more white settlers, who numbered 70,000 by the early 1950s. But the white settlers' hopes ran counter to British policy in Southern Africa, which was that self-government could not be granted to colonies containing white settlers until their African inhabitants could participate in government equally with the settlers.

White settler demands for the amalgamation of the two colonies with a constitution granting complete self-government led to a British government commission which reported back in 1939. It stated that, although the economic case for amalgamation was a good one, the massive native opposition in Northern Rhodesia made the plan politically impracticable.

(c) Africa moves to independence

The empires that were so confidently proclaimed over Africa in the late nineteenth and early twentieth centuries as inevitable and permanent extensions of European power hardly lasted three generations. By the 1960s the colonial system was in full retreat, and by the 1980s only beleaguered South Africa remained as a relic of the old white domination.

The forces making for this rapid development were several. Certainly the growth of the continent's nationalist movements was a central factor. A great spur was given to black political consciousness by Mussolini's invasion of Ethiopia in 1935. As Masrui and Tidy show, 'Black men all over the world were profoundly shaken by the destruction of a country that was the proud symbol of African independence and black achievement amid a sea of colonialism.' Later African leaders, such as Nkrumah and Kenyatta, were outraged, Kenyatta growing a beard as a gesture of support for Ethiopia, with the vow not to shave it until the country was liberated. The black world awoke to the reality that colonialism was not a spent force but a continuing danger to black aspirations.

In the beginning of African nationalism, influences from America were important. The pan-africanism of the West Indian Marcus Garvey found disciples among educated Africans. Azikiwe, Hastings Banda and Nkrumah all studied at colleges in the USA and came under pan-african influence.

Certain other factors ensured that the new nationalism would succeed with relative ease. Firstly, the two world wars and the interwar economic depression undermined Europe's confidence in its civilising mission and its capacity to maintain control of empire. Secondly, colonial control had been educative and therefore carried with it its own solvent. When colonial rulers set up schools, brought in new technology and introduced ideas of independence, it was only natural that Africans would wish to run their own affairs – and many Europeans also believed that independence was a just objective.

Finally, by the 1950s Europeans were realising that it was not in their interest to deny African claims to independence. Part of the purpose of empire – the harnessing of colonial markets and resources for the industrial economies – had been achieved. Such economic links would not be undone by the removal of political controls from Europe, but attempts to maintain controls by force would endanger the economic benefits flowing from Africa. Therefore the need to retain empire was as much weakened as the will to maintain it.

Italy's defeat in the Second World War led to rapid independence for her African colonies of Libya, Eritrea and Ethiopia. Italian and British Somaliland joined in an independent Somali Republic in 1960. Egypt's troubled relations with Britain are recounted in Chapter 19, but in 1956 Sudan rejected her links with Egypt and opted for complete independence. The French empire in North Africa was rapidly dismantled. In 1954 and 1956 self-government was granted to Tunisia and Morocco respectively, but the presence of 1 million French settlers complicated the Algerian question and led to a bloody civil war which De Gaulle solved by holding a referendum in 1962, the result of which led to an independent Algeria.

In Africa south of the Sahara, demands for political change surfaced most swiftly in West Africa. Economic and political organisation there had reached high levels before close contact with European traders. This more advanced area soon organised a nationalist movement, because educated Africans there combined the inspiration of West African history with European techniques of political protest. The region was also particularly open to the influence of international ideologies critical of the colonial system, such as Marxism and Liberalism. From the 1950s a swelling stream of West Africans had studied in Western Europe and the USA and had met negroes from the USA and the West Indies. They learned that the black man need not be an inferior replica of the white; he had his own distinctive culture and history. If Africa united, the African nation could be reborn.

This gospel was propagated above all in the Gold Coast and Nigeria, where many Africans had left traditional village society to become professional men, clerks and shopkeepers. To these were added an important new element, men who had gained education and experience from military service during the Second World War. They gained new perspectives from fighting to free lands such as Burma, India and France from foreign rule, and were inclined to ask why this benefit should be withheld from them.

The programmes of colonial development embarked upon by France and Britain increased the frustrations of the new black élites, because many more European technicians and teachers were brought in to implement the programmes just when Africans were experiencing difficulty in finding suitable employment opportunities, to which they felt their skills and experience entitled them. Frustration first boiled over in the Gold Coast in 1948, and the Ashanti riots caused twenty-nine deaths. The British moved quickly to frame a new constitution which would provide a more rapid advance to self-government via a national assembly. The United Gold Coast Convention, a political association founded in 1947 by a lawyer, J. B. Danquah, accepted this, but one of Danquah's colleagues, Kwame Nkrumah, saw the move as a sell-out to the British and founded a mass party, the Convention People's party. Despite spells in prison, Nkrumah's influence grew, and in 1957 he led the Gold Coast into independence. The European name Gold Coast was replaced by the name Ghana, after the first West African state known to history.

Nkrumah remained in power until 1966. He was a great pan-african, but Masrui and Tidy assert that, as a kind of Leninist tsar, he did great harm to Ghana by setting up a one-party state and imprisoning opponents such as Danquah. He created his own personality cult and damaged the economy by heavy expenditure on socialist schemes. His tyranny and incompetence led to a coup by police and troops in 1966, and Kofi Busia led a civilian government until 1972, when discontent increased at his increasingly dictatorial style and a growing economic crisis. A second military coup then occurred and the following decades saw a pattern of unstable regimes, with further coups in 1978, 1979 and 1981. The latter two were led by Flight Lieutenant Jerry Rawlings as a protest against corruption in government.

Once the principle of a rapid advance to self-government had been accepted for the Gold Coast, it could not be denied to Britain's other West African colonies, and Sierra Leone and the Gambia became independent in 1961 and 1965 respectively. The rapid decolonisation of British West Africa had some effect on France's policy towards her colonies in West Africa, French Guinea becoming independent in 1958 and French Sudan (Mali), Senegal and French Togoland in 1960.

It was in Nigeria that one of the most typical African problems of the independence period was first fully manifested. Three ethnic sub-nationalisms emerged – the Yoruba nationality in the West, Ibo nationality in the East and the Hausa-Fulani nationality in the north.

Britain granted Nigeria independence in 1960 after creating a federation embracing all the three ethnic groups. The conflict that soon occurred was not only political but military, vocational and religious in nature. In January 1966 a coup by Ibo army officers who felt that their promotion was being unfairly blocked led to the death of the prime minister, Sir Abubakar Tafewa Balewa, who was from the Muslim north. Though order was restored by an Ibo, General Aguiyi Ironsi, he was unable to dispel the fears of the Yoruba and Hausa that he would favour the appointment of fellow Ibos, and a second coup led to his death in July 1966. Nigeria was now governed by General Yakubo Gowon, a Northerner, who was unable to prevent Hausa and Ibo pogroms on each other, which caused 30,000 deaths and a flood of refugees. In May 1967 the Ibos under Colonel Odumegwu Ojukwu proclaimed independence as the state of Biafra, a move that led to a tragic civil war. Most Nigerians supported the ideal of one Nigeria, which would be a large multi-ethnic and powerful state. Over the next 3 years Biafran resistance was ground down by larger, more experienced and better armed forces before Ibo resistance ended with Ojukwu's flight in January 1970. The most conspicuous victims were Ibo civilians, who died of famine in their hundreds and thousands.

To his credit Gowon, by dividing the country into twelve states, weakened the old division of Nigeria into 'three' Nigerias, and his clemency helped to reconcile the Ibos. The 1970s saw the Nigerian economy expand until she became black Africa's economic giant through a series of development plans financed by oil revenues. Transport, heavy industry and the social services developed, but agriculture failed to prosper, and the beneficiaries of the boom were not ordinary Nigerians but a small élite of professional men, businessmen and military officers.

Gowon was an indecisive leader in peacetime and was replaced in a bloodless coup in 1975 by Murtala Muhammed. After Muhammed's assassination in 1976, General Olusegun Obasanjo gradually restored the country to civilian rule by 1979. This rule was so corrupt that it provoked a further military coup in December 1983 by Major General Buhari. In August 1985 he was replaced by General Ibrahim Babingida, who adopted a populist style of government, repealed some of the harsh laws introduced by Buhari, and opened up the problems of economic policy to public debate.

The process of decolonisation had its most tragic manifestation in the Belgian Congo. In 1956 the Belgians stated that a 30-year plan would prepare the colony for independence, but the pace of change became much more rapid. Belgian Congolese such as Patrice Lumumba had begun to travel outside the Congo and become inspired by other African independence movements. Thus the traditional Belgian policy of total isolation for the Congo began to break down. In January 1959 the urban proletariat of the capital, Leopold-ville, took to the streets, seeing independence from Belgian domina-tion as the only possible relief for its social and political grievances. The official casualty list of those killed in the riots was forty-nine. The Belgian authorities promised independence for the Congo; in May 1960 elections were held for a national assembly and in July the independent Congo Republic (Zaire) was born.

The Belgians had taken a massive gamble, calculating perhaps that the Congo had been so little prepared for independence that their continued presence would be seen to be vital to the country's survi-val. The new state did indeed lack trained administrators, but, more tragically, no political leader or party in the vast territory comman-ded a national following. Lumumba, who became prime minister, and his Mouvement National Congolais came nearest to this, but he himself lacked confidence or consistency and his party held only a quarter of the seats in the Assembly.

Tribal differences soon shattered the fragile peace. The central government of President Kasavubu and Lumumba was challenged by a separatist movement from Katanga, led by Moise Tshombe. When the left-wing Lumumba asked for Russian help in August, he was dismissed. A UN peacekeeping force was sent, but found its task hopeless as the country degenerated into full-scale civil war. Lumumba was murdered in February 1961, probably in the very presence of Tshombe. The central government, now led by a social-ist, Cyrille Adoula, and backed by a UN force of 20,000, fought secessionists in Katanga and other provinces, both sides carrying out atrocities. It was in flying out in an attempt to solve the issue that Dag Hammarskjold, the UN Secretary General, was killed in a plane crash. Only in 1964 did the central government crush resistance. By then real power lay with the army under General Sese Mobutu, who seized power in 1965 and eliminated such enemies as Tshombe. Rebellions against his authority were ruthlessly crushed in 1967 and 1978. The tragedy of the Belgian Congo was that no politician combined vision with political skill. Tshombe possessed political adroitness but lacked political conscience, while Lumumba held the right views but lacked the necessary political skills.

In East Africa Tanganyika moved to independence with relative ease in 1961, partly because European occupation had done little damage to tribal institutions and the widespread quality of the Swahili language and culture made it easy for the Tanganyika African National Union, founded in 1954 by Julius Nyerere, an Edinburgh University graduate, to etablish a sense of national purpose. Nyerere did well to win the confidence of both the settlers and the British administrators. When nearby Zanzibar experienced a communist revolution in 1964 which ousted the Sultan, Nyerere himself faced a mutiny in the Tanganyikan army. However, he survived with the help of the British, and effected the union of Zanzibar with his own republic, which was renamed Tanzania.

Nyerere became a leading figure in African politics. He established one-party rule in Tanzania, created links with communist China and implemented the collectivisation of agriculture and a national plan to develop the railways. He was not afraid to take a strong line in condemning British policies towards Rhodesia and South Africa.

In Uganda the Kabaka (King) of Buganda (part of southern Uganda) joined in a coalition with the national party led by Milton Obote, and in 1962 the British granted Uganda its independence. Obote never felt secure so long as the Kabaka had an independent source of traditional power in Buganda. In 1966 he established one-party rule and suppressed the Bugandan kingdom by force, the Kabaka fleeing to die in exile. Obote now made an error in relying too much on the army under General Idi Amin. In 1971 Amin overthrew Obote and brought in an appalling reign of terror with the help of Gaddafi of Libya. Amin's aim was Muslim Nubian domination of the country, and in 1972 he expelled 50,000 Ugandan Asians. Amnesty International reported in 1977 that 300,000 people were murdered in this period. Amin consistently attempted to humiliate Britain and eradicate Christian influences by massacre. By 1978 his regime was isolated and faced massive economic chaos. Amin's solution was a war against Tanzania, but Nyerere's troops expelled the Ugandans and their Libyan allies and occupied the capital, Kampala, in 1979. Amin was forced to flee to Libya and Obote returned to power in 1980 helped by his friend Nyerere.

In 1986 Obote was again toppled from power by Yoweri Musevini, but Northern Ugandans from Obote's army continued armed resistance as the Uganda People's Army. In 1988 peace talks were in progress but by then Northern Uganda was in ruins.

In Kenya the process of decolonisation was complicated by the presence of European settlers, whose ownership of the best farmland created resentment among the Kikuyu tribe. Many Kikuyu by 1950 were joining a secret society, Mau Mau, which murdered settlers and any Kikuyu lucky enough to have land or reasonable jobs. British troops intervened to crush Mau Mau by 1959, but the movement helped to convince the British government that measures were needed to alleviate African land hunger and to give Africans a role in the Kenyan government. By then the strongest party in Kenya was the Kenya African National Union (KANU), led by Jomo Kenyatta, a graduate of the London School of Economics, who was compromised in British eyes by his supposed complicity in the Mau Mau movement. Kenyatta was imprisoned by the British, but after Kenya gained independence in 1962 he produced a coalition between KANU and other groups to win an electoral victory in 1963. Kenyatta ruled Kenya until his death in 1978, and in African terms Kenya has been a stable country, despite tribal differences and Kenyatta's expulsion of 60,000 Asians in 1968.

Finally, mention should be made of Spanish and Portuguese colonies. Spain granted independence to equatorial Guinea and the Spanish Sahara in 1968. Portugal attempted to hold on to her three colonies of Guinea, Mozambique and Angola, but faced full-scale guerrilla warfare, actively supported by adjacent independent states. By 1974 half of Portugal's national budget was going to support her military forces in Africa; the Portuguese army and people had had enough and rose in revolt. The new government immediately recognised the claims of the African nationalists for the independence of their territories.

(d) Contemporary Rhodesia and South Africa

Northern Rhodesia and Nyasaland moved to independence with relative tranquillity in 1964, when Kenneth Kaunda and Hastings Banda became the heads of the independent states of Zambia and Malawi respectively. No such easy solution was found for Southern Rhodesia. The failure of the Federation made the settlers determined to go it alone. In 1962 the general election returned a new right-wing party, the Rhodesian Front, to power under Ian Smith. It demanded complete independence from Britain, but the British prime minister, Harold Wilson, believed that he could persuade Smith to make concessions to the African majority as the price to be paid for such independence. Wilson had, however, misjudged both Smith and the mood of most white settlers, and in 1965 Smith's government made a unilateral declaration of independence. Britain and the UN termed the action illegal and no country, not even South Africa, recognised the Smith regime.

The Rhodesia issue faced Britain with difficult choices if she were to retain influence in a multi-racial Commonwealth. African Commonwealth members demanded military force against Smith's regime, but Wilson chose to impose economic sanctions, backed by the UN, in 1966. Shipments of arms, oils, aircraft and vehicles were embargoed, but the sanctions were easily evaded because Rhodesia could be supplied through South Africa, and, until 1974, through Mozambique. In 1970 a new constitution was introduced and Rhodesia proclaimed a republic.

From 1965 on both the Wilson and Heath governments attempted to negotiate a settlement with Smith, but to no avail. What did put real pressure on the Rhodesian regime was the increase in guerrilla warfare, from 1972 on organised by two nationalist groups, the Zimbabwe African National Union (ZANU) and the Zimbabwe African People's Union (ZAPU). The leader of ZANU was Robert Mugabe, a well-educated Marxist member of the Shona-speaking people, who made up 75 per cent of black Rhodesians. ZANU received aid from both Tanzania and China. ZAPU was led by Joshua Nkomo, a member of the Kalanga tribe, and most of his ZAPU recruits were members of the ethnically related Ndebeles, who formed 20 per cent of Rhodesia's black population. ZANU and ZAPU formed a Patriotic Front in 1976, angered by the actions of Bishop Abel Muzorewa, a Shona whose United African National Council believed in cooperation with the Smith government. The Patriotic Front was soon recognised as the rightful government by the so-called Front Line states (Angola, Mozambique, Tanzania, Zambia and Botswana), which bordered on Rhodesia.

Increasing guerrilla activity forced Smith to concede in 1976 that black majority rule would have to come to Rhodesia. An Anglo-American plan was put to him, but the talks collapsed and Smith sought a settlement with Muzorewa. In 1978 they agreed an arrangement which guaranteed only 28 per cent of seats for whites in the Rhodesian parliament, and in April 1979 elections resulted in Muzorewa becoming prime minister. However, the whites still controlled the army and police and could exercise a veto in parliament. Naturally the Patriotic Front, which had not been allowed to fight in the elections, regarded them as invalid, as did the USA and the UN.

With guerrilla actions disrupting agriculture and with white departures now exceeding arrivals by over 500 a month, Smith was finally forced into real negotiations. At the end of 1979, the new Conservative foreign secretary, Lord Carrington, reached an agreement with the Rhodesian government at Lancaster House whereby Britain would supervise new elections, which would now include the Patriotic Front, with the whites guaranteed 20 of the 100 seats. The elections held in March 1980 led to ZANU winning 57 seats and ZAPU 20 seats; Muzorewa's UANC won only 3 seats. Mugabe and Nkomo formed a coalition government and Rhodesia was renamed Zimbabwe, after the massive eleventh-century granite ruins that rise on a hilltop south of the capital Salisbury (renamed Harare).

Zimbabwe's problems are, however, all too modern. In 1981 Mugabe drove Nkomo out of office and gradually established a dictatorship. In 1987 he tore up the British constitution and replaced one-man one-vote with one-party government. The position of the white settlers and Nkomo's supporters remains precarious.

In South Africa Malan's Nationalist Party began to implement a battery of laws imposing restrictions on non-whites after its 1948 electoral victory. The philosophy behind the new laws was well expressed by the Transvaal leader of the Nationalist Party, Strijdom, who later succeeded Malan. 'Our policy is that the Europeans must stand their ground and must remain baas (master) in South Africa. If we reject the herrenvolk (master race) idea . . . if the franchise is to be extended to the non-Europeans, how can the European remain baas?' Thus the laws deprived all South African non-whites of the right to vote and banned the main African political parties. The death penalty was extended to several offences. Government powers to detain without trial and to censor publications were increased. Working conditions for blacks were rigorously controlled, with the banning of strikes. To prevent the congregating of blacks in towns, squatting was forbidden, and in 1954 50,000 blacks in the Johannesburg area were forcibly resettled and black entry into towns controlled by an elaborate system of passes and permits. In 1950 an Immorality Act forbade sex between people of different races, and public segregation acts banned blacks from using the same transport, churches or beaches as whites or meeting in the same schools or universities.

South African governments in the 1950s gave much attention to what was claimed to be the positive side of apartheid (or separate development, as it became called). Steps were taken to make the African areas more genuinely homelands, with their own local self-government and universities. But the homeland (Bantustan) policy was flawed from the start. The 3 million Europeans had 411,000 square miles of the country's 472,000 square miles of land, and 10 million Africans were limited to 61,000 square miles. The Asians, who numbered nearly half a million, and the 136,000 Coloureds, who had emerged from centuries of earlier interaction between the Europeans, their slaves and the Africans, were not catered for at all. The Bantustans were too poor and small to support the Africans, because the native areas were already overcultivated and overgrazed, deficient in water, fertile land or mineral wealth. No sound economic base therefore existed.

The protagonists of apartheid argued that such problems could be solved by attracting industry to the Bantustans and improving agricultural techniques. But the owners of capital, the Europeans, preferred to employ it in the development of the white areas. The most glaring contradiction was that the white economy was dependent on black labour, so that it was not in the European interest for Africans to work in the nine Bantustans (such as the Transkei) in great numbers. European dependence on black labour was vastly increased by a postwar industrial revolution which saw the development of many basic industries. Consequently the African masses were ever more integrated into the white economy, both as workers and consumers. They were needed in more skilled jobs and had to have their purchasing power increased if they were to be significant consumers. A single economy developed in South Africa, and in the last resort it was dependent on the cooperation of the non-European majority.

South African governments have found it difficult to make the concessions that might win that cooperation. After Malan retired in 1954, J. G. Strijdom became premier, and after his death in 1958, he was succeeded by H. F. Verwoerd, a right-wing former editor of a

Broederbund newspaper. After Verwoerd's assassination in 1966, another hardliner, B. J. Vorster, took over the leadership until 1978. Since 1978 P. W. Botha has tried to make modest concessions over the sex and pass laws, but has been forced to move slowly, owing to the opposition of white extremists.

Meanwhile apartheid has continued as a caste system based on racial prejudice, white domination and police force. The black unemployment rate is around 20 per cent, compared with 1 per cent for whites. The pass laws have undermined black family life. The overwhelming majority of African children stop schooling at the primary level, only about 5.5 per cent moving up into secondary schools. The frustration caused has led to the South African crime rate being one of the highest in the world, two and a half times that of the USA.

Opposition to apartheid, which has come from home and abroad, has been resented by South African governments. A non-racial and moderate African National Congress was founded as early as 1912, but in 1959 a more radical movement, the Pan African Congress, was started. When in 1960 the government tried to destroy both organisations, sixty-nine people were killed at Sharpeville when the police opened fire. When both organisations were banned, the leader of the ANC, Nelson Mandela, formed 'The Spear of the Nation' to disrupt the life of the country by sabotage and guerrilla tactics. In 1963 he was arrested with seven others and sentenced to life imprisonment. International pressure to have him released in the 1980s was unavailing.

Since the 1970s violence in the black townships has become endemic, as black opposition to apartheid has become more open and divisions within the black community have increased. In 1976 174 persons, all but two of them black, were killed in a week of protests in Soweto and other black townships surrounding Johannesburg against the compulsory use of Afrikaans in black schools. In 1977 the murder in police custody of Steve Biko, the black consciousness leader, encouraged more violence. Many young Africans became guerrillas, and, to attack their hideouts in neighbouring states, the South African government has carried out reprisal raids.

Over the years the growth of international opposition to apartheid has had only a limited impact on the regime, because South Africa is a rich and relatively self-sufficient country and has been able to evade economic sanctions. Many advanced industrial countries, particularly the USA and Britain, have significant investments and trading links with South Africa. Nevertheless the pressure has tightened since 1962, when the UN proclaimed an economic boycott, followed by an arms embargo and an end to sporting links. Public opinion in the 1980s has forced many large companies to modify or terminate their activities in South Africa, and the isolation of the regime has grown.

After Rhodesia became Zimbabwe, South Africa was confronted by a ring of hostile states.

In some ways international pressure was undermined by its internal contradictions. The South African regime is unpleasantly right-wing and racialist, but its opponents include communist and black African regimes which have been more totalitarian, as guilty of racialism (though not based on colour) and more guilty of genocide. The call from Commonwealth countries for economic sanctions has sounded odd when the Front Line states continue to trade vigorously with South Africa, and when such sanctions would harm the living standards of ordinary Africans. The opponents of apartheid were strangely quiet over the Russian invasion of Afghanistan or the atrocities of Amin. At times the anti-apartheid movement itself has seemed guilty of shabby persecution, as with the hounding of the runner Zola Budd in 1988.

Where the UN was able to develop a strong legal position was over South-West Africa (Namibia). The League of Nations had placed the territory under South African mandate after the First World War. In 1966 the UN General Assembly voted to terminate the mandate on the grounds that South Africa had failed to fulfil its mandated obligations. Vorster responded by integrating Namibia fully into South Africa. A nationalist guerrilla force, the South West Africa People's Organisation (SWAPO), developed from 1962 on in opposition to South African rule, and was recognised as the rightful government by the UN in 1973.

The future for South Africa looks bleak, given white opposition even to changes in the apartheid system that fall far short of black majority rule. As domestic and international pressure mounts, the extreme white nationalist parties, having learnt the wrong lesson from Zimbabwe, seem more likely to move further into their laager or encampment and resort to military methods. Ultimately a final bloody struggle appears to be the most likely outcome. If so, South Africa's weaknesses will be laid bare – its vulnerability over oil, and its manpower crisis, for there are simply not sufficient whites to guard economic installations, to control black townships and run the country's civil and military administration. A third weakness is the growing division in the white population between those who would embrace real change, those like Botha (now retired) who would give grudging change and the diehards who oppose all change.

As the writer Alan Paton, the author of *Cry the Beloved Country* who died in 1988, once commented, 'I write not to express my detestation of the policies of apartheid, not because my government has cruelly and ruthlesly treated its more articulate opponents but because I fear for the future of Afrikanerdom. I fear it is going to be destroyed.' When a sustained black challenge does arise, South

Africa will be the setting for the continent's greatest and final confrontation.

(e) The continent's continuing problems

By the standards of Western Europe, Africa remains a very poor continent, over-dependent on fluctuating world prices for primary products. Yet the rapid transition to independence raised the expectations of the rapidly growing populations, and the new leaders faced a formidable task in trying to develop their economies so that such expectations could be fulfilled. The task became an impossible one in the 1970s and 1980s, as the oil crisis added to most African countries' import bills, as international bank lending led to more indebtedness and as protectionism by advanced industrial countries blocked Africa's exports. The continuing political instability of many African countries made them unattractive as locations for multi-national investment, and the resources of world organisations were inadequate to fill the investment gap. In 1975 an OECD analysis of the world's twenty-nine poorest countries included seventeen from Africa.

The Sahara desert has advanced 60 miles in 17 years, not because droughts have been worse than in previous years but because more land has been put under cultivation for such cash crops as cotton and more watering places drilled for farmers and herdsmen. Human and livestock populations have multiplied rapidly, and the consequent overgrazing, overcultivation and deforestation have led to the process called desertification. Better land husbandry, whereby the grazing of livestock is reduced and reforestation programmes implemented, is urgently needed.

Africa as a continent is still a prey to major diseases. African countries south of the Sahara form the epicentre of the disease malaria, which kills a million children a year. Oncho-cerciasis – river blindness, caused by a parasitic worm and spread by blackfly – infects about 30 million people in Africa. In the 1970s Kenya suffered an outbreak of cholera. Many Africans suffer from malnutrition, which gives rise to such specific deficiency diseases as anemia (iron deficiency), as well as increasing susceptibility to communicable diseases. The AIDS virus is particularly prevalent in Africa.

Africa has also one of the worst refugee problems in the whole world. The causes are several: sometimes the refugee problem arises from a civil war such as in Ethiopia, from wars between states, from the effects of a coup d'état, from periodic tribal massacre or from the expulsion policies of an Amin or Kenyatta. Consequently there are about 2 million African refugees.

One European legacy which had a fatal consequence for Africa was the arbitrary imposition of colonial boundaries by European rulers.

Therefore the new states often contained within them different ethnic groups, whose rivalries provoked civil wars. Such civil wars appear likely to continue for the rest of the century, though, after the failure of the Biafran bid to secede from Nigeria, there may be fewer civil wars caused by secessionists.

Fundamental to the continent's problems was the attempt by Europeans to graft European practices of government on to African stock. Parliamentary government has failed to take root in Africa and African armies are particularly prone to attempting military coups. By 1987 military coups had occurred in twenty-seven African countries in the independence period. When such armies find themselves idle and without a definite mission, the generals haunt corridors of power and threaten government. Such armies need political education to transform them into people's militia or instruments of national development, but few African governments have attempted to implement such a transition, because such policies might lead to their own overthrow.

FURTHER READING

Austin, D., *Politics in Africa*, University Press of New England, Boston, 1984

Davenport, T. R. H., *South Africa: A Modern History*, Macmillan, London, 1987

Martin, D. and Johnson, P., *The Struggle for Zimbabwe*, Faber and Faber, London, 1981

Mazrui, A. A. and Tidy, M., *Nationalism and the New States in Africa*, Heinemann, London, 1984

Oliver, R. and Fage, J. D., *A Short History of Africa*, Penguin, Harmondsworth, 1988

QUESTIONS

1. Was European rule in Africa merely a catalogue of exploitation?
2. Why was a system of apartheid implemented in South Africa and what are its prospects of survival?
3. Why was the process of decolonisation in most of Africa a relatively rapid development?
4. Account for the ultimate failure of the white minority in Southern Rhodesia to hang on to power.
5. In what ways does the history of Nigeria and Uganda since the 1960s typify the difficulties faced by newly independent African countries?

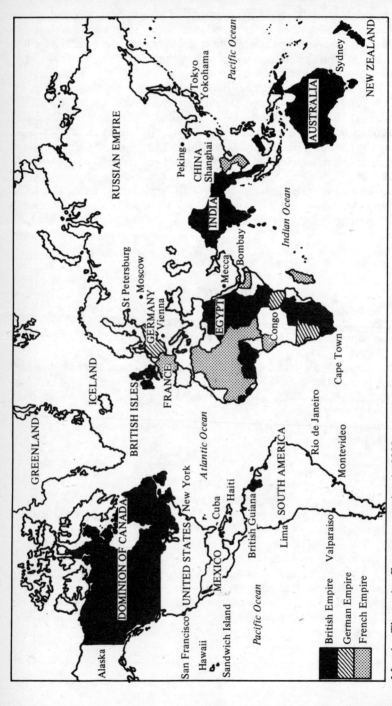

Map 1   *The major European empires in 1900*

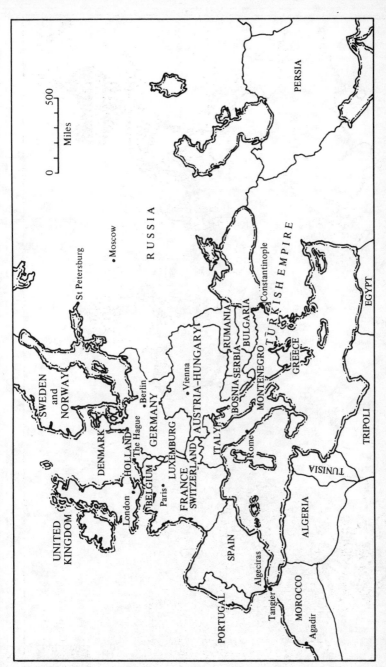

Map 2 *Europe in 1900*

Map 3   *The Balkans, 1880–1914*

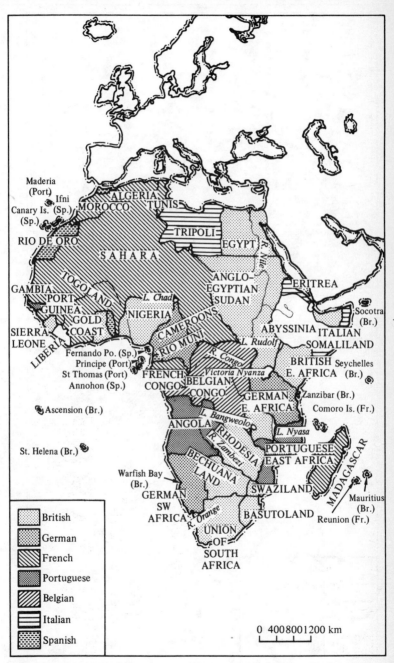

British
German
French
Portuguese
Belgian
Italian
Spanish

0 400 800 1200 km

Map 4   *Africa in 1914*

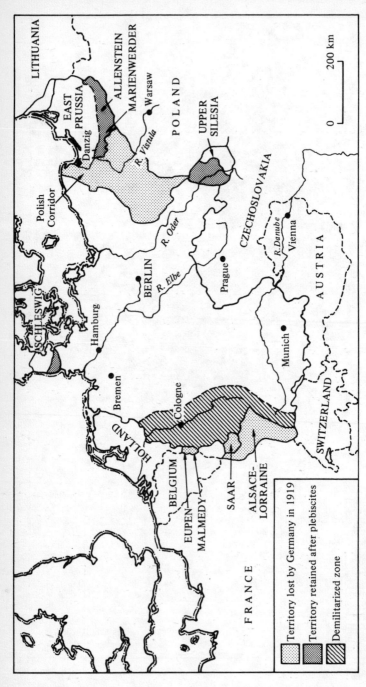

Map 5   *Europe in 1919*

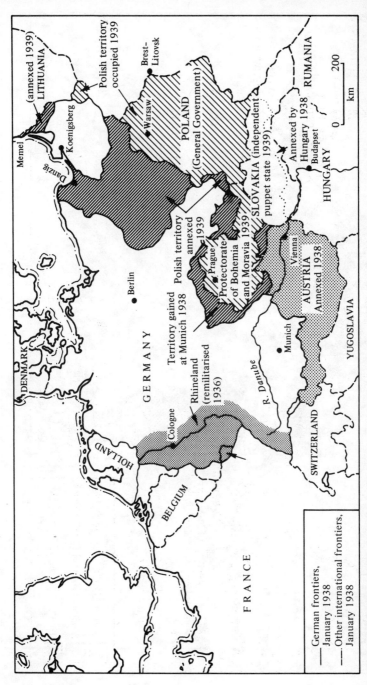

Map 6 *German expansion, 1933–40*

Map 7 *Europe in 1945*

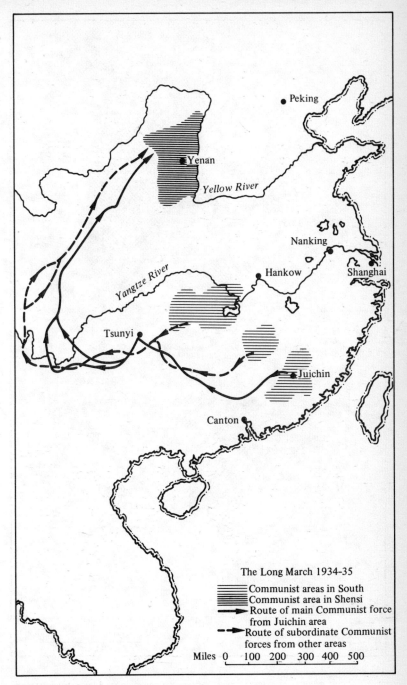

The Long March 1934-35

Communist areas in South
Communist area in Shensi
Route of main Communist force
from Juichin area
Route of subordinate Communist
forces from other areas

Miles 0 100 200 300 400 500

Map 8 *The Long March*

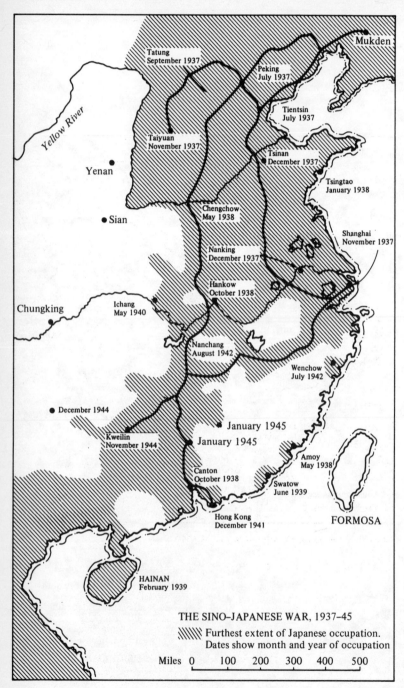

Tatung
September 1937

Peking
July 1937

Mukden

Tientsin
July 1937

Yellow River

Taiyuan
November 1937

Tsinan
December 1937

Tsingtao
January 1938

Yenan

Shanghai
November 1937

Sian

Chengchow
May 1938

Nanking
December 1937

Hankow
October 1938

Chungking

Ichang
May 1940

Nanchang
August 1942

Wenchow
July 1942

December 1944

January 1945

Kweilin
November 1944

January 1945

Amoy
May 1938

Canton
October 1938

Swatow
June 1939

Hong Kong
December 1941

FORMOSA

HAINAN
February 1939

THE SINO–JAPANESE WAR, 1937–45

\\\\\\ Furthest extent of Japanese occupation.
Dates show month and year of occupation

Miles 0   100   200   300   400   500

Map 9   *The Sino-Japanese War, 1937–45*

Map 10   *China and her neighbours, c.1950*

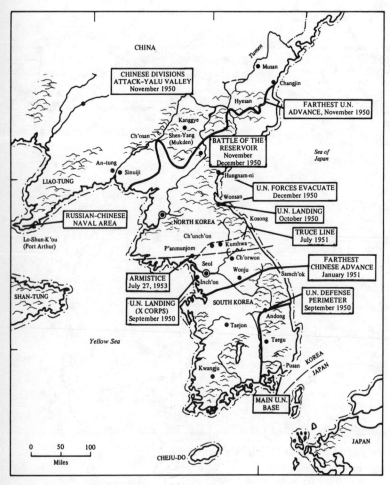

Map 11   *The Korean War, 1950–3*

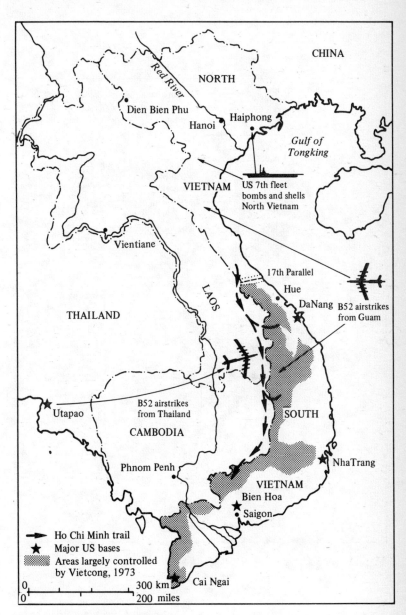

Map 12   *The war in Vietnam*

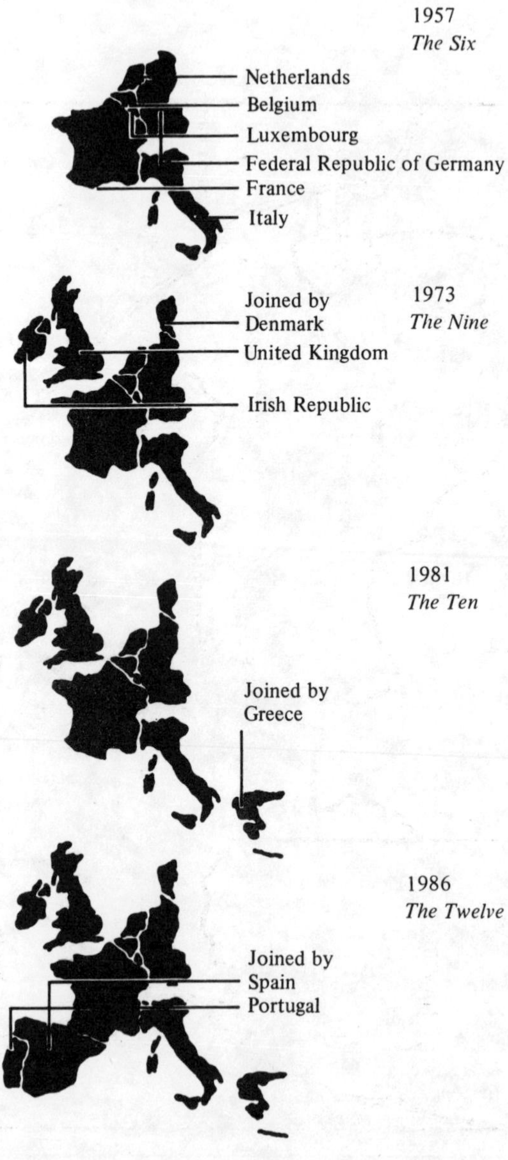

1957
The Six

Netherlands
Belgium
Luxembourg
Federal Republic of Germany
France
Italy

1973
The Nine

Joined by
Denmark
United Kingdom

Irish Republic

1981
The Ten

Joined by
Greece

1986
The Twelve

Joined by
Spain
Portugal

Map 13   *The evolution of the European Community*

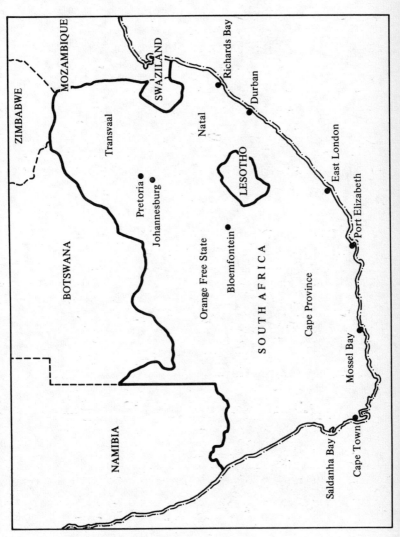

Map 14   *Beleaguered South Africa*

Index